Encyclopedia of Business and Finance

SECOND EDITION

Editorial Board

Encyclopedia of Business and Finance

SECOND EDITION

VOLUME 2
J–Z

Burton S. Kaliski

EDITOR IN CHIEF

MACMILLAN REFERENCE USA

An imprint of Thomson Gale, a part of The Thomson Corporation

THOMSON

GALE

Detroit • New York • San Francisco • New Haven, Conn. • Waterville, Maine • London • Munich

Encyclopedia of Business and Finance, Second Edition
Burton S. Kaliski, Editor in Chief

LIBRARY OF CONGRESS CATALOGING-IN-PUBLICATION DATA

Encyclopedia of business and finance / Burton S. Kaliski, editor-in-chief.— 2nd ed.
     p. cm.
     Includes bibliographical references and index.
     ISBN 0-02-866061-7 (set hardcover : alk. paper) — ISBN 0-02-866062-5 (volume 1 : alk. paper) — ISBN 0-02-866063-3 (volume 2 : alk. paper)
     1. Business—Encyclopedias. 2. Commerce—Encyclopedias. 3. Finance—Encyclopedias. 4. North America—Commerce—Encyclopedias. 5. Finance—North America—Encyclopedias. I. Kaliski, Burton S. II. Macmillan Reference USA.

     HF1001.E466 2007
     650.03—dc22   2006005185

This title is also available as an e-book.
ISBN 0-02-866081-1
Contact your Thomson Gale representative for ordering information.

Printed in the United States of America
10 9 8 7 6 5 4 3 2 1

J

JAPANESE MANAGEMENT METHODS

SEE *Management/Leadership Styles*

JOB ANALYSIS AND DESIGN

Job analysis is the term used to describe the process of analyzing a job or occupation into its various components, that is, organizational structure, work activities, and informational content. The process results in a relevant, timely and tailored database of job-related information that can be used in a variety of ways: to develop conventional, individualized, computer-based and/or critical incident education and training programs and materials; to create and classify job titles; to write job descriptions; to prepare organization charts; to conduct time and motion studies; to determine quality assurance standards; and to write both knowledge- and performance-related employee evaluation measures. Also, job analyses are basic to the preparation of such government publications as the *Occupational Information Network (O*Net), Standard Industrial Classification (SIC), Standard Occupational Classification (SOC), Occupational Outlook Handbook*, and other informational resources describing the job situation (See Figure 1).

Two terms often used interchangeably with job analysis are occupational analysis and task analysis. In the literature, job and occupational analysis most often are viewed as the same. The process focuses on the analysis of a job into its occupational structure, work activities, and informational content. Later, the data provided by the analysis guides the organization and development of the occupational training program.

In contrast, task analysis is an integral part of the job analysis process. More specifically, task analysis addresses the process of analyzing a particular task into its various elements, that is, performance steps; performance step details; technical information topics; career and occupational guidance information topics; standards of performance; frequency, importance, and complexity; and tools, equipment, materials, supplies and technical references. The information resulting from the task analysis provides a basis for developing the knowledge- and performance-based learning activities of the training program.

PROCESS

A number of individual authors and organizations have detailed the process of conducting job analyses (Blank, 1982; Bortz, 1981; Finch and Crunkilton, 1999; Fryklund, 1965; Mager and Beach, 1967; Norton, 1997; U.S. Department of the Air Force, 1998–99; U.S. Department of the Army 1990; U.S. Department of Labor, 1998). The analytical approaches of the various authors and groups differ somewhat in organization and procedural logic. Nonetheless, each analyzes a job or occupation with the intent of identifying its components and incorporating the findings into the development of related "products," that is, training programs and materials, job descriptions, job classifications, and so forth.

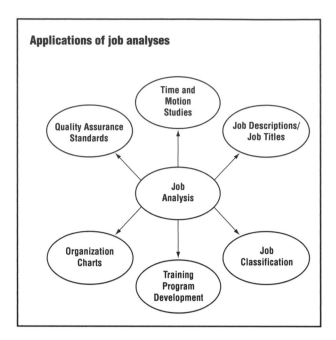

Applications of job analyses

- Time and Motion Studies
- Quality Assurance Standards
- Job Descriptions/ Job Titles
- Job Analysis
- Organization Charts
- Training Program Development
- Job Classification

Figure 1

Three questions seem to be basic to the majority of the authors. These questions address the issues of organization, activity, and informational content:

- What is the *structure* of the occupation?
- What does the worker *do*?
- What does the worker *need to know*?

ORGANIZATIONAL STRUCTURE

The first question concerns the structure or framework of the occupation being analyzed (Bortz, 1981). If the data derived from the job analysis are used in a situation where organizational structure is important to the product being developed, then the structure of the occupation can serve as a basis from which the organizational structure of the product is developed. For example, the hierarchical order of occupational titles in a functionally related family of occupations can serve as a basis for ordering and naming the units and courses of the training program resulting from the job analysis.

WORK ACTIVITIES

The second question addresses the activities of the worker in terms of both tasks and performance steps. Once identified, the tasks, or completed units of work, serve in various capacities ranging from the writing of learning objectives of a yet-to-be-developed competency-based training program to the classification of job titles and writing of job descriptions.

The performance steps for completing each task also will be used in the development of a variety of related materials. Whenever procedure is an issue, the performance steps of the tasks come into play. To use an example from the training of employees in psychomotor skills, the sequence of performance steps guides the instructor through a demonstration of the steps of the learning objective, to the student's practice of the procedural steps, to a final determination of the student's ability to perform the process on a performance test. In each of the three performance-related learning activities, procedure is fundamental to identification and development.

INFORMATION CONTENT

The third question involves identifying the knowledge or informational component of the occupation. Depending on the author, the three types of information most often referred to are technical information, general information, and career and occupational guidance information.

Technical information is that information the worker must know to perform a specific task or group of tasks. Technical information gives the worker the judgment-forming, decision-making ability to perform the task(s) in a safe and correct manner. It is the knowledge base from which the worker can make informed decisions affecting and controlling his/her on-the-job performance.

General information, although related to the job itself or to the individual tasks that comprise the job, does not have direct bearing on the performance of either the job or its component tasks. General information complements the activities of the workers but is not crucial to their outcome. For example, detailed knowledge about the manufacture of computer chips has no direct bearing on the performance of a computer programmer or systems analyst.

Career and occupational guidance information allows workers to make decisions about themselves and the workplace. It includes information on such topics as the short-, intermediate-, and long-range employment needs of the community; the career interests and abilities of individuals; work, work roles and responsibilities; job-seeking skills; the employment outlook; and local, state, national, and global economic trends.

APPLICATION

Each of the following are specific applications of the information gained from a completed job analysis. In some cases, most or all of the information is used in the development of the final product, in other cases, only a portion of the job analysis data is used. (See Figure 1.)

Training Program Development. The organizational structure, work activities, and informational content identified in a job analysis serve as the basis for developing both the structure and content of a training program. The structure of the occupation determines the organization of the curricular components of the training program. The content of the training program depends on the activities and information needed to perform in the occupation. In a competency-based training program, the titles of the tasks become the titles of the corresponding learning objectives. The technical information topics and performance steps of the tasks, respectively, serve as the basis for identifying and organizing the knowledge- and performance-related learning activities of the learning objectives.

Critical incident training is the result of applying the activities and content of a job analysis in a specific training situation. As discussed by Davies (1981), the critical incident method of instruction "focuses upon collecting information on key tasks, particularly on those where problems occur" (p. 131). For these tasks, special training can be devised using the activities and informational content first identified in the job analysis and later, translated into learning objectives, curricula and instructional materials.

Job Classification. A job classification is used to group occupations by function level or ability. To classify jobs by function means to categorize them by similarity of function or activity. For example, titles such as marketing, accounting, production, management, and human resources development imply that all people working in the one of these defined areas are performing a similar type of activity. Functional job classifications are regularly used in organizational development and in the preparation of organization charts.

In contrast, to classify occupations by ability level involves using terms that designate amount of on-the-job experience, skill level, and types of education and training. Terms such as apprentice, journeyman, master, entry-level, technician, and specialist all reflect a classification of jobs by ability level. The classification of employees by ability levels also guides organizational management in establishing the wage and salary schedules of employees.

Job Descriptions/Job Titles. A job description is a narrative statement defining a job, that is, what the employer expects of the employee in terms of on-the-job performance. As stated by Winning (1996), "A job description [or position description] is a list of responsibilities and functions … required in a particular position" (p. 1). A job description categorizes and defines the activities of a worker in more general terms then those used in a job analysis. The description is intended to provide a profile of the job rather than describe the occupation in the detail found in most job analyses. The entries in a well-written job description are introduced by a descriptive verb and closed by a noun defining the activity, for example, "maintains bank records."

Complementing the job description is the job title. Job titles are general in nature, in that they reflect all the activities contained in a job description. In one sense, a job title is more an extension of the job description than of a completed job analysis.

Organization Charts. Organization charts visually depict the line/staff relationships and responsibilities of departments/units and individuals working in an organization. The information gleaned from a job description, together with that found in the accompanying job classification, serves as the basis for determining the final configuration and content of a completed organization chart.

Time and Motion Studies. Time and motion studies address the issues of industrial production and efficiency, since they attempt to measure time on task, product quality, and worker safety. These studies are conducted in the workplace under normal working conditions. A completed job analysis provides the researcher with the necessary list of tasks and performance steps, that is, work activities performed by employees in the completion of their jobs. The focus of a time and motion study is to eliminate wasted motion and determine the most efficient way of performing a particular task.

Quality Assurance Standards. As defined by Peach (1997), "Quality assurance includes all the planned and systematic activities implemented within the quality system" (p. 38). A job description provides the quality assurance professional with the list of tasks performed in a particular job and the performance steps (procedures) required to perform each of the tasks. Also, in a comprehensive job analysis, standards of performance for both the tasks and performance steps are included. The two sets of criteria assist in determining the quality outcomes of both the task (product) and procedural steps (process).

The same two sets of quality standards are also applicable in the education and training of people for the workplace. Again, the content of the completed job analysis would provide instructors with the standards used in preparing students for employment.

SEE ALSO *Job Enrichment*

BIBLIOGRAPHY

Blank, William E. (1982). *Handbook for Developing Competency-Based Training Programs.* Englewood Cliffs, NJ: Prentice-Hall.

Bortz, Richard F. (1981). *Handbook for Developing Occupational Curricula.* Boston: Allyn & Bacon.

Davies, Ivor K. (1981). *Instructional Technique.* New York: McGraw-Hill.

Finch, Curtis R., and Crunkilton, John R. (1999). *Curriculum Development in Vocational and Technical Education.* Boston: Allyn & Bacon.

Fryklund, Verne C. (1965). *Analysis Technique for Instructors.* Milwaukee, WI: Bruce.

Mager, Robert F., and Beach, Kenneth M., Jr. (1967). *Developing Vocational Instruction.* Palo Alto, CA: Fearon.

Norton, Robert E. (1997). *DACUM Handbook.* Columbus: Ohio State University Press.

Peach, Robert W., ed. (1997). *The ISO9000 Handbook* (3rd ed.). Chicago: Irwin Professional Pub.

U.S. Department of the Air Force, Air Force Officer Accession and Training School (1998–99). *Curriculum Catalog.* Alabama: Maxwell Air Force Base.

U.S. Department of the Army, Combined Arms Center and Fort Leavenworth (1990). *Training the Force—Battle Focused Training FM 25-101.* Kansas: Fort Leavenworth.

U.S. Department of Labor. (1998). *O*NET—The Occupational Information Network.* Retrieved October 26, 2005, from http://www.bls.gov/oco/home.htm

U.S. Department of Labor, Bureau of Labor Statistics (1998–99). *Occupational Outlook Handbook.* Washington, DC: U.S. Government Printing Office.

U.S. Department of Labor, Employment and Training Administration O*NET 98 (1998). *Keeping Pace with Today's Changing Workplace* [CD-ROM].

U.S. Department of Labor, Bureau of Labor Statistics (2000). *Standard Occupational Classification Manual.* Washington, DC: U.S. Government Printing Office.

Winning, Ethan A. (1996). "The Many Uses of the Job Description." Retrieved October 26, 2005, from http://www.all-biz.com/articles/jd.htm

Richard F. Bortz

JOB ENRICHMENT

Job enrichment is a way to motivate employees by giving them increased responsibility and variety in their jobs. Many employers traditionally believed that money was the only true motivating factor for employees and that if you wanted to get more work out of employees, offering them more money was the only way to do it. While that may be true for a small group of people, the majority of workers today like to work and to be appreciated for the work they do. Job enrichment, which allows the employ-ees to have more control in planning their work and deciding how the work should be accomplished, is one way to tap into the natural desire most employees have to do a good job, to be appreciated for their contributions to the company, and to feel more a part of the company team.

Job enrichment has its roots in Frederick Herzberg's two-factor theory, according to which two separate dimensions contribute to an employee's behavior at work. The first dimension, known as hygiene factors, involves the presence or absence of job dissatisfacters, such as wages, working environment, rules and regulations, and supervisors. When these factors are poor, work is dissatisfying and employees are not motivated. However, having positive hygiene factors does not cause employees to be motivated; it simply keeps them from being dissatisfied. The second dimension of Herzberg's theory refers to motivators, which are factors that satisfy higher-level needs such as recognition for doing a good job, achievement, and the opportunity for growth and responsibility. These motivators are what actually increase job satisfaction and performance. Job enrichment becomes an important strategy at this point because enriching employees' jobs can help meet some of their motivational needs. There are basically five areas that are believed to affect an individual employee's motivation and job performance: skill variety, task identity, task significance, autonomy, and feedback. Job enrichment seeks to find positive ways to address each of these areas and therefore improve employee motivation and personal satisfaction.

Skill variety involves the number of different types of skills that are used to do a job. This area is important because using only one skill to do the same task repeatedly can be quite boring, typically causing the employee's productivity to decrease after a period of time. However, using a variety of skills in a job will tend to keep the employee more interested in the job and more motivated.

One way businesses are focusing on this area is through job rotation, that is, moving employees from job to job within the company, thereby allowing employees a variety of tasks in their work and helping prevent boredom. While this process can be costly to the company because employees must be trained in several different areas, the cost tends to be balanced by the increase in morale and productivity. Job rotation also gives each employee the opportunity to see how the different jobs of a company fit together and gives the company more flexibility in covering tasks when workers are absent. However, while job rotation is a good way to enrich employees' jobs, it can also hinder performance: Having to know several different jobs in order to rotate can prevent employees from becoming proficient at any of the jobs. Therefore, the advantages and disadvantages of job rotation as an enrichment strategy have to be carefully weighed.

Task identity is a matter of realizing a visible outcome from performing a task. Being able to see the end result of the work they do is an important motivator for employees. One way to make task identity clearer is through job enlargement, which means adding more tasks and responsibilities to an existing job. For example, instead of building just one component part of a humidifier, a team of employees builds the entire product from start to finish. When using job enlargement as an enrichment strategy, it is important that enlarging the job gives the employee more responsibility and more variety, not just more work.

Task significance involves how important the task is to others in the company, which is important in showing employees how the work they do fits in with that done in the rest of the organization. If employees can see how their work affects others, it will be a motivator to do the best job they can.

Many companies take new employees on a tour of the company and provide training sessions on how each part of the company works together with the other parts. In order to accept and handle responsibility, it is important that employees know how the various areas of the company work together; without this knowledge, it is very difficult for them to handle decision-making responsibilities. Putting employees from different areas of the company into planning teams can also help them see the significance of the tasks they perform.

Autonomy involves the degree of freedom, independence, and decision-making ability the employee has in completing assigned tasks. Most people like to be given responsibility; it demonstrates trust and helps motivate employees to live up to that trust. Responsibility can also help speed up work processes by enabling the employee to make decisions without having to wait for management approval. Autonomy is a very important part of job enrichment because it gives the employee power and a feeling of importance.

A type of job enrichment that restructures work to best match the employee to the job is job redesign. Job redesign can focus on combining existing jobs, forming work groups, and/or allowing closer contact between employees and individual suppliers or customers. The idea behind job redesign is to match employees with a job they like and are best qualified to perform. Self-managed teams are a type of job design whereby employees are grouped into teams and given certain guidelines to follow as well as goals to accomplish and are then left alone to accomplish those goals. Self-managed teams demonstrate the company's faith in the employees and give employees a feeling of power and pride in the work they accomplish.

Feedback describes how much and what type of information about job performance is received by the employee. It is one of the most important areas for motivation. Without feedback, employees have no way of knowing whether they are doing things correctly or incorrectly. Positive feedback helps to motivate employees by recognizing the efforts they have put into their work. While monetary rewards for doing a good job can be a strong incentive, sometimes saying "you did a really good job on that project" can mean just as much. Corrective feedback is also important because it lets employees know what areas need improvement.

There are many different types of job-enrichment activities and programs that companies can implement to encourage worker participation and enhance motivation. The team atmosphere is one way to enrich jobs. Grouping employees into teams and allowing the team the freedom to plan, make decisions, and accomplish their goals gives employees a feeling of importance and responsibility. It can also help employees come up with creative ideas on ways to improve work activities by giving them the opportunity to work closely with others. Asking for and encouraging employees to give input on company strategies and plans is another way to enrich jobs. Often employees have the best input because they are the ones actually performing the activity on a daily basis. Holding company award ceremonies can also help to enrich jobs and motivate employees by recognizing individual employees for their contributions to the company.

The purpose of job enrichment is to improve the quality of an employee's job and therefore motivate the employee to accomplish more. However, in order for job enrichment to work, the employee has to desire and accept new ways of accomplishing tasks. Some employees lack the skills and knowledge required to perform enriched jobs, while others are quite happy doing routine jobs because they feel the current work situation is relatively stress-free. It is likely that these types of employees would not like job-enrichment activities and would not accept the new way of doing things. Therefore, asking for employee input and keeping communication lines open is essential to the success of job-enrichment programs.

SEE ALSO *Job Satisfaction; Management*

BIBLIOGRAPHY

Boone, Louis E., and Kurtz, David L. (2006). *Contemporary Business*. Mason, OH: Thomson/South-Western.

Bounds, Gregory M., and Lamb, Charles W., Jr. (1998). *Business*. Cincinnati, OH: South-Western College Publishing.

Fletcher, Jerry L. (1993). *Patterns of High Performance: Discovering the Way People Work Best*. San Francisco: Berrett-Koehler.

French, Wendell L. (2003). *Human Resources Management*. Boston: Houghton Mifflin.

Kolberg, William H., and Smith, Foster C. (1992). *Rebuilding America's Workforce*. Homewood, IL: Business One Irwin.

Madura, Jeff (2004). *Introduction to Business*. Belmont, CA: Thomson/South-Western.

Nickels, William G., McHugh, James M., and McHugh, Susan M. (2005). *Understanding Business* (7th ed.). Boston: McGraw-Hill/Irwin.

Pride, William M., Hughes, Robert J., and Kapoor, Jack R. (2002). *Business* (7th ed.). New York: Houghton Mifflin.

Rosenbaum, Bernard L. (1982). *How to Motivate Today's Workers*. New York: McGraw-Hill.

Marcy Satterwhite

JOB SATISFACTION

Job satisfaction is a worker's sense of achievement and success on the job. It is generally perceived to be directly linked to productivity as well as to personal well-being. Job satisfaction implies doing a job one enjoys, doing it well, and being rewarded for one's efforts. Job satisfaction further implies enthusiasm and happiness with one's work. Job satisfaction is the key ingredient that leads to recognition, income, promotion, and the achievement of other goals that lead to a feeling of fulfillment.

WHAT WORKERS NEED IN JOB SATISFACTION

Major specifics of what workers need in job satisfaction include self-esteem and identity. A significant portion of job satisfaction often comes just from the sheer fact of being employed. If work creates positive features about being employed, unemployment almost invariably lowers self-worth. Genuine job satisfaction comes from a feeling of security whereby one's performance is judged objectively by the quality of work performance rather than artificial criteria such as being related to highly placed executives or to relatives in the firm. Yet at the same time, monotonous jobs can almost shatter a worker's initiative and enthusiasm. Employees have definite needs that they feel are essential to activate as they spend their working hours and years expending their efforts on behalf of their employers.

IMPORTANCE TO BOTH WORKER AND ORGANIZATION

For the organization, high levels of job satisfaction of its workers strongly suggest a workforce that is motivated and committed to high-quality performance. Increased productivity—quantity and quality of output per hour worked—would seem to be almost an automatic by-product of improved quality of workmanship. It is important to note, however, that the literature on the relationship between job satisfaction and productivity is neither conclusive nor consistent. Studies dating back to Frederick Herzberg's (1957) have shown surprisingly only a low correlation between high morale and high productivity. But this is contrary to easily formed logic that satisfied workers tend to add more value to an organization.

Unhappy employees, motivated by fear of job loss, will give 100 percent of their effort for a while, but not for very long. Though fear is a powerful motivator, it is also a temporary one. As soon the threat is lifted, the performance declines.

Tangible ways in which job satisfaction benefits the organization include reduction in complaints and grievances, absenteeism, turnover, and termination, as well as improved punctuality and worker morale. Job satisfaction also appears to be linked to a healthier workforce and has been found to be quite a good indicator of longevity. Although only low correlation has been found between job satisfaction and productivity, some employers have found that satisfying or "delighting" employees is a prerequisite to satisfying or delighting customers, thus protecting the "bottom line." No wonder Andrew Carnegie is quoted as saying: "Take away my people and soon grass will grow on the factory floors. Take away my factories, but leave my people, and soon we will have a new and better factory" (quoted in Brown, 1996, p. 123). Job satisfaction and occupational success can result not only in job satisfaction but also in complete personal satisfaction.

PROMOTING JOB SATISFACTION

Job satisfaction does not come automatically to business organizations. In a broad sense, the job satisfaction program needs to exist and should have activities carefully designed to achieve the intended job satisfaction goals. It must be an action program. And it should be carefully monitored to ensure that changes are periodically made as needed.

Most large organizations now include human resource departments within their management structure. At one time human resource departments were limited to handling the acquisition of new workers. Today, however, many human resource programs take the worthwhile initiative of helping to develop complete programs of personnel practices, such as conducting research on current wage structures.

Most human resource departments learn about employees through interviews, administration of insurance policies, study of legislation that deals with workers, and participation in decisions that affect employees' jobs. These activities must be carefully designed to concentrate in a positive manner on job satisfaction so that employees feel that all the personnel activity is for their benefit.

A primary reason for the emergence of labor unions during the early 1920s was to develop safety measures for working conditions and equipment. Throughout the years labor unions appear to have played an uncertain role in achieving job satisfaction. In some cases, employees join labor unions primarily because they are the only organizations that bring health insurance benefits and increased legal benefits. Sometimes union members get better vacation and retirement benefits than do nonunion members.

ADDITIONAL FACTORS RELATING TO JOB SATISFACTION

When considering job satisfaction, probably the most important point to bear in mind is that many factors that affect it. What makes workers happy with their jobs varies from worker to worker and from day to day. Apart from the factors previously mentioned, job satisfaction is influenced by the employee's personal characteristics, the manager's personal characteristics and management style, and the nature of the work itself. Managers who want to maintain high levels of satisfaction in the workforce must understand the needs of each member of the workforce.

JOB ENRICHMENT

Managers who are serious about the job satisfaction of workers can also take other deliberate steps in increasing a stimulating work environment. One such step is job enrichment, a deliberate grading of responsibility, scope, and challenge in the work itself. Job enrichment usually includes increased responsibility, recognition, and more opportunities for growth, learning, and achievement. Large companies that have used job enrichment include IBM and DaimlerChrysler.

STEPS TO ACHIEVING JOB SATISFACTION

What are the elements of jobs that increase job satisfaction? Organizations can help to increase job satisfaction by putting systems in place that will ensure that workers are being rewarded for being successful. Arthur P. Brief wrote: "If a person's work is interesting, the pay is fair, the promotional opportunities, and the supervisor is support-ive, and the coworkers are friendly, then employees will be satisfied" (1999).

The following list of suggestions may contribute to job satisfaction:

- Flexible work arrangements, possibly including telecommuting

- Training and other professional growth opportunities

- Interesting work that offers variety and challenge and allows the workers to put their "signature" on the finished product

- Opportunities to use one's talents and to be creative

- Opportunities to take responsibilities and direct one's own work

- A stable, secure work environment that includes job security and continuity

- An environment in which workers are supported by an accessible supervisor who provides timely feedback as well as congenial team members

- Flexible benefits, such as child-care and exercise facilities

- Up-to-date technology

- Quality health insurance

If the pleasures associated with one's job outweigh the pains, there is some level of job satisfaction.

SEE ALSO *Management/Leadership Styles; Motivation*

BIBLIOGRAPHY

Brief, Arthur P. (1999). *Attitudes in and around organizations.* Thousand Oaks, CA: Sage.

Brown, Mark G. (1996). *Keeping score: Using the right metrics to drive world-class performance.* New York: Quality Resources.

Daft, Richard L. (2005). *Management* (7th ed.). Mason, OH: Thomson South-Western.

Herzberg, Frederick, Mausner, B., Peterson, R. O., et al. (1957). *Job attitudes: Review of research and opinion.* Pittsburgh: Psychological Service of Pittsburgh.

Sirota, D., Mischkind, L. A., & Meltzer, M. I. (2005). *The enthusiastic employee: how companies profit by giving workers what they want.* Indianapolis, IN: Wharton School Pub.

G. W. Maxwell

L

LABELING

SEE *Packaging*

LABOR

SEE *Factors of Production*

LABOR UNIONS

A labor union has been defined as "a group of workers who have banded together to achieve common goals in the key areas of wages, hours, and working conditions" (Boone and Kurtz, 2005). Originally, labor unions were primarily made up of male, blue-collar workers, but as the economy of the United States evolved from production industries to service industries, union membership has seen a dramatic increase in white-collar and female workers.

HISTORY AND EVOLUTION

Labor unions began to evolve in the United States in the 1700s and 1800s because of the need for safety and security for workers. Workers formed labor unions in response to intolerable working conditions, low wages, and long hours. In the wake of the Industrial Revolution, men, women, and even children worked in unsafe factories from dawn to dark every day of the week for only pennies a day. These oppressive conditions forced workers to look for ways to improve their situation. They gradually learned that by banding together and bargaining as a group, they could pressure employers to respond to their demands.

The progression of the Industrial Revolution and the formation of labor unions go hand in hand. The Industrial Revolution brought about specialization of employees in the workplace and a dramatic increase in production. This factory system, which developed in the nineteenth and early twentieth centuries, brought to workers both prosperity (steady employment in good economic times) and hardship (bad working conditions and unemployment) during depressions. Thus, the Industrial Revolution changed the American class structure, turning skilled tradesmen into the working class, who found it very difficult to escape factory life.

As more and more workers united to improve their situation, two types of labor unions emerged. Craft unions were made up of workers who were skilled in a specific trade. Many craft unions were organized in the 1790s, such as the Philadelphia shoemakers in 1792, the Boston carpenters in 1793, and the New York printers in 1794.

Beginning in 1827, laborers who worked in the same industry, regardless of their specific job, formed industrial unions, such as the United Steel Workers and the Teamsters. The 1837 depression nearly wiped out these unions, but they were reborn shortly before the Civil War (1861–1865) and became strong enough to survive recessions.

Five major labor organizations emerged between 1866 and 1936. The National Labor Union was organized in 1866. Though it became a political party and collapsed within six years, it did successfully bring together into a

Officials from the National Labor Relations Board watch as workers at the Jones and Laughlin steel mill vote whether the Steel Workers Organizing Committee will be their sole bargaining agency May 20, 1937. © **BETTMANN/CORBIS**

national federation both craft unions and reform groups. The Noble Order of the Knights of Labor, founded in 1869, sought to unite all workers, both skilled and unskilled. In 1886, when its membership had reached more than 700,000, it split into two groups. The revolutionary socialist group wanted the government to take over production; the traditional group wanted to remain focused on the economic well-being of its members.

This second group merged with a group of individual craft unions in 1886 to become the American Federation of Labor (AFL). This was the beginning of modern union structure. The AFL's first president, Samuel Gompers (1850–1924), kept the improvement of wages, hours, and working conditions as the objectives of the union. AFL membership grew rapidly until the 1920s, when there were few skilled craftworkers yet to be organized. By that time, three-fourths of the organized workers in the United States were members of the AFL.

In 1905 an organization called the Industrial Workers of the World was established. Though it was short-lived, this union introduced the sit-down strike and mass picketing. In the early 1920s, workers in the steel, aluminum, auto, and rubber industries formed many individual industrial unions (groups of employees working in the same industry, yet not using the same skills). These unions did not agree with the craft union concept (grouping workers with the same specific skill), which was the organizational structure of the AFL. Therefore, in 1936 they split with the AFL and became a new group of affiliated unions called the Congress of Industrial Organizations (CIO). Organizing complete industries instead of individual crafts proved a successful way to deal with mass-production industries, and the CIO's membership soon grew to nearly that of the AFL.

GROWTH

Even with so much union organization activity going on, there were fewer than 1 million union members in the United States in 1900. Membership in labor unions grew slowly from 1920 to 1935, but the modern labor movement was born in the decade between 1933 and 1944. The combination of New Deal labor legislation, competition between the AFL and the CIO, and World War II (1939–1945) quadrupled union membership, which by 1937 was more than 5 million. Union membership continued to increase from 1943 through 1956, reaching more than 15 million in 1950. One-fourth of the labor force were union members at that time, when the government officially sanctioned unions.

In 1955 the AFL and CIO settled their differences and merged into one extremely large labor organization. All the major national unions in the United States today except the National Education Association are affiliated with the AFL-CIO.

Union membership declined from 1956 to 1961, when white-collar workers outnumbered blue-collar workers for the first time, women were entering the workforce in large numbers, and the economy was changing from a production to a service industry orientation. In 1961 growth resumed; from 1964 to 1974, especially during the time of the Vietnam War, unions gained 4 million members, largely public-sector employees and professionals.

DECLINE

The percentage of U.S. workers who are union members has fallen since the 1980s. This decline is largely due to the decrease in the number of blue-collar jobs, labor legislation protecting workers, better employee-management relationships, and the shift from a manufacturing to a service economy (bringing into the workforce more women and young people, who are not easily organized). During the 1990s and the early years of the twenty-first century, despite the decline in the percent of workers who were unionized, nearly 16 million U.S. workers, between one-eighth and one-sixth of the labor force, belonged to labor unions.

ORGANIZATION

Labor unions are organized on several different levels. Local unions represent members in a specific geographic area, such as a city, state, or region. These local unions make up the base of a national union, which unites all its affiliated local unions under one constitution. The Teamsters and the United Steel Workers of America are two examples of large national unions, each uniting many local unions. The decision-making process of national unions is decentralized, which allows decisions to be made at the local level, by those best qualified to make them. Thus, the national union recognizes the autonomy of each local union yet unites them under one set of rules and grants each local union its charter.

Some unions have an international level. These international unions have members both inside and outside the United States, such as in Canada. Their organization is similar to national unions, with local unions being the base of the union structure. The primary emphasis of national unions is economic. Their main function is collective bargaining, though much of the negotiation process occurs at the local union level. Bargaining labor-management contracts, which deal with wages, hours, and working conditions, and settling labor-management disputes are the primary roles of the local and national union leadership.

The top level of labor union organization is the federation, such as the AFL-CIO. Such a federation is made up of many national and/or international unions. The purpose of the federation level is to coordinate its affiliated unions, settle disputes between them, and serve as the political representative of the union members.

MEMBERSHIP POLICIES

Various employment policies have been used in business and industry to determine union membership. The closed-shop policy, which was outlawed by the Taft-Hartley Act in 1947, forced workers to join the union in order to be hired at a company and to remain a union member in order to continue employment. The union-shop policy requires all current employees of a company to join the union when it is certified as their bargaining agent (voted in by the majority of the workers). New employees must also join the union under the union-shop policy. The Taft-Hartley Act, however, allows individual states to outlaw the union-shop policy. Most union contracts negotiated in the 1990s operated under the union-shop policy.

The agency-shop policy allows both union and nonunion workers to be employed by an organization, but the nonunion employees must pay a union fee equal to union dues. This policy requires nonunion workers to pay their "fair share" of the expenses of the union's representing them in negotiations, but none of the cost of the union's political activities. The open-shop policy allows voluntary union membership or nonmembership for all workers. It does not require nonunion workers to pay any union dues or fees.

LABOR LEGISLATION

Both labor unions and management have been affected by federal legislation since 1932, when the Norris-LaGuardia Act was passed. This law protects union activities such as strikes and picketing by making it difficult for management to obtain injunctions against them. In 1935 the Wagner Act (also known as the National Labor Relations Act) made collective bargaining legal and forced employers to negotiate with union officials. The National Labor Relations Board was established by this act. The board oversees union elections and guards against unfair labor practices.

The Fair Labor Standards Act of 1938 set a maximum of forty hours for a basic workweek, outlawed child labor, and set a minimum wage. The Taft-Hartley Act limited the power of unions by prohibiting unions from such activities as coercing employees to join unions, charging excessive fees, refusing to bargain collectively with an employer, and using union dues for political contributions. The Taft-Hartley Act was amended in 1959 by the Landrum-Griffin Act, which requires a union to have a constitution and bylaws, secret-ballot elections of officers, and a financial reporting procedure. Management procedures are also regulated by legislation, such as the Plant-Closing Notification Act of 1988, which requires employers to give workers a sixty-day warning of mass layoffs or plant closings.

OUTLOOK

Labor unions were born out of necessity, to protect the health and well-being of American workers. Through the years, they have provided a unified voice for workers and obtained fair treatment of them in the workplace. During the twentieth century, however, laws were passed that guarantee employees many of the rights that once had to

be negotiated in labor-management contracts. An increase in employee-management teamwork and communication has also reduced the need for workers to be represented by labor unions. Thus, labor unions no longer play the vital role they once did in American labor-management relations.

SEE ALSO *Collective Bargaining; Negotiation*

BIBLIOGRAPHY

Boone, Louis E., and Kurtz, David L. (2005). *Contemporary business* (11th ed.). Mason, OH: Thomson South-Western.

Chaison, Gary N. (2006). *Unions in America*. Thousand Oaks, CA: Sage.

Estey, Marten (1981). *The unions: Structure, development, and management* (3rd ed.). New York: Harcourt Brace Jovanovich.

Masters, Marick F. (1997). *Unions at the crossroads*. Westport, CT: Quorum.

Wray, Ralph D., Luft, Robert L., and Highland, Patrick J. (1996). *Fundamentals of human relations*. Cincinnati: South-Western.

G. W. Maxwell

LAND

SEE *Factors of Production*

LAW IN BUSINESS

Law governs and regulates virtually all aspects of the business process, from the right to engage in a business or trade, to the legal form of a business, to agreements for buying and selling merchandise or rendering services. Law regulates the quality of products sold and the advertising of products for sale. Law governs the employment relationship, protects business property, and taxes business income. This article explores the relationship of business and law in several of these areas.

BUSINESS LAW AND LAWYERS

Business in the United States is regulated by federal and state laws as well as by local ordinances. State law regulating forms of business, business agreements, and some taxes is the most important. Federal law regulates such things as advertising, civil rights, and protection of such property as inventions. Local law typically regulates business hours, where one can do business (zoning), and health and safety.

To qualify as a lawyer, a person must usually earn both a college degree and a three-year law degree and then pass a rigorous examination (the bar exam). Lawyers are normally certified in one or possibly two states. Thus lawyers certified in Massachusetts would not be qualified to answer a question about law in Texas or even a question about local law in a distant city within their own state. The rules and ethics of law practice are governed by the supreme court of each state.

Most lawyers do not have degrees in business. Their expertise is law, not business. All businesses need lawyers from time to time, but it is important for the businessperson to know as much as possible about the law to better weigh the legal advice and the needs of business.

FORMS OF BUSINESS

There are three basic legal forms of business: proprietorship, partnership, and corporation.

Proprietorship. Many businesses begin with an idea worked out at the kitchen table, in a garage workshop, or today, on the computer. There are no legal impediments to or requirements for starting most businesses. One needs only an idea, perhaps inventory, and customers. When one simply starts a business with nothing more, it is called a sole proprietorship. For some business, licenses are necessary. Plumbers, beauticians, and, of course, lawyers and physicians must be licensed by the state. Carpenters, psychologists, tax advisers, and bookkeepers, while they often have professional qualifications, do not need to be legally certified or licensed.

The sole proprietor is responsible for all the debts of the business and in turn receives, after taxes, all of the profits. The sole proprietor may hire employees. A sole proprietorship tends to have no more than up to twelve to fifteen employees. If the number of employees increases beyond this, the business normally evolves into another form.

Partnership. The Uniform Partnership Act, recognized by more than forty states, states that "a partnership is an association of two or more persons to carry on as coowners a business for profit" (UPA 6[11]). A number of factors differentiate this form of business from a sole proprietorship. More than one person is involved, and they are co-owners of the business. A partnership, like a sole proprietorship, may employ workers who are not owners.

Business may be defined as "every trade, occupation, or profession." A partnership may be made up of members of any occupation. The goal of the partnership is profit; therefore, an organization of persons whose purpose is to encourage recycling or advocate a political cause is not a partnership.

A partnership can be created very easily. If Sam and Mike are mechanics and put on a sign "Sam and Mike's Garage—Open for Business," they have formed a partnership under the law. Any income or losses are split half and half in the absence of an agreement that says otherwise. Normally a partnership is created by written document with the help of a lawyer. Suppose Jill and Joan wanted to start a sporting-goods store. Suppose Jill could work only half time but could contribute $50,000 to start the business, while Joan had no money but knew the business and could work full time. With the help of a lawyer, they might agree as follows: The business would operate month to month. If there was income, Joan would draw the first $1,500 as salary. Then Jill would draw $750 as salary. Additional income would pay Jill 6 percent per year on the $50,000 she contributed. Finally, any additional income, if available, would be split evenly between the partners.

If Sam and Mike call their business "Quality Mechanics" or Jill and Joan call their business "Sports Unlimited," the names must be registered with the state and may not be the same as a name previously registered. The purpose of registration is to let the public know Quality Mechanics really means Sam and Mike.

A partnership is easy to create, but its drawback is liability. Suppose Joan buys a large inventory that will not sell. Each partner is fully responsible for company debts. It may cost them their life savings. Accounting or law partnerships may have hundreds of partners. The limited liability partnership and the limited liability company, now recognized in all states, provides the simplicity of partnership and protection from wrongful or negligent acts of other partners. Any business may be called a company. A corporation, which also provides protection from personal liability, is different.

Corporations. A corporation is the form of most large businesses and increasingly small ones. The corporate name is registered with the state and must include the words *corporation, incorporated, limited,* or *professional corporation.* The latter is most commonly used for corporations rendering legal, medical, or other services. The owners or shareholders contribute money, property, or services for shares. If the shares are traded on an exchange the corporation is public. Shares in private—usually smaller—corporations are often held by a few individuals or a single person.

Shareholders elect a board of directors, which in turn appoints corporate officers who hire employees. After salaries and other expenses are paid, the profits may be distributed to the shareholders in the form of dividends or reinvested in the corporation to allow it to grow. The corporation insulates the owners from liability. If Jill and Joan's sporting-goods store was a corporation and declared bankruptcy, Jill and Joan would not have to pay any remaining debt from their own money.

Those wishing to start a business may consult with a lawyer to determine which legal form the business should take.

CONTRACT LAW

Contract law regulates the day-to-day business of buying and selling goods or performing services. A contract is defined in law as an agreement between two parties with an offer, acceptance, and consideration. Assume Jill and Joan have a corporation named Sports Unlimited, Inc. Ed comes in and decides to buy a tent priced at $225. He offers $225 to Sports Unlimited, which accepts the offer by ringing it up on the cash register. The consideration is what is exchanged; that is, $225 and the tent. When the store accepts the price, there is a binding contract. Suppose a sign clearly in Ed's view says "All returns must be made within thirty days with cash receipt." This sign becomes part of the agreement. If Ed brings the tent back twenty-nine days later, he can get his money back; if he brings it back thirty-one days later, it would be too late. Even though it is not stated by either party, if Ed used the tent on a camping trip, it would not be returnable. If, however, the tent leaked, it is not "fit for the purposes for which it was intended" and Ed could get his money back within a reasonable time.

Suppose Sam and Mike form the partnership Quality Mechanics and Mary comes in and says, "The brakes aren't right. Please fix them by 5 P.M." Mike says, "It will be done!" A contract now exists, even though many terms are missing. Sam and Mike have agreed to fix what is wrong with the brakes, and Mary has agreed to pay a reasonable price. The brakes may need a simple adjustment or a complete overhaul. If Sam and Mike see that additional work is necessary, it would be best to call Mary and extend the contract to include more work. Note that while writing can help avoid misunderstanding, oral contracts are valid for business services.

WARRANTIES AND PRODUCT LIABILITY

Warranties and guarantees may be implied or express. If nothing else is said, it is implied that a product is guaranteed to be fit for the purposes for which it is intended. A tent will not leak for a reasonable time and an article of clothing will stand up to reasonable wear and tear. Most products come with express warranties. Most common among express warranties are limited warranties, whereby the manufacturer guarantees all parts and workmanship for a period of one year. If the product breaks down or wears out after that, the customer is responsible, although extended warranties can be purchased on many products, such as cars and appliances. Occasionally products are clearly labeled "Sold as is. No warranty of any kind."

Product liability is a further step in consumer protection. Products must by law be free from hidden defects. A hidden defect may come from a poor design or poor manufacturing. If a hidden defect injures someone, the maker must pay damages. If manufacturers deliberately or recklessly put defective products on the market, they are liable for additional damages, called punitive damages. To protect themselves, makers warn buyers of possible dangers. Major issues have included the side effects of drugs and, in the auto industry, vehicles that roll over too easily or have gas tanks placed in dangerous positions.

EMPLOYMENT LAW

As a business grows, employees are normally hired, and the legal aspects can become very complicated. An agreement to employ is a contract of offer and acceptance. The consideration is an exchange of services for a wage or salary. In the United States, contracts of employment can be quite simple. Bob agrees to work for Sports Unlimited, Inc., for $500 a week. He agrees to work under the direction of Jill and Joan for a set number of hours. He, in the words of the law, is an employee at will. He may quit or be fired at any time. Sports Unlimited is not required to give a reason if it fires him. Bob may request a raise at any time and has no legal right to health benefits, pension, or even vacation.

The law does, however, require a number of things of employers. Sports Unlimited must pay Bob at least the hourly minimum wage. In addition Sports Unlimited must withhold income taxes and pay social security taxes for Bob. Sports Unlimited must also pay workers' compensation and unemployment insurance in case Bob is injured on the job or laid off. The law also makes a distinction between an employee and an independent contractor. If Sports Unlimited hires a painter to paint the building or a lawyer to draw up the corporation papers, the service is done by an independent contractor. Typically, a gardener who cuts the grass and trims the hedges is an independent contractor and is simply paid. A cleaning person working inside the house under the direction of the owner is an employee, and thus the law requires additional paperwork and taxes.

Federal law allows employees of larger companies to form unions and make a single employment contract. The process is known as collective bargaining. If employees wish, the National Labor Relations Board will conduct an election; if a majority of workers want a labor union, the employer must recognize the union. A typical contract spells out wages, benefits such as health insurance and vacation, rights to compete for promotions, and the circumstances in which employees may be laid off or fired. In the United States in 2005, unions represented only about 15 percent of employees.

CIVIL RIGHTS LAWS

It is well known that almost all workers are protected by the Civil Rights Act of 1964, the Equal Pay Act of 1963, and the Americans with Disabilities Act (ADA) of 1990. These acts apply to companies large and small, unionized or not. The law says that employees may not be discriminated against in terms of conditions of employment including hiring and promotion because of race, religion, creed, national origin, sex, and disability. In the not too distant past, many companies would not hire members of racial or religious minorities for positions of authority regardless of their ability. Women were discouraged from entering many trades, such as construction, or professions, such as law and medicine. State laws often forbid women from "dangerous" jobs such as mining although the jobs were no less dangerous for men. These civil rights acts have been very successful in expanding opportunity in America.

Affirmative action is not a federal law but an executive policy (ordered by the president) that requires companies that do business with the government, or institutions such as schools that receive federal funds, to work to increase numbers of workers (or students) from underrepresented classes. This can be tricky because companies are required to seek out and promote members of certain minority groups without discriminating against others. This is not an easy task, but it was part of American policy in 2005.

BFOQ stands for "bona fide occupational qualification" and represents an exception to civil rights laws. One may discriminate if there is a good reason to do so. Since people have a right to privacy, an attendant in a restroom can be required to be of the same sex. Models for a line of dresses can be exclusively young, slim females, and casting for a movie or play may discriminate on any basis. In a 1977 U.S. Supreme Court case, the Court held the state could require guards in a male maximum-security prison to be male. Some questions remain open. Could a Chinese restaurant wishing to create the atmosphere of China have only Chinese servers? That is an open question.

In the 1970s Congress added older workers to the list of protected classes. Legal protection is given only to persons over the age of forty. A company may refuse to hire a twenty-five-year-old as being "too young" or, in an actual case, a thirty-seven-year-old as being "too old" for a job. Persons with disabilities received protection from discrim-

ination in 1990 with the passage of the ADA. The ADA represents a strong national policy that opportunity to achieve to the limit of one's ability should extend to all.

All businesses need to know a few basics about civil rights law. In interviews, no question may be asked about a person's health history or physical or mental condition except "is there any reason physical or otherwise that would prevent you from doing this job?" Reasonable accommodation must be made for those with disabilities. A simple example would be that a desk would be built a little higher for an employee in a wheelchair. The extent of "reasonable" remains an open question. A person subject to occasional seizures would be qualified to work for Sports Unlimited, Inc., as a clerk but probably not for Quality Mechanics as a test driver.

A business must also make sure it is accessible to customers with disabilities. This includes both access to facilities and equal service as a customer. Many open questions remain. For example, to what extent must an Internet sales company provide access to those with vision or hearing impairments? All companies should consult lawyers or specialists on ADA compliance.

There are exceptions. Someone with a history of drug problems need not be hired as an airline pilot or railroad engineer. If drug or alcohol problems come to light, employees must be given reasonable treatment—but if they do not respond, they may be fired.

PROTECTION OF PROPERTY AND INTELLECTUAL PROPERTY

Local authorities, of course, provide police protection from theft of inventory and other company property by customers, employees, and outsiders. Yet, other properties that many businesses have are at least as valuable, and are also protected by law. Among them are business secrets, patents, copyrights, and trademarks/names.

Business Secrets. Businesses frequently keep secret information that is the heart of their business. Customer lists for an insurance company or a stockbroker are examples. State and federal law severely punish anyone who steals or makes use of such property. The most famous secret in the world might be the formula for Coca-Cola. If any person or company can duplicate Coca-Cola, they may produce and sell it under their own name. The law protects the secret from theft but not from duplication.

Patents. Patents are a protection given by the federal government for inventions. A patent gives the inventor the exclusive rights for seventeen years to use or license the invention. Anyone infringing on the patented product is subject to fine and imprisonment. A drug company's new pharmaceuticals enjoy patent protection, but when the patent expires, the drug becomes generic and anyone can make and sell it.

Copyrights. Copyrights give authors protection for their works for their lifetime plus seventy years. Works include literary works, musical compositions, and computer software. While there are exceptions, it is illegal to copy tapes, compact disks, or software. This is theft and is punishable by fines. It is important for business today to set high legal standards for employees for proper business use of copyrighted material.

Trademarks and Trade Names. Substantial growth has been made in the area of trademarks and trade names since the 1990s. Trademarks and trade names can be of enormous value, and businesses work hard to protect their property. Coca-Cola and Coke, both the names and the distinctive script, are among the best known of these. Names and logos are valuable property. Universities, for example, often make substantial money by licensing use of their name, logo, and other associated symbols on clothing and other items. Trademarks and trade names are registered with the federal government. Exclusive use of them lasts as long as they are used.

SEE ALSO *Careers in Law for Business; Ethics in Law for Business*

BIBLIOGRAPHY

Barnes, James A., Dworkin, T. M., Richards, E. L. (2006). *Law for business* (9th ed.). Boston: McGraw-Hill.

Charley, Robert N. (2006). *The legal and regulatory environment of business* (13th ed.). New York: McGraw-Hill.

Cheeseman, Henry R. (2006). *Contemporary business and online commerce law: Legal, Internet, ethical, and global environments* (5th ed.). Upper Saddle River, NJ: Pearson/Prentice Hall.

Jennings, Marianne M. (2006). *Business: Its legal, ethical, and global environment* (7th ed.). Mason, OH: Thomson West.

Mann, Richard A., and Roberts, Barry S. (2006). *Smith and Roberson's business law* (13th ed.) St. Paul, MN: West.

Carson H. Varner

LEADERSHIP

Leadership is a fascinating subject for many people. The term conjures up a familiar scene of a powerful, heroic, triumphant individual with a group of followers returning home after winning a national championship or a war against the evil enemy. They all march through town surrounded by a crowd waving flags. An enthusiastic orator may deliver an energetic speech, hands waving in the air, to thousands of people gathered in a plaza.

The widespread fascination with leadership may be because of the impact that leadership has on everyone's life. Stories of heroic leadership go back thousands of years: Moses delivering thousands of Hebrews from Egypt or Alexander the Great building a great empire. Why were certain leaders able to inspire and mobilize so many people, and how did they achieve what they achieved? There are so many questions that beg answers, but many remain as puzzling as ever. In recent decades, many researchers have undertaken a systematic and scientific study of leadership.

Leadership is defined in so many different ways that it is hard to come up with a single working definition. Leadership is not just a person or group of people in a high position. Understanding leadership is not complete without understanding interactions between a leader and his or her followers. Neither is leadership merely the ability or static capacity of a leader. The dynamic nature of the relationship between leader and followers must be researched. In these unique social dynamics, all the parties involved attempt to influence each other in the pursuit of goals. These goals may or may not coincide as participants actively engage in defining and redefining the goal for the group and for themselves.

Thus, leadership is a process in which a leader attempts to influence his or her followers to establish and accomplish a goal or goals. In order to accomplish the goal, the leader exercises his or her power to influence people. That power is exercised in earlier stages by motivating followers to get the job done and in later stages by rewarding or punishing those who do or do not perform to the level of expectation. Leadership is a continuous process, with the accomplishment of one goal becoming the beginning of a new goal. The proper reward by the leader is of utmost importance in order to continually motivate followers in the process.

What does leadership do for an organization? If leadership is defined as a process involving interactions between a leader and followers, usually subordinate employees of a company, leadership profoundly affects the company. It defines or approves the mission or goal of the organization. This goal setting is a dynamic process for which the leader is ultimately responsible. A strong visionary leader presents and convinces followers that a new course of action is needed for the survival and prosperity of the group in the future. Once a goal is set, the leader assumes the role of ensuring successful accomplishment of the goal. Another vital role of leadership is to represent the group/organization and link it to the external world in order to obtain vital resources to carry out its mission.

When necessary, leadership has to defend the organization's integrity.

CHARACTERISTICS OF SUCCESSFUL AND EFFECTIVE LEADERSHIP

What does it take to make leadership successful or effective? Early students of leadership examined great leaders throughout history, attempting to find traits that they shared. Among personality traits that they found were determination, emotional stability, diplomacy, self-confidence, personal integrity, originality, and creativity. Intellectual abilities included judgmental ability, knowledge, and verbal communication ability. In addition, physical traits cannot be ignored, such as age, height, weight, and physical attractiveness.

It is not only inborn personality traits that are important but also styles and behaviors that a person learns. Strong autocratic leaders set their goals without considering the opinions of their followers, then command their followers to execute their assigned tasks without question. Consultative leaders solicit the opinions and ideas of their followers in the goal-setting process but ultimately determine important goals and task assignments on their own. Democratic or participative leaders participate equally in the process with their followers and let the group make decisions. Extremely laid-back leaders, so called laissez-faire leaders, let the group take whatever action its members feel is necessary.

Inspired and led by Renis Likert, a research team at the University of Michigan studied leadership for several years and identified two distinct styles, which they referred to as job-centered and employee-centered leadership styles. The job-centered leader closely supervises subordinates to make sure they perform their tasks following the specified procedures. This type of leader relies on reward, punishment, and legitimate power to influence the behavior of followers. The employee-centered leader believes that creating a supportive work environment ultimately is the road to superior organizational performance. The employee-centered leader shows great concern about the employees' emotional well-being, personal growth and development, and achievement.

A leadership study group at The Ohio State University, headed by Harris Fleishman, found similar contrasts in leadership style, which they referred to as initiating structure and consideration. The leadership style of initiating structure is similar to the job-centered leadership style, whereas consideration is similar to the employee-centered leadership style. It was the initial expectation of both research groups that a leader who could demonstrate both high initiating structure (job-centered) and high consideration (employee-centered) would be successful and effective in all circumstances.

Many students of leadership in the twenty-first century believe that there is no one best way to lead, believing instead that appropriate leadership styles vary depending on situations. Fred Fiedler (1967), for instance, believes that a task-oriented leadership style is appropriate when the situation is either extremely favorable or extremely unfavorable to the leader. A favorable situation exists when the relationship between the leader and followers is good, their tasks are well-defined, and the leader has strong power. When the opposite is true, an unfavorable situation exists. When the situation is moderately favorable, a people-oriented leadership style is appropriate. Some theorists suggest that situational factors—the type of task, nature of work groups, formal authority system, personality and maturity level of followers, experience, and ability of followers—are critical in determining the most effective leadership style. For instance, when followers are inexperienced and lack maturity and responsibility, the directive leadership style is effective; when followers are experienced and willing to take charge, supportive leadership is effective.

LEADERSHIP IN A MULTICULTURAL SETTING

One major situational factor is the cultural values of the followers. People who have different cultural norms and values require different leadership styles. In a highly collective society such as Japan, the Philippines, Guatemala, or Ecuador, where the social bond among members is very strong and people look out for one another, a strong patriarch at the top of the social hierarchy tends to emerge as an effective leader. Such a leader is not only accepted by the followers but is also expected to protect their interests. China's Deng Xiao-Ping, whose influence continues even after his death, is a case in point.

On the other hand, in an extremely individualistic society, such as the United States (Hofstede, 1984), where the social bonds are loose and individuals are expected to take care of themselves, success and achievement are admired, and a competitive and heroic figure is likely to emerge as a leader. It is no surprise that John F. Kennedy became such a charismatic figure in the United States. His energetic and inspirational speeches are still vividly remembered.

CHARISMATIC AND TRANSFORMATIONAL LEADERSHIP

Regardless of culture and time, however, a great leader is remembered for his or her charisma, which means "divinely inspired gift" in Greek. Charismatic leaders have profound effects on followers. Through their exceptional inspirational and verbal ability, they articulate ideological goals and missions, communicate to followers with passion and inspiration, set an example in their own behaviors, and demand hard work and commitment from followers, above and beyond normal expectation.

Building on charismatic leadership, Bernard Bass (1985) proposed a theory of transformational leadership. Bass views leadership as a process of social exchange between a leader and his or her followers. In exchange for desired behaviors and task accomplishment, a leader provides rewards to followers. This nominal social exchange process is called transactional leadership. In contrast, a transformational leader places a higher level of trust in his or her followers and demands a much higher level of loyalty and performance beyond normal expectations. With unusual charismatic qualities and inspirational person-to-person interactions, a transformational leader transforms and motivates followers to make extra efforts to turn around ailing organizational situations into success stories. Lee Iacocca, when he took over Chrysler as CEO in 1979 and turned around this financially distressed company, was considered an exemplary transformational leader. He was able to convince many people, including employees and the U.S. Congress, to support the ailing company and to make it a success.

WAYS WOMEN LEAD

Leadership qualities such as aggressiveness, assertiveness, taking charge, and competitiveness are traditionally associated with strong, masculine characters. Even women executives tended to show these characteristics in the traditional corporate world. In fact, many of these women executives were promoted because they were even more competitive and assertive than their male counterparts. These successful women executives often sacrificed a family life, which their male counterparts did not necessarily have to do.

The business world is changing, however. Today, much research has found that women leaders are different from their male counterparts in management style. Women leaders tend to be more concerned with consensus building, participation, and caring. They often are more willing than men to share power and information, to empower employees, and to be concerned about the feelings of their subordinates.

Such an interactive and emotionally involved leadership style is not necessarily negative in the business environment. Indeed, some researchers find it to be highly effective. Internally, a culturally diverse work force demands more interactive and collaborative coordination. Externally, culturally diverse customers demand more personable and caring attention. A caring and flexible man-

agement style serves such diverse employees and customers better than traditional methods of management.

LEADERSHIP AND MANAGEMENT

John Kotter (1988) distinguishes leadership from management. Effective management carefully plans the goal of an organization, recruits the necessary staff, organizes them, and closely supervises them to make sure that the initial plan is executed properly. Successful leadership goes beyond management of plans and tasks. It envisions the future and sets a new direction for the organization. Successful leaders mobilize all possible means and human resources; they inspire all members of the organization to support the new mission and execute it with enthusiasm. When an organization faces an uncertain environment, it demands strong leadership. On the other hand, when an organization faces internal operational complexity, it demands strong management. If an organization faces both an uncertain environment and internal operational complexity, it requires both strong leadership and strong management.

SEE ALSO *Management/Leadership Styles*

BIBLIOGRAPHY

Bass, Bernard M. (1985). *Leadership and Performance Beyond Expectation*. New York: Free Press.

Bass, Bernard M. and Avolio, Bruce, J., eds. (1994). *Improving Organizational Effectiveness Through Transformational Leadership*. Thousand Oaks, CA: Sage.

Bennis, Warren G. (1959). Leadership Theory and Administrative Behavior: The Problem of Authority. *Administrative Science Quarterly* 4, 259-260.

Conger, Jay A., and Kanungo, Rabindra (1987). Toward a Behavioral Theory of Charismatic Leadership in Organizational Settings. *Academy of Management Review* 12, 637-647.

Daft, Richard L. (1999). *Leadership: Theory and Practice*. New York: Dryden Press.

Fiedler, Fred E. (1967). *A Theory of Leadership Effectiveness*. New York: McGraw-Hill.

Graef, C. L. (1993). The Situational Leadership Theory: A Critical Review. *Academy of Management Review* 8, 285-296.

Hall, Richard H. (1982). *Organizations: Structure and Process*. Englewood Cliffs, NJ: Prentice-Hall.

Hofstede, Geert (1984). *Culture's Consequences: International Differences in Work-Related Values*. Beverly Hills, CA: Sage.

Howell, Jane M. (1988). Two Faces of Charisma: Socialized and Personalized Leadership in Organizations. In Jay A. Conger and Rabindra N. Kanungo (Eds.), *Charismatic Leadership: The Elusive Factor in Organizational Effectiveness*. San Francisco: Jossey-Bass.

House, Robert J. (1996). Path-Goal Theory of Leadership: Lessons, Legacy and a Reformulated Theory. *Leadership Quarterly* 7, 323-352.

Hughes, Richard L., Ginnet, Robert C., and Curphy, Gordon J. (2006). *Leadership: Enhancing the Lessons of Experience.* Boston: McGraw-Hill/Irwin.

Kirkpatrick, S.A., and Locke, Edwin A. (1996). Direct and Indirect Effects of Three Core Charismatic Leadership Components on Performance and Attitudes. *Journal of Applied Psychology* 81:, 36-51.

Kotter, John P. (1988). *The Leadership Factor.* New York: Free Press.

Meindl, James R. (1990). On Leadership: An Alternative to the Conventional Wisdom. In B. M Staw and L.L. Cummings (Eds.), *Research in Organizational Behavior*, vol. 12. Greenwich, CT: JAI Press.

Meindl, James R., Ehrlich, S.B., and Dukerich, J.M. (1985). The Romance of Leadership. *Administrative Science Quarterly* 30, 78-102.

Trice, Harry M., and Beyer, Janis M. (1991). Cultural Leadership in Organizations. *Organization Science* 2, 149-169.

Yukl, Gary (1998). *Leadership in Organizations* (6th ed.). Upper Saddle River, NJ: Pearson/Prentice Hall.

Lee W. Lee

LIFESTYLES

As the twenty-first century advances, consumers are demanding better servicing in business operations to help simplify their harried lifestyles. The progression of lifestyle changes, in combination with technological and global evolution, will influence the way business and marketing operations function. This article focuses on how family, job, cultural background, social class, social activities, and employment have revolutionized business and marketing operations.

FAMILY INFLUENCES ON BUSINESS OPERATIONS

Family life continues to evolve. In the 1950s in America, it was common to see larger families with several siblings. It was also common at that time for the mother to stay home to take care of the household and children while the father worked to support the family.

In American culture in the twenty-first century, one is more likely to see smaller families. It is also common for both parents to work outside the home to support the family and household. The role of the "traditional" mother has changed whereby she is out in the workforce pursuing a career and helping to support the family. In addition, there are many more single-parent homes. Because of both of these trends, many preschool children stay with day-care providers and many older children are at home alone for two or three hours after school until a

parent gets home from work, making today's children more self-reliant than children in the recent past. The cultural shift in America directly correlates with U.S. Department of Labor statistics that estimated that employment of child-care workers would increase 36 percent or more for all occupations through 2012.

The amount of time that families spend together thus has changed significantly from previous generations. Working couples have lost an average of twenty-two hours a week of family and personal time between 1969 and 1999. This trend has opened up a market known as e-commerce as parents do not have the time to do the tasks necessary that were once part of their everyday life and still have time to spend with their children. Because of technological advances, however, businesses are providing time-saving services. For example, retail shopping from purchasing clothes to groceries may all be accomplished online, with those purchases being delivered right to one's door. According to the U.S. Department of Commerce, in the first quarter of 2005 e-commerce estimates increased 23.8 percent over the numbers from the first quarter of 2004, while total sales increased 7.8 percent during the same period.

JOB INFLUENCES ON BUSINESS OPERATIONS

In the past, businesses were managed very differently than they are today. Technology and its rate of advancement have revolutionized the way job objectives are met in business operations. For example, higher education has changed drastically because of technology. Online education, by providing flexible class schedules, reducing the time-taking courses, and making educational opportunities more affordable, is one response to the needs of adult learners. Because students can attend classes from their homes, the jobs of faculty and the business operations of higher education have changed notably.

The advancement in technology has taken over a large share of the e-commerce business in the everyday homes across America and global society. According to a survey conducted in July 2005 by AC Nielsen, a leading research firm, an amazing 724,000 Americans responded that they relied on eBay for their main support for income. Furthermore, the study identified another 1.5 million eBay users who stated that additional income was generated from selling consumer goods. Reported in 2004, 150 million eBay users bought and/or sold consumer goods valued at over $34 billion.

With this growing trend, the U.S. Postal Service and eBay launched a national tour to support small business and entrepreneurs since many eBay sellers use the U.S. mail for shipping. As the global job structure continues with the paradigm shifts that influence the way business

Online sites, like eBay, have affected how people work, play, and shop in the 21st century © **LANCE IVERSEN/SAN FRANCISCO CHRONICLE/CORBIS**

operations function, such partnerships will continue to be forged.

CULTURAL INFLUENCES ON BUSINESS OPERATIONS

Business operations in the twenty-first century need to be especially conscious of the cultural differences and/or similarities of all countries. Advances in technology have made the world a global business operation. With one click of the mouse one can immerse oneself in a culture very different from one's own. Business conducted on the Internet and e-commerce is the melting pot of ideas, culture, and people that is not just limited to American society.

Language and Communication. According to Stefan Lovgren, a writer for the *National Geography News,* "The next four major languages—English, Spanish, Hindi/Urdu, and Arabic—are likely to be equally ranked by 2050, with Arabic rising as English declines." Corporations need to act on this trend, as this will surely influence business operations in the global marketplace.

The overall culture of an organization is reflected in behaviors that are considered the "norm" in both verbal and nonverbal communication. Americans tend to speak directly to one another, maintaining eye contact with the person to whom they are talking. Hand gestures are commonly used while making presentations or in one-on-one conversation to better explain a point.

Corporate Culture and Clothing. Generally, corporations determine any organization's corporate culture by defining a corporate mission statement and following this statement in their day-to-day practices. Proper business attire was once considered suits and ties for men and business suits for women. That is no longer the case in many organizations, especially in the high-tech industry where the business environment is more casual and jeans and slacks are now considered acceptable.

Gender. Jobs are no longer gender-specific in the American culture. Women, once relegated to administrative and support-staff roles, are now in upper-level management positions alongside or above men. According to the Bureau of Labor Statistics, between 1983 and 2002, the share of women working in the automobile body and repair industry tripled. Furthermore, the share of men participating in the field of dressmaking also increased dramatically during the same period. Gender is no longer a predetermination of a person's role in business and as the twenty-first century continues, more and more occupations should become gender-neutral.

THE INFLUENCE OF SOCIAL CLASS ON BUSINESS OPERATIONS

What comprises social class? Is it the neighborhood in which one lives? The occupation one has? The income one earns? The wealth one has acquired? There is no generally agreed-upon definition of social class, but most people agree that social class does exist. Grouping people together and assigning them a status in society is as old as society itself.

The social class of a particular group of people influences the role of business and marketing operations. The key to success in business and in marketing operations is twofold. First, identify the market for the product. Second, identify the social class one is dealing with in that market. Businesses must become familiar with the customs and culture of the particular social class with which they are trying to do business.

THE INFLUENCE OF SOCIAL ACTIVITIES ON BUSINESS OPERATIONS

Marketing to a particular group often incorporates depictions of social activities as a part of the advertising campaign. For example, Mountain Dew commercials once portrayed young teenagers riding mountain bikes and engaging in extreme sports. A commercial for Grey Poupon mustard portrayed upper-class adults using the product while being chauffeured in a luxury car. In both examples, the companies needed to verify who constituted the market for their product first. Second, they had to learn the characteristics of those people.

Playing golf is reinforced in the corporate culture in many organizations as an important social activity. Instead of remaining inside on a beautiful afternoon, the executives get to conduct business while on the greens. The social activity is an advantage for executives looking to "close a deal," or make a connection in other business circles.

EMPLOYMENT INFLUENCE ON BUSINESS OPERATIONS

Jobs have changed significantly because of technological advances and global influences. Many corporations do business at an international level, which requires travel abroad for many of their employees. With virtual conferencing becoming more widespread, business travel as it is known today will evolve and change. The technological development of the Internet will have major implications and influences on global business and marketing procedures.

Business operations must integrate new and different marketing procedures to keep current with the changing job market. The trend of online education has opened up the market for the consumer and the employee to teach and learn at home. The consumer of the twenty-first century has less time to dedicate to a brick-and-mortar postsecondary educational institution; schools that understand this trend will benefit. Changes in the corporate and postsecondary educational marketplace require lifelong learning by both employees and employers in order to service the consumer.

Marketing operations must embrace e-commerce, internal links via Intranets, and Internet marketing and retailing because these tools can extend business operations and create new opportunities for growth. As technology, lifestyle, and employment change, business and marketing operations must also change in innovative ways as a matter of survival.

CONCLUSION

Consumers today require businesses to provide them with convenience to help simplify their harried lifestyles. This requires business and marketing operations to be aware of the impact of such demographic variables as family, job, cultural background, social class, social activities, and employment. All these demographic variables play an essential role in business operations. Lifestyles and technology have both changed radically, and the global marketplace is a reality. The key to business success is to understand the diversity that exists in the global marketplace and to respond innovatively and swiftly to society's changing needs. Corporations that understand the lifestyle changes of the twenty-first century global marketplace will be able to thrive and continue to service their consumers.

SEE ALSO *Consumer Behavior; Fads*

BIBLIOGRAPHY

Alexander, William M. (1999). An efficiency measure for a sustainable quality of life. Global Ideas Bank. Retrieved November 18, 2005, from http://www.globalideasbank.org/SD/SD-94.HTML

Lovgren, Stefan (2004, February 26). English in decline as a first language, study says. *National Geographic News*. Retrieved November 18, 2005, from http://news.nationalgeographic.com/news/2004/02/0226_04 0226_language.html

U.S. Department of Commerce. U.S. Census Bureau. http://www.census.gov

U.S. Department of Labor. http://www.dol.gov

U.S. Postal Service. (2005, July 21). New study reveals 724,000 Americans rely on eBay sales for income. Retrieved November 18, 2005, from http://www.usps.com/communications/news/press/2005/pr05_062.htm

Michelle Voto

LISTENING SKILLS IN BUSINESS

Expressive skills and receptive skills make up the two skills of communication. Speaking and writing are generally referred to as expressive skills; they provide the means by which people express themselves to others. The receptive skills, listening and reading, are the ways in which people receive information.

LISTENING IMPROVES PRODUCTIVITY

It has been reported that senior officers of major North American corporations spend up to 80 percent of their working time in meetings, discussions, face-to-face conversations, or telephone conversations. Most employees spend about 60 percent of the workday listening. Since such a large percentage of one's waking time is consumed by listening activities, it is clear that one's productivity could be increased through listening training.

Listening consumes about half of all communication time, yet people typically listen with only about 25 percent of their attention. Ineffective listening is costly, whether it occurs in families, businesses, government, or international affairs. Most people make numerous listening mistakes every day, but the costs—financial and otherwise—are seldom analyzed. Because of listening mistakes, appointments have to be rescheduled, letters retyped, and shipments rerouted. Any number of catastrophes can arise from a failed communication, regardless of the type of industry. Productivity is affected and profits suffer.

Research indicates that people hear only 25 percent of what is said and, after two months, remember only one-half of that. This is not true at all stages of one's life. First graders listen to 90 percent of what is said, second graders 80 percent, seventh graders 43 percent, and ninth graders only 25 percent.

It is imperative that people strive to improve their listening skills. When having difficulty understanding a document while reading, it can be reread for clarification. Oral messages, however, unless they are mechanically recorded, cannot be heard more than once. The listener may misunderstand, misinterpret, or forget a high percentage of the original message. With proper training, though, listening skills can be improved. It has been proven that with extended, focused training in listening, one can more than double one's listening efficiency and effectiveness.

RECEPTION AND INTERPRETATION

Communication involves message reception and interpretation. Studies of communication have routinely found that almost all people listen more than they talk, read more than they write, and spend a lot more time receiving messages than sending them. The average person speaks at a rate of 100 to 200 words per minute. An average listener, however, can adequately process 400 words per minute. Given this differential between what is normally heard and what potentially can be processed, it is little wonder that people tend to "tune out" at certain times. Mental tangents are the obvious product of this differential, and managers who believe that subordinates are listening intently to every word they utter are deluding themselves.

Listening can be compared to exercising or wearing seat belts: Everybody knows it is desirable, but everybody finds it difficult to do on a regular basis. Most people yearn to talk and want to be center stage. If one listens to any casual conversation between friends, one will probably note that most people spend much of the conversation paying maximum attention to what they are going to say next. As people listen to others, they spend much of the time thinking about the next thing they will be saying.

SKILLED LISTENING

Listening is more than just hearing what a speaker says. Hearing is simply the reception of sounds by one's ears; listening is interpreting, or making sense of, the sounds that one hears. Hearing is a physical perception; listening is a mental activity. Listening requires concentration, cooperation, and an open mind.

Many situations at work demand skilled listening. Conferences, interviews, receiving instructions, and handling complaints, all call for alert, sensitive listening. Whether one is listening in order to learn how to do a task, make a decision, or achieve friendly relations with one's coworkers, it is important to make a concentrated effort to understand what the speaker is saying.

TYPES OF LISTENING

Three types of listening exist. The first type is casual, or informal. One usually does not need to remember details. The second type of listening is active, or formal. This type of listening takes concentration and requires that the listener absorb details. The last type of listening is nonverbal listening.

Speakers have the responsibility to communicate as effectively as they can, but listeners also have responsibilities. They cannot sit back and contentedly assume they have nothing to do. Like speakers, listeners also need to prepare themselves. As they listen, they must concentrate on both the verbal and nonverbal message of the speaker. Listeners are influenced by the speaker, the message, other listeners, physical conditions, and their emotional state at the time of the listening activity. While the first three cannot be controlled by the listener, the last two can.

Body Language. To give complete attention to the speaker and the speaker's message, the listener should choose a position that allows a full view of the speaker's gestures. Fifty-five percent of a person's message involves nonverbal communication, 38 percent of the message derives from the speaker's voice inflection, and only 7 percent of the message involves the actual words spoken.

In addition to the verbal message, the listener should also concentrate on the speaker's nonverbal messages—communicated through gestures, tone of voice, and physical movements. Do the speaker's gestures seem to reinforce or contradict the words? If the speaker is trying to paint herself as a sincere, dedicated woman, or do you detect elements of dishonesty? Is the speaker actually timid even though he is trying to play the role of a man full of confidence? Only by carefully watching and analyzing a presenter's body language and thoughtfully listening to his or her words can one receive the full impact of the message.

As with the spoken word, body language has its own special pace, rhythm, vocabulary, and grammar. Just as in verbal language, there are "letters" that, when correctly joined, form unspoken "words." Such words are then linked to create the "phrases" and "sentences" by which messages are exchanged. Relaxed gesturing on the part of the speaker, for example, is usually associated with confidence, while jerking and abrupt motions display nervousness and discomfort. Putting learned information about nonverbal communication to practical use can spell the difference between success or failure in many business and social encounters.

BENEFITS OF ACTIVE LISTENING

Whether one is involved in a serious negotiation, job interview, company meeting, or personal interaction, the need to listen more effectively is vital. Active listening is important because listening enables people to:

- Gain important information
- Be more effective in interpreting a message
- Gather data to make sound decisions
- Respond appropriately to the messages they hear

To become a better listener, one should:

1. *Look the part:* Face the speaker and display feedback that the message is being heard and understood. Lean toward the speaker to show interest. Maintain eye contact at least 80 percent of the time. Do not distract the speaker with strange facial expressions and fidgeting.
2. *Listen for nonverbal messages:* Observe the speaker's body language, gestures, and the physical distance. Observe the speaker's facial expressions, eyes, mouth, and hands for hidden messages.
3. *Listen for the main points:* Filter out the nonessential and look for the principal message of the words.
4. *Be silent before replying:* Be certain that the speaker is completely finished speaking before attempting to speak. Resist the temptation to interrupt unnecessarily.
5. *Ask questions:* It is appropriate to question the speaker in order to clarify meanings and reinforce messages heard.
6. *Sense how the speaker is feeling:* To receive the complete message, it is important to sift out any feelings the speaker is trying to convey. Determine what the speaker is not saying.
7. *Take notes:* Jotting down important ideas allows one to review the message at a later time and reinforces the information heard/learned.
8. *Be available:* To be spoken to, one must be available. Stop working and concentrate totally on the speaker.

Encourage others to listen by doing the following:

- Do not speak loudly. It forces others to listen.
- Make what is said interesting. Focus on the listeners' favorite subject—themselves. Encourage others to participate by bringing them into the conversation.
- Create the right environment. Speak where one can be easily heard and understood.
- Be human to the listeners. Address people by name whenever possible; it helps to get their attention.

Good listening habits are an important ingredient in one's journey to success. By practicing careful listening, one will become more efficient in one's job and more knowledgeable about all topics. Responsible, patient listening is a rare thing, but it is a skill that can be developed with practice.

SEE ALSO *Communication Channels; Communications in Business; Reading Skills in Business; Speaking Skills in Business; Writing Skills in Business*

Jan Hargrave

M

MACROECONOMICS/ MICROECONOMICS

Economics is a broad subject that can be divided into two areas: macroeconomics and microeconomics. To differentiate between the two, the analogy of the forest and the individual trees can be helpful. Macroeconomics is the study of the behaviors and activities of the economy as a whole; hence, the forest. Microeconomics looks at the behaviors and activities of individual households and firms, the individual components that make up the whole economy; hence, the individual trees.

MACROECONOMICS

Macroeconomics, the study of the behaviors and activities of the economy as a whole, looks at such areas as the Federal Reserve System, unemployment, gross domestic product, and business cycles.

The Federal Reserve System was created by the Federal Reserve Act of 1913, which divided the United States into twelve districts with a Federal Reserve Bank located in each. Each of these banks is owned by the member banks located within that district. The Federal Reserve System's most important function is to control the supply of money in circulation. Monetary policies made by the Federal Reserve System's Board of Governors have a tremendous impact on the total economy. These policies influence such factors as the amount of money member banks have available to loan, interest rates, and the overall price level of the economy. Three ways in which the Federal Reserve Board regulates the economy are by changing reserve requirements, changing the discount rate, and buying and selling government securities.

Macroeconomists also study unemployment, which simply defined is a very large work force and a small job market, to determine methods to control this serious economic problem. The U.S. Department of Labor estimates the level of unemployment in the economy by using results from monthly surveys conducted by the Bureau of the Census.

Unemployment means lost production for the economy and loss of income for the individual. One type of unemployment is frictional unemployment, which includes those people who are not employed because they have been fired or have quit their job. Cyclical unemployment follows the cycles of the economy. For example, during a recession, spending is low and workers are laid off because production needs are reduced. Structural unemployment occurs when a job is left vacant because a worker does not have the necessary skills needed or a worker does not live where there are available jobs. Some unemployment is due to seasonal factors; that is, employees are hired only during certain times of the year. To help lessen the problem of unemployment, the government can use its powers to increase levels of spending by consumers, businesses, and the government itself and by lowering taxes or giving tax incentives, which makes available more money with which to purchase goods and services. This in turn puts more laid-off workers back to work. The Federal Reserve System can also increase spending by lowering interest rates.

Total economic spending, which includes consumer, business, and government spending, determines the level of the gross domestic product (GDP), which is the market value of all final products produced in a year's time. GDP is one of the most commonly used measures of economic performance. An increasing GDP from year to year shows that the economy is growing. The nation's policy makers look at past and present GDPs to formulate policies that will contribute to economic growth, which would result in a steady increase in the production of goods and services. If GDP is too high or growing too rapidly, inflation occurs. If GDP is too low or decreasing, an increase in unemployment occurs.

Fluctuations in total economic activity are known as business cycles, and macroeconomists are concerned with understanding why these cycles occur. Most unemployment and inflation are caused by these fluctuations. There are four phases of the business cycle: prosperity (peak), recession, trough, and recovery. The length and duration of each cycle varies. From its highest point, prosperity, to its lowest point, trough, these phases are marked by increases and decreases in GDP, unemployment, demand for goods and services, and spending.

MICROECONOMICS

Microeconomics looks at the individual components of the economy, such as costs of production, maximizing profits, and the different market structures.

Business firms are the suppliers of goods and services, and most firms want to make a profit; in fact, they want to maximize their profits. Firms must determine the level of output that will result in the greatest profits. Costs of production play a major role in determining this level of output. Costs of production include fixed costs and variable costs. Fixed costs are costs that do not vary with the level of output, such as rent and insurance premiums. Variable costs are costs that change with the level of output, such as wages and raw materials. Therefore, total cost equals total fixed costs plus total variable costs ($TC = TFC + TVC$). Marginal cost, which is the cost of producing one more unit of output, helps determine the level at which profits will be maximized. Marginal cost (MC) measures the change (Δ) in total cost when there is a change in quantity (Q) produced ($MC = \Delta TC/\Delta Q$). Firms must then decide whether they should produce additional quantities.

Revenue, the money a firm receives for the product it sells, is also a part of the profit equation because total revenue minus total costs equal profit ($TR - TC$ = profit). Marginal revenue, which is the additional revenue that results from producing and selling one more unit of output, is also very important. As long as marginal revenue exceeds marginal cost, a firm can continue to maximize profits.

There are four basic categories of market structures in which firms sell their products. Pure competition includes many sellers, a homogeneous product, easy entry and exit, and no artificial restrictions such as price controls. A monopoly is the opposite of pure competition and is characterized by a single firm with a unique product and barriers to entry. An oligopoly has few sellers, a homogeneous or a differentiated product, and barriers to entry such as high start-up costs. Where products are differentiated, nonprice competition occurs; that is, consumers are persuaded to buy products without consideration of price. The fourth market structure is monopolistic competition. It includes many sellers, differentiated products, easy entry and exit, and nonprice competition.

SEE ALSO *Economic Analysis; Economics*

BIBLIOGRAPHY

Gottheil, Fred M. (2005). *Principles of Economics* (4th ed.). Mason, OH: Thomson.

Lisa S. Huddlestun

MANAGEMENT

Throughout the years, the role of a manager has changed. Years ago, managers were thought of as people who were the boss. While that might still be true in the early twenty-first century, many managers view themselves as leaders rather than as people who tell subordinates what to do. The role of a manager is comprehensive and often very complex. Not everyone wants to be a manager, nor should everyone consider being a manager.

A DEFINITION OF MANAGEMENT

Some would define management as an art, while others would define it as a science. Whether management is an art or a science is not what is most important. Management is a process that is used to accomplish organizational goals. That is, it is a process used to achieve the goals of an organization. An organization could be a business, a school, a city, a group of volunteers, or any governmental entity. Managers are the people to whom this management task is assigned, and it is generally thought that they achieve the desired goals through the key functions of (1) planning, (2) organizing, (3) directing, and (4) controlling. Some would include leading as a managing function, but for the purposes of this discussion, leading is included as a part of directing.

The four key functions of management are applied throughout an organization regardless of whether it is a business, a government agency, or a church group. In a business, many different activities take place. For example, in a retail store there are people who buy merchandise to sell, people to sell the merchandise, people who prepare the merchandise for display, people who are responsible for advertising and promotion, people who do the accounting work, people who hire and train employees, and several other types of workers. There might be one manager for the entire store, but there are other managers at different levels who are more directly responsible for the people who perform all the other jobs. At each level of management, the four key functions of planning, organizing, directing, and controlling are included. The emphasis changes with each different level of manager.

Planning. Planning in any organization occurs in different ways and at all levels. A top-level manager, such as the manager of a manufacturing plant, plans for different events than does a manager who supervises a group of workers who are responsible for assembling modular homes on an assembly line. The plant manager must be concerned with the overall operations of the plant, while the assembly-line manager or supervisor is only responsible for the line that he or she oversees.

Planning could include setting organizational goals. This is usually done by higher-level managers in an organization. As a part of the planning process, the manager develops strategies for achieving the goals of the organization. In order to implement the strategies, resources will be needed and must be acquired. The planners must also then determine the standards, or levels of quality, that need to be met in completing the tasks.

In general, planning can be strategic planning, tactical planning, or contingency planning. Strategic planning is long-range planning that is normally completed by top-level managers in an organization. Examples of strategic decisions managers make include who the customer or clientele should be, what products or services should be sold, and where the products and services should be sold.

Short-range or tactical planning is done for the benefit of lower-level managers, since it is the process of developing very detailed strategies about what needs to be done, who should do it, and how it should be done. To return to the previous example of assembling modular homes, as the home is nearing construction on the floor of the plant, plans must be made for the best way to move it through the plant so that each worker can complete assigned tasks in the most efficient manner. These plans can best be developed and implemented by the line managers who oversee the production process rather than managers who sit in an office and plan for the overall operation of the company. The tactical plans fit into the

Douglas McGregor (1906–1964). © BETTMANN/CORBIS

strategic plans and are necessary to implement the strategic plans.

Contingency planning allows for alternative courses of action when the primary plans that have been developed do not achieve the goals of the organization. In the economic environment of the early twenty-first century, plans may need to be changed very rapidly. Continuing with the example of building modular homes in the plant, the plant might be using a nearby supplier for all the lumber used in the framing of the homes but the supplier loses its entire inventory of framing lumber in a major warehouse fire. Contingency plans would make it possible for the modular home builder to continue construction by going to another supplier for the same lumber that it can no longer get from its former supplier.

Organizing. Organizing refers to the way the organization allocates resources, assigns tasks, and goes about accomplishing its goals. In the process of organizing, managers arrange a framework that links all workers, tasks, and resources together so the organizational goals can be achieved. The framework is called organizational structure. Organizational structure is shown by an organizational chart. The organizational chart that depicts the structure of the organization shows positions in the organization, usually beginning with the top-level manager (normally the president) at the top of the chart. Other managers are shown below the president.

There are many ways to structure an organization. It is important to note that the choice of structure is important for the type of organization, its clientele, and the products or services it provides—all of which influence the goals of the organization.

Directing. Directing is the process that many people would most relate to managing. It is supervising, or leading workers to accomplish the goals of the organization. In many organizations, directing involves making assignments, assisting workers to carry out assignments, interpreting organizational policies, and informing workers of how well they are performing. To effectively carry out this function, managers must have leadership skills in order to get workers to perform effectively.

Some managers direct by empowering workers. This means that the manager does not stand like a taskmaster over the workers barking out orders and correcting mistakes. Empowered workers usually work in teams and are given the authority to make decisions about what plans will be carried out and how. Empowered workers have the support of managers who will assist them to make sure the goals of the organization are being met. It is generally thought that workers who are involved with the decision-making process feel more of a sense of ownership in their work, take more pride in their work, and are better performers on the job.

By the very nature of directing, it should be obvious that the manager must find a way to get workers to perform their jobs. There are many different ways managers can do this in addition to empowerment, and there are many theories about the best way to get workers to perform effectively and efficiently. Management theories and motivation are important topics and are discussed in detail in other articles.

Controlling. The controlling function involves the evaluation activities that managers must perform. It is the process of determining if the company's goals and objectives are being met. This process also includes correcting situations in which the goals and objectives are not being met. There are several activities that are a part of the controlling function.

Managers must first set standards of performance for workers. These standards are levels of performance that should be met. For example, in the modular home assembly process, the standard might be to have a home completed in eight working days as it moves through the construction line. This is a standard that must then be communicated to managers who are supervising workers,

and then to the workers so they know what is expected of them.

After the standards have been set and communicated, it is the manager's responsibility to monitor performance to see that the standards are being met. If the manager watches the homes move through the construction process and sees that it takes ten days, something must be done about it. The standards that have been set are not being met. In this example, it should be relatively easy for managers to determine where the delays are occurring. Once the problems are analyzed and compared to expectations, then something must be done to correct the results. Normally, the managers would take corrective action by working with the employees who were causing the delays. There could be many reasons for the delays. Perhaps it is not the fault of the workers but instead is due to inadequate equipment or an insufficient number of workers. Whatever the problem, corrective action should be taken.

MANAGERIAL SKILLS

To be an effective manager, it is necessary to possess many skills. Not all managers have all the skills that would make them the most effective manager. As technology advances and grows, the skills that are needed by managers are constantly changing. Different levels of management in the organizational structure also require different types of management skills. Generally, however, managers need to have communication skills, human skills, computer skills, time-management skills, and technical skills.

Communication Skills. Communication skills fall into the broad categories of oral and written skills, both of which managers use in many different ways. It is necessary for a manager to orally explain processes and give direction to workers. It is also necessary for managers to give verbal praise to workers. Managers are also expected to conduct meetings and give talks to groups of people.

An important part of the oral communication process is listening. Managers are expected to listen to their supervisors *and* to their workers. A manager must hear recommendations and complaints on a regular basis and must be willing to follow through on what is heard. A manager who does not listen is not a good communicator.

Managers are also expected to write reports, letters, memos, and policy statements. All of these must be written in such a way that the recipient can interpret and understand what is being said. This means that managers must write clearly and concisely. Good writing requires good grammar and composition skills. This is something that can be learned by those aspiring to a management position.

Human Skills. Relating to other people is vital in order to be a good manager. Workers come in every temperament that can be imagined. It takes a manager with the right human skills to manage the variety of workers effectively. Diversity in the workplace is common. The manager must understand different personality types and cultures to be able to supervise these workers. Human skills cannot be learned in a classroom, but are best learned by working with people. Gaining an understanding of personality types can be learned from books, but practice in dealing with diverse groups is the most meaningful preparation.

Computer Skills. Technology changes so rapidly it is often difficult to keep up with the changes. It is necessary for managers to have computer skills in order to keep up with these rapid changes. Many of the processes that occur in offices, manufacturing plants, warehouses, and other work environments depend on computers and thus necessitate managers and workers who can skillfully use the technology. Although computers can cause headaches, at the same time they have simplified many of the tasks that are performed in the workplace.

Time-Management Skills. Because the typical manager is a very busy person, it is important that time be managed effectively. This requires an understanding of how to allocate time to different projects and activities. A manager's time is often interrupted by telephone calls, problems with workers, meetings, others who just want to visit, and other seemingly uncontrollable factors. It is up to the manager to learn how to manage time so that work can be completed most efficiently. Good time-management skills can be learned, but managers must be willing to prioritize activities, delegate, deal with interruptions, organize work, and perform other acts that will make them better managers.

Technical Skills. Different from computer skills, technical skills are more closely related to the tasks that are performed by workers. A manager must know what the workers who are being supervised are doing on their jobs or assistance cannot be provided to them. For example, a manager who is supervising accountants needs to know the accounting processes; a manager who is supervising a machinist must know how to operate the equipment; and a manager who supervises the construction of a home must know the sequence of operations and how to perform them.

MANAGEMENT THOUGHT

There are many views of management, or schools of management thought, that have evolved over the years. Some of the theories of management that have greatly affected how managers manage today include classical, behavioral, contemporary, closed, and open management thought.

Classical Thought. The classical school of management thought emerged in the late 1800s and early 1900s as a result of the Industrial Revolution. Since the beginning of time, managers have needed to know how to perform the functions discussed earlier. The Industrial Revolution emphasized the importance of better management as organizations grew larger and more complex. As industry developed, managers had to develop systems for controlling inventory, production, scheduling, and human resources. It was the managers who emerged during the Industrial Revolution, many of whom had backgrounds in engineering, who discovered that they needed organized methods in order to find solutions to problems in the workplace.

Classical management theorists thought there was one way to solve management problems in the industrial organization. Generally, their theories assumed that people could make logical and rational decisions while trying to maximize personal gains from their work situations. The classical school of management is based on scientific management, which has its roots in Henri Fayol's work in France and the ideas of German sociologist Max Weber. Scientific management is a type of management that bases standards upon facts. The facts are gathered by observation, experimentation, or sound reasoning. In the United States, scientific management was further developed by individuals such as Charles Babbage (1792–1871), Frederick W. Taylor (1856–1915), and Frank (1868–1924) and Lillian (1878–1972) Gilbreth.

Behavioral Management Thought. It was because the classical management theorists were so machine-oriented that the behavioralists began to develop their thinking. The behavioral managers began to view management from a social and psychological perspective. These managers were concerned about the well-being of the workers and wanted them to be treated as people, not a part of the machines.

Some of the early behavioral theorists were Robert Owen (1771–1858), a British industrialist who was one of the first to promote management of human resources in an organization; Hugo Munsterberg (1863–1916), the father of industrial psychology; Walter Dill Scott (1869–1955), who believed that managers need to improve workers' attitudes and motivation in order to increase productivity; and Mary Parker Follett (1868–1933), who believed that a manager's influence should come naturally from his or her knowledge, skill, and leadership of others.

In the behavioral management period, there was a human relations movement. Advocates of the human relations movement believed that if managers focused on employees rather than on mechanistic production, then workers would become more satisfied and thus more productive laborers. Human relations management supported the notion that managers should be paternalistic and nurturing in order to build work groups that could be productive and satisfied.

The behavioral science movement was also an important part of the behavioral management school. Advocates of this movement stressed the need for scientific studies of the human element of organizations. This model for management emphasized the need for employees to grow and develop in order to maintain a high level of self-respect and remain productive workers. The earliest advocates of the behavioral science movement were Abraham Maslow (1908–1970), who developed Maslow's hierarchy of needs, and Douglas McGregor (1906–1964), who developed Theory X and Theory Y.

Contemporary Management Thought. In more recent years, new management thoughts have emerged and influenced organizations. One of these is the sociotechnical system. A system is a set of complementary elements that function as a unit for a specific purpose. Systems theorists believe that all parts of the organization must be related and that managers from each part must work together for the benefit of the organization. Because of this relationship, what happens in one part of the organization influences and affects other parts of the organization.

Another contemporary approach to managing involves contingency theories. This approach states that the manager should use the techniques or styles that are most appropriate for the situation and the people involved. For example, a manager of a group of Ph.D. chemists in a laboratory would have to use different techniques from a manager of a group of teenagers in a fast-food restaurant.

Closed Management Systems. Within the classical and behavioral approaches to management, managers look only within the organization to improve productivity and efficiency. This is a closed system—the organization operates as though it is in its own environment. Outside influence and information are blocked out.

Open Management Systems. Another perspective is the open system. As one would expect, here the organization functions in conjunction with its external environment, acting with and relying upon other systems. Advocates of an open system believe that an organization cannot avoid the influence of outside forces.

SUMMARY

Management is a very complex process to which this article is but a brief introduction. Other articles in this encyclopedia provide extensive insight into the many styles and theories of management.

SEE ALSO *Careers in Management; Ethics in Management; Management: Authority and Responsibility; Management: Historical Perspectives; Management/Leadership Styles*

BIBLIOGRAPHY

Nickels, William G., McHugh, James M., and McHugh, Susan M. (2005). *Understanding Business*. Boston: McGraw-Hill/Irwin.

Pierce, Jon L., and Dunham, Randall B. (1990). *Managing*. Glenview, IL: Scott, Foresman/Little, Brown Higher Education.

Roger L. Luft

MANAGEMENT: AUTHORITY AND RESPONSIBILITY

How can people be influenced to make commitments to the goals of the organization? In part, this question can be answered by how managers define and use power, influence, and authority. Deciding what type of authority system to create is part of the managerial responsibility of organizing. Compare, for example, two managers. One accepts or rejects all ideas generated at lower levels. The other gives the authority for making some decisions to employees at the level where these decisions will most likely affect those employees. How managers use their power, influence, and authority can determine their effectiveness in meeting the goals of the organization.

RESPONSIBILITY

Responsibility is the obligation to accomplish the goals related to the position and the organization. Managers at all levels of the organization typically have the same basic responsibilities when it comes to managing the work force. They must direct employees toward objectives, oversee the work effort of employees, deal with immediate problems, and report on the progress of work to their superiors. Managers' primary responsibilities are to examine tasks, problems, or opportunities in relationship to the company's short- and long-range goals. They must be quick to identify areas of potential problems, continually search for solutions, and be alert to new opportunities and ways to take advantage of the best ones. How effectively goals and objectives are accomplished depends on how well the company goals are broken down into jobs and assignments and how well these are identified and communicated throughout the organization.

INFLUENCE AND POWER

Formal job definitions and coordinating strategies are not enough to get the work done. Managers must somehow use influence to encourage workers to action. If they are to succeed, managers must possess the ability to influence organization members. Influence is the ability to bring about change and produce results; people derive influence from interpersonal power and authority. Interpersonal power allows organization members to exert influence over others.

Power stems from a variety of sources: reward power, coercive power, information power, resource power, expert power, referent power, and legitimate power. Reward power exists if managers provide or withhold rewards, such as money or recognition, from those they wish to influence. Coercive power depends on the manager's ability to punish others who do not engage in the desired behavior. A few examples of coercion include reprimands, criticisms, and negative performance appraisals. Power can also result from controlling access to important information about daily operations and future plans. Also, having access to and deciding to limit or share the resources and materials that are critical to accomplishing objectives can provide a manager with a source of power. Managers usually have access to such information and resources and must use discretion over how much or how little is disseminated to employees. Expert power is based on the amount of expertise a person possesses that is valued by others. For example, some people may be considered experts with computers if they are able to use several software programs proficiently and can navigate the Internet with ease. Those who do not have the expert knowledge or experience need the expert's help and, therefore, are willing to be influenced by the expert's power. When people are admired or liked by others, referent power may result because others feel friendly toward them and are more likely to follow their directions and demonstrate loyalty toward them. People are drawn to others for a variety of reasons, including physical or social attractiveness, charisma, or prestige. Politicians like John F. Kennedy were able to use their referent power to effectively influence others. Legitimate power stems from the belief that a person has the right to influence others by virtue of holding a position of authority, such as the authority of a manager over a subordinate or of a teacher over a student.

In some respects, everyone has power to either push forward or obstruct the goals of the organization by making decisions, delegating decisions, delaying decisions, rejecting decisions, or supporting decisions. However, the effective use of power does not mean control. Power can be detrimental to the goals of the organization if held by those who use it to enhance their own positions and thereby prevent the advancement of the goals of the organization.

Truly successful managers are able to use power ethically, efficiently, and effectively by sharing it. Power can be used to influence people to do things they might not otherwise do. When that influence encourages people to do things that have no or little relationship to the organization's goals, that power is abused. Abuses of power raise ethical questions. For example, asking a subordinate to submit supposed business-trip expenses for reimbursement for what was actually a family vacation or asking a subordinate to run personal errands is an abuse of power. People who acquire power are ethically obligated to consider the impact their actions will have on others and on the organization.

Employees may desire a greater balance of power or a redistribution of authority within the existing formal authority structure. People can share power in a variety of ways: by providing information, by sharing responsibility, by giving authority, by providing resources, by granting access, by giving reasons, and by extending emotional support. The act of sharing information is powerful. When people do not share information, the need to know still exists; therefore, the blanks are filled in with gossip and innuendo. When people are asked to take on more responsibility, they should be provided with tasks that provide a challenge, not just with more things to increase their workload that do not really matter. People need the legitimate power to make decisions without having to clear everything first with someone higher up in the organization. People who have power must also have the necessary range of resources and tools to succeed. Access to people outside as well as inside the organization should be provided and encouraged. People should be told why an assignment is important and why they were chosen to do it. Emotional support can come in the form of mentoring, appreciation, listening, and possibly helping out.

Sharing power or redistributing authority does not necessarily mean moving people into positions of power; instead, it can mean letting people have power over the work they do, which means that people can exercise personal power without moving into a formal leadership role. The ability to influence organization members is an important resource for effective managers. Relying on the title "boss" is seldom powerful enough to achieve adequate influence.

AUTHORITY

Authority is seen as the legitimate right of a person to exercise influence or the legitimate right to make decisions, to carry out actions, and to direct others. For example, managers expect to have the authority to assign work, hire employees, or order merchandise and supplies.

As part of their structure, organizations have a formal authority system that depicts the authority relationships between people and their work. Different types of authority are found in this structure: line, staff, and functional authority. Line authority is represented by the chain of command; an individual positioned above another in the hierarchy has the right to make decisions, issue directives, and expect compliance from lower-level employees. Staff authority is advisory authority; it takes the form of counsel, advice, and recommendation. People with staff authority derive their power from their expert knowledge and the legitimacy established in their relationships with line managers. Functional authority cuts across the hierarchical structure to allow managers to direct specific processes, practices, or policies affecting people in other departments. For example, the human resources department may create policies and procedures related to promoting and hiring employees throughout the entire organization.

Authority can also be viewed as arising from interpersonal relationships rather than a formal hierarchy. Authority is sometimes equated with legitimate power. Authority and power and how these elements are interrelated can explain the elements of managing and their effectiveness. What is critical is how subordinates perceive a manager's legitimacy. Legitimate authority occurs when people use power for good and have acquired power by proper and honest means. When people perceive an attempt at influence as legitimate, they recognize it and willingly comply. Power acquired through improper means, such as lying, withholding information, gossip, or manipulation, is seen as illegitimate. When people perceive the authority of others as illegitimate, they are less likely to willingly comply.

DELEGATION

In order for managers to achieve goals in an efficient manner, part of their work may be assigned to others. When work is delegated, tasks and authority are transferred from one position to another within an organization. The key to effective delegation of tasks is the transference of decision-making authority and responsibility from one level of the organization to the level to which the tasks have been delegated. In order to effectively delegate work, some guidelines should be followed: Determine what each worker can most effectively accomplish; decide whether the worker should just identify a problem or also propose a solution; consider whether the person can handle the challenge of the task; be clear in the objectives of the task; encourage questions; explain why the task is important; determine if the person has the appropriate resources—time, budget, data, or equipment—to get the job done on a deadline; create progress reviews as part of the project planning; and be prepared to live with less than perfect results. Authority should be delegated in terms of expected results. Generally, the more specific the goal, the easier it is to determine how much authority someone needs.

Some employees resist delegation for a variety of reasons. Initiative and responsibility involve risk that some people try to avoid. People tend to play it safe if risk results in criticism. Those who feel they already have more work than they can do avoid new assignments. Some people doubt their own abilities and lack the self-confidence to tackle new assignments. Delegation is an excellent professional development tool so long as it expands a worker's expertise and growth. Delegation can also compensate for a manager's weakness. A successful team is developed by building on the strengths of its members.

People develop most when stimulated to broaden themselves—when challenged. More authority can add challenge, but too much challenge can frustrate people and cause them to avoid new responsibilities. Delegation should involve acceptable challenge—enough to motivate but not so much as to frustrate.

In today's workplace, managers are compelled to rely more on persuasion, which is based on expert and referent power rather than reward, coercive, or inappropriate use of power. A manager who shares power and authority will be the one with the greatest ability to influence others to work toward the goals of the organization.

SEE ALSO *Management; Management/Leadership Styles*

BIBLIOGRAPHY

Bartol, Kathryn M., and Martin, David C. (1998). *Management.* Boston: McGraw-Hill.

Hirschhorn, Larry (1997). *Reworking Authority.* Cambridge, MA: MIT Press.

Lucas, James R. (1998). *Balance of Power.* New York: AMACOM, American Management Association.

Marshall, Don R. (1999). *The Four Elements of Successful Management.* New York: AMACOM, American Management Association.

Cheryl L. Noll

MANAGEMENT BY OBJECTIVES (MBO)

SEE *Human Resource Management; Strategic Management*

MANAGEMENT: HISTORICAL PERSPECTIVES

Since the beginning of time, humans have been managing—managing other people, managing organizations, and managing themselves. Management has been dealt with in this publication as a process that is used to accomplish organizational goals. To some, management is thought of as an art; to others, as a science. Each of those perspectives is grounded in the early writings and teaching of a group of managerial pioneers.

INDUSTRIAL REVOLUTION

While it can be argued that management began well before the Industrial Revolution, it is often felt that what emerged as contemporary management thought began with the beginning of industrial development. The Industrial Revolution began in the mid-eighteenth century when factories were first built and laborers were employed to work in them. Prior to this period, most workers were active in an agrarian system of maintaining the land.

Adam Smith (1723–1790), the economist who wrote *The Wealth of Nations*, was an early contributor to management thought during the Industrial Revolution. He was considered a liberal thinker, and his philosophy was the foundation for the laissez-faire management doctrine. His thoughts about division of labor were fundamental to current notions of work simplification and time studies. His emphasis on the relationship between specialization of labor and technology was somewhat similar to the later thinking of Charles Babbage.

Another early pioneer of management thought regarding the factory system was Robert Owen (1771–1858), an entrepreneur who tried to halt the Industrial Revolution because he saw disorder and evil in what was happening. Owen founded his first factory at the age of 18 in Manchester, England. His approach to managing was to observe everything and to maintain order and regularity throughout the industrial facility.

Owen moved on to a venture in Scotland, where he encountered a shortage of qualified laborers for his factory. His approach to handling disciplinary problems with his workers was to appeal to their moral sense, not to use corporal punishment. He used silent monitors, a system whereby he awarded four types of marks to superintendents, who in turn awarded workers. The marks were color-coded in order of merit. Blocks of wood were painted with the different colors and placed at each workstation. Workers were rated at the end of each day, and the appropriate color was turned to face the aisle so that anyone passing by could see how the worker had performed the previous day. The system was an attempt to motivate laggards to perform better and good workers to maintain high performance.

Charles Babbage (1792–1871) was noted for his application of technological aids to human effort in the manufacturing process. Babbage invented the first computer, in the form of a mechanical calculator, in 1822. Many more modern computers used basic elements of his design. Supervising construction of this invention led Babbage to an interest in management, particularly in the concept of division of labor in the manufacturing process. Babbage invented equipment that could monitor the output of workers, which led to a profit-sharing system in which workers were compensated based on the profits of the company as well as for suggestions that would improve the manufacturing processes in addition to being paid a wage.

SCIENTIFIC MANAGEMENT

Scientific principles for the management of workers, materials, money, and capital were introduced between 1785 and 1835. Scientific managers made careful and rational decisions, kept orderly and complete books, and were able to react to events quickly and expertly. Some of the men discussed above were important early contributors to the scientific management movement before others came along to solidify the thinking. Scientific management of the twenty-first century was introduced by several more contemporary thinkers.

Frederick Taylor (1856–1915) was an engineer who had an innovative approach to management. His approach was for managers, rather than being taskmasters, to adopt a broader, more comprehensive view of managing and see their job as incorporating the elements of planning, organizing, and controlling. His ideas of management evolved as he worked for different firms. As a result of his experiences as both a worker and a manager, he developed the concept of time and motion studies.

In what became the origin of contemporary scientific management, Taylor set out to scientifically define what workers ought to be able to do with their equipment and resources in a full day of work. In his process of time study, each job was broken into as many simple, elementary movements as possible, and useless movements were discarded. The quickest and best methods for each elementary movement were selected by observing and timing the most skilled workers at each. His system evolved into the piece-rate system.

Frank (1868–1924) and Lillian (1878–1972) Gilbreth refined the field of motion study and laid the foundation for modern applications of job simplification, meaningful work standards, and incentive wage plans. The Gilbreths were interested not only in motion studies

Lillian Evelyn Gilbreth (1878–1972) and Frank Gilbreth (1868–1924). *The Gilbreths refind the fields of time and motion study.* © UNDERWOOD & UNDERWOOD/CORBIS

but also in the improvement of the totality of people and the environment, which they believed could be done through training, better work methods, improved environments and tools, and a healthy psychological outlook. Lillian Gilbreth had a background in psychology and management. Frank Gilbreth's fame did not come until after his death in 1924.

BEHAVIORAL MANAGEMENT

The behavioral school of management grew out of the efforts of some to recognize the importance of the human endeavor in an organization. Followers of this school felt that if managers wanted to get things done, it must be through people—the study of workers and their interpersonal relationships.

Henry L. Gantt (1861–1919) was one of the earliest of the behavioral theorists. Although he could be classified in multiple categories, his passionate concern for the worker as an individual and his pleas for a humanitarian approach to management exemplify the behavioral approach. His early writing called for teaching and instructing workers, rather than driving them.

Mary Parker Follett (1868–1933), although trained in philosophy and political science, shifted her interests to vocational guidance, adult education, and social psychology. These led to her lifetime pursuit of developing a new managerial philosophy that would incorporate an understanding of the motivating desires of the individual and the group. She emphasized that workers on the job were motivated by the same forces that influenced their duties and pleasures away from the job and that the manager's role was to coordinate and facilitate group efforts, not to force and drive workers. Because of her emphasis on the group concept, the words "togetherness" and "group thinking" entered the managerial vocabulary.

Elton Mayo (1880–1949), best known for his Hawthorne experiments, introduced rest pauses in industrial plants and in so doing reduced employee turnover from 250 percent to 5 percent in some cases. He was concerned about human performance and working conditions. The work pauses, better known as breaks, reduced employee pessimism and improved morale and productivity.

MANAGEMENT PROCESS

The father of the management process school of thought was the Frenchman Henri Fayol (1841–1925), a mining engineer. He spent his entire working career with the same company, involved with coal mining and iron production. From his experiences as the managing director of the company, Fayol developed his general principles of administration. He thought that the study, analysis, and teaching of management should all be approached from the perspective of its functions, which he defined as forecasting and planning, organizing, commanding, controlling, and coordinating. He thought that planning was the most important and most difficult of these. Much of contemporary management thought revolves around the functions of management.

James D. Mooney (1884–1957), whose writings and research lent credence to the management process school of thinking, is credited with the notion that all great managers use the same principles of management. He emphasized a tight engineering approach to the manager's job of getting work done through others. He gave little thought to the human element, but instead was exclusively process-oriented. His approach to organizational analysis became classic.

CONCLUSION

There are diverse opinions about the people who were the earliest developers of management thought. Although there are many other theorists who can be credited with expanding or enhancing their teachings, the basics of each of the schools of thought can be credited to the individuals discussed.

SEE ALSO *Management*

BIBLIOGRAPHY

Duncan, W. Jack (1989). *Great Ideas in Management.* San Francisco: Jossey-Bass.

George, Claude S., Jr. (1972). *The History of Management Thought.* Englewood Cliffs, NJ: Prentice-Hall.

Wren, Daniel A. (1994). *The Evolution of Management Thought* (4th ed.). New York: John Wiley.

Wren, Daniel A. (2005). *The history of management thought* (5th ed.). Hoboken, N.J.: Wiley.

Roger L. Luft

MANAGEMENT INFORMATION SYSTEMS

Before management information systems can be understood, the terms systems, information, and management must briefly be defined. A system is a combination or arrangement of parts to form an integrated whole. A system includes an orderly arrangement according to some common principles or rules. A system is a plan or method of doing something.

The study of systems is not new. The Egyptian architects who built the pyramids relied on a system of measurements for construction of the pyramids. Phoenician astronomers studied the system of the stars and predicted future star positions. The development of a set of standards and procedures, or even a theory of the universe, is as old as history itself. People have always sought to find relationships for what is seen or heard or thought about.

A system is a scientific method of inquiry, or observation, of the formulation of an idea, the testing of that idea, and the application of the results. The scientific method of problem solving is systems analysis in its broadest sense. Data are facts and figures. However, data have no value until they are compiled into a system and can provide information for decision making.

Information is what is used in the act of informing or the state of being informed. Information includes knowledge acquired by some means. In the 1960s and 70s, it became necessary to formalize an educational approach to systems for business so individuals, work groups, and businesses who crossed boundaries in the various operations of business could have appropriate information. Technical developments in computers and data processing

Blaise Pascal (1623–1662) *French mathematician and philosopher Blaise Pascal invented the first mechanical adding machine.*

and new theories of systems analysis made it possible to computerize systems. Much of this computerization of systems was an outgrowth of basic research by the federal government.

Management is usually defined as planning, organizing, directing, and controlling the business operation. This definition, which evolved from the work of Henri Fayol in the early 1900s, defines what a manager does, but it is probably more appropriate to define what management is rather than what management does. Management is the process of allocating an organization's inputs, including human and economic resources, by planning, organizing, directing, and controlling for the purpose of producing goods or services desired by customers so that organizational objectives are accomplished. If management has knowledge of the planning, organizing, directing, and controlling of the business, its decisions can be made on the basis of facts, and decisions are more accurate and timely as a result.

Management information systems are those systems that allow managers to make decisions for the successful operation of businesses. Management information systems (MIS) consist of computer resources, people, and procedures used in the modern business enterprise. MIS also refers to the organization that develops and maintains most or all of the computer systems in the enterprise so that managers can make decisions. The goal of the MIS organization is to deliver information systems to the various levels of corporate managers. MIS professionals create and support the computer system throughout the company. Trained and educated to work with corporate computer systems, these professionals are responsible in some way for nearly all of the computers, from the largest mainframe to the desktop and portable PCs.

BACKGROUND

Management information systems do not have to be computerized, but with today's large, multinational corporations, computerization is a must for a business to be successful. However, management information systems began with simple manual systems such as customer databases on index cards. As early as 1642, the French mathematician and philosopher Blaise Pascal (1623–1662) invented the first mechanical adding machine so that figures could be added to provide information. Almost two hundred years later, Charles Babbage (1791–1871), a professor of mathematics at Cambridge University in England, wanted to make a machine that would compute mathematical tables. He attempted to build a computing machine during the 1880s. He failed because his ideas were beyond his technical capabilities, not because the idea was flawed. Babbage is often called the father of the computer. With the advent of the computer, management information systems became automated.

In the late 1890s, because of the efforts of Herman Hollerith (1860–1929), who created a punch-card system to tabulate the data for the 1890 census, it was possible to begin to provide data-processing equipment. The punch card developed by Hollerith was later used to form a company to provide data-processing equipment. This company evolved into International Business Machines (IBM). Mainframe computers were used for management information systems from the 1940s up until the 1970s. In the 1970s, personal computers were first built by hobbyists. Then Apple computer developed one of the first practical personal computers (PC). In the early 1980s, IBM developed its PC, and since then, the personal computer industry has mushroomed. Almost every management information system revolves around some kind of computer hardware and software.

Management information systems are becoming more important, and MIS personnel are more visible than they were in the 1960s and 1970s, when they were hidden away from the rest of the company and performed tasks behind closed doors. So remote were some MIS personnel from the operations of the business that they did not even know what products their companies made. This has changed because the need for an effective management information system is of primary concern to the business organization. Managers use MIS operations for all phases of management, including planning, organizing, directing, and controlling.

THE MIS JOB IN THE EARLY TWENTY-FIRST CENTURY

MIS personnel must be technically qualified to work with computer hardware, software, and computer information systems. Colleges and universities could not produce enough MIS personnel for business needs, and job opportunities were great in the mid-2000s. MIS managers, once they have risen through their technical ranks of their organization to become managers, must remember that they are no longer doing the technical work. They must cross over from being technicians to become managers. Their job changes from being technicians to being systems managers who manage other people's technical work. They must see themselves as needing to solve the business problems of the user, and not just of the data-processing department.

MIS managers are in charge of the systems development operations for their firm. Systems development requires four stages when developing a system for any phase of the organization:

Phase I is systems planning. The systems team must investigate the initial problem by determining what the problem is and developing a feasibility study for management to review.

Phase II identifies the requirements for the systems. It includes systems analysis, user requirements, necessary hardware and software, and a conceptional design for the system. Top management then reviews the systems analysis and design.

Phase III involves the development of the systems. This involves developing technical support and technical specifications, reviewing users' procedures control, designing the system, testing the system, and providing user training for the system. Management again reviews and decides on whether to implement the system.

Phase IV is the implementation of the system. The new system is converted from the old system, and the new system is implemented and then refined. There must then be ongoing maintenance and reevaluation of the system to see if it continues to meet the needs of the business.

TYPES OF SYSTEMS

Management information systems can be used as a support to managers to provide a competitive advantage. The system must support the goals of the organization. Most organizations are structured along functional lines, and the typical systems are identified as follows:

Accounting management information systems. All accounting reports are shared by all levels of accounting managers.

Financial management information systems. The financial management information system provides financial information to all financial managers within an organization including the chief financial officer. The chief financial officer analyzes historical and current financial activity, projects future financial needs, and monitors and controls the use of funds over time using the information developed by the MIS department.

Manufacturing management information systems. More than any functional area, operations have been impacted by great advances in technology. As a result, manufacturing operations have changed. For instance, inventories are provided just in time so that great amounts of money are not spent for warehousing huge inventories. In some instances, raw materials are even processed on railroad cars waiting to be sent directly to the factory, eliminating the need for warehousing.

Marketing management information systems. A marketing management information system supports managerial activity in the area of product development, distribution, pricing decisions, promotional effectiveness, and sales forecasting. More than any other functional area, marketing systems rely on external sources of data. These sources include competition and customers, for example.

Human resources management information systems. Human resources management information systems are concerned with activities related to workers, managers, and other individuals employed by the organization. Because the personnel function relates to all other areas in business, the human resources management information system plays a valuable role in ensuring organizational success. Activities performed by the human resources management information systems include, work-force analysis and planning, hiring, training, and job assignments.

The above are examples of the major management information systems. There may be other management information systems if the company is identified by different functional areas.

SEE ALSO *Information Processing; Information Systems*

BIBLIOGRAPHY

Rochester, Jack B. (1996). *Using Computers and Information: Tools for Knowledge Workers.* Indianapolis, IN: Que E&T.

Stair, Ralph M., and Reynolds, George W. (2003). *Principles of Information Systems: A Managerial Approach* (6th ed.). Boston: Thomson/Course Technology.

Lloyd W. Bartholome

MANAGEMENT/ LEADERSHIP STYLES

Leading should not be considered the same as managing. Business leaders who do not understand the difference between the functions/roles of leading and managing are quite likely to misinterpret how they should carry out their duties to meet organizational goals. While some managers are high-quality leaders, others manage only resources and do not lead their subordinates. Leadership is one of the four primary activities that are used to influence others. As such, it is a subcategory of the management concept that focuses mainly on behavioral issues, influence, and engaging opportunities. Managing is more comprehensive than leading. It involves dealing with resource issues as well as behavioral factors. Generally speaking, not all managers are necessarily leaders, yet the most effective managers, over the long term, are leaders.

Leadership is the process of guiding the behavior of others toward an organization's goals. Guiding, in this context, means causing individuals to behave in a particular manner or to follow a specific set of instructions. Ideally, the behavior exhibited is perfectly aligned with such factors as organizational goals, culture, policies, procedures, and job specifications. The main goal of leadership is to get things done through other people, making it one of the main activities that can enhance the management system. It is accomplished to a great degree through the use of effective communication.

Because leadership is a prerequisite for business success, to be a successful business manager one must have a solid understanding of what leadership includes. Indeed, such issues as the increased capabilities afforded by enhanced communication technology and the rise of international business have made leadership even more important in today's business environment. The following sections describe the major theories underlying the most commonly accepted management/leadership practices and the concepts on which they are based.

LEADERSHIP BASED ON TRAITS

The trait theory of leadership is based on research that implies that the abilities and dispositions necessary to make a good leader are inborn, not capable of being developed over time. The central thrust of this research is to describe leadership as accurately and analytically as possible. The reasoning is that a description of the full spectrum of managerial leadership traits would make it possible to easily identify individuals who possess them. An organization could then hire only those individuals who possess these traits and thus be assured of always having high-quality leaders.

Current management thoughts, however, suggests that leadership ability cannot be explained by an individual's inherited characteristics. To the contrary, business analysts believe that individuals can learn to be good or even exceptional leaders. Thousands of employees each year complete training to improve their leadership skills. Corporations and not-for-profit organizations continue to do this as an investment, which pays dividends.

IDENTIFYING LEADERSHIP BEHAVIORS

Since trait theory proved not to be aligned with leadership skill, researchers have analyzed other angles to explain leadership success or failure. Rather than looking at the traits successful leaders supposedly should possess, researchers began to investigate what good leaders really do. This behavioral approach was concerned with analyzing how a manager completed a task and whether the manager focused on such interpersonal skills as providing moral support and recognizing employees for their successes. Based on these research efforts, leaders can be accurately described by either their job-centered behavior or their employee-centered behavior, since this research indicated two primary dimensions of leader behavior: a work dimension (structure behavior/job-centered behavior) and a people dimension (consideration behavior/employee-centered behavior).

In addition, effective leaders are skilled coaches and mentor those around them. They build team thinking and behavior, as well as communicate formative developmental feedback. They also illustrate the visible meaning of the organization's vision and mission, including shared values, as well as being a boundaryless thinker. Successful leaders build networks within and outside their organizations searching for solutions, opportunities, and synergies. In their day-to-day work, they exemplify diplomacy while being an interpreter and spokesperson of the organization's vision.

From a different standpoint, what perspectives and behaviors typically align with poor or ineffective leaders? Behaviors and patterns of thinking that contribute to ineffective leadership include lacking knowledge and skill related to the main activities of the organization and leadership, generally considered incompetence. Being rigid, intemperate, and callous clearly cause difficulties in leading others. Although the next types of poor leadership are obvious, they continue to shackle organizational success. These negative attributes include corruptness, insularity, and being evil. Unfortunately, one often reads or see stories about leaders who have taken the leap to the "dark side."

WHICH LEADERSHIP STYLES ARE MOST EFFECTIVE?

Caution should be exercised when considering what style of leadership is best. Research suggests that no single leadership style can be generalized as being most effective. Organizational situations are so complex that one particular leadership style may be successful in one situation but totally ineffective in another.

CONTINGENCY THEORY

Contingency theory, as applied to management/leadership, focuses on what managers do in practice, because this theory suggests that how a manager operates and makes decisions depends upon, or is contingent upon, a set of circumstances. It is centered on situational analysis. Using contingency theory, managers read situations with an "if-then" mentality: If this situational attribute is present, then there is an appropriate response that a manager should make. This theory takes into consideration human resources and their interaction with business operations. Managers may take different courses of action to get the same result based on differences in situational characteristics.

In general, contingency theory suggests that a business leader needs to outline the conditions or situations in which various management methods have the best chance of success. This theory thus runs directly counter to trait theory, discussed earlier. Some of the challenges to successfully using contingency theory are the need to accurately analyze an actual situation, then to choose the appropriate strategies and tactics, and finally to implement these strategies and tactics.

Managers encounter a variety of leadership situations during the course of their daily activities, each of which may require them to use leadership styles that vary considerably, depending on the situation. In using the contingency model, factors of major concern are leader-member relations, task structure, and the position power of the leader. The leader has to analyze these factors to determine the most appropriate style of response for meeting overall work-unit and organizational goals.

Leader-member relations refer to the ongoing degree to which subordinates accept an individual leader or group of leaders. Task structure refers to the degree to which tasks are clearly or poorly defined. Position power is the extent to which a leader or group of leaders has control over the work process, rewards, and punishment. Taking these factors into consideration, leaders can adjust their style to best match the context of their decision making and leadership. For those leaders who have a breadth of leadership styles, knowing when to change styles gives them the tools to successfully deal with the varying nature of business decision making. For those leaders who have a limited repertoire of leadership styles, they and their superiors can use this information to better match work situations with the styles that a specific leader possesses.

Within this continuum, or range, of leadership behaviors, each type of behavior also relates to the degree of authority the manager can display, and inversely, to the level of freedom that is made available to workers. On one end of this continuum, business leaders exert a high level of control and allow little employee autonomy; on the opposite end, leaders exert very little control, instead allowing workers considerable autonomy and self-direction. Thus leadership behavior as it progresses across the continuum reflects a gradual change from autocratic to democratic leadership.

In today's business environment there are more complicated contexts and relationships within which managers and subordinates must work than existed in previous eras. And, as contexts and relationships become increasingly complicated, it becomes significantly more difficult for leaders to determine how to lead. In addition, there are major societal and organizational forces that add confusion about how to approach leadership.

THEORY X AND THEORY Y

Based on the work of psychologists, organizational theorists, and human relations specialists in the 1960s and 1970s, two distinct assumptions, called Theory X and Theory Y, evolved about why and how people work for others. Theory X posits that people do not like to work and will avoid doing so if the opportunity presents itself. Because of this, most people need to be coerced into completing their required job duties and punished if they do not complete the quantity of work assigned at the level of quality required. Again, because of their dislike for work, most people do not want responsibility, prefer to be directed by others, and have little ambition; all they want is job security.

With an almost completely opposite perspective, Theory Y posits that people like to work and see it as a natural event in their lives. Therefore, punishment and threats are not the only means of motivating them to complete work assignments. People are willing to work hard for an organization; indeed, they will use self-direction and control to work toward goals that are understandable and communicated clearly. In this theory of human behavior and motivation, people are seen as seekers of learning and responsibility who are capable of and willing to be engaged with creative problem-solving activities that will help the organization reach its goals. According to Theory Y, leaders need to develop ways to expand the capabilities of their workers so that the organization can benefit from this significant potential resource.

Although Theory Y has much to offer and is widely followed, many organizations still use a variety of policies and practices that are based on Theory X principles. A further development in explaining human work behavior and then adjusting management/leadership practices to it is Theory Z.

THEORY Z

Probably the most prominent of the theories and practices coming from Japan is the Theory Z approach, which combines typical practices from the United States and Japan into a comprehensive system of management/leadership. This system includes the following principles of best management/leadership practice:

- Seek to establish a long-term employment culture within the organization
- Use collective decision making as much as possible
- Increase and reinforce the importance of individual responsibility
- Establish a slow and long-term process for evaluation and promotion
- Employ implicit, informal control that uses explicit, formal measures/tools of performance
- Institute and use moderately specialized job descriptions and career paths
- Develop policies and practices that support a holistic concern for and support of the individual both at work and at home (as regards family issues)

Theory Z has had a marked impact on the manner in which companies are led today. Theory Z strategies have been instrumental in building stronger working relationships between subordinates and their leaders because of the increased level of worker participation in decision making as well as leaders' higher level of concern for their subordinates.

MANAGERIAL GRID

Business researchers at the University of Texas developed a two-dimensional grid theory to explain a leadership style based on a person's (1) concern for production and (2) concern for people. Each axis on the grid is a 9-point scale, with 1 meaning low concern and 9 meaning high concern. "Team" managers, often considered the most effective leaders, have strong concern both for the people who work for them and for the output of the group/unit. "Country club" managers are significantly more concerned about their subordinates than about production output. "Authority-compliance" managers, in contrast, are singularly focused on meeting production goals. "Middle-of-the-road" managers attempt to balance people and production concerns in a moderate fashion. Finally, "impoverished" managers tend to be virtually bankrupt in both categories, usually not knowing much or caring much about either. Grid analysis can be quite useful in helping to determine managers' strengths, weak points, areas where they might best be used, and types of staff development they might need to progress.

PATH-GOAL LEADERSHIP THEORY

In path-goal leadership theory, the key strategy of the leader is to make desirable and achievable rewards available to employees. These rewards are directly related to achieving organizational goals. The manager articulates the objectives (the goal) to be accomplished and how these can and should be completed (the path) to earn rewards. This theory encourages managers to facilitate job performance by showing employees how their work behaviors directly affect their receiving desired rewards.

SYSTEMS THEORY AND THE LEADERSHIP/MANAGEMENT FUNCTION

A system is a group of interrelated and dependent components that function holistically to meet common goals. Systems theory suggests that organizations operate much like the human biological system, having to deal with entropy, support synergy, and subsystem interdependence. The law of entropy states that there are limited resources available and that as they are used/consumed, their beneficial features are dispersed and are not available to the same degree as they were originally. The other two considerations in a systems approach are the achievement of synergy, or the creation of a total value greater than the value of separate parts, and of subsystem interdependence or the

linkage of components in such a way that synergy can take place.

In the effort to enhance system performance, managers/leaders must consider the openness and responsiveness of their business organization and the external environment in which it operates. In this environment, leaders must consider the four major features of business system theory: inputs, organizational features, outputs, and feedback. The input factors for most systems include human labor, information, hard goods, and financing. Organizational features include the work process, management functions, and production or service technology. Output results include employee satisfaction, products or services, customer and supplier relationships, and profits/losses. In guiding a unit or the whole organization, business leaders need to consider features of their organization's system as it interacts with and responds to customers, suppliers, competitors, and government agencies.

TRANSFORMATIONAL AND TRANSACTIONAL LEADERSHIP

Transformational leadership inspires organizational success by dramatically affecting workers' attitudes about what an organization should be as well as their basic values, such as trust, fairness, and reliability. Transformational leadership, which is similar to charismatic or inspirational leadership, creates in workers a sense of ownership of the organization, encourages new ways of solving problems, and promotes lifelong learning for all members of the organization. Although the topic of transformational leadership is both appealing and exciting, more research is needed to develop insights regarding how one becomes a successful transformational leader.

Transactional leadership refers to the transactions that play out between the leader and the follower. This mindset supports leaders in motivating followers by appealing to their own self-interest. Its principles are to motivate by the exchange process. Transactional behavior focuses on the accomplishment of tasks and good worker relationships in exchange for desirable rewards. Leaders using transactional processes are most likely to adapt their style and behavior to that of their followers. Some researchers suggest that transactional leadership encompasses four types of behavior.

1. *Contingent reward*—The leader uses rewards or incentives to achieve results when expectations are met

2. *Passive management by exception*—The leader uses correction or punishment as a response to unacceptable performance

3. *Active management by exception*—The leader actively monitors work and uses corrective methods

4. *Laissez-faire leadership*—The leader is indifferent and has a "hands-off" approach, often ignoring the needs of others

Transactional leadership behavior is used to one degree or another by most leaders. Using transactional leadership behavior as a singular tool to motivate others can create a few common problems. For instance, it can place too much emphasis on the "bottom line" and by its very nature is short-term oriented, with the goal of simply maximizing efficiency and profits. The leader can pressure others to engage in unethical or amoral practices by offering strong rewards or punishments. Transactional leaders seek to influence others by exchanging work for wages, but this does not build on the worker's need for meaningful work. In addition, transactional leadership may lead to an environment permeated by position, power, and politics. This is why transformational leadership is seen as a more productive way to long-term success.

CONFLICT MANAGEMENT

Of all the skills that a manager/leader needs, none is more important than managing the conflicts that inevitably arise in any organization. Conflicts can arise between members in the same work unit, between the work group and its leader, between group leaders, and between different work groups. Some of the most common causes of conflict are communications breakdowns, personality clashes, power and status differences, goal discrepancies, disputed authority boundaries, and allocation of resources.

The following processes are among those usually suggested to eliminate, reduce, and prevent conflict:

• Focus on the facts of the matter; avoid unsupported assertions and issues of personality

• Develop a list of all possible resolutions to the conflict that will allow the adversarial parties to view the issue from a different perspective

• Maintain a balance of power and accessibility while addressing the conflict

• Seek a realistic resolution; never force a consensus, but do not get bogged down in a never-ending debate to achieve one

• Focus on the larger goals/mission of the organization

• Engage in bargaining/negotiating to identify options to address the conflict

• If needed, use a third party to mediate the differences; bringing in an outside person can add objectivity and reduce personality issues

• Facilitate accurate communications to reduce rumors and to increase the common understanding of the facts and issues

A two-dimensional model for understanding how individuals approach situations involving conflict resolution is widely accepted. On one axis is the dimension of cooperativeness; on the other, the dimension of assertiveness. As discussed earlier, effective leaders vary their style to meet the needs of a specific situation. Hence, during a conflict situation in which time is a critical concern, an assertive style is needed to resolve the conflict so that time is not lost during a drawn-out negotiation process. Oppositely, when harmony is critical, especially when relationships are new or in their early stages, a collaborative and cooperative approach to conflict resolution is needed. This model for conflict resolution fits well with and supports the notion of contingency and situational leadership.

JAPANESE MANAGEMENT/LEADERSHIP METHODS

Since the end of World War II (1939–1945), business leaders around the world have marveled at the ability of Japanese managers to motivate and successfully lead their subordinates to levels of outstanding performance in terms of both the quantity and quality of production. Therefore, Japanese approaches to management and leadership have been studied intensely to find similarities and differences. Among the approaches that have been cited as contributing to Japanese success are:

1. Japanese corporations make the effort to hire employees for a lifetime, rather than a shorter period. This helps workers to feel a close relationship with the organization and helps build employee ownership of the organization's success.

2. Employees are elevated to a level of organizational status equivalent to that of management by leveling the playing field with regard to such items as dress, benefit packages, support services/amenities, restrooms, and stock ownership plans.

3. Employees are shown that they are valued and a critical part of the company. This is accomplished by having ceremonies to honor employees, providing housing at nominal cost to employees, having facilities for social activities that are sponsored by the organization, offering competitive salaries, and so forth.

4. A significant effort is made to build positive and strong working relationships between leaders and their subordinates. This includes making sure that leaders take time to get to know their employees and become cognizant of their main concerns. Such a relationship can have a marked impact on the extent to which employees value the organization and their leaders.

5. Collective responsibility is looked to for the success of the organization. Individual accountability is played down, in contrast to the climate that prevails in U.S. organizations.

6. Implied control mechanisms are based on cultural values and responsibility.

7. Nonspecialized career pathways are typical. Employees work in a number of job categories over the course of their tenure so that they can gain a broader sense of the nature of all the work that is done in the organization.

8. There is a holistic concern for the welfare of every employee. Organizations and their leaders take the time to assist employees with personal issues and work opportunities.

9. The Japanese are generally concerned with how the company performs and how individual work groups perform, rather than how an individual performs. Therefore, incentives for individuals are less likely to be effective than incentives associated with the performance of a work group or of a whole unit. In addition, Japanese leaders and workers focus much less on monetary rewards than on esteem and social rewards.

Another major practice used in the manufacturing and handling of goods was developed in Japan—*kanban*, or what in the United States is known as the just-in-time inventory and materials handling system. In this system, managers/leaders locate high-quality suppliers within a short distance of their operations. They also establish specific quality standards and delivery requirements, as well as materials handling procedures, that these suppliers are contractually obligated to adhere to.

Although these techniques have proven to be successful in Japan, attempts to duplicate them in another culture may have disappointing results. The importance of cultural mores cannot be underestimated. What may work in Japan, France, or the United States may not work anywhere else simply because of cultural factors. Yet Japanese management/leadership principles have taught managers around the world to consider new approaches in order to achieve the higher standards of organizational effectiveness necessary in today's global economy. Business leaders around the world are examining their practices in light of the success that the Japanese and others have had in the areas of strategy building, organizational development, group/team cooperation, and establishing competitive advantage.

SEE ALSO *Job Satisfaction; Leadership; Management*

BIBLIOGRAPHY

Bennis, Warren G. (2003). *On becoming a leader: The leadership classic* (rev. ed.). Cambridge, MA: Perseus.

Blake, Robert R., Mouton, Jane S., and Allen, Robert L. (1987). *Spectacular teamwork.* New York: Wiley.

Blake, Robert R., Mouton, Jane S., and Allen, Robert L. (1990). *Managerial grid IV.* Houston, TX: Gulf.

Burns, James MacGregor (1978). *Leadership.* New York: Harper and Row.

Certo, Samuel C. (2003). *Modern management* (9th ed.). Upper Saddle River, NJ: Prentice Hall.

Dotlich, David L., Noel, James L., and Walker, Norman (2004). *Leadership passages.* San Francisco: Jossey-Bass.

DuBrin, Andrew J. (2005). *Coaching and mentoring skills.* Upper Saddle River, NJ: Pearson/Prentice Hall.

Gardner, John W. (1990). *On leadership.* New York: Free Press.

Goldsmith, Marshall, Govindarajan, V., Kaye, B., and Vicere, A. A. (2003). *The many facets of leadership.* Upper Saddle River, NJ: Prentice Hall.

Kanter, Rosabeth Moss (2003). Introduction. In *Best practice: Ideas and insights from the world's foremost business thinkers* (pp. 1–10). Cambridge, MA: Perseus.

Kellerman, Barbara (2004). *Bad leadership: What it is, how it happens, why it happens.* Boston: Harvard Business School Press.

Koestenbaum, Peter (2002). *Leadership: The inner side of greatness* (rev. ed.). San Francisco: Jossey-Bass.

Kuhnert, Karl W., and Lewis, P. (1987, October). Transactional and transformational leadership: A constructive/developmental analysis. *Academy of Management Review, 12,* 648–657.

Norstrom, K. (2003). Meaningful leadership. In *Best practice: Ideas and insights from the world's foremost business thinkers* (pp. 262–266). Cambridge, MA: Perseus.

Sashkin, Marshall, and Sashkin, Molly G. (2003). *Leadership that matters.* San Francisco: Berrett-Koehler.

Thomas Haynes

MANAGERIAL GRID

SEE *Management/Leadership Styles*

MANUFACTURING

One can trace the origins of modern manufacturing management to the advent of agricultural production, which meant that humans did not constantly have to wander to find new sources of food. Since that time, people have been developing better techniques for producing goods to meet human needs and wants. Since they had additional time available because of more efficient food sources, people began to develop techniques to produce items for use and trade. They also began to specialize based on their skills and resources. With the first era of water-based exploration, trade, and conflict, new ideas regarding product development eventually emerged, over the course of the centuries, leading to the beginning of the Industrial Revolution in the mid-eighteenth century. The early twentieth century, however, is generally considered to mark the true beginning of a disciplined effort to study

Flywheel assembly line at the Ford Motor Company's Highland Park, Michigan, plant ca. 1913. **ASSOCIATED PRESS, FORD MOTOR COMPANY**

and improve manufacturing and operations management practices. Thus, what we know as modern manufacturing began in the final decades of the twentieth century.

The late 1970s and early 1980s saw the development of the manufacturing strategy paradigm by researchers at the Harvard Business School. This work focused on how manufacturing executives could use their factories' capabilities as strategic competitive weapons, specifically identifying how what we call the five P's of manufacturing management (people, plants, parts, processes, and planning) can be analyzed as strategic and tactical decision variables. Central to this notion is the focus on factory and manufacturing trade-offs. Because a factory cannot excel on all performance measures, its management must devise a focused strategy, creating a focused factory that does a limited set of tasks extremely well. Thus the need arose for making trade-offs among such performance measures as low cost, high quality, and high flexibility in designing and managing factories.

The 1980s saw a revolution in management philosophy and the technologies used in manufacturing. Just-in-time (JIT) production was the primary breakthrough in manufacturing philosophy. Pioneered by the Japanese, JIT is an integrated set of activities designed to achieve high-volume production using minimal inventories of parts that arrive at the workstation "just in time." This philosophy—coupled with total quality control (TQC), which aggressively seeks to eliminate causes of production defects—is now a cornerstone in many manufacturers' practices.

As profound as JIT's impact has been, factory automation in its various forms promises to have an even greater impact on operations management in coming decades. Such terms as computer-integrated manufacturing (CIM), flexible manufacturing systems (FMS), and factory of the future (FOF) are part of the vocabulary of manufacturing leaders.

Another major development of the 1970s and 1980s was the broad application of computers to operations problems. For manufacturers, the big breakthrough was the application of materials requirements planning (MRP) to production control. This approach brings together, in a computer program, all the parts that go into complicated products. This computer program then enables production planners to quickly adjust production schedules and inventory purchases to meet changing demands during the manufacturing process. Clearly, the massive data manipulation required for changing the schedules of products with thousands of parts would be impossible without such programs and the computer capacity to run them. The promotion of this approach by the American Production and Inventory Control Society (APICS) has been termed the MRP Crusade.

The hallmark development in the field of manufacturing management, as well as in management practice in general, is total quality management (TQM). Although practiced by many companies in the 1980s, TQM became truly pervasive in the 1990s. All manufacturing executives are aware of the quality message put forth by the so-called quality gurus—W. Edwards Deming, Joseph M. Juran, and Philip Crosby. Helping the quality movement along was the creation of the Baldrige National Quality Award in 1986 under the direction of the American Society of Quality Control and the National Institute of Standards and Technology. The Baldrige Award recognizes up to five companies a year for outstanding quality management systems.

The ISO 9000 certification standards, issued by the International Organization for Standardization, now play a major role in setting quality standards, particularly for global manufacturers. Many European companies require that their vendors meet these standards as a condition for obtaining contracts.

The need to become or remain competitive in the global economic recession of the early 1990s pushed companies to seek major innovations in the processes used to run their operations. One major type of business process reengineering (BPR) is conveyed in the title of Michael Hammer's influential article "Reengineering Work: Don't Automate, Obliterate." The approach seeks to make revolutionary, as opposed to evolutionary, changes. It does this by taking a fresh look at what the organization is trying to do, and then eliminating non-value-added steps and computerizing the remaining ones to achieve the desired outcome.

The idea is to apply a total system approach to managing the flow of information, materials, and services from raw material suppliers through factories and warehouses to the end customer. Recent trends, such as outsourcing and mass customization, are forcing companies to find flexible ways to meet customer demand. The focus is on optimizing those core activities in order to maximize the speed of response to changes in customer expectations.

Based on the work of several researchers, a few basic operations priorities have been identified. These priorities include cost, product quality and reliability, delivery speed, delivery reliability, ability to cope with changes in demand, flexibility, and speed of new product introduction. In every industry, there is usually a segment of the market that buys products—typically products that are commodity-like in nature like sugar, iron ore, or coal—strictly on the basis of low cost. Because this segment of the market is frequently very large, many companies are lured by the potential for significant profits, which they associate with the large unit volumes of the product. As a

Automated automobile assembly line in Durban, South Africa. © **CHARLES O'REAR/CORBIS**

consequence, competition in this segment is fierce—and so is the failure rate.

Quality can be divided into two categories: product quality and process quality. The level of a product's quality will vary with the market segment to which it is aimed because the goal in establishing the proper level of product quality is to meet the requirements of the customer. Overdesigned products with too high a level of quality will be viewed as prohibitively expensive. Underdesigned products, on the other hand, will result in losing customers to products that cost a little more but are perceived as offering greater benefits.

Process quality is critical since it relates directly to the reliability of the product. Regardless of the product, customers want products without defects. Thus, the goal of process quality is to produce error-free products. Adherence to product specifications is essential to ensure the reliability of the product as defined by its intended use.

A company's ability to deliver more quickly than its competitors may be critical. Take, for example, a company that offers a repair service for computer-networking equipment. A company that can offer on-site repair within one or two hours has a significant advantage over a competing firm that only guarantees service only within twenty-four hours.

Delivery reliability relates to a firm's ability to supply the product or service on or before a promised delivery due date. The focus during the 1980s and 1990s on reducing inventory stocks in order to reduce cost has made delivery reliability an increasingly important criterion in evaluating alternative vendors.

A company's ability to respond to increases and decreases in demand is another important factor in its ability to compete. It is well known that a company with increasing demand can do little wrong. When demand is strong and increasing, costs are continuously reduced because of economies of scale, and investments in new technologies can be easily justified. Scaling back when demand decreases may require many difficult decisions regarding laying off employees and related reductions in assets. The ability to deal effectively with dynamic market demand over the long term is an essential element of manufacturing strategy.

Flexibility, from a strategic perspective, refers to a company's ability to offer a wide variety of products to its customers. In the 1990s companies began to adjust their processes and outputs to dynamic and sometimes volatile customer needs. An important component of flexibility is the ability to develop different products and deliver them to market. As new technologies and processes become widespread, a company must be able to respond to market demands more and more quickly if it is to continue to be successful.

Manufacturing strategy must be linked vertically to the customer and horizontally to other parts of the enterprise. Underlying this framework is senior management's strategic vision of the firm. This vision identifies, in general terms, the target market, the firm's product line, and its core enterprise and operations capabilities. The choice of a target market can be difficult, but it must be made. Indeed, it may lead to turning away business—ruling out a customer segment that would simply be unprofitable or too hard to serve given the firm's capabilities. Core capabilities are those skills that differentiate the manufacturing from its competitors.

In general, customers' new-product or current-product requirements set the performance priorities that then become the required priorities for operations. Manufacturing organizations have a linkage of priorities because they cannot satisfy customer needs without the involvement of R&D and distribution and without the direct or indirect support of financial management, human resource management, and information management. Given its performance requirements, a manufacturing division uses its capabilities to achieve these priority goals in order to complete sales. These capabilities include technology, systems, and people. CIM, JIT, and TQM represent fundamental concepts and tools used in each of the three areas.

Suppliers do not become suppliers unless their capabilities in the management of technology, systems, and people reach acceptable levels. In addition, most manufacturing capabilities are now subjected to the "make-or-buy" decision. It is current practice among world-class manufacturers to subject each part of a manufacturing operation to the question: If we are not among the best in the world at, say, metal forming, should we be doing this at all, or should we subcontract to someone who *is* the best?

The main objectives of manufacturing strategy development are (1) to translate required priorities into specific performance requirements for operations and (2) to make the necessary plans to assure that manufacturing capabilities are sufficient to accomplish them. Developing priorities involves the following steps:

1. Segment the market according to the product group.

2. Identify the product requirements, demand patterns, and profit margins of each group.

3. Determine the order winners and order qualifiers for each group.

4. Convert order winners into specific performance requirements.

It has been said that America's resurgence in manufacturing is not the result of U.S. firms being better innovators than most foreign competitors. This has been true for a long time. Rather, it is because U.S. firms are proving to be very effective copiers, having spent a decade examining the advantages of foreign rivals in product development, production operations, supply chain management, and corporate governance then putting in place functional equivalents that incrementally improve on their best techniques. Four main adaptations on the part of U.S. firms underscore this success:

1. New approaches to product-development team structure and management have resulted in getting products to market faster, with better designs and manufacturability.

2. Companies have improved their manufacturing facilities through dramatic reductions of work-in-process, space, tool costs, and human effort, while simultaneously improving quality and flexibility.

3. New methods of customer-supplier cooperation, which borrow from the Japanese *keiretsu* (large holding companies) practices of close linkages but maintain the independence of the organizations desired by U.S. companies, have been put in place.

4. Better leadership—through strong, independent boards of directors who will dismiss managers who are not doing their jobs effectively—now exists.

In sum, the last few decades of the twentieth century witnessed tremendous change and advancement in the means of producing goods and the manner of managing these operations that have led to higher levels of quality and quantity as well as greater efficiency in the use of resources. In the new millennium, because of global competition and the expansive use of new technologies, including the Internet, a successful firm will be one that is competitive with new products and services that are creatively marketed and effectively financed. Yet what is becoming increasingly critical is the ability to develop manufacturing practices that provide unique benefits to the products. The organization that can develop superior products, sell them at lower prices, and deliver them to their customers in a timely manner stands to become a formidable presence in the marketplace.

SEE ALSO *Factors of Production*

Thomas Haynes

MARKDOWNS

SEE *Pricing*

MARKET ECONOMICS

SEE *Economic Systems*

MARKET SEGMENTATION

Market segmentation is one of two general approaches to marketing; the other is mass-marketing. In the mass-marketing approach, businesses look at the total market as though all of its parts were the same and market accordingly. In the market-segmentation approach, the total market is viewed as being made up of several smaller segments, each different from the other. This approach enables businesses to identify one or more appealing segments to which they can profitably target their products and marketing efforts.

The market-segmentation process involves multiple steps (Figure 1). The first is to define the market in terms of the product's end users and their needs. The second is to divide the market into groups on the basis of their characteristics and buying behaviors.

Possible bases for dividing a total market are different for consumer markets than for industrial markets. The most common elements used to separate consumer markets are demographic factors, psychographic characteristics, geographic location, and perceived product benefits.

Demographic segmentation involves dividing the market on the basis of statistical differences in personal characteristics, such as age, gender, race, income, life stage,

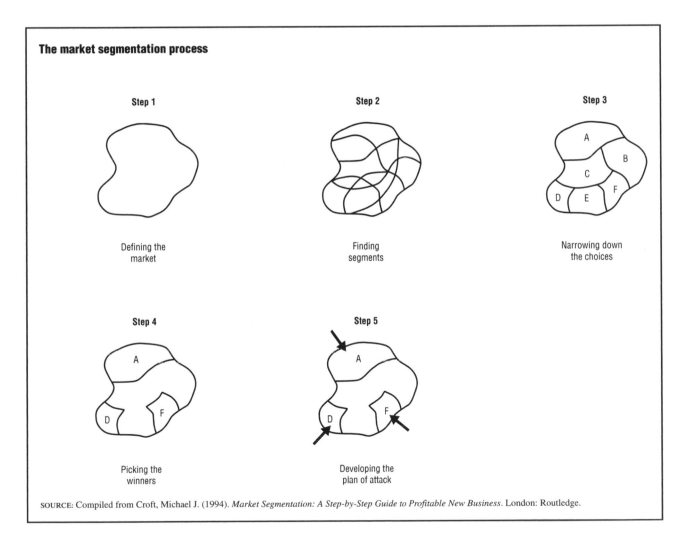

The market segmentation process

Step 1

Defining the market

Step 2

Finding segments

Step 3

Narrowing down the choices

Step 4

Picking the winners

Step 5

Developing the plan of attack

SOURCE: Compiled from Croft, Michael J. (1994). *Market Segmentation: A Step-by-Step Guide to Profitable New Business*. London: Routledge.

Figure 1

occupation, and education level. Clothing manufacturers, for example, segment on the basis of age groups such as teenagers, young adults, and mature adults. Jewelers use gender to divide markets. Cosmetics and hair care companies may use race as a factor; home builders, life stage; professional periodicals, occupation; and so on.

Psychographic segmentation is based on traits, attitudes, interests, or lifestyles of potential customer groups. Companies marketing new products, for instance, seek to identify customer groups that are positively disposed to new ideas. Firms marketing environmentally friendly products single out segments with environmental concerns. Some financial institutions attempt to isolate and tap into groups with a strong interest in supporting their college, favorite sports team, or professional organization through logoed credit cards. Similarly, marketers of low-fat or low-calorie products try to identify and match their products with portions of the market that are health- or weight-conscious.

Geographic segmentation entails dividing the market on the basis of where people live. Divisions may be in terms of neighborhoods, cities, counties, states, regions, or even countries. Considerations related to geographic grouping may include the makeup of the areas, that is, urban, suburban, or rural; size of the area; climate; or population. For example, manufacturers of snow-removal equipment focus on identifying potential user segments in areas of heavy snow accumulation. Because many retail chains are dependent on high-volume traffic, they search for, and will only locate in, areas with a certain number of people per square mile.

Product-benefit segmentation is based on the perceived value or advantage consumers receive from a good or service over alternatives. Thus, markets can be partitioned in terms of the quality, performance, image, service, special features, or other benefits prospective consumers seek. A wide spectrum of businesses—from camera to shampoo to athletic footwear to automobile marketers—rely on this type of segmentation to match up with customers. Many companies even market similar products of different grades or different accompanying services to different groups on the basis of product-benefit preference.

Factors used to segment industrial markets are grouped along different lines than those used for consumer markets. Some are very different; some are similar. Industrial markets are often divided on the basis of organizational variables, such as type of business, company size, geographic location, or technological base. In other instances, they are segmented along operational lines such as products made or sold, related processes used, volume used, or end-user applications. In still other instances, differences in purchase practices provide the segmentation base. These differences include centralized versus decentralized purchasing; policy regarding number of vendors; buyer-seller relationships; and similarity of quality, service, or availability needs.

Although demographic, geographic, and organizational differences enable marketers to narrow their opportunities, they rarely provide enough specific information to make a decision on dividing the market. Psychographic data, operational lines, and, in particular, perceived consumer benefits and preferred business practices are better at pinpointing buyer groupings, but they must be considered against the broader background. Thus, the key is to gather information on and consider *all* pertinent segmentation bases before making a decision.

Once potential market segments are identified, the third step in the process is to reduce the pool to those that are (1) large enough to be worth pursuing, (2) potentially profitable, (3) reachable, and (4) likely to be responsive.

The fourth step is to zero in on one or more segments that are the best targets for the company's product(s) or capacity to expand. After the selection is made, the business can then design a separate marketing mix for each market segment to be targeted.

Adopting a market-segmentation approach can benefit a company in several specific areas. First, it can give customer-driven direction to the management of current products. Second, it can result in more efficient use of marketing resources. Third, it can help identify new opportunities for growth and expansion. At the same time, it can bring a company the broad benefit of a competitive advantage.

Adopting the market-segmentation approach can also be accompanied by some drawbacks. Both production and marketing costs can be more expensive than mass marketing, particularly when multiple segments are targeted. Different product models, for example, are required for each segment. Separate inventories must be maintained for each version. And different promotion may be required for each market. In addition, administrative expenses go up with the planning, implementation, and control of multiple marketing programs.

During the late 1960s, market segmentation moved ahead of mass marketing as the predominant marketing approach. In the following decades, societal changes and wider economic opportunity continually expanded the number of groups with specialized product needs and buying power. In response, businesses increasingly turned to the segmentation approach to capture and/or hold market share.

SEE ALSO *Marketing*

BIBLIOGRAPHY

Cahill, Dennis J. (2006) *Lifestyle market segmentation.* New York: Haworth Press.

Croft, Michael J. (1994). *Market Segmentation: A Step-By-Step Guide to Profitable New Business.* London: Routledge.

Dibb, Sally, Simkin, Lyndon, and Bradley, John (1996). *The Market Planning Workbook: Effective Marketing for Marketing Managers.* London: Routledge.

Michman, Ronald D. (1991). *Lifestyle Market Segmentation.* New York: Praeger.

Weinstein, Art (2004). *Handbook of market segmentation: strategic targeting for business and technology firms* (3rd ed.). New York: Haworth Press.

Earl C. Meyer
Patrick M. Graham

MARKET SHARE

SEE *Marketing Research*

MARKETING

Marketing pertains to the interactive process that requires developing, pricing, placing, and promoting goods, ideas, or services in order to facilitate exchanges between customers and sellers to satisfy the needs and wants of consumers. Thus, at the very center of the marketing process is satisfying the needs and wants of customers.

NEEDS AND WANTS

Needs are the basic items required for human survival. Human needs are an essential concept underlying the marketing process because needs are translated into consumer wants. Human needs are often described as a state of real or perceived deprivation. Basic human needs take one of three forms: physical, social, and individual. Physical needs are basic to survival and include food, clothing, warmth, and safety. Social needs revolve around the desire for belonging and affection. Individual needs include longings for knowledge and self-expression, through items such as clothing choices.

Wants are needs that are shaped by both cultural influences and individual preferences. Wants are often described as goods, ideas, and services that fulfill the needs of an individual consumer. The wants of individuals change as both society and technology change. For example, when a computer is released, a consumer may want it simply because it is a new and improved technology. Therefore, the purpose of marketing is to convert these generic needs into wants for specific goods, ideas, or services. Demand is created when wants are supported by an individual consumer's ability to purchase the goods, ideas, or services in question.

Consumers buy products that will best meet their needs, as well as provide the most fulfillment resulting from the exchange process. The first step in the exchange process is to provide a product. Products can take a number of forms such as goods, ideas, and services. All products are produced to satisfy the needs, wants, and demands of individual buyers.

The second step in the satisfaction process is exchange. Exchange occurs when an individual receives a product from a seller in return for something called consideration. Consideration usually takes the form of currency. For an exchange to take place, it must meet a number of conditions:

1. There must be at least two participants in the process.

2. Each party must offer something of value to the other.

3. Both parties must want to deal with each other.

4. Both participants have the right to accept or to reject the offer.

5. Both parties must have the ability to communicate and deliver on the mutual agreement.

Thus, the transaction process is a core component of marketing. Whenever there is a trade of values between two parties, a transaction has occurred. A transaction is often considered a unit of measurement in marketing. The earliest form of exchange was known as barter.

HISTORICAL ERAS OF MARKETING

Modern marketing began in the early 1900s. The marketing process progressed through four distinct eras: production, sales, marketing, and relationship. In the 1920s, firms operated under the premise that production was a seller's market. Product choices were nearly nonexistent because firm managers believed that a superior product would sell itself. This philosophy was possible because the demand for products outlasted supply. During this era, firm success was measured totally in terms of production.

The second era of marketing, ushered in during 1950s, is known as the sales era. During this era, product supply exceeded demand. Thus, firms assumed that consumers would resist buying goods and services deemed nonessential. To overcome this consumer resistance, sellers had to employ creative advertising and skillful personal selling in order to get consumers to buy.

The marketing era emerged after firm managers realized that a better strategy was needed to attract and keep customers because allowing products to sell themselves was not effective. Rather, the marketing concept philosophy was adopted by many firms in an attempt to meet the specific needs of customers. Proponents of the marketing concept argued that in order for firms to achieve their goals, they had to satisfy the needs and wants of consumers.

The relationship era began in the 1990s and continues today. The thrust of the relationship era is to establish and foster long-term relationships with both customers and suppliers. These long-term relationships with both customers and suppliers add value to the marketing process that benefits all affiliated parties.

MARKETING IN THE OVERALL BUSINESS

There are four areas of operation within all firms: accounting, finance, management, and marketing. Each of these four areas performs specific functions. The accounting department is responsible for keeping track of income and expenditures. The primary responsibility of the finance department is maintaining and tracking assets. The management department is responsible for creating and implementing procedural policies of the firm. The marketing department is responsible for generating revenue through the exchange process. As a means of generating revenue, marketing objectives are established in alignment with the overall objectives of the firm.

Aligning the marketing activities with the objectives of the firm is completed through the process of marketing management. The marketing management process involves developing objectives that promote the long-term competitive advantage of a firm. The first step in the marketing management process is to develop the firm's overall strategic plan. The second step is to establish marketing strategies that support the firm's overall strategic objectives. Lastly, a marketing plan is developed for each product. Each product plan contains an executive summary, an explanation of the current marketing situation, a list of threats and opportunities, proposed sales objectives, possible marketing strategies, action programs, and budget proposals.

The marketing management process includes analyzing marketing opportunities, selecting target markets, developing the marketing mix, and managing the marketing effort. In order to analyze marketing opportunities, firms scan current environmental conditions in order to determine potential opportunities. The aim of the marketing effort is to satisfy the needs and wants of consumers. Thus, it is necessary for marketing managers to determine the particular needs and wants of potential customers. Various quantitative and qualitative techniques of marketing research are used to collect data about potential customers, who are then segmented into markets.

MARKET SEGMENTATION

In order to better manage the marketing effort and to satisfy the needs and wants of customers, many firms place consumers into groups, a process called market segmentation. In this process, potential customers are categorized based on different needs, characteristics, or behaviors. Market segments are evaluated as to their attractiveness or potential for generating revenue for the firm. Four factors are generally reviewed to determine the potential of a particular market segment. Effective segments are measurable, accessible, substantial, and actionable. Measurability is the degree to which a market segment's size and purchasing power can be measured. Accessibility refers to the degree to which a market segment can be reached and served. Substantiality refers to the size of the segment in terms of profitability for the firm. Action ability refers to the degree to which a firm can design or develop a product to serve a particular market segment.

Consumer characteristics are used to segment markets into workable groups. Common characteristics used for consumer categorizations include demographic, geographic, psychographic, and behavioral segmentation. Demographic segmentation categorizes consumers based on such characteristics as age, ethnicity, gender, income level, and occupation. It is one of the most popular methods of segmenting potential customers because it makes it relatively easy to identify potential customers.

Categorizing consumers according to their locations is called geographic segmentation. Consumers can be segmented geographically according to the nations, states, regions, cities, or neighborhoods in which they live, shop, and/or work. Psychographic segmentation uses consumers' activities, interests, and opinions to sort them into groups. Social class, lifestyle, or personality characteristics are psychographic variables used to categorize consumers into different groups. In behavioral segmentation, marketers divide consumers into groups based on their knowledge, attitudes, uses, or responses to a product.

Once the potential market has been segmented, firms need to station their products relative to similar products of other producers, a process called product positioning. Market positioning is the process of arranging a product so as to engage the minds of target consumers. Firm managers position their products in such a way as to distinguish them from those of competitors in order to gain a competitive advantage in the marketplace. The position of a product in the marketplace must be clear, distinctive, and desirable relative to those of its competitors in order for it to be effective.

COVERAGE STRATEGIES

Marketing managers use three basic market-coverage strategies: undifferentiated, differentiated, and concentrated. An undifferentiated marketing strategy occurs when a firm focuses on the common needs of consumers rather than their different needs. When using this strategy, producers design products to appeal to the largest number of potential buyers. The benefit of an undifferentiated strategy is that it is cost-effective because a narrow product focus results in lower production, inventory, and transportation costs.

A firm using a differentiated strategy makes a conscious decision to divide and target several different market segments, with a different product geared to each segment. Thus, a different marketing plan is needed for each segment in order to maximize sales and, as a result, increase firm profits. With a differentiated marketing strategy, firms create more total sales because of broader appeal across market segments and stronger position within each segment.

The last market coverage strategy is known as the concentrated marketing strategy. The concentrated strategy, which aims to serve a large share of one or a very few markets, is best suited for firms with limited resources. This approach allows firms to obtain a much stronger position in the segments it targets because of the greater emphasis on these targeted segments. This greater emphasis ultimately leads to a better understanding of the needs of the targeted segments.

MARKETING MIX

Once a positioning strategy has been determined, marketing managers seek to control the four basic elements of the marketing mix: product, price, place, and promotion, known as the four Ps of marketing. Since these four variables are controllable, the best mix of these elements is determined to reach the selected target market.

Product. The first element in the marketing mix is the product. Products can be either tangible or intangible. Tangible products are products that can be touched; intangible products are those that cannot be touched, such as services. There are three basic levels of a product: core, actual, and augmented. The core product is the most basic level, what consumers really buy in terms of benefits. For example, consumers do not buy food processors, per se; rather, they buy the benefit of being able to process food quickly and efficiently.

The next level of the product is the actual product—in the case of the previous example, food processors. Products are typically sorted according to the following five characteristics: quality, features, styling, brand name, and packaging. Finally, the augmented level of a product consists of all the elements that surround both the core and the actual product. The augmented level provides pur-

chasers with additional services and benefits. For example, follow-up technical assistance and warranties and guaranties are augmented product components. When planning new products, firm managers consider a number of issues including product quality, features, options, styles, brand name, packaging, size, service, warranties, and return policies, all in an attempt to meet the needs and wants of consumers.

Price. Price is the cost of the product paid by consumers. This is the only element in the marketing mix that generates revenue for firms. In order to generate revenue, managers must consider factors both internal and external to the organization. Internal factors take the form of marketing objectives, the marketing-mix strategy, and production costs. External factors to consider are the target market, product demand, competition, economic conditions, and government regulations.

A number of pricing strategies are available to marketing managers: skimming, penetration, quantity, and psychological. With a price-skimming strategy, the price is initially set high, allowing firms to generate maximum profits from customers willing to pay the high price. Prices are then gradually lowered until maximum profit is received from each level of consumer.

Penetration pricing is used when firms set low prices in order to capture a large share of a market quickly. A quantity-pricing strategy provides lower prices to consumers who purchase larger quantities of a product. Psychological pricing tends to focus on consumer perceptions. For example, odd pricing is a common psychological pricing strategy. With odd pricing, the cost of the product may be a few cents lower than a full-dollar value. Consumers tend to focus on the lower-value full-dollar cost even though it is really priced closer to the next higher full-dollar amount. For example, if a good is priced at $19.95, consumers will focus on $19 rather than $20.

Place. Place refers to where and how the products will be distributed to consumers. There are two basic issues involved in getting the products to consumers: channel management and logistics management. Channel management involves the process of selecting and motivating wholesalers and retailers, sometimes called middlemen, through the use of incentives. Several factors are reviewed by firm management when determining where to sell their products: distribution channels, market-coverage strategy, geographic locations, inventory, and transportation methods. The process of moving products from a manufacturer to the final consumer is often called the channel of distribution.

Promotion. The last variable in the marketing mix is promotion. Various promotional tools are used to communicate messages about products, ideas, or services from firms to their customers. The promotional tools available to managers are advertising, personal selling, sales promotion, and public relations. For the promotional program to be effective, managers use a blend of the four promotional tools that best reaches potential customers. This blending of promotional tools is sometimes referred to as the promotional mix. The goal of this promotional mix is to communicate to potential customers the features and benefits of goods, ideas, or services.

INTERNATIONAL MARKETING

International business has been practiced for thousands of years. In modern times, advances in technology have improved transportation and communication methods; as a result, more and more firms have set up shop at various locations around the globe. A natural component of international business is international marketing. International marketing occurs when firms plan and conduct transactions across international borders in order to satisfy the objectives of both consumers and the firm.

International marketing is simply a strategy used by firms to improve both market share and profits. While firm managers may try to employ the same basic marketing strategies used in the domestic market when promoting products in international locations, those strategies may not be appropriate or effective. Firm managers must adapt their strategies to fit the unique characteristics of each international market. Unique environmental factors that need to be explored by firm managers before going global include trade systems, economic conditions, political-legal systems, and cultural conditions.

The first factor to consider in the international marketplace is each country's trading system. All countries have their own trade system regulations and restrictions. Common trade system regulations and restrictions include tariffs, quotas, embargoes, exchange controls, and nontariff trade barriers. The second factor to review is the economic environment. Two economic factors reflect how attractive a particular market is in a selected country: industrial structure and income distribution. Industrial structure refers to how well developed a country's infrastructure is, while income distribution refers to how income is distributed among its citizens.

Political-legal environment is the third factor to investigate. For example, the individual and cultural attitudes regarding purchasing products from foreign countries, political stability, monetary regulations, and government bureaucracy all influence marketing practices and opportunities. Finally, the last factor to be considered before entering a global market is the cultural environment. Since cultural values regarding particular products will vary considerably from one country to another around the world, managers must take into account these differences in the planning process.

Just as with domestic markets, managers must establish their international marketing objectives and policies before going overseas. For example, target countries will need to be identified and evaluated in terms of their potential sales and profits. After selecting a market and establishing marketing objectives, the mode of entry into the market must be determined. There are three major modes of entry into international markets: exporting, joint venture, and direct investment.

Exporting. Exporting is the simplest way to enter an international market. With exporting, firms enter international markets by selling products internationally through the use of middlemen. This use of these middlemen is sometimes called indirect exporting.

Joint Venture. The second way to enter an international market is by using the joint-venture approach. A joint venture takes place when firms join forces with companies from the international market to produce or market a product. Joint ventures differ from direct investment in that an association is formed between firms and businesses in the international market.

The four types of joint venture are licensing, contract manufacturing, management contracting, and joint ownership. Under licensing, firms allow other businesses in the international market to produce products under an agreement called a license. The licensee has the right to use the manufacturing process, trademark, patent, trade secret, or other items of value for a fee or royalty. Firms also use contract manufacturing, which arranges for the manufacture of products to enter international markets. In the third type of joint venture, management contracting, the firms supply the capital to the local international firm in exchange for the management know-how.

The last category of joint venture is joint ownership. Firms join with local international investors to establish a local business. Both groups share joint ownership and control of the newly established business.

Direct Investment. Direct investment is the last mode used by firms to enter international markets. With direct investment, a firm enters the market by establishing its own base in international locations. Direct investment is advantageous because labor and raw materials may be cheaper in some countries. Firms can also improve their images in international markets because of the employment opportunities they create.

MARKETING VIA THE INTERNET

Advances in digital technology have revolutionized the way companies satisfy the needs and wants of customers through marketing. The term *e-commerce* is used to describe the broad range of activities associated conducting business via telecommunication networks. *E-marketing* is the term used to describe the activities associated with the four Ps of marketing for goods and services sold via the Internet.

E-marketing offers a number of advantages to consumers such as convenience, comparison pricing, and personalization. Buyers have the convenience of shopping at businesses located around the world at anytime. For instance, via the General Motors Web site (http://www.gm.com), potential buyers can build custom vehicles, print window stickers, determine monthly payments, and search dealer inventories. Through e-marketing, shoppers can look for the lowest price for products they want to purchase. At certain Web sites, such as Price-Grabber.com (http://www.pricegrabber.com), buyers can compare prices for the same product from many different sellers at the same time and in one location. Personalization is another important advantage of e-marketing. For example, American Airlines provides customers with personalized frequent-flier account summaries, as well as special airfare promotions via electronic mail.

E-marketing offers a number of advantages to sellers, including enhanced speed and efficiency, flexibility, and worldwide reach. Enhanced speed and efficiency is achieved for sellers through the virtual link created with customers via the Internet. This virtual link with buyers results in lower operating cost that can be passed along to customers. E-marketing's flexibility allows changes to be made to product offerings or promotional activities on short notice. Lastly, the worldwide reach of the Internet makes anyone in the world with Internet access a potential customer. This access to a worldwide customer base levels the playing field for small businesses. For example, the Vermont Country Store, with two physical locations, in Rockingham and Weston, Vermont, is able to sell its products to customers worldwide via e-marketing.

SEE ALSO *Careers in Marketing; Ethics in Marketing; Marketing Concept; Marketing: Historical Perspectives; Pricing*

BIBLIOGRAPHY

Boone, Louis E., and Kurtz, David L. (2005). *Contemporary marketing 2006* (12th ed.). Eagan, MN: Thomson South-Western.

Churchill, Gilbert A., Jr., and Peter, Paul J. (1998). *Marketing: Creating value for customers* (2nd ed.). New York: Irwin McGraw-Hill.

Farese, Lois, Kimbrell, Grady, and Woloszyk, Carl (2002). *Marketing essentials* (3rd ed.). Mission Hills, CA: Glencoe/McGraw-Hill.

Kotler, Philip, and Armstrong, Gary (2006). *Principles of marketing* (11th ed.). Upper Saddle River, NJ: Pearson Prentice-Hall.

Pride, William M., and Ferrell, O. C. (2006). *Marketing concepts and strategies.* Boston: Houghton Mifflin.

Semenik, Richard J., and Bamossy, Gary J. (1995). *Principles of marketing: A global perspective* (2nd ed.). Cincinnati: South-Western.

Allen D. Truell

MARKETING CONCEPT

Business philosophy has experienced three major shifts during the history of commerce in the United States. It has moved from a production orientation to a sales orientation to the current consumer orientation. Each of these philosophies has reflected the economic environment of its time.

From the early years of the country into the late 1920s, businesses had limited production capacity and continuous demand for their products. Under those circumstances, it was inevitable that the prevailing philosophy would be "produce as much as you can and it will sell." Business goals based on that belief naturally focused on production. Marketing concerns were limited to order taking and product distribution.

With the introduction of mass production in the late 1800s, the gap between production and the demand for goods and services began to narrow. By the 1930s, production capacity had caught up with and, in many areas, exceeded demand. In order to maintain or regain production and sales levels, businesses adopted a sales-oriented philosophy. This philosophy held that "if you do enough advertising, promotional activities, and direct selling, you can persuade the market to buy all of your output." Initially, companies capitalized on the emergence of the radio as an advertising vehicle and the employment of large sales forces to reach prospective customers in new markets. In the 1940s, the introduction of television enabled them to expand sales efforts even further.

After the end of World War II (1939–1945), two forces combined to create an explosion in demand for goods and services. One was the pent-up demand for products resulting from wartime shortages. The other was the enormous added demand generated by the return of GIs who were establishing new homes and families. The spending boom caused by these forces was sustained by the baby boom and the increased standard of living that followed. At the same time, wartime production capacity and technological developments were shifted to civilian applications, production continued to increase, and new ventures were formed to take advantage of the opportunities.

The net result of all this economic activity was heavy competition for the consumer dollar. Businesses quickly came to realize that if they were going to get their share of those dollars, they were going to have to become more consumer-oriented. This change in philosophy became known as the marketing concept.

ORIGIN OF THE TERM

Although this philosophy had been taking shape for nearly seven years, it was not articulated until it appeared in the 1952 annual report of General Electric. One widely used definition evolving from the report's description is "an organization-wide consumer orientation with the objective of achieving long-range profitability." As this definition implies, there are three parts to the marketing concept. They are:

(1) *A customer focus:* The marketing concept begins with the premise that the starting point for business decisions is the customer's needs and wants. Those needs and wants are carefully researched and thoroughly analyzed. Then, goods and services are identified and/or developed to satisfy them.

In many cases, a consumer's stated needs and desires are limited by a very narrow perception of what is possible. Firms often need to determine what "futuristic" products and services would satisfy latent needs and wants of which consumers are not yet aware. Many popular products such as the iPods, cell phones with cameras, and singing birthday cards were not envisioned by consumers twenty years ago. To successfully implement the marketing concept an organization must research the short-term desires and the long-term needs and wants of their potential customers.

(2) *Long-term organizational success:* The marketing concept dictates that goods and services made available by a business must be produced and marketed so as to meet the long-term goals of the organization. In most businesses this would include the profit objective that is integral to the survival and growth of a business. Without it, the business would not be available to serve the needs and wants of customers. Other objectives, however, may include market share, sales growth, or new product success. Many successful nonprofit organizations, such as the Red Cross, effectively use the marketing concept.

(3) *A total company effort:* Effective implementation of the marketing concept requires involvement of employees from all departments at all levels of the business. Train-

ing must be provided and employees must be motivated to achieve the common goals of maximum customer satisfaction and the long-term organizational objectives.

EXECUTING THE CONCEPT

Businesses that have embraced the marketing concept have found that this concept has had a strong impact on sales. They have also found that, in many respects, this concept has changed the way they operate.

Most of the changes in management practice have been related to changes in thinking inherent in the marketing concept. These include making decisions on the basis of customer needs and wants instead of production schedules and sales goals, encouraging every employee to take an active interest in all aspects of the business, and forcing managers to think through what they are going to do and their reasons for doing it.

Changes in marketing activities that have occurred under the concept involve both marketing strategies and marketing functions. Market research has become a prominent tool. Data gathered to determine customer needs and wants and to provide feedback on company performance are used more effectively. Special attention has been paid to product quality and to tailoring services, as well as products, to customer preferences. The customer's interest has been designated as the first priority in all marketing activities. In selling, for example, helping the customer has been given greater emphasis than getting the sale. In addition, the search for innovative ways to reach and serve the customer has become an ongoing enterprise.

Changes in production brought about by use of the marketing concept, such as closely controlled inventories, have centered on efficiency. Changes in operations, such as extended hours and immediate delivery, have focused on convenient product availability. Additional changes in business practice have been aimed at cost control to give customers maximum value for the price they pay.

A growing interest in the societal marketing concept recognizes the possible conflict between short-term consumer wants and the long-run welfare of consumers and society. Lawsuits against the tobacco industry and, in some cases, the fast food industry, along with other firms, demonstrate this conflict. Although these firms were satisfying the wants of consumers at the time, the long-term harmful results of using the products on those consumers and society have caused many to promote the societal marketing concept. This concept is based on satisfying consumers' needs and wants in a manner that would also maintain or improve the long-term welfare of the consumers as well as the well-being of society.

SEE ALSO *Marketing*

BIBLIOGRAPHY

Hoffman, K. Douglass (2006). *Marketing principles and best practices* (3rd ed.). Mason, OH: Thomson South-Western.

Kotler, Philip, and Armstrong, Gary (2005). *Principles of marketing* (11th ed.). Upper Saddle River, NJ: Pearson Prentice Hall.

Pride, William M., and Ferrel, O. C. (2006). *Marketing: Concepts and strategies.* Boston: Houghton Mifflin.

Thomas Baird
Earl C. Meyer
Winifred L. Green

MARKETING: HISTORICAL PERSPECTIVES

Marketing is one of the major functional areas of a business firm. In this introduction to marketing, this article will describe and define the concept. Then, an account of the evolution of marketing in the United States is presented. The evolution of marketing includes several eras including the simple trade era, the production era, the sales era, the marketing department era, the marketing company era, and the relationship marketing era.

WHAT IS MARKETING?

"Marketing is advertising, like those false or deceptive ads on television that try to get you to buy something that you don't really want."

"Marketing is like those pushy car salespeople, or those salespeople that come to our front doors selling overpriced vacuum cleaners."

"I hate those rude telemarketers calling at all times of the day and night."

Some people think that marketing involves deceptive, high-pressure tactics to get them to buy something they do not really want. This is incorrect. While marketing usually involves advertising or personal selling, marketing—practiced correctly—should not try to get people to buy things they do not want, nor should marketers use deceptive or pushy tactics to get people to buy. Marketing is really the process of developing products to satisfy customers through proper pricing, promotion, and distribution.

The basic premise behind marketing is to satisfy the customer. Satisfied customers are much more valuable than customers who have been deceived into buying something. For example, satisfied customers are more likely to purchase products repeatedly. Furthermore, satisfied customers are more likely to relate positive word-of-mouth to friends and acquaintances, which can increase the chance that they, in turn, will buy the firm's product. Indeed, marketing is really the process of developing and maintaining long-term exchange relationships. Nevertheless, companies have not always practiced this philosophy. The following section describes how company beliefs have changed over time.

THE EVOLUTION OF MARKETING

Marketing, as it exists today, is a relatively recent phenomenon that really began prior to the twentieth century. In the early nineteenth century a woman who wanted a new dress had two choices, either to make her own or to hire someone to make one for her. If she decided to hire someone, the woman needing the dress would pick out the fabric, get measured and the dress would be custom-made to her proportions. There were no standard sizes such as a size six, eight, or ten dress. Standard sizes, such as shoe sizes, are the result of modern mass-manufacturing processes.

The Simple Trade Era. Prior to the industrial revolution, people made most of what they consumed. Any excess household production could be brought to town and sold or traded for other goods. This type of economy is commonly referred to as a pure subsistence economy. In a pure subsistence economy, there is little need for marketing (to facilitate exchanges) since each household produces what it consumes.

With the advent of the industrial revolution, however, the producers of many types of goods were not households but businesses. When the producers of products are not the consumers of those products, exchanges must take place. The following section describes general company business thinking about the exchange process beginning with the period of the industrial revolution.

MODERN-DAY MARKETING EVOLUTION

The evolution of marketing into the most important business function within many business firms was first recognized by Robert Keith, an executive at Pillsbury, in 1960, and was substantiated by other business leaders at other firms. According to Keith, marketing evolved into its present-day prominence within firms during four distinct eras throughout American history. These eras include the production era, the sales era, the marketing era, and the marketing company era.

The Production Era. The production era is so named because the main priority of many companies was the reduction of the cost of production. Companies believed that exchanges could be facilitated merely by lowering manufacturing costs, and in turn, passing along the cost savings to customers in the form of lower prices.

This focus on production (which lasted from just after the Civil War [1861–1865] and continued into the 1920s) was fueled by milestones such as Henry Ford's employment of the assembly line and more-efficient work principles advanced by Frederick W. Taylor's scientific management movement. These two innovations made business managers aware that mass production resulted in steeply declining unit costs of production. In turn, the declining unit costs of production made profit possibilities look fabulous.

The rationale for mass production seemed sound at the time of the production era. According to Michael Porter, reduced production costs can lead to reduced selling prices and thus appeal to the largest segment of customers. Unfortunately, turbulent economic conditions associated with the late 1920s through the 1940s caused many companies to fail even though they had adopted this production-oriented philosophy of doing business. As a result, companies looked for other ways to facilitate the exchange process.

The Sales Era. The next era of marketing evolution is called the sales era because many companies' main priority was to get rid of or move their products out the factory door using a variety of selling techniques. During the sales era, companies believed that they could enhance their sales by using a variety of promotional techniques designed to inform and/or persuade potential customers to buy their products. This type of thinking was initiated by the economic climate of the time.

Herbert Hoover was elected president in 1928 and the mood of the general public was one of optimism and confidence in the U.S. economy. Few people had any reason to believe that prosperity would not continue. In his acceptance speech for the Republican presidential nomination, Hoover said, "We in America today are nearer to the final triumph over poverty than ever before in the history of any land. The poorhouse is vanishing from among us."

Nevertheless, Tuesday, October 29, 1929, Black Tuesday, marked the beginning of the Great Depression. This was the single most devastating financial day in the history of the New York Stock Exchange. Within the first few hours that the stock market was open, prices fell so far as to wipe out all the gains that had been made in the previous year. Since the stock market was viewed as the chief indicator of the American economy, public confidence was shattered. Between October 29 and November 13 (when stock prices hit their lowest point) over $30 billion disappeared from the American economy (comparable to the total amount America spent on its involvement in World War I [1914–1918]).

The amount of disposable and discretionary income that consumers had to spend on necessities and luxuries also decreased dramatically as the unemployment rate approached 25 percent. Companies found that they could no longer sell all the products that they produced, even though prices were lowered via mass production. Firms now had to get rid of their excess production in order to convert products into cash.

In order to get rid of products, many firms developed sales forces and relied on personal selling, advertising signs, and singing commercials on the radio to "move" the product. Theodore Levitt, a prominent marketing scholar, noted that these firms were not necessarily concerned with satisfying the customer, but rather selling the product. This sales orientation dominated business practice through the 1930s until World War II (1939–1945), when most firms' manufacturing facilities were adapted to making machinery and equipment for the war effort. The war, of course, dramatically changed the environment within which business was conducted. This also changed companies' philosophies of doing business.

The Marketing Department Era. After the war, most of the manufacturing capability of industrialized countries was destroyed, except for that in the United States. U.S. firms once again found it relatively easy to sell the products they manufactured because there was little competition from abroad. Armed with sales concepts developed during the sales era, as well as new manufacturing capabilities and large research and development departments developed during the war, firms realized that they could produce hundreds of new and different products.

Firms determined that they needed a set of criteria to determine which products would be manufactured and which would not, as well as a new management function that would incorporate many related functions such as procurement, advertising, and sales into one department, the marketing department. It was also at this time that many firms realized that the company's purpose was no longer to manufacture a variety of products, but to satisfy their customers.

Changing company thinking or purpose from that of manufacturing products to that of satisfying customers was truly evolutionary and had many implications for firms. Firms that see themselves as manufacturers of products use selling techniques that are preoccupied with converting products into cash. Firms that see themselves as marketers focus on satisfying the needs of the buyer through the products that are sold, as well as all of those functions associated with developing the product, delivering the product and consuming the product. In short, selling focuses on the needs of the seller; marketing focuses on the needs of the buyer.

The popular insight by Levitt concerning Ford's adaptation of the assembly line illustrates the difference between firms that focus on production (i.e., a production orientation) and those that focus on customers (a customer orientation). Ford is widely known as a production genius for incorporating the assembly line into automobile production. Many incorrectly believe that the assembly line reduced the cost of manufacturing automobiles and therefore Ford could sell millions of $500 cars (a production orientation).

Ford's thinking, however, was actually the reverse. He employed the assembly line because he concluded that millions of buyers would be willing to pay $500 for an automobile (a customer orientation). His main task was to reduce manufacturing costs (in whatever way possible) so that he could sell cars at $500 and still make a profit. The assembly line was the result, not the cause of his low price. As Ford himself put it:

> we first reduce the price to the point where we believe that more sales will result. Then we go ahead and try to make the prices. We do not bother about the costs. The new price forces the cost down ... because what earthly use is it to know the cost if it tells you that you cannot manufacture at a price at which an article can be sold? But more to the point is the fact that, although one may calculate what a cost is, and of course all of our costs are carefully calculated, no one knows what a cost ought to be. One way of discovering ... is to name a price so low as to force everybody in the place to the highest point of efficiency. (Ford, 1923, pp. 146–147)

In short, during the marketing department era, many companies changed their thinking or purpose from that of manufacturing products to that of satisfying customers. Firms with a customer orientation attempt to create value-satisfying products that customers will want to buy. Some firms have implemented this customer-oriented philosophy to the point where the marketing department sets the agenda for the entire company. These types of firms are referred to as marketing companies.

The Marketing Company Era. Firms that have moved from simply having a marketing department that follows a customer orientation to one where the marketing department guides the company's direction are called marketing companies. In marketing companies, the marketing department sets company operating policy, including technical research, procurement, production, advertising, and sales. An excerpt from Amazon.com's 2004 annual report exemplifies the strategy of a marketing-driven firm:

From the beginning, our focus has been on offering our customers compelling value. We realized that the Web was, and still is, the World Wide Wait. Therefore, we set out to offer customers something they simply could not get any other way, and began serving them with books. We brought them much more selection than was possible in a physical store (our store would now occupy 6 football fields), and presented it in a useful, easy-to-search, and easy-to-browse format in a store open 365 days a year, 24 hours a day. We maintained a dogged focus on improving the shopping experience, and in 1997 substantially enhanced our store. We now offer customers gift certificates, 1-Click℠ shopping, and vastly more reviews, content, browsing options, and recommendation features. We dramatically lowered prices, further increasing customer value. Word of mouth remains the most powerful customer acquisition tool we have, and we are grateful for the trust our customers have placed in us. Repeat purchases and word of mouth have combined to make Amazon.com the market leader in online bookselling. (Amazon.com)

As can be seen with Amazon.com, marketing is the basic motivating force for all activities within the corporation, with the objective of satisfying the needs of the customer. Firms that practice this philosophy of bringing all departments together with the objective of satisfying their customers are practicing the marketing concept.

The marketing concept states that if all of the organization's functions are focused on customer needs, profits can be achieved by satisfying those needs. The satisfaction of customer needs can be accomplished through product changes, pricing adjustments, increased customer service, distribution changes, and the like.

Today, some firms take the marketing concept one step further by establishing long-term relationships with their customers. The following section discusses how firms attempt to satisfy their customers even further by entering into long-term relationships with them.

The Relationship Marketing Era. Relationship marketing takes the marketing concept one step further by establishing long-term, satisfying relations with customers in order to foster customer loyalty and encourage repeat buying of the firm's products. Philip Kotler, a noted author of several books and articles on marketing, pointed out that the need for customer retention is evident because the cost of attracting a new customer is estimated to be five times the cost of keeping a current customer happy.

CONCLUSION

Marketing in the United States has evolved since the Civil War and continues to evolve in the twenty-first century. Many companies have determined that in order to be successful, they must become less internally focused and more externally focused (on the customer). This trend in company thought has extended to the point where many firms now see themselves as long-term partners with their customers.

As information technology becomes more advanced, marketers will be able to become more acutely aware of their customers' needs and more quickly able to provide goods and services to satisfy those needs. A new trend in marketing that incorporates advances in information technology is mass customization. Mass customization is the customization and personalization of goods and services for individual customers at a mass production price. One example of a firm pioneering in mass customization is Nike. With Nike's iD Web site, the masses can buy self-customized sneakers.

SEE ALSO *Marketing*

BIBLIOGRAPHY

Amazon.com. (2004). Obsess over customers. *Annual report.* Retrieved December 6, 2005, from http://library.corporate-ir.net/library/97/976/97664/items/144852/DEX991.htm

Ford, Henry (1923). *My life and my work.* New York: Doubleday.

Haber, Samuel (1964). *Efficiency and uplift.* Chicago: University of Chicago Press.

Keith, Robert J. (1960). The marketing revolution. *Journal of Marketing, 24,* 35–38.

Kinnear, Thomas C., Bernhardt, Kenneth L., and Krentler, Kathleen A. (1995). *Principles of marketing* (4th ed.). New York: HarperCollins.

Kotler, Philip, and Keller, Kevin (2006). *Marketing management: Analysis, planning, implementation, and control* (12th ed.). Upper Saddle River, NJ: Pearson Prentice Hall.

Levitt, Theodore (1960, July–August). Marketing myopia. *Harvard Business Review,* 45–56.

Porter, Michael E. (1980). *Competitive strategy.* New York: The Free Press.

Schultz, Stanley K. (1999). *Crashing hopes: The Great Depression.* Retrieved December 6, 2005, from http://us.history.wisc.edu/hist102/lectures/lecture18.html

James E. Stoddard

MARKETING MIX

The term *marketing mix* refers to the four major areas of decision making in the marketing process that are blended to obtain the results desired by the organization: product, price, promotion, and place. The four elements of the marketing mix are sometimes referred to as the four Ps of marketing. The marketing mix shapes the role of marketing within all types of organizations, both profit and nonprofit. Each element of the four Ps consists of numerous subelements. Marketing managers make numerous decisions based on the various subelements of the marketing mix, all in an attempt to satisfy the needs and wants of consumers.

PRODUCT

The first element in the marketing mix is the product. A product is any combination of goods and services offered to satisfy the needs and wants of consumers. Thus, a product is anything tangible or intangible that can be offered for purchase or use by consumers. A tangible product is one that consumers can actually touch, such as an automobile, a computer, a newspaper, or a window. An intangible product is a service that cannot be touched, such as an automobile repair, a doctor's office visit, or income tax preparation.

Other examples of products include places and ideas. For example, the New Hampshire Division of Travel and Tourism Development might promote New Hampshire as a great place to visit and by doing so stimulate the economy. Cities also promote themselves as great places to live and work. For example, the slogan touted by the Chamber of Commerce in San Bernardino, California, is "It's a great day in San Bernardino." The idea of wearing seat belts has been promoted as a way of saving lives, as has the idea of recycling to help reduce the amount of garbage placed in landfills.

Typically, a product is divided into three basic levels. The first level is often called the core product, what the consumer actually buys in terms of benefits. For example, consumers do not just buy 4×4 pickup trucks. Rather, consumers buy the benefit that 4×4 pickup trucks offer, such as being able to get around in deep snow and ice in the winter. Next is the second level, or actual product, that is built around the core product. The actual product consists of the brand name, features, packaging, parts, and styling. These components provided the benefits to consumers that they seek at the first level.

The final, or third, level of the product is the augmented component. The augmented component includes additional services and benefits that surround the first two levels of the product. Examples of augmented product components are technical assistance in operating the product and service agreements. Buyers of technical products such as computers and video cameras are frequently provided with operating assistance as well as optional service agreement plans.

Durable and Nondurable Goods. Products are classified by how long they can be used—durability—and their tangibility. Products that can be used repeatedly over a long period are called durable goods. Examples of durable goods include automobiles, furniture, and houses. By contrast, goods that are normally used or consumed quickly are called nondurable goods. Some examples of nondurable goods are food, soap, and soft drinks. In addition, services are activities and benefits that are also involved in the exchange process but are intangible because they cannot be held or touched. Examples of intangible services included eye exams and automobile repair.

Categorizing Products by Their Users. Another way to categorize products is by their users. Products are classified as either consumer or business goods.

Consumer goods. Consumer goods are purchased by final consumers, sometimes called end users, for their personal consumption. The shopping patterns of consumers are also used to classify products. Products sold to the final consumer are arranged as follows: convenience, shopping, specialty, and unsought goods. Convenience goods are products and services that consumers buy frequently and with little effort. Most convenience goods are easily obtainable and low-priced, items such as bread, candy, milk, and shampoo.

Convenience goods can be further divided into staple, impulse, and emergency goods. Staple goods are products—such as bread and milk, coffee, and toothpaste—that consumers buy on a consistent basis. Impulse goods such as magazines and candy are products that require little planning or search effort because they are normally available in many places. As impulse goods, candy and magazines are frequently located near checkout counters in grocery stores. Emergency goods are bought when consumers have a pressing need for a product, such as during a natural disaster. An example of an emergency good would be the purchase of a generator when the electricity is expected to be out for a considerable time, such as after a severe ice storm.

Shopping goods are those products that consumers compare during the selection and purchase process. Typically, factors such as price, quality, style, and suitability are used as bases of comparison. With shopping goods, consumers usually take considerable time and effort in gathering information and making comparisons between products. Major appliances such as refrigerators and televisions are typical shopping goods. Shopping goods are further divided into uniform and nonuniform categories. Uniform shopping goods are goods that are similar in quality but which differ in price. Consumers will try to justify price differences by focusing on product features.

Nonuniform shopping goods are those goods that differ in both quality and price.

Specialty goods are products with distinctive characteristics or brand identification for which consumers expend exceptional buying effort. Specialty goods include specific brands and types of products. Typically, buyers do not compare specialty goods with other similar products because the products are unique. Unsought goods are those products or services that consumers are not readily aware of or do not normally consider buying. Burial plots and life insurance policies are examples of unsought goods. Often, unsought goods require considerable promotional efforts on the part of the seller in order to attract the interest of consumers.

Business goods. Business goods are those products used in the production of other goods. Examples of business goods include accessory equipment, component parts, installations, operating supplies, raw materials, and services. Accessory equipment refers to movable items and small office equipment items that never become part of a final product. Office furniture and fax machines are examples of accessory equipment. Component parts are products that are turned into a component of the final product which does not require further processing. Component parts are frequently custom-made for the final product of which they will become a part. For example, an automatic transmission could be produced by one manufacturer for use in an automobile made by another manufacturer.

Installations are capital goods that are usually very expensive but have a long useful life. Mainframe computers, power generators, and trucks and other heavy equipment are examples of installations. Operating supplies are similar to accessory equipment in that they do not become part of the finished product. Operating supplies include items necessary to maintain and operate the overall firm, such as cleaners, file folders, paper, and pens. Raw materials are goods sold in their original form before being processed for use in other products. Crops, crude oil, iron ore, and logs are examples of raw materials in need of further processing before being used in products.

The last category of business goods is services. Organizations sometimes require the use of services, just as individuals do. Examples of services sought by organizations include maintenance and repair and legal counsel.

PRICE

Price is the second element of the marketing mix. Price is the value exchange that occurs between buyers and sellers for a product or service. Factors related to price include legal and regulatory guidelines, pricing objectives, pricing strategies, and options for increasing sales.

Among the legal and regulatory guidelines affecting pricing are the Sherman Antitrust Act of 1890, the Clayton Antitrust Act of 1914, the Robinson-Patman Act of 1936, and various unfair- and fair-trade laws. The Sherman Antitrust Act was enacted to prevent a business from becoming a monopoly. The Clayton Antitrust Act was established to prevent practices such as price discrimination and the exclusive or nearly exclusive dealing between and among only a few companies that would result in reduced competition. The Robinson-Patman Act prohibits a business from selling its product at a price so unreasonably low as to eliminate its competitors. Unfair-trade laws protect special markets by setting minimum retail prices for a product, theoretically protecting specialty businesses from larger businesses that could drive smaller stores out of by selling the same products below cost. Fair-trade laws allow producers to set a minimum price for products.

Four frequently used objectives are competitive, prestige, profitability, and volume pricing. Competitive pricing is to simply match the price established by a leader in the industry for a product and to attract and retain customers by other means such as superior customer service. Prestige pricing involves pricing a product high so as to make it available only to the higher-end customer as a product image enhancing strategy. Profitability pricing seeks to maximize profit while at the same time remaining competitive. Volume pricing seeks sales maximization within established profit guidelines. Higher sales volume is expected to make up for the lower than normal selling price.

Companies can chose from a variety of pricing strategies such as penetration and skimming. Penetration-pricing strategy is used to build market share by obtaining profits from repeat sales. Occasionally, high sales volume allows sellers to further reduce prices. A price-skimming strategy uses different pricing phases over time. Initially, prices are set high to maximize profits and then gradually reduced to generate additional sales.

Companies have several options available for increasing the sales of a product: coupons, prepayment, price shading, seasonal pricing, term pricing, segment pricing, and volume discounts.

- *Coupons:* Offered by almost all companies, reflecting their numerous advantages—enhancing market share, increasing sales on mature products, or reviving old products; coupons are distributed via the Internet, newspapers, and point-of-purchase dispensers

- *Prepayment plan:* Typically used with customers who have no credit or poor credit; these do not as a rule provide customers with a price break

- *Price shading:* Allowing salespeople to offer discounts on a product's price

- *Seasonal pricing:* Adjusts price based on seasonal demand for a product or service; used to move products when they are least salable

- *Term pricing:* Offering a discount to customers paying promptly for purchases; occasionally, companies offer an additional small discount to customers who pay cash

- *Segment pricing:* Discounts offered frequently to children, senior citizens, and students

- *Volume discounting:* Customers purchasing a large volume of a product are offered lower prices

PROMOTION

Promotion is the third element in the marketing mix. Promotion is a communication process that takes place between a business and its various publics. Publics are those individuals and organizations that have an interest in what the business produces and offers for sale. Thus, in order to be effective, businesses need to plan promotional activities with the communication process in mind.

The elements of the communication process are: sender, encoding, message, media, decoding, receiver, feedback, and noise. The sender refers to the business that is sending a promotional message to a potential customer. Encoding involves putting a message or promotional activity into some form. Symbols are formed to represent the message. The sender transmits these symbols through some form of media. Media are methods the sender uses to transmit the message to the receiver. Decoding is the process by which the receiver translates the meaning of the symbols sent by the sender into a form that can be understood. The receiver is the intended recipient of the message. Feedback occurs when the receiver communicates back to the sender. Noise is anything that interferes with the communication process.

There are four basic promotion tools: advertising, sales promotion, public relations, and personal selling. Each promotion tool has its own unique characteristics and function.

Advertising. Advertising is paid, nonpersonal communication by an organization using various media to reach its various publics. The purpose of advertising is to inform or persuade a targeted audience to purchase a product or service, visit a location, or adopt an idea. Advertising is also classified as to its intended purpose. The purpose of product advertising is to secure the purchase of the product by consumers. The purpose of institutional advertising is to promote the image or philosophy of an organization. For example, Ball State University, located in Muncie, Indiana, touts the tag line: "Everything You Need."

Advertising can be further divided into six subcategories: pioneering, competitive, comparative, advocacy, reminder, and cooperative advertising. Pioneering advertising aims to develop primary demand for the product or product category. Competitive advertising seeks to develop demand for a specific product or service. Comparative advertising seeks to contrast one product or service with another. Advocacy advertising is an organizational approach designed to support socially responsible activities, causes, or messages such as helping feed the homeless. Reminder advertising seeks to keep a product or company name in the mind of consumers by its repetitive nature. Cooperative advertising occurs when wholesalers and retailers work with product manufacturers to produce a single advertising campaign and share the costs.

Advantages of advertising include the ability to reach a large group or audience at a relatively low cost per individual contacted. Further, advertising allows organizations to control the message, which means the message can be adapted to either a mass or a specific target audience. Disadvantages of advertising include difficulty in measuring results and the inability to close sales because there is no personal contact between the organization and consumers.

Sales Promotion. Sales promotions are short-term incentives used to encourage consumers to purchase a product or service. There are three basic categories of sales promotion: consumer, trade, and business. Consumer promotion tools include such items as free samples, coupons, rebates, price packs, premiums, patronage rewards, point-of-purchase coupons, contests, sweepstakes, and games. Trade promotion tools include discounts and allowances directed at wholesalers and retailers. Business promotion tools include conventions and trade shows. Sales promotion has several advantages over other promotional tools in that it can produce a more immediate consumer response, attract more attention and create product awareness, measure the results, and increase short-term sales.

Public Relations. An organization builds positive public relations with various groups by obtaining favorable publicity, establishing a good corporate image, and handling or heading off unfavorable rumors, stories, and events. Organizations have at their disposal a variety of tools, such as press releases, product publicity, official communications, lobbying, and counseling to develop image. Public relations tools are effective in developing a positive attitude toward the organization and can enhance the credibility of a product. Public relations activities have the drawback that they may not provide an accurate measure of their influence on sales as they are not directly involved with specific marketing goals.

Personal Selling. Personal selling involves an interpersonal influence and information-exchange process. There are seven general steps in the personal selling process: prospecting and qualifying, preapproach, approach, presentation and demonstration, handling objections, closing, and follow-up. Personal selling does provide a measurement of effectiveness because a more immediate response is received by the salesperson from the customer. Another advantage of personal selling is that salespeople can shape the information presented to fit the needs of the customer. Disadvantages are the high cost per contact and dependence on the ability of the salesperson.

For a promotion to be effective, organizations should blend all four promotion tools together in order to achieve the promotional mix. The promotional mix can be influenced by a number of factors, including the product itself, the product life-cycle stage, and the budget. Within the promotional mix there are two promotional strategies: pull and push. Pull strategy occurs when the manufacturer tries to establish final-consumer demand and thus pull the product through the wholesalers and retailers. Advertising and sales promotion are most frequently used in a pulling strategy. Pushing strategy, in contrast, occurs when a seller tries to develop demand through incentives to wholesalers and retailers, who in turn place the product in front of consumers.

PLACE

The fourth element of the marketing mix is place. Place refers to having the right product, in the right location, at the right time to be purchased by consumers. This proper placement of products is done through middlemen called the channel of distribution. The channel of distribution is comprised of interdependent manufacturers, wholesalers, and retailers. These groups are involved with making a product or service available for use or consumption. Each participant in the channel of distribution is concerned with three basic utilities: time, place, and possession. Time utility refers to having a product available at the time that will satisfy the needs of consumers. Place utility occurs when a firm provides satisfaction by locating products where they can be easily acquired by consumers. The last utility is possession utility, which means that wholesalers and retailers in the channel of distribution provide services to consumers with as few obstacles as possible.

Channels of distribution operate by one of two methods: conventional distribution or a vertical marketing system. In the conventional distribution system, there can be one or more independent product manufacturers, wholesalers, and retailers in a channel. The vertical marketing system requires that producers, wholesalers, and retailers to work together to avoid channel conflicts.

Physical Distribution. How manufacturers store, handle, and move products to customers at the right time and at the right place is referred to as physical distribution. In considering physical distribution, manufacturers need to review issues such as distribution objectives, product transportation, and product warehousing. Choosing the mode of transportation requires an understanding of each possible method: rail, truck, water, pipeline, and air.

Rail transportation is typically used to ship automobiles, chemicals, farm products, minerals, and sand. Truck transportation is most suitable for transporting clothing, gasoline and diesel fuel, food, and paper goods. Water transportation is good for oil, grain, sand, gravel, metallic ores, coal, and other heavy items. Pipeline transportation is best when shipping products such as oil or chemicals. Air transport works best when moving technical instruments, perishable products, and important documents.

Product Distribution. Another issue of concern to manufacturers is the level of product distribution. Normally, manufacturers select from one of three levels of distribution: intensive, selective, or exclusive. Intensive distribution occurs when manufacturers distribute products through all wholesalers or retailers that want to offer their products. Selective distribution occurs when manufacturers distribute products through a limited, select number of wholesalers and retailers. Under exclusive distribution, only a single wholesaler or retailer is allowed to sell the product in a specific geographic area.

SEE ALSO *Marketing; Pricing; Promotion*

BIBLIOGRAPHY

Boone, Louis E., and Kurtz, David L. (2005). *Contemporary marketing 2006* (11th ed.). Eagan, MN: Thomson South-Western.

Churchill, Gilbert A., Jr., and Peter, Paul J. (1998). *Marketing: Creating value for customers* (2nd ed.). New York: Irwin McGraw-Hill.

Farese, Lois, Kimbrell, Grady, and Woloszyk, Carl (2002). *Marketing essentials* (3rd ed.). Mission Hills, CA: Glencoe/McGraw-Hill.

Kotler, Philip, and Armstrong, Gary (2006). *Principles of marketing* (11th ed.). Upper Saddle River, NJ: Pearson Prentice-Hall.

Pride, William M., and Ferrell, O. C. (2006). *Marketing concepts and strategies.* New York: Houghton Mifflin.

Semenik, Richard J., and Bamossy, Gary J. (1995). *Principles of marketing: A global perspective* (2nd ed.). Cincinnati: South-Western.

Allen D. Truell

MARKETING RESEARCH

Accelerating product cycles, easy access to information on products and services, highly discerning consumers, and fierce competition among companies are all a reality in the world of business. Too many companies are chasing too few consumers. Therefore, knowing, understanding, and responding to one's target market is more important than ever. And this requires information—good information. Good information can lead to successful products and services. Good information is the result of market research. Marketing gurus Kevin Clancy and Peter Krieg in their book, *Counterintuitive Marketing,* wrote, "Marketing research, we believe, poses many dangers and many opportunities. Bad research can, and often does, lead companies in the wrong direction. Good research, on the other hand, is the sine qua non of the counterintuitive approach to great marketing" (quoted in DeVries, 2005).

WHAT IS MARKETING RESEARCH?

According to the Marketing Research Association, "Marketing research is a process used by businesses to collect, analyze and interpret information used to make sound business decisions and successfully manage the business" (2005). Marketing research is a $6-billion-a-year industry. Marketing research provides, analyzes, and interprets information for manufacturers on how consumers view their products and services and on how they can better meet consumer needs. The ultimate goal is to please the consumer in order to get, or keep, the consumer's business.

HISTORY OF MARKETING RESEARCH PIONEERS

Marketing research as an organized business activity began between 1910 and 1920. The appointment of Charles Collidge Parlin as manager of the Commercial Research Division of the Advertising Department of the Curtis Publishing Company in 1911 is generally noted to be the beginning of marketing research. Parlin's success led several industrial firms and advertising media to establish research divisions. In 1915 the U.S. Rubber Company hired Dr. Paul H. Nystrom to manage a newly established Department of Commercial Research. In 1917 Swift and Company hired Dr. Louis D. H. Weld from Yale University to become manager of their Commercial Research Department.

In 1919 Professor C. S. Duncan of the University of Chicago published *Commercial Research: An Outline of Working Principles,* considered to be the first major book on commercial research. In 1921 Percival White's *Market Analysis* was published; the first research book to gain a large readership, it went through several editions. *Market*

Call center in Philadelphia, Pennsylvania, October 8, 2004. **AP IMAGES**

Research and Analysis by Lyndon O. Brown, published in 1937, became one of the most popular college textbooks of the period, reflecting the growing interest in marketing research on the college campus. After 1940, numerous research textbooks were published and the number of business schools offering research courses grew rapidly.

Following World War II (1939–1945), the growth of marketing research increased dramatically. By 1948 more than 200 marketing research organizations had been created in the United States. An estimated $50 million was spent on marketing research activities in 1947. Over the next three decades this expenditure level increased more than tenfold.

Methodological Development. Major advances in marketing research methodology were made from 1910 to 1920. Questionnaires, or surveys, became a popular method of data collection. With the growth of survey research came improvements in questionnaire design and question construction. During the 1930s sampling became a serious methodological issue. Modern

approaches to probability sampling slowly gained acceptance in this period.

From 1950 through the early 1960s, methodological innovations occurred at a fairly steady pace. At this time, a major development occurred: the commercial availability of large-scale digital computers. The computer was responsible for rapidly increasing the pace of methodological innovation, especially in the area of quantitative marketing research. As the field of marketing research attracted increasing interest, two new journals began publication in the 1960s: the *Journal of Marketing Research* and the *Journal of Advertising Research*. Technological advances have had a major impact on many aspects of the marketing research profession. These innovations have included checkout scanners in supermarkets, computer-assisted telephone interviewing, database marketing, data analysis by computers, data collection on the Internet, and Web-based surveys.

The second decade of the Internet age has confirmed the Internet as a consumer and business communications medium. In 2005 companies were projected to spend more than $1.1 billion on online market research, a 16 percent increase over 2004. The advantages of online research are self-evident: There is no need for data entry or interviews, and responses are collected automatically, saving time and money while eliminating coding errors and interviewer bias. Also, respondents may feel more comfortable in answering sensitive questions with their anonymity ensured. Ultimately, the Internet, if used properly, can provide the quickest path to valuable insight into a customer's mind.

TYPES OF MARKETING RESEARCH

Marketing research can be classified as exploratory research, conclusive research, and performance-monitoring research. The stage in the decision-making process for which the information is needed determines the type of research required.

Exploratory Research. Exploratory research is appropriate for the early stages of the decision-making process. This research is usually designed to provide a preliminary investigation of the situation with a minimum expenditure of cost and time. A variety of approaches to this research are used, including use of secondary data sources, observation, interviews with experts, and case histories.

Conclusive Research. Conclusive research provides information that helps the manager evaluate and select a course of action. This involves clearly defined research objectives and information needs. Some approaches to this research include surveys, experiments, observations, and simulation. Conclusive research can be subclassified into descriptive research and causal research.

Descriptive research, as its name suggests, is designed to describe something—for example, the characteristics of consumers of a certain product; the degree to which the use of a product varies with age, income, or sex; or the number of people who saw a specific television commercial.

Causal research is designed to gather evidence regarding the cause-and-effect relationships that exist in the marketing system. For example, if a company reduces the price of a product and then unit sales of the product increase, causal research would show whether this effect was due to the price reduction or some other reason. Causal research must be designed in such a way that the evidence regarding causality is clear. The main sources of data for causal research are interrogating respondents through surveys and conducting experiments.

Performance-Monitoring Research. Performance-monitoring research provides information regarding the status

of the marketing system; it signals the presence of potential problems or opportunities. This is an essential element in the control of a business's marketing programs. The data sources for performance-monitoring research include interrogation of respondents, secondary data, and observation.

THE MARKETING RESEARCH PROCESS

The marketing research process is comprised of a series of steps called the research process. To conduct a research project effectively, it is important to anticipate all the steps and recognize their interdependence.

Need for Information. The first step in the research process is establishing the need for marketing research information. The researcher must thoroughly understand why the information is needed. The manager is responsible for explaining the situation surrounding the request for information and establishing that the research information will assist in the decision-making process. Establishing the need for research information is a critical and difficult phase of the research process. Too often the importance of this initial step is overlooked, which results in research findings that are not decision-oriented.

Research Objectives. Once the need for research information has been clearly defined, the researcher must specify the objectives of the proposed research and develop a specific list of information needs. Research objectives answer the question "Why is this project being conducted?" The answer could be as broad as the determination of the amount of effort needed to increase the company's market share by 5 percent or as specific as the determination of the most preferred of five moisturizers by women in southern California. Only when the researcher knows the problem that management wants to solve can the research project be designed to provide the pertinent information.

The difficult part of establishing research objectives is the conflict that often exists between the value of information and the research budget. Because each piece of information has some cost associated with it, whether it is the cost of the account manager's travel expenses or the cost of having an outside agency perform a telephone survey, each piece must be evaluated in terms of its value with respect to the needed decision.

Research Design and Data Sources. The next step in the research process is to design the formal research project and identify the appropriate sources of data for the study. A research design is the framework that specifies the type of information to be collected, the sources of the data, and

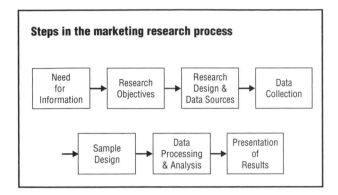

Steps in the marketing research process

Need for Information → Research Objectives → Research Design & Data Sources → Data Collection

→ Sample Design → Data Processing & Analysis → Presentation of Results

Figure 1

the data-collection procedures. Although there are many different ways to classify designs, one that gives a clear overview of the various procedures is based on three methods of generating primary data: experimentation, observation, and survey.

Experimentation involves establishing a controlled experiment or model that simulates the real-world marketing situation being investigated. In the observation method, the primary data result from observing the respondents doing something. The survey method involves collecting the primary data by questioning a certain number of people. Survey questioning may be done in-person, over the phone, through the mail, or online.

To determine the data sources for the research project, an assessment must first be made of the amount and type of data currently available. These data are called secondary data—data already gathered and available, having been accumulated previously for a different purpose. Although these data are assembled quickly and often at a low cost, sometimes they do not satisfy the research objectives.

There are two types of secondary data: internal (data originating within the firm) and external (published data originating outside the firm). Internal secondary data are all the data originating within the firm that were collected for some purpose other than the objective currently being addressed. Two of the most important types of internal data are sales and cost data.

After the internal secondary data have been examined, additional information can be obtained from published external secondary data. The main sources of external data are the Internet; the government; trade, business, and professional associations; the media; trade journals; universities and foundations; corporate annual reports; and commercial data services. Information obtained from any of these sources must be examined carefully to make sure that it fits the particular needs of the researcher.

- *Internet*—The Internet can provide links to many sources of information, quickly and easily. Searching the Web or visiting a business library's Web site are ways to become familiar with the types of resources available. Two Web sites that are useful in evaluating potential research resources are the New York Public Library's Science, Industry, and Business Library (http://www.nypl.org/research/sibl/index.html) and the University of Michigan's Documents Center (http://www.lib.umich.edu/govdocs).

- *Government*—The federal government is by far the largest source of marketing data. Although the data are available at a very low price, if any, once they are located there is often a cost and time commitment in obtaining the data. Some government publications are highly specialized, referring to specific studies of products. Other data are more general in nature. State and local governments also provide information. Data such as birth and death records and information on real estate sales and assessed values are public information and can be obtained from the specific state or local agency.

- *Associations*—Trade, business, and professional associations also have general data on the various activities and sales of their constituency. For example, the National Kitchen & Bath Association has general information on kitchen and bath design professionals, research design strategies, and remodeling. Although such data will not be company-specific, they are useful in gaining an overall perspective on the industry. Address and membership information for all associations can be found in the *Encyclopedia of Associations,* updated annually.

- *Media*—Most magazines, newspapers, and radio and television stations have marketing data available on their audience. Also, media perform periodic market surveys of buying patterns and demographic information in their market area. For example, the *Boston Globe* does a demographic study of its readers in order to give advertisers a better understanding of the marketing potential of their area.

- *Trade journals*—Trade journals also provide a wide variety of marketing and sales data on the areas they cover. For example, if market research were needed in the area of computers, then trade journals such as *Computerworld, InfoWorld,* and *ZDNet* should be checked for any pertinent information.

- *Universities and foundations*—Universities and foundations perform a variety of research projects. In addition to special studies supported by grants from the government, universities publish general research findings of interest to the business community through their research bureaus and institutes.

- *Corporate annual reports*—Corporate annual and 10-K reports are also useful sources of information on specific companies or general industry trends. These reports may not provide great detail; nevertheless, a general picture of the nature and scope of the firms in an industry as well as their general direction can be constructed.

- *Commercial data services*—Many firms offer marketing research and commercial data services. Some provide custom research; they design the research project specifically to meet the client's needs. This can be expensive. Others, such as Nielsen Media Research, offer standardized information, compiled regularly and made available to clients on a subscription basis.

After all the secondary data sources have been checked and the needed data have not been found, the third aspect of a research projected begins—the collection of data through primary research. Primary research can be best looked at in terms of three areas: data collection, sample design, and data processing and analysis.

Data Collection. If it has been determined that the required data are not currently available, then the next step is to collect new data. To develop the data-collection procedure, the researcher must establish an effective link between the information needs and the questions to be asked or the observations to be recorded. The process of collecting data is critical because it typically involves a large proportion of the research budget. The most widely used methods of data collection are focus groups, surveys, or interviews.

Focus groups are often used to collect primary data. A focus group consists of a discussion, usually lasting one and a half to two hours, with eight to twelve individuals and a moderator who is intent on encouraging in-depth discussion of a topic or product. The discussion allows for flexibility and provides broad, in-depth knowledge that cannot be obtained through any other research method.

Surveys, also known as questionnaires, are the most common instrument for data collection. A survey consists of a set of questions presented to respondents for their answers. Surveys need to be carefully developed, tested, and debugged before they are used; they can be administered over the phone, through the mail, via e-mail, or online. Web-based surveys and other forms of online research are popular choices because of their many advantages—timely, reliable data collection providing real-time, instant access to target audiences' opinions at reduced costs. Web surveys do not replace the traditional tech-

niques, but they can be an effective choice for companies big and small.

Primary research data are often obtained by interviews, either in person or over the telephone. For example, one might personally interview consumers to determine their opinions of a new line of low-fat foods or personally interview a few executives to determine their opinions of a nationally known advertising agency. An advantage of personal interviews is that the interviewer can adapt the question to the specific situation at hand. A limitation to this method is that the interviewer can introduce bias into the process by asking leading questions or by giving some indication of the preferred answer. A lot of time, supervision, and interviewer training are needed to implement personal interviews successfully.

Sample Design. When research is being conducted, it is important to determine the appropriate target population of the research—the group of people possessing characteristics relevant to the research problem from whom information will be obtained. Although this may appear to be easy, it is often one of the most difficult tasks in a marketing research project because of the wide variety of factors entering into the determination. For example, it might be important that only recent users of the product be surveyed. Or perhaps the purchasers of the product, not the users, should be the focus of the research.

Once the target population is determined, a decision is needed on how best to represent this population within the time and cost constraints of the research budget. Because there are many different methods used to draw this sample—the group of units composed of nonoverlapping elements that are representative of the population from which it is drawn—the best one needs to be chosen for the specific research project.

Data Processing and Analysis. After the data are collected, the processing begins, which includes the functions of editing and coding. Editing involves reviewing the data forms to ensure legibility, consistency, and completeness. Coding involves establishing categories for responses or groups of responses so that numerals can be used to represent the categories.

It is important that the data analysis be consistent with the requirements of the information needs identified when the research objectives were defined. Data analysis is usually performed with an appropriate software application. This data analysis, whether done by simple numeric counting or by complex computer-assisted analytical techniques, should provide meaningful information appropriate for managerial decisions.

Presentation of Results. After the data have been collected and analyzed, the final aspect of the research project can be generated—the development of the appropriate conclusions and recommendations. This is the most important part of the project, but it does not always receive the proper attention. The research results are typically communicated to the manager through a written report and oral presentation. The research findings should be presented in a clear, simple format and be accompanied by appropriate support material. The best research methodology in the world will be useless to managers if they cannot understand the research report. Some preparation guidelines for the written and oral reports are:

- Consider the audience
- Be concise, yet complete
- Be objective, yet effective

The findings should address the information needs of the decision situation. The final measure of the value of the research project is whether the findings are successfully implemented in the company.

THE VALUE OF MARKETING RESEARCH

Marketing research has, in a way, pioneered the move toward the broader view of marketing. Marketing research serves as a coordinating factor between marketing and the other functions of a business, such as engineering, manufacturing, accounting, and finance. This integration has the effect of enhancing the importance of marketing research to the corporation as a whole.

Marketing research continues to play a key role in organizations in the twenty-first century. Technology does and will continue to enable marketing research to take the lead in providing useful information for effective business decisions. The Internet's role in marketing research will continue to grow because it provides a quick, cost-effective way of collecting and disseminating data. Market researchers will continue their evolution from supplying "market and opinion research" to a more strategic position of supplying information, consulting, and exchanging information with consumers. Companies that take advantage of marketing research and view it as a valuable business component will be the companies that survive and thrive.

SEE ALSO *Marketing; Research in Business*

BIBLIOGRAPHY

Burns, Alvin C. & Bush, Ronald F. (2006). *Marketing research* (5th ed.). Upper Saddle River, NJ: Pearson/Prentice Hall.

Chadwick, Simon (1998). The research industry grows up—and out. *Marketing News, 32*(12), 9–17.

DeVries, K. (2005). Make your choice. *Marketing Health Services, 25*(3), 20–24.

Hirt-Marchand, Jennifer (2005). Online research captures audience insight, competitive data. *Managed Healthcare Executive, 15*(7), 30–32.

Honomichl, J. (2005). Strong progress. *Marketing News, 39,* pp. H3–H57.

Kinnear, Thomas C., and Taylor, James R. (1996). *Marketing research: An applied approach* (5th ed.). New York: McGraw-Hill.

Kottler, R. (2005). Eight tips offer best practices for online MR. *Marketing News, 39*(6), 24–25.

Marketing Research Association. (2005). Glossary of terms. Retrieved January 24, 2006, from http://www.mra-net.org/resources/glossary_terms.cfm?ID=K

Christine F. Latino

MARKUPS

SEE *Pricing*

MASLOW'S HEIRARCHY OF NEEDS

SEE *Behavioral Science Movement; Motivation*

MASS MARKETING

Mass marketing is a marketing approach in which the marketer addresses all segments of the market as though they are the same. The approach results in a single marketing plan with the same mix of product, price, promotion, and place strategies for the entire market.

The appeal of mass marketing is in the potential for higher total profits. Companies that employ the system expect the larger profit to result from (1) expanded volume through lower prices and (2) reduced costs through economies of scale made possible by the increased volume. In order for the system to work, however, certain conditions must exist. One is that the product must have broad appeal and a few features that distinguish it from competing products. Another is that it must lend itself to mass production. In addition, the opportunity must exist, and the marketer must have the ability to communicate and distribute to the aggregate market.

THE EVOLUTION INTO MASS MARKETING

Mass marketing first emerged as a workable strategy in the 1880s. Prior to that time, local markets in the United States were geographically isolated, few products had brand recognition beyond their local area, and continuous process technology had not yet come into its own. Profits in the fragmented markets were based on a low volume/high price strategy.

Between 1880 and 1890, several things occurred that eliminated the barriers and enhanced the appeal of mass marketing. The railroad and telegraph systems were completed, thus providing the potential for nationwide distribution and communication. Mass-production techniques and equipment were refined and adapted to a variety of products. Additionally, the population was growing rapidly, the country was recovering from the Civil War, and the largest depression in U.S. history until that time was ending.

These favorable circumstances by themselves did not create mass marketing. Entrepreneurial vision, drive, organization, and resources had to be added to implement the strategy. From 1880 to 1920, early innovators in many different industries stepped forward to seize the opportunity. Although the total number was relatively small—one or a few per industry—the impact on the U.S. economy was enormous. Many of these pioneering marketers built national reputations for their brands and companies that continued into the early twenty-first century.

Two of the most widely recognized examples are Ford and Coca-Cola. Henry Ford applied the concept in the automobile industry. His Model T was conceived and marketed as a "universal" car that would meet the needs of all buyers. By adopting mass-production techniques and eliminating optional features, he was able to reduce costs and sell his product at an affordable price. The combination catapulted the Model T to the top of the market. Asa Candler was equally successful at using mass marketing in the soft-drink industry. Like Ford, he also viewed his product as being the only one that consumers needed. His initial mass-marketing efforts focused on an extensive national advertising campaign. As product recognition grew, he established a network of bottling operations throughout the county to facilitate sales and distribution. No product in history has matched Coca-Cola's total sales.

Other mass marketers of this era achieved success by focusing on one aspect of the approach. Manufacturers such as Quaker Oats, Proctor and Gamble, and Eastman Kodak used refined mass-production techniques to establish consistent product quality. Still other manufacturers, such as Singer Sewing Machine, developed integrated distribution systems to ensure reliable delivery to the market.

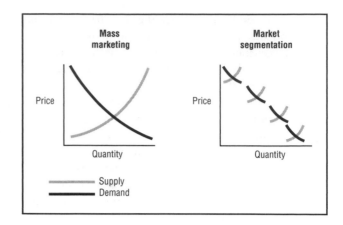

Figure 1

In general merchandise retailing, Sears and Montgomery Ward developed a mass-marketing niche through mail order. Grocery retailer A&P, on the other hand, established its mass market through private branding and systematic operation of multiple stores.

Mass marketers continued their domination in major industries well into the 1960s. Many of them maintained essentially the same mix, while others expanded their use of the strategy. Sears and Montgomery Ward, for example, added store retailing in the 1920s. In the 1930s, supermarkets appeared with a different emphasis than previous grocery retailers—national brands. Over the next several decades, large discount stores came into prominence with a format similar to the supermarkets.

THE EVOLUTION FROM MASS MARKETING

The successes of mass marketers led to the appearance of an alternate approach to marketing. Potential competitors wanting a share of the large market had two options. One was to replicate the organization, promotion, and distribution systems of the company that had created the mass market. The other was to go after a part of the market that had unique needs by developing products specifically for them. For nearly all of the challengers, building an operation to parallel that of an entrenched industry giant was not profitable or realistic. As a result, most of them gravitated to the more attractive market-segmentation approach. (Figure 1 shows the different demand curves for mass marketing and market segmentation.)

General Motors used market segmentation as early as the 1920s when it produced different models for different groups of customers to compete with Ford. Pepsi made a series of attempts, beginning in the 1930s, to crack into

Coca-Cola's market share through changes in product and targeted promotion strategy. In the 1940s, television provided a powerful tool for both new and old companies to reach segmented markets. By the 1960s, market segmentation had surpassed mass marketing as the primary approach.

MASS MARKETING NOW AND IN THE FUTURE

In spite of the shift to market segmentation, mass marketing continues to be used in many situations and has potential for others. Products with broad appeal and few distinguishing characteristics, such as household cleaners, potato chips, and pain relievers, lend themselves to mass marketing just as they always have. At the same time, businesses that use mass marketing for their goods and services continue to look for ways to enlarge their markets by designing different appeals for noncustomers. Chewing gum, for example, is presented as an alternative to smoking. Utilities and credit cards offer special rates to entice potential high-volume customers, while discount retailers, such as Wal-Mart, match their mix of mass-marketed products to local customer bases.

Any product that has mass-marketable attributes will likely be marketed by some form of the approach. In addition, the Internet provides a new medium for mass-marketing initiatives, and newly opened international markets offer a possible arena for mass-marketing opportunities.

SEE ALSO *Market Segmentation; Marketing*

BIBLIOGRAPHY

Gardner, Dana (1998, June). E-Mail Status Is Elevated as Mass Marketing Tool. *InfoWorld*, 1, 84.

Lakelin, Philip (1999, April). Mass Marketing the Internet. *Telecommunications* (International Edition), 59-62.

Tedlow, Richard S. (1996). *New and Improved: The Story of Mass Marketing in America*. Boston: Harvard Business School Press.

Tedlow, Richard S. (1997, Fall). The Beginning of Mass Marketing in America: George Eastman and Photography as a Case Study. *Journal of Macromarketing*, 67-81.

Earl C. Meyer
Lori A. Dailey

MATRIX STRUCTURE

SEE *Organizational Structure*

MEETING MANAGEMENT

Meetings have been considered very important from time immemorial. In fact, it could be said that virtually all of the great events in history resulted from meetings. Meetings undoubtedly started when the first cave dwellers met to make crude hunting plans. Today, meetings are essential means for achieving the communication necessary for the operation of virtually all organizations, large and small.

Just exactly what is a meeting? A meeting is a number of people assembled together, usually at a prestated date and time, to discuss a topic for the purpose of presenting information, swaying opinion, formulating a decision, practicing a skill, and/or developing a plan of action. Those at the meeting may belong to the same group, to different groups, or perhaps not to any group at all. A meeting might be called by an individual or by an organization. Usually the people meeting convene together physically within a designated area. Sometimes, however, meetings are held by people thousands of miles apart via telephone conference calls or video conferencing.

MAJOR TYPES OF MEETINGS

Many kinds of meetings are held in business. Probably the most common are staff meetings, project team meetings, process and procedure meetings, and quarterly meetings. In most large companies, hundreds of these meetings may occur weekly. Employees of all levels, including many below top-management level, attend them.

Staff meetings. Most supervisors and managers hold weekly or biweekly staff meetings with their "direct reports." In these meetings, they communicate higher-level decisions that have been made, discuss progress of the team toward departmental or company goals, and answer any staff members' questions.

Project team meetings. In most large companies, there are often project teams developed and facilitated by project managers. They are often comprised of people from different departments whose purpose is to design, develop, and/or implement a new product, process, or system. Project team members are assigned certain tasks to complete within stipulated time frames. Many of these people serve as part-time project resources in addition to performing their "regular" jobs.

Process and procedure meetings. These meetings are usually called to communicate new processes and/or procedures to a group of people who are affected. The communication includes an overview of the new process or procedure, the effect on that particular group of people, and steps to follow. A presentation-style format is used, with the presenter serving as the facilitator. At the end, a question-and-answer period usually follows.

Quarterly meetings. Quarterly earnings are announced at these meetings, along with detailed information on the financial status of the entire company and progress made toward strategic and departmental goals. Strategic direction changes are also communicated. A team of high-level executives ordinarily preside, using a presentation-style format.

METHODS OF ACHIEVING EFFECTIVE MEETINGS

In order for meetings to be successful, careful attention must be paid to a myriad of details. Two kinds of details are the most important: (1) thorough planning of premeeting activities and (2) skillful leadership during the meeting itself.

Premeeting planning. These steps should be taken before the meeting starts:

1. Determine whether a meeting really needs to be held or whether the objectives could be achieved through phone calls or written communication.

2. Prepare an agenda that includes the objective and the desired outcome of the meeting. Date, location, time of meeting, and a list of attendees should be included. A typical agenda includes the following: (a) call the meeting to order; (b) read the minutes of the previous meeting for approval, then correct errors and omissions; (c) hear reports of officers and committees; (d) discuss unfinished business; (e) take up new business; (f) adjourn. Announcements and other business not requiring a vote may come at the beginning or end of the meeting. If possible, the estimated time for each agenda item should be listed.

3. Distribute the agenda to the participants, providing ample time for them to review the agenda/prework prior to the meeting. Any applicable prework should be attached to the agenda. Roles should be clear to the participants: input providers, decision makers, or both. Persons who will be presenting reports should be contacted to ensure that they will be ready.

4. Determine who will facilitate (preside over) the meeting. This could be anyone present, not necessarily the highest-level attendee. The roles of facilitator and of note-taker may be rotated. The name and position of this person should be announced before the meeting starts.

5. Limit attendance to those with subject-matter knowledge who will make valuable contributions and have decision-making authority.

6. Ensure the availability of the materials/equipment necessary to run the meeting effectively and that the equipment is working. Such materials/equipment may include:

   • extra copies of agenda and prework
   • overhead projector and/or LCD panel/projector
   • easel/flip-chart pads
   • markers, extra pencils
   • name tags
   • extension cords
   • transparencies
   • Light refreshments should be available for people as they arrive; this creates a good feeling and may contribute to the success of the meeting.

Conducting meetings. Once the meeting is underway, following these guidelines will enhance its effectiveness:

1. The facilitator should start the meeting on time. If a gavel is used, it should be rapped once to declare order at the beginning and as necessary throughout the meeting. The facilitator should welcome those present and, if appropriate, have them introduce themselves. After some informal remarks, the facilitator should restate the meeting objectives, establish the ground rules of the meeting, and ask for any additions to the agenda.

2. A quorum (usually a majority of the members) is ordinarily required to conduct business. If the existence of a quorum is questioned, it must be determined that one exists for the meeting to continue.

3. The role of the facilitator is to keep the meeting on track, follow the agenda and time schedule, identify and assign tasks, and listen and ask questions. If the discussion drifts away from the agenda, the facilitator should diplomatically but firmly declare the errant remarks "out of order" and return discussion to the agenda.

4. Any member recognized by the facilitator may make a motion. Following a second, the group discusses the motion. When discussion ends, the motion is voted on. A majority vote is ordinarily required for a motion to pass. A successful vote approves "immediate action" or "tables" the motion (that is, refers one

motion to a committee or postpones discussion until the next meeting).

5. The facilitator must know the degree of formality expected. If informality has prevailed in the past, it should be continued. Informality often permits decision by consensus rather than formal vote. However, if formality prevails, parliamentary procedure must apply. The worldwide reference to this is the publication *Robert's Rules of Order*.

6. Good meeting facilitators try to get as many people as possible to participate in the discussions. It is difficult but necessary to discourage someone who monopolizes the discussion.

7. Special skill is required to manage a meeting if a heated debate breaks out. In such instances, the facilitator must forcefully limit the number and time allotted to those on each side of the issue. Above all, interruptions should not be permitted.

8. There are few things worse than a boring meeting. Good facilitators often find that occasional witty remarks take away hum-drum feelings. Another good practice is to laugh heartily at genuinely funny comments.

9. During the meeting, the facilitator must see to that there is agreement on any next steps or assignments and their target completion dates.

10. At the end of the meeting, the facilitator thanks attendees and, if earned, recognizes their good participation. It is often appropriate to get consensus on the date, time, and place of the next meeting.

MEETINGS OF CORPORATION BOARDS OF DIRECTORS

At the top level of corporations are the meetings of the board of directors. Directors generally have authority over all corporate matters. The articles of incorporation, as amended, determine the number of directors.

Boards meet at regularly scheduled times, including during and immediately after shareholder meetings. If special board meetings are called, notice, in most cases, must be given at least ten but not more than sixty days in advance.

Corporation presidents generally preside at board meetings. If the president is unable to do so, the vice president ordinarily presides. Most large corporations use written meeting agendas.

Quorum requirements ordinarily require a majority of the directors to be in attendance. If at least a quorum attends, whatever decisions are made by those present

constitute an action by the board. Bylaws seldom permit voting by proxy.

Corporation bylaws ordinarily presume that directors approve of any act passed by the board even if they voted against it unless they file a dissenting statement at or immediately after the meeting.

MEETINGS OF CORPORATE SHAREHOLDERS

State statutes and corporation bylaws require annual shareholder meetings. In addition to topics requested by shareholders, three major agenda items are usually covered:

1. Election of board of directors

2. Financial and competitive "state of the corporation"

3. Plans for the future

Special shareholder meetings can be called if a major corporation change is pending, such as a new line of products or a hostile takeover bid by another corporation. Bylaws usually stipulate that notice of a special meeting must be given at least ten but not more than sixty days in advance.

Every item on the agenda must be checked meticulously for any inaccuracies. The Federal Trade Commission, an independent U.S. governmental agency, has the authority to issue cease-and-desist orders against companies that engage in any misleading practices in any shareholder meetings or publications sent to shareholders.

Unlike at meetings of board of directors, proxies can vote at shareholder meetings. A quorum generally consists of shareholders holding a majority of the voting stock (usually common stock).

SEE ALSO *Listening Skills in Business; Speaking Skills in Business*

BIBLIOGRAPHY

Sniffen, Carl R.J. (2001). *The Essential Corporation Handbook.* (Directors' Meetings, pp. 6, 227; Shareholders' Meetings, pp. 161–171.) Central Point, OR: Oasis Press/PSI Research.

Brenda J. Reinsborough

MERGERS AND ACQUISITIONS

Mergers and acquisitions (M&A) are often the means chosen by company boards of directors to meet strategic goals such as expansion of products, services, or revenues.

As the terms imply, a merger is a combination of two existing businesses; an acquisition is a purchase of a company by another company. Since both processes legally unite companies, the transactions are called consolidations. Since the two processes are similar, the term *mergers and acquisitions* is the typical reference used for consolidations in the United States. The detailed differences of such transactions, though, influence the accounting treatment in the company's records. The Financial Accounting Standards Board (FASB) has promulgated rules and practices for the accounting treatment for each of the four variations of consolidations recognized in U.S. accounting standards.

The sections that follow include: consolidation movements in the United States, motivations for M&A, the process, accounting for M&A, and after the merger or acquisition. The range of strategies used by companies to undertake cooperative ventures is not discussed here. Furthermore, the potential tax effects of consolidations are beyond the scope of the discussion provided in this article.

CONSOLIDATION MOVEMENTS IN THE UNITED STATES

Distinct periods for consolidations have been identified in the United States. J. Fred Weston and Samuel C. Weaver, for example, identified four periods with the circumstances that initiated each:

1. 1893–1903—Fueled by consolidation of railroads and industrial enterprises

2. 1920s—Motivated by interest in vertical consolidation to control the entire supply chain

3. 1960s—Spurred by interest in diversification, the building of conglomerates

4. 1980s—Stimulated by availability of junk-bond financing

Writers in the early twenty-first century identified a fifth wave that began in the mid-1990s. For example, Patrick Gaughan noted that by "1993 we were once again in the throes of a full-scale merger wave" (2002, p. 3). The literature about events since 2000 has demonstrated mixed judgment, with some writers indicating that the fifth wave was continuing (as of 2006).

CONTEMPORARY MOTIVATIONS FOR M&A

Consolidations that began in the 1990s have had common motivations identified in the press and in empirical reviews of M&A activity in the United States.

To Enhance Market Position Quickly. The board of directors, viewing a high level of cash reserves and high market value for the company stock, may determine that acquiring a company that has a particular product line or customer base will heighten its position in the market. For example, ConocoPhillips, formed through a series of mergers, continued to grow through mergers through 2005. As of November 2005, it realized that it could become the third-largest oil company with the contemplated purchase of one of the largest independent oil companies in the United States. The target of their interest, Burlington Resources, was attractive owing to Burlington's use of new drilling technologies and because of the possibilities of expanding internationally by gaining access to this company's inroads in countries such as Canada and Ecuador. The outcome of a possible acquisition is seldom clear because other interested parties could appear before the completion of the process.

Larger Size Can Meet Perceived Demand. Businesses such as banks, accounting firms, law firms, and management consulting firms have all experienced mergers and acquisitions during the economic development of the United States. Banks, for example, undertake mergers and acquisitions as customers and potential customers required larger pools of funds than available in a bank with limited resources.

Technological Shifts. A period of intense technological changes encourages mergers and acquisitions. It is not uncommon for a mature company to identify the innovation of an emerging company as a good match to extend their product lines or provide new services. In December 2005 the New York Stock Exchange (NYSE), a traditionally functioning stock exchange that began operations in 1792, concluded that expansion of services electronically was critical for its future. Thus, their acquisition of Archipelago, an electronic trading network, is illustrative of this motivation. As of early 2006, the newly formed NYSE Group Inc. was scheduled to shift from a not-for-profit organization to a publicly owned entity with extended services for clients.

Growth in Revenues. Sometimes competitors realize that they can achieve far more together than separately. The extensive number of mergers and acquisitions during the final decade of the 1800s and the first years of the 1900s is often cited as a key factor in the establishment of a national economy in the United States.

THE PROCESS

There are many aspects to the achievement of a successful merger or acquisition. The process may take a relatively brief period or an extended period of several years. The nature of the initial interest influences the initial process. Experts in the field of M&A who are able to meet the reporting phases mandated by legal requirements in the United States are generally needed. Company charters and bylaws provide policies and procedures that must be met in the event of a sale or merger. For certain types of mergers or acquisitions, the shareholders have the right to cast a vote to support or reject the bid.

Initial Attitudes of Participants. Interested parties—the target company executives and the potential buyer—may be friendly or hostile to each other. If friendly, the leaders of two companies may engage in informal discussion that leads to a more serious assessment of the advantages to each if their company resources were combined.

If the company executives of the target company do not find the efforts of the potential buyer appealing, strategies to undermine the potential takeover may be introduced. The use of poison pills (securities issued to shareholders that become available if purchases of stock reach a specified level) raises the cost of acquisition. Changes in the company bylaws and charter, including the issuances of gold or silver parachutes—high payouts to current executives of target companies—impede progress in hostile takeover efforts. The business press often reports the types of strategies in use by major companies facing hostile takeovers.

The potential buyer, to overcome the reluctance of the target company, may make a tender offer, which is to advertise its interest in buying the target company stock from current stockholders at an attractive price.

Need for Expert Assistance. Companies that engage in mergers and acquisitions on a relatively regular basis may have professional staff members in house that participate in the process. Even with in-house staff, however, the engagement of outsiders is common. Investment bankers are frequently engaged to serve as the key drivers of the total process. Additionally, the companies involved seek the guidance of lawyers, accountants, and proxy solicitation companies, as well as public relations firms.

Review by Regulatory Agencies. Companies with publicly traded securities participating in mergers or acquisitions must submit documents to relevant governmental agencies at the federal and state levels. All such companies must meet federal securities laws that deal with adherence to provisions of the Securities Act of 1933 and the Securities Exchange Act of 1934, which deal with disclosure requirements and the regulation of tender offers. The U.S. Department of Justice and the Federal Trade Commission are responsible for enforcing antitrust laws. Regulated industries, such as banking, insurance, communications, utilities, airlines, and railroads, must meet special regulatory requirements beyond the general rules.

The purposes of such review reflect the interest of the U.S. government in ensuring that the business environment in the United States is favorable to an open, competitive, fair style of behavior by business entities. Furthermore, such reviews include gaining assurance that laws related to employee benefits and environmental requirements are honored by participants in a merger or acquisition.

ACCOUNTING FOR M&A

Mergers and acquisitions fall under the general technical description of "business combinations" in accounting terminology. Two financial accounting standards govern the accounting for business combinations. They are the Statement of Financial Accounting Standards No. 141, "Business Combinations," and the Statement of Financial Accounting Standards No. 142, "Goodwill and Other Intangible Assets," both of which were issued by the FASB in 2001.

The definition of a business combination from FASB Statement No. 141 is: "a business combination occurs when an entity acquires net assets that constitute a business or acquires equity interests of one or more other entities and obtains control over that entity or entities."

The most frequent method for entering into a business combination is acquisition of an equity (common stock) interest of over 50 percent of the outstanding stock of the acquired company. The acquired company does not go out of business. The acquiring company (now called the parent) usually has complete control of the acquired company (now called the subsidiary). Because of this controlling relationship, accounting standards require that consolidated financial statements be prepared for the parent and subsidiary as if they were a single entity. The parent may have many subsidiaries, in which case all would be consolidated with the parent in the consolidated financial statements.

Commonly, the parent acquires the stock of the subsidiary with cash, exchange of stock, and/or debt. The total paid (the cost) is then compared to the book value acquired. Normally, there is an excess of cost over book value acquired for two reasons—book value of long-lived assets is based on historical cost less accumulated depreciation, and intellectual assets are not permitted to be on the balance sheet of the newly acquired subsidiary according to generally accepted accounting principles.

An appraisal of the subsidiary is made and a part of the excess of cost over book value acquired is allocated to all identifiable assets. Nevertheless, because intellectual assets—such as value of employees—are not permitted to be recorded as assets, there is generally a residual value of the excess of cost over the book value acquired after the allocations to bring net assets of the acquired subsidiary to fair value. This residual value is called goodwill. When consolidated statements are prepared, both the fair values of the subsidiary's assets and the goodwill are shown.

There are three other methods for achieving business combinations. One method is for one company to acquire the assets of another. The other two methods use statutory mergers and statutory consolidations. Note that although in common language *mergers* and *acquisitions* are used as synonymous terms for *consolidations,* in accounting these are technical terms. A statutory merger occurs when Company A acquires Company B and dissolves Company B. A statutory consolidation occurs when Companies A and B create Company C and dissolve companies A and B. The accounting for business combinations achieved via asset acquisitions, statutory mergers, and statutory consolidations is similar to the accounting for a business combination via equity acquisition.

AFTER THE MERGER OR ACQUISITION

After the legal functions have satisfactorily concluded, the new entity has the demanding task of integrating the components of the new entity so that the goals anticipated at the time of consolidation are realized. The evidence on the success of mergers meeting their goals is ambiguous. In a summary of several empirical studies, Günter Stahl and colleagues noted, "Despite their popularity and strategic importance, the performance of most M&A has been disappointing" (Stahl, Mendenhall, Pablo, and Javidan, 2005, p. 1).

There are many instances of earlier mergers and acquisitions being spun off. For example, First Data Corporation, which acquired Western Union in 1995, announced in January 2006 that it planned to spin off its purchase of more than a decade earlier. This decision was made even though Western Union had been a fast-growing money-transfer business for the acquirer.

Both Cendant and Tyco, which expanded through mergers and acquisitions over a decade, announced plans to split their companies. In October 2005 Cendant reported it would become four independent companies. In early January 2006 Tyco International reported plans to split itself into three publicly traded companies.

Reconsideration of company strategy leads to mergers and acquisitions as well as to the undoing of earlier mergers and acquisitions. The dynamic characteristic of contemporary business is clearly reflected in these two seemingly contradictory processes that are evident in the economic environment at the same time.

BIBLIOGRAPHY

Dash, Eric (2006, January 27). Western Union, growing faster than its parent, is to be spun off. *The New York Times,* Section C, p. 3.

DePamphilis, Donald M. (2003). *Mergers, acquisitions, and other restructuring activities* (2nd ed.). Amsterdam: Academic.

Gaughan, Patrick A. (2002). *Mergers, acquisitions—Corporate restructuring* (3rd ed.). New York: Wiley.

Stahl, Günter K., Mendenhall, Mark E., Pablo, A. L., and Javidan, M. (2005). Sociocultural integration in mergers and acquisitions. In Günter K. Stahl and Mark E. Mendenhall (Eds.), *Mergers and acquisitions: Managing culture and human resources.* Stanford, CA: Stanford Business Books.

Statement of Financial Accounting Standards No. 141. (2001). Business combinations. Stamford, CT: Financial Accounting Standards Board.

Statement of Financial Accounting Standards No. 142. (2001). Goodwill and other intangible assets. Stamford, CT: Financial Accounting Standards Board.

Weston, J. Fred, and Weaver, Samuel C. (2001). *Mergers and acquisitions.* New York: McGraw-Hill.

Bernard H. Newman
Mary Ellen Oliverio

MICROECONOMICS

SEE *Macroeconomics/Microeconomics*

MISSION STATEMENT

SEE *Strategic Management*

MIXED ECONOMIC SYSTEMS

SEE *Economic Systems*

MONETARY EXCHANGE

SEE *Currency Exchange*

MONETARY POLICY

The central agency that conducts monetary policy in the United States is the Federal Reserve System (the Fed). It was founded by the U.S. Congress in 1913 under the Federal Reserve Act. The Fed is a highly independent agency that is insulated from day-to-day political pressures, accountable only to Congress. It is a federal system, consisting of a board of governors, twelve regional Federal Reserve Banks (FRBs) and their twenty-five branches, the Federal Open Market Committee (FOMC), the Federal Advisory Council and other advisory and working committees, and 2,900 member banks, mostly national banks. By law, all federally chartered banks, that is, national banks, are automatic members of the system. State-chartered banks may elect to become members.

The seven-member board of governors, headquartered in Washington, D.C., is the core agency of the Fed, overseeing the entire operation of U.S. monetary policy. The FRBs are the operating arms of the system and are located in twelve major cities, one in each of the twelve Federal Reserve Districts around the nation. The twelve-member FOMC is the most important policy-making entity of the system. The voting members of the committee are the seven members of the board, the president of the FRB of New York, and four of the other eleven FRB presidents, each serving one year on a rotating basis. The other seven nonvoting FRB presidents still attend the meetings and participate fully in policy deliberations.

MONETARY POLICY AND THE ECONOMY

Being one of the most influential government policies, monetary policy aims at affecting the economy through the Fed's management of money and interest rates. The narrowest definition of money is M1, which includes currency, checking account deposits, and traveler's checks. Time deposits, savings deposits, money market deposits, and other financial assets can be added to M1 to define other monetary measures, such as M2 and M3. Interest rates are simply the costs of borrowing. The Fed conducts monetary policy through bank reserves, which are the portion of the deposits that banks and other depository institutions are required to hold either as vault cash or as deposits with their home FRBs. Excess reserves are the reserves in excess of the amount required. These additional funds can be transacted in the reserves market (the federal funds market) to allow overnight borrowing between depository institutions to meet short-term needs in reserves. The rate at which such private borrowings are charged is the federal funds rate.

Monetary policy is closely linked with the reserves market. With its policy tools, the Fed can control the reserves available in the market, affect the federal funds rate, and subsequently trigger a chain of reactions that influence other short-term interest rates, foreign-exchange rates, long-term interest rates, and the amount of money and credit in the economy. These changes will then bring about adjustments in consumption, affect saving and investment decisions, and eventually influence employment, output, and prices.

GOALS OF MONETARY POLICY

The long-term goals of monetary policy are to promote full employment and stable prices and to moderate long-term interest rates. Most economists believe price stability should be the primary objective, since a stable level of prices is key to sustained output and employment, as well as to maintaining moderate long-term interest rates. Relatively speaking, it is easier for central banks to control inflation (i.e., the continual rise in the price level) than to influence employment directly, because the latter is affected by such real factors as technology and consumer tastes. Moreover, historical evidence indicates a strong positive correlation between inflation and the amount of money.

While the financial markets react quickly to changes in monetary policy, it generally takes months or even years for such policy to affect employment and growth, and thus to reach the Fed's long-term goals. The Fed, therefore, needs to be forward-looking and to make timely policy adjustments based on forecasted as well as actual data on such variables as wages and prices, inflation, unemployment, output growth, foreign trade, interest rates, exchange rates, money and credit, and conditions in the markets for bonds and stocks.

IMPLEMENTATION OF MONETARY POLICY

Since the early 1980s, the Fed has been relying on the overnight federal funds rate as the guide to its position in monetary policy. The Fed has at its disposal three major monetary policy tools: reserve requirements, the discount rate, and open-market operations.

Reserve Requirements. Under the Monetary Control Act of 1980, all depository institutions, including commercial banks and savings and loans, are subject to the same reserve requirements, regardless of their Fed member status. As of October 2005, the structure of reserve requirements was 0 percent for all checkable deposits up to $7 million (the exemption), 3 percent for such deposits from above $7 million to $47.6 million (the low-reserve tranche), and 10 percent for the amount above $47.6 million. Both the exemption and the low-reserve tranche are subject to annual adjustment by statute to reflect changes in reservable liabilities at all depository institutions. No reserves are required for nonpersonal time deposits and Eurocurrency liabilities.

Reserve requirements affect the so-called multiple money creation. Suppose, for example, the reserve requirement ratio is 10 percent. A bank that receives a $100 deposit (Bank 1) can lend out $90. Bank 1 can then issue a $90 check to a borrower, who deposits it in Bank 2, which can then lend out $81. As it continues, the process will eventually involve a total of $1,000 ($100 + $90 + $81 + $72.9 + … = $1,000) in deposits. The initial deposit of $100 is thus multiplied ten times. With a lower (higher) ratio, the multiple involved is larger (smaller), and more (fewer) reserves can be created.

Reserve requirements are not used as often as the other policy tools. Since funds grow in multiples, it is difficult to administer small adjustments in reserves with this tool. Also, banks always have the option of entering the federal funds market for reserves, further limiting the role of reserve requirements. Except for the yearly adjustments of the exemption and the low-reserve tranche, the last change in the reserve requirements was in April 1992, when the upper ratio was reduced from 12 to 10 percent.

The Discount Rate. Banks and other depository institutions may acquire loans through the discount window at their home FRB to meet their short-term needs against, for example, unexpected large withdrawals of deposits. The interest rate charged on such loans is the discount rate. A reduction of the rate encourages more borrowing, and through money creation, bank deposits increase and reserves increase. A rate hike works in the opposite direction. Since it is more efficient, however, to adjust reserves through open-market operations (discussed below), the amount of discount window lending has been unimportant, accounting for only a small fraction of total reserves. Perhaps a more meaningful function served by the discount rate is to signal the Fed's stance on monetary policy, similar to the role of the federal funds rate.

By law, each FRB sets its discount rate every two weeks, subject to the approval of the board of governors. The gradual nationalization of the credit market over the years, however, has resulted in a uniform discount rate. A major revision in the discount window programs took effect in January 2003 to enhance the Fed's lending function. The FRBs began to offer three discount window programs to depository institutions: the primary credit program for financially sound institutions, the secondary credit program for institutions not eligible for primary credit, and the seasonal credit program for small depository institutions that have seasonal fluctuations in funding needs.

Discount-rate adjustments, usually going hand in hand with changes in the federal funds rate, have been dictated by cyclical conditions of the economy, and the frequency of adjustments has varied. For instance, the discount rate moved up from a low of 3 percent in May 1994 to 6 percent in January 2001 to counter possible overheating and inflation from the robust economic growth since the mid-1990s. The rate was then lowered twelve times, to a bare 0.75 percent in two years, to help the economy recover from its 2001 recession. From June 2004 to September 2005, the primary (4.75 percent) and secondary (5.25 percent) credit rates were both raised 11 times to cool off the economy and especially the overheated housing market.

Open-Market Operations. The most important and flexible tool of monetary policy is open-market operations, that is, trading U.S. government securities in the open market. In 2004 the Fed made $7.55 trillion of purchases and $7.51 trillion of sales of Treasury securities (mostly short-term Treasury bills). As of June 2005, the Fed held $721.92 billion of U.S. Treasury securities, roughly 9.2 percent of the total federal debt outstanding.

The FOMC directs open-market operations (and also advises about reserve requirements and discount-rate policies). The day-to-day operations are determined and executed by the Domestic Trading Desk (the Desk) at the FRB of New York. Since 1980 the FOMC has met regularly eight times a year in Washington, D.C. At each of these meetings, it votes on an intermeeting target federal funds rate, based on the current and prospective conditions of the economy. Until the next meeting, the Desk will manage reserve conditions through open-market operations to maintain the federal funds rate around the given target level. When buying securities from a bank, the Fed makes the payment by increasing the bank's reserves at the Fed. More reserves will then be available in the federal funds market and the federal funds rate falls. By selling securities to a bank, the Fed receives payment in reserves from the bank. Supply of reserves falls and the funds rate rises.

The Fed has two basic approaches in running open-market operations. When a shortage or surplus in reserves is likely to persist, the Fed may undertake outright purchases or sales, creating a long-term impact on the supply of reserves. Nevertheless, many reserve movements are temporary. The Fed can then take a defensive position and engage in transactions that impose only temporary effects on the level of reserves. A repurchase agreement (a repo) allows the Fed to purchase securities with the agreement that the seller will buy back them within a short period, sometimes overnight and mostly within seven days. The repo creates a temporary increase in reserves, which vanishes when the term expires. If the Fed wishes to drain reserves temporarily from the banking system, it can adopt a matched sale-purchase transaction (a reverse repo), under which the buyer agrees to sell the securities back to the Fed, usually in fewer than seven days.

SEE ALSO *Federal Reserve System; International Monetary Fund; Macroeconomics/Microeconomics*

BIBLIOGRAPHY

Bernanke, Ben S. (2005, March 30). Implementing monetary policy (Federal Reserve Board Member speech). Retrieved January 23, 2006, from http://www.federalreserve.gov/boarddocs/speeches/2005/20050330/default.htm

Bernanke, Ben S. (2004, December 2). The logic of monetary policy (Federal Reserve Board Member speech). Retrieved January 23, 2006, from http://www.federalreserve.gov/boarddocs/speeches/2004/20041202/default.htm

Bies, Susan S. (2004, October 23). The Federal Reserve System and the economy (Federal Reserve Board Member speech). Retrieved January 23, 2006, from http://www.federalreserve.gov/boarddocs/speeches/2004/20041023/default.htm

The Federal Reserve System: Purposes and functions. (2005, June). Washington, DC: Board of Governors of the Federal Reserve System.

Mishkin, Frederic S. (2006). *The economics of money, banking, and financial markets* (7th ed.). New York: Pearson-Addison-Wesley.

91st Annual Report: 2004. (2005). Washington, DC: Board of Governors of the Federal Reserve System.

Treasury Bulletin. (2005, September). Washington, DC: U.S. Department of Treasury.

Edward Wei-Te Hsieh

MONEY

In the modern world we take money for granted. However, pause for a moment and imagine what life would be like without money. Suppose that you want to consume a particular good or service, such as a pair of shoes. If money did not exist, you would need to barter with the cobbler for the pair of shoes that you want. Barter is the process of directly exchanging one good or service for another. In order to purchase the pair of shoes, you would need to have something to trade for the shoes. If you specialized in growing peaches, you would need to bring enough bushels of peaches to the cobbler's shop to purchase the pair of shoes. If the cobbler wanted your peaches and you wanted his shoes, then a double coincidence of wants would exist and trade could take place.

But what if the cobbler did not want your peaches? In that case you would have to find out what he did want, for example, beef. Then you would have to trade your peaches for beef and the beef for shoes. But what if the person selling beef had no desire for peaches, but instead wants a computer? Then you would have to trade your peaches for a computer—and it would take a lot of peaches to buy a computer. Then you would have to trade your computer for beef and the beef for shoes. But what if … ? At some point it would become easier to make the shoes yourself or to just do without.

THE EVOLUTION OF MONEY

Money evolved as a way of avoiding the complexities and difficulties of barter. Money is any asset that is recognized by an economic community as having value. Historically, such assets have included, among other things, shells, stone disks (which can be somewhat difficult to carry around), gold, and bank notes.

The modern monetary system has its roots in the gold of medieval Europe. In the Middle Ages, gold and gold coins were the common currency. However, the wealthy found that carrying large quantities of gold around was difficult and made them the target of thieves. To avoid carrying gold coins, people began depositing them for safekeeping with goldsmiths, who often had heavily guarded vaults in which to store their valuable inventories of gold. The goldsmiths charged a fee for their services and issued receipts, or gold notes, in the amount of the deposits. Exchanging these receipts was much simpler and safer than carrying around gold coins. In addition, the depositors could retrieve their gold on demand.

Goldsmiths during this time became aware that few people actually wanted their gold coins back when the gold notes were so easy to use for exchange. They therefore began lending some of the gold on deposit to borrowers who paid a fee, called interest. These goldsmiths were the precursors to our modern fractional reserve banking system.

FUNCTIONS OF MONEY

Regardless of what asset is recognized by an economic community as money, in general it serves three functions:

- Money is a medium of exchange
- Money is a measure of value
- Money is a store of value

Money is a medium of exchange. Used as a medium of exchange, money means that parties to a transaction no longer need to barter one good for another. Because money is accepted as a medium of exchange, you can sell

International currency. PHOTODISC/GETTY IMAGES

your peaches for money and purchase the desired shoes with the proceeds of the sale. You no longer need to trade peaches—a lot of them—for a computer and then the computer for beef and then the beef for the shoes. As a medium of exchange, money tends to encourage specialization and division of labor, promoting economic efficiency.

Money is a measure of value. As a measure of value, money makes transactions significantly simpler. Instead of markets determining the price of peaches relative to computers and to beef and to shoes, as well as the price of computers relative to beef and to shoes, as well as the price of beef relative to shoes (i.e., a total of six prices for only four goods), the markets only need to determine the price of each of the four goods in terms of money. If we were to add a fifth good to our simple economy, then we would add four more prices to the number of good-for-good prices that the markets must determine. As the number of goods in our economy grew, the number of good-for-good prices would grow rapidly. In an economy with ten goods, there would be forty-five good-for-good prices but only

ten money prices. In an economy with twenty goods there would be one hundred and ninety good-for-good prices but only twenty money prices. Imagine all of the good-for-good prices in a more realistic economy with thousands of goods and services available.

Using money as a measure of value reduces the number of prices determined in markets and vastly reduces the cost of collecting price information for market participants. Instead of focusing on such information, market participants can focus their effort on producing the good or service in which they specialize.

Money as a store of value. Money can also serve as a store of value, since it can quickly be exchanged for desired goods and services. Many assets can be used as a store of value, including stocks, bonds, and real estate. However, there are transaction costs associated with converting these assets into money in order to purchase a desired good or service. These transaction costs could include monetary fees as well as time delays involved in the liquidation process.

In contrast, money is a poor store of value during periods of inflation, while the value of real estate tends to appreciate during such periods. Thus, the benefits of holding money must by balanced against the risks of holding money.

SUMMARY

Money simplifies the exchange of goods and services and facilitates specialization and division of labor. It does this by serving as a medium of exchange, as a measure of value, and as a store of value.

SEE ALSO *Currency Exchange; Money Supply*

Denise Woodbury

MONEY SUPPLY

Money is a collection of liquid assets that is generally accepted as a medium of exchange and for repayment of debt. In that role, it serves to economize on the use of scarce resources devoted to exchange, expands resources for production, facilitates trade, promotes specialization, and contributes to a society's welfare. This theoretical definition serves two purposes: It encompasses new forms of money that may arise as a result of financial innovations related to technological change and institutional developments. It also distinguishes money from other assets by emphasizing its general acceptability as a medium of exchange. While all assets serve as a store of wealth, only a few are accepted as a means of payment for goods and services.

While this definition provides a clear picture of what money is, it does not specify exactly what assets should be included in its measurement. There are several liquid assets such as coins, paper currency, checkable-type deposits, and traveler's checks, which clearly act as a medium of exchange, and definitely belong to its measurement. Several other assets, however, may also serve as a medium of exchange but are not as liquid as currency and checkable-type deposits. For example, money market deposit accounts have check-writing features subject to certain restrictions, and savings accounts can be converted into a medium of exchange with a negligible cost. To what extent such assets should be included in money's measurement is not clear.

As an alternative, economists have proposed defining and measuring money using an empirical approach. This approach emphasizes the role of money as an intermediate target for monetary policy. As Frederic Mishkin pointed out, an effective intermediate target should have three fea-tures: It must be measurable, controllable by the central bank, and have a predictable and stable relation with ultimate goals. Thus, an asset should be included in money's measurement if it helps satisfy these requirements. As it appears, evidence on which measure of money has a high predictive power is mixed. A measure that predicts well in one period might not perform well in other times, and a measure that predicts one goal, might not be a good predictor of others.

THE FEDERAL RESERVE SYSTEM'S MONETARY AGGREGATES

The Federal Reserve System (also known as the Fed) has incorporated both the theoretical approach and the empirical approach in constructing its measures of the money supply for the United States. The results are four measures of monetary aggregates, M1, M2, M3, and L, which are constructed using simple summations of some liquid assets. M1 is the narrowest measure and corresponds closely to the theoretical definition of money. It consists of six liquid assets: coins, dollar bills, traveler's checks, demand deposits, other checkable deposits, and NOW (negotiated order of withdrawal) accounts held at commercial banks and at thrift institutions. These assets are clearly money because they are used directly as a medium of exchange.

The M2 aggregate adds to M1 two groups of assets: other assets that have check-writing features such as money market deposit accounts and money market mutual funds shares, and other extremely liquid assets such as savings deposits, small denomination time deposits, overnight repurchase agreements, and overnight Eurodollars. Similarly, the M3 aggregate adds to M2 somewhat less liquid assets such as large denomination time deposits, institutional money market funds, term repurchase agreements, and term Eurodollars. Finally, L is a broad measure of highly liquid assets. It consists of M3 and several highly liquid securities such as savings bonds, short-term Treasury securities, banker's acceptances, and commercial paper.

A potential problem with the simple summation procedure, which underlies the construction of the monetary aggregates, is the assumption that all individual components are perfect substitutes. As William Barnett, Douglas Fisher, and Apostolos Serletis pointed out, this procedure is useful for constructing accounting measures of monetary wealth but does not provide reliable measures of monetary services. As a solution, Milton Friedman and Anna Schwartz proposed weighting individual components by their degree of "moneyness," with the weights varying from zero to unity. Another more rigorous solution proposed by Barnett and his colleagues is based on the application of aggregation and index number theory.

Evidence along this line of research suggests that these measures of monetary aggregate are superior to the traditional measures in their predictive contents.

Knowledge of money supply process and information about its behavior are important for two interrelated reasons. First, changes in money growth may have significant effects on the economy's performance. Its short-run variations may affect employment, output, and other real economic variables, while its long-run trend determines the course of inflation and other nominal variables. Second, money supply serves as an important intermediate target for the conduct of monetary policy. As a result, discretionary changes in money growth are instrumental in attainment of economic growth, price stability, and other economic goals.

THE MONEY SUPPLY DETERMINATION PROCESS

Three groups of economic agents play an important role in the process of money supply determination. The first and most important is the Fed, which sets the supply of the monetary base, imposes certain constraints on the set of admissible assets held by banks, and on the banks' supply of their liabilities. Next is the public, which determines the optimum amounts of currency holdings, the supply of financial claims to banks, and the allocation of the claims between transaction and nontransaction accounts. The last is banks, which absorb the financial claims offered by the public, set the supply conditions for their liabilities and allocate their assets between earning assets and reserves subject to the constraints imposed by the Fed. The interaction among the three groups is shaped by market conditions, and jointly determines the stock of money, bank credit, and interest rates.

The level of money stock is the product of two components: the monetary base and the money multiplier. The monetary base is quantity of government-produced money. It consists of currency held by the public and total reserves held by banks. Currency is the total of coins and dollar bills of all denominations. Reserves are the sum of banks' vault cash and their reserve deposits at the Fed. They are the noninterest-bearing components of bank assets, and consist of required reserves on deposit liabilities established by the Fed, and additional reserves that banks deem necessary for liquidity purposes.

The Fed exercises its tight control over the monetary base through open market operations and extension of discount loans. Open market operations are the Fed's authority to trade in government securities. They are the most important instrument of monetary policy and the primary source of changes in the monetary base. An open market purchase expands the monetary base while an open market sale works in the opposite direction. The Fed's control of discount loans is the result of its authority to set the discount rate and limit the level of discount loans through its administration of the discount window.

The money multiplier reflects the joint behavior of the public, banks, and the Fed. The public's decisions about its desired holdings of currency and nontransaction deposits relative to transaction deposits are one set of factors that influence the multiplier. Banks liquidity concerns, and thus their desire to hold excess reserves relative to their deposit liabilities, is another set of factors. The Fed's authority to change the required reserve ratios on bank deposits is the third set of factors. Given the rather infrequent changes in the reserve requirements ratios, the multiplier reflects primarily the behavior of the public, private banks, and the market and institutional conditions.

For example, a decision by the public to increase its currency holdings relative to transaction deposits results in a switch from a component of money supply that undergoes multiple expansions to one that does not. Thus the size of the multiplier declines. Similarly, a decision by banks to increase their holdings of excess reserves relative to transaction deposits reduces bank loans, and causes a decline in deposits, the multiplier, and the money supply. Finally, a decision by the Fed to raise the reserve requirement ratio on bank deposits results in a reserve deficiency in the banking system, forcing banks to reduce their loans, deposit liabilities, the money supply, and the multiplier.

HISTORICAL TREND

Over the 1980–2005 period, the M1 aggregate grew at an average annual rate of 1.6 percent, while the M2 aggregate rate was 1.9 percent. Nevertheless, the growth rates were not stable. They varied between the low of –14.5 percent and high of 17.9 percent for M1, and between the low of –6.2 percent and high of 10.2 percent for M2. What factors contributed to the long-run growth and short-run fluctuations in the money supply? During the same period, the monetary base grew at an average annual rate of 4.6 percent primarily because of open market operations. Thus changes in monetary base and open market operations are the primary source of long-run movements in the money supply. For shorter periods, however, changes in the money multiplier may have also contributed to the fluctuations in the money supply.

SEE ALSO *Federal Reserve System; Money*

BIBLIOGRAPHY

Barnett, William A., Fisher, Douglas, and Serletis, Apostolos (1992, December). Consumer theory and the demand for money. *Journal of Economic Literature 4,* 2086–2119.

Brunner, Karl (1989). Money supply. In John Eatwell, Murray Milgate, and Peter Newman (Eds.), *The new Palgrave: Money* (pp. 263–267). New York: Norton.

Chrystal, K. Alec, and McDonald, Ronald (1994, March–April). Empirical evidence on recent behavior and usefulness of simple sum and weighted measures of the money stock. *Federal Reserve Bank of St. Louis Review 76*, 73–109.

Friedman, Milton, and Schwartz, Anna J. (1970). *Monetary statistics of the United States: Estimates, sources, and methods.* New York: Colombia University Press for the National Bureau of Economic Research.

Mishkin, Frederic S. (2004). *The economics of money, banking, and financial markets* (7th ed.). Boston: Pearson.

Thornton, Daniel L. (2000, January–February). Money in a theory of exchange. *Federal Reserve Bank of St. Louis Review 82*, 35–60.

Hassan Mohammadi

MONOPOLY

A monopoly is a market condition in which a single seller controls the entire output of a particular good or service. A firm is a monopoly if it is the sole seller of its product and if its product has no close substitutes. Close substitutes are those goods that could closely take the place of a particular good; for example, a Pepsi soft drink would be a close substitute for a Coke drink, but a juice drink would not. The fundamental cause of monopoly is barriers to entry; these are technological or economic conditions of a market that raise the cost for firms wanting to enter the market above the cost for firms already in the market, or otherwise make new entry difficult. If the barriers to entry prevent other firms from entering the market, there is no competition and the monopoly remains the only seller in its market. The seller is then able to set the price and output of a particular good or service.

A monopoly—in its pure form—is actually quite rare. The majority of large firms operate legally in a market structure of oligopoly, which means that a few sellers divide the bulk of the market. People often have the impression that the goals of a monopolist are somehow evil and grasping, while those of a competitor are wholesome and altruistic. The truth is that the same motives drive the monopolistic firm and the competitive firm: Both strive to maximize profits. A basic proposition in economics is that monopoly control over a good will result in too little of the good being produced at too high a price. Economists have often advocated antitrust policy, public enterprise, or regulation to control the abuse of monopoly power.

BARRIERS TO ENTRY

For a monopoly to persist in the long run, barriers to entry must exist. Although such barriers can take various forms, they have three main sources:

1. A key resource is owned by a single firm.

2. The government gives a single firm the exclusive right to produce a specific good.

3. The cost of production makes a single producer more efficient than a large number of producers.

Monopoly Resources. The first and simplest way for a monopoly to come about is for a single firm to own a key resource. For example, if a small town had many working wells owned by different firms, no firm would have a monopoly on water. If, however, there were only one working well in town, the firm owning that well would be considered a monopoly. Although exclusive ownership of a key resource is one way for a monopoly to arise, monopolies rarely come about for this reason.

Government-Created Monopolies. In many cases, monopolies have arisen because the government has given a firm the exclusive right to sell a particular good or service. For example, when a pharmaceutical company discovers a new drug, it can apply to the government for a patent. If the patent is granted, the firm has the exclusive right to produce and sell the drug for a set number of years. The effects of such a government-created monopoly are easy to see. In the case of the pharmaceutical company, the firm is able to charge higher prices for its patented product and, in turn, earn higher profits. With these higher profits, the firm is able to complete further research in its quest for new and better drugs. The government can create a monopoly when, in doing so, it is in the interest of the public good.

Natural Monopolies. A natural monopoly occurs when a single firm can supply a good or service to an entire market at a lesser cost than could two or more firms. An example of a natural monopoly is the distribution of water in a community. To provide water to residents, a firm must first put into place a network of pipes throughout the community. If two or more firms were to compete in providing the water distribution, each would have to pay the fixed cost of building a network. In this case, the average total cost of water is lowest when one firm serves the entire market.

MONOPOLY VERSUS COMPETITION

The major difference between a monopoly and a competitive firm is the monopoly's ability to influence the price of its output. Because a competitive firm is small relative to the market, the price of its product is determined by market conditions. On the other hand, because a monopoly is the sole producer in its market, it can often alter the price of its product by adjusting the quantity it supplies to the market.

An example of a company that garnered monopoly power is the case of Microsoft. In 2000, in an antitrust lawsuit brought against Microsoft, a U.S. federal court judge ruled against the company. Microsoft, a computer company, had established first MS-DOS and later Windows as the dominating operating system for personal computers. Once it had achieved a position of strength in the market, would-be competitors faced insurmountable hurdles. Software developers face large costs for every additional operating system to which they adapt their applications. Because Microsoft had the dominant operating system, any rival personal computer operating system would have only a handful of applications, compared to tens of thousands of applications for Microsoft's Windows system. This applications barrier to entry gave Microsoft enduring monopoly power.

The judge's ruling in this case made it clear that, besides being illegal, Microsoft's monopoly was not in the public interest and legal measures would be put into place in order to break the monopoly that Microsoft had created.

For another example, in many cities trash-collecting businesses are invited to bid, perhaps every three years or so, for the exclusive right to operate their business. The successful bidder, selected by the city, has the legal right to own and operate the business, keeping out all competitors for at least three years. Monopoly situations such as this, called utilities, are generally considered to be beneficial for the users and therefore for the public. Some discussion, however, about this issue does occur. In a public letter published by the *Economic Times* on August 22, 1999, among other points, it was stated that utilities profits are constrained. This, of course, may seem a limiting factor in attracting investors.

Laws pertaining to monopolies have been passed. In 1890 the Sherman Antitrust Act was enacted. It forbade mergers of companies that would result in restraint of trade. In 1914 the Clayton Antitrust Act was passed as an amendment to the Sherman act. It made certain practices illegal when their effect was to lessen competition to create a monopoly.

SEE ALSO *Antitrust Legislation; Oligopoly*

BIBLIOGRAPHY

Busted. (1999). *The Economist, 353*(8145), 21, 23.

Heilbroner, Robert L., and Thurow, Lester (1998). *Economics explained: Everything you need to know about how the economy works and where it's going* (rev. ed.). New York: Simon and Schuster.

Jethmalani, Arun (1999, August 22). Of monopolies and utilities [Public letter]. *Economic Times.*

Mankiw, N. Gregory (2006). *Principles of economics* (4th ed.). Mason, OH: Thomson South-Western.

G. W. Maxwell

MORALE

SEE *Job Satisfaction; Motivation*

MORTGAGES

SEE *Personal Financial Planning*

MOTIVATION

Motivation is about individuals' actions and what determines them. The word *motivation* is derived from the Latin verb *movere,* which means "to move." It is a broad theoretical concept used to explain why individuals behave as they do or why they engage in particular actions at particular times. It is a drive that compels one to act because human behavior is directed toward some goal. As defined by Richard Daft, motivation refers to "the forces either within or external to a person that arouse enthusiasm and persistence to pursue a certain course of action" (2003, p. 526). When motivation is intrinsic (internal), it comes from within based on personal interests, desires, and need for fulfillment. Nevertheless, extrinsic (external) factors such as rewards, praise, and promotions also influence motivation. A basic premise about motivation is that individuals approach goals or participate in activities that are considered desirable and avoid situations and events that are likely to be unpleasant.

Motivation theories have their roots in behavioral psychology. They provide a way to examine and understand human behavior in a variety of situations. Even the oldest of motivation theories can be helpful today because they show the importance of human needs and provide the foundation for the development of other theories. Most motivation theories have been developed by researchers in the United States, so they are, therefore, influenced by American culture.

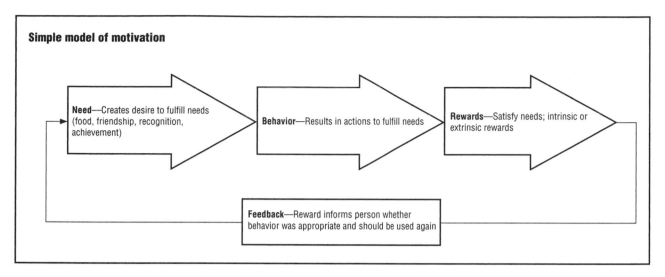

Simple model of motivation

Need—Creates desire to fulfill needs (food, friendship, recognition, achievement)

Behavior—Results in actions to fulfill needs

Rewards—Satisfy needs; intrinsic or extrinsic rewards

Feedback—Reward informs person whether behavior was appropriate and should be used again

Figure 1

From a manager's perspective, it is important to understand what prompts people, what influences them, and why they persist in particular actions. Motivation can lead to high performance in the workplace. People who are committed to achieving organizational objectives generally outperform those who are not committed. Those who are intrinsically rewarded by accomplishments are satisfied with their jobs and are individuals with high self-esteem. Therefore, an important part of management is to help make work more satisfying and rewarding for employees and to keep employee motivation consistent with organizational objectives. With the diversity of contemporary workplaces, this is a complicated task. Many factors, including the influences of different underlying principles, are important to understanding motivation:

• People have reasons for everything they do

• Whatever people choose as a goal is something they believe is good for them

• The goals people choose must be seen as attainable

• The conditions under which the work is done can affect its value to employees and their perceptions of attainability or success

When management was first studied in a scientific way at the turn of the twentieth century, Frederick Winslow Taylor (1856–1915) worked to improve productivity in labor situations so important in those days of the developing Industrial Revolution. Taylor developed efficiency measures and incentive systems. When workers were paid more for meeting a standard higher than their normal production, productivity increased dramatically. Therefore, workers seemed to be economically motivated. At this time in history, social issues involved in human behavior were not yet considered. A more humanistic approach soon developed that has been influencing management ever since.

During the late 1920s and early 1930s, Elton Mayo (1880–1949) and other researchers from Harvard University conducted studies at Western Electric's Hawthorne Works plant in Cicero, Illinois, to measure productivity. They studied the effects of fatigue, layout, heating, and lighting on productivity. As might be expected when studying lighting, employee productivity levels increased as the illumination level was increased; the same effect, however, was noted when the illumination level was decreased.

The researchers concluded that the attention paid to the employees was more of a contributing factor to their productivity level than the environmental conditions. The improvement in the behavior of workers when attention is paid to them came to be called the Hawthorne effect. As a result of this research, it was evident that employees should be treated in a humane way. These findings started the human relations movement—a change in management thinking and practice that viewed increased worker productivity as grounded in satisfaction of employees' basic needs. (Many years later, it was discovered that the workers in the Hawthorne experimental group had received an increase in income; money, therefore, was probably a motivating factor, although it was not recognized as such at the time.)

A simple model of motivation is shown in Figure 1.

Ongoing changes in the workplace require that managers give continuous attention to those factors that influence worker behavior, recognizing that each individual has his or her own values and differing abilities. Being responsive to these differences can help managers work effectively with many different types of employees. Employee performance is influenced in many ways—by how jobs are designed, the conditions of the work environment, and the appropriateness of benefits. Through the use of goals and rewards, managers influence employees, improve morale, and implement incentive and compensation plans.

No one theory can explain all the variances in human behavior, so a wide range of theories have developed over time. The following eight motivation theories can help managers to understand the needs that motivate people and then implement reward systems that fulfill those needs and reinforce the appropriate behavior.

HIERARCHY OF NEEDS

Abraham Maslow (1908–1970), a professor at Brandeis University and a practicing psychologist, developed the hierarchy of needs theory. He identified a set of needs that he prioritized into a hierarchy based on two conclusions:

1. Human needs are either of an attraction/desire nature or of an avoidance nature.

2. Because humans are "wanting" beings, when one desire is satisfied, another desire will take its place.

The five levels of needs are shown in Figure 2. According to Maslow's theory, the lower-level needs must be satisfied before higher-level needs.

- *Physiological needs*—These are basic physical needs for food, water, and oxygen. In the workplace, these needs translate into the survival needs for an ergonomically designed work environment with adequate heat, air, and an appropriate base salary compensation.

- *Safety needs*—People want to feel safe, secure, and free from fear. They need stability, structure, and order. In the workplace, job security and fringe benefits, along with an environment free of violence, fill these needs.

- *Belonging needs*—People have needs for social acceptance and affection from their peers. In the workplace, this need is satisfied by participation in work groups with good relationships among coworkers and between workers and managers.

- *Esteem needs*—People want to be regarded as useful, competent, and important. People also desire self-esteem and need a good self-image. In the workplace, increased responsibility, high status, and recognition for contributions satisfy these needs.

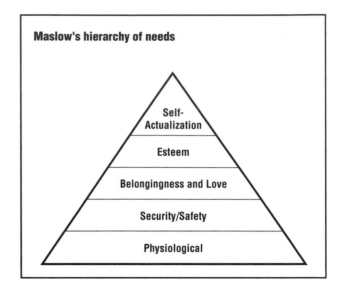

Figure 2

- *Self-actualization needs*—This highest motivation level involves people striving to develop their full potential, to become more of what they are capable of being. They seek to attain self-fulfillment. In the workplace, people satisfy this need by being creative, receiving training, and accepting challenging assignments.

Managers can affect the physical, social, and psychological environment in the workplace, and they have a responsibility to help employees fulfill their needs. Focusing on the needs of retraining for growth and challenge as well as rewards and recognition is important to the quality of work life.

ERG THEORY

In his work, Clayton Alderfer (1940–) expanded on Maslow's hierarchical theory. He proposed three need categories and suggested that movement between the need levels is not necessarily straightforward. Failure to meet a higher-level need could cause an individual to regress to a lower-level need. These ERG theory categories are:

- *Existence needs:* Needs for physical well-being

- *Relatedness needs:* Needs for satisfactory relationships with others

- *Growth needs:* The development of human potential and the desire for personal growth and increased competence

MOTIVATION-HYGIENE THEORY

Frederick Herzberg (1923–2000), a professor of psychology at Case Western Reserve University, studied the attitudes of workers toward their jobs. Herzberg proposed that an individual will be moved to action based on the desire to avoid deprivation. This motivation, however, does not provide positive satisfaction because it does not provide a sense of growth. Herzberg's research found that positive job attitudes were associated with a feeling of psychological growth. He thought that people work for two reasons: for financial reasons to avoid physical deprivation, and for achievement because of the happiness and meaning it provides. Herzberg also identified the concept of job enrichment, whereby the responsibilities of a job are changed to provide greater growth and challenge. His motivation-hygiene theory includes two types of factors, motivation and hygiene.

Motivation. Motivation is based on the positive satisfaction that psychological growth provides. The presence of factors such as responsibility, achievement, recognition, and possibility for growth or advancement will motivate and satisfy people. These factors directly influence how people feel about their work. The absence of these factors will not necessarily demotivate or cause dissatisfaction.

Hygiene. Hygiene is based on an individual's desire to avoid deprivation and the resulting physical and emotional discomfort. Hygiene factors include willingness to supervise; positive working conditions; interpersonal relations with peers, subordinates, and superiors; status; job security; and salary. These factors do not motivate, nor will their presence cause job satisfaction. Their absence, however, will cause dissatisfaction.

Although salary is considered a hygiene factor, it plays an indirect part in motivation as a measure of growth and advancement or as a symbol of recognition of achievement.

THEORY X AND THEORY Y

Douglas McGregor (1906–1964), a professor at the Massachusetts Institute of Technology and a social psychologist, was greatly influenced by the work of Maslow. McGregor recognized that people have needs and that those needs are satisfied at work. He described two sets of assumptions about people that he labeled Theory X and Theory Y.

Theory X. The assumptions of Theory X are that most people will avoid work because they do not like it and must be threatened or persuaded to put forth adequate effort. People have little ambition and do not want

responsibility. They want to be directed and are most interested in job security.

Theory Y. The assumptions of Theory Y are that work is very natural to people and that most people are self-directed to achieve objectives to which they are committed. People are ambitious and creative. They desire responsibility and derive a sense of satisfaction from the work itself.

These assumptions were, at one time, applied to management styles, with autocratic managers labeled as adhering to Theory X and democratic managers to Theory Y. Unfortunately, this fostered a tendency to see people as members of a group rather than as individuals. The important contribution of McGregor's theory was to recognize these two perspectives and to recognize that people can achieve personal objectives through helping organizations achieve their objectives. Their work can be a motivator.

ACQUIRED-NEEDS THEORY

In his studies on personality and learned needs, David McClelland (1917–1998) developed the acquired-needs theory because he felt that different needs are acquired throughout an individual's lifetime. He proposed three needs:

1. *Need for achievement*—The desire to accomplish something difficult, attain a high standard of success, master complex tasks, and surpass others

2. *Need for affiliation*—The desire to form close personal relationships, avoid conflict, and establish warm friendships

3. *Need for power*—The desire to influence or control others, be responsible for others, and have authority over others

McClelland found through his research that early life experiences determine whether people acquire these needs. The need to achieve as an adult is influenced by the reinforcement of behavior received as a child when a child is encouraged to do things independently. If a child is reinforced for warm, human relationships, then the need for affiliation as an adult develops. If a child gains satisfaction from controlling others, then the need for power will be evident as an adult.

McClelland noted that people with a high need for achievement are persistent in striving to reach goals, work harder than people with other needs, and are medium risk takers. He also found these characteristics to be common among college graduates who selected entrepreneurial occupations.

EXPECTANCY THEORY

Victor Vroom (1932–) developed the expectancy theory, which suggests expectancy is the perceived probability that a certain effort or performance will result in the achievement of a particular goal. Perceived probability is important. Individuals' expectations about their ability to accomplish something will affect their success in accomplishing it.

The desirability of outcomes is important, too. The value of or preference for a particular outcome is called valence. To determine valence, people will ask themselves whether or not they can accomplish a goal, how important is the goal to them (in the immediate as well as the long term), and what course of action will provide the greatest reward. An individual's expectation of actually achieving the outcome is crucial to success, and many factors influence this.

The expectancy theory can be applied through incentive systems that identify desired outcomes and give all workers the same opportunities to achieve rewards, such as stock ownership, promotions, or other recognition for achievement.

EQUITY THEORY

The equity theory focuses on individuals' perceptions of how fairly they are treated in comparison to others. It was developed by J. Stacy Adams (1925–), who found that equity exists when people consider their compensation equal to the compensation of others who perform similar work, which is an external standard. People judge equity by comparing inputs (such as education, experience, effort, and ability) to outputs (such as pay, recognition, benefits, and promotion). It can also relate to internal standards when people compare how hard they are working with what they are getting in return.

If people perceive a discrepancy between the inputs and outputs, then they are unhappy. When the ratio is out of balance, inequity occurs. And inequitable pay can create an impossible situation when implementing salary and incentive systems. According to Richard L. Daft (2003), individuals will work to reduce perceived inequity by doing the following:

- *Change inputs:* Examples include increasing or reducing effort

- *Change outcomes:* Such as requesting a salary increase or improved working conditions

- *Distort perceptions:* This occurs when individuals cannot change their inputs or outcomes; one example is artificially increasing the importance of awards

- *Leave the job:* Individuals might do this rather than experience what they perceive to be continued inequity

When administering compensation and incentive programs, managers must be careful to ensure that the rewards are equitable; if programs are not perceived as equitable, then they will not contribute to employee motivation.

REINFORCEMENT THEORY

Reinforcement theory is based on the relationship between behavior and its consequences. In the workplace, reinforcement can be applied to change or modify on-the-job behavior through incentives and rewards and, to some extent, punishments.

B. F. Skinner (1904–1990), a professor at Harvard University, was a highly controversial behavioral psychologist known for his work in operant conditioning and behavior modification. His reinforcement theory takes into consideration both motivation and the environment, focusing on stimulus and response relationships. Through his research, Skinner noted that a stimulus will initiate behavior; thus, the stimulus is an antecedent to behavior. The behavior will generate a result; therefore, results are consequences of behavior.

According to Thomas McCoy:

The quality of the results will be directly related to the quality and timeliness of the antecedent. The more specific the antecedent is and the closer in time it is to the behavior, the greater will be its effect on the behavior. . . . The consequences provide feedback to the individual. (1992, p. 34)

Therefore, the individual more easily associates the behavior with the stimulus.

The four types of reinforcement are:

1. *Positive reinforcement:* The application of a pleasant and rewarding consequence following a desired behavior, such as giving praise. When a behavior is positively reinforced, the individual is more likely to repeat the behavior. People tend to have an intrinsic (internal) need for positive reinforcement. Other examples of positive reinforcers are recognition of accomplishments, promotion, and salary increases.

2. *Negative reinforcement:* The removal of an unpleasant consequence following a desired behavior. This reinforcement is also called avoidance. An example of negative reinforcement is when workers return promptly from a lunch break to avoid being reprimanded by their supervisor or when a manager no longer reminds workers about a weekly deadline

when workers meet the deadline. Negative reinforcement causes the behavior to be repeated.

3. *Punishment:* The application of an unpleasant outcome when an undesirable behavior occurs to reduce the likelihood of that behavior happening again. This form of reinforcement does not indicate a correct behavior, so its use in business is not usually appropriate. Punishment, however, might be an oral reprimand for coming to work late or a demotion for inferior work performance.

4. *Extinction:* The absence of any reinforcement following a behavior. Usually extinction occurs in situations where positive reinforcement was formerly applied. If the behavior is no longer positively reinforced, then it is less likely to occur in the future and it will gradually disappear. And when a behavior is ignored, the behavior tends to go away or become extinct.

In the workplace, positive reinforcement is the preferred approach for increasing desirable behavior and extinction is the preferred approach for decreasing undesirable behaviors. Continuous reinforcement can be effective in the early stages of behavior modification, but partial reinforcement is more commonly used. Reinforcement is most powerful when it is administered immediately.

The appropriateness of a reward depends on the situation. But for managers to apply rewards appropriate for work performance, it is necessary to understand what constitutes a reward. And no single reward will be perceived as positive by all employees. Rewards, however, are important in behavior-based incentive plans because they reward employee behavior that is desirable for the company. Both incentives and recognition provide a reward; nevertheless, incentives drive performance while recognition is an after-the-fact display of appreciation for a contribution.

Financial rewards are certainly important in compensation programs. Social recognition provides employees with a sense of self-worth by acknowledging the contributions they have made. This recognition could be given in the form of a ceremony that helps to validate and is an important compensation—and one that probably costs a company very little in relationship to the benefit to employees.

SUMMARY

The application of motivation theories can help managers to create work situations and employee recognition systems that help workers fulfill their needs. As Maslow wrote, "man has a higher nature ... and ... this higher nature includes the needs for meaningful work, for responsibility, for creativeness, for being fair and just, for

doing what is worthwhile and for preferring to do it well" (1998, pp. 244–245).

Motivation is the key to performance improvement. Some aspects of all jobs may be routine or mundane, but other aspects can be developed to promote job satisfaction and increased productivity. The sharing of responsibility can provide opportunities for growth, renewal, and achievement. This empowerment of workers can heighten employee motivation and improve morale. Both long-term and short-term incentive programs are needed for the employee commitment and effectiveness necessary to achieve organizational objectives. And in all instances, workers must be treated fairly and equitably.

SEE ALSO *Behavioral Science Movement; Management; Management/Leadership Styles*

BIBLIOGRAPHY

Beck, Robert C. (2004). *Motivation: Theories and principles.* Upper Saddle River, NJ: Pearson Education.

Bruce, Anne, and Pepitone, James S. (1999). *Motivating employees.* New York: McGraw-Hill.

Daft, Richard L. (2003). *Management* (6th ed.). Mason, OH: Thomson South-Western.

Hellriegel, Don, Jackson, Susan E., and Slocum, John W. (2002). *Management* (9th ed.). Cincinnati: South-Western.

Maslow, Abraham H. (1998). *Toward a psychology of being* (3rd ed.). New York: Wiley.

McCoy, Thomas J. (1992). *Compensation and motivation: Maximizing employee performance with behavior-based incentive plans.* New York: Amacom.

Nelson, Debra L., and Quick, James Campbell (2002). *Understanding organizational behavior: A multimedia approach.* Cincinnati: South-Western.

Patricia R. Graves

MULTIMEDIA SYSTEMS

Multimedia can be defined as any application that combines text with graphics, animation, audio, video, and/or virtual reality. A computer system is a combination of equipment (hardware), processes and programs (software), and people organized to perform a function. Combining these definitions, a business multimedia system includes equipment, programs, and people organized for the purposes of communication, data storage and retrieval systems (multimedia databases and electronic filing systems), information security, and Internet use (Web pages and electronic-business applications).

Within organizations, multimedia systems are used in all forms of information systems from transaction processing systems to executive decision support systems. These systems also can be found across industries such as accounting, banking, communications, education, entertainment, insurance, manufacturing, medical, retailing, and real estate. Anywhere there is a need for combining text, pictures, sounds, and animation, multimedia systems are found.

Multimedia systems are used for security to keep intruders out of a system and for the protection of stored documents. Scanning devices are available to scan potential user's eyes (retina imaging) or thumb prints to gain access to a computer or site. Other systems can scan a person's signature or capture voice pattern recognition for the same purposes. Stored text, pictures, original document images, sound files, and video files can be protected through encryption methods, read/write protection, password management, and copyright protection that keep intruders from copying or accessing sensitive files.

ANALOG SYSTEMS

Analog multimedia systems use books, documents, films, photographs, records, tapes, videotapes, and many other forms of media to store text, sounds, and pictures. As

technology improves, converting from one medium to another and combining different media formats becomes difficult and cumbersome.

Analog systems are being replaced with systems that digitize the original documents and store them on digital media; nevertheless, analog systems still remain vital for legal, historical, and research purposes. Many new companies have come into existence for the sole purpose of converting analog media into digital formats.

COMPUTER-BASED MULTIMEDIA

Technological advances have changed the hardware and software used for developing multimedia from the traditional analog equipment to computer-based or digital multimedia systems. Computers use 0s and 1s to store and process sounds, still graphics (pictures), and motion video. Text scanning, digital imaging (using digital cameras and scanners), sound cards, and analog video-capturing devices sample, compress, and convert analog media into a series of 0s and 1s (digital) signals for processing by a computer. Once analog media are converted to a digital format, a computer can be used to manipulate the various media. With the development of digital-video cameras

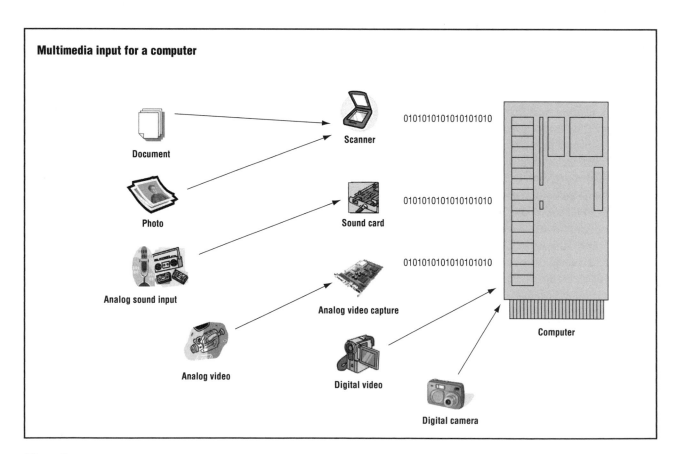

Figure 1

and digital-still cameras, media are already in a form that the computer can process, making it easier to merge text, graphics, video, sounds, and animation into an application.

Multimedia hierarchy is a term that reflects how much computing power is needed to process information. Multimedia systems have different levels of components that handle tasks ranging in difficulty from simple text processing to complex digital-motion video. As more powerful computers are developed, more applications can be used by businesses.

TEXT PROCESSING

Text is the first and simplest level in the multimedia hierarchy. Traditionally, text has been keyed directly into the computer. Scanners equipped with optical character recognition software allow text to be scanned into a computer from printed documents or from Universal Product Codes on products, using wand or handheld scanners.

More complex text input involves voice pattern recognition systems that convert voice to text. These applications find their way into legal, health-care, and other industries and businesses that process vast amounts of text. Text-to-voice systems reverse this process and allow text to be read to the user.

SOUND PROCESSING

Sound in multimedia applications enables a user to describe products, give instructions, enhance a presentation, or provide cues for some action by the viewer. Hardware for capturing and processing sounds includes a card attached to the main motherboard of the computer system.

Sound cards capture analog audio signals from microphones, music compact disks, musical instrument digital interface (MIDI; such as electronic-piano keyboards) devices, and other sound sources through a line-in jack on the card. Computer users can plug in record turntables, cassette tape players, or any other analog device from an audio-out jack on those devices and record sounds. Sound cards also have output jacks for speakers, or the audio-out can be plugged into other sound recording devices. The card contains two computer chips called the AD (analog to digital) and DA (digital to analog) chips. These chips convert sound waves to digits and digits to sound waves.

Sound application software is used to select devices and to capture, edit, and save sounds in digital files. Users can add effects such as fade-in, fade-out, and the echo effect to the digital-sound clip. Several competing file storage standards or extensions exist for computer sound files. These standards depend on the manufacturer of the hardware or developers of the software. The more a given standard is used, the more portable the file is to other users and to Internet applications.

STILL-IMAGE PROCESSING

Various specialized forms of multimedia include image-processing systems designed specifically for handling business forms, images, graphics, or pictures. An example may be found in banking systems that use computer-output microform devices to store images of checks and place several check images on the customer's bank statement or display them on an Internet banking page, rather than returning the canceled checks. Insurance companies use imaging systems to scan insurance applications, claim forms, and pictures of damages to customers' property. The imaging systems provide immediate access to all information stored in a computer for processing of a claim. In transaction-processing systems, companies can digitize customer signatures on sales slips and store the original sales documents for proof of purchase using point-of-sale devices. Other "turnaround documents" may be generated by a computer and scanned into a computer to verify a purchase at a merchandise pickup point.

Scanners and digital cameras can also be used in image processing to capture pictures for printed publications, Internet Web sites, and electronic presentations. A scanner or digital camera can digitize a picture by converting dark and light areas of a graphic to dots or pixels using a charge-coupled device. File sizes can be reduced by saving graphics using compression/decompression (codec) systems such as JPEG (Joint Photographic Experts Group) compression methods. Single images can also be "captured" with a video-capture board from videotape, from a video camera, or directly from broadcast television. In both cases, a file is then saved in computer format for future use.

Photographic editing software lets users add special effects and edit photos or images. Draw and paint computer programs generate graphics and tables for multimedia applications. These programs allow users to draw objects, fill them with colors, and add text and special effects. The user-made images are saved in files and are then incorporated into a multimedia application.

FULL-MOTION VIDEO PROCESSING

In the early twenty-first century, broadcast television and videotapes record moving pictures by using 30 still pictures or frames for every second of motion. Broadcasts and videotapes use a standard developed in the 1950s in the United States, the National Television Standards Committee broadcast standard. Other countries use 25 frames per second and have different image-aspect ratios (ratio of height to width). At the start of the twenty-first century, the high-definition and digital television broadcasting being introduced will change the standards; pictures will have better quality because of an increase in the number of pixels and a change in the aspect ratio of the picture.

More expensive tuner and capture cards on computers allow for "full-motion" capture by saving all of the frames and sound. Because these files become very large (640×480 pixels per frame times 30 frames per second—over 9 million characters for 1 second), several methods have been developed for compressing motion video files. Video is compressed to save it as a smaller file and is decompressed during playback. Several codec systems use hardware including computer chips and software such as MPEG (Motion Picture Experts Group). Since video files are large, they are usually brief recordings or clips from video. The clips are used in business presentations, on Web pages, as product descriptions, or as other media bytes to emphasize an important point in a short time. Advances in storage capacity and speed of newer storage media will eventually allow for smoother and longer clips. Video streaming from Web sites stores large video clips on the host Web site and allows the video to "stream" in smaller segments to the Internet user.

ANIMATION AND VIRTUAL REALITY

The most sophisticated forms of multimedia are animation and virtual reality. These systems combine still graphics, video, sound, and animation to form virtual-reality outcomes. Industries using this technology include entertainment, education and training, legal, architecture and construction, government, and transportation. Animated (anime) movies and computer games have become popular and require all of the multimedia formats for development.

Working with virtual reality requires powerful computers and software to collect, edit, and produce the product or title or presentation. Some examples include computer games, computer-assisted design, home-improvement software that allows users to design and display a proposed project in 3-D, flight simulators, and simulation of a crash for accident investigation.

SUMMARY

Figure 1 summarizes how elements of multimedia are linked to a computer system to develop multimedia applications. Once in a computer (digitized), each element can be used with software to manipulate media files into a multimedia system.

Multimedia systems can be applied to all organizational levels and functional areas of a company and across types of businesses and industries. As technology improves, so will the applications of multimedia.

SEE ALSO *Information Technology; Office Technology*

BIBLIOGRAPHY

Long, L., and Long, N. (2002). *Computers information technology in perspective.* Upper Saddle River, NJ: Pearson Education.

Oz, Effy (2004). *Management Information Systems* (3rd ed.). Boston: Course Technology.

Shelly, Gary B., Cashman, Thomas J., and Vermaat, Misty E. (2003). *Discovering computers 2004: A gateway to information.* Boston: Course Technology.

George A. Mundrake

MUTUAL FUNDS

Mutual funds belong to a group of financial intermediaries known as investment companies, which are in the business of collecting funds from investors and pooling them for the purpose of building a portfolio of securities according to stated objectives. They are also known as open-end investment companies. Other members of the group are closed-end investment companies (also known as closed-end funds) and unit investment trusts. In the United States, investment companies are regulated by the Securities and Exchange Commission under the Investment Company Act of 1940.

Mutual funds are generally organized as corporations or trusts, and, as such, they have a board of directors or trustees elected by the shareholders. Almost all aspects of their operations are externally managed. They engage a management company to manage the investment for a fee, generally based on a percentage of the fund's average net assets during the year. The management company may be an affiliated organization or an independent contractor. They sell their shares to investors either directly or through other firms such as broker-dealers, financial planners, employees of insurance companies, and banks. Even the day-to-day administration of a fund is carried out by an outsider, which may be the management company or an unaffiliated third party.

The management company is responsible for selecting an investment portfolio that is consistent with the objectives of the fund as stated in its prospectus and managing the portfolio in the best interest of the shareholders. The directors of the fund are responsible for overall governance of the fund; they are expected to establish procedures and review the performance of the management company and others who perform services for the fund.

Mutual funds are known as open-end investment companies because they are required to issue shares and redeem (buy back) outstanding shares upon demand. Closed-end funds, on the other hand, issue a certain number of shares but do not stand ready to buy back their own shares from investors. Their shares are traded on an exchange or in the over-the-counter market. They cannot increase or decrease their outstanding shares easily. A feature common of both mutual funds and closed-end funds is that they are managed investment companies, because they can change the composition of their portfolios by adding and deleting securities and altering the amount invested in each security. Unit investment trusts are not managed investment companies like the mutual funds because their portfolio consists of a fixed set of securities for life. They stand ready, however, to buy back their shares.

TYPES OF MUTUAL FUNDS

There are four basic types of mutual funds: money market, stock (also called equity), bond, and hybrid. This classification is based on the type and the maturity of the securities selected for investment. Money market funds invest in securities that mature in one year or less, such as Treasury bills, commercial paper, and certificates of deposits. They are often referred to as short-term funds. Stock, bond, and hybrid funds invest in long-term securities, and as such are known as long-term funds. Hybrid funds invest in a combination of stocks, bonds, and other securities. According to the Investment Company Institute (ICI), the national association of the U.S. investment company industry, there were 8,044 (7,101 long-term and 943 short-term) mutual funds in the United States and 55,528 outside the country at the end of 2004. The total investment by U.S mutual funds amounted to $6.8 trillion (stock=$4.04 trillion, bond=$808 billion, hybrid=$383 billion, money market=$1.61 trillion) and by non-U.S. funds to $3.5 trillion at the end of 1999. The total assets of U.S. mutual funds are less than the total assets of U.S. depository institutions, which stood at $7.5 trillion at the end of 1999.

Mutual funds also differ in terms of their investment objectives, as outlined in their prospectuses. The ICI classifies mutual funds into thirty-three investment objective categories. The main investment objectives within the stock funds include capital appreciation, total return, and world equity. Within each of these objectives, there are subcategories. There are two groups of bond funds: taxable bond funds and tax-free bond funds. Main categories in taxable bond funds are corporate bond funds, high-yield funds, world bond funds, government bond funds, and strategic income funds. The main tax-free bond fund categories are state municipal bond funds and national municipal bond funds. Among money market funds, there are also taxable money market funds and tax-exempt money market funds. As in the case of stock funds, many subcategories exist within each main category of bond and money market funds. In addition to these, there are specialty or sector funds, which invest in a particular segment of the securities market. Examples include biotechnology funds, small-company growth funds, technology funds, index funds, and social criteria funds.

MUTUAL FUND SHARE PRICING

By law, mutual funds are required to determine the price of their shares each business day. They release their prices the same day for publication in the next day's newspapers. Daily prices of mutual fund shares can also be obtained directly from the fund's offices or Web sites of commercial venders of financial information.

The share price represents the net asset value (NAV) per share, which is the current market value of a fund's assets net of its liabilities. The liabilities include securities purchased, but not yet paid for, accrued fees, dividends payable, and other accrued expenses. The NAV per share is obtained by dividing the NAV by the number of shares of the fund outstanding at the end of the day. A buyer of mutual fund shares pays the NAV per share plus any applicable sales load (also known as a front-end load). Sometimes, the sales load is collected when shares are redeemed and is known as a back-end load. Funds that have a sales load are known as load funds and use a sales organization to sell their shares for a fee. Funds that sell shares directly and do not have a sales load are known as no-load funds. The sales load often differs from fund to fund, and it is subject to National Association of Security Dealers (NASD) regulation. When an investor sells a share, it is the NAV that the seller usually receives. Some mutual funds may charge a redemption fee if the shares are held for less than a specified period.

BENEFITS AND COST OF INVESTING IN MUTUAL FUNDS

Mutual funds provide investors with a way to diversify their investment under professional management, which most investors may not be able to obtain on their own. Since the funds operate with a large pool of money, the investors benefit from economies of scale, such as a lower trading cost and a higher yield. Besides delivering attractive yields, many funds provide their investors with such services as check-writing privileges, custody (as a service), and bookkeeping. Investors also benefit from the knowledgeable investment choices of securities and investment objectives that funds offer.

The cost to the shareholder of investing in mutual funds comes in various forms: front-end loads, management fees, cost of maintaining and servicing shareholder accounts (administrative cost), redemption fees, and distribution fees (also known as 12b-1 fees). As mentioned before, a redemption fee is usually levied on shares held for less than a specified period. A distribution fee is a charge on current shareholders to cover the costs of advertising, promotion, selling, and other activities. It is sometimes combined with load charges. All these expenses are aggregated to obtain a single measure of cost to the shareholder. An aggregate measure commonly found in the published data is the expense ratio (expenses as a percent of assets). This measure does not include sales load, if there is one. Rea and Reid (1998) discuss the calculation of an alternative measure of total ownership cost that includes the sales load.

REGULATION AND TAXATION

All U.S. mutual funds are subject to strict regulation by the Securities and Exchange Commission. They are also subject to states's notice filing requirements and anti-fraud statutes. They are required to provide investors a full disclosure of their activities in a written prospectus. They also provide their investors a yearly statement of distribution with the details of the federal tax status of their distribution. Mutual funds in the United States are not subject to corporate income tax, if they meet certain Internal Revenue Code requirements. Instead, mutual fund shareholders are taxed on the distribution of fund's income. For tax purpose, mutual funds distribute their net income to the shareholders in two ways: (1) dividend and interest payments and (2) realized capital gains.

PERFORMANCE AND COMPARISON

The rate of return is widely used for comparing the performance of mutual funds. The rate of return on a mutual fund investment for a period of one year, for example, is calculated by adding the change in the NAV ($NAV_t - NAV_{t-1}$) to income and capital gains distributed during the year and dividing the sum by the NAV at the beginning of the year. The following describes the calculation of return for no-load funds:

$$R_t = \frac{[(NAV_t - NAV_{t-1}) + i + c]}{NAV_{t-1}}$$

where R, i, and c represent rate of return, income, and capital gains, respectively. For load funds, the calculation of return must account for load charges by adding them to the NAV. The performance of a mutual fund is often compared with the performance of a benchmark portfolio that is selected to reflect the investment risk level of the fund's portfolio to see whether the mutual fund had a superior performance.

The rate of return of a mutual fund with a NAV of $15.00 at the beginning of a year and $15.50 at the end of that year, and distributed $0.75 and $0.50 per share as income and capital gain respectively during the year would be:

$$[(\$15.50 - \$15.00) + \$0.75 + \$0.50]/\$15.00 = 11.67\%$$

ANALYSIS AND REPORTING

Key statistics pertaining to a fund—such as the NAV, offer price, sales charges, expense ratio, and performance measure for various categories of funds—are regularly calculated, analyzed, and published. Two firms well known for their analytical service are the Lipper Analytical Services (Lipperweb.com) and the Morning Star Inc. (Morningstar.com). The *Wall Street Journal* and *Barron's* carry the information supplied by Lipper Analytical Services on a regular basis. Investment Company Institute (www.ici.org) also provides a wealth of information on mutual funds, including historical data and Web site addresses of its member funds.

SEE ALSO *Investments*

BIBLIOGRAPHY

Bogle, John (1994). *Bogle on Mutual Funds.* Burr Ridge, IL: Irwin.

Crane, Peter G. (1997). *Mutual Fund Investing on the Internet.* Burlington, MA: AP Professional.

Find the right mutual funds (2005). Hoboken, N.J.: Wiley.

Henriques, Diana B. (1995). *Fidelity's World: The Secret Life and Public Power of the Mutual Fund Giant.* New York: Scribner.

Investment Company Institute website. http://www.ici.org/index.html. Accessed December 1, 2005.

Lavine, Alan, and Liberman, Gail (2001). *The Complete Idiot's Guide to Making Money with Mutual Funds.* Indianapolis, IN: Alpha.

Levy, Haim (1999). *Introduction to Investments.* Cincinnati, OH: South-Western College Publishing.

Rea, John D., and Reid, Brian K. (1998, November). "Trends in the Ownership Cost of Equity Mutual Funds." *ICI Perspective*, 41(3), 2-15.

Sharpe, William F., Alexander, Gordon J., and Bailey, Jeffrey V. (1999). *Investments.* 6th ed., Upper Saddle River, NJ: Prentice Hall.

Anand G. Shetty

N

NAICS

SEE *North American Industry Classification System*

NASDAQ COMPOSITE INDEX

SEE *Stock Indexes*

NATIONAL ASSOCIATION OF STATE BOARDS OF ACCOUNTANCY

More than 100 years ago, in 1896, New York appointed the first board of certified public accountant (CPA) examiners. By 1925 all U.S. jurisdictions were administering CPA examinations. Though all states today administer a single Uniform CPA Examination, there are still fifty-four independent boards of accountancy (for all states, the District of Columbia, Guam, the Virgin Islands, and Puerto Rico) that issue licenses to accountants. These boards set entry requirements for their licensees; enforce measures to support continuing competence, through both professional education and/or peer review requirements for renewal of individual licenses and firm registrations; and insure that technical and ethical standards are upheld via disciplinary proceedings growing out of a complaint-based system. Board-levied penalties for malpractice range from fines, to additional education requirements, to pre-report issuance reviews, to withdrawal of license.

The average CPA is generally more aware of the activities of the professional associations than of those of the state board of accountancy. However, the professional path of all CPAs all begins with the board: they had to apply to the state board of accountancy to take the Uniform CPA Examination; then they took the examination under the auspices of a state board and waited to hear the results of that examination issued by the state board. It is the state board that requires renewal forms and fees to be submitted and the state board that allows licensees from other states to begin to practice within its borders. Fortunately, in the vast majority of cases, the licensee will never see the disciplinary side of the state board's operations. However, that is a vital aspect of the board's operations that protects the public from unqualified practitioners. The wronged consumer needs no legal counsel. A complaint can be brought directly to the board by any individual or organization. In fact, government agencies that uncover inferior performance by licensees are encouraged to refer their complaints to the accountancy boards. With the growth of the Internet, several states accept on-line complaints via their Web sites.

BOARD MEMBERSHIP

For a long time, the CPA profession has prided itself on self-regulation, partially because of the discipline enforced by its professional organizations and partially because the state boards are primarily composed of licensees. Typically members of a board of accountancy are appointed by a state's governor and include both licensed CPAs and public members. The CPA members are often selected by the governor after consulting with the state's CPA society. A small daily stipend for meeting attendance and travel is awarded by some states; others do not provide such compensation. Boards vary in size from five to nineteen members, many with only one public member. In some jurisdictions, there is a limited term of service whereas in others, board members can be reappointed indefinitely. Many of the boards appoint task forces or committees to handle various activities, such as continuing professional education or investigations, which increases the number of volunteer participants. Legal assistance to the boards may come only from the state's attorney general's office or it may also be available from independent counsel. In some states, boards share their administrative staff with other regulatory boards, yet in one jurisdiction the accountancy board has a dedicated staff of over sixty. Similarly, revenues generated by the boards are not treated uniformly: One state will allow the board to use its revenues directly for its licensees; another will have all revenues go into the state's general fund.

As of 1998, the number of licensees in each jurisdiction ranged from Texas, with more than 74,000, to Guam, with 86. Other states with large numbers of licensees include California, with more than 63,000; Ohio, with more than 36,000; and New York, with more than 33,000.

ABOUT NASBA

While the regulation of certified public accountants (and in some jurisdictions public accountants or licensed public accountants) exists on a state-by-state basis, the boards share many concerns and it is from those mutual concerns that the National Association of State Boards of Accountancy (NASBA) was born. Thanks to the efforts of the New Jersey State Board of Public Accountants, the organization was formed in 1908 as the National Association of CPA Examiners, with seventeen examiners from ten states. At that time the New Jersey Board invited all accountancy board members "to confer in regard to matters of mutual interest."

In the early twenty-first century, as in 1908, NASBA provides a forum for the boards to exchange views on professional and regulatory issues and trends affecting regulation. Since 1997 its headquarters have been in Nashville, Tennessee, and a satellite office is maintained in New York City. Committee meetings as well as annual and regional meetings are held at sites throughout the country.

Volunteer leadership includes a chairman, vice chairman, nine directors-at-large, and eight regional directors. The directors-at-large are elected for three-year terms. All others serve one-year terms, and all are elected by the member boards at the annual meeting. Officers are not limited to licensees.

To help the NASBA achieve its mission of "enhancing the effectiveness of state boards of accountancy," the association holds an annual meeting and regional meetings as well as special issue conferences (including those on continuing professional education, ethics, and legislation) for representatives of accountancy boards. It has volunteer committees researching and reporting on issues of concern, such as examinations, relations with government agencies, and international recognition. The committees are composed of members of the state boards of accountancy as well as state board administrators. In addition, a state accountancy board administrators' committee and legal counsel committee work to assist these individuals who specifically work for the member boards.

NASBA's communication efforts include a monthly newsletter, a biennial digest of state laws, an annual Uniform CPA Examination candidates' statistics report, and a Web site (www.nasba.org) that is linked to the Web sites of all of the state boards that maintain sites. Some audio- and videotape production is also done.

NASBA promulgates no laws. Its committees develop model statutes and rules. However, it is the state legislatures and accountancy boards that do the final drafting and implementing of the laws that regulate the practice of public accountancy. NASBA's committees consult with professional organizations, including the American Institute of Certified Public Accountants (AICPA), the National Society of Accountants, and the American Accounting Association, as they develop suggestions. A joint NASBA/AICPA committee developed the Uniform Accountancy Act (UAA) and Rules, which are continually reviewed and updated as necessary. Model contracts and handbooks have also been developed by NASBA committees.

The profession's technical standards are developed by the AICPA. Members of the profession can be brought before the AICPA for disciplinary procedures in cases where such standards have not been met. However, while the professional organization can withdraw membership privileges, it is only the state board of accountancy that can withdraw the license to practice. Since a person's livelihood is involved in such a decision, every effort is made by the boards to ensure that due process is followed throughout all disciplinary proceedings. Formal hearings are held with legal counsel present, if the licensee so desires.

ENTRY-LEVEL REQUIREMENTS

Requirements to become a certified public accountant vary slightly from jurisdiction to jurisdiction. As Internet practice increases cross-border engagements, all states are being encouraged to move in the direction of adopting one set of standards, as detailed in the UAA. This model act calls for 150 hours of education, one year of experience as attested to by a CPA, and successful completion of the Uniform CPA Examination. For those licensees signing audit reports, additional experience is required. To find out the specific requirements for each state, a candidate needs to check with the state board of accountancy.

The required 150-semester-hour education includes a baccalaureate degree with a concentration in accounting, though not necessarily an accounting major. Again, it is necessary to check with the appropriate accountancy board.

Each of the state boards is charged with the responsibility of administering the Uniform CPA Examination, which is developed and graded by the AICPA. Grades are released to candidates through the state boards. The examination as given in May 2000, for example, was a four-part test given over a two-day period. The four sections of the examination were: auditing (AUDIT), business law and professional responsibilities (LPR), financial accounting and reporting—business enterprises (FARE), and accounting and reporting—other areas (ARE).

In November 1997, 20.8 percent of the candidates passed all parts of the exam for which they sat. This does not mean they passed the entire examination, since some candidates retake the examination and consequently only take selected parts. In a few jurisdictions, candidates can choose to take only a limited number of parts at a time. Studies are being conducted to transform the Uniform CPA Examination into a computer-based examination rather than paper-and-pencil test. Such a transformation would shorten the time needed to complete the examination and enable candidates to take the examination on additional dates.

Experience is another requirement carefully defined in each state's accountancy rules. At one time only auditing experience in public accounting firms was acceptable. In many states, work in government, industry, and academia that leads to professional competence is also being accepted.

CONTINUING COMPETENCE

Continuing professional education (CPE) is mandatory for license renewal in all jurisdictions except Wisconsin. Some states have course requirements in auditing and accounting, others have course requirements in ethics, and still others allow licensees to select courses to meet CPE requirements. With more than half of CPAs now not working as public accountants, pressure exists for enlarging the scope of CPE to encompass a broader range of programs and experiences that help ensure the licensee's competence.

In many states CPA firms are required to register with the accountancy board. The firms are then required to participate in quality review programs periodically, which bring the firms' attest services under the review of outside professionals.

AREAS OF COMMITTEE ACTIVITY

The focus of NASBA's committees echoes the areas of the boards' mutual concerns. Examination, for entry-level candidates as well as international licensees seeking U.S. recognition, continues to be a primary area of interest. Ensuring that the examination adequately measures competence is an ongoing concern. The Examination Review Board audits the preparation, administration, and grading of the Uniform CPA Examination to ensure the boards' requirements are met.

Many states call for CPAs to give evidence of "good moral character." This has been interpreted to mean having knowledge of professional ethics as well as having no criminal record that could be related to practicing accounting. NASBA's ethics committee and administrators committee both are concerned with these issues.

Committees on public perception, strategic initiatives, new horizons, and so forth demonstrate the association's continuing concern with keeping in touch with the public's and the profession's expectations and goals. Information about NASBA is available from NASBA at 150 Fourth Avenue North, Suite 700, Nashville, TN 37219-2417; (615) 880-4200; or www.nasba.org.

Licensed public accountants and public accountants are also recognized in a limited number of jurisdictions.

SEE ALSO *American Institute of Certified Public Accountants; State Societies of CPAs*

Louise Dratler Haberman

NATIONAL BUSINESS EDUCATION ASSOCIATION

The National Business Education Association (NBEA) is an organization whose efforts are focused on all major aspects of business instruction, administration, and research. A primary focus of the NBEA is the recognition that specific competency attainment is essential for success and lifelong learning in a business environment. The NBEA provides an important and essential link between both the public and private sectors of business. Its motto is "Educating for Success in Business and Life."

The NBEA is administered by an executive board that includes four officers (president, president-elect, secretary-treasurer, and past president) and an executive director. Additionally, the executive board consists of representatives from each of the five regions (Eastern, Southern, North Central, Mountain-Plains, and Western) and the president of each of its five regional affiliates. The executive board also has representatives from two organizations, the National Association for Business Teacher Education (NABTE) and the International Society for Business Education.

The NBEA's official publication is the *Business Education Forum,* which is published four times a year. Articles are submitted and reviewed by editors from the NBEA membership under one or more of the following topic areas: accounting, basic business and economics, communication, entrepreneurship, international business, marketing, methods, research, student organizations, technology, and NABTE. The NBEA also publishes an annual yearbook as well as several newsletters throughout the year, which focus on a particular business-related topic.

The NBEA holds an annual convention that rotates from region to region. The convention program incorporates a combination of general sessions featuring well-known speakers, group meetings on a variety of topics, and hands-on workshops emphasizing specific uses of technology. One of the features of the convention is an exhibit area offering the latest in publications, equipment and software, and teaching aids. Awards are presented to outstanding business educators, including the most prestigious award, the John Robert Gregg Award, in honor of founder of Gregg Shorthand.

The NBEA may be contacted at its executive office: 1914 Association Drive, Reston, VA 20191-1596; or http://www.nbea.org.

SEE ALSO *Professional Education*

Dorothy A. Maxwell

NATIONAL LABOR RELATIONS BOARD

The National Labor Relations Board (NLRB) is an independent federal agency. Its creation in 1935 by Congress was in response to the National Labor Relations Act (the Wagner Act). Later acts, such as the Taft-Hartley Act, have amended the original NLRB.

The NLRB is made up of three principal parts: the board, the general counsel, and the regional offices. The board is made up of five members who serve five-year terms. It acts as a quasi-judicial body in deciding cases on formal records. The general counsel is independent of the board, and is responsible for the investigation and prosecution of unfair labor practice cases, as well as overseeing the regional offices. Members of the general counsel serve four-year terms. Both the board and general counsel are appointed by the president with Senate approval. The regional offices and its subdivisions serve certain geographic areas, and they are dispersed throughout the United States—mainly in or near large cities.

The function of the NLRB is twofold. First, it determines and implements, through secret ballot elections, the choice by employees as to whether or not they wish to be represented by a union (and if so by which union) in dealing with their employers. Second, it prevents unlawful acts (unfair labor practices), either by employers or by the unions.

Congress, through the National Labor Relations Act, regulates labor-management relations, thereby giving the NLRB its authority. The NLRB, though, has no independent power to enforce its mandates; instead, enforcement is done through the courts of appeals.

One example of what the NLRB does was provided in 1995, when it helped bring a speedy end to the baseball strike. The NLRB secured a 10(j) injunction requiring the owners to withdraw their one-sided imposed changes to the negotiated system of setting baseball wages.

SEE ALSO *Collective Bargaining; Labor Unions; Negotiation*

BIBLIOGRAPHY

Gross, James A. (1981). *The Making of the National Labor Relations Board.* Albany, NY: State University of New York Press.

Tod W. Rejholec

NATIONAL RETAIL FEDERATION

The National Retail Federation (NRF) strives to protect and advance retail industry interests by providing services and conducting programs in government affairs, information technology, education, training, and research. In 2005 NRF members represented more than 1.4 million leading U.S. merchandise, independent, specialty, discount, and mass-merchandise stores; key suppliers to the retail industry; and more than a hundred trade organizations across the globe. NRF's interactive boards and committees, comprised of industry experts in their areas of specialization, are designed to represent and reflect industry's diversity and breadth. These boards and committees formulate and implement policies, standards, guidelines, and strategies that are consistent with retail industry objectives.

The NRF considers itself an advocate for retail organizations across the globe. In December 1997, *Fortune* magazine, one of the premier publications in the business world, ranked the NRF among the top-thirty lobbying organizations in the nation. Additionally, to assist members financially, NRF's member-discount program pools the membership's buying power to negotiate reductions on a variety of services and products.

NRF's information technology component serves as the retail industry's information technology headquarters. NRF's groups—such as the Information Technology Council and the Association for Retail Technology Standards (ARTS)—help configure the retail technology environment. They analyze existing and upcoming technologies, as well as potential regulatory and legislative initiatives, and educate private and government entities about retail technology concerns and needs.

The CIO Council (comprised of highly prominent chief information officers who serve by invitation only) meets spring, summer, and winter to address promising technologies, common-interest issues, and to take proactive positions relating to the creation of new-technology environments. Established in 1991, ARTS is comprised of retailer-driven membership striving to facilitate a barrier-free technology environment for retailers internationally through its four standards (Standard Relational Data Model; Unified Point of Service, POS device interface specification; IX Retail standard XML schemas; and application selection guides through RFPs).

Further, through the NRF's various publications (*STORES Magazine, Management of Retail Buying, Small Store Survival, Retail Industry Indicators 2005,* and many others), valuable information, which can be transformed into best practices, is disseminated. For example, the NRF developed standard color and size codes (used to implement Universal Product Codes) and published them in its *Standard Color and Size Code Handbook.*

More information is available from the NRF at 325 7th Street NW, Suite 1100, Washington, DC 20004; 800-NRF-HOW2, 202-783-7971 (phone numbers); 202-737-2849 (fax); or, http://www.nrf.com.

SEE ALSO *Retailers*

Mary Jean Lush
Val Hinton

NATIONAL TRANSPORTATION SAFETY BOARD

When the National Transportation Safety Board (NTSB) was established in 1967, it was considered an independent federal agency. Nevertheless, NTSB's administrative support and funding were funneled through the U.S. Department of Transportation (DOT). Over time, the need for a totally separate, nonreliant agency was recognized, and the 1975 Independent Safety Board Act severed all DOT ties.

Congress charges NTSB with investigating every U.S. civil aviation accident, as well as significant railroad, highway, marine, and pipeline accidents. NTSB, based on investigation findings, then issues safety recommendations in an effort to prevent future accidents.

NTSB differs from other agencies in that it has no official enforcement or regulatory powers, it is a totally independent agency, and its specially trained staff conducts investigations and determines probable cause. Its investigations are broad, looking more for the "big picture," rather than attempting to focus on a specific detail or category.

With fewer than 400 employees, NTSB is a small agency. It plays a large role, however, in maintaining and/or restoring public confidence in the safety of the nation's transportation systems. NTSB has investigated over 10,000 surface transportation accidents and more than 124,000 aviation accidents since it began operation in 1967.

The most important outcomes of NTSB investigations are the safety recommendations the agency issues based on investigation findings. NTSB has proven itself to be thorough and impartial and has been able to achieve an admirable (more than 80 percent) acceptance rate of recommendations made to various individuals and organizations in positions to effect change.

NTSB also uses accident-investigation findings to identify trends or issues that may otherwise be overlooked. Through proactive outreach efforts (e.g., conferences, symposia, and state advocacy), NTSB makes the public aware of potential safety problem areas, such as child safety seat concerns or accidents related to human fatigue factors.

Further, to address the needs of aviation disaster victims and their families, the role of integrating federal, local, and state authorities' resources with airlines resources was assigned to the NTSB in 1996. To fulfill this essential role, the NTSB established the Office of Transportation Disaster Assistance (originally called the Office of Family Affairs).

Mark Rosenker, vice chairman of the National Transportation Safety Board, on the site of an Amtrak train derailment April 7, 2004.
AP IMAGES

NTSB also enjoys an international leadership role, specifically in regard to accidents involving cruise ships or foreign-flag vessels in U.S. waters, or U.S. planes or U.S.-made aircraft overseas. NTSB has thus contributed significantly to increasing levels of safety for individuals worldwide.

To focus attention on NTSB recommendations with the potential to save the most lives, NTSB has created its "Most Wanted List" of improvements in transportation safety, which includes areas where rapid improvement is considered essential. This list includes requiring railroads to install collision avoidance systems, having natural gas distribution companies install excess-flow valves in high-pressure residential systems, having data recorders with increased parameters installed on ships and airplanes, and requiring fire detection and suppression equipment in airplane cargo compartments.

NTSB's safety recommendations have resulted in many safety improvements, and those in positions to serve as change agents have adopted more than 82 percent of NSTB recommendations. For instance, recommendations stemming from the ValuJet Flight 92 accident in Florida resulted in a DOT's Research and Special Programs Administration Agency (RSPA) rule prohibiting passenger-carrying aircraft from transporting oxygen generators as cargo. In the wake of natural gas pipeline accidents in Catskill, New York, and Allentown, Pennsylvania, cast-iron pipe monitoring and replacement programs were implemented by two major gas-distribution companies. The Federal Aviation Association (FAA) has acted to have Boeing 737 rudder systems modified based on NTSB recommendations stemming from the USAir Flight 427 incident in Pittsburgh. In response to an NTSB-issued emergency recommendation based on its 1996 Child Passenger Protection Study, the automobile industry attached labels and sent warning letters to owners about the dangers posed to children by air bags.

Recognizing a need for highly trained investigators, the NTSB Academy was established on the George Washington University campus in Ashburn, Virginia, in 2003. The academy provides training for both NTSB employees and representatives of the diverse transportation community. The academy curriculum is designed to facilitate objective, technically advanced, and independent investigations of transportation accidents, using critical thought, open and succinct communication, and application of evaluative techniques. This is accomplished through accident reconstruction and the collaborative efforts of first responders and compatible federal and state activities.

Additional information on the NTSB and other actions resulting from NTSB recommendations is available from NTSB at 490 L'Enfant Plaza SW, Washington, DC 20594; 202-314-6000; or http://www.ntsb.gov.

SEE ALSO *Consumer Advocacy and Protection; Transportation*

Mary Jean Lush
Val Hinton

NEGOTIATION

Negotiation is the process of two individuals or groups reaching joint agreement about differing needs or ideas. Oliver (1996) described negotiation as "negotiators jointly searching a multi-dimensional space and then agreeing to a single point in the space."

Negotiation applies knowledge from the fields of communications, sales, marketing, psychology, sociology, politics, and conflict resolution. Whenever an economic transaction takes place or a dispute is settled, negotiation occurs; for example, when consumers purchase automobiles or businesses negotiate salaries with employees.

NEGOTIATION STYLES

Two styles of negotiating, competitive and cooperative, are commonly recognized. No negotiation is purely one type or the other. Instead, negotiators typically move back and forth between the two styles based on the situation.

On one end of the negotiation continuum is the competitive style. Competitive negotiation—also called adversarial, noncooperative, distributive bargaining, positional, or hard bargaining—is used to divide limited resources; the assumption is that the pie to be divided is finite.

Competitive strategies assume a "win-lose" situation in which the negotiating parties have opposing interests. Hostile, coercive negotiation tactics are used to force an advantage, and prenegotiation binding agreements are not allowed. Concessions, distorted communication, confrontational tactics, and emotional ploys are used.

Skilled competitive negotiators give away less information while acquiring more information, ask more questions, create strategies to get information, act firm, offer less generous opening offers, are slower to give concessions, use confident body language, and conceal feelings.

They are more interested in the bargaining position and bottom line of the other negotiating party, and they prepare for negotiations by developing strategy, planning answers to weak points, and preparing alternate strategies.

A buyer-seller home purchase transaction illustrates competitive negotiating. The buyer gathers information to determine home value, quality, expenses, and title status. The seller gathers information to ensure that the prospective buyer qualifies for the loan. The parties negotiate concessions regarding home repairs, items to remain in the house, closing dates, and price. The negotiations stall as the buyer and seller disagree on a closing date; the seller retaliates by keeping the buyer out of the home for several days after the closing date. As a consequence of the competitive strategies used, the relationship between the buyer and seller suffers; however, the end result (sale and purchase of a home) satisfies both parties.

On the other end of the negotiating style continuum is cooperative negotiating, also called integrative problem solving or soft bargaining. Cooperative-negotiation is based on a win-win mentality and is designed to increase joint gain; the pie to be divided is perceived as expanding. Attributes include reasonable and open communication; an assumption that common interests, benefits, and needs exist; trust building; thorough and accurate exchange of information; exploration of issues presented as problems and solutions; mediated discussion; emphasis on coalition formation; prenegotiation binding agreements; and a search for creative alternative solutions that bring benefits to all players. The risk in cooperative negotiating is vulnerability to a competitive opponent.

Cooperative negotiators require skills in patience; listening; and identification and isolation of cooperative issues, goals, problems, and priorities. Additionally, cooperative negotiators need skills in clarifying similarities and differences in goals and priorities and the ability to trade intelligently, propose many alternatives, and select the best alternative based on quality and mutual acceptability.

Cooperative negotiating might be used, for example, in a hiring situation. An employer contacts a candidate to encourage the candidate to submit his or her credentials for a job opening. Trust is built and common interests are explored as the employer and candidate exchange information about the company and the candidate's qualifications. Creative solutions are explored to accommodate the candidate's and employer's special circumstances, including work at home, flexible scheduling, salary, and benefits. The two parties successfully culminate the negotiations with a signed job contract.

THE NEGOTIATION PROCESS

Stages in the negotiation process are (1) orientation and fact finding, (2) resistance, (3) reformulation of strategies, (4) hard bargaining and decision making, (5) agreement, and (6) follow-up (Acuff, 1997). For example, a consumer purchasing an automobile investigates price and performance, then negotiates with an agent regarding price and delivery date. Resistance surfaces as pricing and delivery expectations are negotiated. Strategies are reformulated as the parties determine motivation and constraints. Key issues surface as hard bargaining begins. Problems surface, and solutions—such as creative financing or dealer trades—are created to counter pricing and delivery problems. After details are negotiated, the agreement is ratified. After the sale, the agent may follow up with the buyer to build a relationship and set the stage for future purchase and negotiation. The six stages of the process would be approached differently depending on where the negotiators reside on the style continuum.

Basic strategies, both cooperative and competitive, that can be applied in the negotiation process are:

- Use simple language
- Ask many questions
- Observe and practice nonverbal behavior
- Build solid relationships
- Maintain personal integrity
- Be patient
- Conserve concessions
- Be aware of the power of time, information, saying no, and walking away
- Pay attention to who the real decision maker is, how negotiators are rewarded, and information sources
- Listen actively
- Educate the other party
- Concentrate on the issues
- Control the written contract
- Be creative
- Appeal to personal motivations and negotiating styles
- Pay attention to power tactics
- Be wary of such unethical tactics as raising phony issues; extorting; planting information; and making phony demands, unilateral assumptions, or deliberate mistakes

The following summarize strategies that might be used in various stages of negotiations.

Initial Stages

- Plan thoroughly
- Identify and prioritize issues
- Establish a settlement range
- Focus on long-term goals and consequences
- Focus on mutual principles and concerns
- Be aware that "no" can be the opening position and the first offer is often above expectations
- Be aware of the reluctant buyer or seller ploy

Middle Stages

- Revise strategies
- Consider many options
- Increase power by getting the other side to commit first
- Add credibility by getting agreements in writing
- Be wary of splitting the difference
- To handle an impasse, offer to set it aside momentarily
- To handle a stalemate, alter one of the negotiating points
- To handle a deadlock, bring in a third party
- When asked for a concession, ask for a trade-off
- Be wary if the other party uses a "higher authority" as a rationale for not meeting negotiating points
- Be aware of the "vise" tactic ("you'll have to do better than that")

Ending Stages

- Counter the other party's asking for more concessions at the end by addressing all details and communicating the fairness of the deal in closure
- Counter a persistent negotiator by withdrawing an offer
- Do not expect the other party to follow through on verbal promises
- Congratulate the other side

INTERNATIONAL NEGOTIATING

In international negotiations, obstacles arise when negotiating teams possess conflicting perspectives, tactics, and negotiating styles. Negotiators often assume that shared beliefs exist when, in reality, they do not. Examples are different uses of time; individualism versus collectivism;

different degrees of role orderliness and conformity; and communication patterns, that differ widely worldwide. These cultural factors affect the pace of negotiations; negotiating strategies; degree of emphasis on personal relationships; emotional aspects; decision making; and contractual and administrative elements (Acuff, 1997). The goal of the negotiator should be to "look legitimately to the other side by their standards" (Fisher, 1997).

COLLECTIVE BARGAINING

Collective bargaining frequently requires a third party to help the parties reach an acceptable solution. In these situations, such strategies as mediation, arbitration, and conflict resolution are used.

SUMMARY

Negotiation is the process of two individuals or groups reaching joint agreement about differing needs or ideas. Two styles of negotiating, competitive and cooperative, are commonly recognized, with most negotiators moving back and forth between the two styles based on the situation. A number of strategies were discussed that negotiators might use in negotiation stages. The effectiveness of various strategies can vary based on cultural differences.

SEE ALSO *Collective Bargaining; Labor Unions*

BIBLIOGRAPHY

Acuff, Frank L. (1997). *How to Negotiate Anything with Anyone Anywhere Around the World.* New York: AMACOM.

Fisher, Roger, and Ury, William, with Bruce Patton, ed. (1997). *Getting to Yes: Negotiating Agreement Without Giving In* (2nd ed.). London: Arrow Business Books.

Oliver, Jim R. (1996). A Machine Learning Approach to Automated Negotiation and Prospects for Electronic Commerce. Retrieved October 28, 2005, from http://citeseer.ist.psu.edu/cache/papers/cs/984/http:zSz Szopim.wharton.upenn.eduzSz~oliver27zSzpaperszSzjmis. pdf/oliver97machine.pdf.

Donna L. McAlister-Kizzier

NETWORKING

Computer networks consist of multiple computers and other electrical devices linked together. Networks are classified as local area networks (LANs) or wide area networks (WANs). The difference between LANs and WANs is usually determined by the length of the network. Generally, a LAN's distance includes only several hundred yards. LANs reside mostly in offices, work areas, classrooms, one building, or within several buildings. WANs exist over many miles, across several cities, and even around the world. WANs are multifaceted and complex networks. They require many devices that connect different computers using diverse communication services. WAN communication speed, reliability, and connectivity are more challenging to manage than those of a LAN.

HISTORICAL ACHIEVEMENTS IN COMMUNICATION AND TRANSPORTATION

Networks were developed as a communication method between computers at remote sites. They trace their roots back to nineteenth-century communication and transportation historical achievements. In America, people have always strived for faster travel and communication systems, particularly between the East and West Coasts. These systems included technology and experiments of varying complexity. For example, the Pony Express operated between 1860 and 1861. It provided seven-day mail service between St. Joseph, Missouri, and Sacramento, California.

In 1861 the Western Union Telegraph Company replaced the Pony Express and provided a faster, more reliable communication service. Furthermore, the transcontinental railroad was completed at Promontory, Utah, in 1869. These events improved the telegraph industry. The telephone was invented in 1876, and the first transcontinental telephone line was joined at Wendover, Utah, in 1915. This national telephone network provided a foundation for the wide area computer networks that evolved later in the twentieth century.

NETWORK CHARACTERISTICS

Ownership. LANs consist of computers, scanners, printers, and cables, which are privately owned. WANs connect computers, scanners, printers, and other devices that sometimes may be leased or rented from public and private telephone companies or data communication companies. These networks place high demands on security and reliability.

In addition, the communication line or medium that a company uses for its network is either cable or a wireless technology. When a business creates a WAN, it might not manage all the lines. Sometimes a business leases lines from a communication company. These companies are data and voice carriers such as MCI, Sprint, Verizon, Williams Communications, and AT&T. In these cases, the WAN is not entirely owned by the initial business. The business owns the line up to the point where the handoff with the data carrier occurs. Then, the carrier company handles the transfer of data and hands it back to the business's private LAN network at a location many miles away.

LAN size. The size of a LAN is set by the type of LAN configuration and specifications. For example, a LAN in a building might use an Ethernet technology such as 10Base2, also known as Thin Ethernet. This network technology can have one segment 656 feet (200 meters) in length or five linked segments up to 3,281 feet (1,000 meters) in length. A segment is the length of cable between two computers. For 10Base2, the 10 stands for 10 megabits per second, Base means baseband, and 2 equals 200 meters. Another technology is fiber distributed data interface (FDDI). FDDI networks can be up to 124 miles (200 kilometers) in length; these, however, are mostly used as backbone cables that link several LANs.

WAN size. Because WANs cover large areas, they consist of network technology that extends farther distances than LANs. They incorporate technologies such as FDDI, DSL (digital subscriber line), satellite, and microwave communications. Also, they require routers, switches, and hubs that amplify and direct signals to other routers, switches, and hubs. They can increase their distances nationally and globally.

Speed. Another characteristic of a computer network is speed. Network speeds are measured in bits per second. For example, a byte consists of 8 bits, and one alphabetic character or numeric digit consists of 1 byte. If an average word length is five characters and an average double-spaced page is about 200 words, then a page (counting words and spaces) would consist of about 9,600 bits—((200 words×5 characters)+199 spaces)×8 bits. If a network speed is 9,600 bits per second (bps), then a normal double-spaced page is transmitted every second. If a network speed is 56,000 bits per second (56Kbps), about six pages of information per second would be transmitted.

LANs and WANs, however, are typically faster than 9,600 and 56,000 bps. Many networks are 10, 16, or 100 megabits per second (Mbps). A 100 Mbps network can send 100,000,000 bits in one second—or 10,416 pages per second. Some networks can transmit 2 billion to 8 billion bits per second (gigabits, or Gbps). At 2 Gbps (2,000,000,000/9600), 208,000 pages flash by every second—more than most people read in a lifetime. Network speeds are even reaching terabits per second. One Gbps equals a thousand gigabits—almost unthinkable!

Signal carriers. The medium used to carry signals on a network can be conducted or radiated. Electric signals over wire are conducted. Fiber optic, microwave, infrared, and radio waves are examples of radiated media.

Wire can be shielded (STP) or unshielded (UTP) twisted pair or coaxial cable. UTP is cheaper to install than STP or coaxial cable; therefore, it is a popular network choice. STP or coaxial cable, however, should be used if there is electromagnetic interference on the network. Other networks overcome electromagnetic interference using fiber optic lines and wireless media. They are more expensive, however, than UTP wiring.

Twisted pair wires are rated by the American Wire Gauge (AWG) standard. Smaller numbers mean thicker wires. Regular telephone wire is rated a 28—too thin for most LANs. LANs use AWG ratings between 22 and 26. Another characteristic of twisted pair wires are the number of twists per foot. More twists may reduce cross talk and interference. Cross talk is when one line picks up noise or voices from another line during a conversation or data transmission. Usually 2 twists per foot are a minimum, while 4 are preferred.

Furthermore, the Electronic Industries Association (EIA) has another standard for rating wires. The EIA classifies LAN wires for different uses. For example, Category 3 (Cat 3) must contain 3 twists per foot and is commonly used in creating 10 Mbps LANs. Cat 5 is good for 100 Mbps and has sustained speeds up to 2 Gbps. Cat 7 reliably supports speeds up to 600 Mbps.

Baseband versus Broadband. Currently, most LANs use baseband transmission. Baseband means that there is one signal transmission per line. This means the channel or line is full when one device is sending data. It is easier for baseband LANs than for broadband LANs to have high speeds, behave reliably, and operate with low error rates. Also, baseband LANs are easily monitored by network administrators.

Broadband, on the other hand, means that the line can handle several transmission signals at one time. This is accomplished using different frequencies that act as separate channels. This is called frequency division multiplexing. Broadband networks have the capacity to handle more channels than baseband networks, but they are more expensive and intricate. A single cable that transmits many television channels is an example of broadband technology.

Because of the high interest in obtaining Internet services, broadband technology is becoming more affordable and widespread. For example, some cities are implementing a technology called broadband over power lines (PBL). PBL is a computer network providing Internet data service using broadband transmissions over public power lines. These networks operate at speeds of 90 Mbps.

NETWORK SECURITY

Networks are diverse connections of components that are susceptible to interference, such as unauthorized breaches by attackers. Because of these vulnerabilities, network administrators have ongoing challenges keeping networks secure. Some of the vulnerabilities include eavesdropping, viruses, denial of service (DoS), spoofing, and e-mail bombs. These potential hazards can disrupt and curtail the goals of effective networks. Government networks, financial institutions, educational institutions, and specialty businesses are highly susceptible to attackers. Some of the methods to assure better security are established network firewalls, computer user policies, filter rules, incoming packet inspection mechanisms, and server isolation. While these can be successful, they are not foolproof. Network security planning and implementation is ongoing and constantly improving.

Wireless networks. Wireless LANs are becoming more useful in homes, businesses, and schools. They are also known as Wi-Fi networks. Most of these networks use radio waves for their transmission medium, but some use infrared light waves. Radio waves travel free at the speed of 186,000 miles per second. Unlike light waves, radio waves can travel long distances and can penetrate through nonmetallic objects. Radio waves spread out over vast areas. Because of these advantages, wireless LAN and WAN networks are expanding rapidly.

Interoperability. A concern on wireless networks, interoperability results when vendors produce wireless components that do not work together. Efforts to prevent this from happening have been implemented. One example is the Institute of Electrical and Electronic Engineers (IEEE) 802.11 standard. Most wireless vendors have agreed to follow this standard when producing wireless components. Also, the Wireless Ethernet Compatibility Alliance began certifying vendors who produce components that adhere to 802.11 provisions.

Security on Wi-Fi networks is also a major concern. Security protocols for wireless networks are provided in the 802.11i IEEE data communication standard. This standard defines security protocols that prevent the major security issues such as eavesdropping, spoofing, DoS, and others.

SUMMARY

Networks have become an operational necessity for just about every business, government entity, school, and household. Burgeoning information demands make it necessary to link computers for efficient data sharing, storage, and communication. E-mail services are becoming a communication staple among computer owners. Additionally, enhanced services such as electronic commerce, graphics, and videoconferencing are causing networks to grow and expand. Properly managed networks increase productivity and assist managers and administrators with communication demands. Consequently, networks are an essential component of the information system plan of every business. Networks provide a crucial advantage for end users.

SEE ALSO *Information Systems; Videoconferencing*

Dennis J. LaBonty

NO CHILD LEFT BEHIND LEGISLATION

The No Child Left Behind (NCLB) national legislation was enacted into law in 2001 and represents major changes in public schools at both the elementary and secondary level. NCLB is based on the concept that "no child will be left behind" in every aspect of children's academic education. NCLB legislation has created many detailed and challenging pieces in the process of its implementation.

The NCLB Act reauthorizes the Elementary and Secondary Education Act of 1965 and incorporates strategies and principles of President George W. Bush. These include:

- Increased accountability for individual states, school districts, and individual schools

- More school choice for parents and students, with special emphasis on students attending low-performing schools

- More choice for states and local educational agencies in the use of money from the federal government

- A stronger emphasis on reading instruction, with special emphasis on younger children

INCREASED ACCOUNTABILITY

Accountability for instruction is now being required by all states in that they are required to develop and implement a process of statewide accountability for students attending public schools.

Incorporated into the accountability process is a development and assessment procedure to establish state standards in subject areas, with an initial focus on reading and mathematics. States are responsible for annual testing of all students in grades 3–8, with the overall goal that students will reach proficiency by grade 12. In the process of doing this, results are sorted by race, ethnicity, poverty, disability, and limited English proficiency. School districts that fail to make adequate yearly progress (AYP) toward statewide proficiency goals will be subject to improvement, corrective action, and/or restructuring to get them back on track. Schools that meet or exceed the AYP goals will be eligible for special recognition.

MORE CHOICE FOR PARENTS AND STUDENTS

As a result of the NCLB Act, parents have greater options available to them in determining what schools their children attend. This process may involve restructuring in a variety of configurations to provide a student with the opportunity to attend a school that better meets the student's individual needs. Whenever this occurs, the current school district must provide transportation to the new school using a portion of government funds to do so.

The new law also requires school districts to spend up to 20 percent of their Title I (federal funds) allocations to provide students and parents with choice and additional educational services to eligible students.

GREATER FLEXIBILITY FOR STATES, SCHOOL DISTRICTS, AND SCHOOLS

Funding from four major state grant programs may transfer up to 50 percent of their funding to meet the needs of the NCLB Act. The covered programs include Teacher Quality State Grants, Educational Technology, Innovative Programs, and Safe and Drug-Free Schools. Also included are financial resources dealing with emphasizing reading instruction, with special emphasis for younger children.

READING INSTRUCTION

To ensure that every child can read by the third grade, Bush introduced the Reading First initiative. This initiative has increased federal funds in the early grades to promote more scientific instruction in reading. Reading First provides incentives to schools and teachers who are helping students develop their reading skills at an earlier age through grants and recognition programs. Teachers are also being provided with a multitude of professional development opportunities in the area of reading.

SUMMARY

The NCLB legislation is still in the process of being implemented and presents a wide variety of unique challenges to schools and school districts at both the elementary and secondary level. The long-range effects of the legislation have yet to be determined.

BIBLIOGRAPHY

U.S. Department of Education. (n.d.). No child left behind. Retrieved February 27, 2006, from http://www.ed.gov/nclb/landing.jhtml?src=ln

Dorothy A. Maxwell

NORTH AMERICAN INDUSTRY CLASSIFICATION SYSTEM

The North American Industry Classification System (NAICS) groups establishments into industries according to their primary economic activities. NAICS facilitates the collection, calculation, presentation, and analysis of statistical data by industry. The North American Free Trade Agreement countries—United States, Canada, and Mexico—developed the system to provide comparable statistics among themselves. Federal statistical agencies in these countries use NAICS to produce information by industry on inputs and outputs, productivity, industrial performance, unit labor cost, and employment. Both government and business use this information to understand industries and the economy.

NAICS has a production-oriented conceptual framework. It groups establishments according to similarity in the processes used to produce services or goods. This supply-based framework delineates differences in production technologies. In this system, an industry is not solely a grouping of products or services.

BACKGROUND

NAICS replaced the Standard Industrial Classification (SIC) system in the United States. The SIC system, established in the 1930s and revised through 1987, drew increasing criticism as rapid changes affected both the U.S. and world economies in the late 1980s.

In 1992 the Office of Management and Budget (OMB), an executive office of the president, established the Economic Classification Policy Committee (ECPC). The ECPC was chartered to provide a "fresh-slate" examination of economic classifications for statistical purposes. The ECPC ultimately joined with Mexico's Instituto Nacional de Estadistica, Geografia e Informatica and with Statistics Canada to develop the NAICS. The NAICS codes are revised on a regular five-year cycle.

The U.S. Bureau of the Census, the U.S. Bureau of Economic Analysis, and the U.S. Bureau of Labor Statistics (BLS) continue to develop NAICS. NAICS implementation began for reference year 1997 in the United States and Canada, and for 1998 in Mexico. The U.S. Census Bureau used NAICS to prepare the 1997 Economic Census, which became available in 1999.

Other agencies implementing NAICS include the Federal Reserve Board and federal departments (e.g., Labor, Commerce, Defense, and the Treasury).

STRUCTURE OF NAICS

NAICS uses a six-digit code to identify particular industries, in contrast to the four-digit SIC code. The structure of NAICS is hierarchical. The first two digits of each code indicate the sector. The other digits and what they indicate are:

> Third digit—Subsector
>
> Fourth digit—Industry group
>
> Fifth digit—NAICS industry
>
> Sixth digit—National industry

In the manual *North American Industry Classification System: United States, 2002* (*NAICS: United States, 2002*), there are codes for 1,179 U.S. industries.

NAICS classifies by sectors first. The *NAICS: United States, 2002* manual presents twenty sectors, their two-digit codes, and the distinguishing activities of each, as follows:

11 Agricultural, Forestry, Fishing and Hunting. This sector includes growing crops, raising animals, harvesting timber, and harvesting fish and other animals from farms, ranches, or the animals' natural habitat.

21 Mining. Extracting naturally occurring mineral solids, such as coal and ore; liquid minerals, such as crude petroleum; and gases, such as natural gas; and beneficiating (e.g., crushing, screening, washing, and flotation) and other preparation at the mine site, or as part of mining activity.

22 Utilities. Providing electric power, natural gas, steam supply, water supply and sewage removal (through sewage systems and treatment facilities).

23 Construction. Erecting buildings and engineering projects (e.g., highways), including new work, additions, alterations, or maintenance. Site preparation for new construction and land subdivision are also part of this sector.

31–33 Manufacturing. The mechanical, physical, or chemical transformation of material, substances, or components into new products.

42 Wholesale Trade. Wholesale establishments sell merchandise as an intermediate step in the distribution process and provide services incidental to such sales. Wholesalers can be either merchants or establishments arranging for the purchase or sale of goods owned by others.

44–45 Retail Trade. Retail establishments sell to the general public in the final step of distribution of merchandise and provide services related to such sales.

48–49 Transportation and Warehousing. Providing transportation of passengers and cargo, warehousing and storing goods, scenic and sightseeing transportation, and supporting these activities.

51 Information. Producing and distributing information and cultural products, providing the means to transmit or distribute these products, data or communications, and processing data.

52 Finance and Insurance. Involves the creation, liquidation, or change in ownership of financial assets and/or the facilitation of financial transactions.

53 Real Estate and Rental and Leasing. Renting, leasing, or otherwise allowing the use of tangible or intangible assets (except copyrighted works), and providing related services.

54 Professional, Scientific, and Technical Services. Establishments in this sector provide professional, scientific, and technical services for the operations of other organizations.

55 Management of Companies and Enterprises. Includes: (1) holding securities of companies and enterprises, for the purpose of owning controlling interest or influencing their management decisions, or (2) administering, overseeing, and managing establishments of the company or enterprise, including strategic planning and decision making.

56 Administrative and Support and Waste Management and Remediation Services. Establishments in this sector perform routine support activities for the day-to-day operations of other organizations.

61 Educational Services. Providing instruction and training in a wide variety of subjects.

62 Health Care and Social Assistance. Providing health care and social assistance for individuals.

71 Arts, Entertainment, and Recreation. Operating facilities or providing services to meet varied cultural, entertainment, and recreational interests of their patrons.

72 Accommodation and Food Services. Providing customers with lodging and/or preparing meals, snacks, and beverages for immediate consumption.

81 Other Services (except Public Administration). Providing services not elsewhere specified, including repairs of equipment or machinery, religious activities, grant making, advocacy, laundry, personal care, death care, and other personal services.

91–93 Public Administration. Administration, management, and oversight of public programs by federal, state, and local governments with executive, legislative, and judicial authority.

EXAMPLE

NAICS code 711211 identifies the Sports Teams and Clubs industry in the United States and Canada. It belongs to:

Sector 71—Arts, Entertainment, and Recreation

Subsector 711—Performing Arts, Spectator Sports, and Related Industries

Industry Group 7112—Spectator Sports

NAICS Industry 71121—Spectator Sports

National Industry 711211—Sports Teams and Clubs

The *NAICS: United States, 2002* manual gives a detailed description of the Sports Teams and Clubs industry in the three countries.

ASSIGNMENT OF NAICS CODES

NAICS is a classification system for establishments. *NAICS: United States, 2002* defines an establishment as "the smallest operating entity for which records provide information on the cost of resources—materials, labor, and capital—employed to produce the units of output." In the United States the establishment is generally a single physical location using a distinct process to produce goods or services. An enterprise (company) may consist of more than one establishment. Each establishment within the enterprise is assigned a NAICS code. Statistical agencies such as the Census Bureau and the BLS assign NAICS codes based on information reported to them on administrative, survey, and census reports. The Census Bureau assigns a NAICS code to each establishment based on its primary activity.

INTERNATIONAL COMPARABILITY

Comparable data for the United States, Canada, and Mexico are generally available at the five-digit NAICS industry level. The sixth digit of the NAICS code is used to define national industries, which differ among the three countries because of differences in economic and organizational structures.

Many other countries collect data using the International Standard Industrial Classification (ISIC) system established by the United Nations (UN) in 1948. The

UN's Statistical Commission revised the ISIC structure and codes in 1958, 1968, and 1989.

Similar to NAICS, ISIC primarily classifies establishments (rather than enterprises and firms). The criteria used to classify ISIC division and groups are:

- The type of goods and services produced
- The uses of goods and services produced
- The inputs, process, and technology of production

The third classification criterion of the ISIC is the conceptual foundation of NAICS. Hence, NAICS is aligned more closely with ISIC than the 1987 SIC system. Statistics compiled on NAICS are comparable with statistics compiled according to ISIC, Revision 3.

REVISION OF NAICS

NAICS is more timely than the SIC system it replaced because of its revision process every five years. Revisions to NAICS are made in consideration of its four principles:

1. Production-oriented classification

2. Special attention to new and emerging industries, service industries, and industries involved in the production of advanced technology

3. Time series continuity when possible

4. Compatibility with the two-digit level of the ISIC

As scheduled, *NAICS: United States, 1997* was revised to become *NAICS: United States, 2002. NAICS: United States, 2002* included revisions to the structures of the Construction and Information sectors and additional detail in the Retail Trade sector.

The revision process for the 2007 NAICS began when the OMB published a Federal Register Notice in March 2005 seeking comments on the ECPC proposals, which were due by June 9, 2005. Proposals include separating the Telecommunications subsector into three groups (wired, wireless, and satellite), as well as a fourth group for other telecommunications services. Another proposal creates a separate industry for Biotechnology Research and Development, distinct from Research and Development in the Physical, Engineering and Other Life Sciences. These proposals reflect emerging industries and advanced technology.

NAICS AND THE NORTH AMERICAN PRODUCT CLASSIFICATION SYSTEM

The North American Product Classification System (NAPCS) is a ten-digit code that denotes the principal products and services of an industry. It extends the six-digit NAICS U.S. Industry code to the product level. The seventh digit identifies the product class. The eighth digit signifies the BLS link code. The ninth and tenth digits taken together uniquely designate the product. The Census Bureau uses the codes for its Current Industrial Reports program.

WEBSITES OF INTEREST

For updated information from the Census Bureau about implementation of NAICS: http://www.census.gov/naics

For information on updates to NAPCS: http://www.census.gov/eos/www/napcs/napcs.htm

SEE ALSO *Service Industries*

BIBLIOGRAPHY

Executive Office of the President, Office of Management and Budget. (2002). *North American Industry Classification System: United States, 2002.* Lanham, MD: Bernan.

Office of Management and Budget. (2005, March 11). North American Industry Classification System—Update for 2007. *Federal Register 70*(47), 12390–12399.

Mary Michel

NOT-FOR-PROFIT ACCOUNTING

Not-for-profit organizations (NPOs) are like governmental organizations because they do not seek to earn a profit from their activities, yet NPOs are considered a separate sector for accounting purposes. An NPO differs from a for-profit entity in that its primary purpose is typically to fulfill a social mission instead of generating profits, and it differs from a governmental organization because in the United States it is not owned or controlled by any level of government. The NPO considered in this article is formally defined in the United States as an organization that has officially registered with the Internal Revenue Service (IRS) as a Section 501, tax-exempt organization.

NPOs are given tax-exempt status because as IRS Code Section 501 states, "no part of the net earnings shall inure to the benefit of, or be distributed to, its members, trustees, officers, or other private persons." The Financial Accounting Standards Board (FASB), which provides accounting guidance for NPOs, has a definition that corresponds to that of the IRS's, which describes an NPO as one that receives a significant amount of resources from providers who do not expect a return on those resources, does not operate to earn a profit, and does not have defined ownership interests that can be redeemed, transferred, or sold. NPOs, as identified by both the IRS and the FASB, therefore, exclude governmental organizations.

NPOs encompass a wide range of organizations, including entities as diverse as social service agencies, museums, cemetery organizations, major teaching hospitals, unions, private schools and universities, country clubs, and public radio stations. The sector is a "hybrid" that provides public goods (which is generally the primary function of government) through private organizations (typical of the commercial sector). Although NPOs do not operate to earn a profit and no ownership interest can ever be redeemed, transferred, or sold, they are similar to business organizations in the following ways: (1) They compete for scarce capital resources (whether in the form of loans, donations, or government contracts) and (2) they lack the coercive taxing power of government.

SIZE AND NATURE OF THE NPO SECTOR

NPOs in the United States, according to the Independent Sector (an advocacy group for NPOs), are a major industry: NPOs employ 7 percent of all workers, receive $665 billion in annual revenues, and constitute one of the fastest-growing segments of the U.S. economy. More than 1.5 million NPOs were in existence in the United States in 2006 and the IRS estimated that approximately 50,000 new NPOs were formed each year. NPOs tend to have the following characteristics:

Service Orientation. They exist to provide services rather than to generate profits. Profits measure effectiveness and efficiency of business organizations. The lack of a profit motive in the NPO sector makes measurement of their effectiveness and efficiency extremely difficult.

Diversity. They tend to be diverse in both sources of funding and services provided. Some types of NPOs receive a major portion of their funding from governmental sources and provide services that duplicate or supplement governmental services. For example, the government provides a significant portion of the total revenues of NPOs furnishing residential services for the mentally retarded. Others derive a major portion of their funding from fees for services or dues, and may even compete with for-profit organizations. For example, most of the YMCA's revenue is provided by fees or dues from its health-club facilities.

Multiplicity of Funding. They are subject to a myriad of increasingly complex reporting requirements. Many NPOs are multifunded, receiving funds from such sources as membership fees, local community fund-raising efforts (such as United Way), client fees, governmental grants, private foundations, and individual and/or corporate contributions. One result of the multiplicity of funding sources can be an abundance of complex reporting and accountability requirements. Each resource provider may require different year-ends, distinctive charts of accounts, and unique procedures for allocating indirect costs. (Universities' problems in the allocation of allowable indirect costs to be reimbursed by federal grants have been well documented in the popular media.)

Governmentally Regulated. Although both institutionally separate from government and self-governing, they operate in an atmosphere of increasing governmental regulation. For example, since 2003, fourteen states have increased both the reporting and internal control requirements of NPOs.

Publicly Scrutinized. They exist in an environment of significant public scrutiny. The 1996 Taxpayer Bill of Rights significantly increased NPO disclosure: NPOs are now required not only to supply a copy of their informational tax returns (Form 990) to any requesting party, but to make these returns "widely available." GuideStar—an organization that provides information about the finances, missions, and programs of NPOs—has placed the Form 990s of 1.5 million NPOs on the Internet; the National Center for Charitable Statistics has digitized this information, thus enabling benchmarking and in-depth financial analysis by NPO management, potential donors, external auditors, and investigative reporters. Both GuideStar and the National Center for Charitable Statistics impose fees for some of the information they provide.

Interestingly, NPOs are not, in general, required to supply their audited financial statements to outside parties. There are, however, reporting requirements at the state level.

MANAGEMENT OBJECTIVES

The objectives of NPOs are significantly broader in focus than the objectives of traditional for-profit entities. Since NPOs do not generate profits, evaluative measures that are closely related to profits, such as earnings per share, are not relevant to NPO management. Yet, actual focus of effort finds that many NPO managers focus almost exclusively on meeting budgeted targets. Simply meeting annual financial targets, however, does not mean that an NPO is successful; just the opposite could be the case if these targets have been achieved by minimizing important social and consumer goals that were established by the board of the not-for-profit entity. Like for-profit organizations, the managers of NPOs should begin with a mission statement and incorporate sets of interrelated goals that clearly relate the performance of numerous organizational activities back to the original mission.

FOCUS ON FRAUD

Because of the increased scrutiny under which NPOs are operating, management and board members have become increasingly aware of internal controls needed to reduce the possibility of fraud. The general belief that not-for-profit entities are under the leadership of officers and boards motivated by generous, altruistic individuals who are genuinely committed to the social goals of their organizations has been undermined by disclosures of financial scandals, especially in the post-Enron era, which began in late 2001. NPOs have been found guilty of flagrant violations of laws and fraud. A church-related foundation in Arizona was found guilty of a Ponzi scheme (in which contributions of later participants are used to return "dividends" to earlier participants) in 2002 that fraudulently misdirected tens of millions of dollars from contributors. A superintendent of schools and his colleagues at a school district in New York State in 2004 were found guilty of $11.2 million in fiscal mismanagement.

Boards of not-for-profits are expected to be aware of the potential for fraud in the use of resources. This is important for three major reasons. First, every dollar lost to fraud represents a lost ability to provide needed public services. Second, the sector is facing increased public scrutiny, primarily as a result of detailed financial information becoming more available. Finally, a Gresham's law for nonprofits may be at work—the publicizing of fraud cases may result in an unwillingness of donors to give to any nonprofit. The Association of Certified Fraud Examiners estimated in 2005 that approximately 6 percent of all organization revenues in the United States was lost to fraud every year. Applied to the U.S. NPO sector, this means that more than $40 billion could be lost to fraud annually, a significant amount.

ACCOUNTING STANDARDS

The FASB has jurisdiction over the standards of all private NPOs. The Governmental Accounting Standards Board (GASB) has jurisdiction over government-owned entities. This can result in difficulty in comparing similar organizations. For example, a state university's accounting is governed by the GASB; a private, not-for-profit university's by the FASB.

NPO accounting standards, while similar to the standards for for-profit accounting, do have some differences. External reporting is wholly on the accrual basis, regardless of how NPOs maintain their internal records. In FASB's Statement No. 117, requirements for financial statements prepared according to generally accepted accounting principles are provided. Among the guidance in this statement are the following:

1. Three financial statements are required to be issued: a statement of financial position (balance sheet), a statement of activities (income statement), and a statement of cash flows.

2. Net assets in the statement of financial position must be classified into three categories, based on the presence of donor-imposed restrictions: unrestricted net assets (when no donor restrictions exist), temporarily restricted net assets (for assets that will be used for explicit purposes or periods), and permanently restricted net assets (typically endowments).

3. Revenues must be reported as increases in one of the three categories of net assets (as mentioned in item 2, above). All expenses, however, must be reported as decreases in unrestricted net assets. Thus, an NPO must make two journal entries whenever it expenses a restricted asset: one to record an increase in assets released from restriction (and a decrease in cash or other asset), a second to record a decrease in unrestricted net assets (and an increase in expense).

4. Cash flows must be classified into three categories: (1) cash flows from operations, (2) cash flows from financing, and (3) cash flows from investing. Cash flows from financing must include contributions restricted for long-term purposes and the interest and dividends from these contributions. Contributions not restricted for long-term purposes and the related interest and dividends must be presented in cash flows from operating activities.

5. Voluntary health and welfare organizations (which include most social service organizations) are required to prepare a separate statement of functional expenses in which they classify its expenses by function (such as program, fund-raising, and management) and by object (such as salaries and interest), in a matrix format.

FLEXIBILITY ALLOWED

Because of the variations among NPOs, the FASB has provided flexibility in the presentation of financial information in the statements. For example, the statement of activities (equivalent to the income statement of a for-profit entity) must report expenses by functional classifications, either in the statements or in notes. The guidance, however, does not have a list of required functional classifications. This allows the NPO to determine those classifications that will reflect their activities most accurately. The statement of financial position may be for-matted in one of a number of ways. There are alternatives for recording fixed assets. Additionally, there are some specific requirements for certain types of NPOs, such as universities and health-care organizations.

THE GUIDANCE PROVIDED BY THE AMERICAN INSTITUTE OF CERTIFIED PUBLIC ACCOUNTANTS

From time to time, the American Institute of Certified Public Accountants (AICPA) issues statements of position that relate to NPOs. Among these statements of position are: (1) accounting for advertising costs and (2) costs of activities, which includes fund-raising costs and the handling of joint costs and their appropriate allocation. For example, specific details are provided for determining the allocating of costs to "program" and to "fund-raising" at an event to raise funds when there is a presentation about the organization's program goals.

ANALYSIS OF FINANCIAL DATA

A number of measures are used to assess the performance of an NPO. Among financial measures that are relevant are: (1) the ratio of program expenditures to total expenditures; (2) the ratio of administrative overhead to total expenditures; (3) the ratio of fund-raising expenditures to total expenditures.

SUMMARY

NPOs in the United States provide valuable services to large numbers of individuals and groups. Considered in total, they are successful in securing funds from individuals and business entities as well as from governmental sources. Responsible accounting in accordance with the guidance provided is critical in knowing how effectively such organizations are meeting their missions and goals. Reporting, based on comparable accounting standards and principles, is a valuable means of presenting relevant information to state agencies that provide oversight to such organizations and to individuals and businesses that are selecting those organizations they wish to support with funds.

The Sarbanes-Oxley Act of 2002 is applicable only to publicly owned businesses. Nevertheless, there has been some questioning about its possible value, in some respects, for NPOs. A number of state legislatures (as of January 2006) and attorneys general were considering proposals to increase the accountability of NPOs.

SEE ALSO *Accounting; Government Accounting*

BIBLIOGRAPHY

American Institute of Certified Public Accountants. (n.d.). *Statement of position.* New York: Author.

Copley, Paul A., and Engstrom, John H. (2007). *Essentials of accounting for governmental and not-for-profit organizations* (8th ed.). Boston: McGraw-Hill.

Financial Accounting Standards Board. (1980). *Financial accounting concepts no. 4.* Norwalk, CT: Author.

Financial Accounting Standards Board. (1993). *Financial statements of not-for-profit organizations* [FAS No. 117]. Norwalk, CT: Author.

Greenlee, Janet S. (2000, Spring). Nonprofit accountability in the information age. *New Directions for Philanthropic Fund Raising, 27,* 33–50.

GuideStar. http://www.guidestar.org

Independent Sector. http://www.independentsector.org

Internal Revenue Service. (2005). *Publication 501: Exemptions, Standard Deduction, and Filing Information.* Washington, DC: Author.

National Center for Charitable Statistics. http://www.nccs.urban.org

Janet S. Greenlee
G. Stevenson Smith

O

OCCUPATIONAL SAFETY AND HEALTH ADMINISTRATION (OSHA)

Prior to and during the early 1970s, workplace safety concerns became an issue in the United States. No consistent guidelines required employers to provide safe and healthful working environments. Workers were experiencing job-related injuries, and too often those injuries were fatal. To address these concerns, Congress enacted PL 91-596 (Occupational Safety and Health Act of 1970), which established the Occupational Safety and Health Administration (OSHA), a federal agency headed by an Assistant Secretary of Labor for Occupational Safety and Health. OSHA is functionally structured, with its major programs grouped into eight directorates (Administrative Programs, Construction, Compliance Programs, Federal-State Operations, Health Standards Programs, Policy, Safety Standards Programs, and Technical Support) as well as an Office of Statistics. Senior executive service members head these directorates and offices. Regional offices and subordinate area and district offices or service centers carry out various programs.

OSHA's mission, as set forth in the 1970 legislation, is to "assure...every working man and woman in the nation safe and healthful working conditions." Therefore, OSHA developed and implemented certain standards and enforcement procedures, as well as employers' compliance assistance plans to help employers achieve and maintain healthful and safe workplaces.

Organizations with ten or more employees are subject to OSHA regulation, and those not in compliance may suffer large fines. For instance, OSHA proposed significant fines against a steel firm where alleged safety violations cost two workers their lives. Since OSHA was created, workplace fatalities have decreased by half, but every day about seventeen Americans die on the job.

OSHA strives to create worker awareness of and commitment to resolving workplace safety and health issues by collecting and studying data to identify workplace safety and health problems, as well as achieving problem resolution through regulation, compliance assistance, and enforcement strategies. To enforce regulations, OSHA conducts unannounced, on-site inspections. Data on the OSHA Facts homepage indicate that 34,264 federal and 56,623 state inspections were conducted by OSHA during Fiscal Year 1997, and 87,710 federal and 147,610 state violations were documented. For both federal and state violations, approximately $147 billion in penalties were assessed.

While businesses agree that workplaces should be safe and healthy, many have experienced difficulty in meeting OSHA standards. Because small business owners have found OSHA standards to be financially constricting and consider OSHA penalties harsh, a reform movement is in progress. The House of Representatives has been considering incremental reform of the OSHA Act. On 17 March 1998, two bills (H.R. 2877 and H.R. 2864) concerning OSHA's consultation program and elimination of inspection and penalty quotas were approved; and on 27 March, the Workforce Protections subcommittee heard bills recommending peer review panels to oversee OSHA's rulemaking process, as well as protection from enforcement proceedings for employers meeting certain criteria. Additionally, the Safety Advancement for Employees (SAFE) Act approved in October 1997 exempts small business owners from OSHA fines for two years and allows third-party inspectors. Even with ongoing OSHA reform initiatives, no comprehensive reform bill requiring substantial change in OSHA's structure, procedures, or standards has been enacted.

More information is available from OSHA at U.S. Department of Labor, Occupational Safety and Health Administration (OSHA), 200 Constitution Ave., N.W., Washington, DC 20210; (202) 693-2000, or http://www.osha.gov/html/oshdir.html.

SEE ALSO *Health Issues in Business*

BIBLIOGRAPHY

International Public Management Association. "Government Affairs/Occupational Safety and Health Act (OSHA)." Retrieved October 28, 2005, from http://www.ipma-hr.org/index.cfm?navid=144&id=759&tcode=nws3&search=1.

Fitzgerald, Ted. "Failure to Correct Multiple Hazards Brings Claremont, N.H., Steel Fabricator OSHA Citations and $350,000 in Proposed Penalties." Retrieved October 28, 2005, from http://www.osha.gov/pls/oshaweb/owadisp.show_document?p_table=NEWS_RELEASES&p_id=1316.

National Federation of Independent Business. "OSHA Reform Legislation Summaries". Retrieved October 28, 2005, from http://www.nfib.com/object/IO_21741.html.

Occupational Safety and Health Administration (OSHA). "OSHA Office Directory." Retrieved October 28, 2005, from http://www.osha.gov/html/oshdir.html.

OSHA. "OSHA Strategic Management Plan 2003–2008". Retrieved October 28, 2005, from http://www.osha.gov/StratPlanPublic/index.html.

U.S. Department of Labor, Occupational Safety & Health Administration. "OSHA" Retrieved October 25, 2005, from http://www.osha.gov.

U.S. Department of Labor, Occupational Safety & Health Administration. "OSHA Facts 2004". Retrieved October 25, 2005, from http://www.osha-slc.gov/as/opa/oshafacts.html.

Mary Jean Lush
Val Hinton

OFFICE LAYOUT

Office productivity is influenced by a number of factors, one of which is office layout. Because office layout influences the entire white-collar-employee segment of the organization, its importance to organizational productivity should never be underestimated. Office layout is based on the interrelationships among three primary factors: employees, flow of work through the various work units, and equipment.

Efficient office layout results in a number of benefits to the organization, including the following:

1. It affects how much satisfaction employees derive from their jobs.

2. It affects the impression individuals get of the organization's work areas.

3. It provides effective allocation and use of the building's floor space.

4. It provides employees with efficient, productive work areas.

5. It facilitates the expansion and/or rearrangement of work areas when the need arises.

6. It facilitates employee supervision.

Planning the layout tends to occur in two steps, a preliminary stage and a final stage.

PRELIMINARY PLANNING

When designing office layout, a number of factors need to be taken into consideration during the preliminary planning stage, which is generally carried out by administrative office managers, employees, or consultants. Among the factors to consider during preliminary planning are these:

Work flow: Studying the flow of work vertically and horizontally between individuals and work units is critical in designing office layout. The goal is to design a layout pattern in which work moves in a straight-line direction with minimal, if any, backtracking or crisscrossing patterns. The major source documents found within the various work areas are often considered in analyzing work flow.

Organization chart: Studying the organization chart, which visually depicts who reports to whom as well as the relationships among and between employees, is also considered in the preliminary planning stages. Generally, the organization chart helps determine which units should be physically located near one another.

Projection of number of employees needed in the future: Having a good understanding of the possibility of expansion helps assure that layout is designed to accommodate future growth. Among the factors to be considered are the potential need for additional work units as well as the number of additional employees likely to be needed in both existing work units and new work units.

Communication network: Studying the organization's communication network identifies who within the organization has considerable contact with whom, either face-to-face or by phone. The more contact employees have, the greater the likelihood that they or their work units need to be located physically near one another.

Departmental organization: Studying departmental organization also helps determine which departments should be placed in close proximity to one another. For example, those departments with significant responsibilities for the accounting and financial aspects of the firm should be located near one another; those with frequent contact with outsiders, such as personnel and sales, should be located near the entrance to the structure; and noise-producing departments, such as copying/duplicating and the loading dock, should be located near one another and away from areas where low noise levels are required.

Ratio of private to general offices: Increasingly, many organizations are opting for more general offices and fewer private offices. This trend probably helps reduce the amount of total office space needed, and it facilitates the rearrangement of office areas. A number of advantages result from using general offices rather than private offices. General offices are more economical to build than private offices; general offices make it easier to accommodate change in office layout; and it is easier to design efficient heating, cooling, and lighting systems for general offices.

Space requirements: The total amount of needed space is determined by the amount of space needed for each employee (including projections for growth) in each work unit as well as the amount of space needed for various specialized areas. The amount of space each employee needs is determined by the employee's furniture/equipment requirements, the location of such structural features as windows and pillars, and the employee's job functions and hierarchical position.

Specialized areas: Many organizations have a number of specialized areas that must be taken into consideration in the preliminary planning of office layout. Included are such needs as a reception area, board or conference rooms, a computer center, a mailroom, a printing/duplicating room, a central records area, and a storage area.

Safety considerations: A number of safety considerations play an important role in the preliminary planning of layout, including aisles/corridors of sufficient width, door openings, stairwells, and exits. Providing for quick evacuation of the premises in case of an emergency is a critical aspect of the preliminary planning of office layout.

Barrier-free construction: A number of federal laws require that office layout accomodates individuals with disabilities. The 1990 Americans with Disabilities Act requires "reasonable accommodation" of individuals with disabilities. Perhaps most significant in office layout is designing office/work areas in which individuals can easily maneuver wheelchairs.

Expansion: To stay abreast of developing space needs, many organizations undertake a yearly space analysis, just as they prepare a yearly budget. Doing so enables these organizations to be proactive rather than reactive in anticipating future space needs.

Equipment and furniture needs: The amount of equipment and furniture that needs to be accommodated in an organization must be taken into consideration during the preliminary planning of office layout. Failure to take these needs into consideration often results in inefficient office layout.

PLANNING OFFICE LAYOUT

Perhaps the most critical decision that will be made in planning office layout is whether private offices only or a combination of private and general office areas will be used. The trend is toward a minimum of private office areas and maximum use of general office areas. Typically, the general office areas make use of the open office concept, which overcomes a number of the disadvantages of conventional private offices. Whereas private offices tend to be based on the hierarchical structure of the organization, open office areas are based on the nature of the relationship between the employee and his or her job duties.

Open office planning takes into account the cybernetics of the organization, meaning that information flows and processes are considered in the design process. Information flows pertain to paper flow, telephone communications, and face-to-face interaction.

Three different alternatives are used in designing space around the open office concept. These include the modular workstation approach, the cluster workstation approach, and the landscape approach. In each case, panels and furniture components comprise work areas. Typically, the panels and furniture components are prewired with both electrical and phone connections, which considerably simplifies their installation. Panels are available in a variety of colors and finishes, including wood, metal, plastic, glass, carpet, and fabric.

Modular workstation approach. A prime characteristic of the modular workstation approach is the use of panel-hung furniture components to create individual work areas. Storage cabinets and files of adjustable height are placed adjacent to desks or tables. The design of modular workstations enables employees to have a complete office in terms of desk space, file space, storage space, and work-area lighting. Modular workstations are designed according to the specific job duties of their occupants.

In certain situations, the modular workstation approach is preferred to either of the other two open-space concepts. It is especially well suited for those situations that require considerable storage space, and the work area can be specifically designed around the specific needs of the user. Also, changes in layout can be made easily and quickly.

Cluster workstation approach. An identifying characteristic of the cluster workstation approach is the clustering of employee work areas around a common core, such as a set of panels that extend from a hub, much like the spokes in a wheel. The panels define each employee's work area, which typically includes a writing surface, storage space, and filing space. As a rule, cluster workstations are not as elaborate as either modular workstations or landscaped alternatives. Cluster workstations work well for situations in which employees spend a portion of their workday away from their work area.

Two distinct advantages of the cluster workstation are economics and the ease with which layout changes can be made. The cluster workstation is less expensive than either of the other two alternatives.

Landscape approach. Originally developed in Germany, office landscaping is now used extensively throughout the United States. In a way, office landscaping is a blend of the modular and cluster workstation approaches. One significant difference, however, is the abundant use of plants and foliage in the decor. Plants and foliage, in addition to being aesthetically pleasing, provide a visual barrier. Whereas both the modular and the cluster approaches tend to align the components in rows, landscaping arranges work areas in clusters and at different angles.

In its original form, landscaping eliminated all private offices. However, most organizations that make use of landscaping use a hybrid approach in which a ratio of 80 percent open office areas to 20 percent private offices is common.

In conventional office layout, status was accorded employees through their assignment of a private office. Because the open-space concept removes a considerable number of private offices, employees are accorded status through such other aspects as their work assignments,
their job duties, the location and size of their work area, and the type and amount of furniture they are given.

PREPARING THE LAYOUT

The actual preparation of the layout is carried out using a variety of tools, including templates, cutouts, plastic models, magnetic boards, and computer-aided design (CAD). For more complex layout projects, CAD is most likely the tool of choice. For simple layout projects, any of the others work well. Regardless of which tool is used, a primary concern is making sure every aspect of the layout, including perimeter, structural features, and equipment and furniture components, is scaled properly and consistently.

SEE ALSO *Ergonomics*

BIBLIOGRAPHY

Allcorn, Seth (2003). *The dynamic workplace: present structure and future redesign.* Westport, CT: Praeger.

Rappoport, James E., Cushman, Robert F., and Daroff, Karen, eds. (1992). *Office Planning and Design Desk Reference.* New York: Wiley.

Shumake, M. Glynn (1992). *Increasing Productivity and Profit in the Workplace: A Guide to Office Planning and Design.* New York: J. Wiley.

Turner, G., and Myerson, J. (1998). *New Workspace, New Culture: Office Design as a Catalyst for Change.* Aldershop, Hampshire, England: Gower.

Vischer, Jacqueline (2005). *Space meets status: designing workplace performance.* New York, NY: Routlidge.

Zane K. Quible

OFFICE TECHNOLOGY

Changing technologies—including personal computers (PCs), slide projectors, movie projectors, overhead projectors, television monitors, videocassettes, videodisc players, multimedia systems, and the Internet—have had a major impact on the office environment since the start of the twentieth century. The ability to use technology is an essential skill in the ever changing workforce of the twenty-first century.

The modern office has changed dramatically since the 1990s. Offices in today's society are transmitting information via electronic mail (e-mail), electronic calendars, and teleconferencing, as well as other electronic devices. Communication via technology is just as important as oral and written communication in the work environment. Technology continues to play a vital role in transforming the business environment.

Advances in technology have transformed the world of work. As the work environment has changed, individual workers see how their work connects not only to their particular work place, but to the entire value chain.

The backbone of technology is the local area network (LAN), a single-site computer network, or the wide area network (WAN), which supports worldwide work groups. Both of these networks provide tools for users to transmit data, graphics, mail, and voice across the network. LANs and WANs enable distributed work teams to complete projects using groupware and decision support systems.

Merging in the fast lane of the information superhighway of the twenty-first century world of work, faster information systems, blink-of-an-eye access to the global marketplace, virtual offices, virtual teams, and virtual organizations are coming into existence. The impetus is technology. The technology explosion has transformed every level of business environment—from the typical office worker to the chief executive officer (CEO), providing a challenge for all. Technology is creating whole new genres of content. Office technology focuses upon office information functions such as word processing, data processing, graphics, desktop publishing, and communication.

OFFICE SYSTEMS

The invention of the PC in the 1980s altered the way computing power was distributed within an organization—changing how companies were run, the ways in which information was created, and the ways in which information was used by individuals in carrying out their jobs. The use of word processing and spreadsheet packages made it possible for professional staffs to create their own reports without having to go to a central typing pool or computer center. Prior to the advent of the PC, secretaries typed letters, created reports, and organized information in files. The nature of secretarial positions changed with the arrival of the PC, from a focus on document creation and production to a focus on other kinds of administrative functions, as reflected in the changing work patterns of the office.

Office systems consist of tasks to be performed, procedures to complete the tasks, sets of automated technologies designed to enhance productivity, and personnel working within the framework of a business organizational structure. Office systems exist in facilitating and retaining communications, and creating, processing, and distributing information. Integrated hardware components and integrated software applications enhance the productivity and efficiency of the overall organization to the success of the business.

TYPES OF TECHNOLOGIES

The variety of technologies available continues to change. Some of the technologies used in today's offices are:

Intranets and Internets. Messages can be transmitted electronically within an office (intranet) as well as around the universe (Internet, or Net). Workers are able to exchange information over the computer via the Net through e-mail. E-mails can be sent simultaneously to many individuals around the world.

The intranet is an internal computer network that is used within a company, whereby pertinent information—such as telephone directories, calendars of events, procedure manuals, job postings, and human resources information—can be posted and updated. With the intranet, one is able to communicate online with individuals within a designated work environment.

The Internet is a global computer network that permits millions of computers around the world to communicate via telephone systems and other communication lines. It is also known as the digital information superhighway and is a part of the World Wide Web. With the Internet one can communicate to anyone online throughout the world. The Internet is a public worldwide computer network full of information comprising interconnected networks that span the globe.

Web Pages. Web pages make it possible for businesses, organizations, and anyone who wishes to post information or sell products to do so on the World Wide Web. Web page programs—such as Macromedia, Dreamweaver, and Site Rack—enable users to create their own Web pages.

Web-Based E-Mail. Web mail is a popular Internet service that allows one to send messages and files to anyone around the world from any computer that is connected to the Internet. With an account, users can send and receive messages, images, and any other type of information. Users can access e-mail even if they do not have a computer, simply by using small, inexpensive devices that fit in the palm of one's hand.

E-mail is keyed messages sent from one computer screen to another, using a network linking the units. Transmitting messages from one computer to another offers office workers the ability to communicate quickly through written messages with colleagues, coworkers, and friends.

Voice Mail. Voice mail is an outgrowth of e-mail. Information is spoken into the phone. Words are converted or digitized into electronic computer language. This form of communication is transmitted electronically by phone lines for immediate delivery or can be stored in a computer mailbox. The recipient is able to retrieve the message by dialing a code number to access the mailbox. The computer reconverts the message to the caller's voice and the recipient is able to hear the voice message.

Electronic Calendars. Office tasks are being accomplished and redefined by computers. Computers can keep a calendar of appointments. The computer stores the files of employees' schedules, forthcoming meetings, calendars of events, and conferences, thereby enabling employees to check their central file. Everyone in a particular office has access to electronic calendars and is able to choose a time and place that is available and open on everyone's schedule. Each office employee can be tied into the system by having access to a central electronic file.

Office Suites. Office suites are a group of programs. In the mid-1990s the term *office suite* was considered to be a group of programs that allowed for word processing, spreadsheets, and sometimes data entry. Now *office suite* includes Web design software, presentation software, page layout design, and, in some instances, graphics editors. They are key pieces of productivity software, used in most businesses.

Portable PCs. Portable PCs include personal digital assistants (PDAs), laptop computers, and notebook computers. PDAs are proliferating. Among the most popular PDAs are the Palm and BlackBerry. Laptop computers are used by business travelers to make multimedia presentations, create and send reports and spreadsheets, and do research on the Internet. Notebook computers are similar to laptops, but usually smaller.

Groupware and Decision Support Systems. Groupware is a work group software, such as Lotus Notes. It enables members of a team to share information on a project that they are working on together. Some of the functions of groupware are document formatting, information management, and communication. The group is kept informed via an electronic calendar. It runs an e-mail network that links the work group with remote operations. It also includes an information system that handles all data relevant to the business and provides instant accessibility throughout the organization. Decision support systems facilitate group decisions by providing a formalized process for brainstorming, distilling key concepts, prioritizing or ranking topics, and achieving group consensus.

Teleconferencing. In the business world, many companies hold meetings via teleconferences. Teleconferencing is a method of conducting meetings via telephone lines and/or satellites connecting participants' terminals at two or more locations, with one or more participants per location. There are three types of teleconferences:

1. *Computer conferencing*—Terminals that are connected to a mainframe computer are used by all the participants. Comments or questions can be keyed in on their screens, which are arranged on an interconnected network. Messages are displayed on the participants' screens.

2. *Audio conferencing*—Participants make comments over the phone. They cannot see each other, and they are not able to read body language. Audio conferences are connected by telephone and/or speakerphone.

3. *Videoconferencing*—A CEO in Los Angeles could have a sales conference or interview with a person in Washington, D.C. Both individuals are shown simultaneously or alternately on the screen. The advantage of videoconferencing over audio conferencing is that individuals can see as well as hear each other.

Voice Recognition and Videoconferencing. With the advent of voice recognition, a day may come when human translators are no longer needed. The future of videoconferencing is not only multilingual, but 100 percent real-time—with no delays. Voice recognition software allows humans to talk to a computer. Computers understand the voice. It is an electronic process in which information is printed from voice input, thereby bypassing the keyboarding operations.

At one time, videoconferencing used large, expensive pieces of equipment that provided "room"-based videoconferencing. Participants gathered at a central site in a specially equipped conference room, looking at monitors displaying similar rooms at remote sites.

Computer-based videoconferencing is a new paradigm for videoconferencing. Participants sit at their desk or in a videoconferencing room calling up other participants—similar to making a telephone call. It is a form of communication that uses bandwidth. Bandwidth is interpreted as the speed at which information flows, and communication is the transfer of information from one place to another. The connection between these two remote sites is called communication channels.

Multimedia System. A multimedia system presents information by using a combination of sound, graphics, animation, and video. Multimedia applications are used for business and education. Marketing presentations are developed to advertise and sell products using multimedia. Sales representatives use a computer, a video projector, and a display screen to make their presentations to the audience. Interactive advertisements as well as job applications and training applications can be published on the Internet or in a kiosk display.

Electronic Whiteboard. An interactive "smart" whiteboard with "electronic ink" and touch-sensitive screen can be hooked up to a computer and a projector. The board magnifies images clearly and colorfully. The board has annotation capabilities and notes can be jotted down directly over the projected images, then printed instantly. Thus, there is no need for individuals to take any notes.

The advantage that a whiteboard offers over a simple projection system is that it can be used as a projection screen and a writing surface through its connection with the PC, from which images can be printed out. A whiteboard allows trainers and instructors to operate the computer as if they were using a mouse, moving the cursor around on the computer just by touching a point on the whiteboard. A projector is mounted on the ceiling. The screen should be centered so that all participants have a clear view of the screen.

Smart Board. A smart board is a tool that improves the way people meet, share ideas, and teach. It looks and feels like a regular whiteboard combined with the power of the computer. It lets users save and print notes, collaborate on documents, share information, and run multimedia materials—video or data conferencing across distances.

The smart board becomes a large, touch-sensitive screen when combined with a liquid crystal display panel or projector. It can control Windows or Macintosh applications or multimedia by touching the board with one's finger. By picking up a pen, presenters can draw over their applications in electronic ink to obtain the attention of the audience. Users can e-mail notes to participants and even cut and paste them into other applications.

RECORDS MANAGEMENT

The processing capabilities and storage capacity of computers have made electronic storage and retrieval of information a common practice in business. Computer-generated document management, records management software, and imaging systems assist businesses with large volumes of records. Imaging systems convert all types of documents to digitized electronic data that can be stored and retrieved quickly. With the advent of superhigh-density magnetic storage and online storage, this will be much less of an issue in the future.

A scanner is used in converting paper documents into a digitized form. A processor compresses the image. A retrieval mechanism converts the image for viewing on a monitor, and output devices process the image to a hard-copy format. Laser optical disks are suited for high-volume record management because of their high capacity and durability.

COMMUNICATION IN ORGANIZATIONS

In the business world, technology links employees working in teams; employees are expected to be competent in various software applications and be able to make decisions and multitask. The impetus of newer office technology has transformed the way businesses function in the worldwide marketplace.

In the past, workers acquired a set of skills that became their tools of the trade. Since the mid-1970s, workplace technology has changed swiftly; new technologies have been introduced and replaced. Computer applications are updated continuously. In the twenty-first century, people who work in offices need to be well versed on the use and application of the many emerging technologies. Workers need to adapt to this ever-changing technology. In an increasingly technological world, the expansion of American workers' skills depends upon commitments from the workers themselves, industries, workplaces, and educational and training institutions.

All of these office technologies facilitate communication among people in organizations. All businesses need workers who possess critical thinking skills, problem-solving skills, interpersonal skills, and the ability to communicate effectively—whether in writing or orally. Appropriate choices of communication lead to increased productivity and positive social effects. Workers need to be technologically literate in order to compete in a world that continues to change faster than one can imagine.

SEE ALSO *Desktop Publishing; Information Technology*

BIBLIOGRAPHY

Barrett, Charles F., Kimbrell, Grady, and Odgers, Pattie (2003). *Office skills* (4th ed.). Mason, OH: Thomson South-Western.

Bernard, Ryan (1997). *The corporate intranet: Create and manage an internal web for your organization.* (2nd ed.). New York: Wiley Computer Publishing.

Everard, Kenneth E., and Burrow, James L. (1996). *Business principles and management* (10th ed.). Cincinnati: South-Western.

McGuire, Patrick A. (1988). Wanted: Workers with flexibility for 21st century jobs. *APA Monitor, 29,* 7.

Oliverio, Mary Ellen, Pasewark, William, and White, Bonnie R. (2003). *The office: Procedures and technology* (4th ed.). Mason, OH: Thomson South-Western.

Shelly, Gary B., Cashman, Thomas J., and Vermaat, Misty E. (2003). *Discovering computers 2004: A gateway to information*. Boston: Course Technology.

Anna Nemesh

OLIGOPOLY

An oligopoly is an intermediate market structure between the extremes of perfect competition and monopoly. Oligopoly firms might compete (noncooperative oligopoly) or cooperate (cooperative oligopoly) in the marketplace. Whereas firms in an oligopoly are price makers, their control over the price is determined by the level of coordination among them. The distinguishing characteristic of an oligopoly is that there are a few mutually interdependent firms that produce either identical products (homogeneous oligopoly) or heterogeneous products (differentiated oligopoly).

Mutual interdependence means that firms realize the effects of their actions on rivals and the reactions such actions are likely to elicit. For instance, a mutually interdependent firm realizes that its price drops are more likely to be matched by rivals than its price increases. This implies that an oligopolist, especially in the case of a homogeneous oligopoly, will try to maintain current prices, since price changes in either direction can be harmful, or at least nonbeneficial. Consequently, there is a kink in the demand curve because there are asymmetric responses to a firm's price increases and to its price decreases. That is, rivals match price falls but not price increases. This leads to "sticky prices," such that prices in an oligopoly turn out to be more stable than those in monopoly or in competition; that is, they do not change every time costs change. On the flip side, the sticky-price explanation (formally, the kinked demand model of oligopoly) has the significant drawback of not doing a very good job of explaining how the initial price, which eventually turns out to be sticky, is determined.

Airline markets and automobile markets are prime examples of oligopolies. We see that as the new auto model year gets under way in the fall, one car manufacturer's reduced financing rates are quickly matched by the other firms because of recognized mutual interdependence. Airlines also match rivals' fares on competing routes.

In oligopolies, entry of new firms is difficult because of entry barriers. These entry barriers may be structural (natural), such as economies of scale, or artificial, such as limited licenses issued by government. Firms in an oligopoly, known as oligopolists, choose prices and output to maximize profits. However, firms could compete along other dimensions as well, such as advertising, location, research and development (R&D) and so forth. For instance, a firm's research or advertising strategies are influenced by what its rivals are doing. When one restau-

A billboard at Los Angeles International Airport lists the international flights at Bradley Terminal. © **DAVID BUTOW/CORBIS SABA**

rant advertises that it will accept rivals' coupons, others are compelled to follow suit.

The rivals' responses in an oligopoly can be modeled in the form of reaction functions. Sophisticated firms anticipating rivals' behavior might appear to act in concert (conscious parallelism) without any explicit agreement to do so. Such instances pose problems for antitrust regulators. Mutually interdependent firms have a tendency to form cartels, enabling them to coordinate price and quantity actions to increase profits. Besides facing legal obstacles, cartels are difficult to sustain because of free-rider problems. Shared monopolies are extreme cases of cartels that include all the firms in the industry.

Given that mutual interdependence can exist along many dimensions, there is no single model of oligopoly. Rather, there are numerous models based on different behavior, ranging from the naive Cournot models to more sophisticated models of game theory. An equilibrium concept that incorporates mutual interdependence was proposed by John Nash (1928–) and is referred to as Nash equilibrium. In a Nash equilibrium, firms' decisions (i.e., price-quantity choices) are their best responses, given what their rivals are doing. For example, McDonald's charges $2.99 for a Value Meal based on what Burger King and Wendy's are charging for a similar menu item. McDonald's would reconsider its pricing if its rivals were to change their prices.

The level of information that firms have has a major influence on their behavior in an oligopoly. For instance, when mutually interdependent firms have asymmetric information and are unable to make credible commitments regarding their behavior, a "prisoner's dilemma" type of situation arises where the Nash equilibrium might include choices that are suboptimal. For instance, individual firms in a cartel have an incentive to cheat on the previously agreed-upon price-output levels. Since cartel members have nonbinding commitments on limiting production levels and maintaining prices, this results in widespread cheating, which in turn leads to an eventual breakdown of the cartel. Therefore, while all firms in the cartel could benefit by cooperating, lack of credible commitments results in cheating being a Nash equilibrium strategy—a strategy that is suboptimal from the individual firm's standpoint.

Models of oligopoly could be static or dynamic depending upon whether firms take intertemporal decisions into account. Significant models of oligopoly include Cournot, Bertrand, and Stackelberg. Cournot oligopoly is the simplest model of oligopoly in that firms are assumed to be naive when they think that their actions will not generate any reaction from the rivals. In other words, according to the Cournot model, rival firms choose not to alter their production levels when one firm chooses a different output level. Cournot thus focuses on quantity competition rather than price competition. While the naive behavior suggested by Cournot might seem plausible in a static setting, it is hard to image real-world firms not learning from their mistakes over time. The Bertrand model's significant difference from the Cournot model is that it assumes that firms choose (set) prices rather than quantities. The Stackelberg model deals with the scenario in which there is a leader firm in the market whose actions are imitated by a number of follower firms. The leader is sophisticated in terms of taking into account rivals' reactions, while the followers are naïve, as in the Cournot model. The leader might emerge in a market because of a number of factors, such as historical precedence, size, reputation, innovation, information, and so forth. Examples of Stackelberg leadership include markets where one dominant firm dictates the terms, usually through price leadership. Under price leadership, the leader firm's pricing decisions are consistently followed by rival firms.

Since oligopolies come in various forms, the performance of such markets also varies a great deal. In general, the oligopoly price is below the monopoly price but above the competitive price. The oligopoly output, in turn, is larger than that of a monopolist but falls short of what a competitive market would supply. Some oligopoly markets are competitive, leading to few welfare distortions, while other oligopolies are monopolistic, resulting in deadweight losses. Furthermore, some oligopolies are more innovative than others. Whereas the price-quantity rankings of oligopoly vis-à-vis other markets are relatively well established, how oligopoly fares with regard to R&D and advertising is less clear.

SEE ALSO *Monopoly*

BIBLIOGRAPHY

Cournot, Antoine A. (1971). *Researches into the Mathematical Principles of the Theory of Wealth, 1838.* New York: A.M. Kelley.

Friedman, James W. (1983). *Oligopoly Theory.* New York: Cambridge University Press.

Fudenberg, Drew, and Tirole, Jean. (1986). *Dynamic Models of Oligopoly.* New York: Harwood.

Goel, Rajeev K. (1999). *Economic Models of Technological Change.* Westport, CT: Quorum Books.

Shapiro, Carl. (1989). "Theories of Oligopoly Behavior." In Richard Schmalensee and Robert D. Willig (Eds.), *Handbook of Industrial Organization*, vol. 1, New York: North-Holland.

Rajeev K. Goel

ONLINE EDUCATION

Online education is a flexible instructional delivery system that encompasses any kind of learning that takes place via the Internet. Online learning gives educators an opportunity to reach students who may not be able to enroll in a traditional classroom course and supports students who need to work on their own schedule and at their own pace.

The quantity of distance learning and online degrees in most disciplines is large and increasing rapidly. Schools and institutions that offer online learning are also increasing in number. Students pursuing degrees via the online approach must be selective to ensure that their coursework is done through a respected and credentialed institution.

RATIONALE FOR CONSIDERING ONLINE EDUCATION

Online education has become a viable and exciting method for instructional delivery in the global business society that runs on a 24/7 schedule (24 hours a day/7 days a week) because it provides students with great flexibility.

With the increased availability of the Internet and computer technology, students are able to access information anytime and anyplace that would normally be available only through a traditional classroom. Studies have shown that students learn just as effectively in an online classroom as they do in the traditional classroom.

POSITIVE AND NEGATIVE EFFECTS OF LEARNING ONLINE

Online education offers many positive benefits since students:

- have flexibility in taking classes and working at their own pace and time

- face no commuting or parking hassles

- learn to become responsible for their own education with information available at their fingertips

- find the submission of assignments easy and convenient

- are more apt to voice their own opinions and share and debate issues with other students, as well as learn from other students during the group discussions

Possible negative effects of learning online are that some students:

- may miss the face-to-face interaction with the instructor and among students

- may prefer to attend traditional classes with an instructor who teaches and guides them through the course

- find access to the necessary technology challenging and the availability of technical support limited

In addition, some administrators and instructors who do not understand the workload may display a negative attitude toward online education.

FUTURE OF ONLINE EDUCATION

Online teaching is here to stay. Many students prefer the online classroom since it offers flexibility in their busy schedules. With the proliferation of information and knowledge, students must become lifelong learners in today's world, and online education plays an important role in helping individuals access the learner-centered and self-directed instruction.

With enhanced software, hardware, and Internet access, more options for online education will become available. With student enrollments increasing faster than classrooms can be built, students becoming more proficient with technology, and students pursuing an education that meets their needs, the future of online education will continue to grow. Online degree programs will become more widely accepted as they become a more common practice.

SEE ALSO *Professional Education; Training and Development*

BIBLIOGRAPHY

Center for Online Educators. http://educatoronline.org

NewsweekDistanceLearning.com. http://www.newsweekdistance learning.com

Penn State Online E-Learning Guide. http://www.usnews.com/usnews/edu/elearning/elhome.htm

Carol Larson Jones

OPERATIONAL STRATEGIES

SEE *Strategic Management*

OPERATIONS MANAGEMENT

An important element of any business system is management, whether an individual or a team performs it. In

American society, we no longer think of company management in terms of one person acting as the entrepreneur, but rather as a team effort. Each member possesses specialized knowledge and understanding of one functional area of the business system and is by temperament and training able to work cooperatively with other members of the team toward a common goal.

Whatever the system or organization, the functions of management are always the same: (1) designing, (2) planning, (3) organizing, (4) directing, and (5) controlling. Management establishes the goals and objectives of the firm or organization and plans how to attain them. It is management that organizes the system and directs it so that its goals can be reached. Finally, management must be able to analyze the working of the system in order to control it and to correct any variations from the planned procedures in order to reach the predetermined goals. These functions interact with one another and managers must be skilled in these coordinating processes and functions if they are to accomplish their goals through the efforts of other people.

The concepts of managerial functions has some hidden difficulties when one attempts to apply them to a specific managerial job. First, one cannot tell which functions are most important and how much time must be allocated to each. All functions are important parts of a manager's job, but the significance attached to each one may vary at different times, such as at different stages of a product life cycle. Furthermore, the significance of each function varies at different management levels in the same organization. Operations management, for example, is more focused on directing and controlling than on planning or organizing.

All organizations have operations. Operation management, or technical management, is comprised of department managers and persons with professional technical competence. This level is oriented downward to basic operations, such as producing goods and moving them out the door. A manufacturing company may conduct operation in a mill or factory. The driving force in operations management must be an overriding goal of continually improving service to customers, where customer means the next process as well as the final external user. Since there is an operations element in every function of the enterprise, all people in all jobs in every department of the organization should work together for the improvement of their own operations management elements. It is important to note that the technical expert often seeks recognition from peers and colleagues rather than from managers at the administrative level.

INPUT

The input of a system depends on its specific objective. What raw materials will yield the desired output? If one were to visually illustrate a system, the input would be shown as the components vital to it. A television repairperson needs a diagram of a TV set in order to repair it, or an auditor might need a flowchart of a company's accounting system to check for possible diversion of funds. If a system is designed to maintain a state, the input is information or feedback concerning the essential variable that must be maintained. If the purpose of a system is to make a decision, the input is relevant information about the problem. In a production system, the input consists of raw material, labor, and other manufacturing costs that are combined in the final product.

TRANSFORMATION

After input is established, it is necessary to transform it into a desirable output. In business, the transformation operation is extremely important. Manufacturing, marketing, and distribution must be studied and known in detail. However, there are some areas in which little is known. In a business system, for example, one must consider the way people act and react. Often behavior is placed in this gray area because so little is known about what motivates it. Also, for some people in an organization it may not matter how something works, while others may be vitally interested. A manager may not care how a report gets to him or her, but an accountant would be concerned with all the steps in gathering data, preparing the report, and communicating it to the manager. Thus, in studying any transformation operation, it is important to know the reliability of the process and who is interested in it. This system will vary depending on the output.

OUTPUT

In one sense, output is the quality and quantity of the services and goods produced. In another sense, output may be thought of as the payments made for all the factors of production used. In the first sense, the entire system of the firm is designed to produce something that is desired in a market. Consumers want and seek out goods and services that will make their lives happier, more comfortable, healthier, longer, and so on. In order to produce those goods and services, the firm needs inputs. What may be output for one business may be input for another.

In the second sense, output is converted into revenue for the firm that is used to compensate the owners for the risks they have taken, management for its role in producing the revenue, and employees for their role in producing the good or service. It is also used to pay interest for the use of borrowed capital and wages for labor. Rent must be paid for the use of land; goods and materials used in production must be paid for; and taxes must be paid to the government. The output is the result of the system and is closely related to its objective. Output will accomplish or help to accomplish the specific objective if the system has been designed correctly.

FEEDBACK

All systems should include feedback. When an input is received in the system and undergoes a transformation operation, the result or output is then monitored and transmitted for comparison with a standard. If there is variation between the output and the standard, suitable action can be taken to correct the variation.

A business organization with many systems that range from very simple to very complex requires a much more complicated feedback network. Information must be communicated from person to person and from one part of the organization to another. In fact, the original data may be transformed many times before it reaches its final destination. Each of these transformations is subject to feedback.

Feedback can be defined as knowledge of results. Three basic types of feedback are needed: informational feedback, corrective feedback, and reinforcing feedback. The flow of information in an organization should be two-way from managers to workers as well as vice versa. In contrast to informational feedback, corrective feedback is evaluative and judgmental. An effective manager will not only point out mistakes but also get the individual worker headed in the right direction by means of corrective feedback. Positive consequences or reinforcements are one key to desired performance. In other words, reinforcing feedback is a prime means of achieving growth in job performance.

PRODUCTION MANAGEMENT

Products can be classified in many ways and their distribution can take many forms. However, the essence of production management is that the factors of production—land, labor, and capital—are transformed by management from raw materials into something finished, something to be used, or something to be sold profitably in order to keep the business in operation.

Before production can be started, the firm must determine what kind of product it can profitably produce. Management must decide what markets the product will satisfy, what materials it will contain, what processes will be required to form it, by what means it can be transported, and what quality and quantity of labor will be needed to produce it. Knowledge of all this provides direction to the planning and organization of manufacturing.

Once the firm has decided on the basic product or service to produce, design and development can begin.

Planning the product involves all parts of the business system. The marketing department may discover the need for a new or improved product, and the production department may then determine whether it can manufacture the product for sale at a given price. The finance department then decides whether the venture will be profitable and whether financing is available to cover the costs of development, manufacturing, and distribution. Such product planning determines whether development and design will go forward.

The process of refining a product to a finished form sheds further light on the problems of manufacture: the equipment, raw materials, and fabricated parts that will be required, as well as the flow of production. Planning for production actually starts as soon as the decision is made to develop and design a product.

Production management makes suggestions for manufacturing that will save time, effort, and money without impairing the design of the product. Production management is very complex. Decisions must be made about labors, money, machinery, and materials. Inventories of parts must be maintained, and proper machinery and equipment must be combined with labor. All these activities, although performed within the production system, must be closely coordinated with the overall system of the firm.

Production managers are involved in many diverse areas. They are concerned with all the peripheral aspects of production and must be able to manage workers, materials, and machines in a changing environment.

Why is productivity so important? The basic reason is that productivity is a measure of the efficiency with which a person, business, or entire economy produces goods and services. It is a key indicator of a nation's economic strength. In general, the concept of productivity refers to a comparison of the output of a production process with one or more of its inputs. Thus, productivity may mean different things in different situations.

Manufacturing is simply a special form of production by which raw and semifinished materials are processed and converted into finished products needed by consumers. In a broader and more basic sense, production is the transformation of inputs from human and physical resources into outputs desired by consumers. These outputs may be either goods or services. The production of services is often called operations management.

At the beginning of the twenty-first century, production and corporate management are becoming recommitted to one of the basics of business: making a better product faster and cheaper. This effort is important because the great bulk of assets used in manufacturing companies, including capital invested, people employed, and management time, are allotted to the production function of the business rather than to marketing or finance. This situation is also true in service firms.

The organization for manufacturing depends on the complexity of the products manufactured and the size of the company. In a large company the manufacturing organization has divisions such as engineering, production control, inspection, and purchasing. The success of a product depends on the proper development and management of the product.

CONCLUSION

Management is universal. When more than one person is concerned with a goal, there is need for a process by which this goal can be attained. Management is active in every part of business and at every level. Its functions are performed in every department and in every function of the business. The practice of operations management is a continuous process of problem solving and decision making. The functions of management are based on the ability to make decisions and then to carry out all the implications of those decisions.

SEE ALSO *Productivity*

BIBLIOGRAPHY

Kusiak, Andrew (1999). *Engineering Design: Products, Processes, and Systems.* San Diego: Academic Press.

Moody, Patricia E. (1999). *The Technology Machine: How Manufacturing Will Work in the Year 2020.* New York: Free Press.

Williams, Blair R. (1996). *Manufacturing for Survival: The How-to Guide for Practitioners and Managers.* Reading, MA: Addison-Wesley.

Janel Kupferschmid

OPPORTUNITY COST

One of the lamentable facts of life is that nobody can have everything that he or she wants. This is due, in part, to scarce resources. Whether a teenager with a part-time job or a wealthy businessperson, no single person owns all of the money in the world. Furthermore, there are only twenty-four hours in a day, and seven days in a week. Time and money are only two of the many resources that are scarce in day-to-day living.

Unfortunately, because of these limits, individuals have to make choices in using scarce resources. One can use his or her time to work, play, sleep, or pursue other options or, one can select some combination of possible activities. People cannot spend twenty-four hours a day working, twenty-four hours a day playing, and twenty-four hours a day sleeping. People can choose to spend

their salary on a nice house, an expensive vacation, or on a yacht, but they probably cannot afford all three. They must make choices with their limited resources of money.

In making choices for using limited resources, it is reasonable to evaluate the costs and benefits of all possible options. For instance, suppose one has been trying to decide how to spend the next few years of one's life. He or she has narrowed the options down to two: (1) working at a full-time job, or (2) becoming a full-time student. Going to school will cost approximately $12,000 per year in tuition, books, and room and board at the local state university for the next four years. In addition, he or she will forego the salary of a full-time job, which is $24,000 per year. This makes the total cost of going to school $36,000 per year. In return he or she gets the pleasure, social interaction, and personal fulfillment associated with gaining an education, as well as the expectation of an increase in salary through the remainder of his or her work life.

The question that must be answer is, "Do the benefits of education outweigh the costs?" If they do, school should be selected. If the costs are greater than the benefits, the full-time job should be kept.

An "opportunity cost" is the value of the next-best alternative. That is, it is the value of the option that was not selected. In the example, if the person had chosen to keep the job, then the opportunity cost is the benefit of going to school, including the intangible benefits of pleasure, social interaction, and personal fulfillment as well as the tangible benefit of an increased future salary for the person's remaining working life. If the person had chosen to go to school, then the opportunity cost is the $24,000 per year that would have been earned at the full-time job.

One way of visualizing this concept is through the use of a production possibilities curve—a graph that relates the tradeoff between two possible choices, or some combination of the possibilities. Consider a very simple possible economy for a country. This country can produce two goods: guns (i.e., defense) or butter (i.e., consumer goods). If this country has historically used all of its resources to produce guns then it may be willing to consider allocating some of its resources to the production of butter. Initially, the resources that are least effective in producing guns (e.g., farmland) will be reallocated to the production of butter. Thus, the country does not forfeit many guns to produce a relatively large amount of butter. However, as the country reallocates more resources to the production of butter it is decreasingly productive. At the extreme, when the country gives up the last of its production of guns, the resource is very good for producing guns and not very useful in the production of butter (e.g., a high-tech armaments production facility). Figure 1 demonstrates this situation graphically in showing an example of the production possibilities curve.

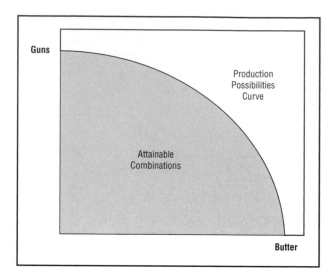

Figure 1

In Figure 1, everything on the curved line or in the gray area is a possible production combination of guns and butter in the simple economy. Any combination on the line uses all of the available resources, while any combination in the gray area is considered inefficient since it does not use all of the available resources. Any combination in the white area is impossible to achieve, given the country's resource limitations.

The idea that the country will initially reallocate its least productive resource to the production of the other good is known as the law of increasing opportunity cost. Thus, if the production of the initial ton of butter costs five hundred guns, then the next ton of butter, which uses resources that are better at producing guns, will cost more guns. The next ton of butter will cost still more guns, and so on. This is represented in Figure 1 by the changing slope of the production possibilities curve.

SUMMARY

Because resources are limited, choices must be made. When evaluating choices in this decision-making process, one attempts to select the best option. That is, one selects the option that offers the most benefit for the costs incurred, and which are possible given any constraints. This is true for individuals, businesses, or countries, though the decisions that each entity makes are vastly different. The second best option is called the opportunity cost and is what is given up when decisions are made.

SEE ALSO *Costs*

Denise Woodberry

ORGANIZATIONAL BEHAVIOR AND DEVELOPMENT

The discipline of organizational behavior is concerned with identifying and managing the attitudes and actions of individuals and groups, looking particularly at how people can be motivated to join and remain in the organization, how to get people to practice effective teamwork, how people can accomplish their jobs more efficiently, and how employees can be encouraged to be more flexible and innovative. Attention is brought to these attitudes and actions in order to help managers identify problems, determine how to correct them, and change behavior so that individual performance and ultimately organization effectiveness increase.

As a field of study, organizational behavior is built on a succession of approaches or ways of thinking about people. Since the early 1900s those who studied behavior in organizations have attempted to prescribe ways to effectively manage employees in order to achieve the organization's goals. The early approaches, referred to as the classical view, promoted increased management coordination of tasks, strict specialization and standardization of work tasks, a strict chain of command, and centralized decision making at the manager level. During the 1920s and 1930s the next new school of thought began to emerge, which was referred to as the human relations movement. By and large this movement began with the famous Hawthorne studies at the Western Electric plant that demonstrated how psychological and social processes could affect productivity and work behavior. This new way of thinking looked at organizational behavior by advocating a more people-oriented style of management that was more participative and oriented toward employee needs.

Contemporary organizational thought has shifted to a more integrative systems approach, which includes the consideration of external influences; the relationship of the organization with managers and employees; and organizational processes, which are the activities through which work gets accomplished. In other words, the best solution for the situation depends on many factors. The organization is depicted as a number of interrelated, interdependent, and interacting subsystems that are continually changing.

Those who managed by the classical approach emphasized the critical role of control and coordination in helping organizations to achieve goals. Those who managed by the human relations approach considered the risks of high levels of control and coordination, focusing instead on the need for flexibility. So where do today's managers fit in? A contemporary approach to management recognizes that there is no one best way to manage. Instead, management approaches need to be tailored to fit the situation.

The manager's role is to effectively predict, explain, and manage behavior that occurs in organizations. Particularly, managers are interested in determining why people are more or less motivated or satisfied. Managers must have a capacity to observe and understand the behavior patterns of individuals, groups, and organizations; to predict what responses will be drawn out by managerial actions; and ultimately to use this understanding and eventual predictions to effectively manage employees. Behavior can be examined on three levels—the individual, the group, and the organization as a whole. Managers seek to learn more about what causes people, individually or collectively, to behave as they do in organizational settings. What motivates people? What makes some employees leaders and others not? How do people communicate and make decisions? How do organizations respond to changes in their external environments?

Although it may be said that the responsibility for studying organizational behavior rests with researchers, assessing and increasing organizational effectiveness is a primary responsibility of managers. They need to collect data about the environment in which people work and describe events, behaviors, and attitudes in order to develop plans for changing and improving behavior and attitudes. Managers can begin to understand organizational behavior by accurately describing events, behaviors, and attitudes. How can this be accomplished?

Data can be gathered by observing situations, surveying and interviewing employees, and looking at written documents. These methods help to objectively describe events, behaviors, and attitudes—a first step in determining their causes and then acting on them.

By direct observation, for example, managers can attend meetings and then describe what is happening, such as who talks most often, what topics are discussed, or how frequently those attending the meeting ask for the managers' viewpoint on the topic. In addition, survey questionnaires could be sent to employees; these might provide concrete data about the situation, proving more useful than relying solely on personal perception of events. Sending the same questionnaire to employees each year could provide some insight into changes in behavior and attitude over time. Employees could also be interviewed in order to examine attitudes in greater depth. Some valuable information about attitudes and opinions may also be gathered by talking informally with employees.

Finally, data could be gathered from organizational documents, including annual reports, department evaluations, memoranda, and other nonconfidential personnel files. An analysis of these documents might provide some insight into the attitudes of employees, the quality of management, group interactions, or other possible reasons behind the problems or situation.

ORGANIZATIONAL DEVELOPMENT

Organizational development (OD) is a planned, ongoing effort by organizations to change in order to become more effective. The need for organizational change becomes apparent when a gap exists between what an organization is trying to do and what is actually being accomplished. OD processes include using a knowledge of behavioral science to encourage an organizational culture of continual examination and readiness for change. In that culture, emphasis is placed on interpersonal and group processes. The fact that OD links human processes such as leadership, decision making, and communication with organizational outcomes such as productivity and efficiency distinguishes it from other change strategies that may rely solely on the principles of accounting or finance.

The fact that OD is planned distinguishes it from the routine changes that occur in the organization, particularly through a more effective and collaborative management or organization culture with special emphasis on forming work teams. The focus on interpersonal and group processes to improve performance recognizes that organizational change affects all members and that their cooperation is necessary to implement change.

The forces compelling an organization to change can be found both inside and outside the organization. Internal forces toward change can affect changes in job technology, composition of the work force, organization structure, organizational culture, and goals of the organization. There are a variety of external forces that may require managerial action: changes in market conditions, changes in manufacturing technology, changes in laws governing current products or practices, and changes in resource availability.

An organization can focus OD change efforts in several areas: changes to structure, technology, and people using a variety of strategies for development. Some of the more common techniques for changing an organization's structure include changes in work design to permit more specialization or enrichment, clarification of job descriptions and job expectations, increase or decrease of the span of control, modification of policies or procedures, and changes in the power or authority structure. Another general approach to planned change involves modifications in the technology used as tools to accomplish work. The assumption behind enhancing technology is that improved technology or work methods will lead to more efficient operations, increased productivity, or improved working conditions. Examples of technological approaches to change include changing processes for doing work, introducing or updating computers or software, and modifying production methods. The third general approach to change focuses on the people in the organization. This approach is intended to improve employee skills, attitudes, or motivation and can take many forms, such as introducing training programs to enhance work skills, increasing communication effectiveness, developing decision-making skills, or modifying attitudes to increase work motivation.

ORGANIZATIONAL DEVELOPMENT STRATEGIES

Choosing the appropriate approach to organizational change depends on the nature of the problem, the objectives of the change, the people implementing the change, the people affected by the change, and the resources available. Several strategies are often thought of as effective techniques for organization development: reengineering, team building, total quality management, job enrichment, and survey feedback.

Reengineering is the sweeping redesign of organizational processes to achieve major improvements in efficiency, productivity, and quality. What makes reengineering so far reaching is that it goes beyond just modifying and altering existing jobs, structures, technology, or policies. This approach asks fundamental questions, such as: What is the purpose of our business? If this organization were being created today, what would it look like? Jobs, structure, technology, and policies are then redesigned according to the answers to these questions.

As part of the OD process, teams are used as a way of responding quickly to changing work processes and environments; they are encouraged and motivated to take the initiative in making suggestions for improving work processes and products. The term team can refer to intact work groups, new work units, or people from different parts of an organization who must work together to achieve a common goal. Often team building begins with a diagnostic session, held away from the workplace, where the team's members examine their strengths and weaknesses. The goal of team building is to improve the effectiveness of work teams by refining interpersonal interactions, improving communication, and clarifying goals and tasks in order to improve overall effectiveness in accomplishing goals. In ideal circumstances, team building is a continual process that includes periodic self-examination and development exercises. Managers must continually develop and maintain strategies for effective team performance by building trust and keeping lines of communication open.

Effective teams generally are attractive to others and are cohesive. The extent to which people want to belong to the team makes the team more attractive to others. If others see the team as cooperative and successful, they are more willing to belong. Teams are seen as less appealing if the group's members feel that unreasonable demands are made on them, if the group is dominated by a few members, or if competition exits within the group. A cohesive team exhibits strong interpersonal interaction among its members as well as, increased performance and goal accomplishments.

Reengineering efforts place a strong emphasis on teamwork with the intent of fostering collaboration to accomplish a goal, to resolve problems, and to explore alternatives. These teams can be traditionally managed by an appointed leader or manager or self-managed. Self-managed teams work without an official leader and therefore share responsibility for managing the work team. Managers continue to coach the team, develop strategies for improving performance, and provide resources even though they may not direct the daily activities of the team.

Total quality management (TQM) is the term used to describe comprehensive efforts to monitor and improve all aspects of quality within a firm. Teamwork plays a major role in quality improvement. Total quality management efforts could include employee training, identification and measurement of indicators of quality, increased attention to work processes, and an emphasis on preventing errors in production and service. What is the connection between TQM and OD? Both require a high degree of employee commitment, involvement, and teamwork. Many decisions must be made at the level where the work is accomplished, and managers must be willing to give employees this power. Managers empower employees to make decisions and take responsibility for their outcomes.

Job enrichment is often thought of as a technique of OD. It involves changing a job by adding additional tasks and by adding more responsibility. The widespread use of self-managed teams results in significant job enrichment. By the mere definition of self-managed teams, employees are now being asked to perform new tasks and exercise responsibilities within the team that they have not had to perform before.

Survey feedback involves collecting data from organizational members; these data are then shared with the members during meetings. In these meetings suggestions for formulating change are made based on the trends that emerge from the data. Survey feedback is similar to team building; however, the survey strategy places more emphasis on collecting valid data than on the interpersonal processes of work teams.

OD EFFORTS AND CHANGE

The success or failure of planned change depends not only on the correct identification of the problem but also on recognition of possible resistance to change. It is critical to the successful achievement of organizational development efforts for the manager to recognize the need for change, diagnose the extent of the problems that create this need, and implement the most effective change strategy. Successful OD efforts require an accurate analysis of the needed changes and an identification of the potential resistance to the proposed changes. Two critical points should be addressed concerning the areas in which organizations can introduce change. First, changes made in one area often trigger changes in other areas as well. Managers and those proposing the change must be aware of this systemic nature of change. Second, changes in goals, strategies, technology, structure, process, and job design require that people change. Serious attention must be given to the reactions of employees and possible resistance to changes in these areas.

People may be resistant to change for a number of reasons. They may feel that they will lose status, power, or even their jobs. People react differently to change; even if no obvious threat to their jobs exist, some people's personalities make them more uncomfortable than others with changes in established routines. The reasons for the change or the exact change that will take place may not be understood. However, even if the reasons for the change are understood, employees may not have a high level of trust in the motives of those proposing the change. Also, those who are the targets of the change may genuinely feel that the proposed change is not necessary.

Organizational culture could also influence people's reactions to OD efforts. Organizational culture can be thought of as the organization's personality. The culture is defined by the shared beliefs, values, and patterns behaviors that exist in the organization. In other words, "the way we do things around here." Some organizational cultures may even reward stability and tradition while treating those who advocate change as outsiders. Sometimes the definition and strength of an organization's culture are not evident until it undergoes change.

How can managers deal with resistance to change? An individual's low tolerance for change is largely a personal matter and can often be overcome with support and patience. Open communication can go a long way toward overcoming resistance to change based on misunderstanding, lack of trust, or different viewpoints. Those who will be affected by the change must be identified, and the reasons for and details about the change must be conveyed accurately to them. Keeping this information secret is bound to cause resistance. Also, the people who are the targets of the change should be involved in the change process. This is particularly important when true commitment to, or ownership of, the change is critical and those affected have unique knowledge about the processes or jobs that may be altered.

DOES ORGANIZATION DEVELOPMENT WORK?

Genuine efforts at organizational development require an investment of time, human effort, and money. Do the benefits of OD outweigh these costs? Reviews of a wide variety of OD techniques indicate that they tend to have a positive impact on productivity, job satisfaction, and other work attitudes. These reviews have also pointed out that OD efforts seem to work better for supervisors and managers than for blue-collar workers and that changes that use more than one technique seem to have more impact. There are several factors that increase the likelihood of successful OD efforts:

- Recognition of organization problems and influences. Before changes can be proposed, correct identification of the gaps between what an organization is trying to do and what is actually being accomplished must be made.

- Strong support from top-level managers. If managers at the higher levels in the organization do not provide obvious and open support for the OD efforts, the program is likely to fail.

- Action research that provides facts, not opinions, for decision making. Action research includes an identification of the attitudes and behaviors of employees and is part of an ongoing assessment of organizational behavior.

- Communication of what OD is and is not and awareness of why it is being used. The culture of the organization should be such that employees are aware of what organizational development is and is not so that it is not seen as a threat.

To thrive in the business environment of the twenty-first century characterized by a dynamic work force, rapid changes in technology, and the increasing volatility of the global environment, organizational development must be an ongoing effort. Encouraging continual examination and readiness for change must be part of the organization's culture.

SEE ALSO *Management; Management/Leadership Styles*

BIBLIOGRAPHY

Conner, Daryl R. (1998). *Managing at the Speed of Change: How Resilient Managers Succeed and Prosper Where Others Fail.* New York: John Wiley & Sons.

Hammer, Michael, and Champy, James (2003). *Reengineering the Corporation: A Manifesto for Business Revolution.* New York: HarperBusiness Essentials.

Hunt, V. Daniel (1996). *Process Mapping: How to Reengineer Your Business Processes.* New York: Wiley.

Johns, Gary (1996). *Organizational Behavior: Understanding and Managing Life at Work* (4th ed.). New York: HarperCollins College.

Kotter, John P. (1996). *Leading Change.* Boston, MA: Harvard Business School Press.

Schein, Edgar H. (1999). *The Corporate Culture Survival Guide: Sense and Nonsense About Culture Change.* San Francisco: Jossey-Bass.

Senge, Peter M. (1999). *The Dance of Change: The Challenges of Sustaining Momentum in Learning Organizations.* New York: Currency/Doubleday.

Cheryl L. Noll

ORGANIZATIONAL STRUCTURE

One of the most challenging tasks of a business may be organizing the people who perform its work. A business may begin with one person doing all the necessary tasks. As the business becomes successful and grows, however, there is generally more work, and more people are needed to perform various tasks. Through this division of work, individuals can become specialists at a specific job. Because there are several people who are often in different locations working toward a common objective, "there must be a plan showing how the work will be organized. The plan for the systematic arrangement of work is the organization structure. Organization structure is comprised of functions, relationships, responsibilities, authorities, and communications of individuals within each department" (Sexton, 1970, p. 23). The typical depiction of structure is the organizational chart. The formalized organizational chart has been around since 1854, when

Daniel McCallum became general superintendent of the New York and Erie Railroad, which is one of the world's longest railroads. According to McCallum, since the railroad was one of the longest, the operating costs per mile should be less than those of shorter railroad lines. However, this was not the case. To remedy management inefficiencies, McCallum designed the first organizational chart in order to create a sense of structure. The organizational chart has been described as looking like a tree, with the roots representing the president and the board of directors, while the branches symbolize the various departments and the leaves depict the staff workers. The result of the organizational chart was a clear line of authority showing where subordinates were accountable to their immediate supervisors (Chandler, 1988, p. 156).

TRADITIONAL STRUCTURES

Traditional organizational structures focus on the functions, or departments, within an organization, closely following the organization's customs and bureaucratic procedures. These structures have clearly defined lines of authority for all levels of management. Two traditional structures are line and line-and-staff.

LINE STRUCTURE

The line structure is defined by its clear chain of command, with final approval on decisions affecting the operations of the company still coming from the top down (Figure 1). Because the line structure is most often used in small organizations, such as small accounting offices and law firms, hair salons, and "mom-and-pop" stores, the president or CEO can easily provide information and direction to subordinates, thus allowing decisions to be made quickly (Boone and Kurtz, 2006, p. 259).

Line structures by nature are fairly informal and involve few departments, making the organizations highly decentralized. Employees are generally on a first-name basis with the president, who is often available throughout the day to answer questions and/or to respond to situa-

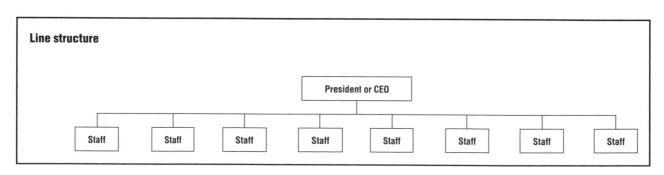

Figure 1

ENCYCLOPEDIA OF BUSINESS AND FINANCE, SECOND EDITION

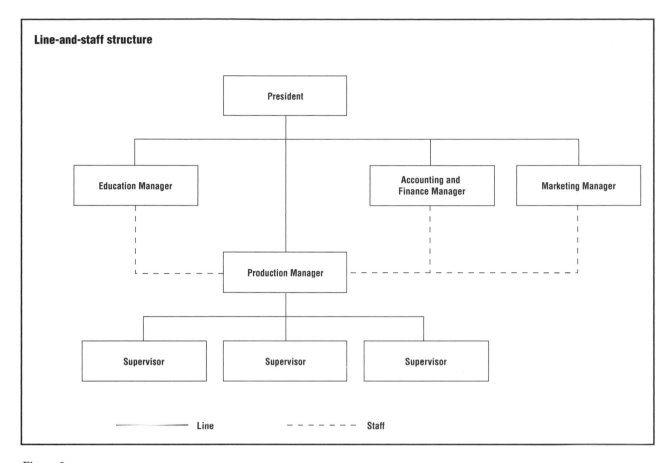

Figure 2

tions as they arise. It is common to see the president or CEO working alongside the subordinates. Because the president is often responsible for wearing many "hats" and being responsible for many activities, she or he cannot be an expert in all areas (Figure 1).

LINE-AND-STAFF STRUCTURE

While the line structure would not be appropriate for larger companies, the line-and-staff structure is applicable because it helps to identify a set of guidelines for the people directly involved in completing the organization's work. This type of structure combines the flow of information from the line structure with the staff departments that service, advise, and support them (Boone and Kurtz, 2006, p. 259).

Line departments are involved in making decisions regarding the operation of the organization, while staff areas provide specialized support. The line-and-staff organizational structure "is necessary to provide specialized, functional assistance to all managers, to ensure adequate checks and balances, and to maintain accountability for end results" (Allen, 1970, p. 63).

An example of a line department might be the production department because it is directly responsible for producing the product. A staff department, on the other hand, has employees who advise and assist, making sure the product gets advertised or that the customer service representative's computer is working (Boone and Kurtz, 2006, p. 259).

Based on the company's general organization, line-and-staff structures generally have a centralized chain of command. The line-and-staff managers have direct authority over their subordinates, but staff managers have no authority over line managers and their subordinates. Because there are more layers and presumably more guidelines to follow in this type of organization, the decision-making process is slower than in a line organization. The line-and-staff organizational structure is generally more formal in nature and has many departments (Figure 2).

MATRIX STRUCTURE

A variation of the line-and-staff organizational structure is the matrix structure. In today's workplace, employees are hired into a functional department (a department that

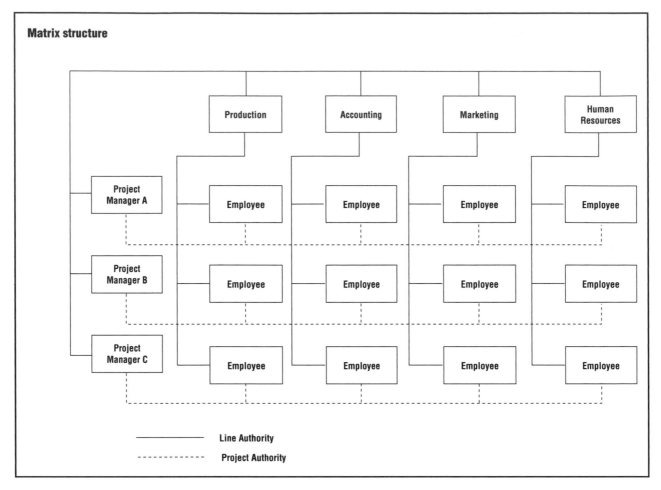

Figure 3

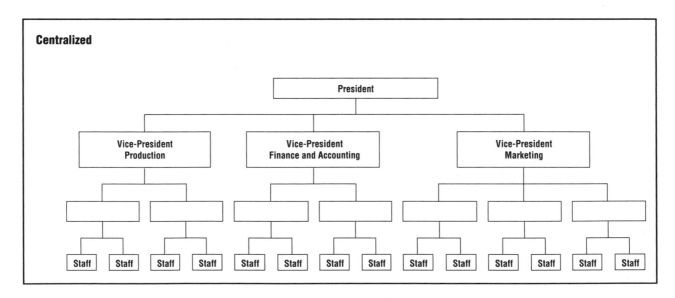

Figure 4

ENCYCLOPEDIA OF BUSINESS AND FINANCE, SECOND EDITION

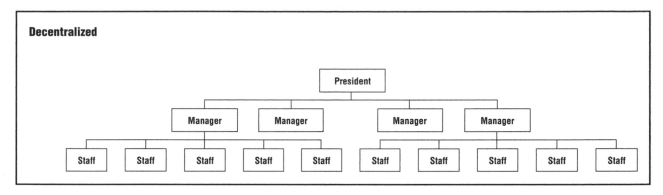

Decentralized

```
                            President
        ┌──────────┬──────────┴──────────┬──────────┐
     Manager    Manager              Manager      Manager
   ┌───┼───┐  ┌───┴───┐           ┌───┬───┐   ┌───┬───┬───┐
 Staff Staff Staff  Staff Staff  Staff Staff Staff Staff Staff
```

Figure 5

performs a specific type of work, such as marketing, finance, accounting, and human resources) but may find themselves working on projects managed by members of another department. Organizations arranged according to project are referred to as matrix organizations. Matrix organizations combine both vertical authority relationships (where employees report to their functional manager) and horizontal, or diagonal, work relationships (where employees report to their project supervisor for the length of the project). "Workers are accountable to two supervisors—one functional manger in the department where the employee regularly works and one special project manager who uses the employee's services for a varying period of time" (Keeling and Kallaus, 1996, p. 43).

Since employees report to two separate managers, this type of organizational structure is difficult to manage—especially because of conflicting roles and shared authority. Employees' time is often split between departments and they can become easily frustrated if each manager requires extra efforts to complete projects on similar timelines.

Because the matrix structure is often used in organizations using the line-and-staff setup, it is also fairly centralized. However, the chain of command is different in that an employee can report to one or more managers, but one manager typically has more authority over the employee than the other manager(s). Within the project or team unit, decision making can occur faster than in a line-and-staff structure, but probably not as quickly as in a line structure. Typically, the matrix structure is more informal than line-and-staff structures but not as informal as line structures (Figure 3).

CENTRALIZATION

Organizations with a centralized structure have several layers of management that control the company by maintaining a high level of authority, which is the power to make decisions concerning business activities. With a cen-

tralized structure, line-and-staff employees have limited authority to carry something out without prior approval. This organizational structure tends to focus on top-down management, whereby executives at the top communicate by telling middle managers, who then tell first-level managers, who then tell the staff what to do and how to do it. Since this organizational structure tends to be fairly bureaucratic, employees have little freedom. Centralized organizations are known for decreased span of control—a limited number of employees report to a manager, who then reports to the next management level, and so on up the ladder to the CEO (Figure 4).

DECENTRALIZATION

Because individual creativity can be stifled and management costs can be greater in a centralized organization, many organizations continue to downsize into a more decentralized structure. Decentralization seeks to eliminate the unnecessary levels of management and to place authority in the hands of first-line managers and staff—thus increasing the span of control, with more employees reporting to one manager. Because more employees are reporting to a single manager than before, the managers are forced to delegate more work and to hold the employees more accountable. Downsizing has also helped to change the flow of communication, so that top management hears staff concerns and complaints in a more direct manner and management has a more hands-on approach. The hands-on approach involves less bureaucracy, which means there is a faster response to situations that demand immediate attention. This structure also takes advantage of bottom-up communication, with staff issues being addressed in a timely manner.

The restructuring generally takes place at the midmanagement level. Because some middle managers have lost their jobs, been laid off, or simply taken advantage of early retirement and severance packages, their positions have been phased out, thus helping to reduce unnecessary

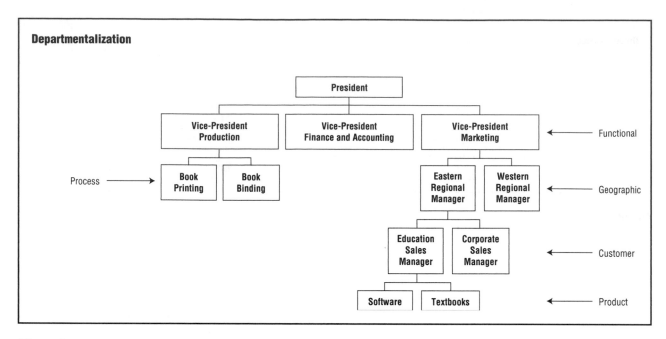

Departmentalization

Figure 6

---

costly salaries and increasing employee span of control. Many middle managers who stayed in their current "positions" found that their jobs have changed to being coaches, or team leaders, who allow their employees greater freedom in completing their work responsibilities (Csoka, 1995, p. 3).

The chain of command is the protocol used for communication within organizations. It provides a clear picture of who reports to whom. Quick decisions can be made in decentralized organizations because approval usually has to come only from the manager one level higher than the person making the decision. The chain of command involves line-and-staff employees, where the staff's job is completing the actual work and the line functions to oversee the staff (Figure 5).

DEPARTMENTALIZATION

Organizations can be divided into various departments, or units, with individuals who specialize in a given area, such as marketing, finance, sales, and so forth. Having each unit perform specialized jobs is known as departmentalization. Departmentalization is done according to five major categories (Figure 6): (1) *product*, which requires each department to be responsible for the product being manufactured; (2) *geographic*, which divides the organization based on the location of stores and offices; (3) *customer*, which separates departments by customer type, such as textbook companies that cater to both grade schools and community colleges; (4) *functional*, which breaks departments into specialty areas; and (5) *process*,

which creates departments responsible for various steps in the production process (Boone and Kurtz, 2006).

SEE ALSO *Management: Authority and Responsibility; Organizational Behavior and Development*

BIBLIOGRAPHY

Boone, Louis E., and Kurtz, David L. (2006). *Contemporary Business 2006*. Mason, OH: Thomson/South-Western.

Chandler, Alfred D., Jr. (1988, March/April). "Origins of the Organization Chart," *Harvard Business Review*, 88, 2, 156.

Csoka, Louis. (1995). Redefining the Middle Manager. *HR Executive Review*, 2(2), 3–5.

Keeling, B. Lewis, and Kallaus, Norman F. (1996). *Administrative Office Management*, 11th ed., Cincinnati, OH: South-Western Educational Publishing.

Litterer, Joseph A. , ed. (1980). *Organizations: Structure and Behavior*. New York: Wiley.

Sexton, William P. (1970). Organization Structure. In William P. Sexton, ed., *Organization Theories*. Columbus, OH: Charles E. Merrill.

Christine Jahn

OSHA

SEE *Occupational Safety and Health Administration (OSHA)*

OUTPUT

SEE *Operations Management*

OUTSOURCING IN THE BUSINESS ENVIRONMENT

Outsourcing (or contracting out) is a procedure involving the delegation of noncore operations or jobs from internal production to an outside resource. Outsourcing is a business decision that is often made to focus on core competences. A subset of the term, offshoring, also implies transferring jobs to another country, either by hiring local subcontractors or building a facility in an area where labor is cheap.

At one time, companies used outsourcing as a way to solve problems of high costs, redundant positions, and poor job skills. In the 1990s the reasons for outsourcing changed. Companies started to outsource to gain an advantage over their competitors. They wanted to improve their processes and build long-term relationships with their overseas partners. Currently, many companies see outsourcing as an indispensable business practice engrained in their corporate philosophy. Research has found that the next wave of globalization will be focused on outsourcing information technology (IT) departments.

When an organization decides that more personnel are needed, it must consider whether to hire more employees, contract workers, or outsource the functions. The focus is on efficiency and cost-effectiveness when deciding whether to outsource. This decision-making process involves internal analysis and evaluation, needs assessment and vendor selection, and implementation and management.

The procurement of services or products from an outside supplier or manufacturer in order to cut costs, outsourcing is one of the hottest emerging trends in business. Public and private sector agencies, lacking a clear, accurate way to measure the number of jobs in the United States that have been lost to outsourcing, or how many might be lost in the future, have yet to agree on the number of jobs that have been or will be affected. According to the Center for American Progress in 2004, the variation in the estimates shows the uncertainty and the difficulty in measuring these numbers.

As white-collar jobs move away with increasing regularity, a debate that once focused on the loss of manufacturing to foreign outsourcing once again became rampant. As companies rush to shed costs, outsourcing remains one of the fastest-growing solutions. Start-ups, encouraged by

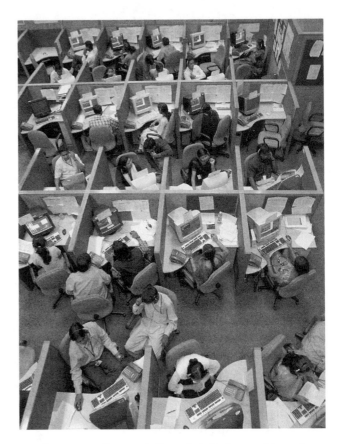

Employees at a call center in Bangalore, India, provide service support to international customers. © SHERWIN CRASTO/REUTERS/CORBIS

their venture investors, were turning to outsourcing just like some big multinational companies. While 15 percent of the 145 large companies surveyed by Forrester Research Inc. early in the twenty-first century revealed that outsourcing was a permanent part of the offshore strategy, an informal survey of venture capitalists suggested 20 to 25 percent of the companies invested had a comparable commitment.

The changing face of business and the need to stay ahead in the game forced companies to look for ways to reduce costs. As a result, outsourcing has become the solution for both the private and public sectors. The growing market and the globalization of business at the start of the twenty-first century have resulted in many changes for businesses all over the world. In 2004 Toyia Bulla wrote that the information age has created an increased level of competition in response to competitive pressures. Both private and public sector institutions have turned their attention to the core competencies relevant to their business or industry.

WHY OUTSOURCE?

The reasons for outsourcing are more than just reducing costs. Bulla suggested that companies outsource in order to:

- improve company focus
- gain access to world-class capabilities
- manage difficult or out-of-control functions
- reduce or control operating costs
- gain resources not otherwise available

Of course, another reason is to free internal resources for other purposes. For example, Datasweep Inc. (which was acquired by Rockwell Automation in 2005), a company whose software helps manufacturers manage factories more efficiently, hired eight programmers in India and China to translate its product into Japanese and connect its programs with software from SAP, a German software maker. Many other companies are reaping the same benefits from outsourcing through the use of educated but lower paid overseas employees performing the routine business tasks. Companies are able to use their U.S.-based staff to focus on innovation.

ADVANTAGES OF OUTSOURCING

Outsourcing is one of the most popular trends in business today because of the benefits it offers. For the company sending work out, the consumer, the economy in general, and for the country and company receiving the work, the economic benefits are clearly seen. The benefits of free trade are enormous: Companies pay less for goods and services, creating more wealth for shareholders, and causing prices to go down or remain the same for consumers, raising the standard of living for the whole country. For the country receiving the work, there is higher employment, more competition for skilled employees, higher revenues for the government in the form of payroll taxes, and a higher standard of living overall.

Companies saving as much as 80 percent on salaries lead to more wealth going to shareholders. This frees up valuable resources to be used in more productive ways. The cost savings enabled by these moves lower prices for consumers, increasing their buying power. Many people are concerned about the future and current implications of outsourcing, as the results of the surveys show. In some cases jobs, estimated at around 2 percent so far, are actually lost. Thus, supporting proponents of outsourcing suggest that this process hardly contributes to the unemployment problems caused by a weak economy. The findings of the U.S. Bureau of Labor Statistics showed that, in the first quarter of 2004, 70 percent of all job losses were a result of internal company restructurings,

such as bankruptcy, business ownership change, financial difficulty, and reorganization.

Next in the chain of benefits comes the company who contracts the work in a foreign country. The company benefits because it can increase its production, and hire more workers. The workers compete for higher paying jobs than they would have otherwise, raising their standard of living. The tremendous growth potential in some areas has the attention of PricewaterhouseCoopers, which pointed to the city of Coimbatore, India, as a center for growth because of its plan for a new IT park. The country and the city benefit from the new income, thus enabling improved infrastructure for the benefit of all.

One group of people often overlooked in this benefits discussion is the population of female workers with moderate education who are able to gain higher-paying positions because of the influx of business process outsourcing and IT-enabled services. This new ability has enabled a social empowerment previously denied young women, and eventually leads to a more equitable position in society.

DISADVANTAGES OF OUTSOURCING

Even though there are numerous advantages to outsourcing, there are just as many disadvantages. One main issue surrounding outsourcing is the number of American jobs being moved overseas. Another issue regarding outsourcing is the inefficiencies that it creates for businesses because of communication barriers. For example, customers may have a hard time getting their technical-support questions answered because of language differences. In some cases the vendor and customer are not available at the same time because of the difference in time zones. Unqualified employees and incompetent vendors are other problems that arise with outsourcing. Customers are not always satisfied with the quality or price of their services and companies can incur losses for their production and IT support. Outsourcing can cause a company to lose control of the part of the project that they have outsourced, especially if the company does not hire an experienced manager when outsourcing.

When IT security is outsourced, contractors overseas are given access to a company's business environment. Companies must control the level of access given to providers and verify that the employees hired overseas meet the company's screening standards. Companies that outsource must ensure that their data and networks are protected.

Outsourcing certain jobs in a business takes a great deal of time and planning and should be carefully evaluated. Eric Wahlgren found that the process of outsourcing can be burdensome for some small companies because they might "lack established processes that can be easily taught through a training manual" (2004, p. 41). The primary disadvantage of outsourcing for the countries overseas is the potential economic fallout of war. During the crisis between India and Pakistan in 2002, there was a decline in offshore contracts for several months.

FUTURE TRENDS

Predictions made by Forrester Research in 2002 indicated that about 3.3 million U.S. service jobs would be moved offshore by 2015. By the use of outsourcing, it was believed that 516,000 software and service industry jobs would be created from 2004 to 2009. Of these jobs, 272,000 would be offshore and 244,000 would stay in the United States. If outsourcing were not used, only about 490,000 jobs would be created. The next wave of globalization will be focused on sending entire IT departments overseas.

SUMMARY

At one time outsourcing was limited to such services as housekeeping, architectural design, food service, security, and relocation. Today, however, outsourcing has become a popular choice in business and industry. Although outsourcing began with small businesses, both large and small organizations are now outsourcing.

Outsourcing is no longer solely a domestic concern. Globally, organizations are considering and using outsourcing. With electronic commerce playing a significant role in the economy, outsourcing is expected to play a considerable role in the growth of electronic commerce.

BIBLIOGRAPHY

Ante, Spencer E., and Hof, Robert D. (2004, May 17). Look who's going offshore. *BusinessWeek Online*. Retrieved January 26, 2006, from http://www.BusinessWeek.com/@@cID9vo QQiqMVbBcA/magazine/content/04_20/b3883090_mz063. htm

Atkinson, Robert D. (May 2004). *Understanding the Offshoring Challenge*. Progressive Policy Institute, Policy Report. Retrieved February 15, 2006, from http://www.ppionline. org/documents/Offshoring_0504.pdf

Bulla, Toyia (2004). Outsourcing ain't what it used to be. *Wichita Business Journal*. Retrieved January 26, 2006, from http://www.aghlc.com/library/articles/outsourcing.htm

Duffy, Daintry (2004, March 1). Outsource with caution. *CSO*. Retrieved January 26, 2006, from http://www.keepmedia. com/pubs/CSO/2004/03/01/460202?from=search

Krishnakumar, Asha (2004, January 30). Growing confidence. *Hindu Online, 21*, 2. Retrieved January 26, 2006, from http://www.flonnet.com/fl2102/stories/2004013000360 9900.htm

Miller, Michael J. (2004, April 28). The benefits of offshore outsourcing. *PCmag.com*. Retrieved January 26, 2006, from http://www.pcmag.com/article2/0,1759,1573729,00.asp?kc= PCNKT0209KTX1K0100360

Outsourcing Institute. http://www.outsourcing.com

Outsourcing statistics in perspective. (2004, March 16). Retrieved January 26, 2006, from Center for American Progress Web site: http://www.americanprogress.org/site/ pp.asp?c=biJRJ8OVF&b=38081

Tesler, Basil (n.d.). Outsourcing IT development: Advantages and disadvantages. Retrieved January 26, 2006, from Intetics Web site: http://www.webspacestation.com/it-outsourcing-news/articles/outsourcing.html

Wahlgren, Eric (2004, April). The outsourcing dilemma. *Inc. Magazine*, p. 41.

Carolyn H. Ashe

P

PACKAGING

Product packaging used to be regarded as a rather utilitarian marketing activity whose functions were to protect the product and to provide a convenient way to transport and store the product along the marketing channel. Since the late twentieth century, packaging has evolved into one of the more important marketing tools to enhance sales of a product. Product packaging, including the labels on the package, is the last opportunity to influence the purchase decision of the consumer at the point of purchase.

Supermarket shelves are cluttered with multiple brands competing for the attention of shoppers. Some estimates are that the average consumer passes approximately 300 items per minute during a shopping trip to the supermarket. Depending on the product category, up to 70 percent of all brand purchase decisions are made at the point of purchase. Thus, the product package should be considered one of the most important components of a marketing effort. As such, it should be designed to attract the attention of the consumer and promote the sale of the product.

Product packaging can be defined as all the activities that:

- are involved in developing and producing the covering(s) and/or container(s) that provide protection for the product;
- facilitate product handling and storage;
- assist in the marketing and promotional efforts; and
- enhance the use of the product by the consumer.

The U.S. Department of Agriculture (USDA) estimated that over 8 cents out of every consumer food dollar was spent on packaging. In fact, many "companies spend more on packaging than on advertising" (Hoffman, 2006, p. 299). In 2004 the total global market for consumer packaging exceeded $350 billion, with a growth rate of about 4 percent annually over the previous ten years. With $98 billion in sales, North America accounted for 28 percent of the market. Food and beverages accounted for approximately 70 percent of all consumer packaging.

Most consumer products, large and small, require some packaging. Refrigerators and other large appliances are normally shipped in a cardboard carton to protect the finish of the unit, and may include internal packing material to protect the mechanical components. On the other hand, small screws are packaged in small plastic boxes or plastic pouches. Some packaging requires minimal information (refrigerator carton), some have selected informational copy (bread), and others have a significant amount of marketing promotional design and copy (branded cookies).

Often a given product will have several layers of packaging each with different functions. The product's primary container is the immediate package that holds the product (such as the plastic tube that contains the toothpaste). The primary container may then be placed in a secondary package for easier stacking, promotional communication, and display on merchandising shelves (the colorful box that holds the tube of toothpaste). Finally, there is the shipping carton—usually corrugated boxes—which will hold a quantity of the products for easy identification, transportation, handling, and storage (six-

577

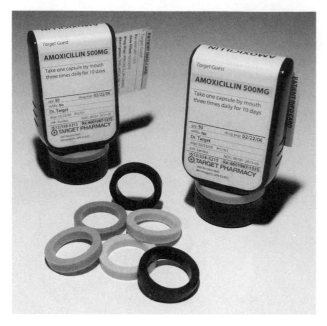

Prescription bottles and colorful rings make up the ClearRx prescription system. The bottle is flattened with easier-to-read lables and rings that can be color-coded for each family member.
AP IMAGES

dozen boxed tubes of toothpaste to a carton). It is easy to see that, in some cases, the cost of packaging a product (toothpaste) may far exceed the value of the actual product (the paste).

FUNCTIONS OF PACKAGING

Packaging is designed to serve one or more of several functions: product protection; easy and efficient handling and storage; providing useful identification and information; and contributing to the marketing and promotional efforts. Products need to be protected from rough handling, the environment, and spoilage. Most products need to move through a marketing channel from the end of the production line to the home of the final consumer. A number of different people and machines will physically handle (or mishandle) the product as it flows through the channel, which will likely involve loading and unloading, transporting, storing, and stocking the product on the vendors' shelves. The shipping containers must be designed to withstand all of the rough handling to which a package and product may be exposed.

The environment poses other dangers to products. Light (which affects milk and beer), moisture (chips and dried soups), temperature (ice cream and meats), and excessive movement (soft drinks) are a few of the environmental concerns for certain products. Another major con-

cern is to protect the product from tampering and, in some cases, shoplifting.

Size, weight, dimensions, and stackability are just a few of the factors that need to be considered in designing packaging for easy and efficient handling of the product. Some automated product handlers have limitations that may influence the package dimensions or weight. How efficiently the product uses allotted space in the tractor trailer can reduce shipping costs. How much space a product uses and how easy it is to stack on the shelf may determine if a retailer carries certain products. These are just a few of the logistical concerns that need to be considered when creating the packaging for a product.

Certain basic identification and information will need to be included on the various layers of packaging required for a product. The shipping cartons will need to identify such things as the product, the brand/company, the quantity, handling instruction, and any dangers associated with handling the product. The primary package and/or the secondary package, if that is what the consumer sees on the shelf, will need information such as: the brand name; quantity; contents or ingredients; suggested usage and instructions for use; any legally required information; "use-before" dates; and the Universal Product Code.

Finally, the marketing and promotional function should definitely be considered in designing the primary product packaging. This function is concerned with two characteristics of the package: attracting attention and the marketable attributes of the product. It is vital that the product's package attract the attention of shopping consumers. The use of color, shape, size, and graphic design are some of the common elements used to attract attention.

There are four situations when the ability of the package to attract the attention of shoppers is beneficial. In some cases the design, particularly the color graphics, allows for more efficient shopping by consumers who are looking for a brand they normally purchase. Shoppers do not initially read brand names, but rather they look for the familiar package and then confirm the brand name (such as Tide in the bright orange box). Being able to find preferred brands quickly will significantly reduce the chance of shoppers buying competing brands.

The second situation is when the package design is recognized from previous exposure of the consumer to promotional advertisements. Seeing the package on the shelf could cause consumers to consciously, or subconsciously, recall a favorable attitude toward the product and increase the likelihood of purchasing the product. It is also a common occurrence that the shopper wants to buy a given item but is not familiar with any of the brands. The package then becomes the primary source of informational and promotional communications, with the brand selection being based on the package. The fourth situation is the pure impulse purchase. In this case shoppers had not considered buying the product until the package attracts their attention and they are enticed to purchase the product.

In addition to drawing the attention of the shopper, the package itself may have attributes that significantly increase the attractiveness of buying a given brand. These are attributes that make the product easier to transport, store, and use, such as multiunit packaging; package dimensions that fit in the refrigerator door or on standard height shelves; and packaging which is easy to open, resealable, reusable, microwaveable and/or pourable. Some consumers also have a strong preference for environmentally friendly packaging that is recyclable or biodegradable. Any of these features may persuade a shopper to purchase a given brand of a product and should be considered when designing product packaging.

SEE ALSO *Marketing; Promotion*

BIBLIOGRAPHY

Arens, William F. (2006). *Contemporary advertising* (10th ed.). Boston: McGraw-Hill.

Hoffman, K. Douglass (2006). *Marketing principles and best practices* (3rd ed.). Mason, OH: Thomson South-Western.

Kotler, Philip, and Armstrong, Gary (2006). *Principles of marketing* (11th ed.). Upper Saddle River, NJ: Pearson Prentice Hall.

Lane, W. Ronald, King, Karen Whitehill, and Russell, J. Thomas (2005). *Kleppner's advertising procedure* (16th ed.). Upper Saddle River, NJ: Pearson Prentice Hall.

Lascu, Dana-Nicoleta, and Clow, Kenneth E. (2004). *Marketing frontiers: Concepts and tools.* Cincinnati: Atomic Dog.

Omega Research Associates. (2004). Executive summary. *Packaging Digest.* Retrieved March 4, 2006, from http://www.packagingdigest.com/pdf/Sum_RigidFlex.pdf

Pride, William M., and Ferrell, O. C. (2006). *Marketing concepts and strategies* (Rev. ed.). Boston: Houghton Mifflin.

Solomon, Michael R., Marshall, Greg W., and Stuart, Elnora W. (2006). *Marketing: Real people, real choices* (4th ed.). Upper Saddle River, NJ: Pearson Prentice Hall.

U.S. Department of Agriculture. (2000). Food marketing and price spreads: USDA marketing bill. *The economics of food, farming, natural resources, and rural America.* Retrieved February 28, 2006, from http://www.ers.usda.gov/Briefing/FoodPriceSpreads/bill/components.htm.

Wells, William, Moriarty, Sandra, and Burnett, John (2006). *Advertising: Principles and practice* (7th ed.). Upper Saddle River, NJ: Pearson Prentice Hall.

Thomas Baird

PARTNERSHIPS

The Uniform Partnership Act (UPA) defines a partnership as "an association of two or more persons who operate as coowners a business for profit." The creation, organization, and dissolution of partnerships are governed by state law. Many states have adopted the UPA. Partnerships that are created under the UPA are referred to as general partnerships. Business partners are fiduciaries to each other under the UPA. The law recognizes the partnership to be all of the partners acting together and does not recognize it as a separate distinct entity. It is a form of business enterprise.

PARTNERSHIP AS DISTINGUISHED FROM OTHER ENTITIES

General partnerships are distinguished from other types of entities. It is an association between two or more people who are seeking a profit. The partners share ownership, profits, losses, and liability. The partners decide who will manage the day-to-day affairs of the partnership. Each shares equally in the profits, losses, and liability for damages that may be incurred by employees or members of the partnership. Equal shares are assumed by the partners unless there is a written agreement that designates it differently.

Common law partnerships, joint ventures, and business trusts are examples of for-profit unincorporated associations. Nonprofit associations include benevolent associations, religious entities, and other organizations/associations that are organized for charitable, humanitarian, or educational purposes. A nonprofit organization focuses upon providing services to the general public, often while relying on government grants, private grant money, and/or donations from businesses or individuals—such as, for example, the American Red Cross. Nonprofit organizations have to register with the government as they do not have to pay taxes because of the benefits they contribute to society. They do not make any profits from this type of business and are usually run by a board of directors.

A partnership can be created by an express agreement or can be created on an informal basis based upon a handshake agreement. In civil law, partnership is a contract between individuals who agree to carry on an enterprise, combine their assets, and share the profits.

There are two types of partners. General partners have joint liability depending upon circumstances whereas liability of limited partners is limited to their investment in the partnership.

GENERAL PARTNERSHIPS

As stated previously, general partnerships can be formed with little formality. As more than one person is involved in this type of business, it is suggested that one should have a written partnership agreement which stipulates the terms of the partnership; authority of the partners; dissolution of the partnership; distribution of the profits and/or losses; amount of each partner's investment in the business whether it is cash, property, or services; and how disputes will be resolved. General partners are subject to unlimited personal liability with regard to the obligation of the partnerships. The partners are liable for any debts that may occur and any legal actions. The partnership can be created by agreement, proof of existence, and estoppels.

A partnership can be formed with an oral or written agreement. In order to avoid any misunderstandings among the partners, a written agreement is recommended. All powers, liabilities, and authorities of the partners are limited and controlled by the partnership agreement. Provisions are provided by the UPA, which governs the relationship of the partners to each other. These provisions can be in writing or inferred from a course of dealings. It is strongly recommended that the partners have a partnership agreement outlining the duties and responsibilities for each of the partners, how decisions will be made, and the dissolution of the partnership. For example, two individuals may enter a partnership by beginning to make dolls in their basement, selling the dolls to others, and splitting the profits and expenses. They have formed a partnership, even if neither of them has ever uttered the word *partnership*. The partnership agreement outlines the responsibilities and rights of the individual partners and is therefore considered a contract.

Unlike the other for-profit entities, no organizational documents must be filed with a public office, and the partnership agreement is not a public document. The only public documents that need to be filed by the partners are the registration of the business name. This requirement applies only if a name is used other than the real names of the partners.

PARTNERSHIPS AS A DISTINCT ENTITY

In most states, a partnership is a distinct entity. A partnership may sue, may be sued, and may own, hold, and/or convey real or personal property. The U.S. Bankruptcy Code treats partnerships as distinct entities. All forms of partnerships share some tax advantages as in many cases profits and losses can be passed directly to the partners without being taxed at the partnership level. For purposes of federal income tax, the partnership is not a distinct entity. Even though the partnership is required to file a federal tax return for informational purposes only, the partnership has no federal tax liability.

LIABILITY OF PARTNERS

Under a general partnership, each partner is liable for debts of the business. Based upon the percentage of ownership of each partner, all profits are taxed to the individual partners. Each partner is liable for debts, obligations, acts, or omissions of the other partners. The main drawback to a general partnership is the unlimited liability of each partner for the acts of the other.

Each partner may be held jointly liable for another partner's wrongdoing or tortuous act; an example is the misapplication of another person's money or property. If a partnership's assets are insufficient to satisfy a creditor's claim, the partners' personal assets are subject to attachment and the possibility of liquidating the business to pay off the business debts. Therefore, each partner is deemed the agent of the partnership and is held liable for a partner's debts.

DUTIES AND LIABILITY OF PARTNERS

Each partner has an equal right to participate in the management of the partnership and control of the business. Partners transact with one another and are not considered to be individuals but to be fiduciaries of one another. Any decisions and actions made should be agreed to by all partners. Each partner owes the other partners the obligation to act in good faith and loyalty. Every partner is an agent of the partnership; therefore, the acts and words of a partner may be imputed to the partnership.

DISSOLUTION OF THE PARTNERSHIP

Unless there is a partnership agreement outlining the circumstances on how the partnership comes to an end, a partnership will automatically terminate under the following conditions:

- the term fixed for existence expires
- a partner gives notice of his/her intention to dissolve the partnership
- a partner becomes insolvent or dies
- the court orders it to do so under certain circumstances of the UPA

Generally speaking, when any of the individuals of the partnership ceases to be associated with the partnership, the partnership is dissolved. This can be triggered by withdrawal, retirement, death, disability, or bankruptcy of a general partner. If there is a partnership agreement, the agreement will stipulate for these types of events with the share of the departed partner being purchased by the remaining partners in the partnership.

LIMITED PARTNERSHIPS

Limited partnerships are an association of one or more general partners and one or more limited partners with limited liability and with little or no managerial control. The limited partner is an investor only. The limited partners have limited liability as they are only liable to the extent of their investments. Limited partnerships must have at least one general partner who is responsible for all debts, liabilities, and any other obligations of the partnership. A limited partnership is a creation of the legislature and each state has statutes that permit and govern them. Limited partnerships are required to file documents with the state government, similar to the filing documents of a corporation. In most states, organization of a limited partnership requires statutory formalities and execution and filing of a certificate with the appropriate state authorities.

An advantage of a limited partnership over a general partnership is that partners limit their liability while preserving their rights to participate in profits and/or tax advantages. The statute shields a general partner's personal assets from obligations arising from the acts, omissions, or negligence of other partners and/or employees of the partnership. The limited partners may not participate in the management of the limited partnership, but they receive limited liability protection.

LIMITED LIABILITY PARTNERSHIP

The limited liability partnership (LLP) is a form of business organization combining elements of partnerships and corporations. Each individual state has its own laws governing the formation of LLPs. LLPs are available only in some states and only to professionals such as engineers, physicians, architects, lawyers, and accountants.

The liability of a LLP varies from state to state. The UPA, Section 306(c), serves as a guideline upon which many state laws are based, granting LLPs a form of limited liability similar to that of a corporation. Partners in an LLP can personally be liable for contract and intentional tort claims brought against the LLP. Profits of an LLP are distributed among the partners for tax purposes and the LLP is not taxed separately.

CONCLUSION

Partnerships offer a variety of structures to meet a variety of individual needs in organizing a business. Studying individual needs to best determine which partnership structure best fits for the situation is crucial in both organizing and building the business.

BIBLIOGRAPHY

Adamson, John E. (2006). *Law for business and personal use* (17th ed.). Mason, OH: Thomson South-Western.

Brown, Betty, and Clow, John E. (2003). *Introduction to business* (5th ed.). New York: Glencoe/McGraw-Hill.

Brown, Gordon W., and Sukys, Paul A. (2003). *Understanding business and personal law* (11th ed.). New York: Glencoe/McGraw-Hill.

Eggland, Steven S., Dalbay, Les R., and Burrow, James L. (2005). *Introduction to business* (5th ed.). Mason, OH: Thomson South-Western.

Anna Nemesh

PATENTS

A patent is the grant of a property right for an invention from the United States Patent Office to the inventor. A patent is granted for a twenty-year term beginning with the date on which the patent was filed in the United States, and U.S. patents are only effective in the United States, its territories, and its possessions. The language of the statute gives the inventor the right to exclude others from making, using, offering for sale, or selling the invention in the United States or importing the invention into the United States. Thus, the inventor is guaranteed the right to exclude others from making, using, offering for sale, selling or importing the invention.

The U.S. Constitution gives Congress the power to enact laws relating to patents in Article I, Section 8, which reads "Congress shall have power…to promote the progress of science and useful arts, by securing for limited times to authors and inventors the exclusive right to their respective writings and discoveries." Under this power, Congress has from time to time enacted various laws relating to patents. The first patent law was enacted in 1790. The law now in effect is a general revision that was enacted on July 19, 1952, came into effect on January 1, 1953, and is codified in Title 35 of the United States Code. The patent law specifies the subject matter for which a patent may be obtained and the conditions for patentability. The law established the United States Patent Office to administer the law relating to the granting of patents and contains various other provisions relating to patents.

In the language of the statute, an individual who "invents or discovers any new and useful process, machine, manufacture, or composition of matter, or any new and useful improvement thereof, may obtain a patent," subject to the conditions and requirements of the law. The term process, as defined by law, is a process, act, or method, and primarily includes industrial or technical

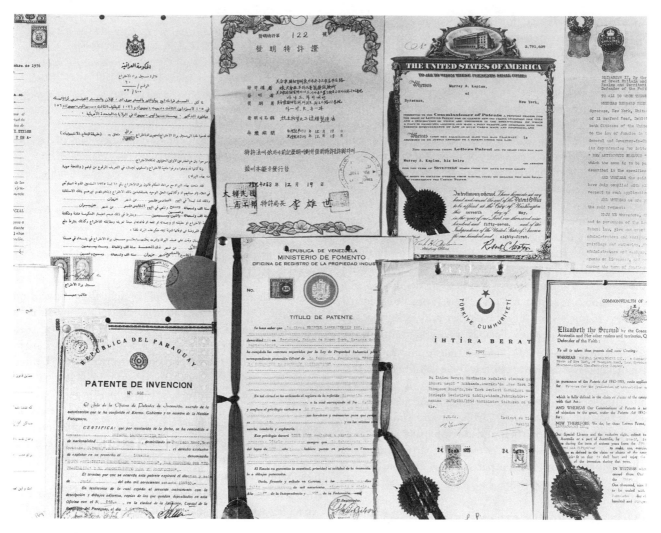

Patents certificates from different countries for many of the same compounds, a necessity for international production and distribution.
© **CHARLES E. ROTKIN/CORBIS**

processes. The term machine, as used in the statute, needs no explanation; the term manufacture refers to articles that are made and includes all manufactured articles. The term composition of matter relates to chemical compositions, which may include mixtures of ingredients as well as new chemical compounds. These classes of subject matter taken together include practically everything that is made by humans and the processes for making them. Consequently, the Atomic Energy Act of 1954 excludes the patenting of inventions useful solely in the utilization of special nuclear material or atomic energy for atomic weapons. The patent law further specifies that the subject matter must be useful. The term useful, in this context, refers to the condition of the subject matter having a useful purpose and also being operable. That is, a machine that will not operate to perform the intended purpose would not be called useful; therefore, the inventor would not be granted a patent. Recent interpretations of the statute by the courts have defined the limits of the field of subject matter that can be patented. Thus the courts have held that the laws of nature, physical phenomena, and abstract ideas are not patentable subject matter.

A patent may only be granted for the creation of a new machine, manufacture, and so on—not for the mere idea or suggestion of the new machine. A complete description of the actual machine or other subject matter for which a patent is sought must be filed with the U.S. Patent Office.

The U.S. Patent Office administers the patent laws as they relate to the granting of patents for inventions and performs other duties relating to patents. Examiners with the office review patent applications to determine if the applicants are entitled to patents under the law. If the inventor is so entitled, the Patent Office approves and issues the patent. Further, the Patent Office publishes not only a list of issued patents but also various other information concerning patents as well as records of assignments of patents. The U.S. Patent Office has no jurisdiction over questions of infringement and the enforcement of patents.

The major purpose of the U.S. Patent Office as an agency of the U.S. Department of Commerce is to grant patents for the protection of inventions and to register trademarks. Further, the Patent Office advises the Department of Commerce and other governmental agencies concerning intellectual property—patents, trademarks, and so on—as well as assisting inventors and businesses in matters concerning their inventions and corporate products. In essence, the United States Patent Office encourages the scientific and technical advancement of the country.

For further information see the United States Patent and Trademark Office website, http://www.uspto.gov/.

Randy L. Joyner

PEER REVIEW

SEE *Performance Appraisal; Performance Audits*

PENETRATION PRICING

SEE *Marketing; Marketing Mix; Pricing*

PERFORMANCE APPRAISAL

Performance appraisal (PA) is one of the important components in the rational and systemic process of human resource management. The information obtained through performance appraisal provides foundations for recruiting and selecting new hires, training and development of existing staff, and motivating and maintaining a quality work force by adequately and properly rewarding their performance. Without a reliable performance appraisal system, a human resource management system falls apart, resulting in the total waste of the valuable human assets a company has.

There are two primary purposes of performance appraisal: evaluative and developmental. The evaluative purpose is intended to inform people of their performance standing. The collected performance data are frequently used to reward high performance and to punish poor performance. The developmental purpose is intended to identify problems in employees performing the assigned task. The collected performance data are used to provide necessary skill training or professional development.

The purpose of the performance appraisal must be clearly communicated both to raters and ratees, because their reactions to the appraisal process are significantly different depending on the intended purpose. Failure to inform about the purpose or misleading information about the purpose may result in inaccurate and biased appraisal reports.

CRITICAL CRITERIA OF DEVELOPING A PA SYSTEM

In order for performance appraisal information to be useful, the PA system must be able to consistently produce

---

Partial graphic rating scale

Instructions: Carefully review employee's work performance during the period indicated above and write in the space an appropriate rating as described below.

1. Unsatisfactory. Performance outcomes are generally unacceptable.
2. Needs Improvement. Performance is deficient in certain areas and improvement is necessary.
3. Average. Performance results consistently meet requirements.
4. Good. Performance outcomes frequently exceed requirements.
5. Excellent. Performance outcomes consistently exceed requirements. Performance is of high quality in every aspect.

Evaluation Factors:

_____ 1. Quantity of work: Considering the volume of work achieved, is he/she at the acceptable level?
_____ 2. Quality of work: Considering accuracy, precision, completeness, and other quality of work, is he/she at the acceptable level?
_____ 3. Job knowledge: Does he/she have adequate skills and knowledge to perform the job?

Figure 1

reliable and valid results. Measurement items in the performance appraisal system must be designed in such a way that the results of rating are consistent regardless of the raters and the timing of the assessment.

Another critical criterion in developing a PA system is the validity of the measurements. It is important to make sure that the appraisal items are really measuring the intended performance or target behavior. If they are not, the PA system encourages the wrong kind of work behaviors and produces unintended, frequently negative, organizational outcomes. For instance, if the number of traffic violation tickets issued is an item in performance appraisal of police officers, it encourages them to sit on a corner of a street and pull over as many violators as possible during heavy traffic hours. The true purpose of a police force, which is public safety, may become secondary to issuing a large number of tickets for many officers.

WHAT TO EVALUATE

The first important step in developing a PA system is to determine which aspects of performance to evaluate. The most frequently used appraisal criteria are traits, behaviors, and task outcomes.

Traits. Many employees are assessed according to their traits, such as personality, aptitudes, attitudes, skills, and abilities. Traits are relatively easy to assess once a rater gets to know ratees. But traits are not always directly related to job performance. Trait-based assessment lacks validity and thus frequently raises legal questions.

Behaviors. For many jobs, performance is so broadly defined or so conceptual in nature—such as ensuring public safety in the police department—that it is hard to come up with reliable performance measures. In such cases, desirable behaviors can be identified and assessed in the belief that such behaviors lead to successful performance. Such behavior-focused assessment encourages employees to adopt desirable behavioral patterns in the workplace.

Task Outcomes. When information about task outcomes is readily available, it is the most appropriate factor to use in evaluating performance. When an organization has a clear and measurable goal as in the case of a sales force, this approach is recommended. However, it has its own pitfalls. There is a problem if employee behaviors are not directly related to the task outcome. Too narrow a focus on measuring outcome only sometimes results in unintended negative consequences. When sales staff narrowly focus on target sales figures to increase their performance measure, for example, they are encouraged to help a few large-volume customers and to ignore many smaller buyers. This may result in poor customer service on the floor.

WHO EVALUATES?

The most common raters of performance are employees' immediate supervisors, who are usually in the best position to know and observe the employees' job performance. They are also responsible for employees' work. Their evaluation is a powerful tool in motivating employees to achieve successful and timely completion of tasks. However, as a result of working together over a long time with the same employees, the immediate supervisor may build up a fixed impression about each employee and use it every time he or she has to evaluate performance.

Some companies find that subordinates are in an excellent position to observe and evaluate their managers' performance, especially when it comes to measuring effective management of their department. While there is merit in asking subordinates to evaluate how they are managed, such evaluation may turn into a popularity contest. Accurate and objective assessment may not be obtained if employees are fearful of possible retaliation from their supervisors. Anonymity of the evaluators is key to the successful use of subordinates for objective evaluation.

Other raters who are frequently used in some companies include peers, customers, and the employees themselves. Peer evaluation is particularly useful when teamwork and collegiality are important to successful task performance. Peer pressure is sometimes a powerful motivator in encouraging teamwork among members. Customer satisfaction is vital to a company's success and can be used in performance appraisal. Many companies systematically collect performance information from customers, typically through anonymous surveys and interviews. Self-assessment is also a useful means, especially when the performance appraisal is intended to identify the training and development needs of potential employees.

Each of these raters contributes to assessing certain aspects of performance. Since job performance is multidimensional in nature, it is important to use different raters or a combination of multiple raters depending on the goal of a performance appraisal system. This multirater evaluation, or so-called 360-degree feedback system, is becoming increasingly popular among many American corporations, including General Electric, AT&T, Warner Lambert, and Mobil Oil.

PA METHODS

To ensure the reliability and validity of a PA system, a company must design the evaluation process carefully and

---

Behaviorally anchored rating scale

Job: Project Manager

Scale values	Anchors
9	Develops a comprehensive schedule, documents it, obtains required approvals, and distributes it to all concerned.
8	Plans, communicates, and observes target dates and updates the status of operations relative to plans, making schedule modifications as quickly as necessary
7	Experiences minor operational problems but still communicates effectively, laying out all parts of the job and schedules for each
6	Usually satisfies time constraints, with time and cost overruns coming up infrequently
5	Makes list of due dates and revises them but is frequently surprised by unforeseen events
4	Has a sound plan but neglects to keep track of target dates or to report schedule slippages or other problems as they occur
3	Plans poorly, with ill-defined, unrealistic time schedules
2	Has no plan or schedule of work and no concept of realistic due dates
1	Fails consistently to complete work on time because of no planning; expresses no interest in how to improve

Figure 2

---

develop appropriate measuring scales. Among the many assessment methods developed by human resource management experts, commonly used ones include the Graphic Rating Scale, Behaviorally Anchored Rating Scale, Narrative Technique, Critical-Incident Method, Multiperson Comparison Method, Forced Choice Method, and Forced Distribution Method.

The Graphic Rating Scale is the simplest and most popular method for performance appraisal. As shown on Figure 1, the Graphic Rating Scale offers a list of areas related to job performance. A manager rates each employee on the listed areas according to a numerical score. Although this method is relatively simple and quick to complete, some experts question its validity and reliability. Without elaborate description, appraisal items and scores are subject to various interpretations of raters.

In order to overcome pitfalls of the Graphic Rating Scale, numerous other methods have been developed. The Behaviorally Anchored Rating Scale (BARS), illustrated in Figure 2, offers rating scales for actual behaviors that exemplify various levels of performance. Because raters check off specific behavior patterns of a ratee, PA results of BARS are more reliable and valid than those of the Graphic Rating Scale. Human resource managers must carefully analyze each job and develop behavior patterns pertinent to various levels of performance for the job before they use the BARS.

The Narrative Technique is a written essay about an employee's job performance prepared by a rater. The essay typically describes the rate's job-related behaviors and performance. Without standard performance description, it is a cumbersome task for raters to write an essay for several employees. For example, a rater can be asked to describe the activities, achievements, and level of performance of the employee in a completely open-ended format (unstructured narration). Alternatively, the rater can be provided with some structure to use in the evaluation; for example, "Describe briefly the activities, achievements, and level of performance of the staff member in the following areas: (1) work habits, (2) planning and organizing the tasks, (3) management skills, communications, and development of others."

The performance review form at a college asks an evaluator to describe the activities, accomplishments, and creative works of the professors in the areas of (1) teaching and (2) research/creative activity. A dean of the college writes about the professor's teaching performance: "Dr. Michael Johnson has been nominated by his students for the Outstanding Teacher Award several times during his service. He introduced many teaching innovations into his classes. His teaching record is exemplary." In the area of creative activity, the dean writes, "Dr. Johnson has a strong and productive research record with a defined focus in organizational leadership. His research has been recognized with several awards given by professional organizations. His creative activity is exemplary."

Similar to the Narrative Technique is the Critical-Incident Method, which involves keeping a running log of

Paired comparison method of employee evaluation

For the quality of work: Performance in meeting quality standards

	Employees that are rated:				
As compared to:	**Amy**	**Barbara**	**Charlie**	**Dave**	**Elaine**
Amy		+	+	−	−
Barbara	−		−	−	−
Charlie	−	+		+	−
Dave	+	+	−		+
Elaine	+	+	+	−	

Note: Barbara ranks the highest.

Figure 3

effective and ineffective job performance. For example, the PA log of an employee, Mr. Campbell, contains Unsatisfactory Incidents as follows: 1/28/2000: "Refused to try a new work procedure," and 2/15/2000: "Argued with a customer about the origin of error in the paperwork." The log also contains Satisfactory Incidents as follows: 1/20/2000: "Volunteered to help Charlie complete his assignment in time"; 2/19/2000: "Trained new employees in safety regulations."

The Multiperson Comparison Method asks raters to compare one person's performance with that of one or more others. It is intended to effectively eliminate the possibility of giving the same rating to all employees. In order to separate performance scores among multiple employees, the Forced Choice or Forced Distribution Methods are adopted. Raters must choose one high performer from the list of employees or distribute certain scores to employees at different ranks. For example, only one top person will get 40 percent, two second-rank persons 20 percent, and the bottom one person 10 percent. The Paired Comparison Method is a special case of the Multiperson Comparison Method. Everyone in the evaluation pool is compared against everyone else as a pair and recorded "plus" or "minus" when the target ratee is better or worse, respectively, than his/her comparison. The final performance ranks are determined by the number of positives. Figure 3 provides an example.

SUBJECTIVITY AND OBJECTIVITY

Accuracy is critical to performance appraisal. In order to obtain accurate performance information, raters must provide objective and unbiased ratings of employees. However, because it is almost impossible to develop a perfectly accurate performance checklist, managers' subjective opinions are frequently called for. Many companies use some combination of subjective and objective assessment for actual performance appraisal.

Yet there are numerous problems in the actual assessment of employee performance, mainly due to rater bias. Some raters tend to rate all employees at the positive end rather than to spread them throughout the performance scale; this is called leniency. Alternatively, central tendency, which places most employees in the middle of the scale, also raises concern about possible appraisal error.

Another common error in performance appraisal is the halo effect. This occurs when a manager's general impression of an employee, after observing one aspect of performance, influences his/her judgment on other aspects of the employee's performance.

Researchers have found that personal preferences, prejudices, appearances, first impressions, race, and gender can influence many performance appraisals. Sometimes raters' personal opinions or political motives creep into the performance appraisal process. They intentionally inflate or deflate performance ratings of certain employees as a way to punish them or promote them out of the department.

Using unreliable and unvalidated performance appraisals may cause a legal problem. A number of court cases have ruled that the performance appraisal systems used by many companies were discriminatory and in violation of Title VII of the Civil Rights Act.

In order to avoid legal problems, companies must develop an appraisal system based on careful job analysis and establish its reliability and validity. They must give clear written instructions to raters for completing evaluations and provide them adequate training if necessary. The company must allow employees to review the results of the appraisals. Human resources departments must play a key role in the development and implementation of an effective performance appraisal system.

SEE ALSO *Management; Motivation*

BIBLIOGRAPHY

Bernardin, H. J., Kane, J. S., Ross, S., Spina, J. D., and Johnson, D. L. (1996). Performance Appraisal Design, Development, and Implementation. In Gerald R. Ferris, Sherman D. Rosen, and Darold T. Barnum (Eds.), *Handbook of Human Resource Management*, Cambridge, MA: Blackwell, 462–493.

Cascio, W. F. , and Aguinis, Herman (2005). *Applied Psychology in Human Resource Management* (6th ed.). Upper Saddle River, NJ: Pearson Prentice-Hall.

Cawley, B. D., Keeping, L. M., and Levy, P. E. (1998). Participation in the Performance Appraisal Process and Employee Reactions: A Meta-Analytic Review of Field Investigations. *Journal of Applied Psychology*, 83(4), 615–633.

DeNisi, A. S., Robbins, T. L., and Summers, T. P. (1997). Organization, Processing, and Use of Performance Information: a Cognitive Role for Appraisal Instruments. *Journal of Applied Social Psychology*, 27, 1884–1905.

Greller, M. M. (1998). Participation in the Performance Appraisal Review: Inflexible Manager Behavior and Variable Worker Needs. *Human Relations*, 51:8, 1061–1083.

Grote, D. (1996). *The Complete Guide to Performance Appraisal*, New York: AMACOM Book Division.

Illgen, Daniel R., Barnes-Farrell, Janet L., and McKellin, David B. (1993). Performance Appraisal Process Research in the 1980s: What Has It Contributed to Appraisals in Use? *Organizational Behavior and Human Decision Processes*, 54, 321–368.

Jawahar, I. M., and Stone, T. H. (1997). Influence of Raters' Self-Consciousness and Appraisal Purpose on Leniency and Accuracy of Performance Ratings. *Psychological Reports*, 80: 323–336.

Jourdan, J. L., and Nasis, D. B. (1992). Preferences for Performance Appraisal Based on Method Used, Type of Rater, and Purpose of Evaluation. *Psychological Report*, 70: 963–969.

Kaplan, R. E. (1993). 360-Degree Feedback Plus: Boosting the Power of Co-Worker Ratings for Executives. *Human Resource Management*, 32, 299–314.

Kravitz, D. A., and Balzer, W. K. (1992). Context Effects in Performance Appraisal: a Methodological Critique and Empirical Study. *Journal of Applied Psychology*, 77, 24–31.

Mount, M. K., Judge, J. A., Scullen, S. E., Sytsma, M. R., and Hezlett, S. A. (1998). Trait, Rater, and Level Effects in 360–Degree Performance. *Personnel Psychology*, 51(3), 557–577.

Peach, E. B., and Buckley, M. R. (1993). Pay for Performance. In H. J. Bernardin and J. Russell (eds.), *Human Resource Management: An Experiential Approach* (482–515). New York: McGraw-Hill.

Sanches, J. I., De La Torre, P. (1996, December). A Second Look at the Relationship Between Rating and Behavioral Accuracy in Performance Appraisal. *Journal of Applied Psychology*, 81, 3–10.

Schneier, C. E. and R. W. Beatty (1979, August). Developing Behaviorally Anchored Rating Scales (BARS). *The Personnel Administrator*, 59–68.

Smith, H. P., and Brouwer, P. J. (1997). *Performance Appraisal and Human Development*, Reading, MA: Addison-Wesley.

Lee Wonsick Lee

PERFORMANCE AUDITS

Performance audits, the public version of operational audits, are conducted to determine if an entity's operations, programs, or projects are functioning effectively and efficiently to achieve goals established. All levels of public administration in the United States—from municipalities to the federal agencies—undergo performance audits. Since all levels of government in the United States have some federal funding, the professional standards for performance audits established by the U.S. Government Accountability Office (GAO) are required for auditors who perform such engagements. Government auditing standards include the following definition for a performance audit:

> An objective and systematic examination of evidence to provide an independent assessment of the performance and management of a program against objective criteria as well as assessments that provide a prospective focus or that synthesize information on best practices or cost-cutting issues. (GAO, 2003, p. 21)

Accountability is the key motivation for performance audit engagements. The performance audit, therefore, is perceived to be a valuable means of determining if goals have been achieved, as well as valuable in identifying what is needed to improve program operations.

The specific objectives of such audits, as noted in the GAO standards, are varied. Among objectives are those relating to program effectiveness, economy and efficiency in the use of resources, internal control, extent of compliance with legal requirements and policies, and prospective analyses.

NATURE OF PROFESSIONAL GUIDANCE PROVIDED

The GAO professional standards for performance audits are categorized as general, field, and reporting. The general standards established by the GAO apply to not only performance audits, but also to financial and attestation engagements. There are field and reporting standards, however, specifically for performance audits. The authority of the standards is identified in a footnote that states:

Requirements in generally accepted government auditing standards (GAGAS) are identified by statements that include the word "should." Auditors are expected to comply with these requirements if they apply to the type of work being performed. (GAO, p. 5)

General Standards. The general standards that guide government auditors, as well as other independent auditors, stated in summary style, are:

- *Independence:* The auditor and his/her firm must be free, in both fact and appearance, from all types of impairments of independence.

- *Professional judgment:* The auditor should use professional judgment in planning and performing all audits.

- *Competence:* Those individuals assigned to the audit must possess adequate professional competence for the tasks required to complete the engagement.

- *Quality control and assurance:* Audits must be performed by auditors whose organizations maintain an internal quality control system and have an external peer review on a regular basis.

As noted, these general standards are the same for all types of audits that are GAO engagements. These general standards impose responsibility on both the audit entity and the individual auditors to ensure that those who participate in such audits are independent in fact and appearance, able to make good judgments, and qualified for engagement tasks. Furthermore, it is expected that the entity that employs auditors for such audits maintains oversight of the work performed to be assured that the quality of performance is adequate and the tasks have been completed.

Field Standards. The field standards deal with planning; supervising staff; collecting evidence that is sufficient, competent, and relevant; and preparing adequate audit documentation.

Planning: All aspects of the work of the audit must be adequately planned. While planning for a performance audit is a continuous process, initial planning is important. Decisions to be made initially include determining:

1. Audit objectives, which state operationally what is intended to be accomplished, must be recorded. Audit objectives, for example, may be the cost-effectiveness of program performance or the extent to which specific organizational goals are being achieved.

2. The scope, which is established by determining the boundaries for the engagement and should reflect the audit objectives.

3. The methodology, which comprises what is to be done to gather and analyze data to achieve the objectives.

Supervision: During an audit, staff must be properly supervised. The tasks of supervision primarily include providing appropriate guidance to staff members, maintaining alertness to significant problems that arise, reviewing the work while it is in progress, and providing useful on-the-job training.

Evidence: The major task of the auditors' work relates to gathering evidence that is sufficient, competent, and relevant to the data for meeting the objectives of the audit. Ultimately, it is the evidence that supports the judgments and conclusions relevant in the report.

Auditors, to meet the objectives of their audits, are able to use different types of evidence. Commonly used evidence sources include: direct observation of individuals, properties, events; documents, such as memoranda, charts, reports; inquiries, interviews, questionnaires; and analytical evidence that includes computations and disaggregating information for detailed assessment. Auditors must make a professional judgment about the sufficiency of their evidence in relation to the objectives earlier identified. There are no quantified requirements for the amount of evidence.

Audit Documentation: Auditors are expected to prepare and maintain sufficient documentation to provide a complete account of the planning, conducting, and reporting related to the audit. Everything from planning to conclusions must be documented. The supervision, as well as other reviewers of documentation, must determine if the work performed is satisfactory or needs to be extended. Quality control at the firm, which is confirmed through periodic outside peer reviews, is primarily based on audit documentation. A framework for the assessment of audit documentation is the standards established by the GAO.

Reporting. There are two reporting standards, communicating results and content.

Communicating Results. An audit report is to be appropriate for its intended recipient and is to be provided in writing or in some other retrievable form. Since the government has responsibility for maintaining public accountability, all audit reports must be retrievable, and, therefore, available to the citizens.

Content. A report of a performance audit is expected to include the objectives, scope, and methodology, as well as the audit results, with details of conclusions, recommendations, and acknowledgment of adherence to GAGAS. Since a draft of the report is to be shared with management of the agency under audit, the final report includes the responses of those who reviewed the draft and the outcome of the issues, if any, that needed to be resolved. Views of the responsible persons in the audited agency are to be reported. If there is any privileged or confidential information that has been omitted, a disclosure of this matter is to be included in the report.

PERFORMANCE AUDITS AT THE FEDERAL LEVEL

The Office of the Auditor General of Canada reported in a peer review on the performance audit practice in the U.S. GAO office that in 2004 the GAO began work on 773 new performance audit engagements. The report noted: "However, the total number of performance audit products issued in 2004 may be more than 1,000 since some engagements can result in multiple products and some products issued in 2004 were initiated in prior years." The performance audit practice of the GAO was given a "clean opinion" on their quality control system. The review team, however, made some suggestions, which were summarized in these words:

Distinguishing between audit and non-audit services. Provide further guidance to staff on the distinction between audit and non-audit services, the evidentiary standards appropriate for each form of product, and on the process for reconsidering a determination.

Strengthening reporting. Provide additional details on the sources of critical information and the implications of scope and methodological choices.

Reviewing the quality assurance system for further efficiencies. Review all the requirements to identify those that may not contribute significantly to audit quality.

Streamlining the documentation requirements. Expand the use of the streamlined documentation regime.

Making the inspection program more efficient. Focus the inspection program on the management of key risks facing the performance audit practice. (Canada, Office of the Auditor General of, 2005, p. 9)

THE VALUE OF PERFORMANCE AUDITS

Performance audits are potentially valuable to both the agencies for whom such audits are undertaken as well as for the citizens of the governmental unit.

Value to agency audited. As noted earlier, a draft of an audit team's report is presented to officials responsible for management. Such a draft is discussed with management and revised accordingly before it is issued to the appropriate parties. Auditors are expected to return to the agency after giving management sufficient time to implement any recommendations contained in the audit report. The purpose of this follow-up visit is to assess the degree to which management has addressed the findings contained in the audit report.

Value to citizens. Reports of governmental activity are generally available to the citizens, except in infrequent instances where confidentiality is judged necessary because of security or other sensitive matters. Citizens seek accountability for tax revenues. Objective results of performance audits are reliable evidence for enlightening citizens who are asked to vote on legislation related to increasing taxes, for example.

Performance audits are posted at states' Web sites, and are accessible through state government offices (keying "state of" followed by a state's name at a search engine is sufficient for reaching governmental offices). Georgia, Oklahoma, and Washington are examples of states with auditors who post performance audits that are clearly identified as performance audits.

The U.S. GAO does not identify performance audits in the title of such reports or make specific reference to the term *performance audit.* Searching for examples of such audits, therefore, at the GAO Web site is not direct; it is necessary to read the titles and make a judgment. According to staff at GAO in September 2005, most GAO reports are considered to be performance audits, even though explicit identification as such is not included in the report. There is generally a statement that the work was done in accordance with the publication *Government Auditing Standards.* Inasmuch as *Government Auditing Standards* includes attestation engagements that are described as "an examination, review, or agreed-upon procedures," there is some uncertainty in determining if a report is a performance audit report.

A PARALLEL AUDIT IN BUSINESS

Business has a parallel type of audit to the audit herein discussed. Outside of governmental units, however, such an audit is usually called an operational audit. Departments of internal audit in companies are generally responsible for operational audits. The guidance for such audits is similar, to a considerable extent, to that for the performance audit. Guidance for such operational audits is provided by the Institute of Internal Auditors.

The results of such nongovernmental audits, however, are not shared with the public. The results are shared with the unit of the business undergoing the operational audit and possibly with top management and the board of directors. The requirements for disclosure of internal control weaknesses related to financial reporting in annual financial reports that became effective as of December 15, 2005, does mean that some matters that might be operational weaknesses related to financial reporting are disclosed.

SEE ALSO *Human Resource Management*

BIBLIOGRAPHY

Campbell, Mary (2003, Fall). Restoring trust in government: A cost-effective approach to the cry for "accountability." *The Journal for Quality and Participation, 26*(3), 44.

Canada, Office of the Auditor General of. (2005, April). *International peer review of the performance audit practice of the U.S. government accountability office.* Ottawa, Ontario, Canada. Available from http://www.gao.gov/peerreviewrpt2005.pdf, accessed January 6, 2006.

U.S. Government Accountability Office. Comptroller General of the United States. (2003, June). *Government auditing standards (The yellow book).* Washington, DC: GAO.

Mary Ellen Oliverio

PERSONAL FINANCIAL PLANNING

An important investment individuals can make is in planning their use of the financial resources they have. While there are skilled financial advisers in all types of financial services institutions, individuals should have some knowledge about their own affairs. Individuals who take time to learn about money matters will receive a rich reward—dividends in understanding that in the long run will maintain their financial position at a level that is in line with their expectations.

HOW DOES ONE BEGIN A FINANCIAL PLAN?

The first step in creating a financial plan is to identify personal and family financial goals. Goals are based on what is most important to an individual. Short-term goals (up to a year) are related to what is wanted soon (household appliances, a vacation abroad), while long-term goals identify what one wants later on in life (a home, education for children, sufficient retirement income). These short- and long-term goals are the basis for establishing priorities, including an emergency fund as the first item. Then the estimated cost of each goal and the target date to reach it should be determined.

Life-cycle changes influence changes in financial planning. A person's goals must be updated as needs and circumstances change. In one's young adult years, short-term goals may include adequate insurance, establishing good credit, spending for a place to live, and gaining skills needed for work. During a person's middle years, the goals shift from immediate personal expenditures to education for children and planning for retirement. In one's later years, when employment ceases, recreational and personal hobbies may become of primary interest.

Planning is for the future. Therefore, age influences the planning process. Here are some guidelines that reflect general descriptions of financial considerations at different ages:

Age 20 to 40. When a person is young, growth of financial resources should be a primary goal; a relatively high degree of risk is tolerable. Suggestions: Invest in a diversified portfolio of common stocks or in a mutual fund managed for growth of assets, not income. Speculation (in real estate, coins, metals, etc.) is acceptable, if the individual is willing to take such risks.

Age 40 to 60. Stocks are still an attractive choice, but now one needs a more balanced approach. This may be the time to invest in fixed-rate instruments (bonds) and, if income is high, bonds that are tax-free (municipals) may be appealing.

Age 60 and over. By this age range, the majority of an investor's funds should be in income-producing investments to provide safety and maximum current interest.

There is a rule of thumb that may be appropriate here. It suggests that the percentage of one's portfolio in bonds should approximate one's age, the balance going into equities (stocks). For example, at age forty an investor would keep 40 percent in bonds and 60 percent in equities. At age sixty the reverse would be appropriate—60 percent in bonds and 40 percent in equities. Of course, this is a very general idea that may not be appropriate for everyone.

When planning investments for one's age bracket, consider the following:

- *Security of principal:* This refers to the preservation of one's original capital. Treasury bills (T-bills) are guaranteed by the government, while stocks fluctuate greatly.

- *Return:* This means the money one earns on investment (interest, dividends, profit).

- *Liquidity:* This deals with the ease of converting investments into cash.

- *Convenience:* This refers to the time and energy one is willing to expend on maintaining and monitoring one's investment.

- *Tax impact:* Depending on one's tax bracket, each type of investment will have different impact on the taxes owed. Municipal bonds are completely tax-free if issuers are in the state of the investor, while certificates of deposit (CDs) are fully taxable.

- *Individual personal circumstances:* These include such factors as a person's age, income, health, individual circumstances, and ability to tolerate risk.

HOW SHOULD ONE DEAL WITH FINANCIAL RISK IN PLANNING?

The single most important factor in deciding on the best investments for an individual is the level of risk one can afford, and is willing, to take. Thus the first step in formulating an investment plan is a careful self-examination. How much money does a person have to invest? What are the financial needs for the foreseeable future? How much of one's capital can be realistically invested with the possible risk that all of an investment might be a loss? What degree of risk is the individual—and the family—willing to accept psychologically? Each of these factors will be helpful in determining the degree of risk that should be tolerated when making investment decisions. The trade-off is simple: To get larger rewards one has to take greater risks. Yet, greater risks present possibility for greater losses.

A person can achieve a balance by investing in a pyramid fashion: Begin with conservative (safe) investments at the foundation (Treasury obligations, insured money markets, CDs) and then gradually build up, accepting a bit more risk at each step. At the very top, an investor may have high-risk investments (e.g., coins, gold, real estate), but because of the pyramid, these investments will be small compared with the rest of one's holdings. Also, to minimize loss, one should have at least two different types

of investments that perform differently during a specific period. For example, when interest rates are low, stocks usually gain while money markets do poorly.

Every investor must find a comfort-zone balance of security and risk. This is one of the cardinal rules of financial planning. Ironically, the goal is to live in comfort, but the key is not to get too "comfortable." From time to time investors must reconsider their earlier decisions and the results of those decisions to date. Investors must recognize that they should not miss out on profitable opportunities.

HOW DOES AN INVESTOR OVERCOME OBSTACLES TO PLANNING?

Regardless of how well a plan is developed, certain obstacles are likely to arise. Four factors that could have a major effect on successful planning are:

1. *Inflation:* To plan financially, one must receive a return that will outpace any long-term effects of inflation. If, for example, funds for retirement are maintained in a money market account paying 2.5 percent per year and over the same period the inflation rate averaged 3 percent, an investment would have less purchasing power at retirement than it did when it was initially made.

2. *Interest rate risk:* A change in interest rates will cause the price of fixed-rate instruments (bonds) to move in the opposite direction of interest rates. If interest rates go down, the value of bonds goes up, and, conversely, if interest rates go up, the value of the bonds goes down. All types of bonds have interest rate risk. The longer the maturity of the bond, the greater the interest rate risk, so if an investor is concerned about this risk, it is wise to invest in short-term instruments, such as T-bills.

3. *Taxation:* Determining to what extent any tax-advantaged investment would help is a serious consideration. Factors requiring attention are tax bracket, present income, future income, and investment holdings at the point of undertaking financial planning.

4. *Procrastination:* This is an obstacle that is solely the responsibility of the individual. There is nothing gained with the thought: "Someday I'm going to stop procrastinating and do something about my future finances." A well-designed financial plan that is in one's mind is not sufficient. If there is not concrete specification of what is to be done and if the relevant decisions are not implemented, little of value is likely to follow.

Here are some guidelines for handling risk, which should increase an investor's sense of security:

1. Do not invest in any instrument in which one can lose more than one can potentially gain. This factor is sometimes referred to as risk-reward balance.

2. Diversify one's holdings. Spread investment dollars among a variety of instruments, thereby reducing potential risk.

3. When investments fail to perform up to expectations (the period to hold them is based upon one's objectives), sell them. Cutting one's losses is the only sure way to prevent minor setbacks from turning into financial nightmares. A rule of thumb is to sell when the value declines by 10 percent of the original cost.

4. Institute a stop order. A stop order is an instruction given to the broker who sold stock to the investor, directing the broker to sell that stock if it should decline by, say, 10 percent of its original purchase price. The moment the predetermined level is reached, the stock will be sold.

5. Do not discount risk altogether. The rewards may justify "taking a chance." Remember the turtle. It makes progress only when it sticks its neck out.

WHAT FINANCIAL RECORDS SHOULD BE MAINTAINED?

An investor needs a road map, so that all documents and their locations are known to the investor—and ultimately to heirs. Records that should be kept accessible are:

- Professional numbers: telephone numbers of lawyers, doctors, accountants, insurance companies, business associates, and financial advisers or brokers

- Account numbers: brokerages, banks, credit cards, insurance policies (and beneficiaries), and safe-deposit boxes (along with keys and authorized deputies)

- Business records, tax returns, payroll data, etc.

- An updated will and trusts agreements, if any

- Retirement benefits: Social Security, Keogh plans, simplified employee pension plans, 401(k)s, and the like

- Burial arrangements: cemetery plots, deeds

- Listings and details of outstanding liabilities

Financial records should be kept in a secure place and organized for easy review and updating from time to time. Copies of basic financial records are best placed in a safe-deposit box.

HOW IS A FINANCIAL PLANNER CHOSEN?

Once a person has developed an overall plan, the decision might be made to handle the task of implementing the plan alone. Or, the decision might be to seek a professional financial planner. Financial planners are paid for their work in one of three ways: fee only, commission only, or fee plus commission. As investors will quickly discover, financial planners do not all charge the same level of fees. Think about how one selects a physician, a school for one's children, a home for one's family. Investors should choose a financial planner who is well qualified and who shares the same basic beliefs and judgment about financial planning.

One may seek recommendations from friends whose judgment is trusted, from a professional organization that maintains lists of financial planners, or from advertisements. In many instances, preliminary personal appointments with a few financial planners will provide additional insight in making a decision about whether to engage a professional planner and/or which one to select.

Furthermore, once a decision has been made about the type of financial professional that seems best, an investor may want to visit a few to seek information on how other clients' investments have performed under their guidance. It is wise to assess how well the planners have been able to achieve their clients' objectives.

Investors should not delegate all interest in their own financial plans. It is important to maintain considerable attention to plans and related decisions. Wise investors read financial information in newspapers, magazines, annual reports, books, and material available at Web sites. Investors also find that they learn much through seminars, lectures, and courses.

A key point is simple: It is never too early for an individual to begin building a firm financial future. There is a saying that sums up financial planning in ten two-letter words: If it is to be, it is up to me.

SEE ALSO *Bonds; Insurance; Investments; Mutual Funds; Stocks*

BIBLIOGRAPHY

Lerner, Joel (1998). *Financial planning for the utterly confused.* New York: McGraw-Hill.

Orman, Suze (2003). *The road to wealth* (Rev. ed.). New York: Riverhead.

Quinn, Jane Bryant (2006). *Jane Bryant Quinn's smart and simple financial strategies for busy people.* New York: Simon and Schuster.

Joel Lerner

PERSONAL SELLING

Personal selling, sometimes called professional selling or professional personal selling, is the person-to-person interaction between the representatives of a sales organization and the representatives of a buying organization resulting in the sale of a good, such as a product, service, or idea. Selling can take place through a retail transaction, a business-to-business transaction, or through telemarketing. Business-to-business professional selling is a process beginning with the sales representative identifying potential customers and potentially culminating in a long-term, mutually beneficial relationship between the seller and buyer. This process, called the sales process, can be separated into seven specific steps: prospecting, preparation, the approach, the presentation, handling objections, closing the sale, and the follow-up.

PROSPECTING

Prospecting involves identifying and qualifying potential customers. Several techniques are available to sales representatives to help them identify potential customers, such as the endless chain, center of influence, and cold calling methods. The endless chain prospecting method is where the sales representative, at the end of a call, asks the buyer for names of other buyers who might be interested in the product. When the sales representative gains additional contacts by getting to know the most influential buyers in the sales territory, this is known as the center of influence prospecting technique. In the cold calling method, the sales representative goes through the territory knocking on doors to identify potential customers.

When qualifying a prospect, a sales representative needs to determine if there is a want or a need for a product, if the company is financially able to buy, if the company is eligible to buy, and if the person interacting with the sales representative has the authority to buy.

PREPARATION

The second step of the sales process is the preparation step. In this step, the sales representative prepares for the sales call in two ways. First, the sales representative gathers general knowledge that is needed to make any call, such as product information, prices, delivery information, and competitive information. Second, the sales representative prepares a plan for calling on each individual customer. The precall plan is often called a sales call plan, essentially an outline of how the sales representative would like the sales presentation to flow. During a sales representative's early tenure with a company, the sales call plan is often a written process; as a sales representative gains experience, however, planning the call becomes a

Appliance sales is one area where person-to-person selling plays an important role. © DON MASON/CORBIS

mental process. The better prepared sales representatives are for each call, the greater their success.

APPROACH

The third step of the sales process is the approach step. The approach is the sales representative's first face-to-face interaction with the customer. There are several techniques available for effectively approaching customers, such as the premium approach, the question approach, and the product approach. The premium approach, sometimes called the free gift approach, involves the sales representative giving the buyer something of value at the beginning of a call. The question approach is when the sales representative's presentation begins with a question to get the buyer involved. In the product approach, the sales representative hands a sample of the product to the buyer at the beginning of the presentation, once again involving the buyer right away.

An important aspect of the approach step is the concept of personal space. Sales representatives need to be aware of cultural differences and not make the buyer feel uncomfortable during the sales call. In some countries, it may be natural for the buyer and seller to communicate almost nose to nose, while this is completely unacceptable in other countries.

PRESENTATION

The fourth step of the sales process is the presentation. Sales representatives need to realize the importance of presenting the sales information in a professional manner. In the presentation step, the sales representative should relate customer benefits for each product feature presented. The sales representative should also ask questions to assess needs and involve the buyer, and use active listening, which is listening carefully to the buyer and using what the buyer says to help guide the direction of the sales presentation.

HANDLING OBJECTIONS

The fifth stage of the sales process is handling objections. In this stage, sales representatives anticipate objections that can be encountered during a sales call, such as those relating to price, product, source (company), and service. Sales representatives should learn to welcome objections because it shows that the buyer is involved in the presentation and because objections help focus the presentation on the buyer's concerns. If sales representatives successfully overcome a buyer's concerns, they are that much closer to a sale. There are no magical techniques for overcoming objections. Sales representatives overcome objections by being prepared and knowing the appropriate information about the company, products, and related services.

THE CLOSE

The close is the sixth, though not final, step of the sales process. When trying to close the sale, sales representatives need to observe the customer and use active listening to recognize buyers' closing signals. Closing signals can be verbal or nonverbal. Once sales representatives identify a closing signal, they use one of a variety of closing techniques to try to close the sale, such as the alternative choice, extra-inducement, or standing room only close. The alternative choice close is when the sales representative closes by offering the buyer choices, such as "Will that be MasterCard or Visa?" With the extra-inducement close, the sales representative attempts to close the sale by offering to give the buyer something extra of value if the buyer agrees to buy; while in the standing room only close, the sales representative informs the buyer that some future event will change the terms of the product offering, for example, an upcoming price increase.

FOLLOW-UP

The final step of the sales process is the follow-up. The follow-up step is essential for building a long-lasting relationship with the customer. A sales representative can build a good relationship with the buyer in many ways. A sales representative can send the buyer a thank-you note for a purchase or make sure that a purchase is delivered when expected. Follow-ups can be e-mails, telephone calls, letters, or personal interactions. A sales representative can contact the buyer to see if there are any questions or concerns about a purchase, to make sure the buyer received the delivery, to make sure the product was properly installed and in good working condition, or to give the buyer additional requested information.

Follow-ups do not always have to be business related. For example, if a sales representative discovers that the buyer is an avid golfer, the sales representative can mail the buyer an article about an upcoming golf event in the buyer's area. The idea of the follow-up is to satisfy the customer's needs and to build a strong business relationship.

SALES INTERACTIONS

Sales representatives have three basic types of sales interactions with buyers: transactional, consultative, and relationship selling situations. Transactional selling is where the sales representative does not have an established relationship with the buyer. Transactional selling tends to happen when sales representatives are first calling on buyers or when buyers intentionally avoid developing a relationship with the sales representative.

Consultative selling occurs when the sale representative is beginning to build a stronger working relationship with the buyer. The buyer begins to trust the sales representative, but still tends to use the sales representative as just an adviser.

With relationship selling, the sales representative has developed a strong trusting relationship with the buyer. The sales representative becomes almost like a partner with the buyer, working side by side with the buyer to help solve the buyer's problems. In return, the sales representative gains long-run sales from the relationship. As a sales representative progresses from transactional selling to relationship selling, the number of competitive sales representatives seen by the buyer tends to decrease.

SEE ALSO *Marketing*

BIBLIOGRAPHY

Anderson, Rolph E., and Dubinsky, Alan J. (2004). *Personal selling: Achieving customer satisfaction and loyalty.* Boston: Houghton Mifflin.

Futrell, Charles (2005). *ABC's of relationship selling through service* (8th ed.). New York: McGraw-Hill/Irwin.

Manning, Gerald L., and Reece, Barry L. (2004). *Selling today: Creating customer value* (9th ed.). Upper Saddle River, NJ: Pearson Prentice Hall.

Weitz, Barton A., Castleberry, Stephen B., and Tanner, John F., Jr. (2004). *Selling: Building partnerships* (5th ed.). Boston: McGraw-Hill/Irwin.

Joseph D. Chapman

PHISHING

SEE *Cyber Crime; Electronic Mail; Privacy and Security*

PLANNING

SEE *Strategic Management*

POLICY DEVELOPMENT

Companies develop policies generally to help them run efficiently in achieving their objectives. They also develop them to comply with the legal and social environment in which they operate as well as to build goodwill with both their employees and their customers. In this way, policies help shape the culture of an organization. They run the gamut from simple parking policies and dress codes to operational policies to complex policies involving benefits and legal rights. To help companies run efficiently, these policies must be appropriate, well written, and easily accessible. Furthermore, as management tools, they must be updated and maintained regularly to work effectively.

DEVELOPMENT METHODOLOGY

To create appropriate policies, companies must decide who is best for the job of creating policy, ensure that they are written clearly, and make them readily available to employees.

Who makes company policy? Depending on the size and management style of a company, the task of creating and writing policy statements varies widely. A small, growing company may start with unwritten policies created by the owners and move to written ones as the need arises. In the early twenty-first century, many such companies purchase template policy manuals, adapting them as appropriate to their businesses. As companies grow larger, their need for formal policies grows. These policies help ensure consistency and fairness to all employees.

The management style of the company often determines who sets the policies. Typically, companies with a top-down management style tend to delegate the policy making. Boards of directors often create policies for executives, while executives and managers create them for their subordinates. Very large companies not only have written policies; they often have different policies for different groups of employees. A set of travel policies, for example, may apply only to those employees who travel, or there may even be different policies for international and domestic travelers. The policy may even vary by level in the organization.

Original	Improved revision
If a member of your family dies, you will receive three days off.	If a member of your immediate family dies, you will receive up to three days paid leave for travel to and from the funeral or for funeral and estate business. Your immediate family includes spouse or significant other, parents, grandparents, stepparents, step-grandparents, aunts and uncles, sisters and brothers, stepsisters and stepbrothers, first cousins, sisters-in-law and brothers-in-law, and children and stepchildren.
After you work for the company for six months, you are entitled to one day of vacation for every month worked.	After you successfully complete your probationary period, you may begin accumulating paid vacation days. For each month you work after the probation period, you will earn one day of paid vacation. You can accumulate a maximum of 20 paid vacation days.
Employees may use their accumulated sick leave for childcare or eldercare.	You can use your sick leave to take care of your sick children or stepchildren. You can also use it to attend to special needs of your parents, stepparents, grandparents, or step-grandparents.

Figure 1

As organizational structures have flattened, companies are moving toward more employee involvement in policy making. A poll of Fortune 500 companies reported that almost half (47 percent) of these companies involve employees in policy decisions. Sometimes policy ideas are solicited from all employees, and sometimes teams of employees create the policies. When policies affect only one department, the department's members contribute substantially to those policies. When policies affect several groups, cross-functional teams are often formed to create those policies.

How should policies be written? One of the most important aspects of effective policies includes communicating them clearly to all affected by them. Two major objectives of well written policy statements are that they be clear and concise. Writers should use words their readers understand; after all, they want statements to be interpreted as they are intended. Also, the tone should be pleasant and the statements should reflect sound practices on such subjects as hiring and firing, pay, and benefits. Many companies also have policies about practices such as giving and receiving gifts, political and charitable contributions, e-mail privacy, Internet use, and health and safety. Some companies even have written policies for activities outside work hours and personal conduct.

Figure 1 gives some examples of original and improved policy statements. As you can easily see policy statements need to be specific and precise. A vague policy will not only lead to confusion but could also cause hard feelings, not to mention legal problems. Without the specific detail defining how the three days paid leave could be taken, an employee might expect to have three days tagged on to his or her vacation for the death of a spouse's distant uncle, or an employee could be under the false impression that vacation days could be accumulated without a cap. That employee might be not only extremely disappointed to learn that the trip to Europe this summer is off because forty days of vacation had not been accumulated but also extremely angry to learn that twenty vacation days were actually lost because they were not taken earlier.

Companies today are extremely sensitive to discriminatory policies. Law requires that women and men be treated uniformly. Most companies with maternity leave have rewritten their policy statements to include paternity leave, while others have rewritten their disability policies to include pregnancy. Discriminatory policies relating to age, race, and religion policies are illegal. Policies requiring someone to work on their religious holidays without telling them before they are hired are viewed as discriminatory. Of course, companies cannot have a policy that is illegal.

Level of flexibility is another factor to consider in writing policy statements. The objective in writing policy statements is to inform the reader about the content of company policy as clearly as possible. For first-line employees and customers, this usually means being very precise. However, management may want the flexibility to make some decisions on a case-by-case basis. Thus policies written for middle- and top-level management may be purposefully written to allow for flexibility and different interpretations. Also, some types of policies have so many acceptable interpretations that listing them all is both ridiculous and unmanageable. Other times companies will implement a new policy without fully understanding the level of precision it needs. However, there should be a plan to refine the level during rewrites of the policy.

The elder care example above might exemplify a new policy. Initially, an employer might intend that employees use these days to take their elders to doctor and dentist appointments. However, a perfectly acceptable use of this day may be driving elders around to various nursing and/or retirement homes to choose one for their future living. In any case, employers may decide to build in flexibility at the beginning, recognizing that most of their employees will not abuse this use of their accumulated sick days. However, companies might rewrite this policy to decrease its flexibility if they find that some employees are testing its reasonable limits.

What technological tools help in policy creation and dissemination? Many technological tools help writers create and disseminate company policies. Most full-featured word processors include revision features. This tool allows policy writers to share their drafts with others, reviewing changes and suggestions others make and deciding whether or not to accept the change. Companies or groups using intranets can post policy drafts and solicit suggestions directly. Still others prefer to create policies using group software tools that allow users to brainstorm, rank, and create policies anonymously.

Many organizations make company policies available on their intranets. In addition to being readily accessible, these policies should be organized clearly and logically. Word processors include tools that can generate a table of contents and an index, two components that help make the policies more easily accessible. Another good idea is to create a glossary that includes unfamiliar terms, such as legal definitions, acronyms, and jargon.

Writing or revising policies can be a big project, involving many people and tasks. Project management software is an excellent tool for helping identify the tasks and manage them efficiently.

MAINTENANCE OF POLICY

One final but important aspect of policy development is to review policies periodically and revise them as necessary. Revisions are indicated when companies find they are continually being asked to clarify the statements. Keeping a log of questions as they are asked will help in the revision process. Another indication that updating is needed is frequent employee or customer complaints about a particular policy. While sometimes they do not understand the reason behind the policy, often they are complaining about its fairness or its harshness in comparison with the policy of other businesses.

Other reasons for revising and maintaining policies include both external and internal changes. Changes in the business, work, and social environments often influence needs. Sometimes business mergers, acquisitions, or spin-offs cause companies to revise polices for the new company. Technology such as the Internet, for example, has changed the way many companies do business with both their internal and external customers and suppliers, creating the need to add, delete, and revise policy statements frequently.

Another way to keep current with needed revisions is by keeping up with news items, such as government regulations, health and safety regulations, antitrust laws, morals laws, ethics, etiquette, and much more. Through reading, a company learns what other companies are doing or what problems they have experienced with certain policies. This allows it to take precautionary steps, revising its statements to avoid problems that others have encountered. Of course, keeping up with new laws or interpretations is critical. For example, laws have been passed regarding e-mail privacy, and courts have ruled in various ways on the rights of the employer or employee in regard to this issue. Undoubtedly, the courts will be hearing and interpreting more cases on e-mail privacy. Keeping up with current events with an eye to how they might impact a company's policy statements is a good idea.

SUMMARY

Policies are created to help business run more smoothly. Knowing how to develop complete and accurate statements for a specific audience will help organizations succeed in having up-to-date policies that work effectively for them.

SEE ALSO *Management*

BIBLIOGRAPHY

Campbell, Nancy (1998). *Writing Effective Policies and Procedures: A Step-By-Step Resource for Clear Communication.* New York: American Management Association.

Kuiper, Shirley (2005). Writing Policies, Procedures, and Instructions. *Contemporary Business Report Writing* (3rd ed.). Mason, OH: Thomson South-Western.

Marie E. Flatley

POWER

SEE *Division of Labor; Management: Authority and Responsibility; Management/Leadership Styles*

PRESTIGE PRICING

SEE *Pricing*

PRICE FIXING

Price fixing is a conspiracy to artificially set prices for goods or services above or below the normal market rate. The U.S. Justice Department and the Federal Trade Commission (FTC) are the regulatory bodies responsible for determining whether companies are involved in price-fixing tactics. Both bodies have the ability to impose heavy fines on those companies found to be conspiring to fix prices.

The health-care industry has been scrutinized many times for price fixing, especially companies that manufacture vitamins. In 1995 the Justice Department fined three vitamin manufacturers a total of $750 million dollars for conspiring to fix vitamin prices. In addition, three vitamin distributors were also found guilty of price fixing that same year; their fines totaled $137 million for fixing the prices for a handful of popular vitamins, and they had to pay just over $1 billion to 1,000 corporate buyers of bulk vitamins, an amount reflecting overcharges during the years of the conspiracy.

Roche Holdings AG, which held 40 percent of the global vitamins market, agreed to pay a fine of $500 million and as of 1999 was the object of class-action lawsuits and investigation by the European Commission. Because of the various price-fixing scandals, Roche and other vitamin manufacturers could experience trouble when raising prices, or even stabilizing them. The price-fixing conspiracy lasted from 1990 through 1999 and affected vitamins A, B2, B5, C, E, and beta carotene. It also included vitamin premixes, which are added to breakfast cereals and other processed foods. The Justice Department's probe of price fixing continued as the government attempted to build cases against other vitamin manufacturers.

In 1996 the FTC and the Justice Department issued a revised Statement of Antitrust Enforcement Policy in Health Care. Under this new enforcement policy, the FTC and the Justice Department do not necessarily view joint agreements on price between previously competing providers as unlawful price fixing if the integrated delivery system is sufficiently integrated. The enforcement statement does not, however, provide solid guidance on what constitutes integration sufficient to permit joint negotiations. But, it does offer rules of thumb that will allow those involved in integrated delivery systems to better assess whether their joint pricing activities will raise antitrust concerns.

The securities industry was also closely scrutinized in the 1990s for price-fixing tactics. Investigations of the National Association of Securities Dealers and the NASDAQ market by the Department of Justice and the Securities and Exchange Commission during the latter part of the 1990s suggested that market makers colluded to fix prices and widen bid-ask spreads in attempts to increase dealers' profits at the expense of investors. At a minimum, market makers appeared to have adopted a quoting convention that could be viewed as anticompetitive behavior.

In understanding the experience of the U.S. securities market, it is important to consider what sorts of behavior are deemed anticompetitive. U.S. law on overt price fixing is clear: such behavior is illegal. In many cases, however, there is no explicit agreement to fix prices. Based on the Sherman Antitrust Act of 1890, U.S. courts developed the doctrine of conscious parallelism, which means, according to the U.S. Supreme Court, that no formal agreement is necessary to constitute an unlawful conspiracy.

Prior to 1996, market makers were allegedly engaged in many price-fixing scandals. In the late 1990s, the Justice Department found evidence that this practice was still occurring. For example, price quotes on Instinet, a private electronic market, differed from NASDAQ quotes for the same stocks.

In 1999 a California appeals court unanimously ruled that Arco and eight other oil companies were entitled to summary judgment in a price-fixing suit because there was no evidence of an agreement among them to fix prices or limit the supply of the cleaner-burning gasoline mandated by California. The appeals court agreed with the trial court's original conclusion that the evidence provided by the plaintiffs suggested not a complex tangled web, but nine defendants using all available information sources to determine capacity, supply, and pricing decisions. The court ruled that the companies involved made these pricing decisions because they wanted to maximize their own individual profits and were not concerned about the profits of their competitors.

Because price fixing occurs when companies conspire to set an artificially high price for a product, the nature of the food-additive industry makes it easy to create price-fixing cartels. Because of the small number of companies that are involved in the additive industry, it is easier for them to organize and maintain a price-fixing conspiracy. Price fixing of food additives is also easy because a small number of companies means that prices are negotiated via individual contracts, instead of in an open market.

The establishment in the 1990s of international trade associations, which are facilitated by the European Union, is another major cause of price fixing. These trade associations provide data about their industry to association members, including information on the exact size of the market and the growth rate of the industry. That information can lead to establishment of a cartel, because the companies can extrapolate pricing information.

Archer Daniels Midland was prosecuted in 1996 for illegally fixing the prices of lysine (which is used as a nutritional additive in livestock feed) and citric acid. During the time of the conspiracy, Archer Daniels Midland produced 54 percent of the lysine used in the United States and 95 percent of the world's. Annual sales of lysine were $330 million in the United States and $600 million worldwide.

The company pleaded guilty to fixing the price of lysine from 1992 to 1996, and the Justice Department fined it $70 million. The higher prices of animal feed resulted in lost income for hog and poultry farmers, as well as feed companies.

The Department of Justice's Antitrust Division reformed legislation in 2003 by introducing the Antitrust Criminal Penalty Enhancement and Reform Act. This legislation increases the statutory maximum penalty under the Sherman Antitrust Act from $10 million to $100 million. A formula is used to determining price-fixing fines. The multipliers for the formula are set by such factors as the company's antitrust history, its cooperation with investigators, the degree of involvement of senior management, and the existence of an effective compliance program.

SEE ALSO *Antitrust Legislation; Monopoly*

BIBLIOGRAPHY

Ackert, Lucy, and Church, Bryan (1998). Competitiveness and price setting in dealer market. *Economic Review, 83*(3), 4.

Calderwood, James (1995). Antitrust warning. *Transportation and Distribution, 36*(12), 72.

Scheffey, Thomas (2000). Westlaw, Lexis hit with price-fixing claim. *The Connecticut Law Tribune, 20*(5), 1.

Smith, Tefft, and Mutchnik, James (2003, December 12). Finding the right price. *Legal Times,* p. 32.

Patricia A. Spirou

PRICING

Price is perhaps the most important of the four Ps (product, promotion, and place being the others) of marketing since it is the only one that generates revenue for a company. Price is most simply described as the value exchange that occurs for a product or service. Broadly, price is the total of all values exchanged for a product or service. Price is dynamic. When establishing a price for a product or service, a company must first assess several factors regarding its potential impact. Commonly reviewed factors include legal and regulatory guidelines, pricing objectives, pricing strategies, and options for increasing sales. Advances in Internet technology have resulted in the increased use of dynamic pricing by some sellers.

LEGAL AND REGULATORY GUIDELINES

The first major law influencing the price of a company's product was the Sherman Antitrust Act of 1890, passed by the U.S. Congress to prevent a company from becoming a monopoly. A monopoly occurs when one company has total control in the production and distribution of a product or service. As a monopoly, a company can charge higher than normal prices for its product or service, since no significant competition exists. The Sherman Antitrust

Act empowers the U.S. Attorney General's Office to challenge a perceived monopoly and to petition the federal courts to break up a company in order to promote competition.

Another significant piece of legislation that has a major effect on determining price is the Clayton Antitrust Act of 1914, passed by Congress in order to prevent practices such as price discrimination and the exclusive or nearly exclusive dealing between and among only a few companies. Like the Sherman Antitrust Act, this act prevented practices that would reduce competition. The Robinson-Patman Act of 1936, which is technically an extension of the Clayton Act, further prohibits a company from selling its product at an unreasonably low price in order to eliminate its competitors. The purpose of this act was to prohibit national chain stores from unfairly using volume discounts to drive smaller firms out of business.

To defend against charges of violating the Robinson-Patman Act, a company would have to prove that price differentials were based on the competitive free market, and not an attempt to reduce or eliminate competition. Because regulations of the Robinson-Patman Act do not apply to exported products, a company can offer products for sale at significantly lower prices in foreign markets than in U.S. markets.

Another set of laws influencing the price of a company's product are referred to as the unfair-trade laws. Passed in the 1930s, these laws were designed to protect special markets, such as the dairy industry, and their main focus is to set minimum retail prices for a product (e.g., milk), allowing for a slight markup. Theoretically, these laws would protect a specialty business from larger businesses that could sell the same products below cost and drive smaller, specialty stores out of business.

Fair-trade laws are a different set of statutes that were enacted by many state legislatures in the early 1930s. These laws allow a producer to set a minimum price for its product; hence, retailers signing pricing agreements with manufacturers are required to list the minimum price for which a product can be sold. These acts prevent the use of interstate pricing agreements between manufacturers and retailers, grounded in the belief that this would promote more competition and, as a result, lower prices. An important aspect of these acts is that they do not apply to intrastate product prices.

PRICING OBJECTIVES

A critical part of a company's overall strategic planning includes the establishment of pricing objectives for the products it sells. A company has several pricing objectives from which to choose, and the objective chosen will depend on the goals and type of product sold by a company. Four pricing objectives are competitive, prestige, profitability, and volume pricing.

Competitive Pricing. The concept behind this frequently used pricing objective is to simply match the price established by an industry leader for a particular product. Since price difference is minimized with this strategy, a company focuses its efforts on other ways to attract new customers. Some examples of what a company might do in order to obtain new customers include producing high-quality and reliable products, providing superior customer service, and engaging in creative marketing.

Prestige Pricing. A company may chose to promote, maintain, and enhance the image of its product through the use of prestige pricing, which involves pricing a product high so as to make it available only to the higher-end consumer. This limited availability enhances the product's image, causing it to be viewed as prestigious. Although a company that uses this strategy expects to have limited sales, a profit is still possible because of the higher markup on each item. Examples of companies that use prestige pricing are Mercedes Benz and Rolls-Royce.

Profitability Pricing. The main idea behind profitability pricing is to maximize profit. The basic formula for this objective is that profits equal revenue minus expenses (P = R − E). Revenue is determined by a product's selling price and the number of units sold. A company must be careful not to increase the price of the product too much, or the quantity sold will be reduced and total profits may be lower than desired. Therefore, a company is always monitoring the price of its products in order to make sure it is competitive while at the same time providing for an acceptable profit margin.

Volume Pricing. When a company uses a volume-pricing objective, it is seeking sales maximization within predetermined profit guidelines. A company using this objective prices a product lower than normal but expects to make up the difference with a higher sales volume. Volume pricing can be beneficial to a company because its products are being purchased on a large scale, and large-scale product distribution helps to reinforce a company's name as well as to increase its customer loyalty. A subset of volume pricing is the market-share objective, the purpose of which is to obtain a specific percentage of sales for a given product. A company can determine an acceptable profit margin by obtaining a specific percentage of the market with a specific price for a product.

PRICING STRATEGIES

Companies can chose from a variety of pricing strategies, some of the most common being penetration, skimming, and competitive strategies. While each strategy is designed to achieve a different goal, each contributes to a company's ability to earn a profit.

Penetration-Pricing Strategy. A company that wants to build market share quickly and obtain profits from repeat sales-generally selects the penetration-pricing strategy, which can be very effective when used correctly. For example, a company may provide consumers with free samples of a product and then offer the product at a slightly reduced price. Alternatively, a company may initially offer significant discounts and then slowly remove the discounts until the full price of the product is listed. Both options allow a company to introduce a new product and to start building customer loyalty and appreciation for it. The idea is that once consumers are familiar with and satisfied with a new product, they will begin to purchase the product on a regular basis at the normal retail price. Retailers with high sales volumes frequently use the penetration-pricing strategy. High sales volume allows retailers, in some cases, to reduce prices even more.

Price-Skimming Strategy. A price-skimming strategy uses different pricing phases over time to generate profits. In the first phase, a company launches the product and targets customers who are more willing to pay the item's high retail price. The profit margin during this phase is extremely high and obviously generates the highest revenue for the company. Since a company realizes that only a small percentage of the market was penetrated in the first phase, it will price the product lower in the second phase. This second-phase pricing will appeal to a broader cross-section of customers, resulting in increased product sales. When sales start to level off during this phase, the company will price the product even lower. This third-phase pricing should appeal to those consumers who were price-sensitive in the first two phases and result in increased sales. The company should now have covered the majority of the market that is willing to purchase its product at the high, medium, and low price ranges.

The price-skimming strategy provides an excellent opportunity for the company to maximize profits from the beginning and only slowly lower the price when needed because of reduced sales. Price adjustment with this strategy closely follows the product life cycle, that is, how customers accept a new product. Price skimming is a frequently used strategy when maximum revenue is needed to pay off high research and development costs associated with some products. This strategy is effective if product image and quality support the higher price and if

an adequate number of customers exist at that price. Producers of high-definition televisions have used price skimming as a strategy to maximize revenue.

Competitive-Pricing Strategy. Competitive pricing is yet another major strategy. A company's competitors may either increase or decrease their prices, depending upon their own objectives. Before a company responds to a competitor's price change with one of its own, a thorough analysis as to why the change occurred needs to be conducted. An investigation of price increases or decreases will usually result in one or more of the following reasons for the change: a rise in the price of raw materials, higher labor costs, increasing tax rates, or rising inflation. To maintain an acceptable profit margin for a particular product, a company will usually increase the price. In addition, strong consumer demand for a particular product may cause a shortage and, therefore, allow a company to increase its price without hurting either demand or profit.

When a competitor increases its price, a company has several options from which to chose. The first is to increase its price to approximately the same as that of the competing firm. The second is to wait before raising its price, a strategy known as price shadowing. Price shadowing allows the company to attract those new customers who are price-sensitive away from the competing firm. If consumers do switch over in large numbers, a company will make up lost profits through higher sales volume. If consumers do not switch over after a period, the company can increase its price. Typically, a company will increase its price to a level slightly below that of its competitors in order to maintain a lower-price tactical advantage. The airline industry uses the competitive pricing strategy frequently.

When competitors decrease their prices, a company has numerous options. The first option is to maintain its price, since the company is confident that consumers are loyal and value its unique product qualities. Depending on the price sensitivity of customers in a given market, this might not be an appropriate strategy for a company to use. The second option is to analyze why a competitor might have decreased its prices. If price decreases are due to a technological innovation, then a price decrease will probably be necessary because the competitor's price reduction is likely to be permanent. Regardless of its competitor's actions, a company may decrease its price. This price reduction option is called price covering. This option is most useful when a company has done a good job of differentiating the qualities of its product from those of a competitor's product. On the flip side, the advantage of price covering is reduced when no noticeable difference can be seen between a company's product and that of a competitor.

OPTIONS FOR INCREASING SALES

Companies have several options available when attempting to increase the sales of a product, including coupons, prepayment, price shading, seasonal pricing, term pricing, segment pricing, and volume discounts.

Coupons. Almost all companies offer product coupons, reflecting their numerous advantages. First, a company might want to introduce a new product, enhance its market share, increase sales on a mature product, or revive an old product. Second, coupons can be used to generate new customers by getting customers to buy and try a company's product in the hope that these trial purchases will result in repeat purchases. A variety of coupon distribution methods are available, such as the Internet, point-of-purchase dispensers, and Sunday newspapers. Internet coupons may be found at the following Web sites: http://www.couponcraze.com, http://www.couponpages.com, http://www.couponsurfer.com, and http://www.dealcatcher.com.

Prepayment. A prepayment plan is typically used with customers who have no credit history or a poor one. This prepayment method does not generally provide customers with a price break, although sometimes it does. For example, the magazine industry widely uses the prepayment strategy. A customer who agrees to purchase a magazine subscription for an extended period normally receives a discount as compared to the newsstand price. Purchase of gift certificates is another example of how prepayment can be used to promote sales. For example, a company may offer discounts on a gift certificate whereby the purchaser may pay only 90 to 95 percent of the gift certificate's face value. This strategy has several advantages. First, consumers are encouraged to buy from the company offering the gift certificates rather than from other stores. Second, the revenue is available to a company for reinvestment prior to the product's sale. Finally, receivers will not redeem all gift certificates, and as a result, a company retains all the revenue.

Price Shading. One way to increase company sales is to allow salespeople to offer discounts on the product's price. This tactic, known as price shading, is normally used with aggressive buyers in industrial markets who purchase a product on a regular basis and in large volumes. Price shading allows salespeople to offer more favorable terms to preferred business buyers in order to encourage repeat sales.

Seasonal Pricing. The price for a product can also be adjusted based on seasonal demands. Seasonal pricing will help move products when they are least salable, such as air conditioners in the winter and snow blowers in the spring. An advantage of seasonal pricing is that the price for a product is set high during periods of high demand and lowered as seasonal demand drops off to clear inventory to make room for the current season's products. Pricing for seasonal holiday products, such as those connected with Thanksgiving and Christmas, are frequently reduced the day after the holiday to clear inventory.

Term Pricing. A company has another positive reinforcement strategy for use when establishing product price, term pricing. For example, a company may offer a discount if the customer pays for the product promptly. The definition of *promptly* varies depending on company policy, but normally it means the account balance is to be paid in full within a specified period; in return, a company may provide a discount to encourage continuation of this early payment behavior by the customer. This term pricing strategy is normally used with large retail or industrial buyers, not with the general public. Occasionally, a company will offer a small discount to customers who pay for a product with cash. For example, Gill Brothers, a furniture store located in Muncie, Indiana, occasionally offers additional discounts to customers who pay cash. During one promotional event, selected items were marked down as much as 40 percent; in addition, customers who paid by cash or check were given an extra 10 percent discount.

Segment Pricing. Segment pricing is another tactic a company can use to modify product price in order to increase sales. Everyday examples of segment-pricing discounts are those extended to children, senior citizen, and students. These discounts have several positive benefits. First, the company is appearing to help those individuals who are or are perceived to be economically disadvantaged, a perception that helps create a positive public relations image for a company. Second, members of those groups who ordinarily may not purchase the product are encouraged to do so. Therefore, a company's sales will increase, which will likely result in increased market share and revenue. Best Western and Marriott are examples of hotel chains offering discounts to senior citizens.

Volume Discounts. A common method used by a company to price a product is volume discounting. The idea behind this pricing strategy is simple: If a customer purchases a large volume of a product, the product is offered at a lower price. This tactic allows a company to sell large quantities of its product at an acceptable profit margin.

Volume pricing is also useful for building customer loyalty. For example, Stacks and Stacks HomeWares often provides volume discounts to customers ordering $1,000 worth of any one item.

DYNAMIC PRICING

The strategy where price is negotiated between buyers and sellers, dynamic pricing, has been used throughout history, but its use waned when fixed pricing became popular during the later part of the nineteenth century. Dynamic pricing is a strategy where price is set based on the individual customer and situations.

Advances in technology such as the Internet have made modern dynamic pricing possible. Companies selling via the Internet can mine databases to determine customer characteristics and adapt products to match buying behavior and set prices accordingly. Companies selling via the Internet can also adjust pricing based on customer demand and product supply. The speed with which changes can be made on the Internet allows sellers to make pricing changes on a daily or even hourly basis. Buyers can even negotiate prices with sellers via the Internet. For example, buyers can negotiate prices on products such as hotel rooms and rental cars at the Web site Priceline.com (http://tickets.priceline.com).

SEE ALSO *Marketing; Marketing Mix; Supply and Demand*

BIBLIOGRAPHY

Boone, Louis E., and Kurtz, David L. (2005). *Contemporary marketing 2006* (12th ed.). Eagan, MN: Thomson South-Western.

Churchill, Gilbert A., Jr., and Peter, Paul J. (1998). *Marketing: Creating value for customers* (2nd ed.). New York: Irwin McGraw-Hill.

Farese, Lois, Kimbrell, Grady, and Woloszyk, Carl (2002). *Marketing essentials* (3rd ed.). Mission Hills, CA: Glencoe/McGraw-Hill.

Kotler, Philip, and Armstrong, Gary (2006). *Principles of marketing* (11th ed.). Upper Saddle River, NJ: Pearson Prentice-Hall.

Pride, William M., and Ferrell, O. C. (2006). *Marketing concepts and strategies.* New York: Houghton Mifflin.

Semenik, Richard J., and Bamossy, Gary J. (1995). *Principles of marketing: A global perspective* (2nd ed.). Cincinnati: South-Western.

Allen D. Truell
Michael Milbier

PRIVACY AND SECURITY

The use of computers by business, industry, health care, education, and government enhances their ability to collect, analyze, and communicate information quickly and efficiently. The availability and access of this information, however, significantly affects individual privacy and security. Personal information is transmitted and stored every time a credit card is used, a telephone call is made, or an electronic mail (e-mail) message is sent or received. Personal information regarding health care, insurance, and Social Security records is digitized, stored, and maintained in easily accessible computer files. Although computer technology makes data easier to compile, combine, and circulate, it dramatically increases potential violations of personal privacy and security.

Privacy is an individual's ability to be anonymous. It is not a constitutional right; unsanctioned intrusion of privacy, however, is legislated against at various federal and state levels. Once personal information is shared—whether in electronic, written, or oral form—the individual's privacy cannot be assured. Security implies confidentiality, integrity, and the assurance that personal information will remain private. In the information age of the twenty-first century, privacy and security are difficult to maintain. Identity theft is a continuous threat.

IDENTITY THEFT

During 2004 more than 9.3 million Americans were victims of identity theft. This activity resulted in $52.6 billion in damages. On average, victims of identity theft spent 600 hours repairing their credit. As victims of identity theft, individuals reported a temporary loss of credit as well as significant mental anguish. Although personal identities may be stolen by computerized methods, the majority (62.8%) of identity theft occurred by more traditional means (stolen wallets, mail removed from household mailboxes, dumpster diving, and employee theft).

Employee theft occurs in places such as medical offices and human resource departments where confidential personal information is routinely recorded and distributed. Although many people are more comfortable providing their credit cards in face-to-face transactions (e.g., at stores or restaurants) rather than electronically (e.g., online shopping), a level of personal trust is assumed in both cases. Online transactions, however, are often processed without human intervention. The potential risk is the security of the database of customer information stored online. Security engineering attempts to protect customer information from corporate hacking.

PRIVACY ORGANIZATIONS

Privacy advocates assert that electronic record keeping and transmittal of information threatens basic American liberties and rights to privacy. In reaction to the growing use of computerized databases, several groups were formed in the early 1990s in an effort to support efforts to protect social and legal privacy issues in cyberspace.

- Electronic Frontier Foundation—established in 1990 to focus on civil liberties (http://www.eff.org)

- Privacy International—in 1990 emerged as a global watchdog for a wide variety of privacy issues, including data matching and medical privacy

- Internet Society—begun in 1992 as an international organization to develop and implement standards for the Internet, as well as to maintain historical and statistical databases of Internet usage (http://www.isoc.org)

- Privacy Rights Clearinghouse—founded in 1992 as a nonprofit consumer information and advocacy organization (http://www.privacyrights.org)

- Electronic Privacy Information Center (EPIC)—established in 1994 to address civil liberties and privacy issues (http://www.epic.org)

- Privacy.org—A joint project of EPIC and Privacy International, which serves as an outlet for privacy and security news and information

SOCIAL ENGINEERING SCAMS

These privacy organizations seek ways to combat social engineering scams that use the Internet and e-mail. The most popular scams are phishing, pharming, and crimeware.

Phishing (pronounced "fishing"), which is also know as spoofing or carding, is a fraudulent method of stealing personal information. The term *phishing* is used because the perpetrators in effect "throw out bait" to unsuspecting individuals. The scam artists create e-mail messages that appear to come from a bank, credit card company, or other trusted entity. Oftentimes, the scammers will create very convincing e-mail messages that include logos or graphics copied from the real institution's Internet site. The message requests that the recipients confirm their personal information (e.g., credit card numbers and account information) by either replying to the message, or more typically, following the provided link to the "company's" Internet site. The link, of course, is not to the company's site, but to a counterfeit site, which also uses appropriate graphics and text in an attempt to appear official. Some phishing scams indicate that because of recent suspicious activity, the user's account will be suspended until the personal information is confirmed.

Pharming (pronounced "farming") is related to phishing in that users are misdirected to fraudulent Internet sites where they are asked to provide personal information such as usernames, passwords, and Social Security numbers.

Crimeware is defined as any instance of malware (malicious software), adware (advertising software), and spyware (spying/tracking software). For example, a Trojan keylogger (spyware) can be used to either capture personal information as it is keyed in or redirect users when they attempt to login to their Internet banking sites. Both phishing and pharming are the focus of the Anti-Phishing Working Group (http://www.anti-phishing.org), which is "committed to wiping out Internet scams and fraud."

LEGISLATION

Computer crime-related legislation is growing. Several laws have been enacted to protect privacy and security. For example, the Privacy Protection Act of 1996 (42 USC 2000) imposes controls on the databanks owned by federal agencies. Any database maintaining personal information cannot be distributed to other federal agencies without going through proper legal channels. In addition, the Family Education Rights and Privacy Act protects the dissemination of student information. The proposed Identity Theft Protection Act attempts to limit the use of Social Security numbers as identifying data and ensure individuals are notified when their personal data are compromised.

In addition to "taking" information through database access, security issues also include deleting information from databases. Improper use and invasion of privacy through harmful access occurs when people knowingly damage or destroy computer programs by deleting information or installing computer viruses (programs designed to run in the background of a computer's memory, silently destroying data). This improper use is addressed under the Computer Fraud and Abuse Act of 1986 (18 USC 1030), which prohibits the improper use of "federal interest" computers—computers that communicate and share information across state lines or internationally.

Any computer that is connected to the Internet (even through a local network provider) is considered a federal interest computer and subject to the Computer Fraud and Abuse Act. In addition, the Electronic Communications Privacy Act (18 USC 2510) makes it a crime to use a computer system to view or tamper with other people's private messages (e.g., e-mail and data files) stored in an online system.

The Health Insurance Portability and Accountability Act of 1996 ensures health insurance coverage during changes in employment as well as establishes national standards for electronic health-care transactions. This second emphasis addresses the privacy and security of health-care information. Additional privacy requirements were added in 1999 and approved in 2001; compliance was required in 2003.

In response to the increase in phishing and pharming scams, the Anti-Phishing Act of 2005 was proposed. This bill, if enacted, proposes a $25,000 fine and/or a five-year prison sentence for individuals who are found guilty of fraudulently obtaining personal information using corporate Internet sites or e-mails.

CONCLUSION

It is apparent that cyberspace has become and will continue to be a major concern to both individual and organizational privacy and security. Although legislation is becoming more substantial, it severely lags behind the pace of technology, forcing the burden of responsibility onto the individual. To maintain personal privacy and security, experts suggest following certain guidelines when using credit cards and communication devices (including telephones and computers):

1. When conducting business online (e.g., paying bills and shopping), provide only the necessary information to process the transaction. Optional information would be kept in a database and potentially connected to an account for identification purposes.

2. Create unique passwords and personal identification numbers that are not easily determined or based on such obvious information as home address, phone number, or date of birth or anniversary.

3. To surf the Internet without leaving behind a personal trail, use an anonymous connection such as an open computer lab at a school, university, or library. When using a personal computer system, delete cookies and regularly run virus, spyware, and adware tools.

4. Although many consumers are wary of paying routine bills online, research indicates that paper bills and statements are stolen more easily from mailboxes. Online statements are more easily monitored and should be routinely checked on a weekly basis.

5. Everyone is entitled to request a free credit report each year from each of the three credit reporting agencies: Equifax (http://www.equifax.com), Experian (http://www.experian.com), and TransUnion (http://www.transunion.com). This process may be initiated at http://www.AnnualCreditReport.com.

Legislation and organizations make every effort to protect privacy and security, but computerized databases will continue to be the most efficient method of storing and retrieving information. Personal privacy and security are best ensured when individuals take personal responsibility to protect themselves. Being aware of how identities may be stolen, precautions to take when providing sensitive information, and procedures to repair credit will best ensure personal privacy and security.

SEE ALSO *Consumer Advocacy and Protection; Cyber Crime; Identity Theft*

Lisa E. Gueldenzoph
Mark J. Snyder

PRIVATE OWNERSHIP
SEE *Entrepreneurship*

PRODUCT LABELING

The label on a product is an important selling point for a company's product. Of all product purchase decisions, 70 percent or more are made at the point of purchase, and the product label is an important element in assisting consumers to make those decisions. Product labels perform several functions: to identify the product; to promote the product; and to provide essential, often required, information about the product and its use. Thus, the product label may make or break the sale of a product. In addition to the marketing aspect, certain legal requirements must be met in order for the label to be compliant with federal regulations. When a company designs a label it must take all of these factors into consideration.

IDENTIFICATION

The brand name is the central focus on the label for identifying a product. Nevertheless, such elements as the logos, brand marks, color schemes, designs, and graphics may also serve to identify a specific brand. The opportunity to quickly identify a specific product is often important to consumers, because it allows them to choose a brand with which they have had experience or previous knowledge. Additionally, the identification of the manufacturer and/or distributor is often required and may be of interest to the buyer.

PROMOTION

The brand name may be enough to persuade a consumer to buy a particular product, but often the label must also promote the product. Creative, attractive, and colorful

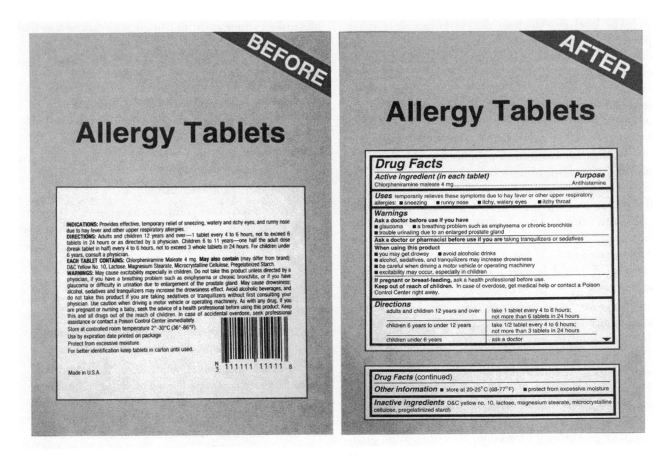

Nonprescription medicine labels shown with warnings printed on them before and after the labeling system changes in 1999. **AP IMAGES**

graphics are needed to allow the product to "pop out" of the wide array of products surrounding it on the shelf and gain the attention of the consumer. Persuasive characteristics or attributes of the product, such as "low fat" or "vitamin enriched," may be prominently displayed on the label to promote the sale of the product.

INFORMATION

Although some products can be identified adequately by brand name alone, many require more complete identification of their nature and use. In short, the purpose of the label is to provide useful and relevant information about the product, as well as to help to market the product. Processed foods, patented drugs, textiles, and numerous other products are required by law to carry a fairly complete list of their ingredients. This specific information is extremely important so that consumers (for example, those who are allergic to certain ingredients) do not use a product that may harm them.

Companies may also provide additional information on their labels that is not legally required. One reason to do so is that consumer groups often publicly protest about the lack of information on labels and request more. Furthermore, when a competitor starts including more information or redesigns its label to make it more user-friendly, a company might decide to modify its own label to prevent losing sales.

Labels may also include a list of ingredients, Universal Product Code, open dating, nutritional labeling, and unit pricing. Ingredients are listed in the order of their prominence, by weight, in the product. The Universal Product Code is a combination of electronically readable lines (the bar code) and numbers identifying the product and providing inventory and pricing information for producers and resellers. Open dating informs consumers about the expected life of the product so they can avoid products that may be spoiled. This information is especially important for such perishable items as milk, eggs, and other products with a short shelf life. Nutritional labeling specifies the amount of calories, total fat, cholesterol, dietary fiber, sodium, minerals, vitamins, and protein in processed foods.

The label also discloses the percentage daily values per serving for each item based on a 2,000-calorie-per-day diet. This information can be useful for consumers who have special dietary needs or are trying to maintain a healthy, balanced diet. Although most often found on the store shelf, unit pricing is occasionally included on the product label and shows the price per unit of standard measure (weight or volume).

Product labels also provide other useful information for consumers. One of the most common features on any label is directions on how the product should be used, or if food, prepared. An example is directions on clothing indicating how to clean and store the items. Another example is directions on either prescription or over-the-counter medications that provide information on how many pills should be taken and warn of possible drug interactions.

Moreover, most products that could be toxic if ingested have a warning about this on the package, as well as instructions on what to do in case of an emergency. This type of label has two main purposes. The first is to help the consumer in case the product is improperly used. The second is to help prevent lawsuits by consumers who misuse products. Generally speaking, more disclosure about the potential hazards of a product provides the company greater legal protection. Nevertheless, no product warning, even a detailed one, can completely prevent all lawsuits.

Most companies also use one or more of three other labels on their products. The first type, known as a grade label, identifies the quality of the product by a letter, such as "grade A," or with a word, such as "prime." The second type, an informative label, uses phrases such as "Keep refrigerated after opening" to help consumers use the product appropriately. The third type, a descriptive label, describes the benefits or positive attributes of the product.

LEGAL ISSUES

The federal government sets forth legal requirements that form a key element of product label design. Federal regulations regarding products and food have become progressively more numerous since the 1960s, due in large part to consumer activism and media attention. The most important of these regulations and laws are discussed here.

At the start of the twentieth century, responding to consumer pressure, the federal government created two government regulatory bodies: the U.S. Food and Drug Administration (FDA), which regulates interstate commerce in foods and drugs, and the Federal Trade Commission (FTC), whose role is to combat deceptive and unfair-trade practices. Both agencies have broad powers to interpret and enforce laws and regulations. Most compa-

nies make a strong effort to comply with federal laws that regulate product labels and advertising.

Numerous laws have been designed to protect consumers, including:

- Wheeler-Lea Amendment (1938) to the Federal Trade Commission Act: Controls deceptive and misleading advertising

- Lanham Trademark Act (1946): Provides protections for and regulations of brand names, brand marks, trade names, and trademarks

- Federal Hazardous Substance Labeling Act (1960): Requires warnings on the labels of all household-use products that contain potentially hazardous ingredients

- Child Protection Act (1966): Strengthens the Federal Hazardous Substance Labeling Act by prohibiting the sale of dangerous toys and other articles that are used by children, especially items containing electrical, mechanical, or thermal hazards

- Fair Packaging and Labeling Act (1966): Primarily outlaws deceptive packaging of certain consumer goods; also requires adequate information on the quantity and composition of product contents, and promotes packaging practices that make it easier to compare prices. In order to comply with the law, the following information must be included on the label: name of commodity and manufacturer, net quantity of contents expressed in the appropriate category (ounces/grams, pints, liters), and relevant ingredient information.

- Cigarette Labeling Act (1965): Requires that all cigarette packages and ads contain the statement: "Warning: The Surgeon General has determined that cigarette smoking is dangerous to your health"

- Consumer Product Safety Act (1972): Established the Consumer Product Safety Commission and gave it broad powers to carry out product tests, set safety standards, ban or seize hazardous products, and issue both civil and criminal complaints against business firms that fail to meet product safety requirements

- Federal Trade Commission Improvement Act (1975): Expanded the authority of the FTC in various ways; in particular, it gave the FTC the power to set rules concerning warranties on consumer products and provide consumers with redress in the form of class-action lawsuits

- Nutrition Labeling and Education Act (1990): Clarified and strengthened the FDA's legal authority to require nutrition labeling on foods and established the circumstances under which claims may be made about the nutrients in foods. The act covers only nutrients or substances in food that "nourish"; it does not in any way regulate nonnutrient substances in foods. Moreover, the act requires that labels disclose the amount of specified nutrients in foods. Every covered food should have a uniform nutrition label disclosing the amount of calories, fat, salt, and other nutrients. In order to make this information meaningful, the act requires the FDA to issue standards providing that uniform servings be noted on the food label. Where the full labeling is impractical, the act provides for an exemption or requires that the information be provided in a modified form. Restaurants, for example, are exempted.

- Federal Trademark Dilution Act (1995): Grants trademark owners the right to protect trademarks and requires relinquishment of names that match or parallel existing trademarks

SEE ALSO *Packaging; Promotion*

BIBLIOGRAPHY

Kotler, Philip, and Armstrong, Gary (2006). *Principles of marketing* (11th ed.). Upper Saddle River, NJ: Pearson Prentice-Hall.

Kotler, Philip, and Keller, Kevin (2006). *Marketing management: Analysis, planning, implementation, and control* (12th ed.). Upper Saddle River, NJ: Pearson Prentice Hall.

Lascu, D. N., and Clow, K. E. (2004). *Marketing frontiers: Concepts and tools.* Cincinnati: Atomic Dog.

Pride, William M., and Ferrell, O. C. (2006). *Marketing concepts and strategies.* Boston: Houghton Mifflin.

Solomon, M. R., Marshall, G. W., and Stuart E. W. (2006). *Marketing: Real people, real choices.* Upper Saddle River, NJ: Pearson Prentice-Hall.

Thomas R. Baird
Michael J. Milbier

PRODUCT LINES

The product mix of a company is the total composite of products offered by that organization. A product line is a group of products within the product mix that are closely related, either because they function in a similar manner, are sold to the same customer groups, are marketed through the same types of outlets, or fall within given price ranges.

Product-line decisions are concerned with the combination of individual products offered in a given line. The responsibility for a given product line resides with a product-line manager (sometimes called a product-group manager), who supervises several product managers who, in turn, are responsible for individual products within the line. A product is a distinct unit within the product line that is distinguishable by size, price, appearance, or some other attribute. Decisions about a product line are usually incorporated into a divisional-level marketing plan, which specifies changes in the product lines and allocations to products in each line. Product-line managers normally have the following responsibilities: (1) Consider expansion of a given product line; (2) consider products for deletion from the product line; (3) evaluate the effects of product additions and deletions on the profitability of other items in the line; and (4) allocate resources to individual products in the line on the basis of marketing strategies recommended by product managers.

One strategy organizations can employ to help sell their products is to use brand-identification strategies. Brand identification is generally defined as creating a brand with positive consumer benefits, resulting in consumer loyalty and repeat purchasing. Other benefits of brand identification include (1) strong in-store recognition, (2) stronger competition against competitors' products, (3) better distribution, and (4) better in-store shelf position. Organizations have four basic types of branding available: individual brand names, family brand names, product-line brand names, and corporate brand names.

Individual brand names can be used to establish brand identification without reference to an integrated product line or to the corporate name. Each brand is sold individually and stands or falls on its own. Family brand names involve the opposite strategy—including the firms' total product mix under one family name. The corporate name, rather than the brand name, is emphasized in order to leverage the high-quality name of the organization. This can reduce advertising and marketing costs. Product-line brand names involve a strategy midway between an individual brand name and a family brand name strategy. All brands within the product line have a common name. Product-line brand names are used when a company produces diverse product lines that require separate identification. Some companies employ the corporate brand name strategy. This strategy associates a strong corporate entity with a brand while maintaining the brand's individuality. If successful, it provides the advantages of both a family brand name and an individual brand name strategy.

An important concept for any product-line manager is the product life cycle, which is defined as the various stages a product goes through (introduction, growth, maturity, and decline). The primary function of the introduction stage is to create a solid brand name for the new product. Television, Internet, radio, and print advertise-

Television personality Tim Allen displays additions to his "Tim Allen Signature Tools" product line in conjunction with his hit television show, Home Improvement, *June 1999.* **AP IMAGES**

ments are coordinated to provide the maximum brand awareness. In the growth stage, the company focuses on creating loyalty to the specific product and also attempts to make minor improvements. Advertising emphasizes the benefits of the product, since the name is already known. When the maturity stage begins, sales start to level off because of increased competition, changes in consumer behavior, or technological advances that make the product less desirable than that of its competitors. In this stage, a company may decide to put limited resources into an advertising campaign to boost sales or create a new image. In addition, minor adjustments might be made to packaging (e.g., a new label) to reattract consumers. The decline stage occurs when sales begin to decline. The company needs to choose between modifying the product to increase sales or discontinuing the product when it finally cannot generate acceptable profits.

The product life cycle is an extremely important element when a company reviews its product line. One of the best ways to extend the life of a product and product line is for a company to use a revitalization strategy. When this tactic is used, the company changes the marketing plan and looks for new markets for the existing product line and the products within it. Here too it is critical that

the company is successful in repositioning the product to new market segments. Another method used to extend the life cycle of a product line is a line-modernization strategy, which focuses on either upgrading the entire product line or modernizing specifics products within the line in order to spark new consumer interest in the product or entire product line.

Other general product-line strategies include product-line additions, product-line deletions, and holding strategy. Product-line additions involve adding new products to a product line so new market segments can be covered. Product-line deletions involve removing a product that has not performed well or is not making enough money. A holding strategy involves maintaining the status quo. The product line stays the same and no major modifications or marketing strategy changes are planned. In order to have a profitable product line, the product line manager will need to employ a variety of the strategies.

SEE ALSO *Marketing*

BIBLIOGRAPHY

Assael, Henry (1985). *Marketing Management: Strategy and Action.* Boston: Kent Publishing Company.

Dickson, Peter R. (1994). *Marketing Management*. New York: Harcourt Brace.

Kinnear, Thomas C., and Bernhardt, Kenneth L. (1983). *Principles of Marketing*. Glenview, IL: Scott, Foresman.

Kotler, Philip, and Armstrong, Gary (2005). *Principles of Marketing*. Upper Saddle River, NJ: Pearson Prentice-Hall.

Myers, James H. (1986). *Marketing*. New York: McGraw-Hill.

Schewe, Charles D., and Smith, Reuben M. (1983). *Marketing: Concepts and Applications*. New York: McGraw-Hill.

Michael J. Milbier

PRODUCT MIX

The product mix of a company, which is generally defined as the total composite of products offered by a particular organization, consists of both product lines and individual products. A product line is a group of products within the product mix that are closely related, either because they function in a similar manner, are sold to the same customer groups, are marketed through the same types of outlets, or fall within given price ranges. A product is a distinct unit within the product line that is distinguishable by size, price, appearance, or some other attribute. For example, all the courses a university offers constitute its product mix; courses in the marketing department constitute a product line; and the basic marketing course is a product item. Product decisions at these three levels are generally of two types: those that involve width (variety) and depth (assortment) of the product line and those that involve changes in the product mix occur over time.

The depth (assortment) of the product mix refers to the number of product items offered within each line; the width (variety) refers to the number of product lines a company carries. For example, Table 1 illustrates the hypothetical product mix of a major state university.

The product lines are defined in terms of academic departments. The depth of each line is shown by the number of different product items—course offerings—offered within each product line. (The examples represent only a partial listing of what a real university would offer.) The state university has made the strategic decision to offer a diverse market mix. Because the university has numerous academic departments, it can appeal to a large cross-section of potential students. This university has decided to offer a wide product line (academic departments), but the depth of each department (course offerings) is only average.

In order to see the difference in product mix, product line, and products, consider a smaller college that focuses on the sciences represented in Table 2. This college has decided to concentrate its resources in a few departments (again, this is only a partial listing); that is, it has chosen a concentrated market strategy (focus on limited markets). This college offers narrow product line (academic departments) with a large product depth (extensive course offerings within each department). This product mix would most likely appeal to a much narrower group of potential students—those students who are interested in pursuing intensive studies in math and science.

PRODUCT-MIX MANAGEMENT AND RESPONSIBILITIES

It is extremely important for any organization to have a well-managed product mix. Most organizations break down managing the product mix, product line, and actual product into three different levels.

Hypothetical state university product mix

WIDE WIDTH, AVERAGE DEPTH

Political Science	Education	Mathematics	Nursing	Engineering	English
Political Theory	Elementary Teaching	Calculus I	Biology	Physics	English Literature
American Government	Secondary Teaching	Calculus II	Chemistry	Advanced Math	European Writers
International Relations	Teaching Internship	Trigonometry	Organic Chemistry	Electrical Concepts	Hemingway Seminar
State Government	Post Secondary Teaching	Math Theory	Statistics	Logic Design	Creative Writing

Table 1

Hypothetical small college product mix

NARROW WIDTH, LARGE DEPTH

Mathematics	Physics
Geometric Concepts	Intermediate Physics
Analytic Geometry and Calculus	Advanced Physics
Calculus II	Topics on Physics and Astronomy
Calculus III	Thermodynamics
Numerical Analysis	Condensed Matter Physics II
Differential Equations	Electromagnetic Theory
Matrix Theory	Quantum Mechanics II

Table 2

Product-mix decisions are concerned with the combination of product lines offered by the company. Management of the companies' product mix is the responsibility of top management. Some basic product-mix decisions include: (1) reviewing the mix of existing product lines; (2) adding new lines to and deleting existing lines from the product mix; (3) determining the relative emphasis on new versus existing product lines in the mix; (4) determining the appropriate emphasis on internal development versus external acquisition in the product mix; (5) gauging the effects of adding or deleting a product line in relationship to other lines in the product mix; and (6) forecasting the effects of future external change on the company's product mix.

Product-line decisions are concerned with the combination of individual products offered within a given line. The product-line manager supervises several product managers who are responsible for individual products in the line. Decisions about a product line are usually incorporated into a marketing plan at the divisional level. Such a plan specifies changes in the product lines and allocations to products in each line. Generally, product-line managers have the following responsibilities: (1) considering expansion of a given product line; (2) considering candidates for deletion from the product line; (3) evaluating the effects of product additions and deletions on the profitability of other items in the line; and (4) allocating resources to individual products in the line on the basis of marketing strategies recommended by product managers.

Decisions at the first level of product management involve the marketing mix for an individual brand/product. These decisions are the responsibility of a brand man-

ager (sometimes called a product manager). Decisions regarding the marketing mix for a brand are represented in the product's marketing plan. The plan for a new brand would specify price level, advertising expenditures for the coming year, coupons, trade discounts, distribution facilities, and a five-year statement of projected sales and earnings. The plan for an existing product would focus on any changes in the marketing strategy. Some of these changes might include the product's target market, advertising and promotional expenditures, product characteristics, price level, and recommended distribution strategy.

GENERAL MANAGEMENT WORKFLOW

Top management formulates corporate objectives that become the basis for planning the product line. Product-line managers formulate objectives for their line to guide brand managers in developing the marketing mix for individual brands. Brand strategies are then formulated and incorporated into the product-line plan, which is in turn incorporated into the corporate plan. The corporate plan details changes in the firm's product lines and specifies strategies for growth. Once plans have been formulated, financial allocations flow from top management to product line and then to brand management for implementation. Implementation of the plan requires tracking performance and providing data from brand to product line to top management for evaluation and control. Evaluation of the current plan then becomes the first step in the next planning cycle, since it provides a basis for examining the company's current offerings and recommending modifications as a result of past performance.

PRODUCT-MIX ANALYSIS

Because top management is ultimately responsible for the product mix and the resulting profits or losses, they often analyze the company product mix. The first assessment involves the area of opportunity in a particular industry or market. Opportunity is generally defined in terms of current industry growth or potential attractiveness as an investment. The second criterion is the company's ability to exploit opportunity, which is based on its current or potential position in the industry. The company's position can be measured in terms of market share if it is currently in the market, or in terms of its resources if it is considering entering the market. These two factors—opportunity and the company's ability to exploit it—provide four different options for a company to follow.

1. High opportunity and ability to exploit it result in the firm's introducing new products or expanding markets for existing products to ensure future growth.

2. Low opportunity but a strong current market position will generally result in the company's attempting to maintain its position to ensure current profitability.

3. High opportunity but a lack of ability to exploit it results in either (a) attempting to acquire the necessary resources or (b) deciding not to further pursue opportunity in these markets.

4. Low opportunity and a weak market position will result in either (a) avoiding these markets or (b) divesting existing products in them.

These options provide a basis for the firm to evaluate new and existing products in an attempt to achieve balance between current and future growth. This analysis may cause the product mix to change, depending on what management decides.

The most widely used approach to product portfolio analysis is the model developed by the Boston Consulting Group (BCG). The BCG analysis emphasizes two main criteria in evaluating the firm's product mix: the market growth rate and the product's relative market share. BCG uses these two criteria because they are closely related to profitability, which is why top management often uses the BCG analysis. Proper analysis and conclusions may lead to significant changes to the company's product mix, product line, and product offerings.

The market growth rate represents the products' category position in the product life cycle. Products in the introductory and growth phases require more investment because of research and development and initial marketing costs for advertising, selling, and distribution. This category is also regarded as a high-growth area (e.g., the Internet). Relative market share represents the company's competitive strength (or estimated strength for a new entry). Market share is compared to that of the leading competitor. Once the analysis has been done using the market growth rate and relative market share, products are placed into one of four categories.

- *Stars*: Products with high growth and market share are known as stars. Because these products have high potential for profitability, they should be given top priority in financing, advertising, product positioning, and distribution. As a result, they need significant amounts of cash to finance rapid growth and frequently show an initial negative cash flow.

- *Cash cows*: Products with a high relative market share but in a low growth position are cash cows. These are profitable products that generate more cash than is required to produce and market them. Excess cash should be used to finance high opportunity areas (stars or problem children). Strategies for cash cows should be designed to sustain current market share rather than to expand it. An expansion strategy would require additional investment, thus decreasing the existing positive cash flow.

- *Problem children*: These products have low relative market share but are in a high-growth situation. They are called "problem children" because their eventual direction is not yet clear. The firm should invest heavily in those that sales forecasts indicate might have a reasonable chance to become stars. Otherwise divestment is the best course, since problem children may become dogs and thereby candidates for deletion.

- *Dogs*: Products in the category are clearly candidates for deletion. Such products have low market shares and unlike problem children, have no real prospect for growth. Eliminating a dog is not always necessary, since there are strategies for dogs that could make them profitable in the short term. These strategies involve "harvesting" these products by eliminating marketing support and selling the product only to intensely loyal consumers who will buy in the absence of advertising. However, over the long term companies will seek to eliminate dogs.

As can be seen from the description of the four BCG alternatives, products are evaluated as producers or users of cash. Products with a positive cash flow will finance high-opportunity products that need cash. The emphasis on cash flow stems from management's belief that it is better to finance new entries and to support existing products with internally produced funds than to increase debt or equity in the company.

Based on this belief, companies will normally take money from cash cows and divert it to stars and to some problem children. The hope is that the stars will turn into cash cows and the problem children will turn into stars. The dogs will continue to receive lower funding and eventually be dropped.

CONCLUSION

Managing the product mix for a company is very demanding and requires constant attention. Top management must provide accurate and timely (BCG) analysis of their company's product mix so the appropriate adjustments can be made to the product line and individual products.

SEE ALSO *Marketing Mix*

BIBLIOGRAPHY

Assael, Henry (1985). *Marketing Management: Strategy and Action*. Boston: Kent Publishing Company.

Kinnear, Thomas C., and Bernhardt, Kenneth L. (1990). *Principles of Marketing*. Glenview, IL: Scott, Foresman/Little, Brown Higher Education.

Dickson, Peter R. (1994). *Marketing Management*. Harcourt Brace College Publishers.

Kotler, Philip, and Armstrong, Gary (2005). *Principles of Marketing*. Upper Saddle River, NJ: Pearson Prentice-Hall.

Myers, James H. (1986). *Marketing*. New York: McGraw-Hill.

Schewe, Charles D., and Smith, Reuben M. (1983). *Marketing: Concepts and Applications*. New York: McGraw-Hill.

Michael J. Milbier

PRODUCTION MANAGEMENT

SEE *Operations Management*

PRODUCTIVITY

Productivity is the result or the sum of all effort that it takes to deliver a product or service. Productivity is frequently referred to as output and, to some degree, can be measured. The output generated by a person, organization, or other entity is measured in terms of (the number of) units or items produced and services performed within a specified time frame. Thus, productivity is the economic value of goods and services. It becomes the value or result of the price of a product or service minus all costs (supplies, materials, human labor, etc., which frequently are monetary) that go into the effort.

PRODUCTIVITY PERFORMANCE MEASURES

Productivity is a performance measure that indicates how effectively an organization converts its resources into its desired products or services. It is a relative measure in that it is used to compare the effectiveness of a country, organization, department, workstation, or individual to itself over time for the same operation, or to other countries, organizations, departments, workstations, or individuals. From a systems perspective, productivity indicates how well an organization transforms its inputs into outputs. In manufacturing, productivity is generally stated as a ratio of output to input. Productivity may be expressed as partial measures, multifactor measures, and total measures. Partial productivity measures are used to analyze activities

in terms of a single input (e.g., units produced per worker, units produced per plant, units produced per hour, or units produced per quantity of material). Multifactor productivity measures take into account the utilization of multiple inputs (e.g., units of output per the sum of labor, capital, and energy or units of output per the sum of labor and materials). A total measure of productivity expresses the ratio of all outputs produced to all resources used.

SYSTEM AND SUBSYSTEM PRODUCTIVITY

An important point in seeking productivity improvements in a subsystem of an organization is to link the subsystem improvements to the total system productivity. Optimization of a subsystem operation that does not affect the overall productivity of the organization is a waste of resources. For example, a manufacturer might improve the productivity of its machining operations, as measured by number of units produced per dollar. But if these units cannot be sold and are warehoused, the productivity of the organization has not increased, since the goal of the manufacturer is to generate revenue through the sale of its products. Activities intended to improve productivity must be carefully selected, and the appropriate measures must be developed to ensure that the organization's efforts result in the improvement of its overall productivity.

Numerous specific components are involved in contributing to and measuring productivity. The most important of these are discussed below.

Return on Investment. Productivity is closely related to, but not dependent on, profit. It can be measured by return on investment (ROI). ROI is determined after the sale of a product or service minus the deductions for the total amount of effort (resources, etc.) put into its design, development, implementation, evaluation, and marketing. The formula for determining ROI is: Price minus Cost divided by Sales.

Productivity Measures for Individuals and Teams. An individual's productivity is measured by that person's potential to reach the highest level of productivity possible. That is, a person has certain skills that determine his or her level of capability (an engineer's skills, banker's knowledge, etc.). An individual's experiences and education usually determine his or her skill level regarding a particular job. Other factors, such as a positive environment (working with a good team, having a good boss, liking the physical surroundings in the workplace, being appreciated, etc.) and how motivated one is to do a job, also contribute to productivity. When several individuals come together to work as a team, the team's productivity or the effectiveness of the team is the sum of individual efforts toward achieving a desired goal. Several factors (motivation, expertise, working conditions, team compatibility, potential, etc.) influence the level of productivity achieved.

Productivity Gap. A productivity, or capacity, gap is the difference between what a person can do and what that person actually does. That is, every person has the ability to achieve at a certain level. If a person is not motivated and is not working up to potential, that person's productivity gap is usually quite large. The same principle applies to a work team, organization, and so on. It is desirable to estimate potential (of a person, work unit, company, etc.) to determine where productivity gaps exist (and how large they are) and find ways to close them. By looking at a person's ability in conjunction with other motivational factors, it is possible to estimate a person's (or a group's) potential to achieve desired results. When all factors operate at optimum, the productivity is said to be at its highest level—the productivity gap has been filled or is minimized.

Motivation. Productivity is directly related to how motivated a person is to perform a task or activity. Many businesses devote much time and effort to finding ways to motivate employees. Worker enhancement programs (for an individual, team, company, etc.) that are built on ways to motivate workers (toward self-motivation and long-term motivation) can optimize productivity. Organizations that are most successful in motivating workers provide a variety of programs (formal and informal avenues within and outside the organization) to meet the needs of their employees. Some organizations offer employees sports and recreational activities, fitness and leisure activities, and family-oriented programs (work- or job-augmented incentives). Incentive programs may be totally separate from or incorporated into work-team meetings, seminars, and education/training programs. Such a comprehensive approach toward enhancing worker performance may capitalize on quality measures (such as value, total quality management [TQM], quality circles, innovation, etc.) and performance standards (such as profitability, efficiency, customer satisfaction, on-time delivery, etc.) and include a wide range of personal and team rewards and incentives.

Mutual Reward Theory. Mutual reward theory (MRT) is based on finding ways for all to benefit. That is, if an organization can assist an employee in reaching some of his or her goals while still meeting the company's production goals, a mutual reward has occurred. When the benefits are at an optimum for all persons involved, the greatest rewards are realized. Productivity is usually directly proportional to the degree of MRT success.

Productivity Benchmarks. Factors that enter into productivity benchmarking for an organization include overall operations, worker training, technology, continuous quality improvement, and management philosophy and strategy. Management strategy includes how and at what level decision making takes place. Usually greater productivity gains are realized when decision making is pushed to its lowest level possible and is still effective. Also, an organization's efficiency may depend just as much on borrowing and lending strategies (e.g., requiring immediate payment on goods sold while practicing delayed payments to creditors) to maximize resource availability as it does on efficient operations and a safe environment. Thus, there are many important factors included in maximizing ROI, most of which depend on making the right decisions at the right time. What is a good decision for one company may be bad or devastating for another.

Productivity Growth and Economics. Productivity growth is defined as a measure of the amount of goods and services that are produced during a specified period of time. Once a standard has been determined, the standard (benchmark or identified level of production) becomes the measure against which all future production can be compared. Since 1950, the U.S. ten-year annual growth rates have been 2.17 percent for the 1950s; 2.85 percent for the 1960s; 1.71 percent for the 1970s; 2.17 percent for the 1980s; and an estimated 1.31 percent for the 1990s. The annual growth rate is of particular interest to individuals, since the productivity growth rate is directly proportional to a person's wealth. That is, as productivity levels go up, so does an individual's buying power. In turn, the total economy benefits from the boost.

Productivity Value Added. While productivity is more easily measured in manufacturing (products produced) than in services, most productivity researchers agree that people are the world's most valuable resources. Many productivity researchers suggest that education and training are the basic foundation for raising productivity levels. The acquisition of expertise through education and training, coupled with the best equipment and resources within an efficient and safe environment, can be maximized by developing employees into people who want to learn, who want to work at their potential, and who want to continuously improve. These factors are best achieved when an employee is motivated to take pride in the work he or she does. A motivated, self-starting employee is one who adds value to an organization and contributes to the overall productivity of him- or herself, a work group, an organization, and the economy.

SEE ALSO *Quality Management; Standard-Based Work Performance*

BIBLIOGRAPHY

Goodstein, Leonard, Nolan, Timothy, and Pfeiffer, J. William (1993). *Applied Strategic Planning: A Comprehensive Guide.* New York: McGraw-Hill.

Hammer, Michael (1996). *Beyond Reengineering.* New York: HarperBusiness.

Jonash, Ronald S., and Sommerlatte, Tom (1999). *The Innovation Premium.* Reading, MA: Perseus Books.

Langdon, Danny (2000). *Aligning Performance: Improving People, Systems, and Organizations.* San Francisco: Jossey-Bass/Pfeiffer.

Lewis, James P. (2000). *The Project Manager's Desk Reference.* New York: McGraw-Hill.

Meyer, Marc H., and Lehnerd, Alvin P. (1997). *The Power of Product Platforms: Building Value and Cost Leadership.* New York: Free Press.

Recardo, Ronald J., Wade, David, Mention, Charles A. III, and Jolly, Jennifer A. (1996). *Teams: Who Needs Them and Why?* Houston, TX: Gulf Publishing.

Reinertsen, Donald G. (1997). *Managing the Design Factory: A Product Developer's Toolkit.* New York: Free Press.

Shim, Jae K., and Siegel, Joel G. (1999). *Operations Management.* Hauppage, NY: Barron's Educational Series.

Smith, Elizabeth A. (1995). *The Productivity Manual* (2nd ed.). Houston, TX: Gulf Publishing.

Tesoro, Ferdinand, and Tootson, Jack (2000). *Implementing Global Performance Measurement Systems: A Cookbook Approach.* San Francisco: Jossey-Bass.

Sharon Lund O'Neil
John W. Hansen

PROFESSIONAL EDUCATION

Professional education is a formalized approach to specialized training in a professional school through which participants acquire content knowledge and learn to apply techniques. Although content is what the participant is expected to learn by attending professional school, such an education also helps the participant acquire the competencies needed for proper practice and behavior. Some common goals of professional education include incorporating the knowledge and values basic to a professional discipline; understanding the central concepts, principles, and techniques applied in practice; attaining a level of competence necessary for responsible entry into profes-

sional practice; and accepting responsibility for the continued development of competence. It is designed to produce responsible professionals and then to ensure their continuing competence in the profession by helping them recognize and understand the significance of advancing professional knowledge and improving standards of practice. It involves the translation of learning to practice and is intended to prevent occupations and professionals from becoming obsolete.

ROLE OF PROFESSIONAL EDUCATION

The essence of professionalism is the delivery of a service in response to a social need. Professional education is a response to society's demands for expert help provided by competent people. The growth and development of a profession is a function of specific needs, and the role of the professional changes because of changes in society. Professional education both responds to changing demands and provides impetus to changing the field itself, balancing a forward look with the realities of the present. Professional education is thus both reactive and initiating. Most problem solving on the job is reactive because decisions need to be made and little time is available for research or consultation with peers.

Special knowledge and skills were once passed on from one professional to others through apprenticeships, were experiential, and came from nonacademic sources. This method became inadequate for preparing competent professionals. Schools were established with the purpose of supplying financial resources and human resources beneficial to society and training the next generation of people. The curriculum attempts to develop discipline and self-awareness in the professional. These schools are charged with planning and delivering a full range of educational services that allow knowledge-based learning through the integration of instruction, research, and technology.

ONGOING AND LIFELONG LEARNING

Professional education determines the quality of services provided. As changes in both practice and theory occur, knowledge increases and beginning levels of competence become insufficient for effective practice. It is not enough merely to collaborate or work closely with peers to find ways to develop new practices and new talents. One way to improve practices and talents is through formal learning opportunities that allow reflection about what is learned with peers. No profession can effectively deal with the pressing changes of standards and ethics surrounding practice without discussing changes and modifying tasks.

Pursuing additional education to satisfy the need for additional information is called lifelong learning.

Lifelong learning is a continuous, seamless effort of training for professionals. Learning occurs through efforts on the part of workers in conjunction with professional schools. It builds on one's current knowledge and understanding and is tailored to reflect interests and goals. Continuing development results in strengthening practices and the development of professionals who assume responsibility for maintaining high standards. Many professionals are self-motivated to learn new competencies required on the job because it enables them to acquire higher degrees of skill and commitment. Training and development creates confident, expert professionals who are motivated to learn and committed to fostering personal growth.

THE INTEGRATION OF TECHNOLOGY EDUCATION

Society has witnessed an explosion in knowledge and technological ability. Changes in job responsibilities and new technologies require specialization in both the profession and the technology. The Internet has changed the nature of professional education by offering an alternative to traditional classroom instruction that delivers the same services as a regular classroom environment.

The Internet is an asset to professional development because of the diversity of resources and ideas it has to offer. In addition, it is readily accessible to most people and user-friendly. The Internet offers a variety of Web-based instructional options, including e-mail, listservs, mailing lists, newsgroups, Web pages, and course management systems.

E-mail is an easy-to-use communication tool used for delivering letters and memos. It usually involves only text and is a fast way to facilitate class interaction and discussion. It allows information such as assignments and announcements to be sent back and forth between instructor and student. Listservs, mailing lists, and newsgroups are simple, convenient, and flexible to use. A listserv is a special-interest discussion group that distributes messages to many users on a mailing list. Users post messages and the listserv software sends the messages to the members. Mailing lists are discussions that allow users to send messages to groups of people as easily as to a single person. Newsgroups are discussion groups organized by topic. Messages are not sent to an e-mail account but are posted to a central location on a network. When users are ready, they select the topics they are interested in and the messages they want to read. Web pages are also an effective tool for exchanging ideas on the Internet. They allow participants to progress through instructional materials to achieve learning outcomes and to participate in electronic discussions during times that are convenient for them, at their own pace, at any time, and from any location. Course management systems are commercially developed software that are designed for classroom management, instructional management, and performance assessment. They allow on-line access, either directly or through Web page links, to course content. These systems monitor participant progress by managing files of participants as they navigate through course content.

Professional development courses on the Internet offer new challenges and new opportunities for professional education. The Internet addresses most professional development needs of the twenty-first century. Other innovative opportunities continue to develop that will offer more services to help with research and keep us informed about topics of special interest. By making use of this technology, instruction is extended beyond the physical limitations of traditional classrooms. Internet technology offers an unlimited database of new knowledge that is available at little or no cost. Attention is directed to professional development at all levels. This new vision of professional development requires a new vision of preparation that includes the ability to relate technology to particular professions and to related fields. It is essential that programs access and integrate technology to facilitate participant learning. This type of cooperation continues to build a new educational system that is based on the traditional concept of lifelong learning.

SUMMARY

Professional education educates the new generation of professionals, expanding the frontiers of knowledge and reaching out in service to society. Professional education is increasingly being called upon to play a significant role in the administration of new programs within continuing and new structures. The rapidly changing society in which professionals exist demands that they attempt to maximize work performance. There is no single model that serves as a prototype program. There are many programs that serve the diverse needs of professionals who are assuming different roles and greater responsibilities. Professional education is a lifelong process and continues to improve, tailoring programs to help shape competent workers for the twenty-first century.

SEE ALSO *Corporate Education; Online Education; Training and Development*

BIBLIOGRAPHY
Abdal-Haqq, Ismat (1998). *Professional Development Schools: Weighing the Evidence.* Thousand Oaks, CA: Corwin Press.
Evers, Frederick T., Rush, James Cameron, and Berdrow, Iris (1998). *The Bases of Competence: Skills for Lifelong Learning and Employability.* San Francisco: Jossey-Bass.

Guskey, Thomas R., and Huberman, A. M. (1995). *Professional Development in Education: New Paradigms and Practices*. New York: Teachers College Press.

Maehl, William H. (2000). *Lifelong Learning at Its Best: Innovative Practices in Adult Credit Programs*. San Francisco: Jossey-Bass.

Connie Anderson

```
Code for computing gross pay for an employee
_____
Machine language
LOAD        GROSSPAY
SUBTRACT    DEDUCTIONS
STORE       NETPAY
High-level language
NetPay=GrossPay-Deductions
```

Figure 1

PROFIT SHARING
SEE *Employee Compensation*

PROFITABILITY PRICING
SEE *Pricing*

PROGRAMMING

A computer can be an extremely efficient technological tool. The use of computers provides humans with the ability to perform a variety of tasks. The actual computer, however, does little on its own. Computer programs enable the computer, or the hardware, to perform a desired function or task. Computer programs are step-by-step instructions written specifically to instruct the computer on how to accomplish a task. The act of writing these computer programs is referred to as programming.

PROGRAMMING LANGUAGES

A programming language includes the rules defining how a computer program is written. Computer programs fall into two major types of programming languages: low-level languages and high-level languages. Low-level languages are more similar to machine language, which is the language that computers understand directly. High-level languages, however, are often more similar to English and easier for humans to understand.

Initially, programmers used machine language to write computer programs. The computer's "native language" is comprised of a series of binary digits. Binary digits, referred to as bits, are the basic units of memory and can store only two different values, 0 or 1. A group of eight bits makes up a byte and is the amount of memory used to store one character of information, such as a letter or number. Each central processing unit (CPU) for a computer has a unique machine language.

For example, the machine language for an IBM computer model is unique compared to that of a Macintosh computer model. Because machine-language programming is extremely time-consuming and cumbersome, programmers began using English-like abbreviations to code the programs. This method of coding resulted in the development of assembly languages. With these languages, assemblers convert or translate the English-like code into machine language, increasing the speed at which programs can be written.

Although assembly languages improved the efficiency of program development, these languages still required many instructions to perform simple tasks. High-level languages were developed to improve programming efficiency by requiring fewer coding statements to accomplish more tasks. These languages use compilers or interpreters that convert high-level code into machine code.

Figure 1 illustrates the distinction between machine and high-level languages.

TYPES OF PROGRAMMING LANGUAGES

The two primary methods of programming are procedural and object-oriented. Procedural programming involves coding a set of statements called procedures that are executed sequentially by the compiler. This method of programming was used considerably when users were interacting with text-based computers. Using this approach, the programmer determines the sequence of actions that occur within the program. Programming languages such as COBOL and FORTRAN are examples of procedure languages.

The object-oriented method of programming (OOP) evolved when operating systems migrated to a more visual environment such as the Microsoft Windows family. Windows-based applications include graphical user interfaces (GUI, pronounce "gooey") to make programs friendlier and easier to use. The elements such as buttons, menus, and windows included in a GUI are called objects. Programmers must provide code that handles the user's interactions with these objects. Because the user can select the objects in any order, the program must respond to the user. Thus, the programmer no longer determines the sequence of execution within the program.

The concept of reusability has increased the popularity of OOP languages as well. OOP languages enable programmers to design and code applications that permit interchangeable software components. These reusable components can be used in other programs. Popular OOP languages are Visual Basic .NET, Java, C++, and Python.

CATEGORIES OF COMPUTER PROGRAMS

Systems programs and application programs are the two main types of computer programs. Systems programs or systems software is typically written in low-level language whereas application software is coded using high-level language. Systems software enables the computer to control and maintain its hardware (mouse, monitor, CPU) and interact with the user. There are three major types of systems software: operating systems, utilities, device drivers.

One of the most important types of systems software is the operating systems software. Operating systems software enables the computer application to communicate with the computer hardware. It also provides an interface or a link between the user and the computer. Utilities, another type of systems software, are specialized programs designed to make computing easier. A common example is antivirus software that protects the computer from harmful files and programs. The third type of system software is device drivers. They are specialized programs designed to allow input/output devices to communicate with the rest of the computer and its software. Device driver software is included with most hardware components. When a printer or scanner is purchased, for example, a device driver that is included must be installed on the computer before it can be used.

APPLICATIONS SOFTWARE

Applications software enables the end user to perform useful tasks or functions. If there is a standard task that needs to be accomplished, such as financial budgeting, application packages or software can be purchased from a software vendor at a retail store. Microsoft Excel, for example, is a popular spreadsheet application package that is used for budgeting. If there is a customized problem that is specific to the needs of an end user or company, an applications programmer can design a software package to solve the problem. Other examples of popular applications include word processors, database managers, spreadsheet programs, graphics applications, and Web browsers.

PROGRAM DEVELOPMENT CYCLE

Regardless of the programming language used, the process of developing a program is similar. The steps are as follows:

1. *Analyzing and determining the program specifications* is the first and most important step to program development. It is defining the problem and determining what the program should accomplish. Failing to complete this step will often result in ineffective and undesired output.

2. *Designing the program* involves planning the solution to the problem by determining a logical sequence of steps. Called an algorithm, this sequence of steps should include precise details of how to solve the problem. Three methods commonly used to develop the algorithm are flowcharts, pseudocode, and hierarchy charts. Flowcharts provide a pictorial representation of logic using diagrams. Pseudocode is written with English-like expressions rather than diagrams. Hierarchy charts are used to show the relationships between sections in a program. Most programmers use pseudocode and hierarchy charts instead of flowcharts to depict their logic.

3. *Choosing the interface* includes designing the GUI. The GUI is a user-friendly interface that allows the user to input data into the application and displays the output to the user. This step is needed only if a user interface is included in the program.

4. *Coding the program* involves translating the algorithm into a programming language and then entering the code into a code editor. This involves using the appropriate programming software to enter the program instructions or code into the computer's memory.

5. *Compiling the program* includes using a compiler or interpreter to convert the code into machine language.

6. *Testing and debugging* the program involves locating and removing any errors in the program. Testing is the process of finding errors and debugging is the process of correcting the errors. During this step, the programmer also does a "walk through" of the program to ensure that the program is functioning properly and that it includes all of the program specifications.

7. *Documenting the program* is a critical step that involves providing detailed descriptions of the pro-

cedures, the variables, and the data names used in the program. It also includes the purpose and objectives of the program. This information is intended to allow another person to understand the program. Internal documentation is found within the code of the program. External documentation is found separate from the program and may include instruction manuals or online help.

POPULAR PROGRAMS

Because of the popularity of applications that provide GUIs for end users which are user-friendly, many programming packages today include a "visual" component. Some of the most commonly used languages by programmers are Visual Basic, NET, Visual C++, and C#. Java, JavaScript, and XML are used for interactive web development.

SEE ALSO *Information Processing; Software*

BIBLIOGRAPHY

Deitel, Harvey M., Deitel, Paul J., and Nieto, Tem R. (2003). *Simply Visual Basic .NET: An application-driven tutorial approach.* Upper Saddle River, NJ: Prentice Hall.

Gaddis, Tony, Irvine, Kip, and Denton, Bruce (2003). *Starting out with Visual Basic .NET.* Boston: Addison Wesley.

Schneider, David (2003). *An introduction to programming using Visual Basic .NET* (5th ed.). Upper Saddle River, NJ: Prentice Hall.

Stern, Nancy, Stern, Robert A., and Ley, James P. (2003). *COBOL for the 21st century* (10th ed.). New York: Wiley, 2003.

Venit, Stewart (2002). *Extended prelude to programming: Concepts and design.* El Granada, CA: Scott Jones.

Ronda B. Henderson

PROMOTION

It would be safe to say that most companies engage in some form of promotional activity every day of the year. Promotion is one of the four Ps of marketing—price, product, place, and promotion. Promotion is generally thought of as a sequence of activities designed to inform and convince individuals to purchase a product, subscribe to a belief, or support a cause. All of the various tools available to marketing managers for promotional activities constitute what is known as the promotional mix.

PROMOTIONAL MIX

Marketing managers use different components of the promotional mix as tools for achieving company objectives—advertising, personal selling, public relations, and sales promotion. Each of these elements can be further divided into additional subcomponents or strategies. The majority of a company's promotional resources are usually spent on these four elements for a simple reason: Companies perceive these methods as the most effective means to promote their products. Other specialized promotional techniques, however, are also used to enhance promotional objectives.

Advertising. Advertising is often thought of as the paid, nonpersonal communication used in the promotion of a cause, idea, product, or service by an identified sponsor. The various advertising delivery methods include banners at sporting events, billboards, Internet Web sites, logos on clothing, magazines, newspapers, radio spots, and television commercials. Among the common forms of advertising are advocacy, comparative, cooperative, informational, institutional, persuasive, product, reminder, point-of-purchase, and specialty.

Personal Selling. Personal selling is considered one of the most effective promotional techniques because it facilitates interaction between consumer and seller. With personal selling, a salesperson can listen to and determine a consumer's needs by asking questions and receiving feedback from the consumer. Furthermore, personal selling activities can generate long-lasting friendships between consumers and sellers that typically generate many repeat purchases. Personal selling can also occur by means of interactive computers, telephone conferences, and interactive videoconferencing. A drawback of personal selling, however, is its high cost. Examples of products promoted through personal selling include automobiles, life insurance, real estate, and many industrial products.

Public Relations. Public relations has been described as building goodwill with a company's various constituencies, including consumers, employees, government officials, stockholders, and suppliers. The overall goal of any public relations effort is to project a positive company image when dealing with such issues as community and government relations, employment practices, and environmental issues.

>   *Consumers.* Public relations efforts are extremely important for maintaining a company's consumer base. Consumers must believe that they are buying from a caring, honest, and trustworthy company. Negative media stories about, for example, exploiting workers or producing substandard products can do enormous damage to a company in the eyes of consumers. Erosion of a company's

Sporting events, such as the FoodCity 500 NASCAR race seen here, are popular venues for advertising. © **SAM SHARPE/THE SHARPE IMAGE/CORBIS**

client base is likely to result in both lost sales and lost market share.

Employees. The most valuable asset a company has is its employees. Therefore, it is essential that employees believe in their company. Public relations communications are extremely important in ensuring that employees receive information about the company before outside media receive and report the information. A good example of providing superior public relations would be to inform company employees that a small reduction in the work force is required but that a full severance package will be provided for laid-off employees. Although this news is not positive, the employees are hearing about it first from the company and are also aware that they will be receiving assistance from the company. If employees read or see negative reports about the employer without a credible public relations explanations, they may find other work or reduce their productivity because of low morale.

Government officials. Maintaining a positive public image is also important because government agencies and offices (e.g., Federal Trade Commission, Federal Communication Commission) monitor the media and have regulatory oversight over company activities. Positive stories in the media obviously help promote a positive image to government regulators, which reduces the chance of being investigated and possibly fined. The opposite is also true as stories about client complaints or other dishonest practices or potentially illegal actions will draw the government's attention and probably some sort of investigation—something that no company wants. An investigation can drag on for months, even years, providing even more negative publicity. Even if the government regulators find no wrongdoing, the public is still likely to be skeptical because the company was investigated. Therefore, every company must make its best effort to answer any questions that regulators have regarding negative media stories or consumer complaints. A strong, well-organized public relations department will ward off potential trouble by being honest, friendly, positive, and helpful to government regulators and members of the news media.

Stockholders. Another key interest group for any company that offers publicly traded securities are the stockholders. If company stockholders generally receive positive news about a company, they are more likely to maintain investment, which helps keep the stock price up. Negative news that is not countered with positive public relations can create uncertainty about how the company is running and encourage stockholders to sell and to invest in other companies. This action can cause the stock value to decrease, making it difficult to attract new investors.

Suppliers. Positive public relations are essential for a company's relation with its suppliers. Suppliers are most concerned about being paid for the product they are selling to a company. Since most suppliers are generally not paid until ten to twenty days after delivery of their product, they must have faith in the ability of a company to pay its bills. Any negative news regarding a company's financial position in the absence of a full and complete explanation from the public relations department may result in a damaged reputation with suppliers. Suppliers could stop shipping their products or demand that payment is made at the time of delivery. Neither option is appealing to a company, and both could cause critical delays in getting its products to market.

Sales Promotion. Sales promotions are marketing practices designed to facilitate the purchase of a product that do not include advertising, personal selling, or public relations. Companies use sales promotion for a variety of reasons, including (1) to attract new product users who will hopefully turn into loyal consumers who keep buying the product; (2) to reward existing consumers with a price reduction, thereby maintaining their loyalty; and (3) to encourage repeat sales from occasional consumers.

SPECIAL PROMOTIONAL ACTIVITIES

Companies use a variety of sales promotion tactics to increase sales, including advertising specialties, cash refund offers/rebates, contests and sweepstakes, coupons, patronage rewards, point-of-purchase displays, premiums, price packs/cents-off deals, samples, and trade shows.

Advertising specialties. Companies frequently create and give away everyday items with their names and logos printed on the items such as bottle/can openers, caps, coffee mugs, key rings, and pencils. Companies prefer to use inexpensive handouts that will yield constant free advertising when used by the recipient.

Cash refund offers/rebates. A cash refund or rebate is similar to a coupon except that the price reduction comes after the product is already purchased. In order to receive the cash refund/rebate, the consumer must send in a proof of purchase with the company offer in order to obtain the refund. Rebates are often an excellent form of sales promotion for a company to use because a high percentage of consumers will not send in the forms for the refund.

Contests and sweepstakes. Many companies use contests and sweepstakes to increase the sales of a product. As a reward for participating, consumers might win cash, free products, or vacations. With a contest, participants are required to demonstrate a skill; for example, entrants might be asked to suggest a name for a new product, design a company logo, or even suggest a company name change. Contest entries are then reviewed by a panel of judges; the originator of the winning entry receives a prize, usually in the form of cash or a vacation. In contrast to the skill required with contests, a sweepstakes winner is determined by chance. For example, consumers maybe given a scratch card in a fast-food restaurants; if three-of-a-kind or another predetermined criterion is achieved, the consumer would be given a free hamburger or some other selected prize.

Coupons. Coupons are certificates that give consumers a price savings when they purchase a specified product. Coupons are frequently mailed, placed in newspapers, or dispensed at the point of purchase. In addition, some companies have coupons generated when an item is scanned at the register. Companies can promote both new and mature products through the use of coupons.

Patronage rewards. Awards provided by companies to promote and encourage the purchasing of their products are called patronage rewards. Airlines use this strategy by awarding frequent-flyer miles to consumers who use their services often. When a consumer has earned enough frequent-flyer miles, he or she can redeem a free ticket. Credit card companies also use patronage rewards by providing a list of free products a person can order based on the number dollars charged in a specified time period.

Point-of-purchase displays. Point-of-purchase promotions can include displays and demonstrations that take place at the point of purchase. The cardboard cutouts of popular movie stars that are put next to merchandise are excellent examples of this method. One drawback to point-of-purchase displays is that stores do not have time to set up all the ones that are offered, so only a handful of them are used. Companies frequently offer assistance in assembling and removing promotional displays to encourages storeowners to use their point-of-purchase displays.

Premiums. A premium is a good offered free or at a low cost to encourage consumers to buy a particular product. Companies can also offer premiums in the form of reusable containers bearing names and logos in order to help promote other products. In addition, a company may also decide to use a self-liquidating premium. The costs associated with self-liquidating premiums are passed along to consumers through the cost of product.

Price packs/cents-off deals. Price packs provide consumers with a reduced price that is marked directly on the package by the manufacture. Companies can offer price packs in the format of two for the price of one or offer products such as a tube of toothpaste and a toothbrush in one package for a lower price than that of the two items purchased separately. Consumers generally react favorably to price packs because they are perceived as a real bargain.

Samples. Some companies offer free samples of their products. The rationale for offering a free product sample is to achieve immediate consumer introduction to the product. Companies have several ways to introduce potential consumers to product samples. Commonly used delivery methods include mailing the product, passing the product out in stores, or door-to-door delivery of the product. The largest drawback of free samples is their high cost. However, it is expected that the associated sales will offset the initial cost of the free samples.

Trade shows. Most industries hold conventions and trade shows each year to show off new technology, assess consumer trends, and review other issues important to the industry. Trade shows provide firms that sell to a particular industry an excellent opportunity to promote new products, make new contacts, renew existing business relationships, maintain or build a reputation, and distribute promotional materials.

PROMOTIONAL OBJECTIVES

There are a number of promotional objectives, some of the most common being information dissemination, product demand, product differentiation, product highlights, and sales stabilization. Regardless of the promotional objective selected, the company's goal is to inform and convince consumers to buy the product.

Information Dissemination. One of the most basic desires of a company is to provide information about a product to potential consumers. Tools available to an organization for informing potential consumers about a product include billboards, flyers, Internet Web sites, magazines, newspapers, radio spots, and television commercials. Normally a variety of these promotional tools are used to communicate a single, coordinated message to potential consumers. These different promotional tools can provide potential consumers with an array of information about a product, such as features, quality, and/or price. The informational focus depends on the makeup of the target audience that the company is trying to reach with its message.

Product Demand. Another organizational goal of promotional activities is to create product demand. A company has several promotional options for fostering product demand. For example, a company may focus on using a primary demand strategy that concentrates on trying to increase demand for a general product or service line. Large companies or cooperatives that have well-known and large product lines normally use the primary demand strategy. Advertisements for these companies carry over to all product categories and, as a result, may improve sales in several product areas. Companies also use another marketing strategy, known as selective demand, which concentrates on promoting a specific brand within a company's product line. Selective demand is often used to help promote a new product so that consumers are aware of the new addition to a large company's product line. A company may also utilize a selective demand strategy when it wants to sell a product that has a high profit margin. A good example of this strategy is the active promotion of sport utility vehicles by major automobile companies.

Product Differentiation. A common challenge faced by companies is increased competition, which often results in the market being flooded with similar products. Consumers may conclude that no substantial difference exists between the products (homogeneous demand) and, therefore, look for the lowest-priced product to purchase. An industry that has experienced the problem of homogeneous demand is the soft-drink industry. With few exceptions, most consumers do not make a distinction among the numerous beverages that are offered. A company that excels at product differentiation can normally demand a higher price for a product because of its perceived higher quality.

Product Highlights. Companies have another tool to employ in order to justify a higher-priced product: A firm can accentuate the product's exceptional quality in detail to convince consumers that the extra cost is worthwhile. Highlighting a product's quality might sound easy, but a company must first develop superior advertisements to promote the product. Moreover, the firm must develop a reputation for making a superior product that is well known to the average consumer. Volvo is one company that has done an excellent job of creating the image of producing only high-quality, safe cars. Thus. Volvo can charge an extra premium for its cars. Caterpillar has also nurtured and promoted a reputation for producing only the best heavy earth-moving equipment in the world. It, too, charges an increased price for its products.

Sales Stabilization. A challenge that companies face is inconsistent demand for their products throughout the year. Reasons for this fluctuation can range from seasonal demand to changing economic conditions. Most companies would rather have a consistent demand for their products throughout the year, since this would allow them to have steady production and distribution facility operations. Ice cream manufacturers often face this dilemma because in the summer months demand for ice cream normally reaches its highest levels while sales decrease substantially in the winter. In order to combat these shifts in product demand, ice cream companies might offer coupons to encourage the purchase of their products during slow sales seasons.

SUMMARY

Companies engage in promotional activities virtually every day of the year. The various tools available to marketing managers for such activities are known as the promotional mix. Elements of the promotional mix include advertising, personal selling, public relations, and sales promotion. Each of these promotional mix elements can be further divided into sub-elements depending upon company objectives.

SEE ALSO *Advertising; Marketing; Marketing Mix*

BIBLIOGRAPHY

Boone, L. E., and Kurtz, D. L. (2005). *Contemporary Marketing* (11th ed.). Mason, OH: Thomson/South-Western.

Churchill, G. A., and Peter, J. P. (1998). *Marketing: Creating Value for Customers.* Boston: Irwin/McGraw-Hill.

Kotler, P., and Armstrong, G. (2006). *Marketing: An Introduction* (8th ed.). Upper Saddle River, NJ: Pearson Prentice-Hall.

Semenik, R. J., and Bamossy, G. J. (1995). *Principles of Marketing: A Global Perspective* (2nd ed.). Cincinnati, OH: South-Western.

Allen D. Truell
Michael Milbier

PSYCHOGRAPHICS
SEE *Lifestyles; Target Marketing*

PUBLIC COMPANY ACCOUNTING OVERSIGHT BOARD

The Sarbanes-Oxley Act of 2002 began with this statement of purpose: to protect investors by improving the accuracy and reliability of corporate disclosures made pursuant to the securities laws, and for other purposes. As stated in the act:

> There is established the Public Company Accounting Oversight Board (PCAOB), to oversee the audit of public companies that are subject to the securities laws, and related matters, in order to protect the interests of investors and further the public interest in the preparation of informative, accurate, and independent audit reports for companies the securities of which are sold to, and held by and for, public investors. The Board shall be a body corporate, operate as a nonprofit corporation, and have succession until dissolved by an Act of Congress. (Sec. 101)

The board provides a structure that is a marked departure from the earlier regulatory structure. Previously, the Securities and Exchange Commission (SEC) had delegated a considerable degree of rule making and oversight to the public accounting profession. Nevertheless, with the initial decisions of the PCAOB in the spring of 2003, rule making for auditing and oversight of auditors and their firms became fully the responsibility of the PCAOB itself.

BOARD MEMBERSHIP

As stated in the act, the board has five members, "appointed from among prominent individuals of integrity and reputation who have a demonstrated commitment to the interests of investors and the public." Furthermore, the members are expected to be knowledgeable of the nature of financial disclosures required of issuers under the securities laws and of the obligations of those who undertake audits of such issuers and issue reports.

Two members, and only two members, are to be certified public accountants (CPAs) or have been CPAs previously. If one of the two members is the chairperson of the board, he or she "may not have been a practicing certified public accountant for at least five years prior to his or her appointment to the Board." Members serve on a full-time basis and may not engage in any other business or professional activity during their service as board members.

Members are appointed for terms of five years and no member may serve for more than two terms, whether or not the terms of service are consecutive.

BOARD DUTIES

The act specifies the duties of board members with responsibility to:

1. Register public accounting firms that prepare audit reports for issuers

2. Establish or adopt, or both, by rule, auditing, quality control, ethics, independence and other standards relating to the preparation of audit reports for issuers

3. Conduct inspections of registered public accounting firms

4. Conduct investigations and disciplinary proceedings concerning, and impose appropriate sanctions where justified upon registered public accounting firms and associated persons of such firms

5. Perform such other duties or functions as the board (or the SEC by rule or order) determines are necessary or appropriate to promote high professional standards among and improve the quality of audit services offered by registered public accounting firms and associated persons thereof, or otherwise to carry out this act, in order to protect investors, or to further the public interest

6. Enforce compliance with this act, the rules of the board, professional standards, and the securities laws relating to the preparation of audit reports and the obligations and liabilities of accountants with respect thereto by registered public accounting firms and associated persons

7. Set the budget and manage the operation of the board and the staff of the board

For the first four duties listed above, there are references to specific sections of the act.

OFFICES AND STAFF

The PCAOB's headquarters are in Washington, D.C. Regional offices in 2005 were in eight locations: Atlanta, Chicago, Dallas, Denver, New York, Northern Virginia, Orange County (California), and San Francisco. The total number of staff at the end of 2004 was 260.

Among the key executives of the staff are the chief of staff, chief accountant, the director of enforcement and inspections, the director of registration and inspections, and director of government operations.

THE IMPACT ON PUBLIC ACCOUNTING

As noted by the American Institute of Certified Public Accountants (AICPA) in a discussion of the impact on the field of accounting, "the relationship between accounting firms and their publicly owned audit clients is different under the new law."

Possibly the most dramatic shift is that professional involvement of practitioners in rule making and monitoring is no longer provided. While earlier auditing standards for publicly owned companies were promulgated by the AICPA's Auditing Standards Board, such standards are now the responsibility of the PCAOB. The SEC continues to have ultimate responsibility and must approve the decisions of the PCAOB. The AICPA's Auditing Standards Board continues to function in developing guidance for nonpublicly owned companies. The inspection of public accounting firms is no longer designed and administered by the member-sponsored organizations.

Auditors now report and are overseen by a company's audit committee, not management. Audit committees must approve all services to be provided by the audit firm. Specified new information must be reported to audit committees. All rules related to independence and quality control are now provided by the PCAOB.

UNRESOLVED ISSUES

The PCAOB has been functioning since the spring of 2003. Much of the guidance provided by the Auditing Standards Board of the AICPA was accepted as interim guidance as the PCAOB reviews the auditing standards and makes determinations about what is to be accepted, what requires revision, and what requires new auditing standards.

As noted earlier, the Auditing Standards Board of the AICPA continues to function to provide guidance for audits of those entities that are not required to report to the SEC under the specifications of the Securities Exchange Act of 1934 in accordance with auditing guidance from the PCAOB. Inasmuch as auditing is a generic process, many critics have raised questions about the wisdom—and complexity—of two sets of standards, as many public accounting firms serve both types of clients.

The new requirement for an audit of internal controls led to much criticism. Section 404 of the act and rules adopted by the SEC require companies that file annual reports with the SEC to report on management's responsibilities to establish and maintain adequate internal control over the company's financial reporting process, as well as management's assessment of the effectiveness of internal controls. Section 404 requires the accounting firm that audits the company's financial statements to perform an audit on management's assessment and on the effectiveness of the company's controls.

Questions have been raised about the value of such an audit related to internal control and the burden imposed by additional costs. Furthermore, there are critics who believe that the scandals related to accounting during the early years of the new century would likely not have been averted by an audit of internal control. Enron, in its 2001 annual report, included an audit report from its audit firm, Arthur Andersen, about its internal controls. (Arthur Andersen had served as the company's internal auditors; thus, they were auditing their own work, which is a violation of the independence required of public accountants at the time.)

This requirement for an audit of internal controls and the submission of an auditor's report became effective with annual reports for fiscal years ending after December 15, 2004. The cascade of questions about the need for the requirement, the nature of the requirement, and the guidance provided led the SEC to convene a Roundtable on Implementation of Sarbanes-Oxley Internal Control Provisions for April 13, 2005. Over 200 letters of comment were submitted to the SEC related to this new requirement. The Roundtable was open to the public. Follow-up of the Roundtable included the provision of additional guidance. Challenges to the value of such an audit continue.

WEBSITES OF INTEREST

For extensive information on activities and plans of the PCAOB: http://www.pcaob.org

The AICPA also provides information about developments at the PCAOB: http://www.aicpa.org

SEE ALSO *Accounting*

Bernard H. Newman

PUBLIC RELATIONS

Public relations (PR) is a profession that includes the functions of communication, community relations, crisis management, customer relations, employee relations, government affairs, industry relations, investor relations, media relations, mediation, publicity, speechwriting, and visitor relations. The first World Assembly of Public Relations Associations, held in Mexico City in August 1978, defined the practice of public relations as "the art and social science of analyzing trends, predicting their consequences, counseling organizational leaders, and implementing planned programs of action, which will serve both the organization and the public interest."

With the advancement of the profession, in 1988 the Public Relations Society of America (PRSA) adopted a short definition, "Public relations helps an organization and its publics adapt mutually to each other." In 1994 the British Institute of Public Relations offered its definition: "Public relations practice is the discipline that looks after reputation with the aim of earning understanding and support, and influencing opinion and behavior." Although these definitions vary to some extent, they all imply that the fundamental functions of PR are communicating and improving the behavior of an organization and the perceptions of that behavior by its clientele.

PUBLIC RELATIONS, ADVERTISING, AND PROPAGANDA

People sometimes confuse public relations with advertising and propaganda. Actually, they are different.

Advertising. The purpose of advertising is to stimulate consumers' desires for a product or service and to motivate them to buy that product or service. Designing advertisements, preparing verbal and graphical messages, and buying time and space from the mass media for their exposure are the tasks of advertising. When necessary, PR professionals will use advertising as one approach to building goodwill and creating proper public attitudes toward their organizations. Tobacco companies' goodwill ads and television commercials are one example of such a use.

Propaganda. The purpose of propaganda is to generate conditioned reflexes among people in order to replace their reasoned actions with the conditioned reflex. Propaganda is used to brainwash people with a doctrine and then mislead them, and obviously the term carries a negative connotation. Some commonly used propaganda devices are:

- Name calling, which creates a positive or negative characterization, such as "he is wise and conscientious," "he is a liar," or "she has character!"

- Emotional stereotyping, which evokes designed images, such as "housewife," "foreigner," or "geek"

- Bandwagon, which creates a theme of "everyone else is doing it, and so should you"

- Card stacking, which provides distorted information by telling only one side of the story

PUBLIC RELATIONS RELATED ACTIVITIES

To carry out its fundamental functions of communicating and improving the behavior of an organization and the perceptions of that behavior by its constituents, PR professionals practice these major activities: researching the market and public opinion, planning and implementing PR campaigns, and counseling management.

Researching the Market and Public Opinion. The foundation of good PR strategies is conducting research on the market, public opinions, and circumstances on which public opinions are formed. Research enables PR professionals to identify an organization's target market and to discover what they think. Survey questionnaires and structured interviews are useful methods for collecting data from the potential market and analyzing and interpreting public opinions, attitudes, issues, and circumstances that might affect the operations of the organization positively or negatively. In some cases, PR professionals can gather information about their market and public opinion from secondary data, that is, data collected and published by others, such as government agencies, industry groups, professional organizations, research institutions, and universities.

Planning and Implementing PR Campaigns. Based on these research findings, a PR professional is able to plan and implement campaigns for bringing an organization's mission and objectives to the attention of its constituency, enhancing two-way communication and mutual understanding, and influencing or changing public opinions and policies. Planning and implementing a PR campaign involves setting objectives, budgeting, recruiting and training staff, developing persuasive messages, selecting appropriate media, working with the media, monitoring the campaign, coordinating various relations, evaluating outcomes, and managing the resources needed to perform all of these activities.

Counseling Management. Experienced PR professionals also act as advisers or counselors to organizations, which are committed to fulfilling their organizational citizenship and social responsibilities. Such professionals have developed reputations for anticipating potential issues that may affect public opinions and policies, helping organizations prepare for and deal with crisis communication, assisting organizations in establishing and maintaining good government relations, and helping organizations improve labor-management relations.

THE VALUE OF PR TO BUSINESS AND SOCIETY

PR serves a purpose for a variety of organizations, including public and private corporations, trade unions, foundations, hospitals, industry groups, professional associations, schools, and universities, as well as government agencies. PR professionals provide organizations with new opportunities because they interact with more internal and external audiences than anyone else in the organizations. They serve as the eyes and ears of top-level executives to keep them informed of what is really happening "out there," thereby overcoming executive isolation. PR professionals also help organizations manage changes through effective communication internally and externally, thereby reducing resistance and criticism from employees and other constituencies and increasing organizational competitiveness.

In addition, PR helps this complex, pluralistic society reach decisions and consensus more effectively by contributing to mutual understanding among individuals and organizations. It serves to bring private and public policies into harmony.

Finally, efficient public relations campaigns protect organizations when they are in crisis. A classic example is when Johnson & Johnson faced a crisis in late 1982 when an unknown murderer laced Extra-Strength Tylenol capsules with cyanide, causing the deaths of seven people in Chicago. With the counsel of Burson-Marsteller (a PR firm), the company responded to the crisis in a very effective and expeditious manner. As a result, Johnson & Johnson's PR campaign was so successful that not only did its Tylenol products make a successful market comeback, but its public image as a socially responsible company was greatly enhanced.

ETHICS AND RESPONSIBILITIES

PR professionals and their organizations have ethical responsibilities to at least these publics: clients, news media, government agencies, educational institutions, consumers, investors, communities, competitors, and critics. As the PRSA Member Code of Ethics 2000 states,

PRSA members are committed to ethical practices. The code is designed as a guide for PRSA members to carry out their ethical responsibilities.

SEE ALSO *Communications in Business; Customer Service; Publicity*

BIBLIOGRAPHY

Marconi, Joe (2004). *Public relations: The complete guide.* Mason, OH: South-Western.

Newsom, Doug, Turk, Judy V., and Kruckeberg, Dean (2004). *This is PR: The realities of public relations* (8th ed.). Belmont, CA: Wadsworth/Thomson Learning.

Public Relations Society of America. (n.d.). About public relations: Official PRSA definition. Retrieved November 21, 2005, from http://www.prsa.org/_Resources/Profession

Public Relations Society of America. (n.d.). PRSA member code of ethics. Retrieved November 21, 2005, from http://www.prsa.org/_About/ethics

Jensen J. Zhao

PUBLICITY

The Publicity Handbook: How to Maximize Publicity for Products, Services, and Organizations, by David Yale, explains that supplying information that is factual, interesting, and newsworthy to media not controlled by oneself is publicity. The media involved can take a variety of forms, including magazines, newspapers, radio, television, and trade journals. *The Random House Handbook of Business Terms* defines publicity as "information designed to appear in any medium of communication for the purpose of keeping the name of a person or company before the public or of creating public interest in their activities" (Nisberg, 1988, p. 229).

Publicity is usually generated from an organization's public relations department and its goal is to gain media coverage. Newsworthy events receiving publicity include ground-breaking ceremonies, press conferences, organized protests, and ceremonial appointments. Successful publicity occurs when an organization has a carefully designed publicity plan, which includes crisis control methods. Media gatekeepers favor publicity events that provide opportunities for photos and video or sound recordings and effectively communicate the source's intended message.

Ethical performance helps a company prevent or counteract negative publicity and gives a company, organization, or individual a competitive edge in gaining airtime or space in publications. In order to gain publicity, a company or individual must have clearly defined and spe-cific goals. Publicity can help a company accomplish many of its goals. Effective publicity can increase sales, bring more customers into a store, and clarify misconceptions. Companies must pick and choose which events deserve media coverage in order to avoid "overkill." Not everything needs full-scale media attention—only events that are most newsworthy and important.

CRISIS PREVENTION AND RESPONSE

Negative publicity can be the result of a mishandled crisis. Anticipating crises and having a solid crisis plan in place, however, can save a company from potentially disastrous situations and enhance its image. A company must first understand the different types of potential crises that exist, avoid common mistakes when handling crises, and be proactive when dealing with a crisis.

The February 5, 2001, article *Can Firestone Get Back on the Road?* in the Brand Debate section of the brandchannel.com Web site points out that the rise of the Internet has made it possible for bad news to travel fast, making it more difficult for companies to react quickly when a crisis strikes. Online discussion groups and chat rooms can spread worldwide bad publicity for a company within minutes. Moreover, consumers have become more skeptical and less trusting than they were even a decade ago and no longer easily buy into the "spin" tactics used by companies in time of crisis. Ratings wars have caused the media to adopt more sensationalized methods of reporting and be always ready to pour more fuel on the fire.

The three major types of potential crises are immediate, emerging, and sustained. An unexpected event, such as a terrorist attack, is an immediate crisis, and does not allow for research and planning. There should be a general consensus among key management on how to react in these situations in order to avoid confusion, delay, or argument. Emerging crises, such as employee dissatisfaction, low morale, or sexual harassment, allow for more research and planning. Management should take corrective action before these issues become critical. Despite the best efforts by management, sustained crises can persist for months or even years. These types of crises can result from media rumors or speculation. Once a company or organization has identified the type of crisis, specific methods should be put into place to control unfavorable publicity.

With effective damage-control methods, any type of publicity can be an advantage for an organization. All organizations should have a crisis management team (CMT) whose job is to anticipate crises and be ready to respond to the worst by upholding the image and reputation of the company if a crisis situation arises. Companies can hire external CMTs or develop and train in-house CMTs.

A company or organization should avoid hesitation in speaking with the press when a crisis occurs. Hesitation may be perceived as callousness, incompetence, or a lack of preparation. Obfuscation, or being unclear, leads the public to believe that the company is insensitive or is not being honest. Retaliation can increase tension and heighten emotions, rather than reduce them. Prevarication, or making false statements, is the biggest mistake a company can make because nothing should substitute for the truth. The use of inflated language—pontification—simply avoids the issue at hand. Confrontation will keep the issue alive, and litigation eliminates all other viable solutions to the crisis.

To combat negative publicity during a crisis, communication lines must be opened. A company spokesperson should be selected, and all employees should send any crisis inquiries directly to this spokesperson. The media should be supplied with information as quickly as possible. The company must be open to the media and tell the full story so that reporters do not look to outsiders to fill in the gaps.

The company must express its concern about the crisis and should show empathy for all who are affected by the problem. Most importantly, the company should tell the public what it is going to do to resolve the crisis and should have a company representative available twenty-four hours a day so long as media interest exists.

Once the crisis is over, the CMT should meet again to summarize the crisis situation, review and evaluate how the plan was implemented, and give open feedback and appropriate recommendations in order to determine where improvements can be made in the crisis-management plan.

CASE STUDIES

The crisis management methods used by four companies—Enron, Firestone, Ford, and Wal-Mart—are examined below.

Enron. Nick Beams, author of *Enron: The Real Face of the "New Economy"* wrote about the 2001 accounting scandal surrounding Texas-based energy trading conglomerate Enron. Before its destruction, Enron had been included six times on *Fortune* magazine's annual list of "most innovating companies." Also destroyed by the scandal was the company's accounting firm Arthur Andersen.

Enron was formed in the late 1980s as a result of a merger between two gas pipeline firms. By 2000 it had accumulated $101 billion in revenue, but by October 2001 the company reported a $638 million loss. Beams

reported, "On November 8, Enron filed documents with the SEC revising its financial statements for the past five years to account for $586 million in losses." The company's bankruptcy was the largest in history and the 21,000 employees with 401K pension plans invested in the company were left with worthless stock. Arthur Andersen waited too long to take responsibility for the tampered financial statements and this hesitation alone ruined the firm's reputation just as badly as Enron's.

Firestone and Ford. In August 2000 Firestone tires found itself in a major crisis. The event caused sales for the 100-year-old brand to drop by 50 percent. Firestone tires could be found on the Ford Explorer, the most popular sport-utility vehicle in the United States, and a tire defect had been linked to 88 road deaths in the United States and a further 46 in Venezuela. After recalls in eighteen countries allegations surfaced that both companies had been aware of the defect since 1997, but rather than warn consumers, the companies withheld important consumer safety information. Initially, 70 percent of consumers believed Ford and Firestone handled the crisis well. After only two weeks, however, that number dropped to 17 percent, severely tarnishing both brands—and leading to the use of derogatory names, such as Gravestone and Tombstone, by some consumers.

Wal-Mart. In 2005, according to the Wal-Mart fact page on the company's Web site, there were six former female employees who had a class-action suit against the company and were claiming the company discriminated against women. To proactively combat this negative publicity, Wal-Mart created a separate diversity office in November 2003. At that time, women made up 60 percent of Wal-Mart associates, but held only 40 percent of management positions.

In addition to these suits, Wal-Mart had 40 pending wage and hour cases in which employees claimed they were working without being paid. Wal-Mart's Web site openly states, "These allegations go against our three basic beliefs—respect for the individual, service to our customers and strive for excellence—and we take these allegations very seriously." Wal-Mart, unlike Ford, Firestone, and Enron, was not hesitating to get their message out into the public and was taking a proactive approach to the negative publicity; as a result, sales for the company were not being adversely affected.

SUMMARY

Publicity is not advertising, public relations, or promotions, because it is not controlled or paid for, but it has many advantages. If used correctly, companies can benefit greatly from publicity. Careful planning, research, and training can reduce negative publicity and can help companies control crises.

SEE ALSO *Advertising; Marketing Mix; Promotion*

BIBLIOGRAPHY

Beams, Nick (2001, December 6). *Enron: The real face of the "new economy."* Retrieved January 3, 2006, from the World Socialist Web Site: http://www.wsws.org/articles/2001/dec2001/enro-d06.shtml

Brand Debate Archive. (2001, February 5). *Can Firestone get back on the road?* Retrieved January 3, 2006, from http://www.brandchannel.com/forum.asp?bd_id=1

Brimm, Dave (2002, March 21). *Enron debacle forcing corporations to evaluate power of reputation management.* Retrieved January 3, 2006, from the Publicity Club of Chicago Web site: http://www.publicity.org/reputation.htm

Carter, Ginger Rudeseal (1999). *Perspectives public relations.* St. Paul, MN: Coursewise.

Cutlip, Scott M., Center, Allen H., and Broom, Glen M. (2006). *Effective public relations* (9th ed.). Upper Saddle River, NJ: Pearson Prentice Hall.

Gender discrimination lawsuit update. (2005). Retrieved January 3, 2006, from the Wal-Mart Web site: http://www.walmartfacts.com/keytopics/default.aspx

Nisberg, Jay N. (1988). *The Random House handbook of business terms.* New York: Random House.

Yale, David R. (1995). *The publicity handbook: How to maximize publicity for products, services, and organizations.* Lincolnwood, IL: NTC Business Books.

Jennifer L. Scheffer

PURE CAPITALISM

SEE *Economic Systems*

Q

QUALITY MANAGEMENT

Quality management (QM), also called total quality management (TQM), evolved from many different management practices and improvement processes. QM is not specific to managing people, but rather is related to improving the quality of goods and services that are produced in order to satisfy customer demands. QM permeates the entire organization as it is being implemented.

TQM has its roots in the quality movement that has made Japan such a strong force in the world economy. The Japanese philosophy of quality initially emphasized product and performance and only later shifted concern to customer satisfaction.

The quality improvement movement began in both the United States and Japan before World War II (1939–1945). Throughout the war, Americans continued to improve concepts related to manufacturing productivity. After the war, the Japanese pursued the idea of quality improvement. It was W. Edwards Deming (1900–1993), an American, who helped the Japanese focus on their fixation with quality.

Rather than trying to inspect the quality of products and services after they have been completed, TQM instills a philosophy of doing the job correctly the first time. It all sounds simple, but implementing the process requires an organizational culture and climate that are often alien and intimidating. Changes that must occur in the organization are so significant that it takes time and patience to complete the process. Just as the process does not occur overnight, the results may not be seen for a long time. Some experts say that it takes up to ten years to fully realize the results of implementing QM.

THE PROCESS

Several steps must be taken in the process of shifting to QM in an organization:

Provide a QM environment. A QM environment is one in which the management-driven culture disappears and a participative culture takes its place. The basic tenets of QM are that employees must be involved and that there must be teamwork. Managers must be willing to involve workers in the decision-making process. Workers who function as a team have much more to offer collectively than do individual workers. Pooled resources are more valuable than just one person's contribution.

Modify reward systems. Reward systems need to be overhauled so as to recognize and encourage teamwork and innovation. The team, not the individual, is the foundation for TQM companies. If a company continues to use traditional compensation plans that create competition between workers, the team concept cannot be implemented. Traditional pay plans are often based on seniority, not on quality and performance. With QM, pay systems focus on team incentives. Each person is paid based on the team's performance. If one person on the team does not perform at the level expected, the team members will normally handle the situation. In

629

W. Edwards Deming (1900–1993). *Dr. Deming introduced U.S. industry to statistical methods needed to measure and improve a range of processes and to compete globally.*
© BETTMANN/CORBIS

some cases, payment is based on the performance of the entire company, which requires an even greater team effort.

Prepare workers for TQM. Workers must constantly be trained with the tools that are needed to upgrade the company's quality. Workers must understand the philosophy of QM before the tools can be used effectively. Managers must be dedicated to transforming their companies into "learning organizations" in which workers want to upgrade their skills and take advantage of the opportunities and incentives to do so. Companies that are successful with TQM allocate up to about 5 percent of their employees' time on training. Some of this training time might include cross-training, that is, schooling workers in the skills to do a different job in the organization.

Prepare employees to measure quality. To ensure gains in quality, the results must be measured objectively as the company progresses toward its quality objectives. This requires that employees be trained to use statistical process control techniques. Without knowledgeable workers using quantitative tools, the organization cannot achieve the intended TQM results.

Identify the appropriate starting place. One of the most difficult tasks in the beginning phases of implementing QM is to determine where to start. One approach to this beginning is to assume that 80 percent of all the company's problems stem from 20 percent of the company's processes (Pareto's law). By identifying the problematic processes that fall in this 20 percent category, one can begin to focus on what needs attention first. Focusing attention on these problems first will return bigger payoffs and build momentum for the future.

Share information with everyone. If a team approach is to be used and if employees are expected to be involved in the decision-making process, it is imperative that information be shared with everyone. The decision-making process requires that workers be fully informed.

Include quality as an element of design. From beginning to end, customer satisfaction should be the focus of the QM system. That means that the goal of customer satisfaction must be included in the planning processes and then maintained day in and day out.

Make error prevention the norm. One approach to producing quality products is to have a group of inspectors who will find the defective items and get rid of them. This is not the QM approach. With QM, the approach is continuous improvement of quality to ensure that there are no products that are defective. The quality is built into the manufacturing process, and workers are continually improving products and processes. This approach is more cost-effective for the organization because it eliminates the waste of materials and workers' time.

Encourage cooperation and teamwork. If mistakes are made, it is the fault of a team of workers, not just one worker. In many organizations that do not use TQM, managers are often on the hunt for someone to blame for problems that are found. This type of environment creates unhealthy stress and discourages innovative thought and practices by workers. The combination of a team approach and QM means seeking to improve the system when problems arise.

Make continuous improvement the goal. Processes and products should continually be improved. The improvement process has no end. This is true for even the best of the best companies. TQM never ends.

Deming created fourteen points for management, which are condensed on the Web site of the Deming Institute (http://www.deming.org/deminghtml/teachings/html) and adapted here:

1. Create constancy of purpose toward improvement of product and service, with the aim to become competitive, to stay in business, and to provide jobs.

2. Adopt a new philosophy. This is a new economic age. Western management must awaken to the challenge, learn their responsibilities, and take on leadership for change.

3. Cease dependence on inspection to achieve quality. Eliminate the need for inspection on a mass basis by building quality into the product in the first place.

4. End the practice of awarding business on the basis of the price tag. Instead, minimize total cost. Move toward a single supplier for any one item, based on a long-term relationship of loyalty and trust.

5. Improve constantly and forever the system of production and service, in order to improve quality and productivity, and thus constantly decrease costs.

6. Institute training on the job.

7. Institute leadership. The aim of supervision should be to help people, machines, and gadgets to do a better job. Supervision of management is in need of overhaul, as is supervision of production workers.

8. Drive out fear, so that everyone may work effectively for the company.

9. Break down barriers between departments. People in research, design, sales, and production must work as a team, in order to foresee problems in production and in use that may be encountered with the product or service.

10. Eliminate slogans, exhortations, and targets for the workforce asking for zero defects and new levels of productivity. Such exhortations create only adversarial relationships, since the bulk of the causes of low quality and low productivity belong to the system and thus lie beyond the power of the workforce. Eliminate work standards (quotas) on the factory floor, substituting leadership. Eliminate management by objective, by numbers, and by numeric goals, also substituting leadership.

11. Remove barriers that rob hourly workers of their right to pride of workmanship. The goals of supervisors must be changed from sheer numbers to quality.

12. Remove barriers that rob people in management and in engineering of their right to pride of workmanship. This means, inter alia, abolishment of the annual or merit rating and of management by objective.

13. Institute a vigorous program of education and self-improvement.

14. Put everybody in the company to work to accomplish the transformation. The transformation is everybody's job.

It is readily apparent that the process of implementing a QM system in an organization is closely aligned with the thinking of Deming.

RECOGNITION

The importance of quality is emphasized with the awards that are presented to companies and organizations that achieve high standards of quality. The Malcolm Baldrige National Quality Award was one of the first given. The 2006 award application identified several categories that must be addressed to qualify for the award—and very few awards are presented. Companies and organizations are rated on seven categories: leadership; strategic planning; customer and market focus; measurement, analysis, and knowledge management; human resources focus; process management; and results. It is a very prestigious honor for a company or organization to be recognized with this award.

Other awards and certifications are also presented. Nevertheless, they constantly change and new ones are added regularly, so they will not be discussed here. QM has become an important philosophy in businesses around the world, and this approach to building better products and services will continue.

WEBSITES OF INTEREST

For a more detailed description of the Deming approach: http://www.managementwisdom.com

For the rating document for the Malcolm Baldrige National Quality Award: http://nqp@nist.gov

SEE ALSO *Manufacturing; Productivity*

BIBLIOGRAPHY

Saylor, James H. (1996). *TQM simplified: A practical approach* (2nd ed.). New York: McGraw-Hill.

Scarborough, Norman M., and Zimmerer, Thomas W. (2005). *Effective small business management: An entrepreneurial approach* (8th ed.). Upper Saddle River, NJ: Prentice Hall.

Weiss, Alan (2000). *"Good enough" isn't enough ... nine challenges for companies that choose to be great.* New York: Amacom.

Roger Luft

QUANTITY DISCOUNTS
SEE *Pricing*

R

READING SKILLS IN BUSINESS

In the business world, workers use special skills to complete their reading tasks. Traditionally, however, business educators have relied on others to develop the job-related reading skills of their students. In 1975, Sticht noted that the overwhelming majority of time in schools is allocated to teaching the reading and interpreting of novels, short stories, dramas, and poetry as opposed to teaching technical reading skills needed in the workplace. The SCANS (Secretary's Commission on Achieving Necessary Skills) report released in 1991 included the reading of technical material as a foundation skill needed by all workers. Workplace reading includes the ability to understand and interpret various documents including diagrams, directories, correspondence, manuals, records, charts, graphs, tables, and specifications.

In the 1970s, two researchers, Ross and Salzman, studied the reading tasks of randomly selected office workers in the Columbus, Ohio, area. Ross completed one-hour observations of one hundred beginning office workers, and Salzman collected 2,659 samples of reading, writing, and mathematical activities from thirty-five beginning and thirty-five experienced office workers. Outcomes of these two studies identified three unique reading skills office workers use: proofreading, verifying, and comprehending detail.

Building on the research that Ross and Salzman completed, Schmidt reported, in 1987, the reading levels of office documents collected for the purpose of developing reading materials aimed at building technical reading skills. One hundred and twenty-one documents collected from ten businesses were analyzed for reading level using the FORCAST formula. The FORCAST formula developed in 1975 by Caylor, Sticht, Fox, and Ford uses the percentage of one-syllable words as the basis for determining reading level, so it eliminates consideration of recurring technical terms, which can artificially raise the reading level of technical materials.

The average reading grade levels for the documents ranged from 11.3 for those collected from a bank to 13.4 for those collected from a university continuing education center office. Other businesses that provided documents and their average reading grade levels included a space industry manufacturer, 11.4; a town administration office, 11.8; a hospital, 12; an insurance company, 12; a chemical industry manufacturer, 12.1; a railroad, 12.8; a country administration office, 13.1; and a school division office, 13.1. Thus, the reading grade level of typical office documents is considerably higher than general interest reading materials. Further, most reading done by adults is technical, job-related reading and not the type of reading emphasized in schools.

Based on a study of two groups of high school students in which one group was enrolled in courses required to complete a business program and the other group enrolled in selected elective business courses, Schmidt reported in 1982 that the first group, composed of 279 students, performed better on a proofreading skills test than the second group, comprising 1,058 students. However, on tests measuring the skills of verifying and comprehending detail, the first group did not score better than the second group. The tests were constructed from actual business documents. From this outcome, Schmidt con-

633

cluded that reading exercises for developing the skills of verifying and comprehending detail were needed.

The National Business Education Association published the exercises that evolved from the studies. In the introduction to the *Office Reading Exercises*, Schmidt describes trial use of the exercises prior to their publication. They were used with experimental and control groups, each with more than 250 high school students. After completing a pretest, the experimental group completed the ten exercises, using 15 to 20 minutes to complete one exercise per day. The students were simply given the exercises and informed of expected outcomes. This group not only scored significantly higher on a post-test administered at the completion of the exercises, but also on a post-test administered after a lapse of three to five weeks. They also scored significantly higher on the post-test than the control group. Thus a research base exists to justify the use of the exercises.

The ten exercises were all developed from actual office documents including a catalog page, a price list, an insurance claim, an enrollment report, a budget allocation form, a meal price schedule, a program confirmation, zoning ordinance information, concentration banking information, and an expense account. Schmidt provides two approaches that can be used for teaching the exercises. One is a holistic approach where the students are simply given the exercises, one day at a time, and told the outcomes desired. This was the approach used in the study described above. They devise, along with their classmates, their own methods for achieving the outcomes. The other approach is instructor-directed and is called a "Guided Approach." It allows the instructor to emphasize the thirteen component skills that are subsets of the two main skills, verifying and comprehending detail.

Verifying requires comparing technical information that has been transferred from one place to another to be sure that it has been transferred accurately. Comprehending detail is reading printed technical information, then determining if statements about it are accurate. The component skills or sub-skills emphasized in the Guided Approach are:

- Following directions
- Perceiving document structure
- Perceiving relationships
- Identifying relevant information
- Locating facts or specifics
- Recognizing comparison/contrasting information
- Interpreting symbols, graphics, or acronyms
- Recognizing sequence of information
- Summarizing or making generalizations

- Selecting relevant information
- Recognizing main idea
- Reading with partner to detect errors
- Recognizing errors: transpositions, typographical and mechanical, additions and omissions

Taylor and Hancock, in a 1993 publication titled "Strategies That Reinforce Academics Across the Business Curriculum," discussed strategies to help introduce, reinforce, and extend students' comprehension, vocabulary, and writing in three reading stages. An overview of the three stages follows.

Pre-Reading Stage. Before students are assigned technical reading, they need to engage in pre-reading strategies to help them in understanding the material. The reading can be broken into smaller segments with a variety of activities that promote student involvement. These might include a graphic organizer, an analogical study guide, or an anticipation/reaction guide. This guide helps focus pre-reading discussion and can also serve for post-reading review.

Reading Stage. At the reading stage, the students need to focus on garnering major ideas as well as important details from the material. A study guide or selective reading guide can help the students achieve this objective. The study guide used should, unlike the text-explicit questions generally supplied by textbook authors, extend the students' thinking beyond mere "parroting" of the text-explicit concepts.

Post-Reading Stage. Once the students have read the material, they need to engage in post-reading activities to assure long-term retention of what they have read. The pre-reading strategies can again be used or students can undertake other activities. These might include vocabulary reinforcement activities, journal writing, or other writing activities that allow the students to apply information from what they have read.

Thus, the reading of technical materials requires the development of unique skills that are not addressed by most teachers. The *Office Reading Exercises* developed by Schmidt and the strategies recommended by Taylor and Hancock provide some approaches that can be used to teach technical reading skills. However, before these approaches are used, instructors should also be concerned with the extent that their students' reading abilities match those required for technical materials. Two methods are available for this purpose: (a) the Cloze procedure developed by Taylor in 1953, which permits the instructor to measure the compatibility of printed materials with the reading ability of students, and (b) a pretest developed from technical terms the material contains.

For classroom use, the following adaptation of the Cloze technique is recommended by Popham, Schrag, and Blockhus.

1. Randomly select reading material in six to nine passages and delete every fifth word in each passage. Stop when 20 words have been deleted.

2. In place of each word deleted, substitute an underscore.

3. Have the material typed, and instruct students to place in each blank a word that makes sense. No guessing or time restrictions permitted.

4. Analyze the answers and give credit for each substitution that approximates the original meaning. Determine a raw score for each student and convert that raw score to a percent by dividing the actual number of correct answers by the possible number of correct answers.

5. Determine the level at which the students comprehend the material by using the following scale. A score of 0 to 30 percent equals the "frustration" reading level, a score of 31 to 49 percent equals the "instructional" reading level, and a score of 50 to 100 percent equals the "independent" reading level.

Some technical materials do not lend themselves to the use of the Cloze test. For these materials a pretest based on technical terms from the material can be developed to provide insight into the extent that students can understand the material. If a student answers less than half of the items on the test correctly, the instructor may assume that the student will have difficulty reading the material.

Students need technical reading skills for the business world. Furthermore, all teachers are expected to reinforce academic competencies in their instruction. The procedures discussed here can help teachers meet the challenge of teaching technical reading skills, those essential for reading in business.

SEE ALSO *Listening Skills in Business; Speaking Skills in Business; Writing Skills in Business*

BIBLIOGRAPHY

Popham, E. L., Schrag, A. F., and Blockhus, W. (1975). *A Teaching-Learning System for Business Education.* New York: McGraw-Hill.

Ross, N. (1977). *An Analysis of the Nature and Difficulty of Reading Tasks Associated with Beginning Office Workers.* Doctoral dissertation. Columbus, OH: The Ohio State University.

Salzman, G. G. (1979). *A descriptive study of the reading, writing, and mathematics tasks of beginning office workers.* Doctoral dissertation. Columbus. OH: The Ohio State University.

Schmidt, B. J. (1982). "Job-related Reading Skills Developed by Business Students." *The Journal of Vocational Education Research*, 7(4), 29-38.

Schmidt, B. J. (1987). "Preparing Business Students to Read Office Documents." *The Delta Pi Epsilon Journal*, (29) 4, 111-124.

Secretary's Commission on Achieving Necessary Skills (1992). *Learning A Living: A Blueprint for High Performance.* Washington, D.C.: U.S. Department of Labor.

Taylor, H. P., and Hancock, D. O. (1993, September). "Strategies That Reinforce Academics across the Business Curriculum." *Delta Pi Epsilon Instructional Strategies*, 9(4).

Taylor, W. L. (1953). "Cloze Procedures: A New Tool for Measuring Readability." *Journalism Quarterly*, 30, 415-433.

B. June Schmidt

RECESSION
SEE *Business Cycle*

RECORDS MANAGEMENT

Advancements in technology and the reproduction of electronic documents have caused organizations to change the way they think about records management. The Emerging Technology Advisory Group of the Association for Information and Image Management (AIIM) identified the top-five emerging technologies entering into the twenty-first century. These technologies have become management concerns and, therefore, concerns of records managers:

1. Electronic-mail (e-mail) management

2. E-mail

3. Knowledge management

4. Records migration

5. Customer relationship management

DEVELOPING AN EFFICIENT SYSTEM

Procedures for maintaining data in some form have been essential for centuries. Records serve important functions, particularly in efforts to minimize risks. Some of these risks include litigation, regulatory noncompliance, natural disasters, criminal activities, and pirating of resources.

Characteristics of an ideal information system

- The system minimizes elapsed time between a user's query and the response from the system

- The more complete the information stored, the more useful the data can be to the end user

- The more completely an information system can prevent "lost" files, the more generally useful the system is to users

- An information system should provide access to the same document or file by more than one user at one time

- The more a retrieval system maximizes pertinence while minimizing redundancy, the more the system services the needs of the user

- Retrieval queries should be possible in the official language(s)

- The information system should make provision for selective security

- The simpler a retrieval system is and the less training required to use it, the more acceptable it is to the user

- Additions, deletions, and updating of files should be as efficient as possible

- Since work hours, particularly of managers, extend beyond prime shift hours, the ideal system should be able to operate in non-regular hours at reasonable cost

Table 1

Unethical practices as well as new regulations demand accountability for actions taken in business and industry. As a result of the risks faced by organizations, Theodore Vander Noot (1998) suggested ten characteristics of an "ideal information system" that should apply whether the system is a computerized database or a file system or library (see Table 1).

There are two basic reasons for the increase in information over the years. The first, modernity, has seen the decline in small businesses as larger and more complex businesses begin to dominate. A more modern democratic government is seen as the second reason for the growth in information. Both public and private organizations tend to collect more information than needed regarding their programs when providing the requested records for the government.

METHODS OF STORING INFORMATION

Four methods are often used for storing information in business and government:

1. A person's brain
2. Paper
3. Microfilm
4. Computer

Technological advances in the record-keeping industry have made it easier to store and retrieve records. Accelerating digital technologies are the storage mode of the twenty-first century. Stored digital information is only as permanent and accessible as the hardware and software that give it intelligibility. The transitory nature of digital technology poses serious questions about how to archive digital documents.

Although migrating is not a practical solution, digital obsolescence or loss can be overcome by periodically migrating electronically to more modern systems. Software used to manage archival collections will change every three to five years. One approach to solving the problem of obsolescence and frequent migration is the online electronic records archive that scientists are developing. Although expensive, this procedure will make it possible to keep up with records that must be stored and ultimately converted.

A provider of collaborative intranet, extranet, and electronic business (e-business) reported the release of a Livelink (IRIMS) module. Livelink Enterprise Server is a highly scalable e-business application. The IRIMS module is a fully integrated function accessed through a Web browser. Its featured enterprise services include virtual team collaboration, business automation, enterprise group scheduling, and information retrieval services.

The major developments affecting the micrographic and hybrid imaging systems field include:

- Consolidation
- Confusion
- Accelerated acceptance of hybrid systems
- Technology substitution, with more applications moving to electronic imaging or the Internet
- Subsequent losses in business volume

Organizations have traditionally relied on paper filing systems for document storage and retrieval. Paper records are extremely difficult to access because they have to be stored in and retrieved from one place. An electronic document management system solves many of the storage and retrieval problems that arise in paper filing systems when more than one person requires the same document at the same time and retrieval rates are high. Indexing has been found to be of significant value to organizations because it facilitates faster retrieval of documents as well as reduces cost.

Careers in records and information management

Job Title	Duties and Responsibilities
Records & Information Supervisor	Maintains uniform records system and procedures throughout the organization. Develops efficient methods, then plans, conducts, and administers them. Selects and supervises staff.
Records & Information Clerk	Maintains specialized records systems, conducts systems analysis. Assists in designing and monitoring established schedules.
Senior records & Information Clerk	Coordinates with records center, retrieves information for users, and maintains logs and indexes. Oversees transfer of records.
Records & Information Clerk	Sorts, indexes, and retrieves files and records. Classifies materials and records and maintains charge-out system for records removal.
Records Center Supervisor	Operates and maintains the records center. Responsible for vital records protection, storage, and disposition. Selects and supervises staff.
Records Center Clerk	Assists in accessing, reference retrieval, and disposal activities of center. Maintains charge-out system for records removed from files.
Micrographics Supervisor	Plans and controls micrographics program. Work closely with records and information analyst and others in developing applications. Selects and supervises staff.
Micrographics Coordinator	Sets priorities and schedules work. Monitors resources and trains personnel.
Micrographics Technician	Provides technical advice, operates microfilm equipment. Develops, maintains, and monitors indexing and retrieval aids. Monitors clerks.
Senior Micrographics Clerk	Receives and logs documents, prepares and handles special projects. Monitors quality control and conducts routine equipment maintenance.
Micrographic Clerk	Prepares documents for microfilming, operates equipment, and prepares indexes. Searches, sorts, and files microforms.
Senior Records Analyst	Analyzes records systems and prepares proposals to change. Designs manual or automated systems, monitors retention program, and directs vital records program.
Records Analyst	Prepares or assists in analyzing existing records systems; writes procedures. Provides staff training and assists in vital records protection program.

SOURCE: Compiled from Ricks, B. R. et al. (1997). *Information and Image Management* (3rd ed.). Scarborough, ON: ITP Nelson, pp. 24–41.

Table 2

Indexing can be field-based, full-text based, or a combination of the two. Indexing fields make unique identification of documents possible and retrieval easier. They may identify documents by their creation date, time, and creator, as well as by fields involving a controlled vocabulary. A full-text document index is important for retrieving specific, accurate files but can be more time consuming.

Offsite storage of inactive records is the most common type of records outsourcing. Records management outsourcing often depends on the quality and cost of the outsourcer. Decision making involves whether to store inactive records offsite or bring in an outsourcing firm to run the entire records management operation.

THE RECORDS MANAGEMENT PROFESSION

Careers in records and information management have often been created or motivated by top-level management personnel who recognize a need for specialization to improve productivity. Many employees hired at the entry level have moved to higher positions partly because of on-the-job-training programs. These programs have helped meet the need for improvement in skills due to new technologies or expansion of the organization.

A successful employee-training program should not be limited to specific functional operations. It should cover all aspects of the organizational system. Fundamentals must be presented in such a manner that employers see themselves as important participants in a highly essential undertaking.

The Institute of Certified Records Managers has determined that a professional records and information manager must have acceptable work experience in three or more of the following categories:

- Management of records program
- Records creation and use
- Active records systems
- Inactive records systems
- Records appraisal
- Retention
- Disposition
- Records protection
- Records and information management technology

The Education Department Committee of ARMA International (formerly the Association of Records Managers and Administrators) created a framework for competency requirements for records and information managers. These basic requirements provide guidance for demonstration and measurement of technical, administrative, managerial, and personal competencies throughout the range of levels of professional development. The following job titles or careers have been identified in records and information management:

- Director
- Manager
- Specialist
- Coordinator
- Analyst/technologist
- Technician
- Senior assistant
- Junior assistant

A need for more specialization in records and information management careers has been initiated by the rapid expansion of information in many fields. Table 2 identifies some of those specialties.

SEE ALSO *Document Processing; Information Processing; Office Technology*

BIBLIOGRAPHY

ARMA International. (2000). *RIM industry competency requirements*. Prairie Village, KS: Association of Records Managers and Administrators.

Ashe, Carolyn, and Nealy, Chynette (2004). *Records management: Effective information systems.* Upper Saddle River, NJ: Pearson Prentice Hall.

The case of hybrid imaging. (2001, March). *Micrographics and Hybrid Imaging Systems Newsletter, 33*(3), 11.

Cisco, Susan, and Wertzberger, Janelle (1997). Indexing digital documents: It's not an option—Play now or pay (more) later. *Inform, 11*(2), 12–20.

Hutchens, Philip H. (1998, October). Information management and the decisionmaker. *Records Management Quarterly 32*(4), 28–30.

Institution of Certified Records Management. (1997). Information sheet no. 1: Introduction to certification. An interactive workshop. *Proceedings of the 42nd Annual Conference of ARMA International,* (p. 469). Chicago.

Perry, A. (2000). Open text releases Livelink IRIMS. *Businesswire.* Waterloo, Ontario, Canada: Business Wire.

Ricks, Betty, Swafford, Ann, Gow, Kay, and Flemming, Glen (1997). *Information and image management* (3rd ed.). Scarborough, Ontario, Canada: Nelson.

Sletten, L. (1998). *Management in Australia: Exploring the information universe.* Paper presented at the meeting of ARMA, Houston, TX.

Vander Noot, Theodore J. (1998, October). Libraries, records management data processing: An information handling field. *Records Management Quarterly, 32*(4), 22–26.

Carolyn H. Ashe

REENGINEERING

The concept of reengineering traces its origins to management theories developed as early as the nineteenth century. The purpose of reengineering is to make all processes the best possible. American efficiency engineer Frederick Winslow Taylor (1856–1915) suggested in the 1880s that managers could discover the best processes for performing work and reengineer them to optimize productivity. Business process reengineering (BPR) echoes the classical belief that there is one best way to conduct tasks. In Taylor's time, technology was not sufficient to allow large companies to design processes in a cross-functional or cross-departmental manner. Reengineering became popular in the early 1990s even though the methodology and approach were not fully understood or appreciated. In the twenty-first century, reengineering is an effective tool for organizations striving to operate as effectively and efficiently as possible. Much attention is given to "best practices" that are the outcome of reengineering strategies.

DEFINITION OF *REENGINEERING*

Reengineering is most commonly defined as the redesign of business processes—and the associated systems and organizational structures—to achieve a dramatic improvement in business performance. BPR has been described as a radical new approach to business improvement, with the potential to achieve dramatic improvement in business performance. BPR should not be considered downsizing, restructuring, reorganization, and/or new technology. It is the examination and change of five components of the business strategy, process, technology, organization, and culture. Many companies continue to experiment with reengineering, even if they have failed in previous attempts.

MOTIVATION FOR REENGINEERING

The motivations for reengineering are many, including to:

- Reduce costs/expenses (the most cited business-driven reengineering project goal)
- Improve financial performance
- Reduce external competition pressure
- Reverse erosion of market share
- Respond to emerging market opportunities
- Improve customer satisfaction
- Enhance quality of products and services

REENGINEERING PROJECT GUIDELINES

A common approach for a BPR project includes the following phases:

Planning and launching—Team selection, objective setting, scope definition, methodology selection, schedule development, consultant selection, sponsor negotiations, change management planning, team preparation

Current state assessing and learning from others—High-level process definition, benchmarking, customer focus groups, employee focus groups, technology assessment

Designing solution—Process design, enabling technology architecture, organizational design, job design

Developing business case justification—Cost and benefit analysis, business case preparation, presentation to key business leaders

Developing solution—Detailed process definition, system requirements writing and system development, training development, implementation planning, operational transition plan, pilots and trials

Implementing solution—Larger-scale pilots and phased implementation, measurement systems, full implementation in all relevant aspects of the company

Instituting continuous improvement strategy—Ongoing improvement and measurement of new processes and systems

FACTORS FOR SUCCESS

Several key factors affect the success of BPR. The objectives of reengineering should be specified clearly, such as improved customer service, reduced costs, and improved quality of work performed. Also required are management support and vision; a strong, committed project leader; clearly established objectives; organized change management; and an effective methodology. Team members must share a clear vision of the objectives and goals, have a common focus and understanding of what is to be done, and support the project. Activities critical for broad acceptance of what is proposed include: (1) constant and relevant communication, (2) employee training for implementation of reengineering outcomes, and (3) transition planning, including reevaluating short-term goals and targets.

FACTORS THAT LEAD TO FAILURE

Factors that contribute to unsuccessful efforts in BPR are failures in:

- *Change management*—insufficient attention to proper design and implementation
- *Technological competence*—inadequate identification of what is needed
- *Strategic planning*—limited view of range of planning prerequisite for strategy
- *Time frame*—inability to predict optimum time required
- *Management support*—range of management involved is too narrow
- *Human resources*—erroneous assessment of quality of in-house personnel
- *Process delineation*—lacks sufficient specificity to be informative
- *Tactical planning and project management*—unskillful in identification of relevant aspects

KEY OBSTACLES TO SUCCESS

Experiences in planning and executing reengineering projects have shown that key obstacles to success are:

1. *Resistance to change*—Failure to understand the extent and nature of involvement of employees throughout the process, a critical prerequisite for effective implementation of changes

2. *Corporate culture*—Traditional operating style that is top-to-bottom and not participatory often dooms a project, even if enthusiastically supported by the project team

3. *Organizational inertia*—Indifference on the part of key executives to the need for comprehensive understanding and participating of all employees

REASONS FOR OUTSOURCING

Among the key reasons companies outsource BPR projects are:

- They are able to negotiate and control costs

- It frees up in-house resources for other purposes

- They can secure resources, especially reengineering management skills not available internally

- Reengineering efforts may be accelerated through the use of such experts

DIFFERENCES BETWEEN CONTINUOUS PROCESS IMPROVEMENT AND BPR

Continuous process improvement begins by documenting what one does today, establishing some measures for process flow, measuring performance, and identifying and implementing improvement. BPR begins with defining the scope and objectives of the reengineering project, learning from customers, employees, competitors, and technology, creating a vision for the future and designing new business processes, creating a plan for action during the transition period, and implementing a solution. BPR efforts are far more comprehensive than those involved in continuous process improvement.

INFORMATION TECHNOLOGY IN REENGINEERING

Most analysts view reengineering and information technology (IT) as irrevocably linked. Wal-Mart, for example, would not have been able to reengineer the processes used to procure and distribute mass-market retail goods without IT. In another well-known example, Ford Motor Company was able to decrease its number of employees in its procurement department by 75 percent by using IT in conjunction with BPR.

Despite studies that indicated that over half of all reengineering efforts were initiated because of a perceived IT opportunity, it has been noted that the actual techno-

logical solution is far less important than educating employees to use IT as both a strategic initiative and as a tool in the reengineering process. IT can prove useful during the reengineering analysis and design process. Graphics software and computer-aided software engineering tools can produce process maps; spreadsheets and costing software allow for activity-based cost analysis; databases can track customer satisfaction and complaints; and "blind" electronic-mail bulletin boards can be used to capture employee suggestions.

During the implementation stage, it is recommended that companies follow these basic rules: recognize that IT is only part of the solution—it allows managers to collect, store, analyze, and communicate and distribute information better; bring in internal or external IT experts because their knowledge, skills, acumen, and experience are invaluable; and, after implementation, continually monitor IT performance and keep up with new IT developments.

SEE ALSO *Management*

BIBLIOGRAPHY

Castano, Silvana, de Antonellis, Valeria, and Melchiori, Michele (1999). A methodology and tool environment for process analysis and reengineering. *Data and Knowledge Engineering, 31*(3), 253–278.

Maull, R. S., Tranfield, D. R., and Maull, W. (2003). Factors characterizing the maturity of BPR programmes. *International Journal of Operations and Production Management, 23*(6), 596–624.

Nashwa George

REINFORCEMENT THEORY
SEE *Motivation*

RESEARCH IN BUSINESS

In the competitive global economy of the twenty-first century, managers are challenged to make tough business decisions, such as how to keep an annual growth rate of 20 percent, how to increase employee productivity, how to improve product quality, how to cut down costs, and how to reduce the employee turnover rate. To make such decisions correctly, managers need research, which is a systematic inquiry that provides scientific findings and conclusions to guide business decisions.

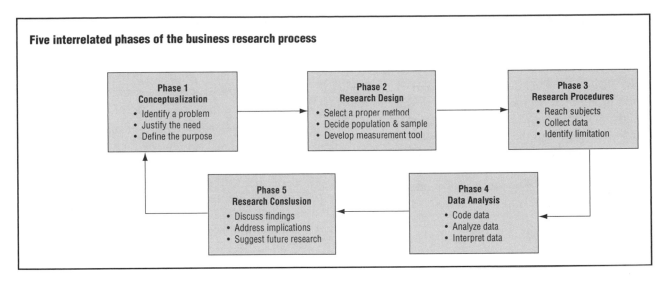

Five interrelated phases of the business research process

Phase 1
Conceptualization
- Identify a problem
- Justify the need
- Define the purpose

Phase 2
Research Design
- Select a proper method
- Decide population & sample
- Develop measurement tool

Phase 3
Research Procedures
- Reach subjects
- Collect data
- Identify limitation

Phase 4
Data Analysis
- Code data
- Analyze data
- Interpret data

Phase 5
Research Conslusion
- Discuss findings
- Address implications
- Suggest future research

Figure 1

CRITERIA OF GOOD BUSINESS RESEARCH

Good business research is a scientific approach that meets the following criteria:

1. The problem of the research should be explicitly stated.

2. The need for the research should be well justified.

3. The purpose of the research should be clearly defined.

4. The research method should be selected according to the nature of the problem and designed scientifically to ensure a valid and reliable outcome.

5. The research procedures should be described in sufficient detail to permit other researchers to replicate the research.

6. The limitations of the research design and procedures should be reported.

7. The analysis and interpretation of data should generate findings that reveal the evidence of scientific measurements.

8. The research conclusions should be drawn based on the findings, and the recommendations should be based on the conclusions.

BUSINESS RESEARCH METHODS

Business research methods refer to the ways researchers gather the evidence needed to make the right decisions. Common business research methods include case studies, the Delphi method, experiments, surveys, and content analysis.

Case Studies. Case studies examine a single, salient business situation or organization by collecting key facts and analyzing them in light of business functions, theories, and best practices. The goal is to generate possible solutions to problems experienced in that particular situation or organization. The case study begins with an explicit problem statement. Based on the problem statement, researchers decide what data need to be collected for analysis. For example, a company case study usually needs to collect both quantitative (e.g., financial and sales figures) and qualitative (e.g., management memos and reports) data to perform the following analyses:

- Industry analysis to understand its growth, market structure, and competition

- Product/service analysis to evaluate the company's market share, product/service portfolio, marketing strategies, and competitive advantage

- Financial analysis to assess the company's profitability, liquidity, leverage, performance, and growth potential

- Management analysis to examine the top-management strategies, short- and long-term objectives, organizational structure, and decision styles

These functional analyses enable researchers to identify the company's *s*trengths, *w*eaknesses, *o*pportunities, and *t*hreats (SWOT). Based on the SWOT analysis, researchers can develop alternative solutions, recommendations, and implementation plans.

The Delphi Method. The Delphi method is a qualitative approach through which a panel of experts is queried repeatedly about possible developments of a particular product/service, technology, workforce, or business strategy in varied scenarios. After the first round of inquiries, the experts review the responses of their peer panelists, revise their own if needed, and then start the second round of inquiries. In most cases, through three to four rounds, the experts' assessments converge toward a set of conclusions that form the basis for solutions to the problem(s). This method is effective for predicting uncertain future business environments and developments, especially when quantitative forecasting based on past trends is not reliable.

Experiments. Experiments are designed to test the cause-and-effect relationships that researchers suspect exist in a business environment. There are two categories of experiments: laboratory and field. A laboratory experiment takes place in an artificial setting created by researchers—such as testing a new drug on mice or testing automobile safety in collisions using dummies. By contrast, a field experiment takes place in a natural setting, such as testing the effect of implementing a total-quality-management system on product quality and employee productivity in a company.

Whether in a lab or in the field, researchers exercise high control when they are able to manipulate independent variables, assign subjects randomly to control and experiment groups, and control extraneous variables. For example, a company wants to know whether newspaper coupons for its product affect sales. The company randomly selects ten communities from the fifty communities having daily newspapers within its sales region and then randomly assigns them to control and experiment groups, with each having five communities. On Tuesday, the control group receives a newspaper advertisement for the company's product without a coupon, while the experiment group gets the same advertisement with a coupon for a 15 percent discount. Sales figures from the two groups are totaled on the following Saturday (the coupon's expiration date). Through a statistical analysis of the sales figures, the experiment shows whether or not the coupon has significantly affected the sales.

Surveys. Survey research is a method of systematically questioning a sample of respondents representing a specific population regarding their beliefs, attitudes, and behaviors. This method is useful for collecting information about a population that is too large for every member to be studied. To ensure the generalizability of the findings, researchers design a survey by taking the following steps:

1. defining the population of the study

2. determining the sample size that is large enough to represent the population yet small enough to be economical

3. selecting a sampling method that ensures that each member in the population has an equal chance to be selected

4. determining whether a questionnaire or structured interview is more appropriate for gathering information

5. developing effective questions by using clear, simple language, nonleading or non-multifaceted questions, mutually exclusive choices, and group categories for sensitive information such as age, salary, and morals

For a questionnaire survey, researchers first decide whether mail, e-mail, or online is the appropriate medium for ensuring a high response rate. Second, researchers need to send a persuasive cover letter with the questionnaire to persuade readers to complete and return the questionnaire. If the first mailing (or e-mailing) generates a low response rate, a follow-up mailing is necessary to remind nonrespondents to complete and return the questionnaire.

For an interview survey, researchers first decide whether a telephone or face-to-face interview is more appropriate. Interviewers must be trained before conducting interviews. The interviewer begins by making the interviewee feel comfortable and important by giving a friendly greeting, explaining the purpose of the interview and the importance of the interviewee's participation, and asking if tape recording is permitted. During the interview, the interviewer should always use an interview guide of predeveloped questions and follow-ups for each interviewee. At the end, the interviewer should express appreciation to each interviewee for participating.

Content Analysis. Content analysis is a method for making inferences by systematically and objectively identifying characteristics of messages embedded in the texts and the causal relationships of message contests and outcomes. This method is widely used in the research of business and managerial communications, negotiations, and Web-based e-business. Content analysis employs a systematic procedure of selecting texts, developing content categories, and coding and analyzing data. Using computers to store and analyze data, researchers are able to conduct large-scaled content analysis with massive amounts of data without much difficulty.

BUSINESS RESEARCH PROCESS

To conduct business research effectively, researchers follow a general research process of five phases and must understand their interrelationships (see Figure 1).

Conceptualization engages researchers in identifying a problem or topic worth studying, reviewing relevant literature to justify the need for the research, defining the purpose of the research, and phrasing the problem in writing as research questions or hypotheses, which set the scope of the research.

Research design requires that researchers transform the research concepts into operational, or measurable, terms by completing these activities: First, select an appropriate research method as discussed in the previous section. Second, determine the population of the study, its sample size, and sampling method. Third, develop an instrument for measuring the existence, characteristics, size, quantity, and quality of the research variables with proper scales.

Research procedures in most studies consist of two common activities: reaching subjects and collecting data. For instance, an experiment reaches subjects by putting them in either control or experiment groups for collecting data, whereas a survey reaches subjects by mailing them questionnaires or telephoning them for collecting data. In addition, researchers need to indicate any limitations in the research design or procedures.

Data analysis requires researchers to sort out nonusable data such as incomplete questionnaires or dropouts in an experiment, code and edit data to meet the computer requirements, and analyze data quantitatively or qualitatively or in combination, thereby transforming data into information, or findings, for interpretation.

Research conclusion includes discussing the significance of the findings such as whether the hypotheses have been accepted or rejected or the research questions have been answered; addressing the theoretical, practical, or pedagogical implications; and recommending future research directions.

ETHICS IN BUSINESS RESEARCH

Business research demands ethical behavior. When research involves human subjects, researchers should first successfully complete an ethics workshop from the U.S. Department of Health and Human Services and then submit for approval a research proposal that ensures ethical compliance with their organization's institutional review boards. When research involves corporate internal documents, researchers should protect owners' rights to privacy and confidentiality.

SEE ALSO *Forecasting in Business; Marketing Research*

BIBLIOGRAPHY

Collis, Jill, and Hussey, Roger (2003). *Business research* (2nd ed.). New York: Palgrave Macmillan.

Cooper, Donald R., and Schindler, Pamela S. (2006). *Business research methods* (9th ed.). Boston: McGraw-Hill.

Sekaran, Uma (2003). *Research methods for business: A skill-building approach* (4th ed.). New York: Wiley.

Zikmund, William G. (2003). *Business research methods* (7th ed.). Mason, OH: Thomson/South-Western.

Jensen J. Zhao

RESPONSIBILITY
SEE *Management: Authority and Responsibility*

RESTRUCTURING
SEE *Reengineering*

RETAILERS

Retailing is the process of selling products and services to consumers for their personal or family use. A retailer is the final business in a distribution channel that links manufacturers with consumers. Although a retailer can also be a manufacturer or a wholesaler in the distribution chain, most retailers direct their efforts to satisfying needs of ultimate consumers.

HISTORY OF RETAILING

Retailing had its raw beginnings in early America with peddlers, a word that comes from the Old English *ped,* which was a pack in which articles to be traded in the streets were stored. One of the earliest records of peddlers in the American colonies is of an itinerant hawker named Richard Graves, who in 1642 shouted his wares from house to house in an attempt to make a deal with whoever would listen to him.

Peddlers traveled throughout America selling their wares, and in the course of this adventure, American peddlers played a part in settling the South and Middle West because of their ability to carry materials to these sparsely populated areas. Although some peddlers had circular routes near home that they serviced each week, most were wanderers, and trips of 1,500 miles (2,414 km) were not uncommon, often with 50-pound (23-kg) loads strapped to their back.

Peddlers sold everything from specialized goods to specialized services. Native Americans in New York, for example, hung carved souvenir plates from their horses and traded them from settlement to settlement. Other specialist peddlers were carpenters, preachers, dentists, artists, and even breeders, who offered farmers the services of stallions for their mares and bulls for their cows. But the true peddler tended to pack his back or wagon with many items, because it was more profitable to carry a large assortment of goods in anticipation of what people might want or need. Somewhere among all these items would be the famous Yankee notions, which were pins and needles, buttons, razors, brooms, books, window glass, and novelties. Most housewives put aside their "pin money" from the sale of eggs and other products in order to buy these notions, but the peddler would often offer credit or barter for furs and other valuable goods with those who did not.

Peddling was a way out of poverty from colonial days onward, and it is surprising how many notable Americans began their careers as peddlers. Like many other frontiersmen in the nineteenth century, Abraham Lincoln's father was a part-time peddler. When he moved his family from Kentucky to Illinois, he took a trunk full of notions to sell from his wagon to help offset the expense of the trip. Inventors John Fitch (1743–1798)—inventor of the steamboat—and Thomas Edison (1847–1931) both began as peddlers.

Countless American fortunes were amassed by men who started their business on the road across America. B. T. Babbitt, America's first soap millionaire, began by peddling his soap in upstate New York, and the company Stanley Tools was founded by a peddler.

Peddlers probably founded the first real American country stores, which are often described as primitive department stores, in remote backwoods areas during the late 1600s. American country stores enjoyed their heyday between 1820 and 1860, at a time when personal income was rising and the population was growing rapidly. Usually located in the middle of town, the country store was the hub of community activity, and it was characterized by its informality, including bare wood shelves, a hodgepodge of goods, and a porch with rocking chairs where the townspeople could sit and socialize. It has been said that the country storekeeper was all things to all men, and he was usually highly respected and self-educated. His store, with the inevitable flour, cracker, and cookie barrels near the counter, carried what was a wonderland of goods to the civilization-starved settlers; and he usually extended credit liberally. For the children, penny candy ranging from licorice whips to all-day suckers were prominently displayed in jars atop the counter.

Country stores were far from fashionable. For more than twenty years after paper bags were invented in 1850, clerks were still wrapping most packages in brown wrapping paper, folded over and tied with a string. Trading in the stores was often conducted by barter, or "country pay" as it was called, with customers exchanging corn, wheat, rye, and flax, or articles of household manufacture such as

Wal-Mart was the world's leading retailer in 2005. **PHOTOGRAPH BY MIRANDA H. FERRARA. THE GALE GROUP.**

blankets and baskets, for goods on the merchant's shelves. Homemade Indian brooms, maple syrup, barrel staves, skeins of wool, dried apples, blackberries and blueberries, churned butter, potash, and charcoal were usually used as cash crops to barter at the country store.

Lincoln clerked in a country store as a youth, and the story of young Abe walking several miles to return a penny to a customer is part of American folklore. As for P. T. Barnum (1810–1891), he ran a general store in Bethel, Connecticut, where he claimed he learned many a trick from country people who cheated him as adeptly as any city slicker could.

Among the founders of great modern-day American department stores who operated and clerked in country stores, Adam Gimbel (1815–1896), J. L. Hudson (1846–1912), Charles A. Stevens, Aaron Montgomery Ward (1844–1913), and Herbert Marcus (1878–1950) should be mentioned. Some of the old country stores became grocery stores, and a few evolved into department stores.

Origins of the Department Store. As far as anyone knows, the first true department store arose in France in the mid-nineteenth century. The best evidence ascribes its beginnings to Bon Marché of Paris. Founded as a small shop in 1838, Bon Marché had begun to assume the proportions of a department store by the early 1850s. Even at that time, Paris had a long history as a retail and fashion center dating back to 1300, and the city was known for large stores, with up to 100 people working in stores called the Lame Devil, the Little Sailor, and the Beautiful Farmer's Wife. Aristide Boucicaut (1810–1877) is credited with starting Bon Marché as well as inventing the retail concept of allowing people to come into the store and browse, with no obligation to buy. He was also the originator of the money-back guarantee, which at the time was a new concept that built up his trade substantially. In addition, he clearly marked all his goods with fixed prices and permitted no haggling between customers and clerks.

Although Bon Marché and native country stores provided American merchants with the inspiration for creating department stores, the great majority of these department stores began as dry-goods stores. Neither Bon Marché nor any of the world's early department stores would have evolved if economic conditions had not been favorable at the time. The American department store is largely a product of the years from 1860 to 1910. More available capital during the Industrial Revolution, low taxes, and cheap labor to build and staff stores contributed to the rise of the department store in America. By the late 1860s or early 1870s, the department store had a firm foothold in America. Although the term *department store* is not recorded in the language until 1887, the idea of separate departments in stores can be found in print at least forty years earlier.

Beginning of Mail-Order Retailing. It was also during this time that mail-order retailing began. The earliest colonists, with no manufacturers of their own, first used mail orders to obtain supplies from the mother country. George Washington ordered goods from England and France, as did Thomas Jefferson. Benjamin Franklin has been called the originator of the mail-order catalog because in 1744 he issued a list of 600 books he would sell by mail. Ward thought he could eliminate the middleman by selling direct to country people by mail from offices in Chicago. In August 1872, Ward, with capital of $1,600 in savings, founded what was to become Montgomery Ward, the world's first great mail-order business, soon to be challenged by Sears.

TYPES OF RETAILERS

Over time, different types of retailers have emerged and prospered because they have attracted and maintained a significant customer base. A retail institution is a group of retailers that provide a similar retail mix designed to satisfy the needs of a specific segment of customers. The most basic characteristic of a retailer is its retail mix, which include decisions and strategies regarding the type of merchandise sold, the price of the merchandise, the assortment of the merchandise, and the level of customer service.

The traditional general-merchandise retail stores are specialty stores, department stores, and discount stores.

Since about 1970, a number of new types of general-merchandise retailers have emerged and are becoming increasingly important to consumers. These include category specialists, home-improvement centers, warehouse clubs, off-price retailers, and catalog showrooms. A traditional specialty store concentrates on a limited number of complementary merchandise categories and provides a high level of service in an area typically smaller than 8,000 square feet (744 sq m).

General-Merchandise Retailers. Department stores are retailers that carry a broad variety and deep assortment, offer considerable customer service, and are organized into separate departments for displaying merchandise. A home-improvement center is a category specialist that combines the traditional hardware store and lumberyard. It focuses on providing material and information that enable do-it-yourselvers to maintain and improve their homes. A warehouse club is a general-merchandise retailer that offers a limited merchandise assortment with little service at low prices to ultimate consumers and small businesses; the stores are large and located in low-rent districts, and the goods usually include food and general merchandise. Off-price retailers offer an inconsistent assortment of brand-name, fashion-oriented soft goods at low prices, in exchange for not using the manufacturer's promotional allowances, return privileges, and delayed-payment options.

Catalog Showrooms. A catalog showroom is a retailer whose showroom is adjacent to its warehouse. These retailers typically specialize in hard goods such as housewares, jewelry, sporting goods, garden equipment, and consumer electronics. Catalog showrooms can offer low prices because they minimize the cost of displaying merchandise, provide minimal service, and are located in lower-rent areas rather than regional malls.

Retail Chains. A retail chain is a company operating multiple retail units under common ownership and usually has some centralization of decision making in defining and implementing its strategy. Some retail chains are divisions of larger corporations or holding companies. Because of scale economies and an efficient distribution system, the corporate chains can sell at lower prices. Since about 1990 there has been considerable restructuring of corporate retail chains. These restructuring activities include consolidation and focus, with consolidation of existing retail chains leaving fewer large chains and focus referring to the expertise in managing a specific retail format rather than operating as a holding company for a diverse set of retail formats.

Franchises. Franchising is a contractual agreement between a franchiser and a franchisee that allows the franchisee to operate a retail outlet using a name and format developed and supported by the franchiser. Approximately one-third of all U.S. retail sales are made by franchisees. Some of the most-well-known franchises in America are McDonald's, Subway, and Dunkin' Donuts.

Mail-Order Retailing. The mail-order retailing of the late 1800s has developed into two types of nonstore retailing: (1) general-merchandise and specialty catalog retailers and (2) direct-mail retailers. General-merchandise catalog retailers offer a broader variety of merchandise in catalogs that are periodically mailed to their customers, while specialty catalog retailers focus on specific categories of merchandise. Direct-mail retailers typically mail brochures and pamphlets to sell a specific product or service to customers at a particular time. Direct-mail and catalog retailing are attractive business opportunities because a business can be started with minimal inventory and can use existing mailing lists to tailor its mailings to a targeted market.

MODERN-DAY RETAILING

Retailing is experiencing international expansion, with many retail organizations opening stores and expanding beyond the borders of the United States. The most commonly targeted countries or regions are Mexico, Europe, China, and Japan. U.S. retailers have strong incentives to expand globally because U.S. markets are saturated in terms of the number of stores, available locations, and competition. Experts believe that some American retailers have a natural advantage when competing globally because of such factors as technology and the emulation of American culture abroad. Like foreign companies entering the United States, however, American companies entering into these countries face specific government regulations, different cultural traditions, and a variety of languages.

Today, the success of small retailers and major retail corporations depends on how much they embrace the retailing concept. The retailing concept is a management orientation that focuses a retailer on determining the needs of its target market and satisfying those needs more effectively and efficiently than its competitors. Three critical environmental factors affect retailing:

1. Competition, because each department store, specialty store, and other type of retail outlet is competing against all others for the consumer's dollar

2. Consumer demographic and lifestyle trends and the impact they will have on retail strategies

3. Needs, wants, and decision-making processes that retail consumers use

Among the list of consumer trends that are greatly affecting retail sales today are the growth of the elderly population, as the baby boomers age; the rapidly growing minority segments of the U.S. population; the importance of shopping convenience, with consumers wanting one-stop shopping; and the rising number of two-income families.

Another response to the changes in consumers' preferences is a form of co-branding in which two retailers share a location. McDonald's has developed partnerships with Wal-Mart and Home Depot, and Starbucks has opened cafés in more than 100 Barnes & Noble bookstores.

ONLINE RETAILING

Since its inception in the mid-1990s, online retailing continues to grow. Online sales in 2004 rose 23.8 percent to $141.4 billion, which represented approximately 5 percent of total retail sales. Online sales of cosmetics and fragrances were expected to grow 35 percent, while the sales of over-the-counter personal care were projected to rise 32 percent. Early in the twenty-first century, retailers have attained growth by launching country-specific sites in order to attract the growing number of international consumers.

SEE ALSO *Channels of Distribution; Discount Stores; Electronic Commerce; Franchising; International Business; Marketing; National Retail Federation; Target Marketing; Wholesalers*

BIBLIOGRAPHY

Berman, Barry, and Evans, Joel R. (2006). *Retail management: A strategic approach* (10th ed.). Upper Saddle River, NJ: Palgrave Macmillan.

Fortune 1000 ranked within industries. (2004, April 5). *Fortune*, p. 54.

Hatch, Denny (1998, September). Eight hundred years young. *Target Marketing, 21*(9), 5.

Hendrickson, Robert (1989). *The grand emporiums.* New York: Stein and Day/Scarborough House.

Levy, Michael, and Weitz, Barton A. (2004). *Retailing management* (5th ed.). Boston: McGraw-Hill/Irwin.

U.S. Department of Commerce, Bureau of the Census. (2003.) Retail trade establishments, employees and payroll. *Statistical Abstract of the United States* (123rd ed.). Washington, DC: Author, p. 660.

Patricia A. Spirou

RETIREMENT PLANNING

SEE *Personal Financial Planning*

REWARD SYSTEMS

SEE *Employee Benefits; Employee Compensation*

RISK MANAGEMENT

Risk management is a term that pervades a number of different areas of human interest. At the ultimate level of risk management, political leaders and government officials must assess the risk of natural disasters, terrorist attacks, and nuclear war—events that threaten human existence. For public health officials and hospital administrators, risk management entails the reduction of mortality due to disease and infection. For transportation safety engineers, risk management focuses on preventing or reducing deaths and injuries caused by accidents. Insurance companies and their customers view risk management as entailing the assessment and mitigation of various types of risks, often with the goal of reducing the costs of insuring against such risks.

For bankers and lenders, risk management involves credit analysis and techniques such as currency hedging and interest rate swaps that reduce credit and lending risks. For the business manager, risk management necessitates the assessment of future market fluctuations both on the sales and supply sides of an enterprise and creating plans to mitigate the effects of these fluctuations. In sum, risk management addresses the possibility that future events may cause adverse effects and entails an attempt to mitigate the impact of these effects.

Risk management draws upon knowledge and skills derived from various disciplines, including statistics, economics, psychology, sociology, epidemiology, biology, engineering, toxicology, systems analysis, operations research, decision theory, and international relations. Because of the wide diversity of risk management topics, this entry addresses only a small portion of the total, concentrating on risk management from the perspective of higher levels of a business enterprise. The specific risk management techniques will not be addressed, but the focus will instead be on components of risk management that are important to business enterprises. Ultimately, risk management can provide assurance to shareholders, creditors, employees, customers, and other interested parties that a business is being well managed, and it can provide

important evidence about compliance with relevant laws and government regulations.

INTERNAL CONTROL

An important contribution to the field of risk management for business enterprises has been provided by the Committee of Sponsoring Organizations (COSO) of the National Commission on Fraudulent Financial Reporting (Treadway Commission). The Treadway Commission was created in 1987 in the wake of several major financial frauds. The sponsoring organizations include the American Accounting Association, American Institute of Certified Public Accountants, Financial Executives International, the Institute of Management Accountants, and the Institute of Internal Auditors.

In 1992 COSO issued the report *Internal Control—Integrated Framework,* which has become the most widely recognized framework for internal control in the United States. Section 404 of the federal Sarbanes-Oxley Act of 2002 requires the management of public companies to issue annual internal control reports which include a statement that management is responsible for establishing and maintaining an adequate internal control structure, as well as procedures for financial reporting, and is to make an assessment of the effectiveness of the internal control structure and the procedures for financial reporting.

Section 404 also requires the company's independent auditor to issue a report on management's assessment of internal control. Public Companies Accounting Oversight Board (PCAOB) Standard No. 2 specifically recognizes the COSO *Internal Control—Integrated Framework* as establishing the criteria for effective internal control over financial reporting.

ENTERPRISE RISK MANAGEMENT

Because the Sarbanes-Oxley Act and the COSO *Internal Control—Integrated Framework* are directed primarily toward internal control and transparency in financial reporting, COSO became concerned that there was a need for a broader framework to identify, assess, and manage enterprise risks. Consequently, in 2004 COSO issued *Enterprise Risk Management: Integrated Framework.* This document is not intended to replace the COSO internal control framework. Rather it incorporates the internal control framework and recommends that companies use the enterprise risk management framework to both satisfy their internal control needs and to develop a more complete risk management process.

According to COSO, the underlying premise of enterprise risk management is that every entity exists to provide value for its stakeholders. Because all entities face uncertainty, the challenge for management is to determine how much risk to accept. COSO defines enterprise risk management as:

> a process, effected by an entity's board of directors, management and other personnel, applied in strategy setting and across the enterprise, designed to identify potential events that may affect the entity, and manage risks to be within its risk appetite, to provide reasonable assurance regarding the achievement of entity objectives. (COSO, 2004)

Several aspects of this definition are underlined, namely that risk management is an ongoing process undertaken by people at various levels of an organization. Furthermore, risk management is a strategic process that looks at the risks facing an entity from a portfolio perspective. Finally, risk management is geared toward providing reasonable assurance to entity management and directors that risks will be managed, and that any risks assumed are related to the objectives of the entity.

OBJECTIVES

COSO believes that enterprise risk management should focus on achieving an entity's strategic, operating, reporting, and compliance objectives. Strategic objectives are defined as high-level goals related to the mission of the entity. Operating objectives focus on effective and efficient use of resources. Reporting objectives deal with reliability of reporting, and compliance objectives involve compliance with laws and regulations. The COSO framework sets forth eight interrelated components for enterprise risk management:

1. *Internal environment*—The tone of an organization and how risk is viewed by the people in the organization

2. *Objective setting*—Objectives must exist before management can identify risks that may affect those objectives

3. *Event identification*—Internal and external events that may pose risks must be identified

4. *Risk assessment*—Risks are analyzed from both the perspective of likelihood and impact

5. *Risk response*—A decision to avoid, accept, reduce, or share the risk

6. *Control activities*—Establishing policies and procedures so that chosen risk response is carried out

7. *Information and communication*—Information about risks and procedures is communicated throughout the organization

8. *Monitoring*—Enterprise risk management is monitored and changes are made as needed

The enterprise risk management framework envisions the objectives of the enterprise and the components of risk management as being arranged in a matrix, so that there is an intersection between each objective and each component. For example, in the area of operations, there is an intersection with internal environment, objective setting, event identification, risk assessment, risk response, control activities, information and communication and monitoring. This matrix is then extended to encompass entity-level, division-level, and business-unit-level risk management objectives and components.

The extent to which the COSO framework will become seen as an exemplar of risk management for business enterprises is still unclear. Nevertheless, the authority of COSO and its sponsoring organizations makes it important for business managers to be aware of the provisions of the framework if they are to be fully conversant with enterprise risk management.

SEE ALSO *Insurance; Investments*

BIBLIOGRAPHY

Beasley, Mark S., and Elder, Randal J. (2005). *The Sarbanes-Oxley Act of 2002: Impacting the accounting profession.* Upper Saddle River, NJ: Pearson Prentice-Hall.

COSO. (1992). *Internal control—Integrated framework.* New York: Committee of Sponsoring Organizations of the Treadway Commission.

COSO. (2004). *Enterprise risk management: Integrated framework.* New York: Committee of Sponsoring Organizations of the Treadway Commission.

National Commission on Fraudulent Financial Reporting. (1987). *Report of the National Commission on Fraudulent Financial Reporting.* Washington, DC: Author.

Rowe, William D. (1988). *An anatomy of risk.* Malabar, FL: Robert E. Krieger.

C. Richard Baker

ROBINSON-PATMAN ACT OF 1936

The Robinson-Patman Act of 1936 is antitrust legislation that amends Section 2 of the Clayton Act of 1914, which was designed to prevent monopolies by catching early-stage practices leading to corporate mergers. Another provision of the Clayton Act prohibits price discrimination by a seller where the effect is to injure the competition. The Clayton Act was directed at firms that sold goods at higher prices in some areas and at lower prices in others to the detriment of a smaller local seller; it confined the prohibition on price discrimination to the impact on the seller. Thus, competition among buyers could be affected adversely when certain buyers received lower prices.

Price discrimination occurs when a firm charges more than one price for goods or services sold to customers and businesses where all other material aspects of the sales are the same. The Robinson-Patman Act is commonly referred to as the "antichain store act" because it prohibits price cutting of commodities for large buyers (chain stores, department stores, and discount houses) designed to eliminate competition from small buyers. The act makes it unlawful for any seller engaged in commerce to discriminate, directly or indirectly, in regard to the price charged to buyers of commodities of like grade and quality sold in interstate commerce for the purpose of resale.

Small businesses implied that their larger competition used their size or market power to gain lower prices from suppliers. This practice enabled the larger competitors to profitably outsell their smaller competitors. The result of this act is that smaller local buyers have restitution against a favored competitor that, because of size, efficiency, or bargaining power, could obtain lower prices from a supplier and, thus, sell products for lower prices. It became illegal for companies engaged in interstate commerce to grant discounts for the same products to large firms without granting similar discounts to smaller independent stores when the selling costs do not vary between the two. The law does permit selling at different prices when costs are based on different methods or quantities involved in the manufacture, sale, or delivery of products. The Robinson-Patman Act was intended to protect competitors as well as competition.

Enforcing the act is a complex task. While both the Federal Trade Commission (FTC) and the U.S. Department of Justice have jurisdiction to enforce the act, most cases are handled by the FTC. Nearly all cases litigated under the act are initiated by private plaintiffs.

SEE ALSO *Antitrust Legislation*

BIBLIOGRAPHY

Dukes, A. J. (2003). Wal-Mart and price discrimination (forum on business and economics). *Phi Kappa Phi Forum, 83,* 4–6.

Garman, E. T. (2004). *Consumer economic issues in America* (8th ed.). Mason, OH: Custom Thomson.

Leiter, J. L., Knight, M., and Scott, C. S. (2001). Lubricants and the Robinson-Patman Act: The limits on price differentiation. *Compoundings, 51,* 16–19.

Meier, K., Garman, E. T., and Keiser, L. R. (2003). *Regulation and consumer protection: Politics, bureaucracy and economics* (4th ed.). Mason, OH: Custom Thomson.

Phyllis Bunn
Laurie Barfitt

S

SALES DISCOUNTS
SEE *Pricing*

SARBANES-OXLEY ACT OF 2002
SEE *Audit Committees; Securities Acts: Requirements for Accounting*

SCARCITY
SEE *Supply and Demand*

SCHOOL TO CAREER MOVEMENT

One of the purposes of education is to prepare students to become productive workers. As occupations within the workforce become more specialized, the development of specific job skills remains on the forefront for educators. The changing labor market dictates that educators prepare all students for future success. To ensure that students are adequately prepared, a transition has taken place from narrow-job-specific vocational programs to programs that reflect the modern workplace. New programs such as biotechnology, the teaching profession, and logistics blend the lines between academic and technical education.

Part of the U.S. Department of Education, the Web site of the Office of Vocational Education (OVAE) states:

> Career and technical education exists in approximately thousands of comprehensive high schools, technical schools, and postsecondary educational institutions. Virtually every high school student takes at least one vocational education course, and one in four students takes three or more courses in a single program area. One-third of college students are involved in vocational programs, and as many as 40 million adults engage in short-term postsecondary occupational training.
>
> Today, eighty-five years after the passage of the first piece of federal vocational education legislation, vocational education is evolving from its original focus on preparing students for work immediately following high school to addressing the needs of all students. With national and state school reform efforts focused on academic achievement and with the fastest-growing occupations now requiring some postsecondary education, vocational education is seeking effective ways to contribute to these goals. (U.S. Department of Education, OVAE)

To better prepare highly qualified career and technical education teachers across the country, the Career and Technical Educational National Dissemination Center provides online resources that enable individuals to participate in discussion boards and to submit initiatives as well as teaching and learning strategies. Strategies include policies, rubrics, frameworks, techniques, procedures, and action plans. These online resources provide documentation and examples of programs that have been successfully implemented.

Educators must continue the implementation of model sequences of courses as well as frameworks for instruction to expand the school to career movement. These frameworks and guidelines provide and support the integration of academic and vocational education to establish specific student learning outcomes and to engage students in the learning process.

HISTORICAL PERSPECTIVE

The Secretary's Commission on Achieving Necessary Skills (SCANS) was formed in 1990 by the secretary of the U.S. Department of Labor to investigate the skills needed by young people to succeed in the world of work. The commission's initial 1991 report identified three foundation areas (basic skills, thinking skills, and personal qualities) and five workplace competencies (resources, interpersonal, information, systems, and technology). The commission's fundamental purpose was to encourage a high-performance economy characterized by high-skill, high-wage employment. The Department of Labor Web site states: "Although the commission completed its work in 1992, its findings and recommendations continue to be a valuable source of information for individuals and organizations involved in education and workforce development" (U.S. Department of Labor).

The School-to-Work Opportunity Act of 1994 (STWOA) resulted from the SCANS report. STWOA was the most comprehensive attempt to implement improved academics skills, the SCANS directive, and a greater emphasis on standards. The primary focus of school to work was on the role of secondary education to prepare young people to enter the workforce. Strategies that included work-based learning, school-based learning, and the integration of academic and vocational education were implemented. Legislators were challenged to connect school-based learning to work-based learning through the use of integrated learning activities. This act was built on a variety of instructional strategies that were already in existence. Through high-profile funding from the federal government these activities were accelerated. "The authors of STWOA had not intended for the programs to become separate entities; therefore, funding for the programs was scheduled to expire in 2001" (Hughes, Bailey, and Karp, 2002, p. 272). The final funding stream for STWOA was administered in October 2001.

LEGISLATION

The reauthorization of the Carl Perkins Act in 2005 was crucial to the school to work movement. In February 2005 the subcommittee on Education and Workforce

Development proposed H.R. 366—The Vocational and Technical Education for the Future Act. The goals addressed in the bill were to advance career and technical education in order to ensure that the United States is able to meet the needs of its employers. In order to meet the goals proposed in H.R. 366, Perkins funding had to be maintained rather than decreased or cut. The bill specifically provided a model sequence of courses, more opportunities for state leaders to ensure the quality of their programs, specific accountability measures, technical assessments, and a simplification of funding streams.

"It is ironic that just as the major federal role in school-to-work has wound down, the flow of evaluation research with positive finding is increasing" (Hughes et al., p. 272). Research studies have indicated that school to career training does provide academic achievement in a variety of ways including the development of skills and abilities needed on the job, increased maturity and psychological development, and encouraged interactions between students and their workplace mentors. Funding for the continuation of career and technical education (CTE) programs is crucial to the school to career movement. "CTE funding may be a very small piece of the federal budget" (Hyslop, 2005, p. 12), but supporters of these programs must ensure that policymakers understand how critical their continuation is to our schools and communities.

SCHOOL TO CAREER AT THE POSTSECONDARY LEVEL

Research and field reports indicate that few college graduates are prepared for the realities of work, and even fewer have the skills for successful organization entry. This is especially true in the human services field, where students may not be effectively prepared to handle the multiple needs of families and communities. One might argue, however, that graduating students have strong technical skills, but cannot work together with other professionals or community residents to solve the complex problems of families and neighborhoods. In either case, graduates need to develop skills in both the technical and clinical arenas to meet the needs of their clientele.

Universities can contribute to the process of interprofessional education and community collaboration through both curriculum and experiential learning. The Association for Experiential Education describes experiential education as "a philosophy and methodology in which educators purposefully engage with learners in direct experience and focused reflection in order to increase knowledge, develop skills, and clarify values" (AEE, p. 47).

When professional development is oriented through experiential learning or direct service, a student begins a process of interaction with professionals and community members. This process embeds technical skills within a larger practice of problem solving in authentic civic life. Furthermore, experiential learning and collaborative work experience enhance the development of problem-solving capabilities of university students beyond their immediate discipline.

L. Michelle Bobbitt, Scott A. Inks, Katie J. Kemp et al. contend that experiential learning techniques create opportunities for students to apply real-life situations to the concepts and theories they have learned. Experiential learning programs can be designed to improve and/or enhance skills in the areas of decision making, problem solving, planning, written and oral communication, and creativity. Experiential learning encompasses a variety of teaching methods, specifically classroom-based (e.g., role-playing, computer simulations, and group projects) and field-based (e.g., internships and practical) techniques. Bettina Lankard Brown supports the use of work-based learning and experiential learning to integrate real-world experiences with classroom curricula learning outcomes. N. T. Frontczak and C. A. Kelly further emphasize the use of experiential learning to integrate theory and practice to improve critical thinking and communication skills.

Many professional graduate programs have long depended on internships and practicum experiences to introduce students to real-life professional practice. According to Steve Jex, the scientist-practitioner model used in graduate education includes opportunities for students to apply information they have learned into real-world settings through internship and field experience. Internships yield high job satisfaction and favorable employment opportunities for participants. Thus, by performing job tasks relevant to chosen vocational fields, students are able to identify personally valued, work-related outcomes and the vocational abilities and interests needed to attain satisfaction from the work arena.

SCHOOL TO CAREER AT THE SECONDARY AND COMMUNITY COLLEGE LEVEL

Secondary educators and community college personnel focus on collaboration to encourage students to pursue technical careers as well as a community college education. Through articulation agreements designed around common course areas and programs of study, students who complete these courses at the high school level are eligible to move directly into a 2 years of secondary education + 2 years of postsecondary education (Tech Prep) or 2 + 4 degree plan at the postsecondary level.

Tech Prep funding and STWOA led "local school districts to reorganize their high school programs according to the locally selected career-cluster areas" (Orr, 2004, p.

24). Work-based learning thus become a "precollege" experience by affording students an opportunity to participate in job shadowing, short- and long-term internships, community service projects, cooperative education, youth apprenticeships, career academies, school-sponsored enterprises, and tech-prep programs. Kenneth Gray states that "the transformation of CTE brought about by Tech Prep has been dramatic" (2004, p.130).

Many of these work-based programs provide students with dual enrollment credits that support an effective transition from secondary education to postsecondary education programs. "Dual enrollment programs give high schools and colleges an opportunity to work together to better link secondary and postsecondary education" (Emeagwali, 2005, p. 16). The use of technology has also increased and continues to become more advanced than in the past. Educators, as well as trainers in business and industry, are required to participate in and develop continuing education activities to ensure that their job skills meet the needs of the industries they represent.

CTE IN MIDDLE SCHOOLS AND ELEMENTARY SCHOOLS

For middle school education, exploration is the primary focus. Students in middle school are often unprepared to make decisions about educational training and/or their career paths. A counselor at a middle school in Utah states that at the middle school level "we don't really pressure students to come up with a specific career" (*Techniques*, 2001, p. 26). Young adolescents are introduced to various careers by participating in a yearlong program called Technology-Life-Careers. Students have the opportunity to learn about careers in business, agriculture, economics, health science, technology, and trade skills. These programs introduce young adolescents to various careers to make students and their parents aware of career opportunities from a broad perspective.

Career cluster programs such as the one identified above can be found throughout the United States. These programs have presented unique opportunities for students to expand their knowledge about various career and technical education opportunities. Broad exposure and self-reflection allow middle school students the chance to cultivate and define their interests. Career and technical education at the middle school level focuses on providing options for students and allowing them to make decisions on their own regarding their career pursuits.

Brown states:

At the elementary school level, this developmental process begins with career awareness, which is initiated to broaden student knowledge about careers and connect academic learning to the workplace.

It establishes school as a foundation for education and workplace connections and requires community involvement and support. (1999)

Career awareness is further enhanced by field trips, guest speakers, and simulations to introduce elementary students to the world of work. Merely introducing students to the concepts of jobs, careers, and the workplace at the elementary level prepares them for the exploration of careers when they enter the middle level grades.

SUMMARY

The challenge for educators at all levels is how to plan and to prepare students for a future workplace where the technological requirements may be far different from those that have been predicted. Consideration of workforce development issues can be found at the elementary, middle, and high school levels as well as at the postsecondary level. Federal, state, and local governments have accepted an active role to identify and to promote the integration of occupational skills in the curricula.

SEE ALSO *Training and Development*

BIBLIOGRAPHY

Association for Experiential Education. (n.d.). About Experiential Education. Retrieved November 22, 2005, from http://www.aee2.org/customer/pages.php?pageid=47

Bobbitt, L. Michelle, Inks, Scott A., Kemp, Katie J., et al. (2000, April). Integrating marketing courses to enhance team-based experiential learning. *Journal of Marketing Education, 22,* 15–24.

Brown, Bettina Lankard (1999). School-to-work and elementary education. Retrieved November 22, 2005, from http://www.cete.org/acve/docgen.asp?tbl=pab&ID=94

Career and Technical Educational National Dissemination Center. http://www.nccte.org/tqi/index.aspx

Emeagwali, N. S. (2005). States' varying policies regarding dual enrollment programs. *Techniques, 80*(1), 16.

Frontczak, N. T., and Kelly, C. A. (2000, April). Special issues on experiential learning in marketing education. *Journal of Marketing Education, 22,* 3–5.

Gray, Kenneth (2004, October). Is high school career and technical education obsolete? *Phi Delta Kappan, 86*(2), 130.

Hughes, Katherine L., Bailey, Thomas R., and Karp, Melinda Mechur (2002, December). School-to-work: Making a difference in education. *Phi Delta Kappan, 84*(4), 272.

Hyslop-Margison, Emery J. (2005). *Liberalizing vocational study: democratic approaches to career education.* Lanham, MD: University Press of America.

Jex, Steve M. (2002). *Organizational psychology: A scientist-practitioner approach.* New York: Wiley.

Littrell, Joseph J., Lorenz, James H., and Smith, Harry T. (2006). *From school to work.* Tinley Park, IL: Goodheart-Willcox.

Orr, M. T. (2004, Spring). Community college and secondary school collaboration on workforce development and education reform. *The Catalyst, 33*(1), 20–24.

A time of exploration. (2001, October). *Techniques, 76*(7), 26.

U.S. Department of Education. Office of Vocational and Adult Education. http://www.ed.gov/about/offices/list/ovae/pi/cte/index.html

U.S. Department of Labor. Employment and Training Administration. (n.d.). What work requires of schools. Retrieved November 22, 2005, from http://wdr.doleta.gov/SCANS/whatwork

Jill T. White

SCIENTIFIC MANAGEMENT

Early attempts to study behavior in organizations came from a desire by industrial efficiency experts to answer this question: What can be done to get workers to do more work in less time? It is not surprising that attempts to answer this question were made at the beginning of the twentieth century, since this was a period of rapid industrialization and technological change in the United States. As engineers attempted to make machines more efficient, it was natural to focus efforts on the human side—making people more productive, too.

The scientific method of management and job design, which originated with Frederick Winslow Taylor (1856–1915), entails analyzing jobs to determine what the worker does and what the requirements are for the job. After this analysis, the job is designed to ensure that employees will not be asked to perform work beyond their abilities. Another aspect of the scientific method is that jobs are divided into small segments for the worker to perform, a method that works well in establishing expected levels of worker performance. While not as popular as in the past, this method of job design is still used in the twenty-first century.

To Taylor, it was obvious that workers were producing below their capacities in the industrial shops of his day. As a foreman in a steel mill, Taylor noticed, for example, that laborers wasted movement when moving pig iron. Believing that productivity could be increased substantially, Taylor carefully analyzed the workers' motions and steps and studied the proper distribution of work and rest. Based on this analysis, he determined a more appropriate method for performing each aspect of the job. He then carefully selected employees and gave them detailed instructions on how to perform the job using the new method. He required that employees follow the instructions precisely. As an incentive, all workers were told that

Frederick Winslow Taylor (1856–1915). The father of the scientific method of management and job design. © BETTMANN/CORBIS

they would receive a substantial pay increase provided they followed instructions. As a result, worker productivity increased substantially.

However, most of the short-sighted management of that time would set certain standards, often paying by piece-rate for the work. Then, when a worker discovered how to produce more, management cut the rate. In turn, the workers deliberately cut down on output, but management could do nothing about this. Taylor came to realize that the concept of division of labor had to be revamped if greater productivity and efficiency were to be realized. His vision included a superefficient assembly line as part of a management system of operations. He, more than anyone else at the time, understood the inability of management to increase individual productivity, and he understood the reluctance of workers to produce at a high rate.

For more than twenty-five years, Taylor and his associates explored ways to increase productivity. Scientific management has often been described as a series of techniques for increasing production rates by means of better cost-accounting procedures, premium and incentive payments, and time and motion studies (which are designed to classify and streamline the individual movement needed to perform jobs with the intent of finding "the one best way" to do them). Even Taylor protested this interpretation. In his view, using these techniques did not in itself constitute scientific management, because, as he put it, the main objective of scientific management was "to remove the causes for antagonism between the boss and the men who were under him." Ironically, at times during his experimentation, Taylor achieved the opposite effect by creating antagonism.

As Taylor made his techniques known, others began to contribute to the body of knowledge of scientific management. These theorists included Carl G. L. Barth (1860–1939), a mathematician and statistician who assisted Taylor in analytical work, and Henry L. Gantt (1861–1919), who invented the slide rule and created the Gantt chart. Another associate, Sanford E. Thompson (1867–1949), developed the first decimal stopwatch. Walter Shewhart eventually transformed industry with his statistical concepts and his ability to bridge technical tools with a management system. Frank G. (1868–1924) and Lillian Gilbreth (1878–1972), aware of Taylor's work in measurement and analysis, chose the ancient craft of bricklaying for analysis. It was assumed that productivity in bricklaying certainly should have reached its peak thousands of years ago and nothing could be done to increase worker productivity. Yet the Gilbreths were able to show that by following Taylor's techniques and using proper management planning, productivity could be raised significantly and workers would be less tired than they were under the old system.

By 1912, the efficiency movement had gained momentum. Taylor was even called before a special committee of the House of Representatives that was investigating scientific management and its impact on the railroad industry, whose members regarded it as a way to speed up work. Little did Taylor realize how workers would perceive his effort at producing more efficiently. Taylor found out the importance of the cooperative spirit the hard way. He was strictly the engineer at first. Only after painful experiences did he realize that the human factor, the social system, and the mental attitude of people in both management and labor had to be adjusted and changed completely before greater productivity could result. He referred to his early experiences in seeking greater output and described the strained feelings between himself and his workers as miserable. Yet he was determined to improve production. He continued his experiments until three years before his death in 1915, when he found that human motivation, not just engineered improvement, could alone increase output.

Unfortunately, the human factor was ignored by many. Shortly after the railroad hearings, self-proclaimed efficiency experts damaged the intent of scientific management. Time studies and the new efficiency techniques were used by incompetent consultants who sold managers on the idea of increasing profit by speeding up employees. Consequently, many labor unions, just beginning to feel their strength, worked against the new science and all efficiency approaches. With the death of Taylor in 1915, the scientific management movement lost any chance of reaching its true potential as the catalyst for the future total quality management system that was to evolve as a key ingredient of organizations of the future.

SEE ALSO *Management: Historical Perspectives; Management/Leadership Styles*

BIBLIOGRAPHY

Benton, Douglas A. (1998). *Applied Human Relations*. Upper Saddle River, NJ: Prentice-Hall.

Greenberg, Jerald (2005). *Managing Behavior in Organizations* (4th ed.). Upper Saddle River, NJ: Pearson Prentice-Hall.

Hersey, Paul, Blanchard, Kenneth H., and Johnson, Dewey E. (2001). *Management of Organizational Behavior*. Upper Saddle River, NJ: Prentice-Hall.

Rue, Leslie W., and Byars, Lloyd L. (2007). *Supervision, Key Link to Productivity*. Boston: McGraw-Hill.

Whetten, David A., and Cameron, Kim S. (2005). *Developing Management Skills*. Upper Saddle River, NJ: Pearson/Prentice Hall.

Wray, Ralph D., Luft, Roger L., and Highland, Patrick J. (1996). *Fundamentals of Human Relations*. Cincinnati, OH: South-Western Educational Publishing.

Yukl, Gary (2005). *Leadership in Organizations*. Upper Saddle River, NJ: Pearson/Prentice-Hall.

Marcia Anderson

SEASONAL DISCOUNTS

SEE *Pricing*

SECURITIES ACTS: REQUIREMENTS FOR ACCOUNTING

Companies issuing securities to the public are required to file registration reports and statements with the U.S. Securities and Exchange Commission (SEC) in accordance with the Securities Act of 1933 and the Securities Exchange Act of 1934. The 1933 act requires that a registration statement be filed and accepted by the SEC before securities are offered for sale. The SEC does not evaluate the merit of the securities, but determines only whether the disclosures provide sufficient information to the investment community.

Companies seeking to issue security offerings rely on specialists in accounting to meet the criteria of the securities acts. The chief accountant of the commission is the principal accounting adviser with respect to difficult or controversial accounting issues. The chief accountant is in charge of establishing, coordinating, and expressing the SEC policy regarding accounting and auditing standards. Policy decisions are published in the SEC Accounting Series Releases (financial reporting releases).

REQUIREMENTS OF THE SECURITIES ACT OF 1933

Under the 1933 act, a company undertakes its first offering of securities to the public market through a process referred to as an initial public offering (IPO). The registration statement submitted to the SEC for the IPO consists of two principal components: Part I is the prospectus, an offering document to be distributed to prospective buyers; and Part II is supplemental information that is available for public inspection at the office of the SEC.

In 1982 the SEC adopted a revised framework for registration as a part of the integrated disclosure system, where the form to be used by the registrant depends on the periodic reporting history and the nature of specific transaction events. In the case of IPOs, for example, Form S-L becomes the forepart of the registration statement and outside front cover page of the prospectus.

Prospectus disclosures must provide the following information: summary of the securities offering, risk factors and the ratio of earnings to fixed charges, the use of proceeds, determination of offering price, dilution, plan of securities distribution, description of securities to be registered, and interests of named experts and counsel. The prospectus must also provide information related to the registrant, such as description of business and property, legal proceedings, market price of equity and dividends, financial statements, supplementary financial information, executive compensation, and management's discussion and analysis (MD&A) regarding disagreements with accountants.

Part II of the IPO covers other information not required in the prospectus such as issuance- and distribution-related expenses, indemnification of directors and officers, recent sales of unregistered securities, exhibits, and financial statement schedules. An accountant's report is required for audited information to be included in this part.

REQUIREMENTS OF THE SECURITIES AND EXCHANGE ACT OF 1934

The 1934 act regulates and controls the securities markets and related matters and practices. This act also includes regulations for reporting and registration forms for the financial statements and audit requirements. The principal annual report to be filed by publicly owned commercial and industrial companies is Form 10-K—which includes financial statements audited by an independent auditor who is registered with the Public Company Accounting Oversight Board—and related information, identified as supplementary data. Additionally, an audit of internal control is required by the independent auditor who provided the financial audit.

Form 10-K requires information about the business, properties, legal proceedings, security holder voting, MD&A regarding financial conditions and operations results, and information about the elective officers of the corporation, their compensation, and their security ownership. Ancillary to the 10-K is Form 8-K, which calls for exhibits, financial statements, schedules, and reports, including a description of loans to officers and directors and their transactions in company equity securities.

The requirements for both Form 10-K and Form 8-K are set forth by SEC Regulation S-X. Under this regulation, the balance sheets at the end of each of the two latest fiscal periods, as well as the income statements and cash flow statements for each of the three latest fiscal years, should be filed within sixty days after the fiscal year ends (a requirement as of December 15, 2005; the deadline remains the same as of December 15, 2006). The principal executive officer, the principal financial officer, the principal accounting officer (the controller), and a majority of the board of directors must sign the Form 10-K.

Issuers of securities registered under the 1933 and 1934 securities acts are required to file Form 10-Q for each of the first three quarters of the fiscal year within forty days after the end of each of the first three fiscal quarters of each year. (A requirement as of December 15, 2005. The deadline is within 35 days of each of the first three fiscal quarters, as of December 15, 2006.) There is also included financial information such as a condensed financial statement, MD&A, financial condition and results of operations as required in Regulation S-K and Regulation S-X; and special event reports occurring during the quarter, such as legal proceedings, defaults upon senior securities, and matters to be voted by security holders. Form 10-Q may be integrated with the quarterly stockholders' report if the combined report contains full and complete answers to all items required by Part I of Form 10-Q.

The Sarbanes-Oxley Act of 2002 introduced a new section, Section 13(j) to the Securities Exchange Act of 1934. This section requires that the MD&A in each annual and quarterly report must disclose:

> all material off-balance sheet transactions, arrangements, obligations (including contingent obligations), and other relationships of the issuer with unconsolidated entities or other persons, that may have a material current or future effect on financial condition, changes in financial conditions, results of operations, liquidity, capital expenditures, capital resources, or significant components of revenues or expenses. (Sarbanes-Oxley Act, Section 401 [a])

THE ROLE OF THE DIVISION OF CORPORATION FINANCE

The SEC Division of Corporation Finance is in charge of reviewing registration statements as well as other annual and periodic reports. The division establishes standards for economic and financial disclosure by determining the nature of information required in the registration statements, reports, and other documents to be filed with the SEC. In addition, the division enforces provisions with respect to securities offered for sale to the public, listed for trading on securities exchanges, or traded in the over-the-counter market. The division is organized into twelve branches of corporate analysis and examination, covering approximately forty industry groups based on standard classification codes.

Preparation of the registration statements and related reports and documents may take three to four months. The lengthy timetable is governed by legal considerations. All parties involved in the preparation—such as the accounting firm, attorneys, and other professionals—may be subject to civil and criminal penalties under the 1933 securities act for any misstatements or omissions.

All reporting companies, both domestic and foreign, must file registration statements, periodic reports, and other forms electronically through the Electronic Data Gathering Analysis and Retrieval system. Filings are made to the Division of Corporation Finance where the statements are reviewed to determine whether the disclosures comply with the 1933 and 1934 securities acts. In cases where deficiencies are identified, the division requests that the registrants complete or explain the items in question.

PRINCIPAL DISCLOSURE FORMS

The principal disclosure forms identified below are intended to provide a convenient point of reference when only a general understanding of their purpose is required. Accountants, after consulting the registrants, determine whether the company meets the criteria for the use of a particular form.

Forms required by the 1933 act include: S-1 through S-3, the general forms for registration; S-4, for business combinations; S-11, for estate entities; and SB-1 and SB-2, for small businesses. Form N-1 is used for open-ended investment companies; N-2, for closed-ended investment companies; N-3 and N-4, for insurance companies offering annuity contracts; and N-5 and N-SAR, for registered international investment companies.

Under the 1934 securities act, the principal forms required of most registrants are 10-K and 10-KSB, with the latter appropriate for small businesses. Other forms are: 11-K, for employee stock purchase or employee option plans; 10-Q, for quarterly reports; 8-K, for certain significant corporate events; 15, to terminate registration; 10-K, for foreign governments; and 18, for the political subdivisions of foreign governments.

DISCLOSURES REQUIRED BY FOREIGN CORPORATIONS

As a general rule, a foreign company intending to offer securities in the United States qualifies as a foreign private issuer, unless: (1) more than 50 percent of its outstanding voting securities are held by U.S. residents; and (2) either the majority of its executive officers are U.S. citizens or residents, or its business is administered or located in the United States.

Under Regulation S-X, foreign issuers are required to provide disclosures under U.S. generally accepted accounting principles (GAAP). SEC Accounting Bulletin 88 allows the foreign issuer to include U.S. GAAP disclosures in the MD&A for information that is not required under its home country GAAP.

Form 20-F is most commonly used for the registration statement and for the annual report. Foreign issuers are also required to furnish reports on Form 6-K instead of Form 10-Q and Form 8-K, which are applicable to U.S. issuers. Some exceptions are possible for Canadian companies that choose to use the multijurisdictional disclosure system (MJDS) forms.

SEE ALSO *Accounting; Financial Statements; Securities and Exchange Commission*

BIBLIOGRAPHY

Arkebauer, J., with R. Schultz (1998). *Going public.* Chicago: Dearborn.

2005 Essential Guide to the Securities and Exchange Commission (SEC) with Comprehensive Coverage of Agency Forms, Regulations, Staff Legal Bulletins, Publications for Investors, Rulemaking, Opinions, Orders, and Reports & Stocks and Bonds, Investment Advisers, Stock Exchanges, Mutual Finds, Accoun-tants, Broker-Dealers, Small Business. (2005). [DVD-ROM]. Progressive Management.

U.S. Securities and Exchange Commission. http://www.sec.gov

Samir Fahmy
Laurence Mauer

SECURITIES AND EXCHANGE COMMISSION

The U.S. Securities and Exchange Commission (SEC) is a regulatory agency responsible for administering U.S. securities laws. The purpose of these laws is to ensure fair markets and to provide accurate information to investors. The major securities laws were enacted in the 1930s after the 1929 stock market crash and the anemic performance of the market in the early 1930s.

The U.S. Congress passed the Securities Act of 1933 (sometimes referred to as the "truth in issuance act") to regulate the primary market—the market for new securities. The act's dual primary purposes related to the sale of securities required companies to submit independently verified financial information, a registration statement, and a prospectus to the Federal Trade Commission to ensure that investors receive credible financial information about companies being offered for public sale, as well as to prohibit fraud and misrepresentation in the sale of securities. Since May 6, 1996, individuals have been able to readily access these statements using the SEC's Electronic Data Gathering, Analysis, and Retrieval System and learn about companies to help them make informed investment decisions.

The Securities Exchange Act of 1934 provided more SEC control, giving it the power to regulate the stock exchanges and the trading practices of the secondary market (a market for currently traded shares). In 1935 the Public Utility Holding Company Act was enacted to regulate all interstate holding companies (a holding company controls other companies by owning their stock) in the utility business. Further, the Trust Indenture Act of 1939 was enacted to allow the SEC oversight in the issuance of bonds, notes, and debentures offered for public sale.

In 1940 Congress passed two laws covering the people working in the security business. The Investment Company Act of 1940 was developed to minimize conflicts of interest by regulating investment companies, including those involved with mutual funds. It focuses on disclosing investment company operations and structure, as well as fund information to the investing public. The Investment Advisers Act of 1940 established regulation of investment advisers and their activities. In 1974 the Employee Retirement Income Security Act gave the SEC jurisdiction over pension funds; and the Sarbanes-Oxley Act of 2002 mandated reforms relating to public accounting fraud and created oversight of the auditing profession through the Public Company Accounting Oversight Board. Other legislation addressed foreign activities, insider trading, and further clarification of existing legislation.

The SEC consists of five presidentially appointed commissioners, only three of whom can be from the same political party. Terms are staggered; thus, each June 5, a person rotates off the commission. To accomplish their duties, the commissioners have office staffs of accountants and lawyers and regional offices in eleven cities.

The organizational structure of the SEC includes four divisions. The Division of Corporation Finance reviews registration statements, tender offers, and mergers and acquisitions. The Division of Market Regulation oversees markets and market participants. The Division of Investment Management is responsible for the enforcement of three statutes: the Investment Company Act of 1940, the Investment Advisers Act of 1940, and the Public Utility Holding Company Act of 1935. The Division of Enforcement is the SEC's investigative arm. After conducting private investigations of possible violations, the Division of Enforcement recommends appropriate commission action either before an administrative law judge or in federal court, and then negotiates settlements.

The commission also has fifteen offices performing duties defined by their titles. For instance, the Office of Compliance, Inspections, and Examinations determines whether all investment organizations are in compliance with federal securities laws.

In enforcing the securities laws, the SEC acts as a guide and adviser whose actions are largely remedial. One common activity of each division is rule making. New rules and rule modifications are usually accomplished in open meetings. Those industries or parties affected by rule changes are allowed to present their positions and make comments in an open meeting. Any SEC investigations are conducted by the Division of Enforcement and the field offices. If the evidence indicates a violation, the SEC can take administrative action (such as suspension) or instigate a civil action in a U.S. district court. If evidence indicates a criminal action, the SEC turns the case over to the U.S. Department of Justice.

More information is available from the Securities and Exchange Commission, 450 Fifth Street NW, Washington, DC 20549; 202-942-7114; or http://www.sec.gov.

SEE ALSO *Securities Acts: Requirements for Accounting*

BIBLIOGRAPHY

Hirt, Geoffrey A., and Block, Stanley B. (2006). *Fundamentals of investment management* (8th ed.). Boston: McGraw-Hill/Irwin.

Levy, Haim (1999). *Introduction to investments* (2nd ed.). Cincinnati: South-Western College.

Securities and Exchange Commission. (2004). *Securities and Exchange Act of 1934*. Retrieved December 9, 2005, from http://www.sec.gov/about/laws/sea34.pdf

Securities and Exchange Commission. (2004). *Trust Indenture Act of 1939*. Retrieved December 9, 2005, from http://www.sec.gov/about/laws/tia39.pdf

Mary Jean Lush
Val Hinton

SERVICE INDUSTRIES

Every year the service industries make significant contributions to the U.S. economy. These contributions appear in a myriad of ways such as a letter carrier delivering the mail, a physician treating a patient, or an airline pilot transporting passengers to their destinations. Taken on an individual basis, these service providers are only a small part of a very big picture. When the service industries as a whole are examined, however, their critical role in the everyday lives of millions of people and businesses throughout the United States and abroad becomes evident.

SERVICE INDUSTRIES DEFINED

The U.S. Department of Commerce's Bureau of Economic Analysis (BEA) offers a broad definition of service industries—service industries provide products that cannot be stored and are consumed at the time and place of purchase. Typically, the "products" sold by the service industry providers are intangible and thus little if anything physical is involved in the transactions. For example, an airline company may sell tickets allowing passengers to occupy seats on an airplane while it flies from one city to another. Upon the completion of the flight, the passengers deplane with no more than what they boarded the flight with, but are indeed in a different location from where they started. In other instances, transactions within the service industries may result in the delivery of something tangible.

For example, every year millions of Americans purchase tax-preparation software on a compact disk (CD) that facilitates the completion of annual federal and state tax returns. The basis for the inclusion of such transactions within the service industry is that the BEA allows tangible items to be included, provided that any tangible

U.S. gross domestic product and service industry product

BILLIONS OF DOLLARS

Year	Gross domestic product	Service industry product	Percentage of GDP from service industry
1960	$526.4	$217.9	41.4%
1970	$1,038.5	$481.9	46.4%
1980	$2,789.5	$1,322.5	47.4%
1990	$5,803.1	$3,113.7	53.7%
2000	$9,817.0	$5,425.6	55.3%
2003	$11,004.0	$6,384.7	58.0%

SOURCE: 2005 Ecomomic Report of the President.

Table 1

Total U.S. employment and service industry employment, 1992, 2002, and projected for 2012

Year	Total employment (in thousands)	Service industry employment (in thousands)	Service industry as percentage of total
1992	123,325	87,510	71.0%
2002	144,014	108,513	75.3%
2012	165,319	129,344	78.2%

SOURCE: Department of Labor, Bureau of Labor Statistics (BLS).

Table 2

item(s) offer minimal contribution to the total cost of the service. In the case of the tax software, the cost of the CD is likely to be extremely low. The item of value in this instance, and what the purchaser is truly paying for, is the programming electronically stored on the CD that allows for easier completion of what can become a very arduous annual task.

SERVICE INDUSTRY PROVIDERS

Within the United States, for-profit businesses, not-for-profit organizations, and the government all provide services. Of these, for-profit businesses are the largest providers of services, followed by the government, and then not-for-profit organizations. Critical in the determination of which sector provides such services are questions such as:

- Can the service be profitably offered for sale?

- Are sufficient levels of services provided by the for-profit market?

- Can nonpaying third parties be excluded from benefiting from the provision of the service?

- Is the service of such vital importance that it must be provided?

Provision of services by for-profit businesses typically occurs where a service can be profitably sold and third-party nonpayers do not directly benefit from the sale. Examples of such include health care, information technology, residential care, and amusement and entertainment services. In instances where the provision of a service to all, regardless of their ability to pay, is of vital importance to society's welfare, the government frequently steps in. Public education and national defense are examples where the government feels that taxpayers and nontaxpay-

ers alike should have access to these services. The government also offers services where it feels the for-profit sector may not be sufficiently self-policing, for instance, with the U.S. Food and Drug Administration and the U.S. Securities and Exchange Commission.

In those areas where services cannot be profitably offered for sale and the government cannot provide sufficient levels of services, nonprofit organizations frequently step forward to fill the void. Some such organizations, for example, may provide assistance to persons during times of environmental disaster or hardship, and some healthcare organizations treat all people regardless of their ability to pay.

ECONOMIC SIGNIFICANCE OF THE SERVICE INDUSTRIES

The economic importance of the service industries can be measured in several ways. One such way is to examine the proportion of the economy's total productivity or gross domestic product (GDP) stemming from the service industry. A second way is to examine the percentage of the labor force employed within the service industries. A third way would be to consider the role that services play in international trade.

A country's GDP represents the total value of all final goods and services produced within that country during the course of a year. According to BEA data reported in the *2005 Economic Report of the President* and shown in Table 1, U.S. GDP in 2003 totaled $11 trillion. Of this of amount, nearly $6.4 trillion stemmed from the productivity within the service industries.

The importance of the service industry in terms of its contribution to GDP continues to grow each year. In 1960 services accounted for just over 41 percent of the total U.S. GDP, as shown in Table 1. By 1990 the service industry's contribution to GDP had swelled to over 50

Predicted fastest growing industries, 2002–2012

Industry	2002 Employment (in thousands)	2012 Predicted Employment (in thousands)	Percentage change 2002–2012
Software Publishers	256.0	429.7	67.9%
Management, scientific, and technical consulting services	731.8	1,137.4	55.4%
Community and residential care facilities for elderly	695.3	1,077.6	55.0%
Computer Systems design	1,162.7	1,797.7	54.6%
Employment Services	3,248.8	5,012.3	54.3%
Individual, family, community, and vocational rehabilitation facilities	1,269.3	1,866.6	47.1%
Ambulatory health care services	1,443.6	2,113.4	46.4%
Water, sewage, and other systems	48.5	71.0	46.4%
Internet Services	528.8	773.1	46.2%
Child Care Services	734.2	1,050.3	43.1%

SOURCE: Department of Labor, Bureau of Labor Statistics (BLS).

Table 3

Export and import of goods and services, 1990–2003

Year	Goods exports	Goods imports	Service exports	Service imports
1990	$367.2	$469.7	$188.7	$142.7
1995	$533.9	$697.6	$245.8	$152.1
2000	$784.3	$1,243.5	$311.9	$232.3
2003	$721.7	$1,307.3	$309.9	$243.3

SOURCE: 2005 Economic Report of the President.

Table 4

percent and in 2003 it surpassed 58 percent. If this trend were to continue, by 2010 more than $3 out of every $5 of final goods and services produced would stem from the service industries.

EMPLOYMENT IN SERVICE INDUSTRIES

The importance of the service industries can also be seen both in the level of employment within the industry and as a percentage of total employment. Total employment and service industry employment for 1992 and 2002 as well as the levels forecasted by the U.S. Department of Labor's Bureau of Labor Statistics (BLS) for 2012 are shown in Table 2.

In 1992 more than 87 million people were employed within the service industry and by 2002 this number had risen to nearly 109 million. By 2012 the BLS expected nearly 130 million persons would be employed in the service industry. More astonishing than the absolute number of persons employed in the service industry is the large and growing percentage of total employment emanating from the service industry. In 1992 nearly 71 percent of all employment was within the service industry. By 2002 more than 75 percent of employment was within the service sector. The BLS forecasted that this percentage would continue to grow, with more than 78 percent of all employment within the service industry by 2012.

Based on the BLS data shown in Table 2, from 1992 to 2012 the total level of employment in the United States was forecasted to increase by approximately 42 million. For the same period, the BLS estimated that service industry employment would increase by 41.8 million. In other words, the service sector was forecasted to be responsible for 99.6 percent of all employment growth from 1992 to 2012.

While the service industry overall is growing substantially, some areas are growing at faster paces than others because of changes in the economy or the country's demographics. Table 3 provides a listing of the ten industries forecasted to have the fastest-growing employment from 2002 to 2012.

The information sector of the service industry is the fastest-growing sector in the economy. Included within this sector is the software publishing industry that is anticipated to be the nation's fastest-growing employer through 2012. Also within this sector is the quickly growing Internet services and data processing industry. The professional and business services industry is another that is expected to experience substantial gains in employment. Within this industry, the employment services sector is experiencing the greatest expansion as companies seek out ways to reduce labor costs and provide greater flexibility in terms of staffing. The gradual but continued aging of the population, together with medical advances that have extended life expectancies, have resulted in the health services industries also exhibiting large growth in employment.

ROLE OF SERVICES IN TRADE

A final point that raises the importance of the service industries within the United States can be found when looking at international trade data. The United States maintains a very large balance of trade deficit due to the importation of large amounts of goods relative to the amount of exportation of goods, as can be seen in Table 4. The balance on services, however, shows a surplus, with the United States exporting more services than it imports.

BIBLIOGRAPHY

Berman, Jay M. (2004, February). Industry output and employment projections to 2012. *Monthly Labor Review, 127*(2), 58–79.

The Economic Report of the President. (2005). Washington, DC: Government Printing Office.

Hecker, Daniel E. (2004, February). Occupational employment projections to 2012. *Monthly Labor Review, 127*(2), 80–105.

Su, Betty (2004, February). The U.S. economy to 2012: Signs of growth. *Monthly Labor Review, 127*(2), 23–36.

Alan G. Krabbenhoft
Amy Lynn DeVault

SEXUAL HARASSMENT

Sexual harassment is defined as unwelcome sexual advances, requests for sexual favors, and other verbal or physical conduct of a sexual nature when submission to or rejection of this conduct explicitly or implicitly (1) affects an individual's employment, (2) unreasonably interferes with an individual's work performance, or (3) creates an intimidating, hostile, or offensive work environment. Sexual harassment charges are among the most frequently litigated workplace claims in the United States.

Although stories of women and men suffering in the workplace by refusing to submit to some sort of sexual activity have appeared in recorded history for centuries, the term *sexual harassment* is relatively new. The term appeared within the feminist movement in the 1960s and entered common usage in 1978 when the federal Equal Employment Opportunity Commission issued guidelines covering such discrimination. Illegal discrimination, typically based on factors such as race and gender, emerged as a key political and social issue during the latter part of the twentieth century; thus, more attention became focused on sexual harassment in the workplace, media, legal profession, academia, and the public.

The legal foundation for the prohibition on sexual harassment can be found in a law chiefly designed to deal with employment discrimination—Title VII of the Civil

Demonstrators in Watertown, Massachusetts, protesting alledged sexual and racial harassment, May 27, 1996. **AP IMAGES**

Rights Act of 1964. The act barred discrimination based on a person's "race, color, religion, sex, or national origin." Making hiring or firing decisions based upon these factors became illegal. This law, however, did not specifically address sexual harassment on the job, leaving the issue in a legal gray area.

This changed when the U.S. Supreme Court, in a unanimous landmark decision in *Meritor Savings Bank v. Vinson* (1986), effectively confirmed the illegality of sexual harassment. The decision's impact was threefold: (1) The ruling confirmed that Title VII outlawed sexual harassment, an issue that had been debated previously. (2) Quid pro quo harassment was defined; that is, harassment implying a trade involving sex, such as a supervisor offering a subordinate a promotion in exchange for sexual favors or denying a job benefit for refusal of the supervisor's advances. (3) The concept of "hostile environment" abuse was established.

A hostile environment occurs when an employee is placed in an uncomfortable or threatening environment because of unwelcome sexual behavior in the workplace. Unwelcome sexual behavior may include telling jokes or stories of a sexual nature, unwelcome touching such as patting or hugging, displaying suggestive posters or calendars, sending letters or electronic mail (e-mail) with text or images of a suggestive or sexually explicit nature, and making suggestive facial expressions. The ruling also cautioned that employers have a responsibility for guarding against harassment, a theme echoed in subsequent decisions. Following *Meritor,* employers throughout the nation began reviewing their personnel policies and practices in the light of these new definitions of sexual harassment.

KEY EVENTS

During the 1990s, two specific events brought the topic of sexual harassment into the national spotlight. The U.S. Navy's Tailhook scandal, in 1991, captured the nation's attention with reports that female naval officers had been assaulted in a hallway "gauntlet" by their fellow officers during the annual convention of naval aviators held in Las Vegas, Nevada.

Also in 1991, the confirmation of Supreme Court nominee Clarence Thomas became the center of a controversial firestorm related to a sexual harassment charge. Anita Hill, a university professor, alleged that Thomas had sexually harassed her from 1981 to 1983 while she worked for him at the Equal Employment Opportunity Commission. Public outcry effectively stopped the confirmation proceedings until the accusations could be examined. Ultimately, Thomas was confirmed for the Supreme Court; the controversy, however, had a lasting effect on the nation's understanding of sexual harassment.

SUBSEQUENT LEGISLATION AND COURT DECISIONS

The Civil Rights Act of 1991, considered a landmark development in the sexual harassment arena, allowed plaintiffs to recover compensatory and punitive damages with a cap of $300,000 on large employers (500+ employees) and $50,000 for smaller ones. Supreme Court decisions on sexual harassment focused more and more on the application of common sense to the particular situation; that is, looking at the situation as a "reasonable" person would. In *Harris v. Forklift Systems, Inc.* (1993), the Court held that if a workplace is permeated with behavior that is severe or pervasive enough to create a discriminatorily hostile or abusive working environment, Title VII is violated regardless of whether the plaintiff suffered psychological harm. Conversely, the decision also held that the mere utterance of an offensive statement would not normally constitute a violation of the law.

Several Supreme Court decisions issued in 1998 are considered among the most significant in defining sexual harassment law: In *Burlington Industries, Inc. v. Ellerth,* the complainant showed that, although she was subjected to offensive, vulgar behavior, she had not suffered in any manner relating to her employment situation. In fact, she had been promoted at the company prior to her resignation. The Court ruled that harassment is defined by the behavior of the harasser, not by what subsequently happens to the worker.

Another key portion of this decision and that of an additional case, *Faragher v. Boca Raton,* addressed employer liability with regard to hostile environment harassment and the employee's responsibility to report the offense to someone with decision-making authority. *Faragher* involved a female lifeguard who claimed she had endured repeated sexual harassment from her male supervisors, yet she had not formally complained because of her fear of retaliation. Evidence showed that although Faragher's employer, the city of Boca Raton, Florida, had a sexual harassment policy, the policy was unknown to both the complainant and her supervisors. The Court indicated that an employer could defend itself successfully if proof was provided that the employer had a known, effective policy against harassment and that the employee failed to take advantage of the policy. Even more importantly, the Court, in defining the elements of this "affirmative defense," outlined to employers how to prevent a hostile work environment from ever arising.

Another 1998 ruling, *Oncale v. Sundowner Offshore Services, Inc.,* defined sexual harassment as "gender neutral." With this decision, the law was expanded to include homosexual situations as well as harassment between two people of the same gender even when neither is homosexual. The Court unanimously declared that sexual harassment is actionable (victims can sue and liability can be found) even when the people involved are of the same gender.

In *Davis v. Monroe County Board of Education* (1999), the Supreme Court addressed student-on-student sexual harassment in academic institutions receiving federal funds. The ruling indicated that behavior could be actionable under discrimination law if the behavior was so severe, pervasive, and objectively offensive that victims were denied equal access to education as guaranteed by Title IX. Key to the liability issue was whether those in authority were deliberately indifferent to the acts of harassment and whether the harasser was under the school's disciplinary authority.

In *Pennsylvania State Police v. Suders* (2004), the Court ruled that an employee facing a situation in which a "reasonable person" would have felt compelled to resign could bring suit regardless of whether that employee had filed a report with the employer before resigning. The ruling also indicated, however, that an accused employer could use the person's failure to file a report, along with evidence of formal policies to prevent harassment, in its defense. If the employer could prove that the employee had not attempted to prevent the harassment, and that safeguards for prevention were in place, the employer would not be liable.

E-MAIL AS EVIDENCE OF SEXUAL HARASSMENT

The majority of workplaces use technology, specifically e-mail, to conduct some portion of business activity. While technology has enabled employees to work faster and more efficiently, e-mail has brought a new risk level to organizations. Many sexual harassment suits are now based primarily on evidence of allegedly inappropriate e-mail messaging and other Internet uses. In a 2001 survey of major companies in the United States, 10 percent reported having responded to a subpoena for employee e-mail. One-quarter of the firms surveyed indicated that they monitor their employees' e-mail via keyword or phrase searches. The monitoring typically focuses on sexual-related or offensive language.

In the area of e-harassment, trends that have emerged in various rulings include the following: (1) courts have been generally less sympathetic in supervisor to employee (as opposed to employee to employee) e-harassment; (2) courts have differentiated between isolated versus continuous incidents; and (3) some employers have successfully established a defense when reasonable care had been exercised to prevent and correct inappropriate use of technology to harass.

PREVENTION AS SOLUTION

Since prevention continues to be the best approach to the sexual harassment problem, the courts consider the actions employers take prior to claims being filed. For employers who wish to make their workplaces free of sexual harassment, various legal and human resources experts recommend the following strategies:

1. Have a written state-of-the-art policy on sexual harassment that explains, in easy-to-understand terms, what behavior is prohibited. Include specific direction related to appropriate e-mail and Internet use. Inform all employees that all messages sent, received, or stored in the e-mail system are business property. Also explain that the employer is entitled to review, monitor, and disclose the stored information. Prior to issuance of the policy, obtain a legal review of the proposed policy. Once the policy is approved, make sure the policy is posted and disseminated to all supervisors and employees, preferably on an annual basis.

2. Commit to the policy at the highest levels. Affirm that employees perceive this issue as important to the company's top managers and to all levels of supervision.

3. Develop an internal complaint process that ensures confidentially and that has multiple access points, not just to the employee's supervisor. Identify management-level personnel of both sexes that are available to those who wish to complain. In some instances, employers have not been found liable if a complaint process was in place and employees failed to use the policy.

4. Investigate complaints promptly and thoroughly, maintaining confidentiality as much as possible. Assure swift action to investigate; courts have found companies liable for sexual harassment in part because they took too long to conduct the investigation. Maintain a firm nonretaliation policy for those complaining or providing information in an investigation.

5. Conduct high-quality training, including refresher training, on antidiscrimination and antisexual harassment policies and practices for three groups: employees, managers, and supervisors. The training must define responsibilities for members of each group and cover the company's sexual harassment policy and complaint procedures. Keep records of such training as tangible evidence of the company's good faith efforts to eliminate sexual harassment.

6. Conduct physical assessments of work areas such as factory floors, warehouses, and remote offices.

Potential problems such as inappropriate posters, cartoon clippings, or improper Internet use may be identified through the physical assessments.

7. Take deliberate, decisive action when the sexual harassment policy is violated and make sure that a solid legal basis for the proposed actions exists.

SEE ALSO *Civil Rights Act of 1964; Diversity in the Workplace*

BIBLIOGRAPHY

Applen, Heather, and Kleiner, Brian H. (2001). An overview of U.S. Supreme Court decisions in sexual harassment. *Managerial Law, 43,* 17–24.

Gutek, Barbara A. (2000). Workplace sexual harassment law: Principles, landmark developments, and framework for effective risk management. *PersonnelPsychology, 53,* 745–749.

Hawkins, Dana (2001, August 13). Lawsuits spur rise in employee monitoring. *U.S. News and World Report, 131,* 53.

Keyton, Joann, Ferguson, Pat, and Rhodes, Steven C. (2001). Cultural indicators of sexual harassment. *The Southern Communication Journal, 67,* 33–50.

Kukec, Anna M. (n.d.). Sexual harassment and bar association policy: Tightening the gaps is key for management. Retrieved November 30, 2005, from the American Bar Association, Division for Bar Services Web site: http://www.abanet.org/barserv/22–3sexhar.html

Male–on–male sex complaints escalating. (2005, March 1). *USA Today,* p. 8.

Petrocelli, William, and Repa, Barbara K. (1999). *Sexual harassment on the job* (4th ed.). Berkeley, CA: Nolo Press.

Stier, William F., Jr. (2005). An overview of sexual harassment. *Strategies, 18,* 13–16.

Towns, Douglas M., and Johnson, Mark S. (2003). Sexual harassment in the 21st Century—E-harassment in the workplace. *Employee Relations Law Journal, 29,* 7.

U.S. Equal Employment Opportunity Commission. (1999). EEOC Notice Number 915.002. Retrieved November 30, 2005, from http://www.eeoc.gov/policy/docs/harris.html

U.S. Equal Employment Opportunity Commission. (2002). Facts about Sexual Harassment. Retrieved November 30, 2005, from http://www.eeoc.gov/facts/fs-sex.html

Warfel, William (2005). SEXED: Insulating yourself from sexual harassment litigation. *Risk Management, 52,* 14–19.

Wyatt, Nancy (2000). Background on sexual harassment. Retrieved November 30, 2005, from http://www.de2.psu.edu/harassment/generalinfo/background.html

Rita Shaw Rone
Clarice P. Brantley

SHERMAN ANTITRUST ACT OF 1890

The Sherman Antitrust Act of 1890, the first and most significant of the U.S. antitrust laws, outlawed trusts and prohibited "illegal" monopolies. The act applies to both domestic companies and foreign companies doing business in the United States. A trust is a relationship between businesses that collaborate through anticompetitive agreements to gain market dominance. Trusts cut prices to drive competitors out of business. Illegal monopolies are those that can be shown to use their power to suppress competition. A monopolist has the power to dominate markets—the ability to set the price by altering supply. Anticompetitive techniques include:

- Buying out competitors
- Requiring customers to sign long-term agreements
- Compelling customers to buy products they do not want in order to receive other goods

The Sherman Antitrust Act, along with the Clayton Antitrust Act of 1914 and the Federal Trade Commission Act of 1914, constitutes a large part of the regulatory umbrella under which U.S. business operates. Through the passage of the Sherman Antitrust Act, the U.S. Congress provided safeguards to prevent firms from merging with other firms if the effect was to substantially lessen competition and create monopolies.

The Federal Trade Commission (FTC) and the Antitrust Division of the U.S. Department of Justice enforce antitrust laws. The FTC has the power to temporarily stop companies from employing suspected anticompetitive practices, while the Justice Department probes and prosecutes businesses.

The Sherman Antitrust Act was passed in response to strong and widespread political pressure to deal with "the trust problem" that reached a peak during the presidential election campaign of 1888. The trusts were corporate holding companies that by 1888 had consolidated a very large share of U.S. manufacturing and mining industries into nationwide monopolies. Some of the most notorious corporate holding companies were the sugar trust, John D. Rockefeller's oil trust, and J. P. Morgan's steel trust. The original legal form of these organizations had been as business trusts.

The Sherman Antitrust Act made trusts and those who violated the act subject to civil remedies and criminal penalties in actions by the Department of Justice and to treble damages in private suits. The act was broad, providing few standards, which meant the executive branch and federal courts had to resolve the trust issues. The act was revised by the Clayton Antitrust Act, which was designed to catch early-stage practices that were thought to lead to

John Pierpont Morgan Sr. (1837–1913). *Steel mogul Morgan was directly affected by the Sherman Antitrust Act.*
GETTY IMAGES

monopolies, such as corporate mergers and acquisitions, price discrimination, tying agreements, and interlocking directorships. Other antitrust acts followed, including the Federal Trade Commission Act of 1914, the Robinson-Patman Act of 1936, and the Celler-Kefauver Antimerger Act of 1950.

Consequences of being found guilty of antitrust activity and being a monopoly are a fine not exceeding $10 million if a corporation, or $350,000 if person, or by imprisonment not exceeding three years, or by both punishments, at the discretion of the court. Furthermore, the court can require breakup of the company and other consequences based on individual cases.

According to Peter Dickson and Philippa Wells it is one of the great ironies in U.S. jurisprudence and free-market capitalism that the Sherman Act became the foundation of modern economic regulation, the legislative promoter and protector of the competitive efficiency of the modern competitive political economy. They posit that the Sherman Antitrust Act has survived in the age of global tariff protection, and now that tariffs are coming down, its reach is becoming even greater, extending into global markets.

Today in the United States monopolistic power means that a business has the ability to raise prices above competitive levels. This typically occurs when an organization has exclusive control over a commercial activity, such as the production or selling of a commodity or service, and thus has the power to fix prices unilaterally because it has no effective competition. Significant antitrust litigation has included the following:

EARLY TWENTIETH CENTURY

- American Tobacco: broken up into separate companies
- Standard Oil: broken up into separate oil-refining and pipeline companies
- U.S. Steel: no illegal monopoly found

FROM THE LATE TWENTIETH CENTURY ON

- IBM: accused of being an illegal monopoly; case dropped
- AT&T: accused of being an illegal monopoly; broken up into one long-distance and seven "Baby Bell" local phone companies
- Microsoft: accused of using monopoly power to sell other products
- Intel: accused of severing business ties with customers who sued it; penalties varied depending on customers bringing litigation
- Weyerhaeuser: federal jury ruled Weyerhaeuser used illegal tactics to force a competing sawmill out of business

SEE ALSO *Antitrust Legislation*

BIBLIOGRAPHY

Dickson, Peter R., and Wells, Philippa K. (2001, Spring). The dubious origins of the Sherman Antitrust Act: The mouse that roared. *Journal of Public Policy and Marketing, 20*(1), 3.

FTC approves Intel deal. (2000, March 6). *The Washington Post.* From http://www.washingtonpost.com/wp-srv/business/longterm/intel/intel.htm, retrieved January 5, 2006.

Garman, E. Thomas (2005). *Consumer economics issues in America* (8th ed.). Mason, OH: Thomson Custom Solutions.

Rivera, D. (2003, April 19). Weyerhaeuser loses lawsuit; jury says timber giant illegally eliminated rival. *The Oregonian* (Portland, OR). Retrieved from http://www.oregonlive.com/search/oregonian/ January 5, 2006.

Phyllis Bunn

SHOPLIFTING

SEE *Crime and Fraud*

SHOPPING

Shopping involves the purchasing of products by consumers, all of which fall into various shopping product categories that are based on the way consumers think of them and purchase them. The two main categories are convenience goods and shopping goods; two lesser categories are specialty items and unsought goods. Although most shopping products are sold in stores, such as retail, grocery, and specialty stores, some consumer purchases are made through other means, such as catalogue shopping, telemarketing, and online purchasing (also known as cybershopping). Cybershopping is the latest trend in consumer shopping. It is estimated that $300 billion worth of online purchases will be made in the first decade of the twenty-first century.

CONVENIENCE GOODS

Convenience goods are goods that consumers purchase frequently, immediately, and with minimal effort. People do not spend a large amount of time shopping for convenience items. They are usually purchases made routinely, such as buying groceries on a weekly basis, or habitually, such as purchasing a daily newspaper. Convenience products include common staples, such as milk and bread. Some convenience goods, however, are not purchased routinely or habitually. They are bought on impulse, such as an ice cream cone on a summer day. Many impulse items are displayed in a manner that encourages quick choice and purchase, such as the candy, magazines, and batteries that are routinely placed near the cash register at checkout counters. Other convenience products may be purchased as emergency items, when the consumers feel there is an urgent need, such as buying candles, water, or canned goods when preparing for a storm. Convenience products can be found in stores such as supermarkets, convenience stores, and department stores.

SHOPPING GOODS

Shopping goods are items consumers will conduct a search for in order to find the one that best suits their needs. They usually require an involved selection process. When purchasing a shopping product, consumers will compare a variety of attributes, such as suitability, quality, price, and style. Automobiles are often bought this way. Consumers may also visit a number of shopping places, such as retail stores, before they make a decision. Because of the importance of these types of purchases, consumers usually invest considerable time and energy before making such a purchase.

Shopping products are broken down into two categories: homogeneous and heterogeneous. Homogeneous shopping goods are those that are similar in quality but different in other characteristics. This difference in characteristics is sufficient for the customer to justify a search for the item. Items that are thought of as homogeneous, or the same, would include television sets, various home appliances, or automobiles. Homogeneous shopping goods are also often evaluated on price. After the consumer has decided on desired characteristics, he or she then looks for the most favorable price.

Heterogeneous shopping goods have product features that are often more important to consumers than price; examples include clothing, high-tech equipment, and furniture. The item purchased must meet certain consumer-set criteria, such as size, color, or specific functions performed. When buying heterogeneous shopping goods, consumers often seek information and advice from salespeople and other experts before purchasing the item. The seller or retailer of heterogeneous shopping goods needs to carry a sufficient variety of the products to suit individual tastes and also needs well-trained salespeople to inform and advise consumers.

SPECIALTY ITEMS

Specialty items have characteristics that compel consumers to make special efforts to find them. Consumers often do not consider price at all when shopping for specialty products, which can include almost any kind of shopping product, including particular types of food, expensive imported cars, or items from a well-known fashion designer or manufacturer that can all be considered specialty goods. Usually, specialty goods have a brand name or other type of distinguishing characteristic. Shopping goods are often classified as specialty products based on the location and need of the consumer. For example, some olive oils or wines may be a convenience product in Italy but a specialty product in the United States. Consumers who favor specialty products may travel considerable distances to purchase a particular item. These types of shopping products can often be found in specialty stores, which carry a large assortment within a small line of goods. An example would be a store that carries only candy, but many different types of candy. Other types of specialty stores include bookstores and sporting goods stores.

Unsought Goods. Unsought goods are products that consumers do not want, use, or even think about purchasing. An unsought shopping good could be a product that a consumer may not even know about—or knows about but has never considered purchasing. In addition, consumers often put off purchasing unsought shopping goods because they do not consider them to be important. Unsought shopping goods are frequently brought to customers' attention through advertising, promotions, or chance. Sometimes they are something new on the market, such as digital telephones. At other times they are fairly standard services that some consumers would not bother shopping for, such as life insurance.

SEE ALSO *Consumer and Business Products*

BIBLIOGRAPHY

"Council of Better Business Bureau." *Better Business Bureau Online.* Retrieved October 29, 2005, from http://www.bbb.org. June 2000.

Encyclopedia Britannica. Britannica.com. May 2000.

Heinzl, John (2000, June). "Year in Review 1998." *Internet Retailing.*

Audrey E. Langill

SHORTAGES
SEE *Supply and Demand*

SHRINKAGE
SEE *Inventory Control*

SIC CODES
SEE *North American Industry Classification System*

SINGLE AUDIT ACT OF 1984 WITH AMENDMENTS

The U.S. Congress adopted the Single Audit Act (SAA; Public Law 98-502) in 1984 to establish entity-wide audit requirements for state and local governments and Indian tribal governments receiving federal financial assistance. The assistance may include grants, contracts, loans, loan guarantees, property, cooperative agreements, interest subsidies, insurance, and direct appropriations from a number of federal agencies. Audits performed under the SAA are intended to satisfy all federal agencies providing assistance to the entity. Before the SAA, federal agencies

had the authority to require an audit of each federally funded program or activity. Thus, audit overlaps and organizational inefficiencies existed as there was no coordination among the federal agencies.

GOAL, OBJECTIVES, AND ADMINISTRATION

The goal of the SAA is that one audit can provide both a basis for an opinion on the recipient entity's financial statement and a basis for determining whether federal financial assistance program resources are being managed and controlled appropriately and used in accordance with legal and contractual requirements.

Also included in the SAA objectives are to:

- Establish uniform audit requirements for federally funded financial assistance programs provided to state and local governments and Indian tribal governments

- Promote the efficient and effective use of audit resources

- Establish uniform requirements for audits of federal funds provided to state and local governments

- Ensure that federal departments and agencies reply upon and use audit work performed pursuant to the SAA to the maximum extent practicable

The director of the U.S. Office of Management and Budget (OMB) is responsible for dictating policies, procedures, and guidelines to carry out the SAA. These policies, procedures, and guidelines were initially contained in OMB Circular A-128, *Audits of State and Local Governments* (1984). Circular A-128 required (1) an audit of the state or local government's (entity's) general-purpose or basic financial statements made in accordance with generally accepted government auditing standards covering financial and compliance audits, and (2) tests of internal accounting and other control systems to provide reasonable assurance that the entity was managing federally assisted programs in compliance with applicable laws, regulations, and the specific provisions of contracts or grants.

During the course of the audit, the auditor must specifically review transactions (expenditures) to determine whether the amounts were used for allowable services and whether the recipients were eligible to receive them. In addition, the auditor must determine if the organization has complied with laws and regulations that may have a material effect on its financial statements and on each major federally assisted program. In 1984 major federal-assisted programs were defined by the SAA as any program for which federal expenditures during the year exceed the larger of $300,000 or 3 percent of such total expenditures.

Upon completion of the audit, the auditor prepares a report that includes (1) the financial statements and a schedule of federal funded programs with a schedule of the total expenditures, (2) an evaluation of internal control systems that identifies the controls evaluated and material weaknesses, if any, and (3) an analysis of compliance stating positive assurance for items tested, negative assurance for items not tested, a summary of cases of noncompliance, and identification of the total amount of expenditures questioned. Since the audit demands skills beyond those necessary for a standard audit, auditors are required to obtain specialized training and expertise. Overall, the audits are a highly rigorous form of oversight.

In 1990 the OMB administratively extended the single audit process to nonprofit organizations by issuing OMB Circular A-133, *Audits of Institutions of Higher Education and Other Non-Profit Organizations.* Thus thousands of additional organizations—including museums, colleges and universities, school districts, hospitals, voluntary welfare and health organizations—are required to have an audit performed in accordance with the SAA. Organizations receiving federal assistance that expend less than $300,000 must maintain records to support federal financial assistance programs and must have a financial audit performed under generally accepted auditing standards.

AMENDMENTS IN 1996

Congress amended the SAA by passing Public Law 104-156, the Single Audit Act Amendments of 1996. The new law extended the statutory audit requirement to all nonprofit organizations and substantially revised various provisions of the 1984 act. The major amendments and changes include:

- Implementation of a risk-based approach to select the major federal programs to be audited rather than selection solely on the basis of total amount of expenditures, thus ensuring greater audit coverage for high-risk programs

- The dollar threshold for single audit coverage increased to $300,000 from $100,000. The amendment also provides for administrative increases to the threshold but decreases are prohibited

- Audit requirements are triggered by federal funds expended rather than funds received

- Auditors must provide a summary of the results of their work concerning the audited entity's financial statement, internal controls, and compliance with laws and regulations

- Auditors must prepare and sign a data-collection form that is submitted to the federal clearinghouse rather than submitting the full audit report

- Audit report due date is reduced from thirteen to nine months

Overall, the SAA Amendments of 1996 address a number of issues that emerged during and after the implementation of the 1984 SAA. The amendments exempt entities receiving a relatively small amount of federal funds, enacts guidelines to ensure that high-risk programs are subject to audit, and simplifies reporting requirements.

In June 1997 the OMB revised and renamed Circular A-133 to implement the SAA's amendments and to extend the circular's coverage to state and local governments, Indian tribal governments, and nonprofit organizations, as well as to rescind OMB Circular A-128. In accordance with the provisions for a periodic review of the audit threshold, a 2003 amendment to A-133 increases the audit threshold to an aggregate federal-funds expenditure of $500,000.

DISADVANTAGE OF SINGLE AUDIT APPROACH

A disadvantage of the single audit approach is that some granting agencies do not receive as much information about their grant programs as when separate grant audits are performed. As a result, some granting agencies require audit work that goes beyond the single audit requirement; the granting agencies, however, must provide additional resources to fund the audit costs.

Studies of single audits began when the Government Accountability Office (which was known as the General Accounting Office until July 2004) reports criticized the quality of audits of governmental entities. Research has found that audit quality suffers when the auditor has an incentive to limit the amount of audit testing to ensure that the engagement remains profitable.

Accountability of the nonprofit organizations receiving federal financial assistance is a concern in light of well-publicized financial scandals, revelations of excessive compensation, and concerns over unethical behavior. A review of single audits found compliance to be quite high for nonprofits receiving substantial federal funding. Nevertheless, smaller nonprofits and those new to federal program assistance and those organizations with prior single audit findings had a significantly higher rate of adverse audit findings.

SEE ALSO *Auditing*

BIBLIOGRAPHY

Brown, C. D., and Raghunandan, K. (1995). Audit quality in audits of federal programs by nonfederal auditors. *Accounting Horizons, 9,* 1–10.

Copley, P., and Doucet, M. (1993). Auditor tenure, fixed fee contracts and the supply of substandard single audits. *Public Budgeting and Finance, 13*(1), 23–35.

Dyson, Robert A. (1997, January). The revised OMB Circular A-133 and the Single Audit Act Amendments. *The CPA Journal,* pp. 46–52.

Keating, Elizabeth K., Fischer, Mary, Gordon, Teresa P., and Greenlee, Janet (2005). The Single Audit Act: How compliant are nonprofit organizations? *Journal of Budgeting, Accounting and Financial Management, 17*(3), 285–309.

Office of Management and Budget. (2003, June 27). *Audits of states, local governments, and non-profits organizations.* Retrieved March 2, 2006, from http://www.whitehouse.gov/omb/circulars/a133/a133.html

Single Audit Act Amendments of 1996 (Public Law 104-156). Retrieved March 2, 2006, from http://www.ignet.gov/single/saamend.html

U.S. General Accounting Office. (1986). *CPA audit quality: Many governmental audits do not comply with professional standards* (AFMD 86-20). Washington, DC: Author.

U.S. General Accounting Office. (2000). *Single audit—Update on the implementation of the Single Audit Act Amendments of 1996* (AIMD 00-293). Washington, DC: Author.

Mary L. Fischer

SITUATIONAL MANAGEMENT
SEE *Management/Leadership Styles*

SKILLSUSA

SkillsUSA is a national organization that promotes and serves students and teachers at both the secondary and postsecondary levels in the areas of technical, skilled, and service occupations. Its major goal is to guarantee that America continues to produce a skilled workforce by working collaboratively with business and industry.

SkillsUSA is organized by chapters, which in 2005 numbered over 13,000 and included representation from fifty-four states and territories; its membership exceeded 264,000. Additionally, nearly 15,000 educators served as SkillsUSA members and instructors.

SkillsUSA programs operate on the concept of using applied learning educational activities while focusing on the development of character, leadership, teamwork, and citizenship. It emphasizes developing eight key workplace readiness skills:

1. Communications
2. Problem solving and critical thinking
3. Information technology applications
4. Business and organization systems
5. Leadership, management, and teamwork
6. Ethics and/or legal responsibilities
7. Safety, health, and environment
8. Employability and/or career development

SkillsUSA holds local, state, and national competitions where students participate and demonstrate occupational and leadership skills. In preparation for competitions, students use a variety of materials and programs offered by national SkillsUSA.

One such program is the Professional Development Program, which teaches eighty-four workplace competencies using a hands-on approach through self-paced lessons. Another program is the Student2Student Mentoring, which provides secondary students the opportunity to serve as a mentor to younger students in the area of career development. A third program, called CareerSafe, offers students a ten-hour online training program in the area of basic safety knowledge, which was developed cooperatively with the Occupational Safety and Health Administration.

SkillsUSA is constantly evaluating its offerings to provide cutting-edge opportunities to meet its goals in providing a wealth of opportunities for young people in the United States. More information is available from: SkillsUSA, P.O. Box 3000, Leesburg, VA 20177-0300; 703-777-8810; 703-777-8999 (fax); anyinfo@skillsusa.org (e-mail); or, http://www.skillsusa.org.

SEE ALSO *Business Professionals of America; DECA; Future Business Leaders of America*

Dorothy A. Maxwell

SKIMMING PRICES
SEE *Pricing*

SMALL BUSINESS ADMINISTRATION

In 2005 small businesses represented 97 percent of all U.S. exporters and 99.7 percent of all employers, created about 75 percent of new jobs, and provided arenas for technological innovation. During the early 1950s, the value of small businesses in providing stability for the U.S. economy was realized.

Prior to that time, big business and industry promises of career success too often proved to be empty, and many disillusioned U.S. workers began to embrace the concept of self-employment. As the number of business entrepreneurs increased, it quickly became apparent that such entrepreneurial endeavors needed a protective umbrella if they were to survive normal start-up difficulties common to small business, not to mention competitive pressures generated by larger organizations.

To address the problem, in 1953 the U.S. Congress approved the Small Business Administration Act, which created the Small Business Administration (SBA). As an independent federal agency, the SBA's mission is to provide postdisaster recovery assistance to communities and to maintain and enhance the national economy by aiding, counseling, assisting, and protecting small business interests based on two principles: quality-focused management and customer-driven outreach.

Throughout its ten regions, the SBA has seventy district offices across the country and program offices in every state, as well as the District of Columbia, the Virgin Islands, Guam, and Puerto Rico. The SBA is considered the government's most cost-effective economic-development engine, with a 2005 loan portfolio of approximately $45 billion, expected to be dispersed to about 219,000 entrepreneurs to foster small-business development and growth. Further, from fiscal year 1999 to fiscal year 2000, the SBA assisted in obtaining loans of approximately $94.6 billion that went to about 435,000 small businesses, and in 2004 lent about $2.5 billion to almost 18,000 women-owned businesses.

The SBA also assists small businesses recover from catastrophic disasters, such as wildfires, hurricanes, and terrorist attacks. While the fiscal year 2005 budget requested $792 million for such disaster recovery funding, since 2001 disaster relief assistance exceeding $3.3 billion has been provided.

The SBA provides financial assistance in the form of loan guarantees, rather than direct loans, through specialized programs that help entrepreneurs attain the appropriate financial position to initiate their business and overcome the first few lean years of infancy. It also provides counseling and training assistance to female, minority, veteran, and socially and/or economically disadvantaged business owners.

The Office of Women's Business Ownership, for instance, has established a women's business owner representative network in every district office, an Online Women's Business Center accessible through the Internet, and nearly seventy women's business centers in forty states; and the Minority Prequalification Loan Program assists qualified minority-owned, for-profit companies to obtain preapproval for a 7(a) loan guaranty. The 7(a) Loan Guaranty Program assists small businesses unable to secure reasonable funding terms through normal lending channels to obtain funding (i.e., microloans) through private-sector lenders on loans guaranteed by the SBA.

The SBA does not provide grants to start or expand a business, but it does coordinate and disseminate information about resources to facilitate awareness of business initiatives, on consulting or mentoring opportunities for managerial novices, and regarding entrepreneurial success strategies. Further, it provides disaster assistance and has established a unit to coordinate and facilitate technology transfer conferences for small businesses. In an effort to centralize access to a full range of technical and financial assistance for small-business owners located in empowerment zones and enterprise communities, the SBA developed One-Stop Capital Shops. These partnerships between the SBA and a local community offer comprehensive small-business assistance from a unique, easy-to-access retail site located in a distressed area, and they generally target underserved communities or the SBA's new markets.

More information is available from the U.S. Small Business Administration Office of Marketing and Customer Service, 409 Third Street SW, Suite 600, Washington, DC 20414; 202-205-6744 or 1-800-8ASK-SBA; or, http://www.sba.gov.

SEE ALSO *Entrepreneurship*

BIBLIOGRAPHY

Office of Management and Budget. (2005). Small Business Administration. Retrieved January 31, 2006, from http://www.whitehouse.gov/omb/budget/fy2005/sba.html

Re: Invention. (2004, October.) Re: Ladies—Go long for a loan. Retrieved January 31, 2006, from http://reinventioninc.blogspot.com/archives/2004_10_01_rei nventioninc_archive.html

Service Corps of Retired Executives. (2005). *Ask SCORE for business advice.* Retrieved January 31, 2006, from http://www.score.org

Small Business Administration. http://www.sba.gov

Mary Jean Lush
Val Hinton

SOCIAL MARKETING

The term *social marketing* was first coined by Philip Kotler and Gerald Zaltman in their 1971 article "Social Marketing: An Approach to Planned Social Change." Social marketing is the application of marketing concepts and principles by government agencies, for-profit businesses, and nonprofit organizations to influence individual behavior to improve the well-being of both the individual and society as a whole.

Traditional and social marketing campaigns differ in three distinct ways: competition, gain, and product. First, with traditional marketing, the competition is identified as those businesses offering similar products and services for sale. By contrast, with social marketing the individual behavior that is to be modified for the well-being of the individual and society is considered to be the competition. Second, monetary gain is the goal of traditional marketing campaigns for businesses involved in selling products and services. In comparison, societal gain is the goal of social marketing.

Lastly, the product of traditional marketing campaigns is the goods and services offered for sale. By contrast the product of social marketing is the social change that occurs because of the campaign. Traditional and social marketing campaigns are similar in that they apply the four Ps of marketing (product, price, promotion, and place), develop marketing campaigns based on market research, and segment target audiences.

Numerous examples of government agencies, for-profit businesses, and nonprofit organizations that have adapted social marketing are available. One government agency that applies social marketing is the U.S. Coast Guard. The Coast Guard applies social marketing with its various boating/water safety programs that are designed to reduce death and injuries. A for-profit business, Anheuser Busch Companies, also applies social marketing through its various responsible-drinking campaigns. Lastly, the American Heart Association, a nonprofit organization, applies social marketing through its various heart health programs.

In addition, the Ad Council of America has developed a number of social marketing campaigns to address a variety of issues such as adoption, blood donation, booster-seat education, bullying prevention, child asthma-attack prevention, obesity prevention, drunk driving prevention, emergency preparedness, emergency preparedness, energy efficiency, environmental conservation, high school dropout prevention, math and science for girls, parental involvement in schools, reducing gun violence, secondhand smoke and children, underage drinking prevention, and wildfire prevention. More information regarding social marketing may be obtained from: The Social Marketing Institute, 1825 Connecticut

Billboard on Interstate 293 near Hookset, N.H., part of Vermont's "Click it or Ticket" campaign, May 16, 2005. **AP IMAGES**

Avenue NW, Suite S-852 Washington, DC, 20009; or http://www.social-marketing.org.

WEB SITES OF INTEREST

For examples of the U.S. Coast Guard boating/water safety social marketing campaigns: http://www.uscgboating.org

For more information regarding the social marketing campaigns of the Anheuser Busch Companies: http://www.anheuser-busch.com/Citizenship/default.htm

For more information regarding the American Heart Association heart health programs: http://www.americanheart.org

For more information about the social marketing campaigns of the Ad Council of America: http://www.adcouncil.org

SEE ALSO *Marketing; Social Responsibility and Organizational Ethics*

BIBLIOGRAPHY

Boone, Louis E., and Kurtz, David L. (2005). *Contemporary marketing 2006* (12th ed.). Eagan, MN: Thomson South-Western.

Davidson, D. Kirk (2002). *The moral dimension of marketing: Essays on business ethics.* Chicago: American Marketing Association.

Goldberg, Marvin E., Fishbein, Martin, and Middlestadt, Susan E. (Eds.). (1997). *Social marketing: Theoretical and practical perspectives.* Mahwah, NJ: Lawrence Erlbaum Associates.

Kotler, Philip, and Armstrong, Gary (2006). *Principles of marketing* (11th ed.). Upper Saddle River, NJ: Pearson Prentice Hall.

Kotler, Philip, Roberto, Ned, and Lee, Nancy (2002). *Social marketing: Improving the quality of life* (2nd ed.). Thousand Oaks, CA: Sage.

Kotler, Philip, and Zaltman, Gerald (1971, July). Social marketing: An approach to planned social change. *Journal of Marketing, 35,* 3–12.

Pride, William M., and Ferrell, O. C. (2006). *Marketing concepts and strategies.* Boston: Houghton Mifflin.

Allen D. Truell

SOCIAL RESPONSIBILITY AND ORGANIZATIONAL ETHICS

The term *social responsibility* means different things to different people. Generally, corporate social responsibility is the obligation to take action that protects and improves the welfare of society as a whole, as well as supports organizational interests. According to the concept of corporate social responsibility, a manager must strive to achieve both organizational and societal goals.

CURRENT PERSPECTIVES

Current perspectives regarding the fundamentals of social responsibility for businesses include the long-standing Davis model of corporate social responsibility, various categories of business social responsibility, and varying positions regarding the role and expectations for business in the social responsibility arena.

First, the Davis model for social responsibility, developed by Keith Davis, suggests that there are five key concepts or propositions that drive business socially responsible behavior. These are:

Proposition 1: Social responsibility arises from social power.

Proposition 2: Business shall operate as an open system, with open receipt of inputs from society and open disclosure of its operation to the public.

Proposition 3: The social costs and benefits of an activity, product, or service shall be thoroughly calculated and considered in deciding whether to proceed with it.

Proposition 4: Social costs related to each activity, product, or service shall be passed on to the consumer.

Proposition 5: Business institutions, as citizens, have the responsibility to become involved in social problems that are outside their normal areas of operation.

The areas in which business can become involved to protect and improve the welfare of society are numerous and diverse. Some of the most publicized of these areas are urban affairs, consumer affairs, environmental affairs, and employment practices. Although numerous businesses are involved in socially responsible activities, much controversy persists about whether such involvement is necessary or appropriate. There are several arguments for and against businesses performing socially responsible activities.

Arguments in Support. The best-known argument supporting such activities by business is that because business is a subset of and exerts a significant impact on society, it has the responsibility to help improve society. Since society asks no more and no less of any of its members, why should business be exempt from such responsibility? Additionally, profitability and growth go hand in hand with responsible treatment of employees, customers, and the community. Only a few studies, however, have indicated a relationship between corporate social responsibility and profitability.

Arguments Against. The distinguished economist Milton Friedman (1912–) advanced one of the better-known arguments against specific social responsibility activities. Friedman argued that making business managers simultaneously responsible to business owners for reaching profit objectives and to society for enhancing societal welfare represents a conflict of interest that has the potential to cause the demise of business. According to Friedman, this demise almost certainly will occur if business consistently is expected to behave in a socially responsible manner when this is in direct conflict with private organizational objectives. He also argued that to require business managers to pursue socially responsible objectives may be unethical, since it requires managers to spend time, money, and other resources that really belong to other purposes and are supported by other individuals (e.g., investors, customers, owners, leaders).

Regardless of which argument or combination of arguments particular managers might support, they must make a concerted effort to perform all legally required socially responsible activities, should consider voluntarily performing socially responsible activities beyond those legally required, and inform all relevant individuals of the extent to which their organization will become involved in performing social responsibility activities.

Milton Friedman (1912–) Economist Friedman, winner of the Nobel Prize in economics in 1976 and the Presidential Medal of Freedom in 1988, in Washington, D.C., May 9, 2002. © **BROOKS KRAFT/CORBIS**

Government Requirements. Federal law requires that businesses perform certain socially responsible activities. In fact, several government agencies have been established and are maintained to develop such business-related legislation and to make sure the laws are followed. The U.S. Environmental Protection Agency does indeed have the authority to require businesses to adhere to certain socially responsible environmental standards. Adherence to legislated social responsibilities represents the minimum performance standard that business leaders must achieve. Managers must ask themselves, however, how far beyond the minimum they should attempt to go. This difficult and complicated question entails assessing the positive and negative outcomes of performing socially responsible activities. An overarching principle is that business should pursue only those activities that contribute to the business's success while contributing positively to the welfare of society.

SOCIAL RESPONSIVENESS

Social responsiveness is the degree of effectiveness and efficiency an organization displays in pursuing its social responsibilities. The greater the degree of effectives and efficiency, the more socially responsive the organization is said to be. The socially responsive organization that is both effective and efficient meets its social responsibilities without wasting organizational resources in the process. Determining exactly which social responsibilities an organization should pursue and then deciding how to pursue them are perhaps the two most critical decision-making aspects of maintaining a high level of social responsiveness. That is, managers must decide whether their organization should undertake the activities on its own or acquire the help of outsiders with more expertise in a specific area.

In addition to decision making, various approaches to meeting social obligations are another determinant of an organization's level of social responsiveness. A desirable and socially responsive approach to meeting social obligations involves the following:

- Incorporating social goals into the annual planning process

- Seeking comparative industry norms for social programs

- Presenting reports to organization members, the board of directors, and stockholders on progress in social responsibility

- Experimenting with different approaches for measuring social performance

- Attempting to measure the cost of social programs as well as the return on social program investments

There are several methods of addressing managerial approaches to meeting social obligations. Three of these are: (1) the social obligation approach, (2) the social responsibility approach, and (3) the social responsiveness approach. Each of these approaches contains behaviors that reflect a somewhat different attitude with regard to businesses performing social responsible activities. The social obligation approach considers business as having primarily economic purposes and confines social responsible activities mainly to conformance to existing laws. The socially responsible approach sees business as having both economic and societal goals. The social responsiveness approach considers business as having both societal and economic goals as well as the obligation to anticipate upcoming social problems and to work actively to prevent their appearance.

Organizations characterized by attitudes and behaviors consistent with the social responsiveness approach generally are more socially responsive than organizations characterized by attitudes and behaviors consistent with either the social responsibility approach or the social obligation approach. In addition, organizations characterized by the social responsibility approach generally achieve higher levels of social responsiveness than organizations characterized by the social obligation approach. As one moves from the social obligation approach to the social responsiveness approach, management becomes more proactive. Leading managers will do what is prudent from a business viewpoint to reduce liabilities whether a law requires an action or not.

In addition to the above-described approaches to social responsibility, managers respond to issues regarding social responsibility in four major ways. First is the reaction strategy, when managers wait until an issue presents itself to the company or to the public and then develop a response strategy to reduce the negative impact of the issue. Second, the avoidance or defense strategy is when managers lead by reducing or avoiding situations that might develop into social responsibility issues. Sometimes this includes legal maneuvers, or lobby government to change laws or regulations.

The third type of managerial approach is the accommodation strategy. In this strategy, managers pursue actions that will address the needs of consumers, employees, government, environmentalists, and so on. Many times this managerial approach is targeted to reduce or eliminate problems with issues that are particularly controversial with specific stakeholders. The fourth type of managerial style is the proactive strategy. This method of social responsibility leadership attempts to address social responsibility topics or issues by using socially responsible behavior without outside pressure or threats. The managers lead by setting a priority on supporting social responsible behavior before issue or problems develop.

AREAS OF MEASUREMENT

To be consistent, measurements to gauge organizational progress in reaching socially responsible objectives can be and are performed. The specific areas in which individual companies actually take such measurements vary, of course, depending on the specific objectives of the companies. All companies, however, probably should take such measurements in at least the following four major areas:

1. *Economic function:* Gives some indication of the economic contribution the organization is making to society

2. *Quality of life:* Whether the organization is improving or degrading the general quality of life in society

3. *Social investment:* The degree to which the organization is investing both money and human resources to solve community social problems

4. *Problem solving:* The degree to which the organization deals with social problems

THE SOCIAL AUDIT: A PROGRESS REPORT

The social audit is the process of taking measurements of the socially responsible activities of an organization. The basic steps in conducting a social audit are monitoring, measuring, and appraising all aspects of an organization's socially responsible performance. Probably no two organizations conduct and present the results of a social audit in exactly the same way.

Another factor that affects many business organizations is the role of social responsibility in an international market environment. Business leaders need to have background and experience working with social issues in different political, geographical, language, and social contexts. International companies have often overlooked this, causing them embarrassment, and lost opportunities and reduced financial resources. Managers in today's business world increasingly need to be aware of two separate but interrelated concerns—business ethics and social responsibility. The next section focuses on business ethics.

BUSINESS ETHICS

Perhaps the most practical approach is to view ethics as a catalyst that causes managers to take socially responsible actions. The movement toward including ethics as a critical part of management education began in the 1970s, grew significantly in the 1980s, and since the late 1990s has seen a significant rise in interest because of scandals at Enron, WorldCom, Archer Daniels Midland, Arthur Andersen, and Tyco. Hence, business ethics is a critical component of business leadership.

Ethics can be defined as concern for good behavior. People feel an obligation to consider not only their own personal well-being but also that of other human beings. This is similar to the precept of the Golden Rule: Do to others, as you would have them do to you. In business, ethics can be defined as the ability and willingness to reflect on values in the course of the organization's decision-making process, to determine how values and decisions affect the various stakeholder groups, and to establish how managers can use these precepts in day-to-day company operations. Ethical business leaders strive for fairness and justice within the confines of sound management practices.

Many people ask why ethics is such a vital component of management practice. It has been said that it makes good business sense for mangers to be ethical. Without being ethical, companies cannot be competitive at either the national or the international levels. While ethical management practices may not necessarily be linked to specific indicators of financial profitability, there is an inevitable conflict between ethical practices and a firm's emphasis on making a profit; the system of competition in the United States presumes underlying values of truthfulness and fair dealing.

ENHANCING CORPORATE HEALTH

The employment of ethical business practices can enhance overall corporate health in three important areas. The first area is productivity. The employees of a corporation are stakeholders who are affected by management practices. When management considers ethics in its actions toward stakeholders, employees can be positively affected. For example, a corporation may decide that business ethics requires a special effort to ensure the health and welfare of employees. Many corporations have established employee assistance programs to help employees with family, work, financial, and legal problems, and with mental illness or chemical dependency. These programs can be a source of enhanced productivity for a corporation.

A second area in which ethical management practices can enhance corporate health is in minimizing regulation from government agencies. Where companies are believed to be acting unethically, the public is more likely to put pressure on legislators and other government officials to regulate those businesses or to enforce existing regulations. For example, in 1990s and the early years of the twenty-first century, hearings and criminal court cases were conducted regarding collusion, fraud, and inaccurate reporting of financial data in a variety of organizations, some of which were already mentioned. The outcomes of these proceedings were of interest to the public because many people thought that these unethical leaders would be able to buy their way out of jail time or major fines and restitution. In the end, most of the indicted were convicted, which showed that big, powerful business leaders could not get away with stealing without consequences.

The third area in which ethical management practices can enhance corporate health is by positively affecting "outside" stakeholders, such as suppliers and customers. A positive public image can attract customers. For example, a manufacturer of baby products carefully guards its public image as a company that puts customer health and well-being ahead of corporate profits, as exemplified in its code of ethics.

A CODE OF ETHICS

A code of ethics is a formal statement that acts as a guide for how people within a particular organization should act and make decisions in an ethical fashion. Of the *Fortune 500* companies, 90 percent—and almost half of all other firms—have ethical codes. Codes of ethics commonly address issues such as conflict of interest, behavior toward competitors, privacy of information, gift giving, and making and receiving political contributions. According to one survey, the development and distribution of a code of ethics within an organization is perceived as an effective and efficient means of encouraging ethical practices within organizations.

Business leaders cannot assume, however, that merely because they have developed and distributed a code of ethics an organization's members have all the guidelines needed to determine what is ethical and will act accordingly. Not all situations that involve decision making in an organization can be addressed in a code. Codes of ethics must be monitored continually to determine whether they are comprehensive and usable guidelines for making ethical business decisions. Managers should view codes of ethics as tools that must be evaluated and refined in order to more effectively encourage ethical practices.

CREATING AN ETHICAL WORKPLACE

Business managers in most organizations commonly strive to encourage ethical practices not only to ensure moral conduct, but also to gain whatever business advantage there may be in having potential consumers and employees regard the company as ethical. Creating, distributing, and continually improving a company's code of ethics is one usual step managers can take to establish an ethical workplace.

Another step managers can take is to create a special office or department with the responsibility of ensuring ethical practices within the organization. For example, management at a major supplier of missile systems and aircraft components has established a corporate ethics office. This ethics office is a tangible sign to all employees that management is serious about encouraging ethical practices within the company.

Another way to promote ethics in the workplace is to provide the workforce with appropriate training. Many companies conduct training programs aimed at encouraging ethical practices within their organizations. Such programs do not attempt to teach what is moral or ethical but, rather, to give business managers criteria they can use to help determine how ethical a certain action might be. According to Saul Gellerman, managers can then feel confident that the general public will consider a potential action ethical if it is consistent with one or more of the following standards:

1. *The Golden Rule:* Act in a way you would want others to act toward you.

2. *The utilitarian principle:* Act in ways that result in the greatest good for the greatest number.

3. *Immanuel Kant's categorical imperative:* Act in such a way that the action taken under the circumstances could be a universal law, or rule, of behavior.

4. *The professional ethic:* Take actions that would be viewed as proper by a disinterested panel of professional peers.

5. *The TV test:* Always ask, "Would I feel comfortable explaining to a national TV audience why I took this action?"

6. *The legal test:* Ask whether the proposed action or decision is legal. Established laws are generally considered minimum standards for ethics.

7. *The four-way test:* Ask whether you can answer "yes" to the following questions as they relate to the decision: Is the decision truthful? Is it fair to all concerned? Will it build goodwill and improve friendships? Will it be beneficial to all concerned?

Finally, managers should take responsibility for creating and sustaining conditions in which people are likely to behave ethically and for minimizing conditions in which people might be tempted to behave unethically. Practices that lead to high-stakes decisions and actions tend to put employees and leaders in positions where they have to weigh the short-term personal benefits against the longer-term organizational and societal outcomes. The higher the stakes, the more likely unethical behavior will be observed. By eliminating high-stakes factors, managers can reduce much of the pressure that people feel to perform unethically.

SEE ALSO *Ethics: An Overview; Ethics in Law for Business; Ethics in Management*

BIBLIOGRAPHY

Cooper, Stuart (2004). *Corporate social performance: A stakeholder approach.* Burlington, VT: Ashgate.

Davis, Keith (1975). Five propositions for social responsibility. *Business Horizons, 18*(3), 19–24.

Dhillon, Gurpreet S. (Ed.). (2002). *Social responsibility in the information age: Issues and controversies.* Hershey, PA: Idea Group.

Friedman, Milton (1989). Freedom and philanthropy: An interview with Milton Friedman. *Business and Society Review, 17,* 11–18.

Gellerman, Saul W. (1989). Managing ethics from the top down. *Sloan Management Review, 30*(2), 73–79.

Kotler, Philip, and Lee, Nancy (2005). *Corporate social responsibility: Doing the most good for your company and your cause.* Hoboken, NJ: Wiley.

McAlister, Debbie Thorne, Ferrell, O. C., and Ferrell, Linda (2005). *Business and society: A strategic approach to social responsibility* (2nd ed.). Boston: Houghton Mifflin.

Sethi, S. Prakash (1975). Dimensions of corporate social performance: An analytical framework. *California Management Review, 17*(3), 58–64.

Treviño, Linda Klebe, and Weaver, Gary R. (2003). *Managing ethics in business organizations: Social scientific perspectives.* Stanford, CA: Stanford Business.

Thomas Haynes

SOCIALISM
SEE *Economic Systems*

SOFTWARE

Software refers to computer programs that are designed by a computer programmer or, more likely, a team of computer programmers, to perform a particular function. The software is either embedded in a device, such as a handheld device or appliance, or installed on a computer.

Software comes in many different types for many different users. Examples of these types include the computer's disk operating system (DOS) software; user interface; programming software; browsers; entertainment software, such as gaming; communications software; and utility software, such as word processing, spreadsheets, databases, and publishing.

OPERATING SYSTEM SOFTWARE
The hardware components of a computer need instructions to order to work transparently to the user. These instructions constitute the operating system of the computer, frequently referred to as DOS, and are the first files to be installed on a hard drive. Several of these files are hidden from the user to prevent file corruption. The instructions in these files inform the various components of the computer system about such tasks as recognition of components, communications, data processing, internal data transfer, and memory management. The operating system also includes utility programs such as media formatting, addition and deletion of new hardware and software, and printing queues.

The operating system of a desktop computer is based on single-user design. When the computer is added to a computer network, another layer of computer operating system is required. This layer, referred to as the network operating system, instructs the computer about the presence of a network interface card installed in the computer and its address, and controls the flow of data and command traffic to and from the computer. This ability allows the computer to share peripherals on the network system and to access outside systems such as the Internet.

USER INTERFACE

Operating systems are complicated and often not intuitive to the user. Therefore, a software program called a graphical user interface (GUI) runs over the operating system to make the operating system easier for the user to operate. More importantly, GUIs allow a "family" or "suite" of products to share the same screen and operational design, making the learning of new software much easier. For example, the screen-design menu system provides identical icons for common commands among software packages, such as save, print, spell-checking, help, and basic document formatting. Microsoft's Windows is an industry leader. The Microsoft Office Suite, for example, offers word processing, spreadsheets, publishing, and database software that share a common interface and, therefore, a common screen design and tool menus.

PROGRAMMING SOFTWARE

Computer programmers program in a variety of computer languages. These languages are actually software that use more intuitive codes than the digital machine languages (0s and 1s) but that actually translate to machine language for use by the computer's central processing unit. C++ and Visual Basic are computer languages that do not require the programmer to know machine language.

Specific computer programming language is necessary to create nonlinear products that can be accessed through the World Wide Web path of addresses used on the Internet. That universal language is the hypertext markup language (HTML). Many software packages, most notably Microsoft's Frontpage and Macromedia's Dreamweaver, are available to make programming in HTML easier and most efficient.

BROWSERS

Access to software produced for access to the Internet requires a browser for searching the Internet from the computer desktop. Software produced in HTML is hosted on computers called servers. The address access path to the respective server and software is called the URL (uniform resource locator). Commercially successful Internet browsers include Netscape Navigator and Microsoft's Internet Explorer.

Software called search engines are also available for searching the Internet for specific items. Google, for example, is a search engine that can search the Internet for virtually any topic. EBay is another software interface that specializes in bidding sales by individuals.

ENTERTAINMENT

Software for the entertainment market has been accelerating in demand since the 1990s, particularly for children and young adults. Specific hardware is often required to operate the software, such as a joystick, handheld device, or console. The handheld GameBoy and console PlayStation, for example, require frequent new software to sustain the market. Much of that software comes on cartridges, using Plug-N-Play technology, so that users can maintain libraries that do not require the installation process required on desktop computers.

COMMUNICATIONS

In addition to browsers and operating systems, users have many other personal communication needs that require desktop-loaded software. One such need involves faxing information from one location to another. That capability has become so routine that taxpayers often submit their tax forms via electronic mail (e-mail) and users employ fax machines for such mundane tasks as renewing memberships, car registrations, and driver licenses.

Another communications need is transfer between personal devices. For example, personal digital assistants and cellular telephones communicate with desktop computers through data transfer. A technology that has become popular are transfers from the photographic feature of a cellular phone to a desktop for color printing. While most handheld devices are manufactured with embedded software, the desktop computer requires software in order to know how to handle and process images.

A frequently used software is for e-mail. E-mail has evolved into a comprehensive tool for communication between individuals and groups. Microsoft's Outlook is a common e-mail facility included in the Microsoft Office Suite. Capacities include creation of e-mail address files, communication with Listservs (online discussion forums), and use of document attachments. The maintenance of e-mail logs of messages is an important part of document retention. Courts now recognize e-mail messages and attachments as legal evidence.

Communication software does pose hazards. Computer viruses can be attached to e-mail messages, address books, and attachments. The hazzards of spam, unsolicited e-mail, and software that allows people to access and track another person's computer equipment require a software solution. Detection software to protect users from these desktop invasions is critical to efficient operation. Another necessary protection is called a firewall, which is software that scrambles the Internet protocol address of the desktop computer so that electronic communications cannot be tracked back to the computer that originated the communication. This is absolutely essential when the users of a particular desktop computer may be children who are vulnerable to predators.

UTILITY SOFTWARE

A number of software packages include tools that are needed by many business users. These packages include word processing, spreadsheets, database management, and publishing. Often bundled into a family or suite of software, such packages can be purchased and installed together.

Word processing is a text-preparation tool. This software allows users to produce such documents as letters, memorandums, and reports. Elements of document style such as line spacing, font selection, paragraph indentions, bolding, italics, and centering can all be accomplished with relative ease. Templates of preset-up documents are also available. The documents are saved to both online and off-line media. Advanced features such as tables, rudimentary spreadsheets, and database structures are not available in word-processing packages.

Word processing has evolved into more than a document-preparation program. Now that spell-checkers are accompanied by grammar and style checking and other advanced features, word processing has become a narrative tool that can aid in the creation process of such artistic works as stories, poems, plays, and portfolios.

Spreadsheet software, such as Microsoft Excel, is an essentially quantitative tool wherein data in cell locations are placed in rows and columns in matrix format. That makes data easy to structure. Rows and columns can be individually designed. Cell contents can be numeric data, alphanumeric data, or algorithms. Algorithms allow new data to be generated through formula results. Advanced features include financial and statistical functions.

Database software, such as Microsoft Access, allows users to maintain records of related information. For example, database software can be used to maintain the records of the customers of insurance companies. Fields of related information might include name, contact information, type and amount of insurance carried, date of last contact, benefit information, and billing information. These fields of information are relational to the key field of name and the fields together represent a record.

This software maintains the integrity of the data structure while allowing printing in many different ways, such as forms, according to the various needs of the user. Another major feature of this software is the ability to search the records for particular needs. In an inventory database, for example, a purchasing query could be done for all merchandise at or near the inventory minimum of the particular item.

Publishing software, such as Microsoft Publisher and Adobe Pagemaker, allow users to create pamphlets, fliers, and other creative documents using layout design. Style elements include such features as imported images, text and graphic boxes, and rich color, as well as portrait and landscape layouts.

An important software design feature referred to as object linking and embedding, allows software to share "objects" that are pieces of other data. For example, a spreadsheet object can be brought into a word-processing document. Any time the spreadsheet object is updated in the original spreadsheet software, the object is automatically updated in the destination document. The word-processing document, in this example, would automatically be updated without even opening the word-processing software or document.

Software serves the limitless needs of business and entertainment. The market for software is as dynamic as the changing needs and wants of users.

SEE ALSO *Information Processing; Programming*

BIBLIOGRAPHY

Blanc, Iris, and Vento, Cathy (2005). *Performing with projects for the entrepreneur—Microsoft Office*. Cincinnati: Thomson.

Bucki, Lisa A. (2005). *Learning computer applications: Projects and exercises* (3rd ed.). New York: Pearson Prentice Hall.

Castro, Elizabeth (2003). *HTML for the World Wide Web* (5th ed.). Berkeley, CA: Peach Tree.

Shneiderman, Ben (2004). *Designing the user interface: Strategies for effective human-computer interaction* (8th ed.). Reading, MA: Addison Wesley Longman.

Douglas C. Smith

SOLE PROPRIETORSHIP

A sole proprietorship is the simplest form of business ownership. Not surprisingly, the vast majority of small businesses begin their existence as sole proprietorships. A sole proprietorship has but one owner. That sole owner may engage in any form of legal business activity any time and anywhere. Other than the various local and state business licenses that every business must purchase regardless of type of ownership, no legal formalities are required to start or operate the business. The owner is responsible for securing and investing the funds for the business. These funds may come from the owner's existing or borrowed financial resources.

The Internal Revenue Service (IRS) permits one exception to the "one sole owner" rule. If the spouse of a married sole proprietor works for the firm but is not classified as either a partner or an independent contractor, the business may still considered to be a sole proprietorship and forgo having to submit a partnership income tax return. Also, the sole proprietorship can avoid self-employment taxes.

If the owner's true name is used, such as "John Smith Auto Repair," there is ordinarily no problem in selecting a name for the sole proprietorship. However, care must be taken if a fictitious name is contemplated. The owner must register the name with the county to see whether the name duplicates that of another business. Even if it does not, the owner must submit a "doing business as (DBA)" form to the county, or, in a few states, to the secretary of state.

ADVANTAGES

An owner of a sole proprietorship gets to keep all profits derived from the operation. The owner may even share any portion of the profits (and losses) with another person or persons.

The owner has the authority to make all the decisions relating to the business. Since there are no co-owners, there is no need to hold policy-meeting sessions or form any group similar to a board of directors. The owner, of course, must bear the responsibilities that accrue from the decisions made.

The owner may hire employees or work with independent consultants and still retain the sole proprietorship form of ownership. Even if these employees or independent consultants are requested to offer their opinions relating to the firm's business decisions, the opinions are considered to be only recommendations. The owner cannot abdicate any responsibility for the outcomes fostered by these recommendations.

DISADVANTAGES

Unlimited liability is the major disadvantage borne by the sole proprietorship. The owner is financially responsible for satisfying all business debts and/or losses suffered by the firm, even to the point of sacrificing his or her personal or other business interests to pay any liabilities. For example, assume a lawsuit inflicts a debt of $190,000 on a sole proprietorship that is able to contribute only $85,000 toward settlement of the liability. Further assume

---

Elements of a business plan

I. Cover sheet
II. Statement of purpose
III. Table of contents
    A. The business
        1. Description of business
        2. Marketing
        3. Competition
        4. Operating procedures
        5. Personnel
        6. Business insurance
    B. Financial data
        1. Loan applications
        2. Capital equipment and supply list
        3. Balance sheet
        4. Break-even analysis
        5. Pro-forma income projections (profit and loss statements)
          • Three-year summary
          • Detail by month, first year
          • Detail by quarters, second and third years
          • Assumptions upon which projections were based
        6. Pro-forma cash flow
    C. Supporting documents
        • Tax returns of principals for last three years
        • Personal financial statement
        • Copy of franchise contract and all supporting documents if appropriate
    D. Copy of proposed lease or purchase agreement for building space
        • Copy of licenses and others legal documents
        • Copy of resumes of all principals
        • Copies of letters of intent from suppliers, and so forth

Figure 1

---

that the proprietor owns a home, equipment, and other business investments totaling $365,000.

The following shows the picture of the owner's liability:

Total liability of the proprietorship $190,000

Capability of the proprietorship in settling the liability $85,000

Extent to which the owner's personal assets (totaling $365,000) must be used to settle the debt $105,000

Owners of sole proprietorships have severe potential liabilities from customers, competitors, lenders, employees, and even government. The cost of liability insurance or of defending against a lawsuit is beyond the financial capability of many business firms. For this reason, most individuals holding somewhat extensive personal assets do not ordinarily use the sole proprietorship form of ownership. Instead, an alternative form of ownership is often used, such as corporation or special forms of partnership, that eliminates the unlimited liability.

TERMINATION OF THE BUSINESS

A sole proprietorship legally terminates immediately upon the death of the owner. Even if a spouse, relative, or friend of the deceased owner assumes ownership and keeps the business operating under the same name, legally a new business enterprise has been formed. It is recommended that owners at least make a will, and preferably a revocable trust, to name the beneficiary of the owner's interest in the business.

A sole proprietorship also terminates if the ownership interest is sold to another person or group of persons, if the business is abandoned by the owner, or if the owner becomes personally bankrupt.

These potential risks of sudden termination place sole proprietorships at a serious disadvantage in attracting top-flight employees who may not to wish to tie their future to a business that may suddenly become inoperative.

INCOME TAXES

When filing an income tax return, no legal distinction exists between a person as a sole proprietor and an individual person. The sole proprietor's personal income tax return (Form 1040) must include calculation of the proprietorship's income tax as well as any income or loss that the owner incurs from any additional entity, such as an employee, investor, or the like.

If, for example, a taxpayer realizes net earnings of $65,000 from a sole proprietorship and $28,000 from investments, the IRS considers the total net income to be $93,000. However, if a sole proprietor suffers a net loss of $42,000 from the business and a $71,000 net income from investments, the IRS would consider the total income to be $29,000.

Sole proprietors use Schedule C of IRS Form 1040 to file their income tax return for the proprietorship section of their income. The details of Schedule C can get very involved, so many sole proprietors require professional advice for this phase of their income tax report.

Where applicable, sole proprietors file Form 4562 to report depreciation and amortization, and Form 8829 to report business use of the owner's residence.

TYPES OF BUSINESS

Proprietorships engage in a wide variety of businesses. Using the major categories of the new North American Industry Classification System (NAICS), the types of business activity that small businesses (including sole proprietorships) are likely to be involved in are:

Accommodation, food services, and drinking places

Administrative and support and waste management remediation services

Agriculture, forestry, hunting, and fishing

Arts, entertainment, and recreation

Construction

Educational services

Health care and social assistance

Information

Manufacturing

Mining

Professional, scientific, and technical services

Real estate and rental and leasing

Religious, grant making, civic, professional, and similar organizations

Retail trade

Transportation and warehousing

Utilities

Wholesale trade

REQUISITES FOR SUCCESS

Success does not come easily for small business enterprises. To achieve success, authorities have recommended a number of characteristics and activities.

Successful sole proprietors should be strong physically and emotionally. It is very important that they be in good health. Attitudes of business owners are critical. They should possess a positive outlook and enthusiasm. They should be receptive to advice. They need to work very hard, particularly during the first several years.

Sole proprietors should possess considerable business experience, especially in the product or service lines offered by their business. Having an appropriate and sufficient education is very valuable. Other capabilities could be added, such as getting along with different kinds of people, having the ability to plan and organize, knowing how to arrive at and carry out decisions, and being a self-starter.

It is often recommended that sole proprietors select a type of business in which they have both skills and interest. The geographic location should be investigated thoroughly regarding its growth potential. And it may be important for a sole proprietor to consider having a partner.

In setting up a business, a new sole proprietor should:

- Learn as much as possible about the product or service being offered for sale

- Make sure there is enough capital available to meet necessary equipment and building needs as well as to pay for the first year's operating expenses

- Determine the amount to be invested and find the sources of any necessary loans

- Secure the assistance of an accountant, attorney, insurance agent, and banker

- Become familiar with licenses required, zoning laws, and other regulations

- Determine the most desirable types of employees; take steps to locate them and interest them in applying; and learn how to handle all withholdings

- Learn the fundamentals of advertising and, if appropriate, store layout

- Make sure that the appropriate forms of accounting and record keeping are established, and see that balance sheets and income statements are prepared

- Learn all aspects of marketing, including the principles of determining market share

In addition, the new sole proprietor should write a thorough business plan. The Small Business Administration provides an outline for the elements of a business plan (see Figure 1).

SEEKING ADVICE

Sole proprietors find it very helpful to consult with other sole proprietors who successfully operate a business. Many also seek the advice of the Small Business Administration (SBA), an independent government agency.

Organized by Congress in 1953, the SBA has offices in nearly every major city in the United States. Its toll-free telephone number is 1-800-UASK-SBA. Among many other services, SBA sponsors the Service Corps of Retired Executives (SCORE), Business Information Centers (BICS), and Small Business Development Centers (SBDC).

BIBLIOGRAPHY

Bustner, Irving (1993). *Start and Run Your Own Profitable Service Business.* Englewood Cliffs, NJ: Prentice-Hall.

Davidson, Robert L. III (1993). *The Small Business Partnership Kit.* New York: Wiley.

Diamond, Michael, and Williams, Julie (2001). *How to Incorporate: A Handbook for Entrepreneurs and Professionals* (4th ed.). New York: Wiley.

United States Small Business Administration. Retrieved October 29, 2005, from www.sbaonline.sba.gov.

G. W. Maxwell

SPAM

SEE *Cyber Crime; Electronic Mail; E-Marketing*

SPEAKING SKILLS IN BUSINESS

Studies show that Americans' number-one fear is public speaking. Actors, television personalities, and public speakers all feel it. So do salespeople, community leaders, and managers who are called on to make seemingly routine presentations.

Experienced speakers, though, know how to combat stage fright. Through careful planning, proper training, and conscious relaxation exercises, these speakers have learned how to channel fear into control and confidence. All people have the actual skills needed for good presentations; using these skills in front of an audience is the area in which training is needed. Good communication and successful speaking skills can be learned.

In defining a presentation, this article begins with one end of the spectrum, something that is loosely called a speech. Most speeches have very little impact because they do not ask the speaker to do anything, whereas the very definition of the word present is "to bring, to give a gift to." This implies that a giver (a presenter) is tuned in to what the recipient (the audience) wants. What response do we get when we give someone a gift of something he or she really wants? What response do we get when we give someone a gift that he or she really doesn't like? The difference between these two is the difference between sharing a meaningful message and delivering a speech. Audiences dislike being talked to; they eagerly await speakers who drive home a point or idea that they can readily use in their personal or professional lives.

When imparting information, two things are happening simultaneously:

1. The presenter is making a commitment to the audience. The presenter is working to prove a point that will win the support of the audience or that will generate action.

2. The audience is making a judgment on the presenter, asking such questions as, "Do I really trust this person?" "Does this information make any sense?" "Are the facts presented accurate?"

A person who has accepted an invitation to speak should answer three questions before beginning to think about what to say and how to say it:

1. Who is the audience?

2. What does the audience want to know?

3. What is the best way to provide the audience with the information they want?

Most presentations are given for one of five reasons: to entertain, inform, inspire, convince, or persuade. Once the purpose is determined, a talk should be organized around three main parts:

1. *Introduction*: This "hooks" the audience, entices people to listen, and previews what is to come. Effective introductory devices include questions, dramatic or humorous statements, jokes, anecdotes, and personal experiences.

2. *Body*: This is the subject—the meat of the speech. It should relate the who, what, when, where, why, and how of the subject. To keep the talk simple and easy to understand, the speaker should stick to three—no more than four—main points, relying on facts, figures, illustrations, specific examples, and comparisons to support these main points.

3. *Conclusion*: This final section should highlight key points that the audience should remember. It should also make people feel they have gained something by listening. The audience might be challenged to act or react to the message within a specific time frame.

The content of the message should be structured in an orderly and logical manner. This makes it easier for people to follow, digest, and retain the information. If the audience has difficulty following the speaker's train of thought, the message will not get or keep their attention.

The skeletal structure of any presentation should be:

I. Introduction
   A. Opening
   B. Objective
   C. Preview
II. Body
   A. Key point 1
     a) Supporting material
     b) Transition statement
   B. Key point 2
     a) Supporting material
     b) Transition statement
   C. Key point 3
     a) Supporting material
     b) Transition statement
III. Closing
   A. Summary
   B. To do

Formulating an achievable and clearly stated objective is crucial. It provides the whole focus for preparation and acts as a guide in determining what to include in the body of the message.

Stating the objective at the beginning of the presentation is equally important. Doing so lets the audience know what to expect. It prepares them for what they are about to hear. Therefore, it should always be stated in conversational terms. It might begin this way: "Today we will explore...." or "I will help you understand...."

With the foundation (objective) in place, one can proceed to outline the body of the presentation. Key points are those that unlock the door to the subject and let the audience in on the most important content areas of the message.

It is said that every great message contains at least one key point but not more than three. The rule of three forces the speaker to think through the material and distill the most significant points. Having three or fewer points keeps it simple for listeners. Usually information is remembered in groups of threes, fours, or sevens. Telephone numbers, for example, are spoken first with two sets of three numbers and then with a set of four: (123)456-7890. Elementary school teachers never present material in groups of more than seven items. The way people store and recall information represents the brain's effort to organize and combine data, making it easier to remember.

This same principle applies to the body of a presentation. Simplifying it provides the audience with a message that they will be better able to assimilate and retain.

Supporting material for each key point can be obtained by using:

- Examples
- Stories
- Quotations
- Findings
- Comparisons

Since supporting material accounts for most of the content of a presentation, it generally takes the most time to identify, collect, and develop. Again, though, the rule of three should be applied. Significant points will get lost in the maze of rambling information if too much supporting material is presented. On the other hand, a presentation will not be convincing if too little supporting material to substantiate key points is included.

A transition statement acts as a minisummary or minipreview within the body of the presentation. It announces the end of one point and introduces the next. Transitions help listeners stay with the speaker, making the message easier to follow and remember. Without transitions, a speaker could be halfway into the next point while some of the listeners are still trying to figure out what this has to do with the previous point. A sample transition statement might be: "Now that we have studied...," or "Let's take a look at..."

People are most readily persuaded by what they heard frequently and recently; therefore, a summary should include a capsule of the key points in brief sentence form. This review drives the message home to the listener.

Most trainers apply the formula T × 3 (tell them three times) when delivering a message:

Preview. Tell them what you are going to tell them.

Body. Tell them.

Summary. Tell them what you told them.

The last point to impress on an audience is how they can use the information presented to bring about meaningful change in their lives. The "To Do" of a message can be accomplished by using statements such as: "I challenge you to..." or "I encourage you to..."

Memorizing a presentation is a bad idea because stumbling or forgetting one word might cause the whole speech to fall apart. Memorized words also tend to sound cold and lifeless instead of warm and genuine. Reading a speech is not a good option either, because doing so prevents having eye contact with the audience. Instead, a speaker should write the main points on note cards and rehearse the speech at least five times, striving for spontaneity, variety, and naturalness in delivery.

To assure a successful presentation, follow these suggestions:

1. Practice mental imagery. Imagine yourself triumphantly succeeding. Tell yourself, over and over again, that you have something important to share and that you will do a great job sharing it.

2. Rehearse privately in front of a mirror and on tape. Critique the pace and tempo of your presentation, as well as your enunciation, articulation, and pronunciation of words. Ask a trusted friend to critique your delivery.

3. Type your talk in large, bold type and number all pages/cards of your presentation. If you drop them, visible numbers will help you put them back together again in the correct order.

4. Conduct extra research. Conducting detailed research on your topic helps you gain a tremendous feeling of mastery and confidence.

5. Dress comfortably, but in good taste, and tuck away a lucky symbol on yourself.

6. Bring along some handouts. Cartoons, objects, or memorabilia that can be passed around the room are very effective interest grabbers. They are especially useful when you must pause to collect your thoughts or calm your nerves.

7. Talk to someone. Before your talk begins, talk to a friend in your audience. Or talk to several. The more people you have a chance to meet before the talk begins. the more easily you will be able to treat your audience as a group of friends.

8. Introduce yourself. Talk a bit about your background. Let your audience know something about your interests. Even frightened speakers have the ability to introduce themselves with style.

9. Speak deeply. Let your comments flow from deep within your body. Your voice will sound more forceful as a result.

10. Position yourself firmly at the lectern or table. Rest your hands firmly but comfortably at the edge of the lectern or table. As your hands gently grasp the lectern, you will boost your sense of command and confidence.

11. Remember that physical action often softens fear. The more you are able to move your body or your major muscle groups, the more likely you will induce a sense of calm.

12. Modulate your voice. Enunciate carefully, pause when appropriate, and accent important points with a change in volume.

13. State your case. Good presentations are forceful presentations. Do not hesitate to express your viewpoint firmly or offer provocative ideas to the audience. The more you are able to express strongly held views, the more you will feel in control of the presentation.

14. Enjoy yourself. You need not be a polished celebrity to deliver a quality talk. Enjoy the experience. To relax yourself and your audience, do not forget to smile!

SEE ALSO *Communications in Business; Listening Skills in Business; Reading Skills in Business; Writing Skills in Business*

BIBLIOGRAPHY

Gelb, Michael J. (1988). *Present Yourself!* Rolling Hills Estates, CA.: Jalmar Press.

Ensman, Richard G., Jr. (1993, Winter). "Stage Fright Bites the Dust." *Communiqué*, 17-22.

Filson, Brent (1994). *Executive Speeches.* New York: Wiley.

Hargrave, Jan L. (1995). *Let Me See Your Body Talk.* Dubuque, IA: Kendall/Hunt.

Lewis, Jan (1996, July/August). "Become a Better Communicator." *Women In Business*, 21-24.

Jan Hargrave

SPECIAL EVENT PRICING

SEE *Pricing*

SPECIALTY GOODS

SEE *Shopping*

SPREADSHEETS

Spreadsheet software is one of the most-used technologies for collecting, computing, and displaying data. Spreadsheets contain a rectangular array of cells in rows and columns that can hold data. Users can create business models, graphs and charts, and reports for financial, statistical, or other data. Most spreadsheet software allows a user to access real-time data from Web sites and to collaborate across teams and workgroups.

SPREADSHEET PACKAGES

Spreadsheet packages are available for various operating systems, such as Windows, Macintosh, UNIX, Java, Linux, and VMS. Spreadsheet capabilities are included in financial management packages and integrated software packages. The best-known spreadsheet software packages are Microsoft Excel, Lotus 1-2-3 from IBM Corporation, and Corel's Quattro Pro. These three packages are included as parts of office suites from Microsoft, IBM, and Corel.

In addition, dozens of other spreadsheet packages are available. Many of these offer users an opportunity to try the product for a limited period and then pay a fee for permission to use the package beyond the evaluation period. Many spreadsheets are listed on the Internet by their developers, either as shareware or for purchase, and some are available for downloading.

SPREADSHEET APPLICATIONS

A spreadsheet is a table representing information in worksheet form. The spreadsheet can be visualized as a large sheet of paper with rows and columns and is based on the worksheets used by accountants for manual computa-

Sales by region for first quarter				
	January	February	March	Total
East	$ 1,200	$1,500	$1,800	$4,500
Midwest	500	1,000	1,500	3,000
South	900	1,500	1,800	4,200
West	2,000	2,100	2,400	6,500
Totals	$4,600	$6,100	$7,500	$18,200

Figure 1

tions. Spreadsheets range from small, simple text tables to large documents that can carry out complex computations and statistical analysis of thousands of data entries.

Simple spreadsheets can be displayed on screen; more complex spreadsheets extend into vast numbers of cells and can be displayed in part on one screen. The power of a spreadsheet is in its ability to store formulas and display their results. A recalculation feature in spreadsheets allows a user to enter new data into the spreadsheet—which can affect other sections of the spreadsheet—and see the results of new calculations. This "What If" feature of spreadsheets is a valuable tool for users.

FORMAT OF A SPREADSHEET

Spreadsheet software packages organize numeric data into table format, vertically in columns and horizontally in rows. Three types of data may be entered into a spreadsheet or worksheet: (1) values or numbers, (2) names or labels, and (3) formulas for calculation. Values may be used for basic arithmetic operations: addition, subtraction, multiplication, or division. Labels identify information in the worksheet and organize the information. Formulas perform calculations on data and display and store the resulting values. A cell, the intersection of a row and column, can contain a label, a value, or a formula for performing calculations. Cells are addressed by column number and row number, and a current cell address is displayed in an address box. The "home" cell is A1, located in column A, row 1.

Only a small part of a complex spreadsheet is displayed on the screen at one time. Spreadsheets can contain millions of cells in each spreadsheet, and a spreadsheet file can include multiple spreadsheets. For example, Lotus 1-2-3 and Microsoft Excel spreadsheets have 256 columns and 65,536 rows, or 16,777,216 cells. A spreadsheet file also may include multiple worksheets. More than one worksheet can be used to render three-dimensional charts of data. Spreadsheets are very powerful, extensive electronic worksheets.

A spreadsheet handles such simple functions as adding, subtracting, multiplying and dividing. Arithmetic operators are used to represent the functions: addition (+), subtraction (–), multiplication (*), and division (/). For example, an entry into cell D3 of "=B3+C3" would instruct the spreadsheet to add the contents of cells B3 and C3 and store the sum in cell D3. A symbol at the beginning of a formula identifies the entry as a formula instead of a label. In an entry of =B3+C3, the equal sign identifies the entry as a formula.

A simple spreadsheet can be enhanced with spreadsheet tools. Font faces (e.g., italic or bold), sizes, and types can be changed, color can be added to the background of cells or labels, and graphs can be used to illustrate data from the spreadsheet.

A spreadsheet is initially set up by default with a given column width, row height, and format for entries. If labels are longer than the column width allowed, the spreadsheet does not "lose" the extra characters; instead they are not displayed if the cell to their right has an entry. The user may change the column width and row height to enhance the appearance of the entries. Values are stored by the spreadsheet in their simplest form initially; an entry of $1,050.00, for example, can be stored as 1050. The user then has tools within the spreadsheet for formatting entries.

Numeric data may be formatted as dollars and cents, with commas separating hundreds and thousands, in various formats for different countries, with a given number of decimal points, in exponential form, or in other formats. When a formula is entered, the cell displays the result of computation and retains the formula. To display the formula, not its results, in a cell, a user can choose a format for "text." A formula that is entered as +=C3+D3–E3, for example, might show a result of 25. If the cell is formatted to the "text" format, the formula will show instead of the computed answer. Spreadsheet packages usually have a "shortcut" keyboard method of displaying the formula version of entries.

A set of data can be described to the spreadsheet as a range by specifying the beginning cell, in the upper left corner of the data, and the ending cell, in the lower right corner of the data. For example, to identify a rectangle that begins with cell A1 and extends down to cell D3, one address for the range would be A1:D3. Spreadsheets identify the range with a symbol that means "through." In the example A1:D3, the format used by many spreadsheets, the range is interpreted as "cell A1 through cell D3."

An example of a spreadsheet is shown in Figure 1. Rows 1 through 7 show a spreadsheet. In row 1, "Sales by Region for First Quarter," the heading for the entire worksheet, is an example of a label. The column headings and items in column A are labels; columns B through D are

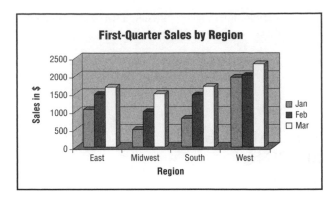

Figure 2

values, which are summed in column E with formulas. The formulas in column E sum the numbers for January, February, and March for each item. Across the bottom of the spreadsheet, the total line is also a result of using formulas to sum the columns. The formula for E3, for example, is =SUM(B3:D3).

The title, "Sales by Region for First Quarter," and the column headings (January, February, March, Totals) show how font changes can enhance the readability and attractiveness of a spreadsheet. Cells can be formatted to bold, underline, or italicize entries; background color or shading can be added; and font faces and sizes can be changed. In the sample worksheet, formatting has been used to aid readability.

Values can be formatted. In the sample spreadsheet, the values in rows 4 through 6 have been formatted to no decimal places with commas. Rows 3 and 7 have been formatted with a dollar sign for readability. A user can select the desired formatting from a menu.

Spreadsheet data can be selected for charts, or visual representations of those data. Cells are selected by highlighting them. Spreadsheet packages may chart one set of data in the form of a pie chart, or two or more sets of data in bar charts (with vertical bars, horizontal bars, or stacked bars), line charts, area charts, or mixed charts, which combine bars and lines to represent data. Data can be displayed in two-dimensional or three-dimensional form. Charts become part of the spreadsheet and may be stored on the same page as the spreadsheet or as a separate page or worksheet. Figure 2 shows a sample chart for the sales spreadsheet described above.

The chart depicts the figures from B3 through D6 in the spreadsheet, categorized by cells A3 through A6 (labels). A column (or bar) chart is only one of several choices of charts that a user can select. The software provides steps for adding a title to the chart, a legend, and/or a listing of labels for the charted data.

MACROS IN SPREADSHEETS

A macro is a series of commands that automate a spreadsheet task, streamline complex procedures, or create applications. A user can enter a macro into a worksheet file or into a macro library, a worksheet file that stores macros. To create a macro, the user enters the steps needed to carry out a task, gives the macro a name, and saves it in a file. To use the macro, the user selects it by name from a menu and runs the macro in the spreadsheet. The steps are carried out automatically. For complex tasks that are used often, a macro makes it easier for a user to avoid mistakes in the task, since the steps are stored as a file and recalled as needed.

SPREADSHEETS IN INTEGRATED PACKAGES

Integrated software packages, which contain several kinds of software within one, include a spreadsheet. Information can be copied from a spreadsheet into other software packages, such as a word-processing package. Spreadsheets can be linked to files in other software in the package so that changes made in the spreadsheet are automatically reflected in the linked document. A table from a spreadsheet can be linked to a word-processing document so that any changes in cell entries in the spreadsheet change the contents of the table in the word-processing document.

Embedded objects, such as a chart from a spreadsheet, can be embedded into a word-processing document. Unlike linking, changes in the embedded chart in the document are not reflected in the source file (spreadsheet file). These features make the spreadsheet a very powerful tool for analysis and reporting of data in various formats.

SUMMARY

Spreadsheets are used by almost every business firm that records data. Spreadsheets have also become a useful tool for personal record keeping. The data organization and graphics capabilities of spreadsheets make them a useful tool for all types of calculations, displays, and analysis.

SEE ALSO *Information Processing; Software*

BIBLIOGRAPHY

IBM Corporation. Lotus. Retrieved December 10, 2005, from http://www-306.ibm.com/software/lotus

Shelly, Gary, Cashman, Thomas J., and Vermaat, Misty (2003). *Microsoft Office 2003: Introductory Concepts and Techniques* (2nd ed.). Boston: Course Technology.

Webopedia. (n.d.). *Spreadsheet.* Retrieved December 7, 2005, from http://www.webopedia.com/TERM/s/spreadsheet.html

Betty J. Brown

STAGGERS RAIL AND MOTOR CARRIER ACTS OF 1980

In enacting the Staggers Rail Act of 1980, the U.S. Congress "recognized that railroads faced intense competition from trucks and other modes for most freight traffic" and that "prevailing regulation prevented railroads from earning adequate revenues and competing effectively" (Association of American Railroads, 2003). Survival of the railroad industry required a new regulatory scheme "that allowed railroads to establish their own routes, tailor their rates to market conditions, and differentiate rates on the basis of demand" (Association of American Railroads, 2003). In the early twenty-first century, Congress was debating the effectiveness and impact the act.

Prior to the Staggers Rail Act and the Motor Carrier Act of 1980, the railroad industry was suffering. Many railroads had financial problems, and the conditions of rail facilities had deteriorated. Public demand for a better rail system caused Congress to take action and pass the Staggers Rail Act, which has resulted in rail profits and improved service. The act marked the most significant change in rail policy since the Interstate Commerce Act of 1887.

"The basic principle of the Staggers Rail Act was simple: Railroads should be permitted to act much as other businesses in managing their assets and pricing their services" (Association of American Railroads, 2003). It eliminated most common-carrier obligations, granted railroads greatly increased commercial freedom, and generally reversed previous policy. The act deregulated the nation's railroads. In deregulating the nation's railroads, Congress intended (1) to return the nation's railroads to financial health, (2) to replace government regulation wherever possible with the powers of competition, and (3) to continue to provide captive shippers with protection from "unreasonable" rates.

The system of economic regulation of railroads in the United States that was put in place by the Staggers Rail Act has provided a balance between allowing railroads the freedom to compete effectively in the marketplace and protecting shippers from abuse of railroad market power. In 2005 W. C. Vantuono reported that twenty-five years after it was passed, the Staggers Rail Act was doing exactly what it was supposed to do: help move the railroads toward revenue adequacy.

Railroads have been able to increase their profitability since passage of Staggers in the face of strong competition from trucks and declining rates only through increased productivity. The flexibility Staggers provided "has enabled railroads to upgrade their systems, reinvest in productive rail infrastructure, generate higher levels of service and greater volumes of traffic, dramatically increase productivity, improve profitability from once anemic levels, and improve safety—while at the same time sharply lowering rates for shippers" (Association of American Railroads, 2003).

Until 1995 the regulating agency for the railroads was the Interstate Commerce Commission (ICC). The intent of the Staggers Rail Act was to replace federal regulation with market competition. The ICC was charged by Congress in the Staggers Rail Act to promote rail-to-rail competition. Unfortunately, the ICC did not fully succeed in its charge.

The ICC's successor, the Surface Transportation Board (STB) of the U.S. Department of Transportation, was created by Congress in 1995. The STB retained authority to set maximum rates or take other actions if a railroad was found to have market dominance or to have engaged in competitive behavior. The STB is also responsible for railroad mergers, consolidations, and track age rights. Railroads largely control their pricing; changes, however, must be approved by the STB and, if they are, the railroad is not subject to antitrust regulations.

Since its beginnings in the 1830s, "the U.S. freight rail industry has seen many market improvements, making today's industry competitive against other modes of transport and vital to the economic health" (Association of American Railroads, 2003) of the U.S. economy. The Staggers Rail Act of 1980 has helped that happen.

SEE ALSO *Transportation*

BIBLIOGRAPHY

Association of American Railroads. (2003). *A trip through railroad history.* Retrieved December 10, 2005, from http://www.tomorrowsrailroads.org/industry/history.cfm

Association of American Railroads. Policy and Economic Department. (2005, June). *Why the rail reregulation debate is important.* Retrieved December 10, 2005, from http://www.aar.org/About_AAR/about_aar.asp

Deregulations anniversary. (2005, October 10). *Traffic World, 269*(41), 8.

Vantuono, W. C. (2005, July 7). Twenty-five years after Staggers: New challenges, huge opportunities. *Railroad Age, 206,* 22–26.

Phyllis Bunn
Laurie Barfitt

STANDARD & POOR'S 500

SEE *Stock Indexes*

STANDARD-BASED WORK PERFORMANCE

Forces in the workplace such as organizational values, work cultures, and business goals shape the structures, strategies, and human resource processes of most successful organizations. One change emerging from these forces is the development and implementation of work standards. Work standards deliver specific goals to employees, helping them understand exactly what is expected of them in order to earn a fair and equitable pay for their job performance. These work standards also provide employers with a reliable performance appraisal system. This compensation process is referred to as standard-based work performance.

Standard-based work performance came into vogue in the 1990s, when many U.S. organizations began using it in some way. Pay-for-performance, at-risk compensation, and merit pay are other terms for standard-based work performance. Standard-based pay is a form of compensation known as incentive pay. With an incentive pay plan, pay increases are granted to employees based on their rated performance in a given period. Pay increases are granted with the goal of motivating future, and, it is hoped, more productive, performance. Some organizations view standard-based work-performance compensation as a way to change behavior; others view it as a reward mechanism. Clearly for many, "incentive compensation is the motivational tool that drives employees to meet their goals which in turn drives the company to new levels of success" (Human Resource Department Ltd.).

Indeed, an effective compensation strategy is crucial to achieve organizational goals. A key element in compensation strategy is monitoring and improving employee performance and productivity. Compensation & Performance Management stated that among other things, an effective compensation strategy helps a firm recruit and retain valuable employees, ensure equitable pay levels, use compensation as a motivator, and manage compensation costs.

STANDARD-BASED WORK-PERFORMANCE PLAN REQUIREMENTS

Key to success with standard-based work performance in an organization is to have the appraisal system backed by a clear sense of corporate purpose. Thus, designing and implementing a new compensation program and appraisal system requires a great deal of planning in deciding what action management wants to elicit from employees. Obviously, organizational and corporate culture and management styles will determine how to implement the changes in compensation. Generally, priority may be given to corporate strategy rather than to industry standards when developing pay plans. A two-tiered approach, however, may be the best choice in order to develop goals appropriate for both management and labor.

Another issue to consider regarding the organizational culture is whether to promote teamwork or individual effort. The goals of each are very different and must be clearly stated. If compensation rewards are to be based on the effectiveness of the team's work rather than individual effort, the organization needs to help employees learn to function as members of a team.

An organization must also decide whether performance-based compensation is practiced at only executive and middle-management levels or at all employee levels. This decision is critical as it determines the type of training required throughout the organization.

Standard-based performance is based on the assumption that performance can be measured. It is difficult to objectively measure job performance in many positions. William Abernathy with Organizational Performance Systems suggested that poor measurement is one of the reasons results vary when organizations implement incentive pay plans. Abernathy suggested five measurement problems that can affect the success of an incentive pay compensation plan. The measurement problems are:

1. *Subjective measures:* Use of subjective versus objective measures fails to provide to the employee important information needed to improve performance

2. *Multiple measures:* Measure fewer and more important job responsibilities

3. *Group measures:* Group measures are more successful with smaller groups (fewer than 15)

4. *Process measures:* Typically, outcomes should be the target of the measurement, not processes

5. *Uncontrollable measures:* Unfair to employees to be measured/evaluated on outcomes over which they have no control

Successful performance-based pay plans have three common qualities. They must be clearly communicated to employees, they must include an annual review of the plan, and they need appropriately ambitious goals. Abernathy suggested that these are common communication problems:

- Employees do not understand the system
- Feedback is delayed
- Recognition is for goal achievement only—none for improvement
- Measures and goals are changed frequently

- Closed-book management—information is not shared with employees
- Employees do not know how to improve—education is critical

Abernathy also suggested that management problems may contribute to a lack of success with standard-based work performance. Failure happens when managers do not manage to measure, do not coach employees, do not support the system, do not negotiate measures and goals, and do not help design performance improvement plans.

In sum, effective communication up and down the chain of command is key to a successful standard-based work-performance plan. The plan is also something that must be jointly developed between manager and employee to not only establish clear goals but also establish appropriate measurement strategies.

STANDARD-BASED WORK-PERFORMANCE THEORIES

Four psychological theories address how work standards relate to work performance. The psychological expectancy theory suggests that standard-based work performance is likely to motivate increased performance when performance is necessary to attain a pay increase. The theory states that for the performance-based pay plan to be successful, performance must be accurately measured, pay must be a valued outcome, pay must be made contingent on performance, and the employee must have the opportunity to have an impact on performance.

The psychological reinforcement theory suggests that standard-based performance should motivate increased performance when the outcomes of favorable performance are clearly defined to the employee, the rewards are contingent on a desired performance, and compensation is increased in a timely manner when performance improves.

The psychological equity theory suggests that standard-based pay will increase employee motivation when it leads to perceptions of equity by the employee. It requires an organization to shift from valuing seniority to valuing performance inputs and basing compensation on performance rather than years of employment.

The psychological goal-setting theory suggests that standard-based performance increases motivation when it is the result of setting more-difficult goals and demonstrating a commitment to reach these goals. Goals should be weighted by difficulty, and compensation rewards should be given based on degree of difficulty of the goal achieved.

As stated earlier, examining performance in terms of measurable outcomes is key to a *pay-for-performance* plan. Employees must know what will determine a pay increase: the manner in which the work performed is being measured, the work itself, or the factor to be measured.

EXAMPLES OF STANDARD-BASED WORK PERFORMANCE

Many examples of work standards exist in business today. Compensation experts say the key is to design a plan that enforces the goals of the organization and to regularly evaluate the effectiveness of the plan. Compensation & Performance Management reported these benefits of pay-for-performance plans:

Increased productivity and efficiency

Better understanding of goals

Clearer communication

Improved collaboration

Successful retention

The standard-based work-performance plan used by the Ford Motor Company measures quality using warranty figures expressed as repairs per thousand vehicles and both short- and long-term customer satisfaction.

In the late 1990s, Sun Microsystems started tracking quality of customer loyalty and customer quality. Employees understand that the corporation's overall success will affect their compensation. Employees know their annual bonus is based on a reduction in customer dissatisfiers (such as late delivery, software defects, and poor product quality) and an increase in customer loyalty. The idea for the Sun Microsystems plan emanated from quality benchmarking strategy meetings of chief executive officers of Sun Microsystems, Federal Express, Motorola, and Xerox. The successful standard-based work-performance plans of these companies have three qualities in common: clear communication with employees, annual plan reviews, and appropriately ambitious goals.

Employees must have a clear idea of the organization's goals, how their jobs factor into meeting those goals, and how they will be rewarded for doing their part to achieve the goals. The degree to which an employee is accountable for results on the job is the amount of control or opportunity available to the employee. Standard-based performance focuses on the importance of providing accountability for work performance. Goals and compensation should be assessed, reviewed, and updated at least once a year.

LAYING THE FOUNDATION

When an organization hires new employees, the assumption is often made that the employees have the requisite technical skills needed to get the job done. Nevertheless, the notion of a skill being performed to a particular standard may not have been part of the novice employees' education and/or training, to say nothing of the employees considering their skill levels being tied to compensation. Thus the notion of developing standards as a route to accountability and increased job performance slowly emerged.

> In 1994, Congress created the National Skill Standards Board (NSSB) to develop a voluntary national system of skill standards, assessment, and certification to enhance the ability of the United States to compete effectively in the global economy and to increase opportunities for America's workers (American Youth Policy Forum)

The American Youth Policy Forum also reported that skill standards were being developed across a number of industries, starting with the manufacturing industry sector and the sales and service industry sector. Skill standards tell the student and teacher not only the specific skill required, but also the level at which the skill must be performed.

The state of Texas, for example, has developed a skill standards program to guide the incorporation of industry-specific skill standards into the curriculum in technical and community colleges throughout the state. The Texas program suggested skill standards are comprised of seven essentials, divided into three parts:

1. **Work-oriented elements:**
   - Critical work functions
   - Key activities
   - Performance criteria

2. **Worker-oriented elements:**
   - Occupational skills, knowledge, conditions
   - Academic knowledge and skills
   - Employability knowledge and skills

3. **Evaluate performance:**
   - Statement of assessment

In summary, standard-based work performance is an extraordinarily useful tool for both management and employees to set both workplace expectations and measurement strategies. Postsecondary education can serve a unique role in including skill standards-based instruction throughout their programs of study.

SEE ALSO *Employee Compensation; Performance Appraisal; Productivity*

BIBLIOGRAPHY

Abernathy, William (n.d.). Obstacles to the effective execution of an incentive pay system. Organizational Performance Systems. Retrieved December 1, 2005 from http://www.organizationalsystems.com/articles/incentive-pay-obstacles.cfm

American Youth Policy Forum. (2002, February 1). National skill standards board: Integrating manufacturing skill standards into education and training programs. A forum brief. Retrieved November 23, 2005, from http://www.aypf.org/forumbriefs/2002/fb020102.htm

Compensation & Performance Management. http://www.compensation.com/servicescompstrategy.cfm

Heneman, Robert L., and Werner, Jon M. (2005). *Merit pay: Linking pay to performance in a changing world* (2nd ed.). Greenwich, CT: Information Age.

Human Resource Department Ltd. (n.d.) Incentive plans (pay for performance). Retrieved November 23, 2005, from http://www.thrd.com/services/incentive_plans.php

Texas Skill Standards Board. (n.d.). A user's guide: Incorporating skill standards into community & technical college curriculum. Retrieved November 23, 2005, from http://www.tssb.org/wwwpages/pdfiles/TSSBUsersGuide1.doc

Wanda L. Stitt-Gohdes

STANDARD COSTING

Standard costing is an objective method of optimizing the use of resources in the provision of goods or services. This is a traditional method for monitoring the use of resources that was initially applied to basic inputs for only basic factory costs of production of goods. In the last two decades of the twentieth century, the technological capabilities of computers initiated innovative ways to identify and monitor costs, but the basic concepts of standard costing have continued to have relevance in many businesses.

Costing is the identification of the value of resources used for specified goods or services. One purpose of costing is to determine what resources, and in what quantities, are required to provide the goods or services. A second purpose is to provide a guide to resource usage monitoring. It is the second purpose that is considered in the following discussion.

METHODS OF COSTING IDENTIFIED IN BUDGETS

Budget figures may be based on actual, budgeted, or standard costs. These categories are not mutually exclusive. For example, while a standard cost is a budgeted cost, a budgeted cost is not always a standard cost. An actual cost for a prior year may be a budgeted cost for the forthcoming year and recorded in the budget.

Budgeted costs are generally described as the best estimate about what should be allowed for forthcoming activity. Some budgeted costs are based on actual costs of the previous year, information from supervisors about where resources might be more efficiently used, and subjective judgments about how much should be allowed for resources. Another basis for recording budgeted costs is to use standard costs.

STANDARD COSTS

Standard costs are determined costs that reflect the effective and efficient use of resources. Standard costs are costs established through identifying an objective relationship between specified inputs and expected outputs. Engineers in laboratories are often involved in establishing standards for manufacturing processes, for example. Standard costs are generally related to carefully analyzed phenomena both in the laboratory and in the workplace. For example, in a factory that produces personal computers, standard costs are often used for direct materials, direct labor, and variable overhead, at the unit level. Resource usage that can be traced exactly to what is to be produced is referred to as direct.

To establish the standard usage of a direct material for the production of the keyboard of the personal computer, the possibilities are analyzed in a laboratory, where conditions are maintained as optimum as possible. Prior attention has been given, generally, to the quality of the metal to be used. There are times, though, that alternative materials that meet company standards for quality have been selected and each is tested to find out if there are differences in quantities needed, since scrap and problems in cutting may not be the same for all the alternatives. At this point, the focus is not on how many minutes are needed by an experienced cutter to meticulously cut the metal so as to minimize usage, but rather on how much of the metal is to be allowed for each keyboard.

What is determined to be the optimum usage of material—the standard usage of material for the production of a single personal computer of a specified type—in the laboratory undergoes another assessment. This then answers the question: "What usage is to be allowed for an adequately qualified worker in the factory?" Often, a technically determined standard in laboratory testing is modified to take into account the conditions of the workplace, which might not be as ideal as those maintained in the laboratory.

The goal of the personnel responsible for setting standard costs is to provide realistic standards. Only standards perceived to be reasonable are likely to motivate workers to adhere to what is prescribed. Workers are motivated to achieve output by meeting specified standards. If standards are unreasonable, either too tight or too loose, the level of discipline expected is seriously undermined. If standards cannot be achieved with reasonable effort, workers may become discouraged and become so indifferent that their work quality deteriorates significantly. If standards are too easy to achieve, there may be an unnecessary waste of resources.

Standard costing has applications to any type of business activity. The process described briefly above can be applied, for example, for processing documents in an insurance company or in a financial services business, as well as in manufacturing firms.

MONITORING STANDARD COSTS

Standard costs are monitored as a basis for determining the extent to which expectations are realized. Before the widespread use of computer-based systems, typical reporting was done weekly or monthly. In contemporary companies, it is not uncommon for a company with factories or stores to monitor on a daily basis their resource usage, thereby allowing modifications, if judged necessary, to be introduced promptly. Computer-integrated production methods, for example, allow for maintaining both the actual cost/usage and the standard cost/usage figures in the records maintained.

A commonly used method is to determine the difference between what was allowed by standard costs, which are the budget allowances, and what was actually spent for the output achieved. This difference is called a variance. For example, assume that the factory producing personal computers completed 10,000 computers where the standard usage of one type of metal, as a direct material, was 2 pounds per computer, or 20,000 pounds. The actual usage of the output achieved, 10,000 units, was 20,430 pounds. Since actual usage of the direct material was greater than the standard allowed, the excess usage is called an unfavorable variance, or 430 pounds unfavorable. The monetary cost of this variance is then determined: The variance in units is multiplied by standard cost per unit for the metal. Therefore, if the standard cost for the metal was $2.95 per pound, the variance would be reported as $1,268.50 unfavorable (430 pounds × $2.95, the standard price).

What has been described for a direct material is the process that is used for each component of production. Resources monitored include, in addition to direct material and direct labor, variable factory overhead and fixed factory overhead. Both standard usage of resources and standard costs for each are established and monitored. The process for variable overhead is somewhat more complex because the components of variable overhead are multiple indirect resources that are related to volume of production processed. For example, while a chain of fast food restaurants may consider ground beef as a direct

material, they will consider the wrapping used for the cooked hamburger an indirect material. Such a chain's controller's office has determined the material costs that cannot be directly tied to each unit and/or those material costs which individually are not significant for direct tracing. This collection of material costs is then analyzed to determine the most appropriate basis for allocating to the goods produced.

Standards are developed for fixed overhead costs, too. Fixed costs are costs incurred in production that are not a function of volume produced. Though in the long run all costs can vary, fixed costs are costs that do not change as activity levels change.

A REVIEW OF ACTUAL RESULTS

Companies have policies about the level of variance that is to be investigated. Some variation from expectations is allowed, and if standards are realistic, much of the variation is eliminated over the period of a year; insignificant favorable variances cancel out insignificant unfavorable variances. Companies monitor the extent to which standards appear to be reasonable by assessing the end-of-year balances in variance accounts.

Variances that are determined to be significant are investigated. Careful observation and discussion with those workers involved in producing the output that led to a significant variance will aid in determining an explanation. The explanation is the basis for considering what changes need to be made.

In an objective review of observations and discussions, questions may arise as to the appropriateness of a standard, if the actual result is unreasonably different from the standard. There may need to be a reconsideration of the earlier analyses that were the basis for the standards used in the budget followed by operational personnel.

For an organization to gain optimum value from standard costing, all employees involved must understand the motivation for such costing and also understand the assessment that will be made. Imposing standard costs without communicating in an honest, candid manner will undermine much of the perceived value of such costing.

CONTEMPORARY DEVELOPMENTS

An Ernst & Young survey in 2003 found that 76 percent of U.S. manufacturing companies reported that they used standard costs. Developments in the global business world, however, are influencing many companies to make changes. For example, in the twelfth edition of a popular German textbook, *Flexible Plankostenrechnung und Deckungsbeitragsrechnung* (Flexible plan cost accounting and contribution margin accounting), a cost system that is widely used in Germany and other European countries is outlined. It can be described as a direct or variable costing system, commonly referred as *Grenzplankostenrechnung,* or in the United States as GPK. A subsidiary of a Germany company in the United States began reporting on a GPK basis by December 31, 2004.

Developments beginning in the twenty-first century reflect the continuing need for more effective methods in cost accounting. Lean accounting, modified activity-based costing, along with GPK, were all getting considerable attention at seminars and conferences attended by practitioners in mid-2005. Considerably more careful studies are needed to determine most effective strategies for costing. There is evidence, though, to support the fundamental concept of standard costing as relevant for effective monitoring of resource usage. Yet, the scope of the fundamental concept requires reconsideration as newer strategies are proposed.

SEE ALSO *Budgets and Budgeting; Cost Allocation; Costs*

BIBLIOGRAPHY
Ernst & Young (2003). *2003 survey of management accounting.* New York: Author.

Fleischman, R., and Tyson, T. (1998, March). The evolution of standard costing in the U.K. and U.S.: From decision making to control. *Abacus,* 92–119.

Merwe, A. V. (2004). Chapter zero in perspective. *Management Accounting Quarterly,* 5(2), 1.

National Association of Accountants (now Institute of Management Accountants) (1974). *Standard Costs and Variance Analysis.* Montvale, NJ: Author.

Offenbacker, S. (2004). Zero: Introduction: Marginal costing as a management tool. *Management Accounting Quarterly,* 5(2), 7.

Smith, C. (2005, April). Going for GPK: Stihl moves toward this costing system in the United States. *Strategic Finance,* 36–39.

Bernard H. Newman
Mary Ellen Oliverio

STANDARD INDUSTRIAL CLASSIFICATION SYSTEM (SIC CODES)

SEE *North American Industry Classification System*

STANDARD METROPOLITAN STATISTICAL AREAS

Since the mid-twentieth century, a population movement from rural to urban areas has occurred. Because many urban areas cross political boundaries, the U.S. Office of Management and Budget has defined three metropolitan statistical areas. Originally, in 1949 the standard designation was the Standard Metropolitan Area; in 1959 it was changed to Standard Metropolitan Statistical Area. In 1983 the name was changed to Metropolitan Statistical Area (MSA) and represented a city of at least 50,000 people, with a surrounding rural population. In 1990 Metropolitan Area was used to refer collectively to MSAs, Primary Metropolitan Statistical Areas (PMSAs; more than a million people with strong internal economic and social links), and Consolidated Metropolitan Statistical Areas (CMSAs). If two or more PMSAs are geographically linked, they are referred to as CMSAs.

The United States has twenty CMSAs, with New York, northern New Jersey, and Long Island being the largest. Further, the term *core based statistical area* (CBSA) has referred collectively to micropolitan statistical areas and MSAs since 2000. At that time, metropolitan areas were defined so that each CBSA includes at least one 10,000-inhabitant urban area; each MSA has at least one 50,000-inhabitant urbanized area; and each micropolitan statistical area has at least one 10,000- to 50,000-inhabitant urban cluster. The U.S. Census Bureau reported that 560 micropolitan statistical areas and 362 MSAs had developed in the United States, as well as 5 micropolitan statistical areas and 8 MSAs in Puerto Rico, by June 2000. This trend toward urbanization has implications for marketing.

In highly industrialized countries, the growth of population has slowed, forcing marketers to adopt segment or target marketing. Segment marketing requires the marketer to break the total market into smaller segments by using certain variables: demographic, geographic, psychographic, and behavioristic.

Demographic variables are objective population characteristics that are easily collected and readily available in the United States. The information that interests marketing people includes: age, gender, race, income, education, occupation, and family size. Demographic variables and geographic variables (such as size, region, and climate) are also important in selecting a market segment.

A number of examples demonstrate of how marketers use some of these demographic variables. In the United States, age is an important variable for market segmentation. For example, since teenagers control a certain amount of spending, specific products are marketed directly to them. The same is true of senior citizens, who constitute a growing segment of the American population.

Gender is another demographic variable. In industrialized countries where people are living longer, women generally outnumber men. Therefore, the needs and buying habits of women must be factored into any marketing plan.

Urbanization and population mobility are two other factors that are considered in marketing plans. Because it is easier to market goods and services in highly urbanized areas, marketing plans are more effective there. Mobility provides opportunities for national advertising for regional branding. For example, some products sold in the northeastern United States have done well in south Florida because many Northeasterners have migrated to Florida.

Other variables that affect market segmentation are occupation and education. In 1960 approximately 30 percent of women were working outside the home; in the early twenty-first century that number has almost doubled—and women own more than one in four of U.S. businesses with paid employees. Marketing implications include work clothes for women, more meals eaten outside the home, and easily prepared convenience food. The list of demographic and geographic variables and their marketing implications are infinite.

Using population data, however, has limitations. They may be dated because of the time lag from collection to availability; also, census data are collected only every ten years. Some data may be too broad and, thus, hide marketing opportunities. Finally, using demographic and geographic variables, which are easily gleaned from data on MSAs, ignores two very important segmentation variables: psychographic and behavioristic variables.

SEE ALSO *Economic Analysis*

BIBLIOGRAPHY

ASDE, Inc. (n.d.). *U.S. geographic definitions.* Retrieved January 31, 2006, from http://www.surveysampler.com/Terminology.htm#21

Evans, Joel R., and Berman, Barry (2004). *Marketing* (9th ed.). Cincinnati: Atomic Dog.

Integrated Public Use Microdata Series. (n.d.). Metropolitan area. Retrieved January 31, 2006, from http://www.ipums.org/usa/hgeographic/metareaa.html

Office of Management and Budget. The Executive Office of the President. (1998, December 21). Alternative approaches to defining metropolitan and nonmetropolitan areas; notice. Retrieved January 31, 2006, from http://www.whitehouse.gov/OMB/fedreg/msa.html

Pride, William M., and Ferrell, O. C. (2004). *Marketing looseleaf* (13th ed.). Boston: Houghton Mifflin.

University of Michigan Documents Center. (2005). Statistical resources on the web: Demographics and housing. Retrieved January 31, 2006, from http://www.lib.umich.edu/govdocs/stdemog.html

U.S. Census Bureau. (2005). About metropolitan and micropolitan statistical areas. Retrieved January 31, 2006, from http://www.census.gov/population/www/estimates/aboutmetro.html

U.S. Department of Labor, Bureau of Labor Statistics. (2005). Wages by area and occupation. Retrieved January 31, 2006, from http://www.bls.gov/bls/blswage.htm

Mary Jean Lush
Val Hinton

STATE SOCIETIES OF CPAS

Independent professional societies for certified public accountants (CPAs) exist in each of the fifty U.S. states and in Washington, D.C., Puerto Rico, the Virgin Islands, and Guam. CPAs may choose to join their state's professional organization, generally known as [state's name] Society of CPAs or [state's name] Association of CPAs. Such societies provide CPAs with common interests and goals a wide range of professional activities. The societies are also avenues for members to become leaders in their profession. In the larger states, the state societies are divided into chapters by geographic location. The relationships between the state societies and the national organization, the American Institute of Certified Public Accountants (AICPA), and also between the state societies and the state and national boards of accountancy, are discussed briefly in this entry.

The societies are run by full-time and/or part-time staff as well as a board of directors, with officers elected from the membership. State societies have executive directors and finance their operations primarily through membership dues.

SERVICES

State societies sponsor education programs and provide resources for members and opportunities for them to network with other professionals. They represent the interests of the profession at the state legislative level and have an array of committees that members can join. The societies provide publications for members and nonmembers, and frequently sponsor public education sessions.

Frequently state societies offer additional benefits to their members, such as access to insurance plans for professional liability, life, and health insurance. State society members often list networking as an important reason to join; often joint meetings/functions are held with other state professionals, such as lawyers, bankers, or educators.

EDUCATION

In many states, practicing CPAs are required to complete continuing professional education (CPE) credits to maintain their license. While licensing is the responsibility of the board of accountancy, state societies often offer a variety of CPE courses. These courses are offered as seminars, online workshops, or through self-study videos and/or workbooks.

Sessions are frequently offered for the public. Topics include programs for the public, such as the Financial Literacy project, whose goal is to help educate the public on the use of information generated by accounting. Programs are designed for students in secondary schools and colleges that inform students of the career opportunities and requirements in public accounting.

ADVOCACY AND PROMULGATION OF PROFESSIONAL STANDARDS

State societies monitor developments that are of interest to their members in their respective state legislatures. Legislation affecting regulation of the profession, tax issues, and other assorted economic issues are of interest to CPAs. The response of the society may range from making members aware of proposed legislation to composing a position paper to hiring lobbyists.

COMMITTEES

Some of the state society committees are common to many states; others may be unique to a state or a region. Some committees exist to provide a forum for discussion among members with similar interests. Other committees enable members to discuss important common topics such as peer reviews, changes or proposed changes in audit standards, or recent changes in tax law. Ethics committees allow the society to provide a vehicle to hear complaints regarding allegations of ethics violations by members. Still other committees plan social events or fund-raising activities.

AICPA AND STATE SOCIETIES

The AICPA is a national professional society founded in 1887. The majority of AICPA members (350,000 in 2005) are licensed CPAs, with some limited specialty categories for non-CPAs. The AICPA and the state societies are unaffiliated. CPAs can join the AICPA and/or their state society. Many members of state societies join the AICPA and some serve on committees at the national level and participate in activities sponsored by the AICPA.

The AICPA provides resources for CPAs and assists state societies with problems or initiatives. The AICPA has responsibility for producing and grading the computer-based Uniform CPA Examination, while the state's board of accountancy is responsible for the distribution of examinations to those who registered in their respective states. The AICPA serves as an advocate for the profession at the national level. Laws that affect CPAs are monitored by the AICPA as well as representatives from the states. The AICPA publishes the monthly *Journal of Accountancy,* and maintains a large professional library. Several state societies also publish their own journals.

The AICPA maintains a code of professional conduct for members' ethical standards. Most state societies also implement this same code through the Joint Ethics Enforcement Program. Members who fail to abide by the code may have their membership terminated and their name published. A member's license, however, can be revoked only by a state board of accountancy.

PUBLIC COMPANY ACCOUNTING OVERSIGHT BOARD

In 2002 the Public Company Accounting Oversight Board (PCAOB) was established to oversee auditors of public companies as a result of the Sarbanes-Oxley Act of 2002. Both the AICPA and state societies make information regarding the PCAOB available to their members.

BOARDS OF ACCOUNTANCY

Each state has a board of accountancy responsible for administering the Uniform CPA Examination, licensing CPAs, and regulating the practice of public accountancy, generally through legislation. State regulations include requirements for the CPA certificate and/or license and rules governing CPE credits. State boards of accountancy are regulatory agencies with no direct ties to the AICPA or the state societies, although they frequently cooperate on projects that benefit the profession.

The National Association of State Boards of Accountancy exists to enhance the effectiveness of the state boards of accountancy. It serves as a forum for the nation's state boards of accountancy and includes a member from each state's board of accountancy.

Although the state's board of accountancy is independent from the state's society and the AICPA, they often form joint task forces. Some examples of cooperation include peer review and attempts to unify the requirements among the states for becoming a CPA. Peer review is a method for relicensing mandated by a state's board of accountancy. These programs are often monitored by the state society, an arrangement generally accepted by the state board of accountancy.

CONCLUSION

The state societies and the AICPA are professional organizations that CPAs may join. The state boards of accountancy are regulatory agencies. The organizations are independent, with each having a different function.

WEB SITES OF INTEREST

American Institute of Certified Public Accountants: http://www.aicpa.org

Public Company Accounting Oversight Board: http://www.pcaob.org

National Association of State Boards of Accountancy: http://www.nasba.org

SEE ALSO *American Institute of Certified Public Accountants; National Association of State Boards of Accountancy; Public Company Accounting Oversight Board; Uniform Certified Public Accountant Examination*

Kathleen Simons

STATEMENTS ON MANAGEMENT ACCOUNTING

Statements on Management Accounting (SMAs) are produced, issued, and implemented to reflect official positions of the Institute of Management Accountants (IMA), the largest and most prominent management accounting organization in the world. The IMA is an organization of accounting professionals that had a membership of approximately 70,000 members in 2005.

HISTORY

One of the chief activities of the IMA is to conduct and sponsor research in management accounting. In 1969 the IMA (which at the time was called the National Association of Accountants) created the Management Accounting Practices (MAP) Committee to serve as its senior technical committee. This committee was charged with the task of promulgating statements on management accounting that reflect the views of the IMA. The MAP Committee membership included twelve representatives—from corporate and public accounting as well as education—appointed by the IMA president. These representatives were widely considered expert authorities in accounting. Past members have included members of other prominent accounting regulatory groups such as the Financial Accounting Standards Board (FASB).

The IMA has merged the MAP Committee with the Foundation for Applied Research (FAR) creating the MAC/FAR Committee. Currently, SMAs are maintained by this MAC/FAR group. This board is comprised of trustees and operates similarly to the MAP Committee in supporting SMA maintenance and other research initiatives.

PURPOSE

The purpose of the MAC/FAR Committee in issuing SMAs is generally twofold: (1) to express the official position of the IMA on accounting and business reporting issues raised by other standard-setting groups, and (2) to provide broad guidance to IMA members and to the wider business community on management accounting concepts, policies, and practices. Regarding the first stated purpose, other standard-setting groups include those such as the FASB, the Governmental Accounting Standards Board, the International Accounting Standards Committee, and government agencies such as the Securities and Exchange Commission. Regarding the second purpose, the work of the MAC/FAR trustees is seen as an effective method of summarizing the wide range of activities that define management accounting.

Some accountants believe that SMAs should be accorded the same considerable authority as generally accepted accounting principles. As of 2005, such authority had not been granted. There is some support for this position. The Auditing Standards Board of the American Institute of Certified Public Accountants (AICPA) in the Statement of Accounting Standards (SAS) No. 5 (later revised as SAS No. 69 in 2005, with amendments in SAS No. 93) stated that principles that are "pronouncements of bodies composed of expert accountants," and are issued only after "a due process procedure, including broad distribution," are authoritative and are to be applied where relevant (American Institute of Certified Public Accountants, 2005, p. 716).

The usefulness of authoritative statements to guide management accounting practice is apparent given the diversity of industries and accounting practices within industries. In addition, the business environment is becoming increasingly complex as technological advances make practices of the past obsolete. The role of external business reporting has expanded. In 1994 the AICPA's Special Committee on Financial Reporting (sometimes referred to as the Jenkins Committee) recommended significant changes in the current financial reporting model to include expanded coverage of both nonfinancial or operating data and more forward-looking or future-oriented data. As of mid-2005, these types of changes were still being recommended, but implementation problems had not been resolved. Problems primarily stem from the reluctance of corporate organizations to reveal what they regard to be proprietary data in the areas of nonfinancial and forward-looking information.

The recommendations of the AICPA Special Committee reflect the needs and desires of investors and other business report users to have increasing amounts of information and information of a nontraditional nature. Obtaining nonfinancial and predictive data requires access to previously nondisclosed or proprietary items traditionally used by management accountants within their companies. Thus the IMA, through their SMA promulgation mechanism, may be in a good position to produce suggestions in these areas of recommended increased disclosure.

While investors and others strive to obtain increased amounts and different types of business information, companies with reporting responsibility are concerned with safeguarding information for which disclosure may affect their competitive position. Recommendations are needed for the control of what information should be released in many cases. This issue is one that will likely be addressed by a convergence of several professional accounting groups. If accounting organizations though SMA promulgation or other means are unable to achieve a satisfactory resolution on demands for increased disclosure, the judicial system may ultimately have to establish these boundaries.

PROCESS

In promulgating statements, the MAP committee historically used a Subcommittee on SMA Promulgation. Generally, each subcommittee member oversaw the process of promulgating a particular SMA. After a proposed statement was drafted, there followed a rigorous exposure process whereby input was solicited from other members of the accounting profession through the selection of two advisory panels.

One panel was composed of a sample of IMA chapter presidents or other individual chapter representatives. (In 2005 the IMA had 250 local chapters organized geographically in cities across the United States and 9 chapters in other countries.) The other panel was composed of representatives nominated from other accounting or accounting-related organizations, including the AICPA, the Financial Executives International, the American Accounting Association, and the Society of Management Accountants of Canada. Although no new SMAs had been produced since the combination into the MAC/FAR group, the MAC/FAR Committee was reviewing the existing SMAs and discussing the prioritization of revisions based on a planned practice analysis that was to be completed in late 2005.

Historically, once the two advisory panels' comments were reviewed by the subcommittee and appropriate modifications to a draft made, a proposed SMA was submitted to the MAP Committee for approval. The committee would then take one of three possible actions: (1) approve the draft as recommended, (2) further modify and then approve the draft, or (3) return the draft to the subcommittee to be developed further. Historically, SMAs were published only after completion of this review process and final approval requiring a two-thirds majority vote by the MAP Committee.

CONTENT

The SMA subcommittee was guided by a framework for management accounting that considered five broad categories: (1) objectives, (2) terminology, (3) concepts, (4) practices and techniques, and (5) management of accounting activities. All SMAs are classified and numbered based on this five-element framework. For example, SMA No. 1A is included in the objectives classification. Dates of publication are indicated parenthetically after each title.

In addition to following the five-element framework, the IMA's approach to the content of future SMAs, as with past statements, is clearly based on, and fully consistent with, the MAP Committee's definition of management accounting as follows:

> Management accounting is the process of identification, measurement, accumulation, analysis, preparation, interpretation, and communication of financial information used by management to plan, evaluate, and control within an organization and to assure appropriate use of and accountability for its resources. Management accounting also comprises the preparation of financial reports for non-management groups such as shareholders, creditors, regulatory agencies, and tax authorities. (Management Accounting Practices Committee, 1981)

The majority of issued SMAs are written for use by accounting practitioners. This perspective is consistent with the fact that the greatest number of statements issued to date have been in the Practices and Techniques category. This is also consistent with the stated purpose of an SMA, which is to supply an in-depth understanding of a management accounting subject that would allow a practitioner to implement the concepts and techniques. Often the application of information included in an SMA is illustrated by studies of companies who have implemented the techniques.

The content of issued SMAs ranges from fundamental issues, such as SMA No. 1A, "Definition of Management Accounting," to restructuring the finance function. A review of titles of the statements reveals the range. Note that statements numbered 1A through 2A deal with fundamental aspects of the field of management accounting that guide the IMA. There are many that provide guidance for handling typical responsibilities of staff under the direction of the controller. A number of statements deal with emerging innovations such as benchmarking, activity-based costing, performance indicators, value-chain analysis, electronic commerce, and lean production. There are no statements related to the third category, Concepts. Since the IMA has not yet developed a conceptual framework for management accounting, this lack of statements related to the term *concepts* is not surprising.

The following list comprises all SMAs issued to date. Statements are revised from time to time. Furthermore, changes in business management and developments in technology affect management accounting in such ways that new statements are required to ensure sufficient guidance for practitioners. Many of these statements can be downloaded without fee by IMA members at the IMA Web site (http://www.imanet.org).

1A "Definition of Management Accounting" (1981). First in the series, SMA 1A sets forth the Framework for Management Accounting and the definition of management accounting that delineates the field.

1B "Objectives of Management Accounting" (1982)

1C "Standards of Ethical Conduct for Practitioners of Management Accounting and Financial Management" (1997). (Originally issued in 1983; revised in 1997, but number of original retained.)

1D "The Common Body of Knowledge of Management Accountants" (1986)

1E "Education for Careers in Management Accounting" (1987)

2A "Management Accounting Glossary" (1990)

4A "Cost of Capital" (1984)

4B "Allocation of Service and Administrative Costs" (1985)

4C "Definition and Measurement of Direct Labor Cost" (1985)

4D "Measuring Entity Performance" (1986)

4E "Definition and Measurement of Direct Material Cost" (1986)

4F "Allocation of Information Systems Costs" (1986)

4G "Accounting for Indirect Production Costs" (1987)

4H "Uses of the Cost of Capital" (1988)

4I "Cost Management for Freight Transportation" (1989)

4J "Accounting for Property, Plant, and Equipment" (1989)

4K "Cost Management for Warehousing" (1989)

4L "Control of Property, Plant, and Equipment" (1990)

4M "Understanding Financial Instruments" (1990)

4N "Management of Working Capital: Cash Resources" (1990)

4-O "The Accounting Classification of Real Estate Occupancy Costs" (1991)

4P "Cost Management for Logistics" (1992)

4Q "Use and Control of Financial Instruments by Multinational Companies" (1992)

4R "Managing Quality Improvements" (1993)

4S "Internal Accounting and Classification of Risk Management Costs" (1993)

4T "Implementing Activity-Based Costing" (1993)

4U "Developing Comprehensive Performance Indicators" (1995)

4V "Effective Benchmarking" (1995)

4W "Implementing Corporate Environmental Strategies" (1995)

4X "Value Chain Analysis for Assessing Competitive Advantage" (1996)

4Y "Measuring the Cost of Capacity" (1996)

4Z "Tools and Techniques of Environmental Accounting for Business Decisions" (1996)

4AA "Measuring and Managing Shareholder Value Creation" (1997)

4BB "The Accounting Classification of Workpoint Costs" (1997)

4CC "Implementing Activity-Based Management: Avoiding the Pitfalls" (1998)

4DD "Tools and Techniques for Implementing Integrated Performance Management Systems" (1998)

4EE "Tools and Techniques for Implementing ABC/ABM" (1998)

4FF "Implementing Target Costing" (1999)

4GG "Tools and Techniques for Implementing Target Costing" (1998)

4HH "Theory of Constraints (TOC) Management System Fundamentals" (1999)

4II "Implementing Integrated Supply Chain Management for Competitive Advantage" (1999)

4JJ "Tools and Techniques for Implementing Integrated Supply Chain Management" (1999)

4KK "Implementing Lean Production Fundamentals" (2000)

4LL "Implementing Capacity Cost Management Systems" (2000)

4MM "Designing an Integrated Cost Management System for Driving Profit and Organizational Performance" (2000)

4NN "Implementing Process Management for Improving Products and Services" (2000)

4-OO "Understanding and Implementing Internet E-Commerce" (2000)

4PP "Implementing Automated Workflow Management" (2000)

5A "Evaluating Controllership Effectiveness" (1990)

5B "Fundamentals of Reporting Information to Managers" (1992)

5C "Managing Cross-Functional Teams" (1994)

5D "Developing Comprehensive Competitive Intelligence" (1996)

5E "Redesigning the Finance Function" (1997)

5F "Tools and Techniques for Redesigning the Finance Function" (1999)

5G "Implementing Shared Service Centers" (2000)

Those charged with the responsibility of developing new statements monitor developments in the field, including the IMA's initiatives in providing a conceptual framework for management accounting, as well as in business generally. Such monitoring assures the practitioners that timely guidance will be available. The results of the monitoring will lead to changes and extension of guidance.

SEE ALSO *Accounting; Institute of Management Accountants*

BIBLIOGRAPHY

Aldridge, C., and Colbert, J. (1997, July). We need better financial reporting. *Management Accounting*, pp. 32–36.

American Institute of Certified Public Accountants. (2005). Statement on auditing standards No. 69. *AICPA Professional Standards*. Vol. 1. New York: Author.

Institute of Management Accountants. (1991, June). [Editorial]. *Management Accounting*, p. 1.

Management Accounting Practices Committee. (1981). Definition of management accounting. *Management Accounting Statements*. Montvale, NJ: Institute of Management Accountants.

Schiff, Jonathan B., and Penino, Charles J. (1990, Winter). The emerging authority of statements on management accounting. *The Journal of Applied Business Research*, pp. 87–91.

Vangermeersch, Richard, and Jordan, Robert (1996). In M. Chatfield and Richard Vangermeersch (Eds.), *The history of accounting*. New York: Garland.

B. Douglas Clinton

STOCK EXCHANGES

A stock exchange is a forum provided by any organization, association, or group of persons for trading in securities representing shares of firms. By providing a trading system, a stock exchange performs two essential services. First, it provides a market for the buying and selling of stock. Second, it provides a way of monitoring the value of a stock investment portfolio.

The statutory definition of *exchange* as specified by the U.S. Securities and Exchange Commission (SEC) is a "market place or facilities for bringing together purchasers and sellers of securities or for otherwise performing with respect to securities the functions commonly performed by a stock exchange." The SEC carefully revised Rule 3b-16 to define these terms to mean any organization, association, or group of persons that: (1) brings together the orders of multiple buyers and sellers; and (2) uses established, nondiscretionary methods (whether by providing a trading facility or by setting rules) under which such orders interact with each other, and the buyers and sellers entering such orders agree to the terms of a trade.

A particular trading system may not be recognized as an exchange, depending on the securities laws of the country. Given that differences across countries may exist with respect to legal definitions, a more detailed discussion of what constitutes a trading system is appropriate.

TRADING SYSTEMS

Trading markets may be defined as systems consisting of an order-routing system, an information network, and a trade-execution mechanism. A trading system is a communications technology for passing allowable messages between traders, together with a set of rules that transform traders' messages into transaction prices and allocations of quantities of stock among market participants.

Floor of the New York Stock Exchange, October 19, 1987. **AP IMAGES**

In the United States, the Securities Exchange Act of 1934, the primary legislation covering the securities markets, undertook to update the regulatory requirements for the buying and selling of securities. After the exposure of a concept release in May 1997 to gather ideas from interested parties, final rules effective as of April 1, 2000, were adopted. The regulations for alternative trading systems were promulgated to strengthen the public markets for securities, while encouraging innovative new markets. These new regulations more effectively integrated the growing number of alternative trading systems into the national market system, accommodated the registration of proprietary alternative trading systems as exchanges, and provided an opportunity for registered exchanges to better compete with alternative trading systems.

Exchanges may offer more than one trading system. Types of trading systems are sometimes differentiated by the form of market intermediation provided by entities with direct access to the system. The nature of competition between exchanges is a defining feature, since exchanges may adopt varying market structures in order to compete in different fashions. A stock exchange is a business entity, and the form of its governance arrangements is important in understanding its nature and conduct.

The nature of allowable messages varies with the trading system's (exchange's) rules and technology. A typical message consists of an offer to buy, or to sell, a given number of shares at a certain price. The New York Stock Exchange (NYSE), for example, permits such messages, as well as orders, to buy some amount of stock at current market prices.

The transformation of messages and information from the system into a price and a set of quantity allocations is governed by another set of rules. In open outcry auctions, bids and offers are orally exchanged by traders standing in a single physical location. The acceptance of a bid or offer by another trader generates a transaction. In dealer systems, such as NASDAQ, dealers accept orders by telephone or computerized routing, and transact at prices they themselves set. In batch auctions, such as that of the Arizona Stock Exchange, price is set by maximizing trading volume, given order submission at the time of the auction. In most computerized markets, traders submit orders to a central limit order book, and a mathematical algorithm determines prices and quantities. Examples include the CAC system of the Paris Bourse and the OM system of the Stockholm Stock Exchange.

MARKET INTERMEDIATION

Investors are generally not given free access to trading systems. Entry into the exchange's systems is intermediated by brokers. Brokers may simply route orders to exchanges. They sometimes make decisions as to what exchange, and what system within the exchange, should process various parts of an order. In open outcry markets, brokers also physically represent orders on the floor of the exchange.

Another class of intermediaries is known as market makers. Market makers trade for their own accounts, usually providing an offer to sell and an offer to buy at the same time, but at different prices. In doing so, they both contribute to the pricing process and supply immediacy to the market by a willingness to be a counterparty to an order for which another investor may not be immediately available.

On some exchanges, most notably the NYSE, there is one primary market maker designated by the exchange, known as the specialist. The specialist obtains consideration for the supply of immediacy and the maintenance of an orderly market by having private access to order-flow information through the order book for the stock.

There may be multiple market makers in a given stock, regardless of the precise form of trading system. The prototype example is that of dealer markets, in which the dealers are the market makers. They post bids and offers, and trade out of their own inventory.

Electronic-limit order-book markets offer the possibility of trading without such financial intermediation. In practice, however, market makers exist on electronic markets as well. Multiple market makers in a security are often designated by an exchange, fulfill obligations not dissimilar to those of a specialist, and receive some consideration for the service. Anyone with direct access to the trading system can function as a market maker, however, simply by continuously offering quotes for stock on both sides of the market.

COMPETITION

Exchanges have two clienteles: companies, which list their shares, and investors, who trade on the exchange. Historically, the product (a listing service) offered to companies was a bundle, consisting of (1) liquidity, (2) monitoring of trading against forms of fraud, (3) standard-form rules of trading, (4) a signal that a listing firm's stock is of high quality, and (5) a clearing function to ensure timely payment and delivery of shares. The product offered to investors consists of a combination of liquidity and pricing information, as well as any benefits accruing to the investor from the bundle offered to companies.

Government regulation and increased competition from automated-trading systems lessen the importance of exchange monitoring and standardized rules. Technological advances in information processing allow better signals about company quality than simple listings, permit wide distribution of pricing information outside exchanges, and enable separation of the clearing function from other exchange operations. The result is that exchanges now compete solely along the dimensions of liquidity and cost of trading.

Competition through liquidity and cost has led to increased automation of the exchange trade-execution process. Automated exchanges are less costly to build and operate, and provide lower-cost trade execution. Liquidity is enhanced by the ability to establish wide networks of traders through communications systems with an automated-execution system at the nexus. The drive for increased liquidity through computerization has led to new developments in the structure of the exchange services industry, most notably including mergers and alliances between automated exchanges for increased order flow.

Communications technology and the computerization of trade execution have also globalized trading. The physical location and boundaries of an exchange floor are no longer important to traders. A company does not need to be listed, or even traded, on a domestic exchange. Not only are there many possible execution services providers, but electronic exchanges place their own terminals on foreign soil, allowing direct access to overseas listings, regardless of the nationality of the companies involved.

GOVERNANCE

The organizational structures commonly found for exchanges are: nonprofit, the consumer cooperative, and for-profit. Historically, most exchanges have been nonprofit organizations, but since the 1990s, there have been trends toward incorporating an exchange as a for-profit organization. Ten such demutualizations globally are listed in Ian Domowitz and Benn Stell's article, "Automation, Trading Costs, and the Structure of the Securities Trading Industry" (1999), and such initiatives are under investigation by many traditional exchanges, including NASDAQ and the NYSE. The NYSE approved its intention of becoming a publicly traded entity after its merger with the Archipelago exchange as of early 2006. (The merger was approved in December 2005.) Archipelago is an electronic trading platform that owns the Pacific Stock

Exchange. Shares of the merged company, to be known as NYSE Group Inc., will trade on the exchange's board under the NYX symbol. There is uncertainty about what changes will be made in the traditional process of buying and selling securities at the NYSE as a result of the merger.

Increased competition between exchanges forces the change in ownership structure. This is the view of the exchange services industry, as well. The industry argument is simply that a corporate structure with a profit motive enables faster initiatives in response to competitive advances than a committee- and voting-oriented membership organization. Efforts for mergers and acquisitions among several stock exchanges throughout the globe were in process as of the end of 2005.

Changes in the contractual relationship between exchanges and listing companies might outweigh competition as a force behind the shift from cooperative to corporate ownership arrangements. The long-term mutual dependency between companies and exchanges no longer exists, and market makers do not make firm-specific investments that might be fostered under a cooperative umbrella.

The third view is that communications and computerized execution technology permit and encourage the change in governance structure. Traditional exchanges are limited by floor space, and access is rationed through the sale of limited memberships. In an automated auction, there are no barriers to providing unlimited direct access with a transactions-fee pricing structure, which in turn lends itself to corporate for-profit operations. All examples of the change in governance begin with a conversion from floor-trading technology to automated-trade execution. For trade-execution services with no prior history of cooperative governance structure, the mutual structure is routinely avoided in favor of a for-profit joint-stock corporation.

One important aspect of the exchange's governance in the United States is the concept of self-regulation, a concept that highlights the American approach to the regulation of securities and futures markets. As a self-regulating organization it is subject to constraints with regard to its governance structure. The Securities Exchange Act imposes four major obligations on exchanges: a fair representation of its members in the selection of directors; one or more directors representing issuers and investors who are not associated with members of the exchange; subject to some exception, only brokers and dealers may become members; and its rules are designed to protect investors and the public interest.

SEE ALSO *Stock Indexes; Stocks*

BIBLIOGRAPHY

Dalton, John (Ed.). (2001). *How the stock exchange works.* Paramus, NJ: New York Institute of Finance.

Domowitz, Ian, and Stell, Benn (1999). Automation, trading costs, and the structure of the securities trading industry. In Robert E. Litan and Anthony M. Santomero (Eds.), *Brookings-Wharton Papers on financial services.* Washington, DC: Brookings Institution.

Hart, Oliver, and Moore, John (1996). The governance of exchanges: Members' cooperatives versus outside ownership. *Oxford Review of Economic Policy 12*, 53–69.

Lee, Ruben (1998). *What is an exchange?: The automation, management, and regulation of financial markets.* New York: Oxford University Press.

Macey, Jonathan R., and O'Hara, Maureen (1999). Globalization, exchange governance, and the future of exchanges. In Robert E. Litan and Anthony M. Santomero (Eds.), *Brookings-Wharton Papers on Financial Services.* Washington, DC: Brookings Institution.

Securities and Exchange Commission. (1998, December 8). Final rules: Regulation of exchanges and alternative trading systems (Release No. 34-40760, File No. S7-12-98). Retrieved March 3, 2006, from http://pages.stern.nyu.edu/~jhasbrou/Teaching/SEC/ATS/Reg%20ATS%20Summary.pdf

Stoll, Hans (1992). Principles of trading market structure. *Journal of Financial Services Research, 6*, 75–107.

Wyss, B. O'Neill (2001). *Fundamentals of the stock market.* New York: McGraw-Hill.

Anand Shetty
Ian Domowitz

STOCK INDEXES

An understanding of the basic characteristics of the different kinds of stocks will be helpful in considering the information in this article. An investor's most important tool is information: information about stock prices, movement in the market, and business trends. Without sound information, investment decisions are pure guesswork. The first place to look for information about any stock is the financial pages of a newspaper, and the best place to start is with the columns listing the current stock prices on one or more of the major organized exchanges. Figure 1 shows a typical listing for a stock traded on one of the major exchanges. The following list explains the information and what it means for prospective investors:

SAMPLE STOCK LISTING

1. *High* and *low.* These are the highest and lowest prices paid for the stock during the previous fifty-two weeks. This item shows that the highest price

paid for this stock during the previous period was $44 per share; the lowest price, $16 per share.

2. *Stock.* Stocks are listed alphabetically by an abbreviated form of the corporate name, in this sample, JLJ.

3. *Dividend (Div).* The rate of annual dividend is shown; it is generally an estimate based on the previous quarterly or semiannual payment. This item shows that JLJ is paying an annual dividend of $2.50 per share, or about 7 percent yield.

4. *Price/Earnings (P/E) ratio.* This is the ratio of the market price of the stock to the annual earnings of the company per share of stock. It is an important indicator of corporate success and investor confidence and cannot be calculated from the information given here as other data are needed to do so.

5. *Shares traded.* This is the number of shares sold for the day, expressed in hundreds. In the example shown, 3,300 shares of JLJ stock were traded. The figure does not include odd-lot sales. Note: If the number in this column is preceded by a "z," it signifies the actual number of shares traded, not hundreds.

6. *High* and *low.* These are the highest and lowest prices paid for JLJ stock during the trading session (that is, the business day). The highest price paid for JLJ stock was $35.25 per share; the lowest price, $34 per share.

7. *Closing price (Last).* The final price of JLJ stock for the day. In this case, it was $35 per share.

8. *Change.* The difference between the closing price of the stock for this session and the closing price for the previous close; yesterday's closing price would have been $34.50 ($35.00 minus $0.50).

Understanding the details of a particular stock is basic to finding value in a stock market index which reflects a critical characteristic—statistically determined—about a group of stocks. What follows is a general introduction to such indexes.

USEFULNESS OF STOCK MARKET INDEXES

The expectations of future growth and profit are captured through computations that are called market indexes. Such indexes provide, in essence, summaries of expectations. There are indexes that cut across industries; there are indexes that deal with one industry only. Indexes include varying numbers of stocks. Additionally, indexes are based on a variety of assumptions about the factors that influence expectations. Factors that might be used in several indexes may be given different weights in each index. Many market indexes will, at times, provide the same, or similar, assessments. Nevertheless, there is considerable difference in the performance of indexes in the long run. The stocks, divisors, and weighting selected for an index lead to long-run difference.

SOME POPULAR STOCK MARKET INDEXES

There are thousands of stock market indexes. Much information is available through accessing Web sites of exchanges and other organizations, such as Dow Jones and Russell Group, that have developed indexes. Details of the assumptions and stocks included are readily provided in materials accessible at Web sites. Some stock exchanges provide custom-designed stock market indexes. There are such indexes in many countries. Some of the most popular U.S. indexes in (alphabetical order) are:

- American Stock Exchange (AMEX) composite index
- Dow Jones Industrial Average (DJIA) index
- NASDAQ composite index
- NASDAQ 100 index
- New York Stock Exchange (NYSE) composite index
- Russell 3000 value index
- Standard & Poor's (S&P) 500 index

Three of the most widely quoted stock market indexes and the types of stocks they include are briefly discussed here.

Sample stock listing

High (1)	Low (1)	Stock (2)	Div (3)	P/E (4)	100S (5)	High (6)	Low (6)	Last (7)	Change (8)
44	16	JLJ	2.50	9	33	35.25	34	35	.50

Figure 1

Stocks that make up the Dow Jones Industrial Average as of 2005

3M	(MMM)	Exxon	(XON)	McDonald's	(MCD)
Alcoa	(AA)	General Electric	(GE)	Merck	(MRK)
Altria Group	(MO)	General Motors	(GM)	Microsoft	(MSFT)
American Express	(AXP)	Hewlett-Packard	(HWP)	Pfizer	(PFE)
American Int. Group	(AIG)	Home Depot	(HD)	Proctor & Gamble	(PG)
Boeing	(BA)	Honeywell Int.	(HON)	SBC Communications	(SBC)
Caterpillar	(CAT)	Intel	(INTC)	United Technologies	(UTX)
Citigroup	(C)	International Business Machines	(IBM)	Verizon Communications	(VZ)
Coca-Cola	(KO)	Johnson & Johnson	(JNJ)	Wal-Mart	(WMT)
Du Pont	(DD)	JP Morgan Chase	(JPM)	Walt Disney	(DIS)

Figure 2

THE DOW JONES INDUSTRIAL AVERAGE

Charles H. Dow (1851–1902) introduced the Dow Jones Industrial Average (DJIA) in 1896 when the market was not considered a respectable venture because of unscrupulous dealers, massive speculation, and the lack of information. His average brought about change at a time when people found it quite difficult to understand the ups and downs of fractionalized points. It is called an average because it originally was computed by taking the stock prices, adding them together, and dividing them by the number of stocks. The first figure came out on May 26, 1896, with an average of 40.94. Dow defended his average by comparing it to the placement of sticks in the sand on the beach. His concept was to determine, after each wave, whether the tide was coming in or receding. If the average of his stocks increased progressively, then he was able to call the period a "bull market." If the average dropped lower, then a "bear market" had taken hold.

The DJIA provides a comparison of industrial stocks to the direction of the average. In attempts to gauge or predict large-scale trends in stock market values, the DJIA is most often cited. The term *industrial* is a bit misleading. In the late nineteenth century, railroads and steel companies were the important corporations. In the twenty-first century, they do not represent any great hold on the DJIA.

The DJIA is the most frequently mentioned of four Dow Jones averages (covering industrial stocks, transportation stocks, utility stocks, and a composite average); it is a barometer of stock market trends based on the stock prices of thirty large U.S. corporations listed on the NYSE. Every day, the fluctuations in the prices of these stocks are combined by adding up the prices of the thirty stocks and dividing the result by the designated factor used to compensate for complicating situations, such as stock splits, spin-offs, and periodic substitutions in the list of stocks used.

The current divisor is published every business day. Over the history of the average, the divisor has been changed many times, mostly downward. This explains why the average can be reported as, for example, 10,000, although no single stock in the average approaches that price level. In 2006, a $1 rise in the price of a component stock would raise the DJIA roughly five points, assuming prices of the other twenty-nine stocks were unchanged. The thirty stocks and their symbols that made up the DJIA during 2005 are shown in Figure 2.

THE STANDARD & POOR'S 500

The Standard & Poor's (S&P) 500 index was created (in its present mode) in 1958 in order to make indexes more popular with the investing public. Rather than keeping its previous index, made up of ninety stocks, it moved to a much broader scale of 500 stocks, making it the S&P 500. In its continuous review, the selection committee replaces about thirty companies annually. The reason for a company's elimination might be its own downsizing (so it can no longer be considered a large-cap [capitalization] stock) or its acquisition by or merger with a different type of company not represented in the S&P.

The reported number (factor) that one sees in the daily paper or hears about on the financial news report, along with the Dow and the NASDAQ, is determined by the price of the 500 stocks in the S&P index. It is also important to mention that the S&P is market-weighted. This is done so that no single company, or small group of companies, will dominate the index or influence its calculations. Market weighting is determined by taking the number of shares of the outstanding stock of a company and multiplying it by its price. This creates a market situation in which no one company's performance can drastically change the overall performance of this index. The DJIA is not calculated in this manner, creating the possibility that the performance of a single stock in the Dow could change the value of the entire index on any given day.

Also, consider the number of businesses involved in the S&P index. With 500 stocks market-weighted, this index becomes a good indicator of market movements because it mirrors the combined knowledge of thousands of analysts and investors who, through their sales and purchases of stocks, determine the market value of the shares of stocks in the index.

THE NASDAQ COMPOSITE

The NASDAQ (originally known as the National Association of Securities Dealers Automated Quotations) was created in 1971 to compete with the S&P 500 and to measure the entire range of the market. With a great proportion of its companies in the high-tech field, however, the NASDAQ is much more volatile than the stock market in general and the Dow and the S&P in particular. The NASDAQ is not involved only in high-tech stocks; the index, however, comprises eight industry subindexes: banking, biotechnology, computers, finance, industrials, insurance, telecommunications, and transportation.

The NASDAQ has been called the "index of the new economy," as compared to the "old economy" of the Dow. This composite index includes 5,500 companies and, like the S&P, is market-weighted, thus providing more meaningful numbers. The index's composite figure is computed by measuring the market value of all common stocks listed on the NASDAQ. Any change in any security in any direction will cause the index to change in that direction, but only in proportion to its market value (the last transaction price multiplied by the total shares outstanding). In 1985 NASDAQ introduced the NASDAQ-100 index, which is made up of the largest and most active nonfinancial domestic and international issues on the NASDAQ stock market based on market capitalization.

It is true that there is no way to tell where the market will be a year or two from now, but by keeping informed and using indexes as a guide, investors stand a better chance in the roller-coaster market that has been experienced.

SEE ALSO *Investments; Stocks*

BIBLIOGRAPHY
Davis, Ned (2005). *Markets in motion.* New York: Wiley.

Ingebretsen, Mark (2002). *NASDAQ: A history of the market that changed the world.* New York: Crown.

Little, Jeffrey B., and Rhodes, Lucien (2004). *Understanding Wall Street* (4th ed.). New York: McGraw-Hill.

Weiner, Eric J. (2005). *What goes up: The uncensored history of modern Wall Street as told by the bankers, brokers, CEOs, and scoundrels who made it happen.* New York: Little, Brown.

Joel Lerner

STOCKS

There is no doubt that investing in the stock market can be one of the most exciting ways of making money. It is rewarding to see the little-known stock one chose become a hot property, perhaps doubling in price—and then doubling again and again. But as with any investment, the potential risks are equal to the rewards, so investors who want to participate in the stock market owe it to themselves to become fully informed before getting involved.

HOW DOES THE STOCK MARKET WORK?

A share of stock represents a unit of ownership in a corporation. When one buys stock, one is becoming a part owner of the business. Therefore, one benefits from any increase in the value of the corporation and one suffers when the corporation performs badly. One is also entitled to share in the profits earned by the corporation.

Stocks are bought and sold in marketplaces known as stock exchanges. The exchange itself does not buy or sell stock, nor does it set the price of stock; the exchange is simply a forum in which individuals and institutions may trade in stocks. Stock exchanges play a vital role in a capitalist economy. They provide a way for individuals to purchase shares in thousands of businesses, and they provide businesses with an important source of capital for expansion, research, and other purposes.

HOW ARE STOCKS TRADED?

Here, in two steps, is what happens when an investor decides to buy or sell a particular stock.

Step 1. An account executive at the brokerage house receives the buy or sell order, which may take any of several forms:

- *Round-lot order:* An order to buy or sell 100 shares, considered the standard trading unit

- *Odd-lot order:* An order to buy or sell fewer than 100 shares

- *Market order:* An order to buy or sell at the best available price

Japan's electronic stock board. AP IMAGES

- *Limit order:* An order to buy or sell at a specified price

- *Stop order:* An order designated to protect profits or limit losses by calling for sale of the stock should its price fall to a specified level

- *Good till canceled (GTC) order:* An order that remains open until it is executed or canceled by the investor

Step 2. After the order is received, it is sent to the floor of the stock exchange. The brokerage firm's floor broker receives the order and executes it at the appropriate trading post. Confirmation of the transaction is reported back to the account executive at the local office, who notifies the investor. Remarkably, the entire process may take as little as two or three minutes.

Not all stocks are traded on any of the fourteen organized exchanges. Those that are not are traded "over the counter" in the so-called unorganized exchange. Not a physical place, the unorganized exchange consists of thousands of brokers and dealers who trade in about 50,000 different unlisted stocks through telephone, facsimile, or electronic communication.

In the over-the-counter market, transactions are negotiated privately rather than on an auction basis. An investor wishing to purchase a particular unlisted security consults a broker, who contacts other brokers dealing in that stock. The broker offering the stock for sale at the lowest price receives the offer.

Prices of over-the-counter stocks are quoted as both bid and asked prices. The bid price is the final price offered by a buyer, while the asked price is the final price requested by a seller. Trades are normally made when the bid and asked prices approach one another. Note the listing in Figure 1.

Increasingly, investors are buying and selling stocks online. There are many firms specializing in providing online services.

WHAT KINDS OF STOCKS ARE AVAILABLE?

The two basic kinds of stocks are common and preferred.

Common Stock. Each year, hundreds of new issues of stock, known as initial public offerings (IPOs), are sold to the public. In an initial offering of common stock, an underwriter is the seller. The underwriter sells the initial issue of stock at a fixed price to a group of initial buyers

Sample OTC stock listing

Stock	Bid	Asked	Bid change
HALMAZ	7	8	+2

Stock: The abbreviated name of the issuing company.

Bid: This is the price at which dealers are willing to buy the stock – in this case, $7.00 per share.

Asked: This is the price at which dealers are willing to sell the stock. It is always higher than the bid price, in this case, $8.00 per share.

Bid Change: This is the difference between the bid price today and the bid price at the close of the previous day. Since today's bid price is up two from the previous day's close, the bid price yesterday was $5.00 per share.

Figure 1

who in turn "farm out" the investment until it reaches the "street," which is the investor. IPOs are appealing to some investors. Some IPOs offer "immediate profit opportunity," although determining when this will happen is not easily predicted, since for some IPOs, there is a quick realization—after the initial sale—that the issue was "overpriced."

A share of common stock represents a unit of ownership, or equity, in the issuing corporation. Each share of common stock usually has a par value, which is a more or less arbitrary value established by the board of directors and which bears little relation to the stock's actual market value. The market value is influenced by many factors, including the corporation's potential earning power, its financial condition, its earnings record, its record for paying dividends, and general business conditions.

Ownership of a share of common stock carries certain privileges:

A share in earnings. Each year, the board of directors of the corporation meets to determine the amount of the corporation's earnings that will be distributed to stockholders. This distribution, known as the dividend, will vary depending on the company's current profitability and accumulated earnings. A dividend may be omitted altogether if the company is earning no current profits or if the board elects to plow back profits into growth.

A share in control. Holders of common stock are invited to attend annual meetings of stockholders and they have the right to vote on matters of corporate policy on the basis of one vote per share held. However, the small investor with only a few shares of stock has little or no practical influence on corporate decisions.

A claim on assets. In the event of the company's liquidation, holders of common stock have the right to share in the firm's assets after all debts and prior claims have been satisfied.

There are four main categories of common stock, each of which is best for a particular investment strategy and purpose.

1. *Blue-chip stocks.* High-grade, or blue-chip, stocks are issued by well-established corporations with many years of proven success, earnings growth, and consistent dividend payments. Blue-chip stocks tend to be relatively high priced and offer a relatively low-income yield. They are a relatively safe investment when compared with other categories of stock.

2. *Income stocks.* Income stocks pay a higher-than-average return on investment. They are generally issued by firms in stable businesses that have no need to reinvest a large percentage of profits each year.

3. *Growth stocks.* Issued by firms expected to grow rapidly during the years to come, growth stocks have a current income that is often low, since the company plows back most of its earnings into company research and expansion. The value of the stock, however, may rise quickly if the company performs in accordance with company expectations.

4. *Speculative stocks.* Speculative stocks are backed by no proven corporate track record or lengthy dividend history. Stocks issued by little-known companies or newly formed corporations, high-flying "glamour" stocks issued by companies in new business areas, and low-priced "penny stocks" all may be considered speculative stocks. As with any speculative investment, there is a slight possibility of tremendous profit—but a substantial risk of losing all as well.

Preferred Stock. Preferred stock, like common stock, represents ownership of a share in a corporation. Holders of preferred stock, however, have a prior claim on the company's earnings as compared with holders of common stock; hence the name *preferred stock.* Similarly, holders of preferred stock have a prior claim in the company's assets in the event of a liquidation, but they have no voting privileges.

Preferred stock also has certain distinctive features related to dividend payments. A fixed, specified annual dividend is usually paid for each share of preferred stock. This fixed dividend may be expressed in dollars (for example, $10 per share) or as a percentage of the stock's par value. The dividend must be paid before dividends are issued to holders of common stock.

Preferred stock dividends, however, are not considered a debt of the corporation—unlike, for example, the interest due on corporate bonds—because the firm is not obligated to meet its dividend payments. The board of directors may decide to withhold the dividend payment for a given year because of limited earnings or other reasons. To protect stockholders against undue losses in dividends, most preferred stock is issued with a cumulative feature. If a dividend is not paid on cumulative preferred stock, the amount is carried over to the following period, and both current and past unpaid dividends must be paid before holders of common stock can receive any dividend.

WHAT ARE THE ADVANTAGES AND DISADVANTAGES OF STOCKS?

Like any investment, stocks have distinct advantages and disadvantages.

Advantages

Growth potential. When a company has the potential for growth in value and earnings, so does its stock. If the investor chooses the right stock—in a company that is highly profitable and continues to be—or a group of such stocks, significant profit can be realized, possibly, in a relatively short time. History reveals that, as a whole, the stock market has had an upward trend in values, with years of gain outnumbering those of decline by better than three to one.

Liquidity. Stocks traded on the major exchanges can be bought and sold quickly and easily at readily ascertainable prices.

Possible tax benefits. Growth stocks, which pay low or no dividends so that company profits can be reinvested, provide an effective tax shelter. As the corporation's value grows, so does the value of the stock, which is a form of tax-deferred income, since no taxes need to be paid on these gains until the stock is sold.

Disadvantages

Risks. There can be no guarantee of making money by investing in stocks. Companies may fail, stock prices may drop, and investors may lose their investments. Remember the saying of one concerned investor: "I am not so concerned with the return *on* my investment as I am with the return *of* my investment."

Brokerage commissions. Most investors need the help and advice of a stockbroker when they become involved in the market. High broker commissions, however, can largely erode profits. Since one fee is charged when the stocks are bought and another when stocks are sold, investors are, in effect, paying twice. Well-informed investors should look into the use of a discount broker, who provides little or no investment counseling but charges greatly reduced commissions when trading stocks.

Complexity. The stock market is complicated, and the amount of knowledge needed to be consistently successful is considerable. Investors who lack the patience, time, or skill to inform themselves about the market often buy and sell on impulse, thereby minimizing their profits and maximizing their losses.

SUMMARY

The only way to approach the stock market is to maintain good, old-fashioned common sense. Here are some points to keep in mind:

- *Avoid hot tips:* If a friend knows about a hot tip, so do hundreds of other people. Remember, hot tips can get one burned.

- *Do not become attached to a company and its stock:* Be objective in viewing a stock even if it is the stock of one's employer, accumulated over the years. Weed out stocks that are not meeting one's objectives, even if it is the first stock ever bought as an investor.

- *Do some portfolio comparisons:* Check on the total return by adding up the stock's price change and dividends for a specific period and divide the total by the price at the start of that period. Then multiply the result by 100. This will result in a percentage that can be compared to what the return in other types of investments would have been.

- *Have some patience:* Except for wild speculation, investors should take their time. Stocks should not be sold on the basis of performance over a short time, but rather on the concept of the long run. Remember that the longer the holding period, the more likely a profit will be gained in spite of the inevitable interim ups and downs. On the buy side, the same rule applies. Do not get bullied into purchasing something that "can't wait." Good investments can wait.

Never forget that whenever a stock is bought, someone else is selling it. Stock may be bought because of a belief that the investment is good and the price will rise. Nevertheless, the person selling that same stock believes the opposite, so only one of these people will be correct. Thinking of it in these terms will make an investor a realistic and conservative player.

SEE ALSO *Investments; Securities and Exchange Commission; Stock Exchanges; Stock Indexes*

BIBLIOGRAPHY

Campbell, Allan B. (2004). *Conquering stock market hype.* New York: McGraw-Hill.

Dalton, John M. (2001). *How the stock market works* (3rd ed.). New York: New York Institute of Finance.

Fontanills, George A., and Gentile, Tom (2001). *Stock market course.* New York: Wiley.

Kelly, Jason (2003). *The neatest little guide to stock market investments.* New York: Penguin.

Stav, Julie, and Adamson, Deborah (2000). *Get your share: The everyday woman's guide to striking it rich in the stock market.* New York: Berkeley Books.

Joel Lerner

STRATEGIC MANAGEMENT

Strategic management is the process of developing and executing a series of competitive moves to enhance the success of the organization both in the present and in the future. These competitive moves are derived from the demands of the external environment in which the firm operates as well as the internal capabilities that it has developed or can reasonably hope to build or acquire. While managers may follow somewhat different strategic management routines, a sound process should include an analysis of the current business situation, the formulation of objectives and strategies based on that analysis, and an implementation and evaluation procedure that ensures progress toward each strategy and objective. This article focuses on the formulation of appropriate strategic objectives based on a sound understanding of the internal and external environments faced by the firm. A brief discussion of implementation is included though this topic is covered in greater detail in other entries.

SITUATIONAL ANALYSIS

In order to create appropriate strategic objectives, organizations work to understand their internal capabilities as well as the environment in which they operate. Further, they also seek to clarify their purpose or mission. The situation analysis firmly focuses management's attention on these issues, allowing it to create a fit between its resources and the demands of the competitive situation.

The steps to be taken in a situational analysis are largely agreed upon, though there does exist some debate as to whether one starts with a mission statement or with an analysis of the state of the organization. Those who believe that a mission statement is the logical starting point argue that management must first think carefully and creatively about the future direction of the company if they are to create and implement effective objectives. In this way, managers can choose their own vision of what the company ought to be rather than be unduly affected by company history or industry exigencies. On the other hand, managers may want to have a keen understanding of the history and current performance of a company as well as important industry factors so as to craft a strategic vision that is attainable in terms of organizational competencies and industry dynamics. While both sides have merit, this article discusses the state of the organization first.

STATE OF THE ORGANIZATION

In analyzing the state of the organization, managers take a candid measure of its recent performance. Typically, they consider such issues as profitability, stock price performance, market share, revenue growth, customer satisfaction, product innovation, and so forth. These measures can vary from industry to industry. Product innovation, for example, is important to the pharmaceutical industry, while the number of new distributors signed may be a more important measure in the multilevel marketing industry.

In addition to this performance review, managers typically examine a company's (s)trengths, (w)eaknesses, (o)pportunities, and (t)hreats (SWOT) by conducting a SWOT analysis. Strengths consist of those things that a company does particularly well relative to its competition and that provide it with some competitive advantage. Strengths can be found in many different areas, including people, such as a particularly competent sales force; systems, such as Federal Express's information systems; locations, like that occupied by a restaurant with sweeping ocean views; and intangible assets, such as a strong brand name. These strengths provide the competitive advantage needed to succeed in the marketplace.

Weaknesses, however, diminish the competitiveness of a company. They, too, can be found in many different areas, including outdated equipment, a poor understanding of customers, or a high cost structure.

Strengths and weaknesses are typically internal to a company and, therefore, largely under a company's control. By contrast, opportunities and threats are usually derived from the external market situation and require some response from a company if it is to perform well. Opportunities can arise in many areas, including geographical expansion, new technologies, and changing customer preferences and tastes. Only when a firm has (or can hope to acquire) the specific skills needed to seize upon some option does it become an opportunity for the company.

Whereas opportunities are chances to be seized, threats can be thought of as concerns that are largely outside of the organization's control but have the potential to disrupt its operations. Probably the biggest threat to many companies is their competition. Other sources of threats include foreign economic crises such as the Asian flu that spread in the latter part of the 1990s, government regulations, natural disasters, and so forth. In creating strategic objectives, management prepares contingency plans to minimize the impact of its most serious threats.

In addition to conducting a SWOT analysis and candid performance review, the executive team may use several other tools to acquire a better understanding of its current situation. They may, for example, identify those forces in the industry that are causing the nature of competition to change for all competitors. One example would be the publicizing of the link between cholesterol and heart disease that made many consumers more aware of the amount of fat in foods. This change made it important for many food manufacturers to either lower the amount of fat in their products or to introduce fat-free or low-fat versions of those products. These forces that change the nature the way companies compete in an industry are known as driving forces.

Another tool used by managers in conducting a state-of-the-organization review is an analysis of key success factors. In this analysis managers examine those things that all companies within a given industry must do well if they are to survive. These might include rapid service for the fast-food industry, producing large numbers of vehicles so as to offset the high cost of specialized equipment in the automotive industry, or having skilled designers in the fashion industry. By understanding such factors, managers are in a position to better allocate resources so as to perform well in the future.

In addition to these tools, managers may also conduct other types of analyses, including ones focused on customers, economic characteristics of the industry, supplier relationships, and so forth. These analyses constitute a first step in the strategic management process as organizational leaders attempt to understand the organization's current situation so as to later be able to identify those strategic objectives most likely to improve performance.

MISSION STATEMENTS

Having thoroughly understood an organization's internal and external environment, managers establish a mission statement to create a five- to ten-year vision of the company. A mission statement documents the service or product the company provides to the marketplace and the unique way in which it distinguishes itself from other companies. It also indicates the target group of customers that the company serves.

An example of this type of mission statement is provided by Courtyard by Marriott. It indicates that Courtyard by Marriott is serving economy- and quality-minded frequent business travelers with a premier, moderately priced lodging facility that is consistently perceived as clean, comfortable, well maintained, attractive, and staffed by friendly, attentive, and efficient people. This mission statement indicates the product and service provided to the target customers and the way in which it will be done.

Mission statements serve several purposes in strategic management. First, they provide direction for the organization. As a firm engages in its strategic planning process it compares its objectives with the path it has set for itself. If any of the goals suggest a deviation from the purpose of the organization, managers must decide if the goal is sufficiently important to warrant a change in the mission statement. Otherwise, the objective might be dropped. With this in mind managers are typically careful to write mission statements that are broad enough to encourage growth but specific enough to give direction.

A second purpose of mission statements is to create a shared sense of purpose and inspiration among employees. In some organizations, employees are required to memorize the mission statement so that they will understand what is appropriate behavior and what is not. For this reason, most mission statements are relatively short so that the purpose of the company remains clearly in the minds of its employees. Furthermore, many companies seek the input of their employees in creating a mission statement so as to create a document that is owned by all.

Finally, mission statements are also external documents. They communicate to the outside world the values and goals of the organization. Unfortunately, some companies create mission statements as a marketing document and then fail to live up to that vision of themselves. For a mission statement to be effective, it must be a living document that motivates behavior.

EXTERNAL ENVIRONMENT REVIEW

Once a company has carefully and frankly understood its situation and has spent time considering the appropriateness of its mission statement, it may choose to do a more thorough review of the external environment. This environment consists of industry, government, competitive, economic, political, and other factors that the organization cannot control but which may have an important impact on the company. For example, the dietary supplements industry in the United States spends large amounts of money to keep abreast of the latest regulations issued by the Food and Drug Administration.

Much of this analysis may be done within a "State of the Organization" report, but some companies choose to address it as a third step in the strategic planning process to ensure that they are not caught off guard by these important factors. While the organization cannot control these forces, it can formulate responses that will minimize the potential damage or even put the firm in a better competitive position should the eventuality actually occur.

KEY OBJECTIVES AND STRATEGIES

Having conducted the previous three steps, managers have sufficient information to choose objectives that are most likely to match the internal capabilities of the firm with the exigencies of the external environment. Thompson and Strickland (1998) state that "objectives represent a managerial commitment to achieving specific performance targets within a specific time frame" (p. 36). While drawing heavily on the previous three steps in the process, objectives rely even more particularly on the SWOT analysis in enhancing certain strengths, overcoming specific weaknesses, capitalizing on opportunities, and addressing the threats. By creating such a fit between the demands of the industry and the skills and competencies of the organization, a firm increases its ability to compete successfully in the marketplace.

Firms may set specific objectives including such things as increasing market share, decreasing customer complaints, cutting costs by 10 percent, or creating a more effective food preparation facility. These broad objectives are then broken down into specific strategies that may, in turn, be broken down into even more specific action steps. It is important that objectives be written in a way that clearly indicates the nature of what is to be achieved, the single individual responsible for the objective, a committee to work on the project, funding assigned, and date to be completed. Based on these requirements, an objective for a rural hospital might take the following form:

Objective 2: Increase revenues from visiting physicians by $500,000.

Person Responsible: Virginia Moody (CEO)

Committee Members: Virginia Moody, Dr. Etta, Erika Boerk (PR director), Sean Ortiz (Facilities Coordinator), and Tristan Roberts (Marketing)

Funding: $125,000

Date Due: June 1, 20XX

Strategies

1. Develop relationship with Dr. Yang (podiatrist).

2. Refurbish existing office space to accommodate visiting physicians.

3. Contract with local newspaper to advertise visits.

4. Find a dermatologist

5. Etc.

In addition, each of the strategies could also be broken down in similar fashion to include the person(s) responsible, funds required, and due dates.

IMPLEMENTATION

Having created detailed objectives and strategies, an organization may find that some internal adjustments in the way a firm is organized or in the competencies of its workers are required to achieve those objectives. These adjustments may be as simple as sending an employee to a seminar to better understand a new information process software or as complex as creating a new international division to take advantage of overseas opportunities. This process requires the identification of those individual and organization competencies needed to facilitate the accomplishment of the stated objectives.

In addition to serving as a guide to the form of the organization, the objectives also serve as the basis of the year's budgets and performance standards. Having set the funding requirements for each objective, these monies are added to the normal operating budget for each division so that they can fulfill these goals. Further, these objectives and strategies are added to the existing performance standards for each division or department and become an integral part of the performance evaluation of the individuals assigned to each task. In this way the progress of each objective is tracked throughout the year and a specific and agreed-upon measuring stick exists for each employee's performance.

Finally, it should be mentioned that in any strategic management process, but particularly in those taking place in dynamic environments, situations change and strategic plans require modification. While five-year plans may remain relatively unchanged in some industries, other industries may make major modifications monthly. For this reason, most firms consider strategic management to be an ongoing process characterized by periodic progress evaluations and major plan analysis on a yearly basis. Such updates allow a firm to continually reconfigure its internal process and capabilities to create a better fit with the demands of the competitive situation.

SEE ALSO *Management; Policy Development*

BIBLIOGRAPHY

Bourgeios, L. J. III, Duhaime, Irene M., and Stimpert, J. L. (1999). *Strategic Management: A Managerial Perspective* (2nd ed.). Fort Worth, TX: Dryden Press.

Hitt, Michael, Ireland, R. Duane, and Hoskisson, Robert E. (2005). *Strategic Management: Competitiveness and Globalization* (6th ed.). Mason, OH: Thomson/South-Western.

Mintzberg, Henry (1987, July-August). "Crafting Strategy." *Harvard Business Review*, 66-75.

Porter, Michael A. (1985). *Competitive Advantage: Creating and Sustaining Superior Performance*. New York: Free Press.

Porter, Michael A. (1998). *Competitive Strategy: Techniques for Analyzing Industries and Competitors*. New York: Free Press.

Porter, Michael E. (1996, November). "What Is Strategy?" *Harvard Business Review*, 61-78.

Prahalad, C. K., and Hamel, Gary. (1990, May-June). "The Core Competence of the Corporation." *Harvard Business Review*, 79-83.

Thompson, Arthur A., Jr., and Strickland, A. J. III (1998). *Strategic Management: Concepts and Cases* (12th ed.). Boston: McGraw-Hill/Irwin.

Norman S. Wright

STRESS

Stress has been defined in a number of ways by a number of different individuals, but everyone agrees that stress is experienced by all workers in the business world no matter what their position. Stress is the body's reaction to any demand placed on it, and health experts agree that some stress is essential for human survival. As demands are placed on a person's body, there will be some kind of automatic reaction. When this reaction is positive, the stress helps individuals perform their jobs better. Positive stress, called eustress, can lead individuals to a new awareness of their abilities and a completely new perspective on their jobs. Negative stress, called distress, upsets individuals and can make them physically sick. It can lead to feelings of distrust, rejection, anger, and depression, which may lead to a number of medical problems, including stroke, heart disease, high blood pressure, cancer, and ulcers.

SYMPTOMS OF STRESS

Because everyone is different, the symptoms of stress are varied and numerous. The symptoms of stress have been placed in different categories, the most common being physical, psychological, behavioral, and mental. Headache, fatigue, grinding teeth, clenched jaws, chest pain, shortness of breath, insomnia, nausea, high blood pressure, muscle aches, constipation or diarrhea, and heart palpitations are all physical symptoms of stress. Anxiety, nervousness, depression, anger, defensiveness, hypersensitivity, apathy, feelings of helplessness, impatience, and short temper are symptoms of psychological stress. Behavioral symptoms include overeating or loss of appetite, procrastination, increased use of alcohol or drugs, pacing, nervous habits (nail-biting, foot-tapping), crying, swearing, poor personal hygiene, and withdrawal or isolation from others. Individuals who experience a decrease in concentration and memory, indecisiveness, confusion, loss of sense of humor, and mind going blank or racing may have mental stress.

Many of these symptoms, when not treated, can lead to serious medical problems as well as loss of time on the job. When individuals experience stress, they often miss work because of illness or arrive late because they dread coming to work. When on the job, they may not performing up to their ability.

REACTION TO STRESS

When individuals perceive or anticipate a threatening or stressful situation, part of the nervous system, the sympathetic nervous system, becomes activated and releases a number of chemicals. One of these chemicals, adrenaline, is a stimulant hormone and is released into the bloodstream. Adrenaline and other hormones, including noradrenaline, produce changes in the body that get the individual geared up for action.

David Posen (1995), who specializes in stress management, indicates that gearing up for action is often called "the fight-or-flight response" because it provides the strength and energy to either fight or run away from danger. These responses increase heart rate and blood pressure in order to get more blood to the muscles, brain, and heart, the organs that are the most important in dealing with danger. This increase in blood flow to the brain, heart, and muscles means that there is a decrease in the blood flow to the skin, digestive tract, kidneys, and liver, where it is least needed in a time of crisis. Individuals will also begin to breathe faster to take in more oxygen, and their muscles will tense so that they are prepared for action. An increased mental alertness and sensitivity of sense organs occurs. As these reactions are taking place, there is also an increase in the blood sugar, fats, and cholesterol and a rise in platelets and blood-clotting factors.

Repeated release of chemicals as a reaction to stress can, over time, cause wear and tear on the heart and blood vessels, eventually leading to heart disease and stroke. Because adrenaline and the other hormones released during stress increase muscle tension, slow digestion, and constrict and dilate arteries, the liver may deliver cholesterol and fat into the bloodstream. The hormone testosterone may increase, which can reduce the levels of high-density lipoproteins (HDL), the good cholesterol.

CAUSES OF STRESS

There are a number of life events, experienced at one time or another by everyone, that cause stress. Some of these are family-related, such as marriage, death of a family member or close friend, divorce or separation, birth or adoption of a child, a personal major illness or illness of a family member, and a major change in a spouse's job or income. An individual's control over the situation will determine the amount of stress these events will cause.

Physical stressors include pollution, excessive noise, physical disability or handicap, weather extremes, smoking, excessive drinking, obesity, overeating, poor nutrition, and lack of rest or relaxation. Many of these physical stressors are beyond an individual's control.

Common workplace stressors include the possibility of dismissal, time pressures, too many responsibilities, unreasonable deadlines, disorganization, adapting to new technology, conflicts with co-workers, information overload, and major changes in job responsibilities.

COMPUTERS AND STRESS

The use of computers in the workplace has introduced new sources of stress. One of the most frequent computer-related stressors is repetitive strain injury (RSI), which occurs when the employee is overworked or when the working environment is not physically conducive to work. Causes of RSI may be repetitious actions such as typing or using a mouse, poor lighting, and poor posture. Another computer-related problem is carpal-tunnel syndrome (CTS), which occurs when the person typing has bad posture and uses incorrect hand movements on the keyboard. Hands and eyes are the main source of communication with the computer. When bad posture and incorrect hand movements are too prevalent, the result is tingling and numbness of the fingers.

Extended time spent working before a computer monitor can produce eye irritation, fatigue, and difficulty focusing, all of which are symptoms associated with eyestrain. Nearsightedness has been associated with eye strain caused by working at a computer monitor.

SOURCES OF JOB STRESS

Job pressures are a major source of stress. Several job conditions have been identified as increasing stress in most employees. Job overload is one such condition. Although some employees may have the ability to do the job, they may not have enough time to do the amount of work necessary. Other employees lack the ability to do the job, being unable to meet the performance standards or expectations set by the employer. Clear job objectives are necessary, and when employees do not know what specific job performance is expected of them, they begin to develop stress.

When jobs are too boring or employees are not challenged to use their abilities, stress occurs. Stress also results from undesirable physical working conditions. Employees experience stress when the work environment is too noisy, too hot, too cold, or too crowded.

A major source of stress involves frequent or significant changes that have a direct effect on the individual's job. These changes can include changes in management, management style, equipment, or job location.

MANAGING STRESS

Just as there are a number of causes for and symptoms of stress, there are a number of ways to manage stress. Individuals vary in their ability to manage stress, and the same techniques do not work for every person. Individuals need to become aware of the stressors they experience and how they react to these stressors.

One stress-management technique that can apply to almost all individuals is learning to manage time more effectively. Managing time more effectively means that individuals learn to prioritize and plan so that they have time for themselves, thus leaving time for listening to music, exercising regularly, mediating, or engaging in whatever type of activity that they find relaxing. Developing an organized time schedule helps ward off tension, which helps reduce stress.

When on the job, employees and managers need to match individual abilities with workload. Managers should be sure that the job objectives are clear so that there is no role ambiguity or role conflict. As employees' work responsibilities change, managers should keep them informed of what is going to happen, why it is going to happen, and when it will happen.

When individuals cannot manage stress on their own or with the help of their managers, medication may be necessary. These medications can, in the short term, moderate physical reactions to stress. Doctors usually prescribe Valium and Xanax for relief from stress. Tranquilizers are suggested for only short periods of time, because individuals can become dependent on them.

SEE ALSO *Employee Assistance Programs; Workers' Compensation*

BIBLIOGRAPHY

"Ever Thought of Calling in Well?" (1998, November 9). *U.S. News & World Report*, 82-83.

Keita, Gwendolyn Puryear, and Hurrell, Joseph J., Jr., eds. (1994). *Job Stress in a Changing Workforce.* Washington, DC: American Psychological Association.

Losyk, Bob (2005). *Get a Grip!: overcoming stress and thriving in the workplace.* Hoboken, NJ: John Wiley & Sons.

Moore, Jo Ellen (1999, January). "Are You Burning Out Valuable Resources?" *HR Magazine*, 1:93-98.

Newton, Tim (1995). *Managing Stress: Emotion and Power at Work.* Thousand Oaks, CA: SAGE Publications.

Posen, David B. (1995). "Stress Management for Patient and Physician." *Canadian Journal of Continuing Medical Education.*

Seaward, Brian Luke (2006). *Managing Stress: principles and strategies for health and wellbeing* (5th ed.). Sudbury, MA: Jones and Bartlett Publishers.

Stranks, Jeremy (2005). *Stress at Work: management and prevention.* Oxford; Boston: Elsevier/Butterworth-Heinemann.

Timm, Paul R., and Peterson, Brent D. (1993). *People at Work: Human Relations in Organizations* (5th ed.). Cincinnati, OH: South-Western College Pub.

Jim D. Rucker

SUPPLIERS

SEE *Channels of Distribution*

SUPPLY AND DEMAND

The market process is generally modeled using the economic concepts of supply and demand. The plans/desires of consumers are embedded in the concept of demand and the plans/desires of producers in the concept of supply. The plans of these two types of economic actors are brought together in markets, which are the entities in which transactions occur. In a modern economy, markets do not require that the buyers and sellers meet in a geographic place, so markets no longer require actual "marketplaces."

The concept of demand represents the market activity of consumers. Demand is defined as the quantity of a good or service that consumers will be both willing and able to purchase at any given price during a specific period of time, holding all other factors constant. Demand is, therefore, a relationship between price and quantity demanded. Many factors other than price affect the amount con-

Widgets		
Quantity supplied	Price	Quantity demanded
50	$13	10
40	$11	20
30	$ 9	30
20	$ 7	40
10	$ 5	50

Table 1

sumers choose to purchase, and these factors are what is being held constant within the concept of demand.

Demand can be illustrated in a schedule that shows how many units of a good or service consumers will purchase at several distinct prices. Table 1 shows how many units of a good (widgets) consumers will purchase at a number of different prices. This relationship between price and quantity demanded can also be represented graphically. A demand curve represents the maximum price that consumers would be willing to pay for a particular quantity of the good. Consumers are willing to purchase something because they value that product more than its opportunity cost. The opportunity cost is the value of the best alternative they could purchase with the same money. That is, when a consumer chooses to spend $2 on a hamburger, he or she has decided that the hamburger provides more satisfaction (at that moment in time) than anything else that could be bought with that $2. Thus, the demand curve represents the value of the product to the consumer. The area under the demand curve provides a measure of the total value that consumers receive from consuming that amount of the product.

The nature of this relationship between price and quantity demanded is so consistent that it is called the law of demand. This law states that the relationship defined by the concept of demand is an inverse or indirect one. When prices rise, other factors held constant, consumers will purchase less of the good, and vice versa. The rationale for the law is that when the price of a product changes relative to the price of other products, consumers will change their purchasing patterns by buying less of the now higher-priced good and purchasing more of other goods which are now relatively less expensive that satisfy the same basic wants. Goods that satisfy the same basic wants are called substitutes. For example, if the price of beef rises relative to the price of pork, chicken, and turkey, consumers will shift some of their purchases from beef to pork, chicken, and turkey.

Supply can be defined as the relationship between the price of a good or service and the quantity producers are willing and able to make available for sale in a given period of time, holding other things constant. A supply schedule showing how many widgets producers will make available for sale at several distinct prices is also shown in Table 1. Supply represents graphically the minimum price that consumers are willing to accept in order to make a given amount of the good or service available for sale. As such, it is the opportunity cost to society of producing that particular good.

The law of supply states that this relationship is a direct one. When the price of a good rises, holding other factors constant, producers will be willing to supply more of the product. The rationale for this law is that resource owners will want to use their resources in the most valuable way possible. For example, if the market price of corn rises relative to that of wheat, farmers will choose to plant more of the land available to them in corn and less in wheat.

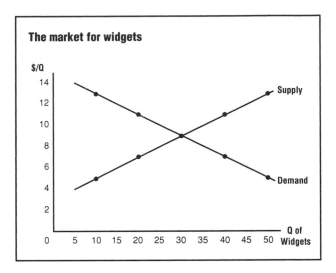

Figure 1

EQUILIBRIUM

A market is a place where suppliers and demanders meet to conduct an exchange. Modern markets do not require these two parties to be in the same place or even to communicate their desires at the same time. The market process can be thought of as a type of "auction process." Given the supply and demand curves shown in Figure 1, if an auctioneer was to call out a price of $5, consumer would be willing and able to purchase 50 units (the quantity demanded), but producers would be willing and able to supply only 10 units (the quantity supplied). If consumers want to buy 50 units and there are only 10 for sale, there is a shortage of 40 units (quantity demanded minus quantity supplied). Whenever there is a greater quantity demanded than supplied, there will be a shortage. Consumers will then attempt to compete for the scarce units. This competition will take the form of bidding up the price.

To continue with the auction illustration, the auctioneer sees that people want to buy more than is available, and so he calls out a new, higher price of $7 per unit. At $7, the consumers who valued the product more than $5, but less than $7, drop out of the market. That is, the quantity demanded falls from 50 units to 40 units. However, the law of supply tells us that the new, higher price will induce producers to increase the quantity supplied. The quantity supplied rises from 10 to 20 units. Consumers still want to buy more than producers want to sell, so there continues to be a shortage, but the shortage has been reduced from 40 units to 20 units. Consumers still must attempt to out-compete other consumers, and the price is bid up again. Only when the auctioneer calls out a price of $9 is the quantity consumers demand equal to the quantity that producers supply. This is called the market clearing price. This price "clears" the market because

everyone who wants to buy at that price is able to and everyone who wants to sell at that price is able to. This makes the market stable because consumers no longer have a need to bid up the price. Thus, the market is at an equilibrium at the price for which the quantity demanded is equal to the quantity supplied.

If the price is above the market clearing price, consumers will be willing and able to buy less than producers are willing and able to make available for sale. For example, if the price is $13 (in Figure 1), quantity demanded will be 10 units and quantity supplied will be 50 units. Whenever quantity supplied is greater than quantity demanded, there will be a surplus. In this case, the surplus is equal to 40 units (quantity supplied minus quantity demanded). If there is a surplus in a market, producers will compete with each other for scarce buyers by bidding down the price. When the price falls to $11, consumers will increase the amount they want to buy to 20 units and producers will reduce the amount they want to sell to 40 units, so that the surplus falls to 20 units. But here, the producers will continue to try to outcompete other producers for the consumers in the market by offering their product for an even lower price. It is not until the price falls to the market clearing level of $9 that the surplus disappears and producers no longer need to bid the price down in order to sell their product.

If the price is below the market clearing price, consumers will up bid the price, and if the price is above the equilibrium price, producers will bid down the price. It is only at the equilibrium price that quantity demanded equals quantity supplied and the market price stabilizes. This is the only price for which consumers have no reason to offer a higher price and producers have no reason to offer a lower price.

NONPRICE DETERMINANTS OF DEMAND

Consumers base their purchasing decisions on several factors other than price. These nonprice determinants of demand are the things that are held constant in the definition of demand. When these factors change, the relationship between price and quantity demanded changes; that is, the demand curve itself shifts. An increase in demand is represented graphically as a shift in the demand curve in a northeasterly direction (for example, from *D*0 to *D*1 in Figure 2), and a decrease in demand is represented as a shift of the demand curve in a southwesterly direction (for example, from *D*0 to *D*2 in Figure 2). The two main nonprice determinants of demand are consumers' incomes and wealth, and the prices of related goods. An increase in income and/or wealth can cause the demand for a good to either increase or decrease. If an increase in income/wealth causes the demand for a good to increase, the good is called a normal good. This increase in demand is illustrated in Figure 2 by a shift from *D*0 to *D*1, causing the market equilibrium to change from *E*1 to *E*2, resulting in an increase in the market price (from $9 to $11) and an increase in quantity bought and sold (from 30 to 40 units). If an increase in income/wealth causes the demand for a good to decrease, the good is called an inferior good. This is illustrated in Figure 2 by a shift in demand from *D*0 to *D*2. The market then clears at *E*3 with a lower market price ($7) and a smaller quantity (20 units). Likewise, the impact of a change in the price of a related good on a good's demand depends on whether the goods are related as substitute goods or complementary goods. Two goods are substitutes if an increase in the price of one causes the demand for the other to increase, and the goods are complements if an increase in the price of one causes the demand for the other to decrease.

NONPRICE DETERMINANTS OF SUPPLY

Producers base their decisions about what to produce with the productive resources they have at their disposal on more factors than just the prices of the different goods. These other factors are called the nonprice determinants of supply. The major nonprice determinants of supply are the prices of the inputs used to produce the product, the state of technology used to produce the product, and the prices of other goods that are related in production. An increase in supply is represented graphically as a shift in the supply curve in a southeasterly direction and a decrease in supply is shown as a shift in a northwesterly direction (see Figure 2). An increase (decrease) in the price of an input into the production of a good, which would increase (decrease) the cost of production, will cause the supply to fall (rise). For example, an increase in the price

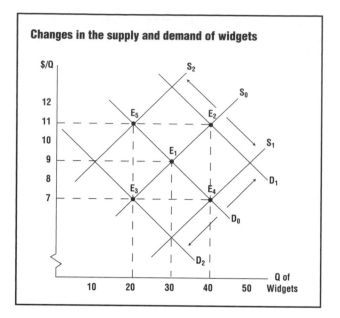

Figure 2

of fertilizer will cause the supply of corn to fall, holding other factors constant. If the supply curve were to shift from *S*0 to *S*2, everything else being equal, the market equilibrium would change from point *E*1 to *E*5, causing the market clearing price to rise (from $9 to $11) and quantity transacted to fall (from 30 to 20 units). An advancement in technology that lowers the cost of production will also cause supply of the good to rise. For example, the discovery of a new chemical agent that increases the yield of an acre of land planted in corn will increase the supply of corn, holding other factors constant. If the supply curve were to shift from *S*0 to *S*1, the market equilibrium would change from point *E*1 to *E*4, causing the market clearing price to fall (from $9 to $7) and the quantity transacted to rise (from 30 to 40 units). An increase (decrease) in the price of a different good that is produced using the same inputs (goods that are related in production) will cause producers to increase their production of the now higher-priced, and hence more profitable, good. In order to do this, resources will need to be reallocated away from the production of other goods. For example, an increase in the price of wheat (relative to the price of corn) will cause producers to shift factors of production toward the production of wheat and away from the production of corn.

SEE ALSO *Macroeconomics/Microeconomics; Pricing*

John L. Conant

T

TARGET MARKETING

A target market is a set of buyers sharing common needs or characteristics that a company decides to serve. A company identifies a target market in order to organize its tasks and cope with the particular demands of the marketplace. Target marketing forms the foundation of a modern marketing strategy because doing it well helps a company be more efficient and effective by focusing on a certain segment of its market that it can best satisfy.

Targeting also benefits consumers because a company can reach specific groups of consumers with offers carefully tailored to satisfy their needs. To do so, a company has to evaluate the various segments and decide how many, and which ones, to target. There is no single way to segment a market. A company needs to research different segmentation variables alone and in combination with others to find its target market. Four main variables can be used in segmenting consumer markets: geographic, demographic, psychographic, and behavioral segmentation.

GEOGRAPHIC SEGMENTATION

Geographic segmentation calls for dividing the market into different geographic units, such as nations, regions, states, counties, cities, or neighborhoods. Many companies localize their products as well as their advertising, promotion, and sales efforts to fit the needs of individual cities, regions, and neighborhoods. For example, clothing stores sell clothes targeted to their geographic markets. In January, the Gap clothing store sells winter clothing in Portland, Maine, such as mittens, scarves, and winter jackets. A Gap located in Clearwater, Florida, will sell more T-shirts, shorts, and bathing suits.

DEMOGRAPHIC SEGMENTATION

Demographic segmentation divides the market into groups based on such variables as age, gender, family size, family life cycle, income, occupation, education, religion, race, and nationality. Demographics is the most popular basis for segmenting customer groups because consumer needs, wants, and usage rates often closely reflect demographic variables. Even when a market segment is first defined using other factors, such as psychographic or geographic segmentation, demographic characteristics must be known in order to assess the size of the target market and to reach it efficiently.

Demographics is also the easiest and least expensive to retrieve because it is secondary data; that is, it comes from research that has already been conducted. For example, a target market for a real estate developer selling luxury vacation homes near Walt Disney World would include professional married couples approximately 30- to 45-years-old with young children, and with incomes of more than $100,000. Another example of targeting through demographics is Liz Claiborne Apparel Company. They have named their target market; her name is Liz Lady. They know Liz Lady's age, income range, professional status, family status, hobbies, and interests. Every decision from marketing to design is based on Liz Lady's profile.

PSYCHOGRAPHIC SEGMENTATION

Psychographic segmentation is the process of dividing markets into groups based on values, social class, lifestyle, or personality characteristics. Individuals in the same demographic group may fall into very different psychographic segments. Psychographic segmentation involves qualitative aspects—the "why" component of consumer buying patterns. Therefore, a company must conduct its own research, which can become very time-consuming and expensive.

Marketers, however, are increasingly focusing on psychographic characteristics. An example of psychographic segmentation is that of the clothing retailer Abercrombie and Fitch. Abercrombie and Fitch has developed a powerful personality that is fun-loving, independent, and sexually uninhibited—a winning formula with teenagers and college students. To remain familiar with teen tastes and to spark ideas for new merchandise, Abercrombie and Fitch sends about thirty staffers to college campuses each month to chat with students about what they play, wear, listen to, and read. This kind of research led to success in the early twenty-first century with wind pants. (These resemble track-and-field pants but are generally made of nylon.) The stores themselves, featuring comfortable armchairs, are designed to be gathering places. They are staffed by high-energy "brand reps" recruited from local campuses and dressed in Abercrombie and Fitch clothes.

BEHAVIORAL SEGMENTATION

Behavioral segmentation divides a market into groups based on consumer knowledge, attitude, use, or response to a product. Many marketers believe that behavior variables are the best starting points for building market segments. Why does one consumer drink Coke, another Pepsi, and a third iced tea? Demographics and psychographics can provide many clues, but it is often helpful to consider additional factors as well. Individuals act differently depending on their situation or the occasion for using the product. For example, a woman who shops only at discount stores for clothing may nonetheless think nothing of spending $100 on a bathing suit at a specialty shop for her Caribbean vacation. Some holidays, such as Father's Day and Mother's Day, were originally promoted partly to increase the sale of flowers, candy, cards, and other gifts. Many food marketers prepare special offers and ads for holidays. For example, Beatrice Foods runs special Thanksgiving and Christmas ads for Reddi-whip in November and December, months that account for 30 percent of all sales of whipped cream.

SELECTING A TARGET MARKET

Identifying a target market allows marketers to develop strategies for designing, pricing, distributing, promoting, positioning, and improving their product, service, or idea. For example, if research shows that a sturdy recyclable package with blue lettering appeals to one's target market and if one is focused on that target market, that type of packaging should be chosen. If, however, marketers are product or profit oriented—rather than people oriented—they might simply make the package out of plain Styrofoam because it protects the product (product oriented) or because it is less expensive (profit oriented). If one knows one's target market is 24- to 49-year-old men who like rhythm and blues, are frequent CD buyers, and live in urban neighborhoods, one can create an advertising message to appeal to those types of buyers. Additionally, marketers could buy spots on a specific radio station or television show that appeal to this type of buyer, rather than buying general media time to cover all the bases.

Many variables can be used to segment and select a target market. Practically any variable—such as age, sex, product usage, lifestyle, or desired benefit—can be used to describe a target market. The number of target markets identified also depends on a marketing strategist's ability to be creative in identifying segments. Target marketing is especially important for specialty products and shops. Target marketing rests on the assumption that differences among customers are related to differences in the purchasing behavior.

SEE ALSO *Marketing; Promotion*

BIBLIOGRAPHY

Clemente, Mark N. (2002). *The marketing glossary: Key terms, concepts, and applications in marketing management, sales, advertising, public relations, direct marketing, market research, sales promotion.* Glen Rock, NJ: Clemente Communications Group.

Kotler, Philip, and Armstrong, Gary (2006). *Principles of marketing* (11th ed.). Upper Saddle River, NJ: Pearson Prentice Hall.

Edward Lowe Foundation. (2003). *How to identify a target market and prepare a customer profile.* Retrieved January 3, 2006, from http://edwardlowe.org/index.peer?page=main&storyid=6378

Small Business Administration. (2003). Target market. Retrieved January 3, 2006, from http://www.sba.gov/starting_business/marketing/target.html

Weinstein, Art (2004). *Handbook of market segmentation: Strategic targeting for business and technology firms* (3rd ed.). New York: Haworth.

Tatum Krause

TARIFFS

SEE *Global Economy; International Investment; International Trade; Trading Blocs*

TAXATION

Taxation is the imposition of a mandatory levy on the citizens and/or the businesses of a country by their government. In almost every country, the government derives a majority of its revenues for financing public services from taxation. Most individuals will feel the impact of quite a number of taxes during their lifetimes. In addition, taxes have become a powerful instrument for policy makers around the world to use in attaining economic and social goals. As a result, the system of taxation in the United States and elsewhere has an impact on almost every business and investment decision that is made.

NATURE AND HISTORY OF U.S. TAXATION

In 1936, the U.S. Supreme Court defined a tax as "an exaction for the support of the Government." In this regard, there is no direct relationship between the exaction of revenue by the government and any benefit to be received by the taxpayer. As a result, a taxpayer, such as a corporate shareholder, cannot trace his or her tax payment to any particular governmental asset or program. Taxes may be distinguished in a similar fashion from licenses and from fees, which are payments made to the government for some special privilege granted or service rendered (such as a marriage license or a camping fee). They can also be distinguished from regulations and from penalties, which are charges imposed by government to eliminate or control a specific activity.

For taxes to pass constitutional muster, they must be levied on the basis of predetermined criteria. Not only must taxes be determined objectively, but also taxpayers must be able to calculate their tax liability ahead of time. Since most taxes are levied on a recurring or predictable basis, individuals can also engage in tax planning or in tax avoidance. In other words, they are free to conduct their lives in a way that minimizes the amount that must be transferred to the government in taxes.

Despite the adage that nothing is certain in the world but death and taxes, taxation has not always been the chief source of revenue for governments. While the primary goal of taxation is to provide the resources necessary to fund governmental expenditures, any taxing authority that has the power to control the money supply, such as the U.S. government, can satisfy its revenue needs merely by creating money. Complete reliance on this governmental power, however, would stimulate excess demand in the economy, which in turn would cause price inflation. Taxes, on the other hand, raise revenue with the opposite effect because they drain money from the private sector, causing a reduction in private consumption or investment expenditures.

Reflecting one of the rallying cries of the American Revolution—"No taxation without representation"—the system of taxation in the United States closely parallels the tax regime of England. At the time of its adoption in 1789, the U.S. Constitution gave Congress the power to levy and collect taxes. Promptly exercising this authority, Congress enacted was the Tariff Act of 1789, imposing a system of duties on imports called excise taxes. As a result, tariffs became the federal government's principal source of revenue.

As the scope of governmental activities and programs increased, additional sources of revenue were necessary to supplement the tariff system. However, the Constitution required that any direct tax imposed by Congress had to be apportioned among the states on the basis of their relative populations. Because the sizes of the states' populations differed, any tax on income would result in a different tax rate for the citizens of each state. Despite the apportionment requirement, Congress enacted the first federal income tax in 1861 to finance the vastly increased expenditures brought on by the Civil War.

While the original federal income tax was allowed to expire after the Civil War, it did lead to the successful effort to amend the Constitution. The Sixteenth Amendment to the Constitution became effective on February 25, 1913, providing that: "The Congress shall have the power to lay and collect taxes on incomes from whatever source derived, without apportionment among the several States, and without regard to any census or enumeration." Without hesitation, Congress enacted the Revenue Act of 1913, on October 3, 1913 and made it retroactive to March 1, 1913.

As historical conditions changed and the federal government's need for additional revenues increased, Congress exercised its income taxing authority by the passage of many new revenue acts. Since each new piece of legislation simultaneously reenacted previous revenue acts and added new amendments to the law, it became necessary to research over one hundred separate statutory sources to determine what tax law was currently in effect. Eventually, in 1939, Congress resolved the confusion by systematically arranging all of the tax laws into the Internal Revenue Code of 1939, a permanent codification of the law that does not require reenactment.

MAJOR TYPES OF U.S. TAXES

Since its establishment in 1913, the income tax has played the dominant role in providing the funds with which the federal government operates. An income tax is an extraction of some of the taxpayer's economic gain, usually on a periodic basis. The federal government and almost every state government impose a tax on the income of individuals, corporations, estates, and trusts. A final tax reckoning, which involves the reporting of income and payment of taxes due, is made at the end of each year. However, in order to ensure tax collections, Congress has created a pay-as-you-go requirement, through a combination of payroll withholdings and estimated tax payments during the year.

Income is generally defined as any permanent increment to wealth. It does not include loans or any other temporary increments. As a general rule, Congress considers any incremental wealth to be taxable income, unless specific statutory authority excludes it. These increments to wealth can take many forms, such as cash, property other than cash, and services that are rendered to the taxpayer. While state governments set their own tax rules and rates, a majority of the states use the same definition of gross income as the federal government.

Unlike federal and state income taxes, wealth-transfer taxes are not significant revenue producers. Historically, the primary function of wealth-transfer taxes has been to hinder the accumulation of wealth by family units. Since 1976, the federal estate tax and the federal gift tax have been combined into one tax, known as the unified transfer tax. This unified system eliminates the distinction previously made between taxable lifetime transfers and transfers at death. Under this system, the value of a decedent's taxable estate is treated as his or her final gift.

Like federal income taxes, the tax rates on unified transfers are progressive. This means that an increasing percentage rate is applied to increasing increments of the tax base. Unlike the annual assessment of federal income taxes, the federal transfer tax is computed cumulatively on gifts made during a lifetime as well as on transfers at death. In addition, many states impose an inheritance tax on the right to receive property at death. Unlike an estate tax, which is imposed according to the value of property transferred at death, an inheritance tax is imposed on the recipient of property from an estate, although many wills provide that the estate should pay any inheritance taxes imposed on recipients of property.

In addition to income taxes and wealth transfer taxes, the federal government and most states impose some form of employment tax. The most common form of state employment tax is levied on wages, with the proceeds used to finance that state's unemployment compensation benefits program. In addition to its own unemployment tax, the federal government also imposes a Social Security tax on employers, employees, and self-employed individuals. The federal government uses proceeds from the Federal Insurance Contribution Act (FICA) tax to finance the payment of Social Security benefits as well as Medicare health insurance. If an employee will be eligible for Social Security and Medicare, the FICA tax is paid by both the employee and by his or her employer. Although subject to

a different tax rate, self-employed individuals are required to pay FICA taxes on their net earnings from self-employment.

With only a few exceptions, state and local units of government in the United States also use the income tax and wealth transfer taxes as a source of revenue. In addition, these taxing jurisdictions have customarily relied on two other tax sources that generally escape taxation by the federal government:

1. The annual assessment of property tax has traditionally been the backbone of the local revenue system. It is a tax on the value of property—usually only real property, such as land and buildings—owned within a jurisdiction by nonexempt individuals or organizations.

2. In addition, most states and many local units of government impose sales taxes. This is a tax on the gross receipts from the retail sale of tangible personal property, such as automobiles and clothing, and certain services. Each taxing authority determines its own tax rate as well as the services and articles to be taxed. The seller collects the tax at the time of the sale, and then periodically remits the revenue to the appropriate taxing authority.

TAX PLANNING

In the United States and other democracies, a majority of citizens—or their duly elected representatives—vote to impose taxes on themselves in order to finance public services on which they place value but which are not adequately funded by market processes. However, determining which individuals or households or businesses actually reduce their private consumption or wealth as a consequence of a tax is not always a straightforward matter. After all, although taxes affect numerous aspects of everyone's lives, their impact is not uncontrollable.

Tax planning is simply the process of arranging one's actions in light of their potential tax consequences. After all, a character in *Gone with the Wind* improves on the earlier adage by observing, "Death and taxes and childbirth! There's never any convenient time for any of them!" Despite the inconvenience that taxes impose, the average individual will feel the impact of quite a number of taxes during his or her lifetime. As a result, almost any attempt to accumulate or preserve wealth requires diligent tax planning.

The process of minimizing the tax liability of an individual or of a transaction is usually referred to as tax avoidance. Not to be confused with tax evasion, tax avoidance is the perfectly legal effort by taxpayers, and by paid tax advisers on behalf of their clients, to take those steps necessary to reduce one's taxes. As a result, anyone interested in minimizing their tax liabilities in the United States should take their cue from a 1947 opinion by Justice Learned Hand: "Over and over again courts have said that there is nothing sinister in so arranging one's affairs so as to keep taxes as low as possible. Everybody does so, rich or poor, and all do right, for nobody owes any public duty to pay more than the law demands: taxes are enforced exactions, not voluntary contributions. To demand more in the name of morals is pure cant."

SEE ALSO *Income Tax: Historical Perspectives*

BIBLIOGRAPHY

Brownlee, W. Elliot (2004). *Federal Taxation in America: A Short History* (2nd ed.). Washington, DC: Woodrow Wilson Center Press.

Graetz, Michael J. (1997). *The Decline (and Fall?) of the Income Tax.* New York: Norton.

Jones, Sally M. (1998). *Principles of Taxation for Business and Investment Planning.* Boston: Irwin/McGraw-Hill.

Richmond, Gail Levin. (2002). *Federal Tax Research: Guide to Materials and Techniques* (2nd ed.). New York: Foundation Press.

Jeffrey L. Jacobs

TEAMS

SEE *Work Groups (Teams)*

TELECOMMUNICATIONS

Telecommunications is long-distance communications in which a conglomeration of information-sharing networks is tied together. The word *tele* in Latin means distance; thus, telecommunication is distance communication. It is the merger of communications and computers. The term *telecommunications* refers to devices and systems that transmit electronic or optical signals across long distances. It is a process by which people around the world contact one another to access information instantly and to communicate from remote areas. It involves a sender of information and a recipient linked by technology, such as a telephone system. It is a medium for delivering news, data, information, and entertainment—locally, nationally, and internationally.

Communication began as early as the existence of humankind. The evolution of communication systems has included primitive sign language, pounding drums, smoke signals, fire signals, the telegraph, the telephone, wireless communication, and satellite communication. To succeed in this world, communication has become a vital tool in everyday living. With telecommunications systems, individuals access information, bank, and shop online; and professionals are linked together by very complex computer networks. Communications technology has reshaped the world. Radio, television, computers, the Internet, and wireless networks have made it easier and more affordable to stay in touch. Communication has become a way of life. Communications technology has revolutionized the way people stay connected.

Telecommunication messages are transmitted in a variety of ways. Messages are sent from one sender to a single receiver (point-to-point) or from one sender to many receivers (point-to-multipoint). Point-to-point transmission includes personal communications such as a telephone conversation or a facsimile (fax).

Telegraphs, phones, radios, and television modify electronic signals; this form of transmission is known as analog transmission, used to transmit electrical voltages representing variations in sound levels. Computers and other electronic equipment transmit digital information. This means that the transmission is sent over wires, cables, or radio waves and then decoded by a digital receiver.

Personal computers (PCs) communicate with each other via networks using the phone network, such as the Internet. Computers rely on broadband networks provided by telephone and cable companies to send music, text, photography, and video over the Internet at high speeds. Different types of transmission media are employed, including copper wires, fiber-optic cables, communication satellites, and microwave radio. Telecommunications media use wire-based or wire-line communications to link phones and phone networks to transmit messages, or use wireless communication that employs technologies such as cordless phones, cell phones, pagers, and satellites.

TELECOMMUNICATIONS RESOURCES

The most widely used resource is the Internet. The Internet enables students and teachers to participate in discussions, conduct research, and access electronic libraries and databases. This tool has been referred to as the "virtual classroom." One major component of the Internet, the World Wide Web, has gained popularity through the use of Web browsers, enabling the end user to access information on a variety of subjects.

The trend of distance learning is growing. The instructor and students participate in an interactive setting separated geographically by time and place. The objective of distance learning is providing equitable access to quality education and yet meets the unique differentiated learning styles and needs of individual students. Technologies used for distance education include satellite delivery, television broadcast, compressed video, computer conferencing, multimedia, audio conferencing, radio, and videotapes. Remote education and training activities in one's home will continue to become increasingly common.

The telephone has become a self-service information-access device. Individuals use a phone and/or the Internet to check bank balances, transfer funds, pay bills, check interest rates, obtain stock quotes, and place trades. One can locate retailers, purchase goods and services, and make flight arrangements—confirming flight information and seat assignments without speaking with an airline agent.

Computers have become an integral part of twenty-first century lives through a variety of ways. The Internet enables users to communicate with friends and colleagues in an efficient manner. It provides the opportunity to provide education and conduct research in innovative and individual ways that are constantly changing.

Electronic business (e-business) is any type of transaction, banking, or investing that occurs online. Consumers can conduct their banking and use credit cards to make purchases, and vendors can accept payments online. Consumers can shop around, investigate and explore, research products and services, and make intelligent buying decisions.

Selling products directly to consumers via the Internet has grown significantly, with telecommunications being used as a sales channel for marketing goods and services. With telemarketing advancing, customer service has increased in importance as a competitive tool for telemarketing companies to provide quick service.

NEW WAYS OF LOOKING AT TELECOMMUNICATIONS

Since the 1990s, government-sanctioned telecommunications monopolies have given way to markets opened to competition yet subject to heavy regulations. Technological advances are causing fragmented markets to converge. Firms face increased competition in their traditional markets even as technology simultaneously offers them new business opportunities. The industry is responding with consolidation, while regulators struggle to keep up the pace.

Growth opportunities in telecommunications have shifted to customized services, such as asynchronous transfer and packet-based on demand. New technologies have transformed the telecommunications business from horizontal services and carrier control of networks to become customer- rather than carrier-centric.

In the coming years the borderless enterprise, using such technologies as real-time Internet applications and data sharing, will be turning business inside out in an effort to improve efficiency and customer service—and changing the rules for the telecommunications industry. To accomplish this, businesses will be using Internet protocol (IP) and broadband. IP powers the consumer Internet, the corporate extranet, and wide area networks of service providers. Moving out of the data world, it has now become a cornerstone of the converged networks, offering combined data and voice over IP implementations. Borderless enterprises are the mobile enterprises, conducting business through mobile personnel using a wide variety of devices to access and process information. In the communications market, mobile and data are the fastest-growing segments.

IMPLICATIONS OF TELECOMMUNICATIONS FOR THE FUTURE

The complex world of telecommunications will continue to be full of challenges and provide one of the most exciting occupational fields in modern society. Development of new technology is constant, and its use in the technical systems that make up a telecommunications network create opportunities for further development of services for the consumer. The telecommunications industry is often referred to as an enabling industry.

The telephone, PC, and television will continue to exist and develop in parallel. The PC is used as a general-purpose office terminal for desktop conferences, data communication, electronic mail (e-mail), and information retrieval. Cordless and mobile telephones will complement the use of the PC.

The U.S. Bureau of Labor Statistics has stated that the telecommunications industry encompasses voice, video, and Internet communication services. Overcapacity, technological advances, mergers, and outsourcing will effect change in the job growth in this industry. The rapid technological changes in telecommunications will demand up-to-date technical skills and education; the individuals possessing these skills will have the best job opportunities.

The expansion of communications networks and the need for telecommunications providers to invest in research and development will create opportunities for electrical and electronics engineers. The use of increasingly sophisticated computer technology, however, will increase the employment of computer professionals, which includes computer software engineers, computer support specialists, and computer systems analysts, thus creating employment for engineering and computer and information systems managers. Rising demands for telecommunication services will result in a resumption of job growth in the industry.

Residential and business demands for high-capacity communications will lead to upgrades of telecommunications networks. Wireless demands and construction of a new generation of wireless systems will help the wireless portion of the industry. Individuals with up-to-date technical skills and communication degrees will have the best employment opportunities.

Implementing universal personal telecommunications requires access to network intelligence. Advanced computer support and coordination of the fixed mobile and paging networks is essential for the network operator to have in place. Universal personal telecommunication means calling a person directly instead of a terminal. Subscribers are assigned a personal number on which they can be reached regardless of their whereabouts.

CONCLUSION

Telecommunications is a technology on which every business depends. It is more than just phones. Technology convergence has advanced, enabling consumers to use phones, browse Web sites, talk to their families over the Internet, buy goods and services via TV, and carry music collections on a flash drive.

Electronic communication such as telephone calls, e-mail, cable TV, and satellite broadcasts is a vital part of personal life and is important to business. Businesses are a part of the telecommunications industry. They are concerned with communications as they build and install communication equipment such as fax equipment, video cameras, compact disk players, PCs, and telephones. Companies that create messages or content that the technologies carry, such as movies, books, and software, are also concerned with telecommunications; they need to communicate and coordinate their products and services to inform others outside their business. They are a part of the media or telecommunications industries. Telecommunications in operations of any business provides effective services and products to customers. It gives individuals access to worldwide information and services.

The Internet and the proliferation of mobile devices such as the mobile phone and personal digital assistants have changed the way businesses communicate. Key challenges that face business enterprises are mobility, customer satisfaction and cost optimization. With emerging technologies—such as Session Initiation Protocol, Voice eXtensible Markup Language, Web services, and speech recognition—a new generation of multimedia applications and services enables business enterprises to face these challenges. New technologies bring new services and business opportunities. Collaboration and communications

have become the cornerstones of successful competition and effective customer service. These changes reshape the requirements for enterprise communications and networking.

SEE ALSO *Communications in Business; Electronic Mail; Telecommuting*

BIBLIOGRAPHY

Brock, Gerald W. (1981). *The telecommunications industry: The dynamics of market structure.* Cambridge, MA: Harvard University Press.

The changing nature of telecommunications/information infrastructure. (1995). Retrieved February 1, 2006, from http://www7.nationalacademies.org/cstb/pub_changingnature.html

Exploring the digital divide: Charting the terrain of technology access and opportunity. (2001). Retrieved February 1, 2006, from http://www7.nationalacademies.org/cstb/whitepaper_digitaldivide.html

Gullickson, Paul (2001, March). The promise and challenge of a connected world. *T.H.E Journal, 27*(8), 50–54.

Kleinrock, Leonard (2005, March 9). *The history of the Internet.* Retrieved February 1, 2006, from http://www.lk.cs.ucla.edu/personal_history.html

Telecommunications research and development. (2005, October 24). Retrieved February 1, 2006, from http://www7.nationalacademies.org/cstb/project_telecomrnd_prospectus.html

The 2006 telecommunications industry review: An anthology of market facts and forecasts. (2005). Boonton, NJ: Insight Research.

Mary Nemesh

TELECOMMUTING

Telecommuting or teleworking, the ability to work remotely with the aid of portable computers, high-speed telecommunication links, and mobile pocket devices, has become increasingly prevalent in the modern business environment. Private and public organizations are adopting telecommuting for a variety of reasons, including global competition, increased productivity, as a recruitment tool, an expanded workforce, staffing flexibility, business continuity if disaster hits, environmental standards, and facility costs.

The key to a successful home-based office is to structure it so that customers and business associates sense no difference in work performed in the home and work done in a regular office. Unlike those who run their businesses exclusively from home, the telecommuter must have

Telecommuting allows people like this father to work in places other than the traditional office setting. © **ROB & SAS/CORBIS**

access to all information and resources required at both locations, and these arrangements must be cost-effective.

This alternative workplace strategy that ensures increased costs savings, more efficient use of space, and higher levels of worker productivity offers a profound opportunity to benefit both the employee and the company. Yet a successful telecommuting program requires the combination of a motivated manager, a motivated employee, and a well-defined task.

DIFFERENT TYPES OF TELECOMMUTING

Several different types of telecommuting are outlined below:

- *Working at home:* The most popular method, in which the employee designates workspace at home to conduct business functions

- *Satellite office:* Remote office location, usually placed near a large concentration of employee residences, which allows employees at a single company to share common office space and reduces the time and expense of the commute to and from the main office facility

- *Neighborhood work center:* Provides workspace for employees of different companies in one location; each company housing employees at such a location is usually responsible for the administrative and technical requirements of its employees

- *Mobile teleworking:* The newest form of telecommuting—the telecommuter's office may be an airport, a hotel, or a car; these mobile telecommuters are constantly on the road and use technology to link to the office

NUMBER OF TELECOMMUTERS IS GROWING

Today's knowledge workers are ideal candidates for splitting time between a central office and a home office. Telecommuting has increased at a brisk pace; about 20 percent of the U.S. workforce telework. According to a survey conducted by the International Telework Association Council, published in 2005, there were approximately 44.4 million teleworkers. Between 2003 and 2004, the number of telecommuters grew at a rate of 7.5 percent.

Research conducted in 2002 on the use of broadband Internet technology indicated that employees equipped with this high-speed access work more flexibly and productively at home and other locations than workers who use dial-up. This rapidly evolving technology has allowed employees to engage more frequently in accessing the Internet for information, exchanging large files, and working as a group.

Some of the "telecommuting-friendly" employers who are open to this work flexible work arrangements include Aetna, American Airlines, AT&T, Bank of America, Baxter Healthcare, Cigna, Cisco Systems, Citibank, IBM, John Hancock Insurance, Lanier Worldwide, MCI, Nike, Oracle, Sprint, Sun Microsystems, Texas Instruments, and Xerox. The companies have indicated that many of their employees telecommute, but the decision for telecommuting must be made jointly between the employer and employee.

WORKPLACE AND WORKFORCE FOR THE NEW MILLENNIUM

The philosophy that people are the most important element of a company has created a new awareness of the necessity to adapt the work facility to the needs of employees. Although telecommuting is one of the fastest-growing business trends, not every line of work is conducive to it. Telecommuting has been common for sales staffs that spend most of their time on the road, but this arrangement can work for many other employees involved with office activities.

Technology-driven corporations are in the forefront of telecommuting. Telecommuting is ideal for such individuals as computer programmers, sales representatives, technical writers, public relations officials, news reporters, clerical assistants, computer systems analysts, engineers, researchers, customer service representatives, pieceworkers, and data-entry clerks.

CHALLENGES

Areas of concern include feelings of isolation, exploitation of workers, working too much, supervision, access to files, and performance evaluation. Union officials do not want telecommuting to lead to "home work" equaling "electronic sweatshops." The implementation of telecommuting in Los Angeles County, California, led to the filing of three notices of alleged unfair labor practices by Local 660 of the Service Employees International Union, which represented half of the county's permanent employees. The fundamental contention was that home workers are less protected from such potential abuses as violations of over-

time standards and payment for work on a piecework basis. In Japan, piecework is done by telecommuters, with a truck coming by once a week to pick up the products.

A major stumbling block for companies is created by managers who do not trust that employees will work unless under direct supervision. The adage "While the cat's away, the mouse will play!" applies. The major problem employees face with telecommuting is fear that they will not be remembered when promotion time comes around. To address these concerns, both employers and employees must be involved in the development of the telecommuting program and learn to measure productivity in terms other than office hours.

BENEFITS

Telecommuting benefits both the company and employees in many ways. The most frequently mentioned advantages of telecommuting include greater productivity, improved information turnaround, better communication, reduced office space requirements, greater staffing flexibility, lower employee turnover, and an expanded employee market. A 2004 research project sponsored by the AT&T Foundation and Cisco Systems, demonstrates how teleworking benefits a company by enabling employees to continue working when faced with disaster-related interruptions.

Telecommuting provides opportunities for new parents, physically challenged individuals, the elderly, people living in remote locations, and individuals taking care of housebound persons to join or remain in the workforce. Telecommuting is seen as a potential means of employing and retaining valuable employees by helping them balance work and home demands as well as reducing commuting costs and time. The major advantages of telecommuting are the reduced time and expense of commuting and the increased flexibility of working hours. Telecommuting is becoming a viable work alternative for many and can attract more individuals into the workforce and retain them. The information age brings a myriad of changes that can be viewed either as a threat or an advantage.

SELECTION OF PERSONNEL

Successful telecommuting requires a cooperative arrangement between managers and employees. Managers must select individuals who are suited to working at home and jobs that can be completed at home. Since it is difficult to monitor the employee and the workplace, the manager must be involved in designing and overseeing the telecommuting program. A trusting relationship between the employer and the employee is essential.

To have potential for success, employees should be self-directed, self-motivated, productive, well organized, and very knowledgeable about their job. Potentially successfully supervisors should trust employees, have a positive attitude toward telecommuting, be flexible, and be able to communicate well.

EQUIPMENT COSTS AND PROCUREMENT

Any equipment that works well in the office also works well in the home office. The costs of the equipment and supplies are usually borne by the employer. According to Cisco, the cost for setting up a teleworker is between $500 and $1,500, depending on the technology needed. If a notebook computer is included, the cost could go up to $2,500.

The recommended equipment includes a notebook computer with a docking station at the office; all-in-one system (scanner, printer, fax machine, copier); quality phone and voice mail; dedicated phone lines; and Internet access. Telecommuters may also be set up with Web-conferencing capabilities allowing them to sit in on office meetings via modem and webcam, or at the very least, a conference call.

IMPLICATIONS FOR TRAINING

As economic and demographic changes force telecommuting to become a reality for organizations and employees, there is a tremendous demand for training. A curriculum for a successful telecommuting program should include the following subjects: keyboarding, work environment, office automation, time management, performance-based evaluation, decision making, and ethics.

According to the City of Los Angeles Telecommuting Task Force report, training for home telecommuters should include how to set up a home office, how to start and stop working, how to control interruptions, and how to develop a results orientation to work assignments. The training for supervisors should include establishing performance standards for telecommuters, troubleshooting potential problems, and selecting the right employee and the right task.

SUMMARY

As the global economy in the information age evolves, telecommuting will increasingly become a popular work style. Many companies are turning to telecommuting to solve the dilemma of recruiting and retaining quality employees, controlling costs of office space, and meeting environmental standards. The major national advantages for telecommuting include savings in gasoline, a reduction in pollution, a decrease in traffic congestion, and lower highway accident rates.

For a successful telecommuting program, top-down support is vital, employee support is necessary, screening is important, training is essential, and guidelines are required. Major capital investments are not necessary. Telecommuting should be customized for each agency, each employee, and each task.

As Peter Drucker summed up telecommuting, "Commuting to office work is obsolete. It is now infinitely easier, cheaper, and faster to … move information … to where the people are" (Drucker, 1993, p. 340).

SEE ALSO *Office Technology; Telecommunications*

BIBLIOGRAPHY

Drucker, Peter F. (1993). *The ecological vision: Reflections on the American condition.* New Brunswick, NJ: Transaction.

Exploring telework as a business continuity strategy: A guide to getting started. (2005). Retrieved December 14, 2005, from http://www.workingfromanywhere.org/telework/twaresearch.htm

Interagency Telework. http://www.telework.gov/index.asp

International Telework Association and Council. (2004, September 2). Work at home grows in past year by 7.5% in U.S. Use of broadband for work at home grows by 84% [Press Release]. Retrieved December 14, 2005, from http://www.workingfromanywhere.org/news/pr090204.htm

Pratt, Joanne H. (2003, April). Teleworking comes of age with broadband. Retrieved December 14, 2005, from http://www.workingfromanywhere.org/pdf/TWA2003_Executive_Summary.pdf

Telecommute friendly companies. (2005). Retrieved December 14, 2005, from http://www.2work-at-home.com/telecommute.shtml

Telecommuting—A practical guide for working at home. (2005). Retrieved December 14, 2005, from http://www.teleworkarizona.com/pdf/teleguide.pdf

Carol Larson Jones

TELECONFERENCING

SEE *Videoconferencing*

TELEMARKETING

Telemarketing is the process of selling goods and services over the telephone. It has been used to successfully market a variety of products ranging from insurance to newspapers to industrial equipment, and it has the potential for selling virtually any product. There are two types of telemarketing: outbound and inbound. Outbound telemarketing calls are those placed by salespeople to homes or

Operators at a telemarketing center in Japan. © TOM WAGNER/CORBIS SABA

businesses. Inbound telemarketing occurs when customers call in to businesses to place orders.

OUTBOUND CALLS

Outbound telemarketing is particularly appealing to businesses whose salespeople have traditionally made outside sales calls. It reduces the cost per contact, increases the number of contacts that can be made per day or week, and still retains the human element. Computerized databases of prospects and automated predictive dialers can further extend the potential number of contacts a telemarketer can make. Outbound calls can be used to canvass for new business, follow up former customers, contact new leads, speed up payments on past due accounts, and raise funds for nonprofit organizations.

Outbound calls present an ideal marketing situation in which the telemarketer has the undivided attention of the prospect and can get immediate feedback. At the same time, the limited window of opportunity requires that the salesperson establish rapport and trust quickly, listen carefully, and provide clear information. Success in outbound

sales is related to product knowledge and presentation skills and, thus, can be enhanced by training.

INBOUND CALLS

Inbound telemarketing is also a very efficient marketing approach that also retains the element of personal interaction. Calls are generated by catalogs mailed to prospective customers or by radio, television, commercial Web sites, or print advertisements. These promotional pieces solicit customers to buy by calling a toll-free number. When customers call in, they may either reach a telemarketer directly or receive an electronic message that gives them the option of being connected to a salesperson. Since inbound callers have entered the buying process when they call in, a customer service orientation is more critical to the success of the telemarketer than sales training.

The use of the telephone as a sales tool dates back to the early 1900s. The full potential of outbound telemarketing, however, was not recognized by business until Wide-Area Telecommunications Service lines came into existence in 1960. Likewise, the full potential for inbound sales did not become apparent until the Sheraton hotel chain implemented the first toll-free 800 lines in 1967. By 2001 telemarketing sales to consumers and businesses exceeded $660 billion, with a projected growth rate of 8.4 percent through 2006. Employment in the teleservices industry surpassed 6 million in 2001, with a projected growth rate of 4.2 percent through 2006.

PERCEPTIONS AND OUTLOOK

Although telemarketing has experienced continued growth, it has not been without problems. Many consumers have a negative perception of it, particularly with outbound telemarketing, because of untimely and annoying calls. This discontent led to the development of the National Do Not Call Registry by the Federal Trade Commission in 2003. The registry listed over 58 million phone numbers in the first eight months. Many states also have instituted do-not-call lists.

Another problem with telemarketing is that it has been the vehicle for a variety of fraudulent schemes, which prompted a crackdown by the U.S. attorney general in 1997. Despite these concerns, the outlook for the industry appears to be positive. Research indicates that businesses are becoming increasingly receptive to doing business with sales representatives by telephone and inbound telemarketing is becoming an even more important component of a direct-marketing campaign.

SEE ALSO *Marketing*

BIBLIOGRAPHY

Direct Marketing Association. (2005). *Teleservices in the United States.* Retrieved September 14, 2005, from http://www.the-dma.org/government/USmap.pdf

Goldstein, Linda (1996, February). Reflections on the past and predictions for the future of telemarketing legislation. *Telemarketing and Call Center Solutions,* 48–50.

Kotler, Philip, and Armstrong, Gary (2006). *Principles of marketing* (11th ed.). Upper Saddle River, NJ: Pearson Prentice-Hall.

Kotler, Philip, and Keller, Kevin (2006). *Marketing management: Analysis, planning, implementation, and control* (12th ed.). Upper Saddle River, NJ: Pearson Prentice Hall.

Lascu, D. N., and Clow, K. E. (2004). *Marketing frontiers: Concepts and tools.* Cincinnati: Atomic Dog.

Pride, William M., and Ferrell, O. C. (2006). *Marketing concepts and strategies.* Boston: Houghton Mifflin.

Solomon, M. R., Marshall, G. W., and Stuart E. W. (2006). *Marketing: Real people, real choices.* Upper Saddle River, NJ: Pearson Prentice-Hall.

Thomas R. Baird
Earl C. Meyer
Winifred L. Green

TELEPHONE SKILLS

Telephones are devices that allow the user to communicate messages across lines electronically. One can easily communicate with those both nearby and far away using the telephone by simply dialing a specially designated number. The word telephone comes from two Greek words meaning "far" and "sound."

Alexander Graham Bell invented the first telephone in 1876 in Boston, an outgrowth of his teaching the deaf and his experimentation with devices to assist in improving the hearing process.

It is difficult to estimate the total number of telephones in existence today. They are ubiquitous because of their extreme importance as a communications tool. Telephones come in a wide variety of shapes, sizes, and colors, as well as with options that can be configured to accommodate almost any conceivable need.

DEVELOPING EFFECTIVE TELEPHONE SKILLS

Effective telephone skills are predicated on strong communications skills. The four major means of communication are speaking, reading, writing, and listening—with listening being the most important part.

Listening involves sensing, interpreting, evaluating, and responding. The major roadblocks to effective listening include distractions and interruptions. Roadblocks to effective listening can be overcome by practicing the following techniques:

- Being ready to listen actively.
- Keeping your emotions in check.
- Listening for specific information.
- Asking questions when necessary.

PARTS OF AN EFFECTIVE TELEPHONE CALL

Telephone calls may be broken into three major parts—(1) the introduction, in which both parties establish their identity and the convenience of the call; (2) the purpose, which involves communicating needs by asking well constructed questions; and (3) the conclusion, whereby both parties reach a verbal agreement on the points made during the call and any specific action that needs to be taken.

QUESTIONING SKILLS

Questions should be asked in such a way as to obtain the desired information. There are three major types of questions:

- *Open questions:* These questions call for more than a yes/no answer and often begin with *who, what, where, when, why* or *how.*

- *Closed questions:* These questions are used primarily to verify information. Often these questions begin with *are you, do you, can, could, did, will,* or *would.*

- *Forced-choice questions:* These questions call for an either/or response. The listener has the choice between at least two options.

It is an excellent idea to write down any questions prior to beginning the call or during the call. During the call, when both parties are asking questions, it is equally important to listen attentively. Attentive listening can be demonstrated by speaking in such a way that the listener knows you are hearing.

SKILLS FOR MAKING EFFECTIVE TELEPHONE CALLS

Before making a telephone call, consider its purpose. Calls could possibly be made to obtain information, return a call, schedule an appointment, or service a customer.

Be ready psychologically to make the call. Have a positive attitude toward making the call while making it. Have all necessary information available when you make the call.

When making a call, be sure to do the following:

- Identify yourself immediately to get the call off to a positive start.

- Tell the person the purpose of the call. Be specific.

- Ask well-stated, appropriate questions to obtain the desired action.

- Close the call in a friendly tone with an understanding between both parties of the action(s) that need to be taken.

TOOLS FOR EFFECTIVELY MAKING TELEPHONE CALLS

Telephone numbers may be obtained from your own record, from directories, or from directory assistance.

Have the telephone number visible when you get ready to make the call. Developing a personal telephone list is very helpful.

Telephone directories that contain both White Pages and Yellow Pages can also be sources of excellent information. Use the White Pages to locate a specific name of a person. Use the Yellow Pages to locate a product or service.

Directory assistance provides access to a telephone number by going through a directory assistance operator. Usually there is a fee for obtaining this information.

Directory information is also available on the Internet.

OPERATOR-ASSISTED CALLS

Operator-assisted calls are the most expensive type of telephone calls. Avoid them if possible. Types of operator-assisted calls include the following:

- *Collect calls:* In collect calls, the person being called must agree to accept the charges for the call.

- *Third-number billing:* Such a call is billed to a third party.

- *Person-to-person:* Such a call involves telling the operator you will speak only to a designated person. If that person is unavailable, you will not have to pay for the call.

INCOMING TELEPHONE CALLS

Be prepared to answer the telephone when it rings. Keep pens and message pads close by as well as telephone directories and other reference materials. Use an answering machine if necessary.

When answering the phone, follow these guidelines:

- Answer the telephone no later than the second ring.

- Identify yourself in a friendly tone.

- Use the caller's name.

- Gather as much information as possible.

- Do not interrupt the caller.

- Give accurate information.

SCREENING CALLS

Screening a call means using judgment to determine whether you should put the caller through to the desired person by being friendly to the caller without revealing embarrassing or unnecessary information.

TRANSFERRING CALLS

Transferring a call means that, for any number of reasons, it would be best for the caller to speak with someone else. It is important to be thoroughly familiar with the specific procedure for transferring a call.

MESSAGE TAKING

Messages may either be left as voice-mail messages for the person being called or written down by someone else. If you are writing down the message, use a telephone message form to fill in the appropriate parts.

HANDLING COMMON TYPES OF SPECIALIZED TELEPHONE CALLS

Handling the wide variety of both incoming and outgoing specialized telephone calls requires in-depth skill. The following are some of the more common types of specialized calls:

- *Information calls*: Calls made to gather information require careful thought to determine exactly *what* information you are trying to obtain.

- *Scheduling appointment calls*: Know exactly when you want an appointment before placing the call. Have all information in front of you when you place the call. If you are making calls for another individual, notify that person of the scheduled appointment. Likewise, be certain you have carefully recorded on an appointment calendar the designated scheduled time as well as any special instructions.

- *Complaint calls*: Often a complaint call can become a negative experience by nature of the call's very existence. Be prepared to deal with emotions in as positive a fashion as possible.

- *Collection calls*: Collecting money over the telephone is a challenging experience. Good questioning skills are of paramount importance in handling a collection call.

- *Telemarketing calls*: Selling a product or service over the telephone is done by a skilled salesperson called a telemarketer. Generally, telemarketers have been trained to deal with a wide variety of responses and situations.

It is wise to follow these steps when dealing with specialized calls:

1. Always respond in a courteous and professional manner.
2. Give accurate information.
3. Be prepared to deal with rejection and negative responses.
4. Offer a variety of positive solutions.
5. End all calls courteously.

CUSTOMER SERVICE ON THE TELEPHONE

Customer service is an extremely important aspect of telephone skills. This is the reason most businesses are in existence—to serve the customer. Good customer service via the telephone shows respect for the customer and builds business over time. Good customer service is provided by maintaining an excellent voice quality that is easy to understand and includes a pleasant tone spoken at a reasonable speed. Selecting appropriate vocabulary is also important. If words are used that are not understood, positive communication will not be conveyed. Listen intently when servicing a customer. Be prepared to offer responses that will be delivered in a positive manner.

TELEPHONE EQUIPMENT AND EMERGING TECHNOLOGY

Choosing telephone equipment is a challenge with the wide variety of choices available. There are many telephone-related pieces of equipment that can be used with the telephone. Some points to consider when selecting telephone equipment include size, location, number of phones, special options, and whether to buy or lease. Careful thought should be given to researching your needs before making a decision.

Cellular telephones are the type of mobile phones used, for example, in cars, on planes, or on the street. These phones are serviced through licensed cellular phone companies with a variety of configurations. Check them out carefully. Often bad weather or other types of interference can make communication by cellular phone difficult.

Cordless telephones are portable and very convenient. They come in a wide variety of styles for easy use. Cordless phones can be used only within a certain range of area. Their base must be attached to a telephone line in order to function.

Pagers are devices that can be used to alert the user that someone is trying to call them. Pagers come with various options. The more options that are selected, the more expensive the pager.

TELEPHONE SKILLS AND THE FUTURE

Telephone skills will undoubtedly continue to be increasingly important as the technology and equipment evolve. Strong communication skills will always be highly essential when using the telephone. Evolving technology will enhance the telephone in the future. Telephone skills must be integrated with that technology to make the process work.

SEE ALSO *Communications in Business*

BIBLIOGRAPHY
Friedman, Nancy J. (2000). *Telephone skills from A to Z: the telephone doctor phone book* (rev. ed.). Menlo Park, CA: Crisp Learning.

Maxwell, Dorothy A. (2006). *Phone skills for the Information Age* (3rd ed.). New York: McGraw-Hill/Irwin.

Neal, D. (1998). *Telephone Techniques* (2nd ed.). New York: Glencoe/McGraw-Hill.

Dorothy A. Maxwell

TEMPORARY EMPLOYMENT

Temporary employment is work that is not a permanent job. Rather, temporary employment allows an individual to work for shorter terms in a variety of jobs utilizing many skills. The scope of temporary employment is wide-ranging. In many cases, temporary employment can lead to permanent positions. Temporary employment is an expanding type of work in the twenty-first century. As America joins the global marketplace in seeking qualified employees for its work force, temporary employment is playing a major part in the process.

Since the middle of the twentieth century, temporary employment has expanded greatly and become a viable and effective tool for American businesses. In 1995, it was estimated that the actual size of the contingent, or flexible, work force was between 2.2 and 4.9 percent of the work force (Bureau of Labor Statistics, 1995).

Clerical workers accounted for approximately 40 percent of the total U.S. temporary payroll in the 1990s. However, the number of contingents includes CEOs, human resources directors, computer systems analysts, accountants, doctors, and nurses. Approximately 20 percent are professionals. About 90 percent of short-term temporary workers are supplied by a staffing company.

When a business can hire temporary help on an as needed basis, costs can usually be controlled. In the twenty-first century, temporary employment plays a major role in expanding jobs in the global marketplace. Employing people on a temporary basis to work in diversified work environments allows businesses worldwide to deal with competition more effectively.

REASONS FOR EXPANSION

There are several major reasons for increased temporary employment. One is company downsizing. Many companies are being forced to downsize because of increased costs of operation. When a company is placed in this position, temporary employment often becomes a realistic option. From the standpoint of cost, it is cheaper, as many fringe benefits do not have to be paid to temporary employees. Companies can hire temporary employees for periods of time necessary to accomplish the project or task at hand. Also minimal training is required for temporary employees.

Another reason is increased global competition. The global marketplace of the early twenty-first century necessitates the use of temporary employment on a worldwide scale. There is a growing acceptance of temporary hiring through Europe. Formerly, many nations did not acknowledge temporary employment. However, governments are beginning to recognize a legitimate need to use all human resources available in dealing with global competition.

Job requirements vary greatly from country to country, thus creating unusual challenges for those considering the use of temporary employees. Benefits also vary greatly. For example, Belgium requires a substantial contribution to health and social security costs for temporaries, a contribution that totals about 35 percent of the gross salary, payable by the temporary help firm. In contrast, the United Kingdom requires very few benefits for temporaries.

In many European countries, temporary employees function as temporary replacements for those on maternity leave. Throughout much of Europe, maternity leaves last much longer than in the United States. For example, in Belgium pregnant employees get four and a half months of leave. In France, employees stop work six weeks before their due date and come back to work eight weeks after the birth of the child. In both countries, the employees' jobs are guaranteed upon return.

VALUES TO FIRMS AND EMPLOYEES

Temporary employment is growing for several reasons. To begin with, technology has provided opportunities for both large and small companies to customize and streamline their tasks. But doing so requires specialized technical competence. Temporary employees can provide state-of-the-art competence.

Professional staffing firms are especially helpful in this area. For example, Manpower has a division called Manpower Technical, whose employees are assigned to many of the world's leading high-technology firms. Specific technology training is provided for them to meet this increasing demand.

In addition, with the workplace constantly undergoing change, temporary employees can bridge the gap when a business experiences a shortage of help. Temporary employment gives companies the opportunity to test patterns of employment trends and gives employees the opportunity to explore various careers. The combination creates a unique opportunity for a win-win situation.

Reasons for considering temporary employment are as individual as the individuals who seek temporary employment. The major reasons individuals become temporary employees include the following:

Additional income: With a continuing trend of more family members needing to work, temporary employment provides additional income.

Career-path mobility: Temporary employment can often lead to full-time temporary positions or to permanent positions. Employers who use part-time employees have the opportunity to try out an individual to see if perhaps a permanent job match would work. The wide variety of firms using temporary employees provides for ample career exploration.

Temporary employment can alleviate the financial and emotional stress involved in the search for a permanent job, thus resulting in a better permanent job.

Skill improvement: Temporary employment provides employees with an opportunity to gain additional training in specific skills, especially in the area of technology. Most large staffing firms provide training to temporary employees on an ongoing basis.

Flexibility: Temporary employment provides flexibility in a variety of ways. This can be both a plus and a minus. Being assigned a temporary job usually means working with different groups of individuals to get a job done in a short period of time. On the other hand, temporary jobs can provide personal opportunities for acquiring knowledge in various fields of work. Temporary employment demands flexibility in being available for work on short notice with a positive attitude toward whatever the assignment may be.

SOURCES

The most common route to temporary employment is through a professional staffing service. One good approach is to look in the Yellow Pages telephone book. Newspapers are also good resources. And the Internet abounds with a wide variety of staffing services. In addition, many companies who have Web sites have a section called "Applying for a Job." Of course, the traditional door-to-door approach can provide opportunities for temporary employment, as can word of mouth.

It is recommended that persons consider these points when seeking a temporary job through use of a staffing service:

1. What is the history of the staffing service?

2. What is its placement record?

3. Do I have to pay a fee if a job is found?

4. What benefits does the temporary staffing service offer?

5. How often am I paid?

6. Is the staffing service affiliated with a national association such as the National Association of Temporary and Staffing Services?

7. What potential is there for growth with the staffing service?

8. What, if any, job restrictions exist?

9. Will I be kept busy with challenging and interesting assignments?

10. Will I be provided with training?

Getting answers to these questions is important for those considering temporary employment, for they often reflect the quality of the staffing service.

THE FUTURE

The future of temporary employment appears extremely good. Temporary work assignments are becoming more challenging and are lasting for longer periods of time.

Temporary employment will probably continue to be a strong training ground for businesses. The effect of downsizing indicates that no job is stable forever. Because of technology, many jobs have become obsolete, and thus employees without technological skills have been separated from companies for which they had been employed for many years. These displaced workers often turn to temporary employment as an opportunity to improve old skills and learn new ones. Although education can be obtained by returning to a formalized school setting, training can also be obtained at a staffing agency.

Professional temporary employees work for a variety of reasons. Many seek only short-term employment to keep busy. Many are semiretired and looking for a sense of involvement while supplementing their retirement incomes.

Temporary employment offers many interesting opportunities, but it definitely is not for everyone. A staffing agency should be investigated carefully before one signs on. Being flexible and assuming a fair amount of risk taking is recommended. Long- and short-term goals should always be kept in mind.

Temporary employment is almost certainly here to stay and should continue to grow in the years ahead. Learning both the obstacles and the opportunities of temporary employment can provide a sense of focus and direction.

SEE ALSO *Human Resource Management*

BIBLIOGRAPHY
Bureau of Labor Statistics (1995). *U.S. Department of Labor, Report 900, Contingent and Alternative Employment Arrangement.*

Burgess, John & Connell, Julia (eds.) (2004). *International perspectives in temporary work and workers.* New York: Routledge.

Dorothy A. Maxwell

THEORY X; THEORY Y; THEORY Z

SEE *Behavioral Science Movement; Management; Management/Leadership Styles; Motivation*

TIME MANAGEMENT

Time is probably the most valuable asset available to people and organizations. Understanding how to manage one's time can contribute mightily to the success of personal and professional lives. However, as with any other asset, it may be wasted if it's not valued.

Unfortunately, it is human nature to waste time. It is true that some people naturally have good time-management skills, having developed good techniques for managing themselves and their time. However, others have developed poor habits related to time. Needless to say, most people do not like to proclaim or admit these kinds of weaknesses.

Wasted time cannot be replaced. With increasing demands both in the workplace and at home, a great need exists for time to become more respected, valued, and balanced.

DEFINITION OF TIME MANAGEMENT

Time management may be defined as the discovery and application of the most efficient method(s) of completing assignments of any length in the optimum time and with the highest quality.

This definition of time management has widespread applications:

- It applies to the entire spectrum of activities ranging from (1) simple "do-it-this-morning tasks" assigned by individuals to themselves or to others (e.g., prepare several short letters) to (2) large projects developed for a large organization by many people with completion contemplated to take a long period of time (e.g., write a book or open a new branch office).

- It denotes the best time, which is usually but not always the shortest time.

- It pertains either to (1) continuing and repetitious activities (e.g., daily logging-in of shipments received) or to (2) occasional activities (e.g., selection of new CEO).

- It includes production of anything, such as manufacture of a tangible product, provision of a service, preparation of a written document, development of a procedure, or arrival at a decision.

- It may include a progress-point assignment (e.g., development of plans for the preliminary testing of a new product) or an end-goal assignment (e.g., a final marketing plan for a new product).

- Development of plans for time management must necessarily presume the existence and application of such desirable personal and work qualities as motivation, discipline, consideration for others, and the desire to succeed.

BENEFITS OF GOOD TIME MANAGEMENT

Many valuable rewards potentially await those willing to develop good time-management practices. In individual careers, increased job performance and promotions may result. In personal lives, individuals may achieve successful marriages, more family time, less debt, and less stress. In addition, all types of organizations—business, civic, school, political, and religious—may receive productive, competitive, and financial benefits from observance of good time-management practices.

ACHIEVEMENT OF GOOD TIME MANAGEMENT

Business firms and other organizations often find it profitable to take tangible steps to learn the best possible time-management strategies. Some or all of the following approaches may be considered:

- Call in an outside person or organization that specializes in time-management consulting and have a detailed evaluative study conducted of the practices being followed.

- Develop task forces within the firm or organization to undertake time-management studies with the goals of finding, analyzing, and "curing" areas experiencing wasteful time procedures.

- Have individuals within the firm or organization engage in educational and research activities related to time management, such as enrolling in college courses, checking the Internet, participating in correspondence courses, and/or attending seminars.

- Check into the possibility of visiting and studying other firms noted for their efficient time-management practices.

ACHIEVING AND APPLYING GOOD TIME-MANAGEMENT PRINCIPLES

In most organizational and personal activities, three areas of endeavor play prominent roles in achieving and applying good time-management principles: (1) development of suitable personal qualities, (2) development of short- and long-range goals, and (3) effective use of computers.

Development of Suitable Personal Qualities. Good time management requires the utmost in organizational ability. Answers to questions such as the following must be found: Does the worker have all the necessary tools located conveniently? Can necessary tools be found without wasting time? Is provision made for replacement of items that routinely get used up? Are necessary lists placed in a handy location? Are lighting, temperature, and noise at proper levels? If reference materials are needed to perform the job, are they placed in accessible locations? Where direct contact with other persons is necessary to obtain information, can these persons be quickly contacted? Have procedures been worked out to reduce clutter and confusion? Is complete clean-up of workstations required daily or at other appropriate time intervals? Have job duties been arranged in order of priority?

Planning is necessary to achieve success in time management. Companies find that production moves more efficiently when procedures have been carefully worked out in detail.

Self-discipline and motivation play key roles in this process. Once a commitment is made to improve, an urge to proceed efficiently tends to follow, and it is necessary to apply this urge to the tasks at hand. Motivation grows as workers begin seeing the results of improved production.

Special efforts need to be paid to procrastination, one of the deadliest enemies of good time management. People who suffer from procrastination wait until the last possible moment to do almost anything. Some find it almost impossible to take the first step in any project. It can seriously affect work quality and heighten personal stress. It may create uninvited feelings of panic and chaos.

Perhaps the best cure for procrastination is imposition of strict time limits either upon one's self or upon others in the chain of command.

Development of good time-management practices may require inauguration of a program of self-evaluation. Personal habits may need to be studied carefully to see if any are faulty and need to be improved.

Development of Short- and Long-Range Goals. Establishing short- and long-range goals is essential to successful time management in both one's personal life and one's work life.

When establishing goals, it is necessary to determine and specify standards that must be achieved within stated dates and/or times. This involves identifying a series of specific steps designed to bring one closer and closer to a stated goal. A good plan must include amounts of time per day or hour (or other time measurement) that will be devoted to work geared to achievement of the goal. It should include estimated time costs that might result from barriers or obstacles encountered along the way.

Prioritizing, or ranking goals in order of importance, is necessary in situations where the most important of the possible goals may not be easily determined. For example, in designing a new refrigerator, there is often a clash between the engineers, who wish it designed to operate at the highest efficiency level, and the marketing people, who wish it to be given a price tag that will maximize its salability. Which is given the highest priority—quality or pricing? A time-management plan may very well be involved in determining the answer.

Effective Use of Computers. Computers can provide essential assistance in helping people to manage their time wisely by tracking details, coordinating schedules, facilitating communication, and securing and organizing data.

Computers greatly assist those who work with others at a considerable geographic distance. Written messages can be transmitted instantly through e-mail. Data can be researched comparatively quickly through the Internet.

In and of themselves, however, computers do not provide an automatic solution for time-management problems. They are most helpful to people who are already both knowledgeable and organized and therefore best able to apply the benefits of computers to time management.

In addition to computers, other technology exists that can contribute to the quality of time-management plans:

- Faxing is the instantaneous transmission of communications from one fax (facsimile) machine to another anywhere in the world.

- Priority mail and overnight-delivery service are offered by the U.S. Postal Service.

- Telephones, which once provided only voice-transmission service, now offer voice-mail recording, beepers, cellular service, and other services.

TIME MANAGEMENT AND LARGE PROJECTS

Complications inevitably arise with a large project that involves management and coordination of several organizations and people who are all contributing to its completion. A classic example is a construction project involving a building, dam, bridge, or road.

Suppose, for example, a building is being constructed for XYZ business firm. Often, in cases like this, the role of time is very critical. It may be that XYZ firm has found it necessary to get heavily involved in activities such as selling or leasing its existing location, making the myriad of moving arrangements for its employees and their equipment, and working out contacts with its customers.

XYZ firm very much desires the building under construction to be completed at the agreed-upon time. If not, XYZ firm could encounter large expenses in having to put up with temporary locations and increase the time spent in making large numbers of alternative arrangements. In fact, time in such situations is so critical that contracts often require builders to forfeit fees if the construction is not completed on schedule.

In cases such as this (and in many other applications), extensive use may be made of the Program Evaluation and Review Technique, usually called PERT. Developed in the 1950s, PERT groups various activities graphically. Activities in the construction of a large building, for example, might include excavations, various foundation workings, windows, air conditioning, heating, painting, and so on. Each activity requires not only estimates of time but also the costs of labor, material, and money. Some of the activities are sequential—the first activity must be completed before the second can begin. Other activities are concurrent—more than one activity can be worked on at a time. Many valuable rewards await people and organizations that are willing to develop good time management practices.

BIBLIOGRAPHY

Fitzwater, Ivan W. (1997). *Finding Time for Success and Happiness Through Time Management*. Austin, TX: MESA Publications.

Frings, Christopher S. (2004). *The hitchhiker's guide to effective time management* (2nd ed.). Washington, DC: AACC Press.

Lapin, Lawrence L. (1994). "Project Planning with PERT." *Quantitative Methods for Business Decisions: with cases* (6th ed.). Fort Worth, TX: Dryden Press.

Mackenzie, Alec (2002). *The Time Trap* (4th ed.). New York: MJF Books.

Mancini, Marc (2003). *Time Management*. New York: McGraw-Hill.

Mayer, Jeffrey J. (1995). *Time Management for Dummies* (2nd ed.). Foster City, CA: IDG Books.

Reynolds, Helen, and Tramel, Mary E. (1979). *Executive Time Management*. Englewood Cliffs, NJ: Prentice-Hall.

Carrie Foley

TIME VALUE OF MONEY

Are you indifferent between receiving $1,000 today and receiving $1,000 one year from today? If your intuition prefers receiving the funds today, rather than one year from today, then your intuition recognizes the time value of money. Owners of cash can permit borrowers to rent the use of their cash. Interest is payment for the use of cash.

Expenditures for an investment most often precede the receipts produced by that investment. Cash received later has less value than cash received sooner. The difference in timing affects whether making an investment will earn a profit. Amounts of cash received at different times have different values. We use interest calculations to make valid comparisons among amounts of cash paid or received at different times.

CONCEPTS

Businesses typically state interest cost as a percentage of the amount borrowed per unit of time. Examples are 12 percent per year and 1 percent per month. When the statement of interest cost includes no time period, then the rate applies to a year; thus interest at the rate of 12 percent means 12 percent per year.

The amount borrowed or loaned is the principal. Compound interest means that the amount of interest earned during a period increases the principal, which is then larger for the next interest period.

If you deposit $1,000 in a savings account that pays compound interest at the rate of 6 percent per year, you will earn $60 at the end of one year. If you do not withdraw the $60, then $1,060 will earn interest during the second year. During the second year your principal of $1,060 will earn $63.60 interest ($60 on the initial deposit of $1,000 and $3.60 on the $60 earned the first year.) By the end of the second year, you will have $1,123.60. Compounded annually at 8 percent, cash doubles itself in nine years. If a twenty-five-year old annually invests $2,000 which earns 8 percent a year, his retirement fund will grow to more than $425,000 by the time he reaches age sixty-five.

When only the original principal earns interest during the entire life of the loan, the interest due at the time the borrower repays the loan is simple interest. Simple interest calculations ignore interest on previously earned interest. Nearly all economic calculations, however, involve compound interest.

Problems involving the time value of money generally fall into two groups:

1. We want to know the future value of cash invested or loaned today.

2. We want to know the present value, or today's value, of cash to be received or paid at later dates.

FUTURE VALUE

If you invest $1 today at 12 percent compounded annually, it will grow to $1.12 at the end of one year, $1.2544 at the end of two years, $1.40493 at the end of three years, and so on, according to the formula:

$$F_n = P(1 + r)_n$$

where

F_n = accumulation or future value

P = one-time investment today

r = interest rate per period

n = number of periods from today

The amount F_n is the *future value* of the present payment, P, compounded at r percent per period for n periods.

Example. How much will $2,000 deposited today at 8 percent compounded annually be worth 40 years from now?

$2,000 will grow to $2,000 × $(1.08)^{40}$ "or"
$2000 × 21.72452 = $434,490 *

*(While you can compute 1.08 can be raised to the 40th power manually, future value tables, calculation, and computers can remove the tedium of such computations.)

PRESENT VALUE

Now consider how much principal, P, you must invest today in order to have a specified amount, F_n, at the end of n periods. You know the future amount, F_n, the interest rate, r, and the number of periods, n. You want to find P. In order to have $1 one year from today when deposits earn 8 percent, you must invest P of $.92593 today. That is, $F_1 = P(1.08)^1$ "or" $1 = $.92593 × 1.08.

The number $(1 + r)^{-n}$ [= $1/(1 + r)^n$] equals the present value of $1 to be received after n periods when interest accrues at r percent per period. The discounted present value of $1 to be received n periods in the future is $(1 + r)^{-n}$ when the discount rate is r percent per period for n periods.

Example. What is the present value of $1 due 10 years from now if the interest rate (equivalently, the discount rate) r is 8 percent per year?

$$(1 + .08)^{-10} × $1 = $.46319 *$$

*(Present value tables and computers simplify such a calculation)

CHANGING THE COMPOUNDING PERIOD: NOMINAL AND EFFECTIVE RATES

"Twelve percent, compounded annually" states the price for a loan. This means that interest increases principal once a year at the rate of 12 percent. Often, however, the price for a loan states that compounding is to take place more than once a year. A savings bank may advertise that it pays 6 percent, compounded quarterly. This means that at the end of each quarter the bank credits savings accounts with interest calculated at the rate 1.5 percent (= 6%/4).

$10,000 invested today at 12 percent, compounded annually, grows to a future value one year later of $11,200. If the rate of interest is 12 percent compounded semiannually, the bank adds 6 percent interest to the principal every six months. At the end of the first six months, $10,000 will have grown to $10,600; that amount will grow to $10,600 × 1.06 = $11,236 by the end of the year. Notice that 12 percent compounded semiannually is equivalent to 12.36 percent compounded annually. At 12 percent compounded monthly, $1 will grow to $1 × $(1.01)12 = $1.12683 and $10,000 will grow to $11,268. Thus, 12 percent compounded monthly provides the same ending amount as 12.68 percent compounded annually. Common terminology would say that *12 percent compounded monthly* has *an effective rate of 12.68 percent compounded annually* or *is equivalent to 12.68 percent compounded annually.* If a nominal rate, r, compounds m times per year, the effective rate equals $(1 + r/m)^m - 1$.

SEE ALSO *Interest Rates; Investments*

BIBLIOGRAPHY

Stickney, Clyde P., and Weil, Roman L. (2006). *Financial Accounting: An Introduction to Concepts, Methods and Uses* (11th ed.). Mason, OH: Thomson/South-Western.

Roman L. Weil

TRADE DISCOUNTS
SEE *Pricing*

TRADE SHOWS

Trade shows provide a forum for companies to display and demonstrate their products to potential buyers who have a special interest in buying these products. The compacted time frame and concentrated location of trade shows are cost-effective for exhibiting companies and convenient for buyers.

Since the 1960s, trade shows have become an increasingly prominent part of the promotional mix. Their relative importance is reflected in the promotional expenditures of U.S. companies. Larger amounts are spent each year on trade exhibitions than on magazine, radio, and outdoor advertising; only newspaper and television advertising receive a larger share of promotional dollars.

The primary role of trade shows in the promotional mix is that of a selling medium. Depending on the type of product being exhibited, selling activities can involve booking orders or developing leads for future sales. If show regulations permit, they can even involve selling products directly at the exhibit. Trade shows also serve as vehicles for advertising and publicity. Exhibits can be very effective three-dimensional ads as well as collection points for names for direct-mail lists. They can also command the attention of the news media, which regularly cover shows in search of stories on new products and new approaches.

Participating companies can also accomplish nonpromotional marketing objectives at trade shows. Market research data, for example, can be collected from show visitors. Competitors' offerings can be evaluated, and contacts can be made with potential suppliers and sales representatives.

More than 10,000 trade shows are held in the United States each year, and the number is growing. Nearly half of those are large business-to-business shows with 100 or more booths. The smaller exhibitions include both business-to-business and consumer shows.

Business-to-business trade shows focus on goods and services within an industry or a specialized part of an industry. They are targeted to wholesalers and retailers with the intent of pushing products through the channel of distribution. Most attendees at these shows are actively looking for products and have the authority to buy. Examples of business-to-business exhibitions are those in the areas of health care, computer products, electronics,

The Detroit Auto Show is one of the premiere trade shows in the United States. © **BARNES ALLAN/CORBIS SYGMA**

advertising specialties, heavy equipment, agriculture, fashions, furniture, and toys.

Consumer trade shows, like business-to-business expositions, also have an industry focus. They are different, however, in that they target the general public and, accordingly, are designed to stimulate end-user demand. The kinds of products exhibited at these open shows include autos, housewares, boats, antiques, and crafts.

Several trade show organizations provide information and assistance to exhibitors and those considering exhibiting. The Center for Exhibition Industry Research (formerly the Trade Show Bureau) is an umbrella organization that represents the entire exhibition and convention field. It sponsors research on the effectiveness and cost-efficiency of trade shows, has a resource center, and serves as a referral point for more specialized groups. The International Association of Exhibit Managers is the association of individuals within companies who are responsible for exhibit arrangements. Others, like the Healthcare Convention and Exhibitors Association, concentrate on the organization and promotion of shows for specific industries.

SEE ALSO *Marketing; Promotion*

BIBLIOGRAPHY

Lamas, Bob (1999, March). Involve Your Staff in Trade Shows for Better Results. *Marketing News*, 9-10.

Miller, S. (1999). *How to Get the Most Out of Trade Shows*. Chicago: NTC Business Books.

Earl C. Meyer
Winifred L. Green

TRADEMARKS

Trademarks, or marks, are words, symbols, designs, combinations of letters or numbers, or other devices that identify and distinguish products and services in the marketplace. When trademarks are presented to the public via advertising, marketing, trade shows, or other means, they become one of a company's most valuable assets—potential customers identify a company by its trademark. Because certain trademarks immediately create an image of quality goods and services to potential buyers, they are valuable assets that should be protected.

When trademarks are registered at the state, federal, or international levels, their owners are provided the maximum legal protection for company names and/or company products. Thus, in creating or selecting company names and trademarks, a major concern is to design names and trademarks that may be registered with U.S.

The Chicago Cubs logo is a registered trademark. © SANDY FELSENTHAL/CORBIS

Patent Office. Today, the feasibility of designing names for products and services as well as trademarks for them is not likely because millions of trademarks are already registered.

The creation of trademarks involves the development of symbols or other devices to identify products and services in the marketplace. Guidelines exist for creating trademarks. Individuals who are developing trademarks must avoid generically descriptive and misleading terms as well as foreign translations. As soon as a tentative trademark has been developed, its creators should consult a patent attorney for assistance making it sufficiently distinctive to be registrable.

After the distinctive trademark has been designed, the creators need to ascertain that it is available for use. That is, it should not be currently used by another company. Thus, a trademark search is recommended by a company specializing in trade and service mark law. Once the availability of the proposed trademark has been certified, applications and related artwork are filed with the U.S. Patent Office. On receipt of the application, examiners in the Patent Office conduct a search to validate that the proposed trademark is not confusingly similar to previously registered trademarks and is thus usable. To receive a filing registration date, the owner must provide all of the following: (1) a written application form; (2) a drawing of the mark on a separate piece of paper; (3) the required filing fee; and (4) if the application is filed based on prior use of the mark in commerce, three specimens for each class of goods or services. The specimens must show actual use of the mark with the goods or services. The specimens may be identical or they may be examples of three different uses showing the same mark.

If the Patent Office search does not yield any conflicting trademarks and the proposed trademark is deemed registrable, it is published for opposition in the Patent Office's *Official Gazette.* Anyone who believes that a company may be damaged by the registration of the proposed trademark has an opportunity to challenge its registration. If no objection to the proposed trademark is filed, then the registration is allowed and issued. Thus, the trademark is distinctive and the ® may be used after it. Once the trademark has been issued by the Patent Office, its owners need to watch for inappropriate use of it. In addition, trademark owners need to monitor proposed trademark registrations for similar trademarks.

Trademark maintenance involves periodic filing of documents with the Patent Office to keep the registration active. Unlike copyrights or patents, trademark rights can last indefinitely if the owner continues to use the mark to identify its goods or services. The term of a federal trademark registration is ten years, with ten-year renewal terms. However, between the fifth and sixth year after the date of initial registration, the registrant must file an affidavit setting forth certain information to keep the registration alive. If no affidavit is filed, the registration is canceled. A U.S. registration provides protection only in the United States and its territories. The owner of a mark who wishes to protect it in other countries must seek protection in each country separately under the relevant laws. The U.S. Patent Office cannot provide information or advice concerning protection in other countries. Interested parties may inquire directly in the relevant country or its U.S. offices or through an attorney.

BIBLIOGRAPHY
International Trademark Association website Retrieved January 31, 2006, from http://www.inta.org/.

Randy L. Joyner

TRADING BLOCS

An evolving trend in international economic activity is the formation of multinational trading blocs. These blocs are made up of a group of contiguous countries that decide to have common trading policies for the rest of the world in terms of tariffs and market access but have preferential treatment for one another. Organizational form varies among market regions, but the universal reason for the formation of such groups is to ensure the economic growth and benefit of the participating countries.

Regional cooperative agreements have proliferated since the end of World War II (1939–1945). Among the more well-known ones are the European Union and the North American Free Trade Agreement (NAFTA). Some of the lesser-known ones include the Mercosur (Southern Cone Free Trade Area) and the Andean Group in South America, the Gulf Cooperation Council in West Asia, the South Asian Agreement for Regional Cooperation in South Asia (SAARC), and the Association of South East Asian Nations (ASEAN). The existence and growing influence of these multinational groupings implies that nations need to become part of such groups to remain globally competitive. To an extent, the regional groupings reflect the countervailing force to the increasing integration of the global economy—it is an effort by governments to control the pace of the integration.

Trading blocs take many forms, depending on the degree of cooperation and interrelationships, which lead to different levels of integration among the participating countries. There are five levels of formal cooperation among member countries of these regional groupings, ranging from a free trade area to the ultimate level of integration, which is political union.

Before the formation of a regional group of nations for freer trade, some governments agree to participate jointly in projects that create economic infrastructure (such as dams, pipelines, and roads) and that decrease the levels of barriers from those that allow little or no trade to those that encourage substantial trade. Each country may make a commitment to financing part of the project, such as India and Nepal did for a hydroelectric dam on the Gandak River. Alternatively, they may share expertise on rural development and poverty-alleviation programs as well as lower trade barriers in selected goods, as did SAARC, which consists of Bangladesh, Bhutan, India, Maldives, Nepal, Pakistan, and Sri Lanka. These types of loose cooperation are considered a precursor to a more formal trade agreement. The evolutionary path for the development of various forms of trading blocs is shown in Figure 1.

FREE TRADE AREA

A free trade area, which has a higher level of integration than a loosely formed regional cooperative, involves a formal agreement among two or more countries to reduce or eliminate customs duties and nontariff trade barriers among partner countries. Member countries, however, are

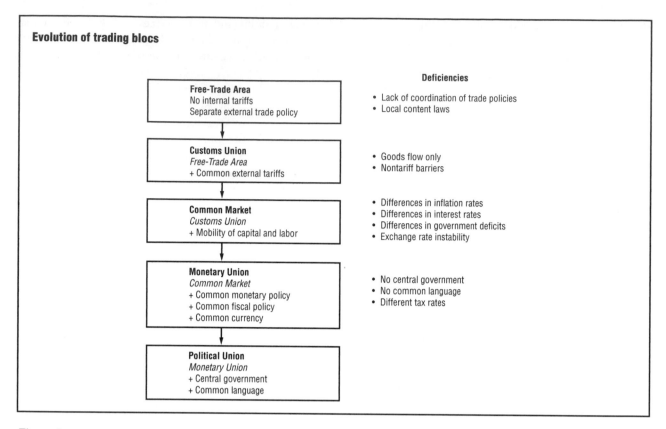

Figure 1

free to maintain individual tariff schedules for countries that do not belong to the group.

One fundamental problem with this arrangement is that a free trade area can be circumvented by nonmember countries, which can export to the member nation having the lowest external tariff and then transport the goods to the destination member nation without paying the higher tariff that would have been applicable if the goods had gone directly to the destination nation. In order to prevent foreign companies from using this export method to avoid tariffs, local content laws are usually introduced. These laws require that in order for a product to be considered "domestic" and thus not subject to import duties, a certain percentage or more of the value of the product should be sourced locally within the free trade area. Thus, local content laws are designed to encourage foreign exporters to set up their manufacturing locations in the free trade area.

A free trade area is not necessarily free of trade barriers among its member countries. Although it is an attempt by treaty to develop freer trade among the member countries, trade disputes and restrictions nonetheless frequently occur.

NAFTA. NAFTA is a comprehensive free trade agreement among Canada, Mexico, and the United States, and is an attempt to progressively eliminate most tariff and nontariff barriers to trade among these countries over a transition period that began on January 1, 1994 and concludes on January 1, 2008. The agreement also facilitates cross-border investment, requires that sanitary and phytosanitary standards for trade be scientifically based, and expands cooperation regarding the environment and labor.

NAFTA was preceded by a free trade agreement between Canada and the United States that went into effect in 1989. The United States has a free trade agreement with Israel as well. Mexico also signed a transatlantic free trade agreement with the European Union in 2000 without U.S. involvement. Likewise, Canada signed a trade deal with the Andean Group in 1999 as a forerunner to a possible free trade agreement.

The three NAFTA countries are very different in their economic structure, development, and size. The U.S. economy boasted a gross domestic product (GDP) of $11.8 trillion and a population of 295 million in 2004. While Canada's per-capita income is similar to that of the United States, its economy is only $1 trillion, or about 9

The North American Free Trade Agreement was initialed in San Antonio, Texas, on October 7, 1992 by Julie Puche of Mexico, Carla Hills of U.S.A., and Michael Wilson of Canada (left to right). Standing behind them are Mexican President Carlos Salinas de Gortari , U.S. President George H. W. Bush, and Canadian Prime Minister Brian Mulroney. © **BETTMANN/CORBIS**

percent that of the United States because of its much smaller population of 33 million. On the other hand, thanks primarily to its NAFTA trade, Mexico's economy, which had been little more than 5 percent of that of the United States in 1998, grew to the size of the Canadian economy, or $1 trillion in 2004, although it has a relatively large population of 106 million.

Despite the different sizes of their economies, Canada and Mexico are the largest and second-largest trading partners of the United States. Nevertheless, trade between Canada and Mexico remains insignificant, while both the Canadian and the Mexican economies are dependent on the U.S. economy as their primary export markets. Both Canada and Mexico shipped about 87 percent of their respective total exports to the United States in 2004. For both countries, almost half of their trade with the United States takes place on an intrafirm basis, with parent companies and their subsidiaries shipping parts and products among their own corporate units.

European Free Trade Association (EFTA). EFTA is another well-known free trade group; established in 1960, in 2005 it consisted of Iceland, Liechtenstein, Norway,

and Switzerland. Although Austria, Finland, and Sweden used to be EFTA member countries, they joined the European Union (discussed later in this entry), and Switzerland has applied to become a member. It appears that EFTA will gradually merge into the European Union.

Southern Common Market (Mercado Común del Sur or Mercosur). Established in 1991, Mercosur is a free trade area consisting of Brazil, Argentina, Uruguay, and Paraguay, with an automatic schedule for the lowering of internal trade barriers and the ultimate goal of creating a customs union. Chile, in 1996, and Bolivia, in 1997, became associate members. More recently, Peru, in 2001, and Venezuela, in 2004, also became associate members.

As can be seen from these free trade areas, their trading relationships are far from stable. Mexico also established a formal transatlantic free trade area agreement with the European Union without U.S. involvement in 2000. On the other hand, on December 11, 2002, the United States and Chile also reached a free trade agreement.

The Proposed Free Trade Area of the Americas. Possibly the most ambitious free trade area plan is also in the works. The Free Trade Area of the Americas (FTAA) was proposed in December 1994, by thirty-four countries in the region as an effort to unite the economies of the Western Hemisphere into a single free trade agreement. A framework similar to that of NAFTA would be extended southward, potentially opening a free trade umbrella over 800 million people who accounted for $17 trillion in GDP in 2004. Whether FTAA will materialize in the near future, however, remains moot. It is quite a challenge to reach an agreement among thirty-four countries (Cuba is excluded at the United States's insistence and French Guiana, officially part of France, is not taking part).

Regional cooperative agreements in the 1990s such as NAFTA and Mercosur have made trading within the continent much easier, but the South America markets are still less open than those of East Asia. Although many people doubted the U.S. government's power to stand up to domestic industries crying for protection, many are seeing FTAA as more than a remote hypothesis and are already preparing for it.

CUSTOMS UNION

The inherent weakness of the free trade area concept may lead to its gradual disappearance in the future, although it may continue to be an attractive stepping stone to a higher level of integration. When members of a free trade area add common external tariffs to the provisions of the free trade agreement, then the free trade area becomes a customs union.

Therefore, members of a customs union not only have reduced or eliminated tariffs among themselves but also have imposed a common external tariff on countries that are not members of the customs union. This prevents nonmember countries from exporting initially to a member country that has a low external tariff with the goal of sending the exports on to a member country that has a higher external tariff. The ASEAN is a good example of a currently functional customs union whose eventual goal is formation of a common market. The Treaty of Rome of 1958, which formed the European Economic Community (which evolved into the European Union), created a customs union made up of West Germany, France, Italy, Belgium, the Netherlands, and Luxembourg.

COMMON MARKET

As cooperation increases among the countries of a customs union, they can form a common market, which eliminates all tariffs and barriers to trade among its members, adopts a common set of external tariffs on nonmembers, and removes all restrictions on the flow of capital and labor among member nations. The 1958 Treaty of Rome that created the European Economic Community

had the ultimate goal of creating of a common market—a goal that was substantially achieved by the early 1990s in Western Europe, known as the European Community (Austria, Belgium, Denmark, France, Germany, Ireland, Italy, Luxembourg, the Netherlands, Portugal, Spain, and the United Kingdom). German banks can now open branches in Italy, for example, and Portuguese workers can live and work in Luxembourg. Similarly, South American countries, led by the Mercosur and the Andean Group, are actively seeking to create a common market of more than 300 million consumers.

MONETARY UNION

A monetary union represents the fourth level of integration among politically independent countries. In strict technical terms, a monetary union does not require the existence of a common market or a customs union, a free trade area or a regional cooperation for development. Nevertheless, it is the logical next step after a common market, because it requires the next higher level of cooperation among member nations.

In Europe, the Maastricht Treaty, which succeeded the Treaty of Rome and called for the creation of a union (and hence the change in name from European Community to European Union), created a monetary union and has the ultimate goal of creating a political union, with member countries adopting a common currency and a common central bank.

The European Union keeps expanding, however. When it was founded in 1993, the European Union originally consisted of twelve countries (Belgium, Denmark, France, Germany, Greece, Ireland, Italy, Luxembourg, the Netherlands, Portugal, Spain, and the United Kingdom). As of mid-2005, the European Union had expanded to twenty-five countries (with the addition of Austria, Finland, and Sweden in 1995; and Cyprus, the Czech Republic, Estonia, Hungary, Latvia, Lithuania, Malta, Poland, Slovakia, and Slovenia in 2004). Bulgaria, Croatia, Romania, and Turkey were likely candidates to join the European Union.

As part of the European Union movement, on January 1, 1999, the eleven countries of the so-called euro-zone (excluding then–European Union members Denmark, Greece, Sweden, and the United Kingdom) embarked on a venture that created the world's second-largest economic zone, after the United States. In 2000 Greece also joined the euro-zone as the twelfth member country. The ten new member countries that joined the European Union in 2004 were not members of the euro-zone in 2005.

The Euro. The seeds for the euro were sown in 1969. That year, Pierre Werner, a former prime minister of Luxembourg, was asked to chair a think tank on how a European monetary union (EMU) could be achieved by 1980. The Werner Report, published in October 1970, outlined a three-phase plan that was very similar to the blueprint ultimately adopted in the Maastricht Treaty, signed on February 7, 1992. Like the Maastricht Treaty, the plan envisioned the replacement of local currencies by a single currency. The EMU, however, was put on hold following the monetary chaos created by the first oil crisis of 1973.

The next step on the path to monetary union was the creation of the European monetary system (EMS) in the late 1970s. Except for the United Kingdom, all member states of the European Union joined the exchange rate mechanism, which determined bilateral currency exchange rates. Currencies of the, by then, nine member states could still fluctuate, but movements were limited to a margin of 2.25 percent. The EMS also led to the European currency unit (ecu)—in some sense the predecessor of the euro, though the ecu never became a physical currency.

The foundations for monetary union were laid at the Madrid summit in 1989, when the European Union member states undertook steps that would lead to free movement of capital. The Maastricht Treaty, signed shortly afterward, spelled out the guidelines toward creation of the EMU. Monetary union was to be capped by the launch of a single currency by 1999. This treaty also set norms in terms of government deficits, government debt, and inflation that applicants had to meet in order to qualify for EMU membership. All applicants, with the exception of Greece, met the norms, though in some cases (e.g., Belgium and Italy) the rules were bent rather liberally. These eleven countries forming the euro-zone surrendered their right to issue their own money starting in January 1999.

Monetary policy for this group of countries is now run by the European Central Bank, headquartered in Frankfurt, Germany. Three of the European Union member states—the United Kingdom, Sweden, and Denmark—decided to opt out and sit on the fence. Until 2002 the euro was in a "twilight zone"—existing as a virtual currency, but not existing physically. During this transition period, stocks, bonds, and government debt were denominated in the euro. Companies could use the euro for their transactions and accounting procedures. In 2002 the euro became a physical reality and went into circulation in all EMU member states. During the first half of 2002, local currencies and the euro coexisted. After July 1, 2002, the euro replaced local currencies, which then were no longer accepted as legal tender.

POLITICAL UNION

The culmination of the process of integration is the creation of a political union, which can be another name for a nation when such a union truly achieves the levels of integration described here on a voluntary basis. The ultimate stated goal of the Maastricht Treaty is a political union. In 2005 Britain remained the principal opponent of ceding any part of the sovereignty of the nation-state to any envisaged political union. Even the leading proponents of European integration—Germany and France—had reservations about a common defense and foreign policy.

Sometimes countries come together in a loose political union for reasons of common history, as with the British Commonwealth, consisting of nations that were once part of the British Empire. Commonwealth members received preferential tariffs in the early days, but when Britain joined the European Union, this preferential treatment was lost. The group now exists only as a forum for discussion and an expression of common historical ties.

The best-known political union that exists today is the United States. The individual states went through a process similar to the evolutionary path for the development of various forms of trading blocs in the early years after declaring independence from Great Britain in 1776.

SEE ALSO *European Union; International Trade*

BIBLIOGRAPHY

Kotabe, Masaaki, and Leal, R. (2001). *Market revolution in Latin America: Beyond Mexico.* New York: Elsevier Science.

Nugent, N. (2003). *The government and politics of the European Union.* Durham, NC: Duke University Press.

Panagariya, Arvind (1997). The regionalism debate: An overview. *World Economy, 22*(4), 477–511.

Masaaki Kotabe

TRAINING AND DEVELOPMENT

The field of training and development changed significantly during the 1990s and early 2000s, reflecting both its role and importance in achieving higher employee performance and meeting organizational goals. This field has become more important because employees need to learn new skills, advance their knowledge, and meet the challenges of technology in achieving high performance.

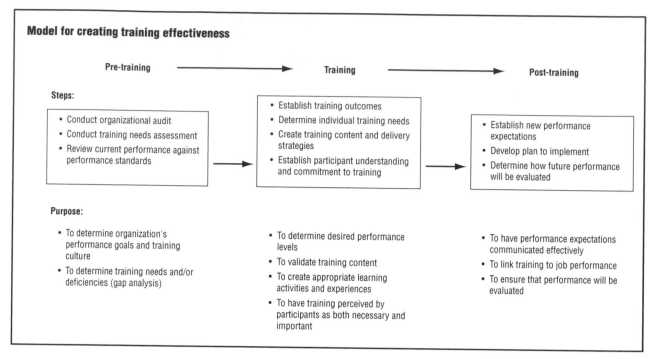

Figure 1

BACKGROUND

Training has traditionally been defined as the process by which individuals change their skills, knowledge, attitudes, and/or behavior (Robbins and DeCenzo, 2006). In this context, training involves designing and supporting learning activities that result in a desired level of performance. In contrast, development typically refers to long-term growth and learning, directing attention more on what an individual may need to know or do at some future time. While training focuses more on current job duties or responsibilities, development points to future job responsibilities. However, sometimes these terms have been used interchangeably or have been denoted by the single term performance consulting, which emphasizes either the product of training and development or how individuals perform as a result of what they have learned.

To be effective, training and development must meet a number of goals. First, they must be focused on individual training needs but still reflect organizational goals in terms of desired or expected performance. Second, training and development must reflect learning goals or outcomes, outlining what will be accomplished by this process. Third, they must be based on sound learning principles, be perceived as important by trainees, and be conducted in a manner that maximizes learning. Last, they must be evaluated to determine effectiveness and to help guide change and improvement.

TRENDS IN TRAINING AND DEVELOPMENT

A number of trends have occurred that reflect the common theme of making training more effective. Some of the most significant trends include the following:

- *A greater emphasis on customized training* reflects the needs of trainees, both in terms of the skills and knowledge they currently have and those that they need, along with identifying the unique learning style of each individual. By having this focus, training can better match each individual's learning goals and needs, and thus be perceived as more relevant and appropriate by the trainee.

- *An increased development of personalized learning objectives* relates to present or future job requirements and reflects past performance appraisal information. This information can be gained, in part, by conducting a needs assessment for each trainee and can help in designing learning activities that encompass the critical skills and content areas needed for future performance.

- *A greater use of instructional technologies,* such as distance learning, allows individuals to customize learning to their job situation—such as location, time, access to technology, and so forth. The use of current training technologies can greatly assist individuals in their learning, since training content and delivery can be standardized, quickly updated, and constructed so as to require learners to demonstrate the desired competencies as they engage in learning activities.

- *A greater integration of training and development into the workplace* links learning to job performance. Training outcomes and learning activities are linked to each individual's job requirements so that what trainees learn will be reflected in their job performance. For example, individuals who have participated in a training program on developing teamwork skills would be expected to demonstrate these skills in their future job performance.

- *A greater use of action or performance plans* requires trainees to develop a plan outlining how they will implement what they have learned and how they will determine whether this plan will, in fact, improve performance. The use of this process further links training to job performance, and it can also be integrated with the performance appraisal process to measure changes or improvements in an individual's performance.

A MODEL FOR CREATING TRAINING EFFECTIVENESS

With training and development becoming more systematic, models describing the process and activities required to achieve successful training are being used more frequently to explain how training should be designed, delivered, and evaluated. One such model, as shown in Figure 1, outlines the steps that should be completed during the pre-training, training, and post-training stages. This model also presents a brief summary of each of these stages, explaining why each step should be performed carefully and accurately.

During the *pre-training* stage, information is gathered to help determine the need for training. An assessment is made regarding what improvements or changes an organization needs to make, along with an assessment of what trainees need to meet their performance expectations. From this information, a decision can be made regarding the *training gap*, for example, the difference between the performance that is desired and the performance that currently exists.

After this assessment is complete, a number of *training* activities can be completed, including developing training goals or outcomes, determining the appropriate learning activities and strategies, and achieving an understanding and commitment from the trainees for the program or activities. When these activities are performed effectively, the likelihood that the training will be successful is greatly enhanced.

During the final stage, *post-training*, a number of activities are required to follow up on the training, ensure that it is integrated into the workplace, and measure performance changes and the effectiveness of the training. Although training can be measured through several techniques, the most important and relevant measurement is one that focuses on changes in performance rather than other factors, such as trainees' satisfaction with the training or what they have learned.

IMPACT OF TRAINING AND DEVELOPMENT ON PERFORMANCE AND ORGANIZATIONAL EFFECTIVENESS

One current method of evaluating the impact and importance of training is to examine the potential—or real—benefits to be achieved through training and development. Although not all benefits can be measured on a strict cost-benefit analysis basis, most benefits can be at least informally measured and used to determine effectiveness. The most significant direct benefits of training are the following:

- It clarifies job duties and responsibilities
- It increases an individual's job competence
- It provides the foundation for further development
- It assists in conducting an accurate performance appraisal
- It produces higher levels of performance

In addition, training may also be evaluated in terms of indirect benefits that can add additional value. These indirect benefits could include the following:

- Enhancing teamwork and team building
- Producing a strong sense of commitment to the organization
- Achieving higher levels of employee motivation
- Assisting in cross-training/job rotation

Although the impact of training can be measured in terms of individual learning and performance, another way to determine its impact is in relation to organizational growth, development, or effectiveness. As organizations have changed in recent times, there has emerged a need to study the critical elements that make organizations prosper and relate these to training and development. It has become common to view organizations in a dynamic sense, noting that they are constantly changing, renewing themselves, and in need of being reflective of current business practices. One current prospective is to view an organization as a "learning culture," reflecting its need to be constantly involved with learning how to become better and to provide significant training opportunities for employees. Accordingly, when organizations adopt this learning culture, they create a variety of training opportunities for all employees and develop performance expectations that instill in all employees the need for and value of training and development on a continual basis.

SUMMARY

Training and development have achieved a high degree of recognition for their importance in helping individuals become better performers and assisting organizations in achieving their goals. The field has become more visible, training processes more clearly defined, and the need for training more evident as societal and technological changes have occurred.

Through designing training and development activities as described in the model presented in Figure 1, the direct and indirect benefits outlined in this article can be achieved. Further, when employees learn new skills and acquire new knowledge, they increase their career potential and add extra value to their employers and others whose work is impacted by their performance.

Following a well-structured plan for designing, implementing, and evaluating training and development programs is helpful in ensuring the effectiveness of the program and achieving a return on investment. To be effective, training should reflect the following guidelines:

- *It should be tied to the organization's culture and goals.* The current mission and goals should guide the development of all training and development activities. Each potential training activity should be reviewed by asking: How will this help achieve the organization's mission or goals?

- *It should be perceived as important by trainees.* Training should be viewed as important and relevant for achieving personal success and high performance levels.

- *It should be relevant to the needs of the trainees.* Some form of assessing the needs of the trainees should be completed prior to training to ensure that the program and learning activities are relevant to what the trainees need to learn or do.

- *It should be linked to the workplace.* Once training is completed, a plan should be completed by all trainees outlining how they will integrate the training results into their job. Some type of action plan that defines what activities will be completed, how they will be done, and when they will be implemented should be used.

- *It should be applied but based on sound learning principles.* Current learning and training theories and principles should be used as the foundation for developing and delivering training programs, but the learning activities should stress how these theories and principles can be used in daily job duties.

- *It should be supported and reinforced.* If training is to be implemented effectively, support should be given by the trainees' supervisor and others who have an impact on the performance of trainees. In addition, policies and performance reward systems should help to support the training efforts and recognize when performance has improved as a result of training.

SEE ALSO *Corporate Education; Professional Education*

BIBLIOGRAPHY

DeCenzo, D. A., and Robbins, S. P. (2006). *Supervision Today!* Upper Saddle River, NJ: Pearson/Prentice Hall, Inc.

Robinson, D. G., and Robinson, J. C. (1995). *Performance Consulting: Moving Beyond Training* San Francisco: Berrett-Koehler Publishers.

Senge, P. M. (1990, Fall). "The Leader's New Work: Building Learning Organizations." *Sloan Management Review*, 32(1), 1–17.

David J. Hyslop

TRANSFER PAYMENTS

Transfer payments are a form of income to individuals for which no current good or service is expected in return. They differ from other payments to individuals for whom either a service (including labor services) is performed in return for such payments or a good is exchanged.

Transfer payments can originate from either business or government sources. Business transfer payments include corporate gifts to nonprofit institutions, payments for personal injury, and taxes paid by domestic corporations to foreign governments. Far more important, in dollar terms and policy significance, are transfer payments originating from government sources. Government transfer payments can be made by any level of government (federal, state, or local) and can take the form of either cash or in-kind benefits. Cash benefits include Social Security; government employee, military, and railroad retirement pensions; unemployment insurance; veterans' benefits; workers' compensation; cash public assistance (including Temporary Assistance for Needy Families [TANF] and Supplemental Security Income [SSI]); and educational assistance. Also included are government payments to nonprofit institutions that do not involve work under research-and-development contracts. Major in-kind government transfer payments include food stamps, medical insurance (Medicaid and Medicare), and housing assistance.

Size and Significance of Transfer Payments. The size of the U.S. government, measured as public expenditures, increased more than threefold from 1940 to 2000, and much of this increase was due to the growth in transfer payment expenditures, especially on Social Security, Medicare, and Medicaid. In the United States at the end of the twentieth century, transfer payments accounted for 44 percent of government spending by all levels of government (*Economic Report of the President*, 1999).

By their very nature, government transfer payments are excluded from the calculation of a nation's gross domestic product (GDP) since they do not represent compensation for the production of currently produced goods and services. Instead, transfer payments represent a redistribution of income, taking money away from some individuals (taxpayers) and giving it to others who are eligible for the various programs noted above. It is also important to recognize that while a considerable amount of transfer payments represent spending on public assistance, such as programs to aid the poor, other transfer payments are for social insurance programs (e.g., Social Security, Medicare, unemployment insurance) that bring significant benefits to the middle class. Public assistance programs are typically "means-tested," implying that the recipient must have household income below some threshold level to qualify and that the amount of the benefit decreases as household income increases.

Rationale for Transfer Payments. Government transfer payments are rationalized in various ways depending on the nature of the programs involved. Public assistance transfer payments are often justified using Richard Musgrave's (1959) "distribution function" of government. Here it is argued the market outcomes may lead to a distribution of income that in the judgment of society is "too unequal." In particular, a government safety net is needed to insure that all members of society, including children and those unable to work, have a minimally adequate standard of living. Most public expenditures on low-income programs involve in-kind benefits, rather than cash assistance, because they allow the public some control over the spending patterns of recipients.

It should be noted that this rationale for government intervention and income redistribution through transfer payments is not without critics. Some would argue that nongovernmental organizations (e.g., churches and other forms of private philanthropy) are better equipped to meet the needs of low-income individuals.

Social insurance transfer-payment programs are rationalized in several ways. One relates to private market failure due to the phenomenon of adverse selection. Consider a private firm selling unemployment insurance to individuals without knowing the details of their employment status. If the firm were able to offer an insurance policy to a large group, the firm could make a reasonable estimate of the fraction of the group that would become unemployed over some period of time and charge rates accordingly to make a normal profit. However, the firm does not have information on the employment status of any single individual. When selling an unemployment insurance policy to a single individual, the firm must assume that individuals prone to unemployment are the most likely participants in this market. Accordingly, the firm would have to charge higher rates to individuals than for the group as a whole to make a profit. The higher cost of insurance would lead many people to choose not to insure, leading to less than the economically efficient amount of insurance being provided.

Social insurance transfer payments can also be rationalized on the grounds that some individuals lack the foresight to purchase sufficient insurance. For example, in the absence of Social Security some individuals might not save adequately for retirement. Society would then be faced with either letting such individuals retire with less-than-adequate resources or coming to their aid. The possibility of the latter further reduces the incentive for individuals to save during their working years.

Effect on Economic Behavior. Critics sometimes charge that major transfer-payment programs have adverse effects on household decisions to work and save. Regarding work effort, the benefits from means-tested programs are reduced as income from labor increases; in some cases the reduction is dollar-for-dollar, implying an implicit tax of 100 percent on the wages of program participants. In 1996 Congress addressed the work disincentive for the major cash transfer-payment program to low-income persons by changing the name of the program from Aid to Families with Dependent Children (AFDC) to Temporary Assistance for Needy Families (TANF) and mandating work requirements for most program participants.

Many economists believe that Social Security contributes to lower saving rates by individuals and influences their retirement decisions. Individuals view Social Security as an alternative saving vehicle for retirement, leading them to save less than they would in the absence of this program. Nationally, this may depress the level of saving because the Social Security system is financed on a pay-as-you-go basis, whereby current workers pay for the benefits of current retirees; benefits are not financed out of any past saving on the part of the retiree. The potential effect that Social Security has on retirement decisions has been mitigated by legislation passed by Congress in 2000 that eliminated the implicit tax (reduced benefits) of individuals over 65 who choose to continue to work while nonetheless drawing Social Security benefits.

SEE ALSO *Balance of Trade; International Trade*

BIBLIOGRAPHY

Council of Economic Advisors (1999). *Economic Report of the President*, Tables B-82, B-94. Washington, DC: U.S. Government Printing Office.

Feldstein, Martin S. (1996, June). "Social Security and Saving: New Time Series Estimates." *Journal of Political Economy*, 151-164.

Moffit, Robert (1992, March). "Incentive Effects of the US Welfare System." *Journal of Economic Literature*, 1-61.

Musgrave, Richard A. (1959). *The Theory of Public Finance*. New York: McGraw-Hill.

Rosen, Harvey S. (2005). *Public Finance* (7th ed.). Boston: McGraw-Hill/Irwin.

Michael Nelson

TRANSFER PRICING

SEE *International Trade*

TRANSFORMATIONAL LEADERSHIP

SEE *Management/Leadership Styles*

TRANSPORTATION

Transportation systems move goods and people around the world. Physical distribution of goods is accomplished by various means: truck, railroad, airplane, ship or boat, and pipeline, or a combination of these methods. Surface and air transportation systems that are widely used to transport people include automobiles, bicycles, rail, air, ship or boat, bus, and rapid-transit systems.

MOVING GOODS

Railroads are a low-cost mode of transportation for large quantities of heavy and bulky items. Since rail lines are stationary, other forms of transportation move goods to

Freight trains wait to load grain in Thunder Bay, Ontario. © PAUL A. SOUDERS/CORBIS

and from the rail site. Piggyback services enable trucking companies and railroads to work cooperatively, loading trailers on rail cars for shipment. Trucks, a flexible transportation method, can handle large or small shipments of almost any type of product, including goods that require special handling. Trucking costs are relatively low for short distances and easy-to-handle products. Ships and boats move large quantities and large products at a low cost. Ships are relatively slow and must be used in combination with trucks or railroads to move goods to shipping centers. On inland waterways, barges handle bulky and nonperishable items such as coal, grain, and cement at relatively low prices. Barges are slow, but they can move large quantities of goods.

For rapid delivery over long distances, air transportation is a logical but more costly choice. Larger products and large quantities of a product are moved by cargo planes while smaller parcels are carried on many types of planes, including commercial flights. Air shipment is suited to highly perishable products or products that are needed quickly. Gas, oil, and water move in large quantities over long distances by pipeline. Pipelines are expensive to construct and difficult to maintain, but once built, they are an inexpensive method for transportation of large volumes.

Using more than one mode of transportation (intermodal freight) improves efficiency in movement. Trucks move trailers to a rail or ship loading site; trucks and railroads move goods from pipelines. This combining of modes increases shipping volume dramatically.

MOVING PEOPLE

Various systems offer choices for transporting people. The automobile is a major "people-mover," but rail systems, bicycles, airlines, ships, and various mass-transit systems move hundreds of millions of people who travel short and long distances each day.

Automobiles. Automobile transport requires an integrated network of roadways and relies on traffic-control systems for efficiency and safety. In many countries, that infrastructure enables people to travel efficiently and economically. Nevertheless, congestion of traffic and bottlenecks contribute to poor air quality, increased energy consumption, and a diminished quality of life. A major concern is how to lessen the impact of transportation systems on the quality of life.

Bicycles and Buses. Because of congestion, bicycles are a popular means of travel in some localities. Within a city, for example, delivery persons find bicycles or motorized bicycles an efficient means of moving small packages. Buses are an economical public transportation system within and between cities. In some areas where auto travel is difficult, buses meet travel needs for millions of people each day.

Rail Systems. The railroad revolutionized transportation in the United States in the nineteenth century, but passenger travel by train declined precipitously after World War II (1939–1945). Amtrak was created in 1971 as a way to reduce automobile traffic congestion. The rail company, however, was not able to maintain ridership and could not revitalize the passenger-train industry in the United States.

High-speed rail passenger systems were pioneered in Japan in 1964. European countries eventually followed, and in 2000 high-speed service in the United States was introduced with the Acela Express, running between Washington, D.C., and Boston. High-speed trains require high-quality track, good roadbeds, and right of way to avoid highway intersections.

Urban areas depend on rapid-transit systems with surface, elevated, or underground (subway) railways, or a combination of these means. Electrically powered, self-propelled rapid-transit systems move large numbers of passengers in a single train, an efficient and environmentally less damaging mode of transportation than automobile travel. Surface or elevated light-rail systems have received renewed support as urban areas seek efficient and energy-saving means of transporting masses of people.

Monorail systems are one type of people-mover system that uses a single track and vehicles wider than the guideway that supports them. Monorails are usually elevated systems, but they may run on the surface, below surface, or in subway tunnels. Subways, surface systems, and elevated systems are widely used for commuting in urban and suburban settings.

Air Transport. Air transport grew dramatically from the 1930s, with the development of a mail-transport system by the U.S. Postal Service. Mail carriers then quickly expanded to carry passengers and cargo to augment their airmail income. After jet service was introduced in 1959, fast, cross-country passenger service became commonplace. Since then, the growth of smaller carriers, the mergers of larger carriers, dramatic increases in the number of passengers, low-fare carriers, and growth in the number of cities served by airlines characterized the air-passenger industry.

Cruise Ships. Passenger travel by boat and ship has evolved primarily into the cruise industry. With increased air travel, many passenger lines lost market share and went bankrupt by the mid-twentieth century. Cruise-ship companies then began to create an image of a "fun ship," which attracted many passengers who had never traveled by ship. The emphasis is on the voyage itself, not transportation to a particular destination. A few superliners, such as those of the Cunard line, provide luxury travel across oceans, but travel by ship is now for vacations, not everyday travel.

THE FUTURE OF TRANSPORTATION

Goals for mass transportation in the future include greater carrying capacities at an affordable cost and in environmentally friendly modes. Intelligent transportation systems will promote better management of routes, electronic payment, crash prevention and safety, and improved emergency management.

SEE ALSO *National Transportation Safety Board; Staggers Rail and Motor Carrier Acts of 1980*

BIBLIOGRAPHY

Monorail Society. (n.d.). Definition of monorail. Retrieved December 14, 2005, from http://www.monorails.org/tMspages/WhatIs.html

Transportation history. (n.d.). Retrieved December 14, 2005, from Duke University Rare Book, Manuscript, and Special Collections Library, Ad*Access Project Web site: http://scriptorium.lib.duke.edu/adaccess/trans-history.html

U.S. Department of Transportation. (2003, September). Strategic plan, 2003–2008. Retrieved December 14, 2005, from http://www.dot.gov/stratplan2008/strategic_plan.htm

Betty J. Brown

TRAVEL CARDS

SEE *Credit/Debit/Travel Cards*

TRIPLE BOTTOM LINE REPORTING

The term *triple bottom line* (TBL) was coined by John Elkington (1949–) and colleagues at SustainAbility, a strategy consultancy firm, in 1994. It is part of a historical progression that included the development of the concept of sustainable development in the Brundtland Report, *Our Common Future,* which proposed the pursuit of financial gains be constrained by the need to maintain social and natural systems at levels sufficient for the needs of future generations.

TBL reporting is a perspective that identifies business performance as affecting three systems that are critical to long-term human survival: economic/financial, social/ethical, and environmental. The term expresses the broadening of accountability for business performance beyond the financial bottom line reported in traditional accounting documents. The term implies the responsibility of businesses for social and environmental, as well as financial, outcomes that result from their operations.

The TBL has become a framework for measuring and reporting business performance. TBL reporting has become formalized and institutionalized by the Global Reporting Initiative, which delineates dimensions for measurement and reporting within each of the environmental, social, and economic domains. TBL reporting is now common for large multinational companies and is often found on their Web sites. Examples of companies using the TBL reporting measures include Anheuser-Busch Companies, Dow Chemical Company, Microsoft Corporation, and Weyerhaeuser Company.

Multiple stakeholders have an interest in triple bottom-line reports: stockholders with an interest in socially responsible investing, employees with a desire to work for a company with exemplary performance in all three dimensions, and customers who wish to purchase from companies they identify as having a social and environmental conscience. Mutual funds that screen for TBL performance are now available. In addition, the Dow Jones Sustainability Indexes and the FTSE4Good Index rate corporate performance on the TBL and accept to their lists only those firms with outstanding performance. These ratings serve as signals to those wishing to invest in companies satisfying TBL criteria.

WEB SITES OF INTEREST

For more information regarding the Global Reporting Initiative: http://www.globalreporting.org

For more information regarding the Dow Jones Sustainability Indexes: http://www.sustainability-indexes.com

For more information regarding the FTSE4Good Index: http://www.ftse.com/ftse4good/index.jsp

SEE ALSO *Financial Statements*

BIBLIOGRAPHY

SustainAbility. http://www.sustainability.com

World Commission on Environment and Development. (1987). *Our common future.* New York: Oxford University Press.

John Vann

U

UNIFORM CERTIFIED PUBLIC ACCOUNTANT EXAMINATION

The certified public accountant (CPA) is a designation awarded by a state or other governmental jurisdiction to individuals to practice as a licensed CPA. The candidate for the CPA must meet education, examination, and experience requirements. The Uniform CPA Examination is required for licensure in the fifty-five U.S. jurisdictions (the 50 states, the District of Columbia, Puerto Rico, the U.S. Virgin Islands, Guam, and the Commonwealth of North Mariana Islands.

BACKGROUND OF THE CPA EXAMINATION

Examinations were used as early as 1884 to test the qualifications of accountants and to issue certificates of proficiency upon passage of the examination. In the 1880s two competing organizations, the Institute of Accounts and the American Association of Public Accounts—the predecessor to the current American Institute of Certified Public Accountants (AICPA)—were issuing certificates based on satisfactory completion of an examination or years or experience as an accountant. Neither organization was able to effectively control the practice of accounting by nonmembers. Consequently, the two rival organizations cooperated to introduce legislation in New York to regulate the practice of public accounting. In 1896 New York State passed the first accountancy law, which required testing the qualifications of those who wished to practice as public accountants. The first examination was adminis-

tered in December 1896. This led to the issuance of a state license to practice as a CPA and the emergence of accounting as a profession with education requirements, professional standards, and a code of professional ethics.

Other states followed this lead, and eventually fifty-five jurisdictions in the United States (50 states and 5 territories) enacted legislation requiring an examination of candidates for licensing as CPAs. The boards of accountancy of each jurisdiction are responsible for administering compliance with the public accountancy laws. Efforts are underway to make the requirements more uniform among the various jurisdictions, so that it would be a relatively simple process for a CPA to participate in the interstate practice of public accounting.

By the 1960s all the jurisdictions in the United States required CPA candidates to pass a Uniform CPA Examination developed and scored by the AICPA. The AICPA has provided this service since 1917. The objective of the examination is to provide reasonable assurance to the boards that candidates passing the examination have the level of technical knowledge, skills, and abilities necessary to protect the public interest. The examination content and format have changed over time as the world in which public accountants function has changed.

The Uniform CPA Examination entered a new era with the introduction of a computer-based test in April 2004, replacing the paper-and-pencil predecessor exam. The AICPA continues to create and grade the examination. The National Association of State Boards of Accountancy is responsible for the national candidate database, which will record information about all persons who apply for the examination. Thomson Prometric, which develops electronic testing products, administers the exam throughout the United States at more than 300 computer testing centers. The fifty-five individual boards of accountancy continue to be responsible for determining eligibility and notifying candidates of their grades. The boards oversee the administration of the CPA exam in their jurisdictions, as was the case with the earlier type of examination.

THE CURRENT EXAMINATION

With the introduction of the computer-based format, candidates can choose to take the examination at a convenient time for much of the year. They may also take the examination at any location throughout the jurisdictions, regardless of where they live or work. The examination is offered five (and sometimes six) days per week during two months of every quarter. These periods are known as "testing windows." For example, the schedule for 2006 provided testing in January and February, April and May, July and August, and October and November; testing was not available in March, June, September, and December.

Emphases. The computer-based examination emphasizes information technology and general business knowledge and reflects a broader approach to testing candidates' understanding of auditing concepts. Also, there is increased testing of skills in areas such as research and analysis.

Some research activity is required, usually involving an electronic search of or access to authoritative literature, the Internal Revenue Code, and income tax regulations. Questions need to be answered and some writing is required, including a letter or memorandum.

Topics. The examination consists of four timed sections, with a total time of 14 hours allowed to complete the exam. The four sections, each of which is considered a separate examination, include:

Auditing and Attestation (AUD; 4.5 hours). This section deals with generally accepted auditing standards, auditing procedures, standards related to attest engagements, and the skills needed to apply that knowledge.

Business Environment and Concepts (BEC; 2.5 hours). This section deals with the general business environment candidates encounter and the concepts needed to comprehend the underlying business reasons for and the accounting implications of business transactions and the skills needed to apply that knowledge.

Financial Accounting and Reporting (FAR; 4 hours). This section deals with generally accepted accounting principles for business enterprises, not-for-profit organizations, and governmental entities, and the skills needed to apply that knowledge.

Regulation (REG; 3 hours). This section deals with federal taxation, ethics, professional and legal responsibilities, and business law, and the skills needed to apply that knowledge.

General Format. While there are variations in the format of the four examinations, the AUD, FAR, and REG examinations are a combination of multiple-choice items, objective questions, and condensed case studies, called simulations. The BEC examination is composed of multiple-choice items only.

Candidates take different, equivalent exams. Each candidate's exam consists of items drawn from a pool of test questions according to defined specifications, so that there is assurance that results of candidates' tests are comparable. The specifications include "exposure controls" to limit the extent to which examinees are administered the same sets of questions.

REQUIREMENTS FOR CANDIDATES

While all jurisdictions use the same examination, the requirements and procedures for applying to sit for the examination differ among the jurisdictions.

Candidates must complete an education requirement, which varies among the jurisdictions. Most require at least a bachelor's degree with a concentration in accounting, but a majority of the jurisdictions have legislated an education requirement of at least 150 semester hours. Normally this includes a bachelor's degree plus thirty semester hours of advanced coursework. The date this requirement becomes effective varies among the jurisdictions.

Some jurisdictions specify the number of required semester hours or courses in accounting and related business subjects. Candidates must first decide on the jurisdiction to which they will apply. International applicants must follow the same procedures. The examination is available only in English. Special accommodations under the Americans with Disabilities Act may be requested as part of the application process. These procedures are included in the application materials provided by the candidate's state board of accountancy.

Other requirements for taking the examination vary among the jurisdictions as to residency, place of employment, and U.S. citizenship.

Candidates should contact the board in the jurisdiction where they plan to sit for the examination or plan to practice for the most current education, residency, and citizenship requirements as such requirements are subject to modification.

As a general rule, eligible candidates may schedule sections in any testing window and in any order. Nevertheless, candidates may not take any single section twice in the same window. Candidates need to check their board's requirements for the rules that apply to them.

While the boards of accountancy determine the time limit for passing the four sections of the examination, most boards allow eighteen months for the remaining three sections, after successful completion of one section.

ASSISTANCE PROVIDED CANDIDATES

The AICPA provides an online tutorial to help potential candidates with the types of questions and responses used in the computer-based test and with moving from one section to another.

The objective of the examination is to test the knowledge and skills that a candidate needs to practice as a CPA in planning and implementing a public accounting engagement. The examination requires candidates to display evaluation, judgment, presentation, and decision-making abilities related to accounting and auditing information.

SECURITY PROVIDED

The computer-based test has been designed with measures to prevent and detect cheating and other dishonest activities. The test's emphasis on simulations and increased number of multiple-choice questions from which there are random selections reduces the value of memorization and it is virtually impossible for candidates to anticipate specific questions.

The computer-based exam has stringent security measures to protect the confidentiality of personal information. The AICPA, the state boards of accountancy, and Thomson Prometric are prohibited from using information from the database for any purpose other than administering the exam. Candidates' personal information, as well as their test scores, is maintained with a high level of security.

WEB SITES OF INTEREST

For further information on the Uniform CPA Examination: http://www.cpa-exam.org

For information from the National Association of State Boards of Accountancy on the examinations: http://www.nasba.org/nasbaweb.nsf/exam

For details about the structure, length, content, skills definitions and content weighting of the CPA exam: http://www.cpa-exam.org/cpa.computer.html

SEE ALSO *American Institute of Certified Public Accountants; National Association of State Boards of Accountancy; State Societies of CPAs*

BIBLIOGRAPHY

American Institute of Certified Public Accountants. (2005). *Uniform CPA Examination Candidate Bulletin.* New York: Author.

Flesher, Dale, Miranti, Paul J., and Previts, Gary John (1996, October). The first century of the CPA. *Journal of Accountancy,* pp. 51–57.

Snyder, Adam (2003, December). The new CPA exam: Meeting today's challenges. *Journal of Accountancy,* p11(2).

Bernard H. Newman
Mary Ellen Oliverio

UNITED STATES GOVERNMENT ACCOUNTABILITY OFFICE

In 2004 the U.S. Congress changed the name of the U.S. government financial management oversight office to the Government Accountability Office (GAO). Since 1921 this nonpartisan office of Congress had been the General Accounting Office (so it retained its initialism, GAO), even though the office did not keep accounts or establish accounting rules. Initially, the GAO did actually review government vouchers and receipts. For decades, though, the GAO's work has been primarily review of federal government financial transactions, covering programs, projects, and activities within the United States and abroad. The GAO does serve, however, as the principal auditor for the U.S. government's annual consolidated financial statements, and in 2005 devoted 15 percent of its workload to financial audits.

The GAO's chief officer is the comptroller general of the United States, who is appointed by the president for a single term of fifteen years with the advice and consent of the Senate. Removal of the comptroller general from office requires the passage of a joint resolution of Congress signed by the president. The protection of office afforded to the comptroller general strengthens the independence of the GAO.

Much of the work that the GAO performs originates as requests from committees of Congress or from members of Congress. Other work fulfills GAO mandates or legislative requirements.

HISTORY AND ESTABLISHMENT BY CONGRESS

The GAO was established by the Budget and Accounting Act of 1921, which transferred powers previously held by the U.S. Department of Treasury to the GAO. This transfer of powers from the executive branch represented a substantial change in federal financial management. As the presidency became the dominant focus of government in the twentieth century, the GAO became a powerful investigative office of Congress, with authority to audit the financial operations of government and to examine matters related to the receipt and disbursement of public funds.

EVOLVING NATURE OF RESPONSIBILITIES

The GAO has broad responsibility for oversight of financial activities in the executive branch and wide discretion in the application of its responsibilities. Over time, the GAO's interpretation of its responsibility has evolved through four phases of dominant orientation: bookkeeping, auditing, evaluation, and systems development. Until the end of World War II (1939–1945), the GAO had a bookkeeping orientation. Its work consisted of checking the accuracy and the legality of transactions. Operations were centralized, and personnel lacked professional credentials.

Following World War II, responsibility for bookkeeping practices was transferred to executive agencies, and the GAO's orientation shifted to auditing. It began to conduct financial audits of government corporations, such as the Tennessee Valley Authority, and to perform economy and efficiency audits of activities within selected agencies. Additionally, the GAO was aggressive in auditing defense contracts for cost overruns. Many of the auditors were military veterans who were educated in accounting.

Starting about 1965 with the adoption of Great Society programs, the GAO's orientation shifted to program evaluation and service to Congress. Staff members with a variety of educational backgrounds were recruited for their expertise in a number of fields, including accounting, information systems, and law.

From the early 1980s, the GAO's focus centered on the development of financial and management systems. As a means of improving management of the government, resources were directed to improving internal control systems, financial reporting systems, and performance-based management systems.

NATURE OF RESPONSIBILITIES AND ACTIVITIES

The GAO has broad responsibilities as noted in 2004 by David Walker, the comptroller general:

> The scope of GAO's work today includes virtually everything the federal government is doing and thinking about doing anywhere in the world.... GAO has become a modern, multidiscipline professional services organization whose 3,200 employees include economists, social scientists, engineers, attorneys, actuaries, and computer experts as well as specialists in areas from health care to homeland security. (Walker, 2004)

Nevertheless, the GAO's authority over the executive branch is limited. In *Bowsher v. Synar* (1986), the U.S. Supreme Court held that the comptroller general could not exercise executive branch decision-making authority. And, in *Walker v. Cheney* (2002), the District Court for the District of Columbia held that the GAO lacked the standing to sue to compel the vice president to disclose information.

Accounting and Auditing. The scope of GAO audits may be broader or narrower than the scope of financial audits in the private sector. To provide the necessary expertise, personnel on GAO audit teams often have disciplinary backgrounds other than accounting. Also, GAO audits tend to be initiated by request and usually are not performed on a routine periodic basis. The GAO is responsible, however, for the annual audit of consolidated government-wide financial statements. Although the number of agencies receiving unqualified audit opinions has increased since government-wide statements were initiated in 1997, material weaknesses at the U.S. Department of Defense and other agencies have precluded the issuance of an unqualified opinion on the consolidated government-wide financial statements (as of the end of fiscal year 2004).

The GAO, although not directly responsible, participates in the development of accounting principles and standards and advises federal agencies about fiscal policies and procedures. Additionally, through the publication *Government Auditing Standards,* commonly known as the *Yellow Book,* and other directives, the GAO proscribes standards for auditing and evaluating government programs, including standards for governmental entities subject to the Single Audit Act of 1984 (and its amendments of 1996). The GAO's auditing standards have been revised from time to time with the latest revision in June 2003.

Legal Advice. The GAO provides legal advice to Congress, reviews legislative proposals, and assists with drafting legislation. Its staff investigates possible civil and criminal misconduct discovered during audits and evaluations. Within its judicial functions, the GAO resolves bid protests that challenge government contract awards, interprets laws governing public expenditure, and adjudicates claims for and against the government.

Reporting. Findings and recommendations of the GAO are published as reports to Congress, delivered as testimony to Congress, or conveyed in oral briefings. Additionally, the GAO publishes comptroller general decisions. All unclassified reports are available to the public and are generally posted at the GAO Web site (http://www.gao.gov) promptly upon publication.

Improvement of Performance. To motivate improvements in the performance of federal agencies, the GAO has developed the High Risk Series and the Performance and Accountability Series. Begun in 1990, the High Risk Series identifies programs that are vulnerable to waste, fraud, abuse, and mismanagement. The 1999 Performance and Accountability Series provides a general report and separate reports on each cabinet department and most other major independent agencies. This series is oriented to understanding ways performance-based management can be applied to achieve economy, efficiency, and effectiveness in government operations.

ROLE ENVISIONED

At the GAO's Web site are the words *accountability, integrity,* and *reliability.* These words are the fundamental concepts that guide the work of the agency. The GAO stated mission is "to support Congress in meeting its constitutional responsibilities and to help improve the performance and ensue the accountability of the federal government for the benefit of the American people."

Walker's comment reflected the mission statement when he wrote:

> At today's GAO, measuring the government's performance and holding it accountable for results is central to who we are and what we do. We continue to believe that the public deserves the facts on all aspects of government operations—from spending to policy making. (Walker, 2004)

SEE ALSO *Chief Financial Officers Act of 1990 and Federal Financial Management Act of 1994; Government Accounting*

BIBLIOGRAPHY

Trask, Roger R. (1991). *GAO History 1921–1991.* Washington, DC: General Accounting Office.

Trask, Roger R. (1996). *Defender of the public interest: The General Accounting Office, 1921–1966.* Washington, DC: General Accounting Office.

Walker, David M. (2004, July 19). GAO answers the question: What's in a name? *Roll Call.* Retreived from http://www.gao.gov/about/rollcall07192004.pdf January 6, 2006.

Walker, David M. (2005, July). Audit profile: Government Accountability Office of the United States. *International Journal of Government Auditing, 32*(3), 18–22.

Jean E. Harris

V

VALUES
SEE *Social Responsibility and Organizational Ethics*

VARIANCE
SEE *Costs*

VIDEOCONFERENCING

George Jetson, a character in the 1970s cartoon, was not terribly futuristic when he used his telephone that enabled him to see the person to whom he was talking. Videoconferencing, as it is known today, has been under development in the research labs at Pacific Bell since the 1920s. The project, referred to as picturephone, is in the form of a desktop videoconferencing system. Videoconferencing rooms have been in existence at AT&T since the 1960s, where they are used to support large corporate meetings, including the annual shareholder's meeting.

It was not until the 1964 World's Fair that the picturephone was introduced to the public. AT&T predicted that the picturephone would replace the telephone by 1970. Although that prediction was wrong, the recession of the 1970s created a wider acceptance of videoconferencing by corporations that were looking for alternative ways to conduct meetings and conferences while cutting travel costs. Videoconferencing was not successful at that time, however, because the technology needed to attain personalized meetings was lacking.

With technology becoming more affordable and economically justifiable, practical and profitable applications of teleconferencing have gained popularity in the business world. With increasing competition and the need for face-to-face contact with customers, videoconferencing has become more popular because it allows face-to-face interaction without wasting travel time. Teleconferencing also allows team meetings without the need to travel hundreds of miles.

WHAT IS TELECONFERENCING?
The earliest form of teleconferencing was the telephone conference call, in which several parties in various parts of the world could simultaneously hold a conversation. Businesspeople could talk with each other while sending and receiving faxes to provide a hard copy of the information being discussed. Today computer technology allows for synchronous, or simultaneous, sharing of data through four means: voice, video, digital whiteboard, and data files.

Several parties are able to share not only voice but also a live camera image of themselves while they talk. The size of the image can be shrunk to occupy only a small portion of the computer monitor or large display screen so that a data file can be accessed, displayed, and edited on the monitor at the same time.

Individuals participating in the conference call have the option of sharing and working with data files from either party's computer. While verbally discussing changes within the document and observing each other's body language, either party can edit the document and give immediate feedback. The digital whiteboard provides an

Videoconferencing allows people around the world to meet face-to-face. © STEVE CHENN/CORBIS

electronic version of the dry erase board mounted on the wall. While viewing each other's actions via the computer monitor, individuals can also write on each other's whiteboard with special markers in the color of their choice. This allows professionals to make decisions and solve problems on the spot.

VIDEOCONFERENCING AND BUSINESS

This type of communicating enables people to work from their home via satellite, which increases family and/or personal time while reducing time spent commuting. It is estimated that in 1999 between 8 million and 15 million of the 120 million U.S. employees worked at home and communicated with their offices and customers using a computer and telephone lines. The number of telecommuters in America was expected to double by 2005.

A business environment requires most corporate employees to collaborate on a routine basis. Videoconferencing allows for face-to-face planned as well as impromptu meetings of workers who are separated by several thousand miles.

Sales presentations are an example of a profitable and easily justified business use of videoconferencing. When conducting the sales presentation at the customer's loca-

tion, a sales representative with videoconferencing equipment on a laptop computer can connect the customer with specialists back at the company's offices to answer specific questions about the product being demonstrated. This allows greater specialization, with the salesperson focusing on closing the sale and the specialists focusing on the technical aspects of the product. The salesperson is able to view the customer's body language and ask the specialist for clarification on customer objections or questions. The customer feels a sense of security by being able to see the individual instead of merely hearing a voice.

Another business application of videoconferencing is the ability to train people without actually traveling to another location. Companies can provide more frequent training to their employees in distant locations for less cost.

The Northrop Grumman Corporation implemented extensive teleconferencing for its 45,000 employees by setting up one hundred Team Communications Centers (TCCs) (teleconferencing rooms) at their offices across the United States. The TCCs are equipped with large digital whiteboards and projector screens. Groups of employees or managers from two or more locations collaborate on, discuss, and edit documents as though they were all in the same room, saving both time and money. The corporation identified airfare savings in 1998 of $150,000. These savings did not include hotels, meals, overtime, or incidentals.

VIDEOCONFERENCING AND EDUCATION

Teleconferencing can bring more educational choice and excellence to remote schools with small student bodies. Specialized courses that individual schools could not offer because of cost or limited student interest can be shared by several schools to provide cost efficiency. Flexibility in scheduling classes to meet either an individual student's or a group of students' need is another major advantage.

Many universities offer courses over the Internet or by means of other teleconferencing capabilities. Known as distance learning, this technology enables thousands of students to take college classes without leaving their community or, in many cases, their home.

The nature of videoconferencing often requires distance-learning classes to present more class material, use better visuals, and show greater preparation of the teaching materials than traditional classes. These classes also hold students more accountable for their own learning. A major drawback for some students is that they must still attend classes (virtually) at preset times and progress at the pace set for the course.

Internet courses often better meet student needs by allowing them to work within their own time schedules and to progress at their own pace. Students sign into the virtual classroom (chat room) when it is convenient for them and respond to instructor questions and other student responses in much the same manner as they would in a traditional classroom discussion. The major differences are that all students must actively participate and the responses are written rather than oral.

Videoconferencing can present barriers to learning when interpersonal skills such as face-to-face interaction, eye contact, gaze, body language, and voice inflection are not transmitted. Another potential barrier is intercommunication delays when the timing of visual and audio signals, which are known to be effective in communication, are sometimes delayed.

For effective videoconferencing, the design of the room and the training of participants are critical factors. In educational settings, the classroom layout should allow all participants, including the instructor, to see and hear one another clearly. Instructors often need training on how best to project enthusiasm using this medium, how to monitor and adjust the camera and audio components, and how to prepare effective materials. Institutions must have a clear plan of how the system will be used to deliver instruction before they offer classes.

TECHNOLOGY

The three major types of videoconferencing involve conference rooms, roll-around units, and desktop units. The conference room facilities provide the user with a meeting room equipped with the audio and video technology needed to conduct an interactive conference. Roll-around units contain the needed audio and video equipment but are designed to be moveable. They provide a degree of flexibility, but the large size of the units often makes them impractical.

Desktop units provide desk or office videoconferencing access at the user's computer. The two essential components in addition to the computer are a small video camera, which usually sits on top of the computer, and a microphone, which can be set on a pedestal or worn as a headset. Telephone network capabilities have limited the quality of the video as well as causing delays in transmission. With the new TV cable hook-ups, however, desktop conferencing is achieving excellent video and audio quality.

Two types of desktop systems are VISIT and TMS. VISIT was an early desktop multimedia system integrating desktop videoconferencing, screen sharing, high-speed data transfer, electronic voice-mail access, and voice call management on a desktop computer. It required a plug-in video board; a black-and-white, fixed-focus CCD camera with an electronic auto iris; and application software.

TMS (Telepresence Media Space System), the newer system, is designed to capture the existing physical, cognitive, and social skills of users to support the same confidentiality, intimacy, and trust that develop in people who are engaged in face-to-face interaction. TMS also provides real-time document sharing and editing, video mail, video receptionist, and video recording of meetings. The technology needed for a TMS system includes a Sun workstation as the central server, computer controlled audio-video switch, PictureTel codec, Sony VCR, and camera mounted on the roof.

KEY TO SUCCESSFUL VIDEOCONFERENCING

The key to successful videoconferencing is effective communication skills. The users must be comfortable with the system, so that it appears as transparent as possible. This will allow the receiver to concentrate on the message and the sender to concentrate on making eye contact, so that participants feel included and are not just observers.

Participants in a videoconference should wear solid-colored clothing in dark or neutral colors to enhance the camera's focus. Movements should be slow and smooth, and caution should be taken not to block the camera's line of sight.

Participants should always maintain appropriate on-camera positioning, adhering to the elbows and wrists rule so that when you stretch out your arms, the edge of the screen falls between your elbows and wrists. It is important that participants see each other's facial expressions, but close-up shots should be used judiciously because the camera is sensitive to movement and will exaggerate blinking eyes, moving hands, or shifting in chairs. Videoconferencing participants will find it difficult to pay attention if the subject is not presented in an interesting and enthusiastic manner. Presenters should get beyond the talking head model and make the session as interactive as possible.

As in any instructional or corporate setting, the use of images, objects, and audio or video clips will greatly enhance the meeting's effectiveness. Visuals should have large, bold text with simple fonts and concise bulleted information. Time should be allowed for all participants to view the graphics. Participants should always speak in a strong, clear voice and avoid interrupting another speaker because the time delay may cause confusion.

Although videoconferencing has been available for more than seventy years, it is only in recent years that its quality has reached the standards needed in business and educational settings. Its popularity has increased because it is able to save individuals and business both time and money, which are valuable and limited resources. As technology improves, the use of videoconferencing will increase as more businesses and individuals embrace it as an effective means of face-to-face communications.

SEE ALSO *Communications in Business; Telecommunications*

BIBLIOGRAPHY

InnoVisions Canada. (n.d.) Retrieved October 29, 2005, from http://www.ivc.ca

Moore, G., and Schuyler, K. (1996). Videoconferencing 90's Style: Sharing Faces, Places and Spaces. *PowerGrid Journal.*

The Telework Coalition (2005). Retrieved October 29, 2005, from http//www.telcoa.org.

James E. Miles

VISUAL MERCHANDISING

SEE *Promotion*

VOICE MESSAGING

Voice messaging is a computerized method of storing and manipulating spoken recorded messages that is accessible to users from any touch-tone phone twenty-four hours a day. A voice-messaging system can be easily accessed by local, remote, or mobile users via land-lines or cellular phones. Messages may be created in a user's voice mailbox and then transported to another voice mailbox in a manner similar to the e-mail process.

Voice-messaging systems include such services as voice messages, voice-mail distribution lists, fax-in and fax-on demand in the mailbox, interactive voice response, and voice forms that any user can access anywhere in the world.

HOW VOICE MESSAGING WORKS

Person A calls Person B, who is not available to take the call. Person B's voice mailbox or answering machine takes the call, replaying it when Person B returns and accesses it. The answering machine can be precise to Person B or can be shared with multiple office personnel. If the company has either a precise or shared system, Person B may retrieve the message by using a digitized code assigned to him or her. This code is called a voice-mail number. The voice mail system is designed to transfer a person's call to another telephone automatically by using call forwarding and to prioritize messages so that a specific phone number from Person A—the recipient—is prepared to communicate to Person B—the caller—for feedback.

HOW VOICE MESSAGING RELATES TO THE COMMUNICATION PROCESS

Voice messaging relates to the communication process by increasing productivity, improving internal communication, enhancing customer service, and reducing message-taking costs. The proper implementation of a voice-messaging system could be linked directly to improved public relations in companies.

In companies where a voice system is in place, users can easily change their greeting and the information in it and invite callers to leave their name, number, and any desired information. Voice-messaging systems in some companies permit users to call from any telephone in the world to change their greeting and to retrieve messages at any time of the day or night. Using a voice-message system ensures accurate messages, reduces the need for receptionists to take messages, and frees users from time zone dependence.

Many different types of companies, from investment services to manufacturers, could possibly attain significant benefits in a short period of time, by using a voice-message system for internal communication between remote sites by means of such of integrated features as fax/voice mailboxes and pager notifications. It appears that the more voice messaging a company uses, the more benefits and revenue savings could be realized.

When using a voice-messaging system, users should especially careful to make their communication clear, concise, complete, and unambiguous. A voice-messaging system can create a first and lasting impression for users. Therefore, the following do's and don'ts may should be observed.

THE DO'S

- Communicate with departments to obtain support.

- Consider training classes for company users so they can effectively handle incoming calls to the voice-messaging system.

- Communicate with customer service representatives about proper handling of calls.

- Test and navigate through the various options in the system to improve or streamline the messages.

THE DON'TS

- Be careful not to overlook company customers. Be sure to know how they want their calls handled.

- In communicating, avoid being insular. Consider what your company's competition is doing and how you can apply their success to your company.

- Do not revise the system unnecessarily. Inquire about added features/applications only if you have maximized the use of those in existence.

VOICE-MESSAGING PRIVACY

As voice messaging become more prevalent, the issue of privacy becomes critical. Companies need to be as protective of their voice-mail system as they are of their computer system. Potential abuses of voice-messaging systems include fraudulent long-distance charges, malicious system intrusion, and corporate espionage. Many such abuses can be prevented by establishing certain policies and procedures that can enhance security, such as making it easy for users to change their passwords, establishing a system of automatic random password creation for new mailboxes, and having a flexible password structure. Nine to eighteen digit passwords are advised.

Two components prevalent to voice messaging are a user's outgoing personal greeting recorded in his/her own words and their message left for a receiver's response.

TIPS ON OUTGOING PERSONAL MESSAGES

- When recording a greeting, speak in a slow, clear, and concise fashion.

- Once a greeting has been recorded, call yourself to see how you sound and to determine whether you should re-record the message.

- Keep the recording to eight to twelve seconds.

- With your best voice, speak in a friendly tone of voice.

- If you will be unavailable for an extended period of time, change your message to let your callers know the time of your return and the name and phone number of someone who can help them until then.

TIPS ON LEAVING A MESSAGE

- Be sure to have a message in mind when you place a call in case you have to leave a message.

- Get to the point: Explain who you are and why you have called. Avoid rambling and repeating yourself.

- If you want to speak with someone about a specific topic that could be long and detailed. leave a "sub-ject-matter-only" message; for example, "Allen, I need to speak to you about the XYZ Project at your convenience." Do not leave a long, drawn-out message.

- Do not leave bad-news messages of a personal nature on the voice-mail system. Such messages are inappropriate.

- Be careful of what you say and how you say it, so you will not regret the message later. Because most voice-mail systems allow messages to be forwarded to others, you never know who might hear your message. Many voice-messaging systems do not allow you to eliminate a message once it's sent.

- While it may not be necessary to give the date and time of your message, it is wise to leave a date and time when you will be available if you want a call-back.

ADVANTAGES AND DISADVANTAGES

With the increasing prevalence of voice messaging, both its advantages and disadvantages have begun to surface.

ADVANTAGES

- It provides twenty-four-hour-a-day answering capability.

- It enhances efficiency and boosts job productivity.

- It saves and generates money for the company.

- It improves the accuracy of message content.

- It enables one to send multiple messages to people.

- It allows messages to be easily updated.

- It reduces the need for administrative/receptionist/secretarial support.

- It serves as an important medium for business communication.

- It makes transferring of phone calls from department to department easier and more efficient.

DISADVANTAGES

- Many people are resistant to technological advancement.

- It can be difficult if users are not trained to use voice-messaging systems.

- A voice-messaging system can be less economical for smaller companies.

- People can "hide behind their mailbox" and not return calls.

- Many people dislike not being able to reach a live person.
- Concern for the sender of message leaving a confusing message and lack of instructions.
- Too many voice-messaging options may make it difficult for people to recall which options they used previously.

WHEN TO USE VOICE MESSAGING

Voice messaging has become a viable alternative to e-mail and fax systems as a business communicating tool, each of these three methods having specific advantages in different situations. (1) If users need to ensure privacy, deliver information quickly, get a quick response, add a personal touch, or send messages quickly, voice messaging is more desirable than e-mail or fax. (2) If users need to send information to many persons, outside the company, e-mail is most desirable. (3) If users want to edit or attach comments, forward messages to others, send information to many persons outside the company, keep or providing a hard copy, and provide a quick review of information, a combination of voice mail and e-mail is most desirable. (4) If users want to keep or provide hard copies of documents and distribute complex, lengthy information, the fax system is most desirable. (5) If users want to ensure privacy, edit or attach documents, and distribute complex or lengthy information, a combination of voice and fax systems is desirable.

SEE ALSO *Communications in Business; Speaking Skills in Business*

BIBLIOGRAPHY

Anderson, Ronald A., Fox, Ivan, and Twomey, David P. (1995). *Business Law & the Regulatory Environment: Principles & Cases.* Cincinnati, OH: West Educational Publishing Company.

Galle, William P., Nelson, Beverly H., Luse, Donna W., and Villere, Maurice (1996). *Business Communication: A Technology-Based Approach.* Chicago: Irwin.

Norman, Donald A. (1998). "Why Voice Messaging Can't Cut It." *Across the Board*, 35(5,17):1.

Okolica, Carol, and Stewart, Concetta M. (1996). "Factors Influencing the Use of Voice Messaging Technology: Voice Mail Implementation in a Corporate Setting." *Central Business Review*, 15(1): 55-59.

Treece, Malra, and Kleen, Betty A. (1998). *Successful Communication for Business and Management.* Upper Saddle River, NJ: Prentice Hall.

Christine M. Irvine

VOLUME PRICING
SEE *Pricing*

W

WHOLESALERS

Wholesaling refers to all of the transactions in which products are bought for resale, for the making of other products, or for general business operations. A wholesaler is the individual or organization that facilitates these wholesaling activities by buying products and reselling them to yet another reseller, government agency, or an institutional user. In 2005 there were approximately 620,000 wholesaling companies in the United States, with more than half of all products sold in the country passing through these wholesaling firms. Approximately 400,000 independent firms handled close to $2 trillion worth of merchandise and employed close to 6 million workers.

Wholesaling is an important aspect of a company's marketing-channel strategy because it essentially involves the planning associated with industrial customers that need to distribute their products to manufacturers, retailers, government agencies, schools, hospitals, and other wholesalers.

SERVICES PROVIDED BY WHOLESALERS

Because wholesalers are in the business of buying in large quantities and delivering to customers in smaller amounts, they are able to perform physical distribution activities more effectively, including materials handling, warehousing, and inventory management. They often offer quick and frequent pickup and deliveries, as needed, which allows both the producers of the goods and wholesale customers to avoid the risks associated with holding large inventories.

Wholesalers support retailers by assisting them in their overall integrated market planning through pricing and promotion assistance. In addition, because they enter into sales contracts with a producer and because they can sell different amounts of the product to retailers, wholesalers serve as an extension of the producer's workforce. They often provide financial assistance and extend credit as needed.

Keeping producers up to date on market conditions is a critical component of wholesalers' services. Their assessment and analysis of changing market conditions are important for producers who are concentrating on market development and strategies for growth.

Because of their position in the marketing channel, wholesalers have closer contact with retail customers than do producers. Wholesalers can spread their sales costs over more products than can most producers, which results in lower costs per product. Because of this, many producers shift their financing and distribution activities to wholesalers. Because they are often specialists in understanding market conditions and experts at negotiating final purchases, wholesalers are a critical component in retail distribution strategies.

The distinction between services performed by wholesalers and those provided by other businesses has changed over the years. Retailers are discovering that they may be able to deal directly with producers and they may also be able to perform wholesalers' functions themselves. Because of the increased use of computers, retailers have been able to expedite ordering, delivering, and handling of goods more effectively than in the past. Nevertheless, not all functions of wholesalers can be eliminated; these

Rice wholesalers in Hong Kong. © **JAMES MARSHALL/CORBIS**

functions still have to be performed by some member of the marketing channel—producer, retailer, or wholesaler—because they are vital components of supply-chain management.

TYPES OF WHOLESALERS

There are three basic categories of wholesalers: merchant wholesalers; agents, brokers, and commission merchants; and manufacturers' sales branches and offices.

Merchant Wholesalers. Merchant wholesalers are independent wholesalers that take title to the products they sell. This type of wholesaling accounts for a large percent of all wholesale establishments in the United States. Since merchant wholesalers take title to the products that they resell, their earnings are obtained through markup of these goods. Merchant wholesalers are often called distributors and can be categorized as either full-service or limited-function wholesalers (see Figure 1).

Full-service wholesalers often provide a wide range of services to the customers for which they purchase products. Customers rely on them for product availability, suitable assortments, breaking of large quantities into smaller ones, financial assistance, and technical advice and service. Although full-service wholesalers often earn higher gross

margins than other wholesalers, their operating expenses are also higher because they perform a wide range of functions.

There are four types of full-service wholesalers:

1. General-merchandise wholesalers
2. Limited-line wholesalers
3. Specialty-merchandise wholesalers
4. Rack jobbers

General-merchandise wholesalers carry an extensive line of products and provide a wide variety of services. Although these wholesalers may carry many different product lines, they do not carry an extensive variety within them. Most general-merchandise wholesalers deal in such products as drugs, nonperishable foods, cosmetics, detergents, and tobacco.

Limited-line wholesalers carry only a few product lines, such as groceries, lighting fixtures, or oil-well drilling equipment, but offer an extensive assortment of products within those lines. They also offer fewer marketing services than general-merchandise wholesalers because they specialize in just a few functions that are associated with the product lines they carry. Limited-line wholesalers often take title to the products, but they may not deliver

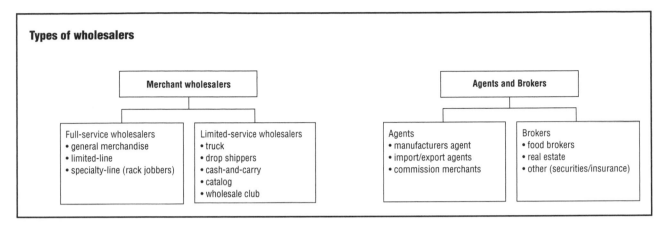

Types of wholesalers

Merchant wholesalers
- Full-service wholesalers
  - general merchandise
  - limited-line
  - specialty-line (rack jobbers)
- Limited-service wholesalers
  - truck
  - drop shippers
  - cash-and-carry
  - catalog
  - wholesale club

Agents and Brokers
- Agents
  - manufacturers agent
  - import/export agents
  - commission merchants
- Brokers
  - food brokers
  - real estate
  - other (securities/insurance)

Figure 1

merchandise, grant credit, provide essential marketing information, or store inventory. This results in smaller profit margins as compared to general-merchandise wholesalers.

The decision as to whether a company should use a limited-line wholesaler depends on the structure of the marketing channel and the need to manage the supply chain in order to obtain a competitive advantage, that is, do a "good" job so that competitors do not "steal" the business. Although the number of limited-line wholesalers is relatively small, they are important in the distribution of such products as specialty foods, perishable items, construction materials, and coal.

Specialty-line wholesalers carry the most narrow product assortment, usually consisting of a single product line or part of one. Because specialty-line wholesalers are product experts, they can offer extensive sales and product support.

Rack jobbers, sometimes considered a subcategory of specialty-line wholesalers, concentrate on retail stores. They set up and maintain displays and stock them with goods that are sold on consignment. Retailers depend on rack jobbers for the provision of health and beauty aids, hosiery, books, greeting cards, and magazines.

The five types of limited-function wholesalers are truck jobbers, drop shippers, cash-and-carry wholesalers, catalog wholesalers, and wholesale clubs. Producers of fast-moving goods, especially those that are perishable and need frequent replenishment, often use truck jobbers because they deliver only within a particular geographic region in order to maintain product freshness. Truck jobbers are often chosen as the wholesaling method because they offer quick and frequent delivery, which is especially crucial for such items as bakery goods, meats, and dairy products.

Drop shippers arrange for shipments directly from the factory to the customer; although they do not physically handle the product, they do take title and responsibility for all the risks associated with the transport of goods. In addition, they offer the necessary sales support for the products they distribute. They operate in a wide variety of industries, including chemicals, industrial packaging, lumber, petroleum, and heating products.

Cash-and-carry wholesalers are intermediaries whose customers are usually small businesses that pay cash and have to arrange the delivery of these products themselves. Cash-and-carry wholesalers usually carry a limited line of products that have a high turnover, such as groceries, building materials, and electrical or office supplies. They do not deliver the products they sell, nor do they extend credit, but they are a vital intermediary for those small businesses that would be unprofitable for larger wholesalers to service.

Catalog wholesalers are an alternative to cash-and-carry wholesalers that serve both major population centers and remote locations. Prepayment for goods is required, and delivery is arranged through delivery services such as UPS and FedEx. A wide range of competitively priced products are offered, such as office furniture and equipment, packaging materials, and shelf and storage systems.

Wholesale clubs are organizations that offer customers a fee-based membership that entitles them to make purchases at below-retail prices. This particular concept is a growing phenomenon in the United States because of the success of such wholesale clubs as Costco and Sam's Club.

Agents, Brokers, and Commission Merchants. The second category of wholesalers is agents and brokers (see Figure 1). Agents represent either buyers or sellers on a permanent basis, whereas brokers are middlemen that buyers or sellers employ temporarily. Both agents and brokers perform fewer functions than limited-service wholesalers but they are usually more specific in their product selection, and thus can provide valuable sales expertise. Using agents and brokers allows companies to benefit from the expertise of a trained sales force, which results in a decrease in personal selling costs. Often called functional middlemen, agents and brokers perform a limited number of services in exchange for a commission that is based on the selling price.

One type of agent is called a manufacturer's agent; this type accounts for half of all agent wholesalers. They are independent middlemen who represent more than one seller and offer complete product lines. A manufacturer's agent is restricted to a particular territory and sells and takes orders year-round. There is a contractual agreement between the agent and the manufacturer that outlines territories, selling prices, order handling, delivery, service, and warranties. In service-based manufacturer's agent companies, the more services that are offered, the higher the commission. These types of agents are commonly used in the sales of apparel, machinery and equipment, steel, furniture, and automotive products.

Two other types of agents, import and export agents, specialize in international trade. Import agents find products in foreign markets and sell them in their home countries. In many countries, it is extremely difficult and sometimes illegal to try to sell products from another country without going through an import agent. Export agents locate and develop markets abroad for products that are manufactured in their home countries.

Selling agents are middlemen who market a whole product line or a manufacturer's entire output. They perform all the functions of wholesaling, except that they do not take title of the product. Frequently, companies opt to use selling agents in place of marketing departments. To avoid conflicts of interest, selling agents represent noncompeting product lines and have the authority for pricing, promotion, and distribution of those products.

Finally, there are commission merchants. These are agents who receive goods on consignment and negotiate sales in large central markets. Their specialty is securing the best price possible under market conditions. These agents are primarily found in agricultural industries, taking possession of truckloads of commodities and arranging for grading, storage, and transportation. Commission merchants deduct commission and the expense of making the sale, and then turn over the profits to the producer. Although they provide planning and assistance with credit, they do not provide any promotional support.

Since brokers are the intermediaries that bring buyers and sellers together, they are paid a commission on the transaction. Brokers do not enter into contracts for extended periods; rather they work on a transaction-by-transaction basis. There are thousands of wholesale brokers in the United States, with most of them concentrated in food and agricultural industries. Brokers are especially useful to sellers of supermarket products and real estate. Food brokers, for example, sell food and general merchandise to retailer-owned stores and merchant wholesalers, grocery chains, food processors, and organizational buyers. Since brokers perform fewer functions than other intermediaries, they are not involved in financing, physical possession, pricing, or risk taking. What they offer instead is expertise in a particular commodity and a network of established products.

Manufacturer-Owned Wholesalers. Thousands of manufacturer-owned wholesalers operate in the United States. These wholesalers maintain inventory and perform a wide variety of functions, such as providing delivery, credit, market feedback, and assistance with promotional planning. Manufacturer's sales offices are the other type of producer-owned wholesaler. They do not maintain inventory, but they assist with sales and service, market analysis, and the billing and collection of funds for products sold. Both sales branches and sales offices are located away from the manufacturing plants and closer to customers because the producers are attempting to reach their customers more effectively in an effort to create a competitive edge in the marketplace.

DEVELOPMENTS IN WHOLESALING

In the early years of the twenty-first century, wholesaling gross profits declined. Because of the economic recession, a decrease in new store construction, and competition, wholesaling growth declined. Chains, which usually prefer to buy directly from manufacturers, grabbed a larger part of the market in areas such as home-improvement products. But, while tough economic conditions can affect wholesalers adversely, a booming economy can do the same thing. Retailers, experiencing rapid sales growth, may opt to buy directly from manufacturers, thus cutting wholesalers from the supply chain.

Both retailers and producers are eager to improve their profitability, and the wholesalers are caught in the middle. Industry observers see the power in the channel shifting more toward the retailer, who may choose to reevaluate the current supply-chain members.

Because of these changing market conditions, wholesalers are concentrating on strategies to improve service by adding more value-added concepts. Even though wholesaling has traditionally involved the handling of goods, the activities and functions of wholesalers are being applied more and more in service industries. Access Graphics in Boulder, Colorado, for example, takes an active role in pursuing new business for its vendors by providing them with customer databases that help resellers in identifying sales prospects. In addition, it also provides in-house graphic departments that produce the promotional materials needed by resellers and their customers. Access Graphics believes in adding value to its supply-chain relationships; as a result, it has established a staff of system engineers who help resellers with installation, system design, and computer-memory testing.

Tough market conditions in the United States have forced many wholesalers to adopt a global perspective. Wholesalers have been encouraged by the North American Free Trade Agreement to expand their operations into Mexico and Canada. It was expected that by 2010, 25 percent of wholesalers' business would come from foreign markets.

International wholesalers will experience stages of growth depending on the economic development of foreign economies. All-purpose wholesale merchants will dominate in simple economic conditions, while an expanding economy will see the emergence of interregional wholesalers. As foreign economic conditions mature, there will be a growth of specialized wholesalers, with product-line and functionally specialized wholesalers dominating the chain. In an advanced economy, channels become controlled by large-scale retailers and manufacturers, thus causing a decline in the need for conventional wholesalers.

Wholesalers that expand through globalization will face the challenge of competition against current wholesalers, new languages, an array of different legal systems, and a multitude of cultural differences. Nevertheless, a decision to stick with domestic markets only could hamper the growth of a wholesaler.

ELECTRONIC MARKETING CHANNELS

Advances in electronic commerce have opened new avenues for reaching buyers and creating customer values. This interactive technology has been made possible by electronic marketing channels, which use the Internet to make goods and services available for consumption for use by both end consumers and business buyers.

SEE ALSO *Discount Stores; Electronic Commerce; Marketing; Retailers*

BIBLIOGRAPHY

Pelton, Lou E., Strutton, David, and Lumpkin, James R. (2002). *Marketing channels: A relationship management approach* (2nd ed.). Boston: McGraw-Hill/Irwin.

Pride, William M., and Ferrell, O. C. (2006). *Marketing concepts and strategies* (Rev. ed.). Boston: Houghton Mifflin.

Rosenbloom, Bert (2004). *Marketing channels: A management view* (7th ed.). Mason, OH: Thomson South-Western.

U.S. Bureau of the Census. (2006). *Statistical abstract of the United States.* Washington, DC: Author.

Patricia A. Spirou

WORD PROCESSING

Word processing refers generally to the creation, editing, formatting, storage, and output of both printed and online or electronic documents. Word processing is undoubtedly the most-used business application for personal computers, perhaps alongside World Wide Web browsers and electronic-mail (e-mail) applications.

Word-processing software includes basic applications designed for casual business or home users and powerful, advanced applications capable of meeting the most-demanding needs of businesses. Many word-processing applications are designed for use as part of a suite or integrated group of word-processing, spreadsheet, and presentation programs. For example, Microsoft Word, probably the most widely used word-processing software, is part of the Microsoft Office suite, which includes Microsoft's PowerPoint presentation program and Excel spreadsheet program. Corel WordPerfect, a less widely used but very popular word-processing program, is part of Corel's WordPerfect Office suite, which includes Quattro Pro spreadsheet software and Presentations multimedia slideshow software.

Some word-processing software is available as shareware for a relatively small fee or as freeware at no cost. For example, Yeah Write, a basic fill-in-the-blank word processor designed for people who do not want to deal with formatting tasks, is available as shareware. OpenOffice.org is a complete office suite that includes a powerful word-processing program, WRITER, which is intended as an open-standard, vendor-neutral alternative to proprietary word-processing programs.

Most word processors include the same essential word-processing functions and a variety of more-advanced features for document production and formatting.

ESSENTIAL WORD-PROCESSING FUNCTIONS

Essential word-processing functions can be grouped into the categories of input, manipulation, formatting, and output of text.

Text Input. Typically, text is entered into the word processor from a keyboard; other input methods include:

- Copying text from other applications (such as from hypertext markup language [HTML] documents, e-mail messages, or online encyclopedias) and pasting it into a word-processing document

- Scanning printed documents and using optical-character-recognition (OCR) software to convert the scanned documents into text characters

- Using voice-recognition software to convert spoken words into text characters

Text Manipulation. Text manipulation refers to the "processing" part of word processing. Word processors provide easy methods of deleting, inserting, copying, and moving individual characters, words, phrases, and paragraphs—even entire pages of information—with a few clicks of a mouse button or with such keyboard shortcuts as Ctrl-C to copy, Ctrl-X to cut, and Ctrl-V to paste or insert text. Text can be automatically checked for spelling and for conformance to basic grammatical principles as the text is entered and edited.

The find-and-replace feature in a word processor allows the user to search for every occurrence of a particular character, word, or phrase within a document and replace it with new text. Most word processors also include automatic correction and automatic formatting of common errors and mechanical conventions as text is entered from the keyboard. For example, commonly misspelled words can be automatically corrected as soon as the misspelled words are entered; two spaces entered after the end of a sentence can be changed automatically to one space; a lowercase letter beginning a new sentence can be capitalized automatically. Proper typographic quotation marks ("smart" or "curly" quote marks—" and ") and apostrophes (') can be inserted automatically instead of the straight typewriter-style quotation marks entered from the keyboard. Fractions and other symbols can be formatted automatically as their keyboard equivalents are entered. For example, when a fraction for one-half is entered as 1/2, it is changed to the symbol ½; two hyphens (--) are changed to a long dash (—); and (c) is changed to ©.

Text Formatting. Word-processing software typically includes "wizards" or "help" features to provide automated formatting of common business documents. For example, a letter wizard can assist the user to properly format a business letter, and a résumé wizard can help the user format a professional-looking résumé. Templates are another automated formatting feature. A template is a type of pre-formatted, fill-in-the-blank document that is useful for maintaining a specific format each time a document is created, especially when multiple word-processing operators are involved. A newsletter template, for example, allows a user to entered the text of newsletter articles, headlines, and graphics without having to re-create the newsletter layout for each issue of the newsletter.

The most-common formatting tasks are typically performed by the user as a document is created. Individual character and word formatting includes selection of type size, type style, and typeface. Size is measured in points, a unit of measure in which 72 points make up an inch. Typically, 11- or 12-point type is used for basic business documents. Newsletters, annual reports, and other such "designed" documents may use type as small as 8 or 9 points for the basic text and as large as 24, 36, or 48 points (or more) for main titles. Type styles, such as *italics*, underline, and **bold,** are easily selected using keyboard shortcuts or by selecting them from the basic font menu. Typefaces (typeface refers to the look or design of the type) are available in thousands of varieties, including such commonly known faces as Times Roman, Arial, Helvetica, and Garamond.

Paragraph formatting includes line spacing, meaning the amount of blank space left between lines of type (single spacing and double spacing, for example); paragraph spacing (the amount of blank space that precedes or follows each paragraph); justification (all lines of type made even at both margins, or left uneven or ragged at the right margin); and indentation (such as a first-line indentation at the beginning of each paragraph).

Page and overall-document formatting includes setting margins (typically 1-inch margins are used on the top, bottom, and both sides of such basic business documents as letters, reports, and memos), creating columns like those used in a newspaper or newsletter, and creating headers and footers (information such as the page number or a chapter title that is repeated at the top or bottom of each page of a document). Most word processors also provide special layout features for formatting outlines, tables, envelopes, and mailing labels.

Text Output. Once text has been created, edited, and formatted into a finished electronic document, it must be put into some tangible form or lasting electronic form to be of practical benefit. That output process usually starts with the saving of the document on the computer's hard drive, a floppy disk, a CD, or a memory device such as a flash drive. Saving the document, in fact, is an activity that should take place frequently during the creation and editing processes to guard against loss due to problems such as electrical-power failure, computer malfunctions, and operator error.

Printing a document on paper is the most common output method; other output methods include faxing a document directly from the word processor by use of a computer modem, sending the document to another person by e-mail, and converting the word-processing document to various other electronic formats for online viewing or for eventual printing from other applications. For example, word-processing documents are frequently converted to HTML for use as Web pages, to portable document format (PDF) files, and to rich text format (RTF) files for use in other computer programs (particularly other word-processing programs).

ADVANCED WORD-PROCESSING FEATURES

Although most word-processing users tend to learn and use primarily the basic word-processing features, numerous more-advanced features are available in most word processors to make word processing much easier to complete in less time. Taking the time to learn some advanced word-processing features and functions usually has a high payoff in terms of productivity and professionalism.

Some of the more-common advanced word-processing features and functions are described briefly below:

Styles. Styles are user-created formatting commands that allow great control over repetitive formatting structures within a document. For example, using a "style" for each type of heading in a report will ensure consistent formatting of the headings and will eliminate the need for a user to manually format each heading as it is created.

Macros and Merging. Macros are stored keystrokes, or sets of editing and formatting commands, that can be replayed whenever needed. Macros can boost productivity and take much of the tedium out of repetitive word-processing tasks. Merging is the process of using lists of such information as names, addresses, phone numbers, product descriptions or model numbers, and so on to fill in designated fields or blanks in documents to create mass mailings, address labels, directories, and catalogs.

Version Control. Version-control features allow a user to track the various stages of editing that a document may pass through, including versions created by multiple users involved in the creation and editing of a document. Related features such as the ability to track changes made in a document enable multiple users to review suggested document changes and to accept or reject proposed changes.

Automatic References and Indexes. Documents that include tables of contents, cross-references, indexes, footnotes, endnotes, and captions will benefit from the capability of a word processor to automatically generate and format these items.

Desktop-Publishing Capabilities. Professional-looking documents such as newsletters, advertisements, annual reports, brochures, and business cards can be designed with most modern word-processing software.

Graphical images from clip-art collections, digital photographs, and scanned images, and drawings created with graphics programs, can be integrated easily into word-processing documents. Pages and paragraphs can be enclosed with decorative borders. Background images and colors can be added to pages within a document. Graphical elements such as lines, boxes, arrows, and artistic textual headings can be created quickly and easily within most word-processing programs.

Although word processors are generally not as sophisticated as desktop-publishing software or page-layout programs in their capabilities for setting type and for working with graphical elements, they can be used to create attractive, professional-looking documents that go beyond the basic layout and formatting of letters, memos, and reports. Using a word-processing program to create designed documents is often preferable to using a high-end desktop-publishing program, however, because word-processing users are not required to become proficient in using another program and because documents within an organization or department are created and maintained using the same application.

SEE ALSO *Information Processing; Office Technology*

BIBLIOGRAPHY

Bucki, Lisa A. (2005). *Learning computer applications: Projects and exercises* (3rd ed.). New York: Pearson Prentice Hall.

O'Leary, Timothy J., and O'Leary, Linda I. (2006). *Computing essentials* (Rev. ed.). Boston: McGraw-Hill.

Shelly, Gary B., Cashman, Thomas J., and Vermaat, Misty E. (2003). *Discovering computers 2004: A gateway to information.* Boston: Course Technology.

Ray L. Young

WORK GROUPS (TEAMS)

Competition in business today has created a desire and need for work groups. The delegation of duties is occurring through this redesign of the work process. The delegation process is in turn creating team environments in organizations. The redesign of the work process is also due to downsizing, a collapsing of the organization's ranks, and the retiring of employees. David Cleland (1996) states that "the traditional model of organizational design is an endangered species" (p. vii). As teams are more readily seen as an effective way to involve employees and solve problems, they have modified the organizational design of many businesses. Consequently, teams are noted as the "common denominator of organizational change" (Cleland, 1996, p. 9).

The team philosophy has become prevalent throughout business. Teams, which began as social-technical-business experiments as part of the total quality management concept, have become an accepted norm in a majority of organizations. Teams can be categorized as steering teams, project teams, task forces, cross-functional teams, and so forth. Villis Ozols (1996) notes that 51 percent of all employees are on teams of one sort or another.

The role of a team is to improve a situation or solve a problem. Teams were initiated because it was believed that "employees will best respond (be productive) when they have a high feeling of self-worth and of identification with the success of the organization" (Ketchum and Trist, 1992, p. 18). Reengineering, empowerment, and restructuring strategies can all give employees more control or hands-on involvement in dealing with their changing jobs. Traditional jobs do still exist, but "jobs are increasingly a patchwork of responsibility fitting into an overall mosaic" (Cleland, 1996, p. 21). Jobs are becoming a collection of responsibilities, and employees need to be more flexible and responsive to changing demands. As individual jobs are changing, so is the manager's role. The manager is not only becoming more of a coach or facilitator but is also charged with developing the self-motivation of employees. These employees should not only set goals for themselves but also evaluate their efforts. Employees are still individually important, but they are more important when they contribute to the whole—to the team.

Elisa Mendzela (1997) notes that although groups and teams are not necessarily synonymous, many people refer to almost any work group as a team. Teams have many definitions, including the following:

1. A unified, interdependent, cohesive group of people working together to achieve common objectives.

2. People with complementary skills, committed to a common purpose approach, who work together effectively and hold themselves mutually accountable.

3. A number of persons associated together in work or activity.

Not all individuals necessarily possess team skills. Because American society is an individualistic one, individuals will need to suppress traditional communication methods and learn new ways to function effectively within a team. When team members receive the necessary train-

ing to learn needed skills, the team becomes more effective and the individual employee wins as well.

TEAM DEVELOPMENT PROCESS

"Team development is the process of unifying a group of people with a common objective into an effectively functioning unit" (Shonk, 1982, p. 1). The team development process includes defining, analyzing, planning, acting, and evaluating. A combination of these stages will help to produce a productive team.

An organization must first define the team and decide whether the team format is the way to proceed. Analyzing team performance and planning for improvement are essential steps in the team development process. Planning for improvements, implementing actions, evaluation, and follow-up should be designed to work in a circular pattern so as to achieve team improvement and productivity. (See Figure 1.)

ADVANTAGES OF TEAMS

Teams are helpful in dividing and organizing work. Advantages include breaking down departmental or branch barriers, improving service, providing more time for other duties, identifying issues, obtaining feedback from others, and, of course, dividing work duties and responsibilities. These are all obviously advantageous to any company.

Teams have also been known to decrease error rates, cut order-processing time, increase manufacturing productivity, and decrease theft and absenteeism. However, even with all these benefits, Mendzela (1997) notes that 60 percent of teams fail.

TEAM FAILURE

Reasons for team failure include internal competition, companies' failure to recognize team performance, lack of clear goals or common cause, a team being inappropriate for a situation, and negativity. The team should not be in competition with the individual; the team works through individuals toward a common goal.

When team members are confused about the team's goal or objective, they are basically saying the following three things:

1. They do not believe in the outcome.

2. They do not believe the outcome is reachable.

3. They cannot figure out what the boss really wants as an outcome.

Several myths, noted by Harvey Robbins and Michael Finley (1995), lead to unsuccessful teams. The

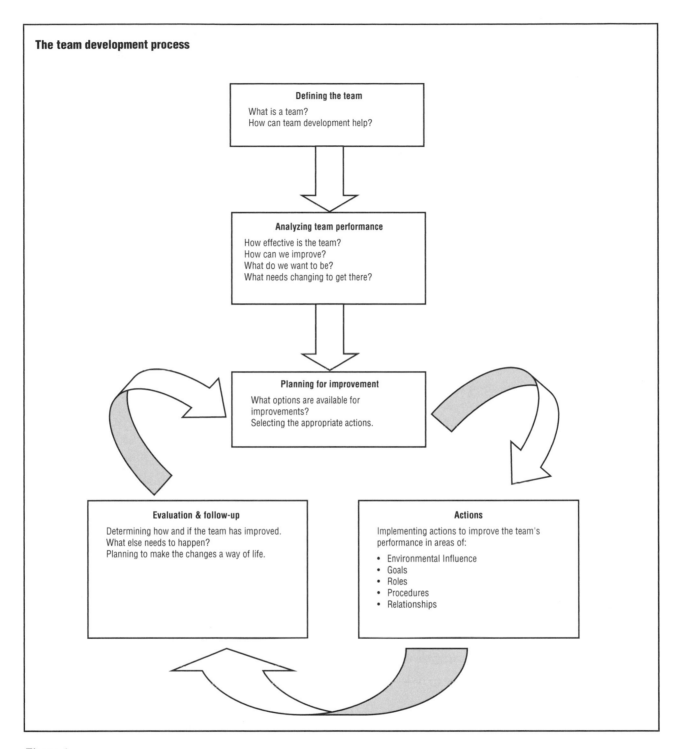

The team development process

Defining the team

What is a team?
How can team development help?

Analyzing team performance

How effective is the team?
How can we improve?
What do we want to be?
What needs changing to get there?

Planning for improvement

What options are available for improvements?
Selecting the appropriate actions.

Evaluation & follow-up

Determining how and if the team has improved.
What else needs to happen?
Planning to make the changes a way of life.

Actions

Implementing actions to improve the team's performance in areas of:

- Environmental Influence
- Goals
- Roles
- Procedures
- Relationships

Figure 1

idea that people enjoy working together is not necessarily true. Many people need their own space and feel confined when assigned to a specific group. It is also untrue that a team can solve any problem. This is not the case if the team is not focused on and knowledgeable about the problem. Just because a manager or the company president is overzealous about teams does not mean that a team approach can immediately or totally solve a problem. Assigning everything to teams and assuming "the more the merrier" does not work in all situations.

Ozols (1996) states that the major reason for team failure is that teams are set up only to achieve management results, not to answer the employee question "What's in it for me?" Employee job satisfaction, recognition, and so forth are essential in reducing team failure.

SUCCESSFUL TEAMS

Characteristics of successful teams include open-mindedness, involvement, ability to deal with conflict, responsibility, trust, respect for others, effective listening, and full participation. Rob Heselbarth (1997) notes that "a strong team is built by distributing responsibility, authority, and information" (p. 5). The individuals working as a team, as well as the team itself, must possess these characteristics. These characteristics can be evaluated through Pollar's (1997) five categories of team evaluation:

1. Purpose and direction
2. Problem solving and decision making
3. Communication
4. Participation
5. Leadership

A major advantage of the team approach is that employees are happier and more productive when they are grouped and, in turn, have input into or control over a certain problem in their organization. The result of the team's work has a direct impact on the individuals and their jobs; therefore, they are more interested in their work. Teams are successful when their individual members are successful.

Many companies have had success with teams. A few examples are noted by Cleland (1996).

- *Federal Express and IDS*: 40 percent boost in production
- *Motorola Corporation*: Teams dedicated to improving quality, cutting costs, and reducing cycle time
- *IBM*: Technology assessment teams to review current and emerging technologies
- *General Electric Company*: Best-practices assessment to determine the basis of the success of competitors

Marilyn Manning and Patricia Haddock (1996) note seven steps to help manage teams:

1. Communicate the mission of the company.

2. Make sure each team member knows what is expected.

3. Encourage open communication among team members.

4. Resolve conflicts quickly and fairly.

5. Encourage interaction among teams.

6. Support your teams.

7. Motivate and reward.

These steps work well in the management of teams and can be incorporated into the team development process.

DISADVANTAGES OF TEAMS

Disadvantages of teams are not always acknowledged. However, when a company is deciding whether to develop teams, the disadvantages, such as potential internal conflict and individual loss, must be weighed against the advantages. (Individual loss refers to individual team members' giving up personal gain; they must share the success.) Power struggles are likely to arise from internal conflict disagreements.

Common problems that may arise include overbearing, dominating, or reluctant participants; floundering; a rush to accomplish goals; digression; acceptance of opinions as facts; and feuding members. The result will be a lack of focus on the common goal.

PRIOR TO TEAM BUILDING

Because weighing the advantages and disadvantages of teams is important, specific questions must be asked. Certain situations do not call for a team and may be better served by another work mode. Mendzela (1997) offers four specific and demanding questions to help companies determine whether a team approach is best:

1. Why would a team approach be helpful?
2. What is unsatisfactory about the current situation?
3. What are possible causes and solutions?
4. Will your organization really support a team approach?

If a team is deemed beneficial and worth implementing, a mission or purpose statement must be carefully developed. It is important that the team be clear and knowledgeable about its purpose to be able to meet the team goal and, in turn, the objectives and goals of the organization.

CONCLUSION

Teams can be effective or ineffective depending on the team environment. Minda Zetlin (1996) notes the following helpful and hindering habits for teams. Helpful habits include open-mindedness, open and immediately dealing with conflict, respect for others' time, listening, low defensiveness, and full participation. Hindering habits include negative body language, false participation, complaining about other team members rather than discussing problems with them directly (triangling), two-way arguments (crosstalk), accumulating grievances (stamp collecting), speaking at length in too much detail (going deep), and destructive humor.

Whether to use teams is an important organizational decision. Advantages and disadvantages in developing and utilizing teams must be researched. Team outcomes are dependent on an effective design and efficient work with recognition of the teams' efforts.

BIBLIOGRAPHY

Cleland, D. I. (1996). *Strategic Management of Teams.* New York: Wiley.

Heselbarth, R. (1997). "Strong Business Teams Share More Than Matching Hats." *Contractor,* 44(3), 5, 29.

Ketchum, L. D., and Trist, E. (1992). *All Teams Are Not Created Equal.* Newbury Park, CA: Sage.

Manning, M., and Haddock, P. (1996). *The NAFE Guide to Starting Your Own Business: A Handbook for Entrepreneurial Women.* Chicago: Irwin Professional Publishing.

Mendzela, E. (1997). "Effective teams." *CPA Journal,* 67(9), 62-63.

Merriam-Webster Online Dictionary. http://www.m-w.com/home.htm. 1999.

Ozols, V. (1996). "Why Teams Don't Work." Rocky Mountain Quality Conference, Denver, CO.

Pollar, O. (1997). "Effective Teams." *Executive Excellence,* 14(7), 18.

Pucel, D. J., and Fruehling, R. T. (1997). *Working in Teams: Interaction and Communication.* St. Paul, MN: EMC Paradigm.

Recardo, R. (1996). *Teams: Who Needs Them and Why?* Houston: Gulf Publishing Co.

Robbins, H., and Finley, M. (2000). *The New Why Teams Don't Work.* San Francisco: Berrett-Koehler Publishers.

Sashkin, M., and Sashkin, M. G. (1994). *The New Teamwork: Developing and Using Cross-Function Teams.* New York: American Management Association.

Scholtes, P. R. (1988). *The Team Handbook: How to Use Teams to Improve Quality.* Madison, WI: Joiner Associates.

Shonk, J. H. (1982). *Working in Teams.* New York: AMACOM: A Division of American Management Association.

Zenger, J. H., Musselwhite, E., Hurson, K., and Perrin, C. (1992). "Managing: Leadership in a Team Environment." *Security Management,* 36(9), 28-33.

Zetlin, M. (1996). "Helps and Hinders: The Habits of Successful Teams." *Getting Results...for Hands-on Manager,* 41(9), 5.

Tena B. Crews

WORK MEASUREMENT

Work measurement is the careful analysis of a task, its size, the method used in its performance, and its efficiency. The objective is to determine the workload in an operation, the time that is required, and the number of workers needed to perform the work efficiently. Work measurement helps to determine the time spent performing any process and offers a consistent, comparable methodology for establishing labor capacities.

Work measurement can be extremely effective at informing supervisors of the working times and delays inherent in different ways of carrying out work. The purpose of a measurement method is to achieve full coverage of the work to be measured.

A good work measurement system has many benefits. It helps to reduce labor costs, increase productivity, and improve supervision, planning, scheduling, performance appraisal, and decision making.

WORK MEASUREMENT COMPONENTS

A work measurement system has three components: preferred methods, time values, and reporting. Preferred methods are not always the most efficient or fastest way to do a task. They should enhance safety, quality, and productivity. Safety for the employee and for the product should be considered. Quality is equally important; it has been proven that good performance and good quality go hand in hand. People who are trained in the proper method and follow that method will produce high-quality work and perform at an acceptable performance level. Time values and reporting should also be considered. The time that a job should take is determined not on the basis of speeding up the motions a worker normally makes but on the normal pace of the average worker, taking into consideration allowances for rest periods, coffee breaks, and fatigue. A reporting system is important to the success of any work measurement method. Supervisors and managers must have access to labor-management information that is both timely and complete. Timely information can be used to manage and shift labor hours to areas where they are needed and to correct problems or at least prevent them from becoming a crisis. Personal computers help to apply work measurement more effectively and more cheaply and provide immediate feedback to the workers, supervisors, and managers.

WORK MEASUREMENT METHODS

Work measurement programs involve the use of a number of techniques, each selected to cover an appropriate part of the task. The purpose of measurement is to collect real data about actual events. To obtain time standards, the data are usually converted to target data or data that apply under known conditions. All work measurement systems are based on the same, simple three-stage procedure: analysis, data collection and measurement, and synthesis. They differ in the nature and degree of analysis, the nature and level of data collection and measurement, and the nature of the synthesis process. However, the three-stage procedure remains common.

Before measurement begins, the task to be measured is analyzed and broken into convenient parts that are suitable for the chosen measurement technique. The purpose of the measurement technique is to derive a basic time for each activity, element, or motion. At the measurement stage, it is necessary to collect descriptive or qualitative data on the nature of the task, the conditions under which it is performed, and other factors, which may have a bearing on the time that the task takes to be complete. When repetitive jobs are measured, data are collected over a number of representative cycles of a job to obtain a mean or typical value. An analysis of the results can be done using statistical techniques to determine the number of observations that must be made to provide a given level of confidence in the final results.

At the synthesis stage, the various parts of the task and their associated basic times are combined together in correct sequence and with the correct frequency to produce the time for a complete job. During this stage, the basic time will be adjusted for allowances to become the standard time for the task.

There are four work measurement methods, each of which has strengths and weaknesses. The historical data method shows the time it actually took to complete a task. Such data have the advantages of being easy to collect, understand, and communicate, but they provide no information for future improvement. For the work sampling method, a large number of random observations are made of the task to determine the steps in its normal performance. This method is easy to learn and use, and it provides more operational detail than historical data. The disadvantage of work sampling is that it requires thousands of samples to establish an accurate measure for each step.

The time study method uses continuous and snapback approaches to record the elapsed time of a task. The snapback approach requires a stopwatch with a reset button that allows the observer to read and record the time at the end of each work element then reset (snapback) the watch to zero. Although popular, the time-study method is subjective and relies heavily on the experience of the time-study analyst. A computerized data collector provides more accurate timing than the stopwatch. However, converting actual time to the expected or normal time remains a problem.

The predetermined motion/time systems method is based on the premises that all work consists of basic human motions and that times can be assigned to these motions if they are defined and classified in a systematic way. A film or videotape records what a job entails and how long it takes. This technique is used most frequently in studying high-volume settings such as a workstation or an assembly line. An observer measures a job by watching and analyzing it into its basic constituent motions. This method requires substantial training and practice to acquire and maintain accuracy. It enables all types of tasks to be assigned time/duration values that can then be extended into cost values. The results are not easy to communicate, but when properly executed, this method yields very accurate times.

SEE ALSO *Productivity; Standard-Based Work Performance*

BIBLIOGRAPHY

Aft, Lawrence S. (2000). *Work Measurement and Methods Improvement*. New York: Wiley.

Gagnon, Eugene J. (2000, February). "How to Measure Work." *Material Handling Management*, 71-77.

Gowan, C. Bruce (1999, March). "Which Work Measurement Tool?" *Manufacturing Engineering*, 18.

Gregson, Ken (1993, July/August). "Do We Still Need Work Measurement?" *Work Study*, 18-22.

Horngren, Charles, Datar, Srikant M., and Foster, George (2005). *Cost Accounting: A Managerial Emphasis* (12th ed.). Upper Saddle River, NJ: Prentice Hall.

Rad, Parviz F. & Levin, Ginger (2006). *Metrics for Project Management: formalized approaches*. Vienna, VA: Management Concepts.

Nashwa George

WORKERS' COMPENSATION

Workers' compensation is a form of insurance that provides medical coverage and/or income replacement for employees who sustain injuries or suffer other disabilities because of workplace conditions or accidents. The cost for workers' compensation is the responsibility of the employer and is regulated by the state and/or country in question. The major purpose of workers' compensation is to assist injured workers and their dependents. Certain workers' compensation laws limit the amount an injured employee can receive in benefits.

Historically, the earliest workers' compensation law was passed in Germany in 1884, with Great Britain following in 1897, and the United States in 1908. Most industrialized countries provide compulsory workers' compensation. In the United States, all fifty states have passed workers' compensation laws and are further regulated in certain aspects from the federal government. The benefits provided are dictated by law.

Workers' compensation was initially intended to provide protection from hazardous types of industrial work. In the early twenty-first century most places of employment that have large numbers of employees, such as schools and factories, also provide workers' compensation benefits. Some situations in agriculture-related employment, as well as small businesses, do not provide workers' compensation.

Although workers' compensation was originally designed as protection from accidental injuries, as time passed, additional types of job-related conditions were added. For example, if a worker acquired a disease as a direct result of the job, the worker would be covered by workers' compensation. Workers' compensation laws today generally cover accidents occurring while working on the job.

State workers' compensation laws provide the framework when the job is a state-related position. At the federal level, the Federal Employment Compensation Act (FECA) provides workers' compensation for nonmilitary and federal employees. The FECA also, in most cases, provides compensation for accidents or other disabilities sustained while employees are performing their duties, as long as the accidents are not willful or caused by intoxication. Medical expenses for disability are also covered. Occasionally, employees may be retrained for another type of job. Disabled employees receive a portion of their monthly salary while they are disabled and may receive more if the injury is permanent or if there are additional dependents. The act also provides compensation to survivors of employees. The FECA is administered by the Office of Workers' Compensation Programs.

Several areas related to workers' compensation are covered by a variety of laws. The Federal Employment Liability Act provides for injuries incurred by interstate railroad employees if the interstate railroad has been negligent. Another is the Merchant Marine Act (also known as the Jones Act), which provides protection against injury for those working in positions on the seas. Certain specified employees who work for private maritime employers are covered against injury by the Longshore and Harbor Workers' Compensation Act. Miners are protected by the Black Lung Benefits Act for this disease, which is supervised by the secretary of the U.S. Department of Labor.

While most injuries are legitimate, it is important to note that workers' compensation claims are scrutinized carefully before awarding benefits. Detailed documentation is an essential requirement before making a judgment in settling a workers' compensation claim.

BIBLIOGRAPHY

Hood, Jack B., Hardy, Benjamin A., Jr., and Lewis, Harold S., Jr. (2005). *Workers' compensation and employee protection laws in a nutshell* (4th ed.). St. Paul, MN: Thomson/West.

McCoy, Doug (2002). *Workers' compensation: The survival guide for business.* Newark, NJ: LexisNexis.

Popow, Donna J. (2004). *Principles of workers' compensation claims* (3rd ed.). Malvern, PA: American Institute for Chartered Property Casualty Underwriters/Insurance Institute of America.

Priz, Edward J. (2005). *Ultimate guide to workers' compensation insurance.* Irvine, CA: Entrepreneur Press.

Workers' compensation: An overview. Retrieved December 13, 2005, from http://www.law.cornell.edu/wex/index.php/Workers_compensation

Dorothy A. Maxwell

WORKPLACE SAFETY

SEE *Occupational Safety and Health Administration (OSHA)*

WRITING SKILLS IN BUSINESS

Business writing has seven purposes:

1. Convey information
2. Explain a situation
3. Request action
4. Seek information
5. Persuade
6. Reply to communication previously received
7. Convey an attitude

The goal of business writing is to have readers understand the message completely, clearly, and accurately. A few recommendations by authorities follow.

EFFECTIVE WRITING

Effective writers use correct grammar, spelling, and punctuation.

EFFECTIVE GRAMMAR

- Use first person personal pronoun (*I*) to indicate who is stating the action: *Sally and I visited the museum.* (not *Me and Sally*).

- Use parallel construction: *Managers' days are spent completing reports, interviewing personnel, and attending meetings.* (not *in meetings.*)

- Make each sentence complete: *Please read the article. You will find it a truly moving experience.* (not *Please read the article. A truly moving experience*).

- Do not run sentences together: *Enter the competition. I think you'll win.* (not *Enter the competition I think you'll win.*)

- Make the meaning of sentences very clear. Assume you wish to declare limits on your work times. *I work only in the mornings.* (not *I only work in the mornings*, which concentrates not on work times, but on activities).

- *Do not* and *does not*, are preferred in formal writing. However, in informal writing *don't* or *doesn't* may be substituted. *Jones does not have any objections to the changes in the project. I don't have time for lunch.*

- Double negatives are illogical. *I don't want any more carrots.* (not *I don't want no more carrots.*).

- The use of *lie* and *lay* determines their meaning. *Lay* takes an object, while *lie* does not. *I need to lie down.* (not *lay* down). *Lay the book on the table.* (here *lay* means to set something down).

- The past tense of *know* is *known. I have known her for a year* (not *knowed*).

- The word *from* (not *than*) usually follows *different. Today is different from yesterday.*

EFFECTIVE SPELLING

Spell all words correctly. Use a dictionary if you are not sure how a word is spelled. Following are correct spellings of words often misspelled:

- accommodation

- judgment

- its (possessive) *vs.* it's (contraction for *it is*)—I dropped the tire off of *its* mounting. *It's* Friday.

- E-mail is now *accessible.*

- accept (take) *vs.* except (excluding)—Will you *accept* my invitation? I want my pizza with everything *except* onions.

- lose (misplace) *vs.* loose (not tight)—I'm afraid I'll *lose* my notes. The nail came *loose.*

- than (comparison) *vs.* then (time)—My light is brighter *than* a spotlight. I went to the bank *then* saw my customer.

- I am *grateful* for your assistance.

EFFECTIVE PUNCTUATION

Use periods to end sentences that:

- State fact or opinion: *I'm reading a book.*

- Suggest or order action: *You should visit Dorothy.*

- Request action in question form: *Will you please go.*

- Are indirect questions: *She asked when school started.*

- End with an abbreviation: *She lives on Palm Ave.* (no double period).

Use question marks to end sentences that:

- Ask questions of fact or opinion: *Are students admitted?*

- Close with abbreviations: *Is it 7:00 p.m.?*

Use exclamation points to end sentences showing strong opinions: *Your house is on fire!*

Use commas:

1. After introductory parts of sentences: *After studying, she got an "A" grade.*

2. After prepositional phrases: *During the meeting, everyone talked.*

3. Before and after "interruptors" within sentences: *Please come in, Mrs. Alexander, before guests arrive.*

4. To separate two independent clauses in one sentence joined by a conjunction. *I saw her Friday, but she's home now.*

5. To separate series of three or more words, phrases, or clauses: *Germans, Russians, and Spaniards were there.*

6. Before and after non-essential interruptors, where meanings would be clear without interruptors: *This clock, as you might have guessed, is an antique.*

7. Do not use commas around interruptors that are essential to the meaning: *The automobile parked in Stall C-16 is mine.*

Semicolons join independent clauses not joined by coordinating conjunctions: *Spring is here; it's finally warm!*

Use colons where:

- Series of items follow: *Four brothers stand before you: Abraham, Benjamin, Charles, and Herman.*

- Long quotations follow: *The mayor said: "…Never before have I experienced the joy of knowing that one of our citizens was elected governor…"*

Use quotation marks at beginning and end of:

- Direct, exact quotations: *"Holidays,' said one speaker, "are students' friends."*
- Titles of book chapters, poems, or magazine articles: *The chapter is entitled "Computers and Clocks."*
- Terms possibly unfamiliar to readers, such as *An IRA is an "Individual Retirement Account."*

Rules for punctuation related to quotation marks include:

- Periods and commas go inside quotation marks: *"I am listening, Father," said Robert, "I am listening."*
- Colons, semicolons, exclamation points, and question marks go outside quotation marks unless part of the quoted material: *You said, "No one can solve this puzzle"; I found three who could.*
- Do not use quotation marks around indirect quotations: *He said he'd leave before 3:00 p.m.*
- Use single quotation marks for quotations within quotations: *Virginia said, "I saw the movie 'Titanic.'"*
- Use underscore, all capitals, or italics (but not quotation marks) for titles of books; pamphlets, long poems, magazines, or newspapers; or performing, musical, literary, or visual art pieces.

Apostrophes have two major rules:

1. To show possession for nouns, not pronouns: *The composer's melody is beautiful.*
2. To substitute for missing letters in "contractions": *You're the winner!*

Some major rules for capitalization are:

- Capitalize first words in sentences. *Eighty-five books were purchased.*
- Capitalize names: *Finally Marie visited Portland, Maine.*
- Capitalize and abbreviate titles: *Here's Mr. Blake.*

EFFECTIVE SENTENCES AND PARAGRAPHS

Writing effectively requires skillfully transforming correct grammar, spelling, and punctuation into sentences and paragraphs.

Effective Sentences. Main ideas can be emphasized by placement in independent clauses at ends of sentences: *From shrewd investments, Martin achieved overwhelming success.* Emphasis also comes by comparing or contrasting: *He speaks with the force of a thunderbolt.* Connecting words emphasize ideas: *She's inexperienced; however, look at her sales reports.* Positive attitudes increase sentence effectiveness: *We appreciate your thoughtful reply. We will study it carefully* (versus *We cannot understand your reply.*)

Effective Paragraphs. Place a central core thought in each paragraph. Central core thoughts may come first followed by supporting sentences.

We're concerned about declines in sales and profits. Two years ago, sales reached $260 million. Last year they dropped to $214 million. Two years ago, our profit rate was 13 percent on sales. This past year, it dipped to 8 percent.

Ending paragraphs with central core thoughts are equally effective:

Two years ago, sales reached $260 million. Last year they dropped to $214 million. Two years ago, our profit rate was 13 percent on sales. This past year, it dipped to 8 ercent. We're concerned about declines in sales and profits.

Skillful repetition makes a paragraph effective:

Bosses forgive occasional tardies. They even overlook mistakes. But they never condone a negative attitude.

Climatic paragraphs can generate excitement by sequencing events in order of occurrence:

On June 14, two girls carrying shopping bags entered our men's furnishings department. While one girl talked to a sales associate, the other slipped around quietly loading her shopping bag. Soon, they left by the front door. However, our security patrol spotted them. When the two girls got outside, security nabbed them and called the police.

VISUAL ASPECTS

Whether transmitted via letter, FAX, e-mail, or interoffice communication, appropriate formats create favorable impressions.

Business Letters. Business letters are mailed to persons outside the writer's company:

- One-inch margins give clean, open appearances.

- Indent first lines of paragraphs five spaces.
- Use 10- or 12-point font sizes for most letters and memos.
- Except for extremely short letters, use single spacing.
- Most business stationery is 8.5 by 10 inches.
- On envelopes, place the return address at upper left and the addressee's address in approximate vertical and horizontal center.

Business Memos. Memos go to persons within the writer's company. Their format, which is often informal, is similar to that of business letters.

Facsimilies. Business faxes (facsimiles), business letters, and memos have similar formats. Faxes, however, have attached cover sheets listing name, title, organization, address of company, and fax number of both addressee and writer. Also shown is number of pages, counting cover sheets.

E-Mail. Formats for e-mail are less formal than for letters.

- Avoid capitalizing all words. It is equivalent to shouting.
- When replying to an earlier e-mail, include a copy of the message you received.
- Always include subject lines.
- Make grammatical structures, typing, numbers, and technical information accurate and clear. Compose lengthy messages off-line.
- Confidentiality cannot be guaranteed with e-mail.

Good Impressions. Always convey a good impression.

- Write sincerely and courteously.
- Avoid big words. Do not try to impress.
- Aim communications to the reader's level.
- Have appropriate-length messages. Short messages may be curt; long messages may lose readers.
- Be correct. If the meeting is Wednesday, November 30, do not write Thursday, November 30.
- Messages should flow smoothly from beginning to end and reach logical conclusions.
- Get to the point early.
- Do not pretend to know readers when you actually do not.
- Avoid gender stereotyped communications.
- Correctly convey company policy. Consult with colleagues if necessary.

SEE ALSO *Listening Skills in Business; Reading Skills in Business; Research in Business; Speaking Skills in Business*

BIBLIOGRAPHY

Aaron, Jane E. (2004). *The Little, Brown Compact Handbook* (5th ed.). New York: Pearson/Longman.

Ellison, Pat Taylor (2007). *Business English for the 21st century* (4th ed.). Upper Saddle River, NJ: Pearson Prentice Hall.

Sabin, William A. (2005). *The Gregg Reference Manual* (10th ed.). Boston: McGraw-Hill.

G. W. Maxwell

Index

ENCYCLOPEDIA OF BUSINESS AND FINANCE, SECOND EDITION

Earnings management, **214–215**. *See also* Fraudulent financial reporting

eBay, 230–232, 459, *460*

Eckert, John Presper, 382, 388

Econometric models, 324

Economic analysis, **215–218,** 307

Economic choice, 225–226

Economic cycles. *See* Business cycle

Economic development, **218–220**

Economic indicators, 66

Economic systems, **220–223**

Economics, **223–227,** *224. See also* Factors of production; Monetary policy

   careers in, 84–87

   education, 86

   ethics, 264–266

   professors, 84

Economics: historical perspectives, **227–229**

Education and training

   accounting, 329, 695

   auditing, 391

   corporate, 158–160, 743–746

   e-learning, 434, 560, 721–722

   economics, 86

   ethics, teaching of, 271–272

   interactive technology and, 399, 401

   Internet and, 428

   No Child Left Behind legislation, 543–544

   on-the-job training, 159

   professional education, 614–616

   school to career movement, 651–654

   videoconferencing, 758

EEC (European Economic Community), 424

EEOC (Equal Employment Opportunity Commission), 205–206

EFTA (European Free Trade Association), 741

Elder care services, 39

Electronic commerce, 39, **229–232,** *230, 231,* 432, 722. *See also* E-marketing

Electronic Communications Privacy Act, 603

Electronic Data Gathering Analysis and Retrieval System, 657, 658–659

Electronic mail, 124, 127, 187–188, **232–234,** 235, 271, 427–428, 555, 595, 602, 635, 664

Electronic whiteboards, 557, 757–758

Embezzlement, 179

Emerging Issues Task Force (EITF), 309, 339, 340

Employee assistance programs, *236,* **236–239**

Employee benefits, **239–242**

Employee compensation, **242–245,** *243, 244*

Employee discipline, **245–248**

Employee evaluation, 246, 370

Employee motivation, 444–446

Employee Retirement Income Security Act, 659

Employee safety and health, 371

Employment and Earnings, 61

Employment law, 273–274, 454–455

Employment statistics, 60–61, 660*t,* 661*t*

Employment tax, 720

ENIAC computer, 361, 382, 388–389

Enron, 41–42, 43, 335, 548, 624, 627, 675

Enterprise resource planning, 13

Enterprise Risk Management: Integrated Framework, 647

Entrepreneurship, 224, **248–252,** 291

Environmental Protection Agency (EPA), **252–254,** 353

Environmentalism, 274, 357

Equal Employment Opportunity Act of 1972, **254–255,** 353

Equal Employment Opportunity Commission (EEOC), 205–206

Equal Pay Act of 1963, **255–256**

Equilibrium, 715

Equity theory, 526

ERG theory, 524

Ergonomics, **256–259,** *257,* 365–366

Ethics. *See also* individual topics

   in business research, 643

   codes of, 675–677

   public relations and, 625–626

Ethics: an overview, **259–261.** *See also* individual topics

Ethics in accounting, **261–264**

Ethics in economics, **264–266**

Ethics in finance, **266–269**

Ethics in information processing, **269–272,** 270*t. See also* Cyber crime

Ethics in law and business, **272–274**

Ethics in management, **275–279**

Ethics in marketing, **279–283**

Euro, 284–285, 743

European Economic Community (EEC), 424

European Free Trade Association (EFTA), 741

European Union, **283–285,** *284,* 407–408, 742–743

Examination (accounting service), 310–311

Executive compensation, 244–245

Expectancy theory, 526

Experiments (business research), 642

Exports, 48, 409, 417, 492, 661*t. See also* International trade

Exposure Drafts, 308

External auditors, 42–43

External environment review, 710–711

Extranet, 433–435

F

Facsimile reproduction, **287–289,** *288*

Factors of production, 224, **289–291**

Fads, *292,* **292–294**

Fair Labor Standards Act of 1938, 452

Fair Packaging and Labeling Act of 1966, **294–295**

Fair-trade laws, 599

Family and Medical Leave Act, 365

FAR (Foundation for Applied Research), 696

Faragher v. Boca Raton, 663

FASB (Financial Accounting Standards Board), **307–309**

   described, 356

   financial statement guidelines, 318–320

   GAAP and, 1, 3, 5, 9, 339–343

   not-for-profit organizations, 548–549

Fayol, Henri, 469, 474, 475

FCC (Federal Communications Commission), 352, 430

FDA. *See* Food and Drug Administration (FDA)

FDIC (Federal Deposit Insurance Corp.), 268, 354

Federal Accounting Standards Advisory Board. *See* (FASB (Financial Accounting Standards Board)

Federal Employment Compensation Act, 775

Federal Insurance Contribution Act (FICA), 720

Federal Management Act of 1994, **112–114**

Federal Open Market Committee (FOMC), 296, 314